THE PERFECT
ACT Tutorial

STUDENT VERSION

BY ERIK KLASS

ST★R Tutors

The Test Prep Experts

Edition 2.0, July 2020

Written by Star Tutors LLC
Copyright © 2020 Star Tutors LLC
All rights reserved.
ISBN-13: 9798679246102

Star Tutors offers classroom, online, and in-person tutoring. For more information about our programs, visit us at www.startutors.net.

Printed in the United States of America.

A NOTE FROM THE AUTHOR

Dear Student,

Congratulations! You now have the most complete and effective ACT tutorial available: *The Ultimate ACT Tutorial*. Unlike many of the techniques found in other tutorials, the methods taught here are easy to learn, clearly presented, and proven to work. These lessons and techniques come from my years of experience. I have tested and perfected every technique in this tutorial. I know they work because I have been watching them work for years.

But this tutorial does not work magic. You must be prepared to work hard, complete your homework assignments, and diligently study the methods and examples. I can't predict how high your score will go. What I can guarantee is that this tutorial will provide you with the strategies and techniques you need to succeed on nearly every problem on the ACT. With practice and effort, you should walk into the testing room prepared and confident.

Study with discipline and diligence as you set your pace toward the college of your dreams.

Best of luck!

Erik Klass

INTRODUCTION

THE ULTIMATE ACT TUTORIAL

This tutorial provides you with the techniques you need to excel on the ACT. These techniques will be displayed using clear example problems, and you will have opportunities to practice and master the techniques on literally hundreds of practice problems.

THE OFFICIAL ACT* PREP GUIDE

You may have noticed that there are no practice tests in this tutorial. We believe that students will benefit from taking *real* ACTs, not ones made up by a test-prep company. While most of our competitors decided to create their own tests, we decided against this for two reasons: (1) it is next to impossible to create a test that truly reflects a real ACT, and (2) we don't have to—there is an excellent book written by the actual test makers. So:

! **In order for this tutorial to be most effective, you should purchase** *The Official ACT Prep Guide*.

So why do you need *The Ultimate ACT Tutorial*? Why not just buy the official ACT book? The ACT book is an excellent source of ACT *tests* but not a great source of ACT *techniques* and *strategies*. That's where we come in—we provide these techniques and strategies, and you can practice and perfect them on real ACT tests. As you work through this tutorial, you will see assignments for every test question in the ACT book.

PRACTICE TESTS

There are five tests in the official ACT book. We will use four of them (Tests 1–4) for *timed* practice. The tests will give you the practice and experience you will need before tackling the real test on "game day." More test-taking information is found on the following pages.

PRACTICE PROBLEMS

We'll use Test 5 in the official ACT book for practice problems. This book also contains a number of additional practice problems for English and Science that are *not* part of the five practice tests. They are found in Chapter 5 (English) and Chapter 8 (Science). Practice problems will be assigned as you work your way through our tutorial. You will usually complete these practice problems untimed and sometimes out of order.

*ACT is a registered trademark of the ACT, Inc., which was not involved in the production of and does not endorse this book.

ACT'S *PREPARING FOR THE ACT* BOOKLET

You can find an additional practice test in the most recent *Preparing for the ACT* booklet, written by the ACT. This booklet is free and can be downloaded at the ACT's website (www.ACT.org).

DISCLAIMER

This tutorial is the most accurate and up-to-date ACT guide that we know of, at the time of this writing. But the ACT has been known to make small changes to the test's format and content from time to time, often with little or no warning. We recommend that you check the *Preparing for the ACT* booklet to see if there have been any recent changes since the publication of this tutorial.

PROGRAMS

We have prepared three general ACT programs that you may follow as you work your way through the tutorial. The hours below are estimates of *actual tutoring times* (including learning techniques, reviewing homework, taking quizzes, and completing lesson problems). **The hours do *not* include time for completing homework and taking practice tests.** To determine the program that is right for you, consider: (1) how much time you have before you plan to take the ACT and (2) your desired level of mastery.

Throughout the tutorial, you will notice notes **in bold** for each of the programs, such as lessons and questions to complete (or skip), tests to take, and so on. Details for each program are found on the following pages (Tutoring Schedules).

20-HOUR PROGRAM

Our shortest standard program should take about 20 hours of lesson time. Rest assured that the 20-hour program still covers most of the important ACT topics.

30-HOUR PROGRAM

For many students, we recommend the 30-hour program. This program covers most of the questions you will find on the ACT. This is our most popular program.

40-HOUR PROGRAM

If you are looking for the highest score possible and if time permits, look at every topic in the tutorial, as covered by the 40-hour program. Students with high starting scores should definitely consider this program (although these students will probably choose to skip easier lessons).

IF YOU'RE FOLLOWING THE 20- OR 30-HOUR PROGRAM

Throughout this tutorial, at the ends of chapters, you will see various assignments for practice problems and practice test corrections. Unless you're following the 40-hour program, some of the questions you will be asked to tackle will *not* be covered by your chosen program. You have two options:

- **Skip a question not in your program**: If you get to a question that you suspect tests a technique you haven't covered, skip it. But make sure to check the solutions (see "Answers" below) to make sure the problem is definitely not covered by your program.
- **Go for it**: Go ahead and try any problems not in your program. You might get some of these correct, so it's good practice. And the questions that you miss may help you pinpoint additional topics to cover, if you have time.

We recommend the second option above (go for it), but if you're running short on time, covering only the questions in your chosen program makes sense.

TUTORING SCHEDULES

As you may have noticed in the Table of Contents, *The Ultimate ACT Tutorial* is divided into four main parts: English, Math, Reading, and Science. You should *not* work straight through this tutorial. The tutoring schedule on the following pages will be your guide.

20-HOUR SCHEDULE

If you're following the 20-hour program, simply stop at the 20-hour mark in the schedule. You'll spend the last lesson reviewing Test 2.

30-HOUR SCHEDULE

If you're following the 30-hour program, simply stop at the 30-hour mark in the schedule. You'll spend the last lesson reviewing Test 3.

TIMES

Take a look at the schedule. You can see that each lesson is scheduled for *two hours*. As described before, these hours are estimates of *actual lesson time* (including learning techniques, reviewing homework, taking quizzes, and completing lesson problems). The hours do *not* include time for completing homework and taking practice tests. For most students, completing one to two lessons per week is a realistic pace. Obviously, consider your final test date as you plan your lessons.

Students have different strengths and weaknesses and work at different paces, so treat the schedules as general guides. Don't worry if your actual times don't match the times on the schedules. You may choose to spend extra time on more difficult topics or skip entire sections that you are already comfortable with.

For each lesson, the schedule gives time breakdowns for each part of the curriculum (English, Math, etc.); see the number in parentheses following each list of lessons. These time estimates also include time that you might spend going over the previous lesson's homework.

HOMEWORK

As you work your way through the tutorial, you will notice assignments labeled with a homework symbol:

The following schedules will include *additional* homework assignments: see the homework (HW) row following each lesson. All homework assignments (those labeled with the symbol above and those on the schedules) should be completed *between* lessons—we recommend you "step away" from the material before completing these assignments.

TUTORING SCHEDULES

Hrs.	English	Math	Reading	Science
	□ Quickly review "The Big Picture" (see https://www.klasstutoring.com/the-big-picture.pdf).			
1/2	□ English Introduction □ Verb Tense □ Subject-Verb Agree. (0.75)	□ Math Introduction □ Calculators □ Basic Concepts □ Percent Problems (1.25)		
	□ Go over "Taking Practice Tests" in the Homework Packet.			
HW	□ **Take Test 1***	□ **Take Test 1*** □ Basic Concepts Worksheet	□ **Take Test 1***	□ **Take Test 1***
3/4	□ Pronouns □ Parallelism (0.50)	□ Proportions □ Ratios □ Averages… □ Rates… (1.25)	□ Reading Introduction □ The Passage (0.25)	
	□ Go over "Correcting Practice Tests" in the Homework Packet.			
HW	□ Study for Grammar Quiz 1 (Sections 1-4)	□ Basic Concepts: Correct Test 1[†]		
5/6	□ Grammar Quiz 1 (Sections 1-4) □ Punctuation □ Fragments (0.50)	□ Exponents □ Tables & Graphs □ Probability □ Arithmetic Word Probs. (0.50)	□ Reading Strategies □ Direct Questions (0.50)	□ Science Introduction □ Data Representation Introduction □ Graph Basics (0.50)
HW		□ Arith. Worksheet 1 □ Arith.: Correct Test 1[†]	□ Tutorial Passage I	□ Data Rep.: Passage I
7/8	□ Run-ons □ Misplaced Words (0.25)	□ Essential Algebra □ Alg. Word Problems □ The Pick Tricks (start) (0.75)	□ Extended-Reasoning Questions (0.50)	□ New Information □ Trends □ Make Connections (0.50)
HW	□ Study for Grammar Quiz 2 (Sections 5-8)		□ Tutorial Passage II	□ Data Rep.: Passage II
9/10	□ Grammar Quiz 2 (Sections 5-8) □ Redundancies □ Apostrophes & Confused Words □ Idiom (0.50)	□ The Pick Tricks (finish) (0.50)	□ Timing (0.50)	□ Tables □ Calculations & Math □ Combining Graphs (0.50)
HW			□ Timing Passage □ Direct and Extended- Reasoning Questions: Correct Test 1[†]	□ Data Rep.: Passage III
11/12	(0.25)	(Skip Advanced Alg. Ch.) □ Geometry Intro. □ Area… (0.75)	□ Purpose Questions (0.75)	□ Timing (0.25)
HW	□ Study for Grammar Quiz 3 (Sections 9-11)	□ Algebra Worksheet 1 □ Algebra (20- & 30- hour programs: add Adv. Alg.): Correct Test 1[†]	□ Tutorial Passage III □ Purpose Qs: Correct Test 1[†]	□ Data Rep.: ACT Passage I*

* These assignments are in **The Official ACT Prep Guide**: Test 1 is near the front, and Tests 2–5 are toward the back. Test 5 will be used for practice problems. **English practice passages** are in Chapter 5. **Science practice passages** are in Chapter 8.

† For corrections and Test 5 practice problems, problem lists for each test are found in the Techniques chapter at the end of this tutorial. Make sure you turn to this section. All work can be done in *The Real ACT Prep Guide*. These assignments are "open book."

Continued →

TUTORING SCHEDULES (continued)

Hrs.	English	Math	Reading	Science
13/14	□ Grammar Quiz 3 (Sections 9-11) (0.25)	□ Triangles □ Angles □ Coordinates (1.0)	□ Main Idea Questions (0.50)	□ Data Representation Odds & Ends (0.25)
HW			□ Tutorial Passage IV □ Main Idea Qs: Correct Test 1[†]	□ Data Rep.: Passage IV
15/16	□ Usage/Mechanics □ Usage/Mechanics: Tutorial Passage I (0.50)	□ Lines □ More Circles □ Solids & Volume (0.75)	□ Comparison Questions (0.50)	(0.25)
HW	□ Usage/Mechanics: Tutorial Passage II □ Usage/Mechanics: Correct Test 1[†]	□ Geom. Worksheet 1 □ Geom.: Correct Test 1[†] □ Basic Concepts: Test 5[†] □ Arith. Probs.: Test 5[†] □ Alg. Probs.: Test 5[†]	□ Tutorial Passage V □ Comparisons Qs: Correct Test 1[†]	□ Data Rep.: Correct Test 1[†] (Remember to correct all Data Rep. *questions*, even ones that show up on other types of passages.)
17/18	□ Timing (0.50)	□ Review Timing (1.00)	□ Review Timing (0.25)	□ Review Timing (0.25)
HW	□ **Take Test 2***	□ **Take Test 2***	□ **Take Test 2***	□ **Take Test 2***
19/20	If you're following the **20-hour program**, correct Test 2 for all subjects during this final lesson. If you're following the **30- or 40-hour program**, go to the next row (you will correct Test 2 later).			
19/20	□ Rhetorical Skills □ Rhetorical Skills: Tutorial Passage I (0.50)	□ Function Basics □ Graphs of Functions (0.50)	□ Tone Questions (0.50)	□ Research Summaries Intro. □ Data Rep. Revisited (0.50)
HW	□ Rhetorical Skills: Tutorial Passage II □ Usage/Mechanics: Correct Test 2[†]	□ Basic Concepts, Arith., Algebra (20- & 30-hour programs: add Adv. Alg.), and Geom.: Correct Test 2[†]	□ Tutorial Passage VI □ Tone Questions: Correct Test 1[†]	□ Data Rep.: Correct Test 2[†]
21/22	(0.50)	□ Basic Trigonometry □ Trig & the Unit Circle (1.00)	□ Words-in-Context (WIC) Questions (0.25)	(0.25)
HW	□ Rhetorical Skills: Correct Tests 1 & 2[†]	□ Functions Worksheet 1 □ Functions: Correct Tests 1 & 2[†]	□ Tutorial Passage VII □ WIC Questions: Correct Test 1	
23/24	Back to Grammar Ch.: □ Adjectives & Adverbs □ Comparisons (0.25)	□ Principle of Counting □ Permutations & Combinations □ Complex Numbers (0.75)	□ Difficult Passages (0.25)	□ Research Methods □ Sci. Sense/Knowledge (0.75)
HW	□ ACT Passage II*	□ Trig. Worksheet 1 □ Trigonometry: Correct Tests 1 & 2[†]	□ Tutorial Passage VIII □ All Question Types: Correct Test 2[†]	□ Research Sum.: ACT Passage II* □ Research Sum.: Correct Tests 1 & 2[†] (Remember to correct all Research Summary *questions*, even ones that show up on other types of passages.)

*/† See first page of Schedule

Continued →

Hrs.	English	Math	Reading	Science
25/26	□ Illogical Comparisons □ Grammar Odds & Ends (0.25)	□ Logarithms □ Patterns □ Matrices (0.75)	(0.50)	(0.50)
HW	□ ACT Passage III*	□ Algebra Worksheet 2 □ Geom. Worksheet 2 □ Odds & Ends Worksheet I	□ Test 5: Passage I	□ Data Rep.: Tutorial Passage I □ Data Rep.: Tutorial Passage II □ Research Sum.: Tutorial Passage I □ Research Sum.: Tutorial Passage II
27/28	(0.25)	(0.75)	(0.25)	(0.75)
HW	□ Take Test 3*	□ Take Test 3*	□ Take Test 3*	□ Take Test 3*
29/30	If you're following the **30-hour program**, correct Test 3 for all subjects during this final lesson. If you're following the **40-hour program**, go to the next row (you will correct Test 3 later).			
29/30	(0.00)	Advanced Algebra Ch.: □ Systems of Equations & Inequalities □ Factoring □ Working with Polynomials (1.00)	(0.00)	□ Conflicting VIewpoints Intro. □ Direct Questions □ Indirect Questions □ Comparisons □ Strengths & Weaknesses (1.00)
HW	□ Correct Test 3: All missed questions	□ Advanced Algebra Worksheet I □ Basic Concepts, Arithmetic, Algebra, Geom., Adv. Alg.: Correct Test 3[†]	□ Test 5: Passage II □ All Question Types: Correct Test 3	□ Conf. VIewpoints: ACT Passage III* □ Conf. VIewpoints: Correct Tests 1–3[†]
31/32	(0.25)	Back to Functions Ch.: □ More Graphs of Functions □ Functions as Models (1.00)	(0.50)	(0.25)
HW	□ Study for Grammar Quiz 4 (Sections 1-15)	□ Geom. Worksheet 3 □ Geometry Probs.: Test 5[†] □ Functions Probs.: Test 5[†] □ Functions: Correct Test 3[†]	□ Test 5: Passage III	□ Data Rep. and Research Sum.: Correct Test 3 □ Data Rep.: Tutorial Passage III □ Conf. VIewpoints: Tutorial Passage I
33/34	□ Grammar Quiz 4 (Sections 1-15) (0.25)	Back to Trig. Ch.: □ Graphs of Sine & Cosine □ The Laws of Sines & Cosines □ Trig. Odds & Ends (1.00)	(0.25)	(0.50)
HW	□ Test 5: Passage I □ Test 5: Passage II	□ Arith. Worksheet 2 □ Algebra Worksheet 3 □ Geom. Worksheet 4 □ Trig. Probs.: Test 5[†] □ Trig.: Correct Test 3[†]	□ Test 5: Passage IV	□ Data Rep.: Test 5: Passage I □ Research Sum.: Tutorial Passage III □ Research Sum.: Test 5: Passage II □ Conf. VIewpoints: Tutorial Passage II

*/† See first page of Schedule

Continued →

TUTORING SCHEDULES (continued)

Hrs.	English	Math	Reading	Science
35/36	(0.25)	Back to Odds & Ends Ch.: □ Parabolas & Ellipses □ Vectors □ Direct & Inverse Variation □ Sets & Groups □ Greatest/Least Possible Values (1.00)	(0.25)	(0.50)
HW	□ Test 5: Passage III □ Test 5: Passage IV	□ Advanced Algebra Worksheet II □ Functions Worksheet 2 □ Trig. Worksheet 2 □ Odds & Ends Worksheet II □ Odds & Ends Probs.: Test 5[†] □ Odds & Ends: Correct Tests 1–3[†]	□ Tutorial Passage IX	□ Data Rep.: Test 5: Passage III □ Research Sum.: Test 5: Passage V □ Research Sum.: Test 5: Passage VII □ Conf. Viewpoints: Test 5: Passage IV □ Conf. Viewpoints: Tutorial Passage III
37/38	□ Review Timing (0.25)	(1.00)	□ Review Timing (0.25)	□ Review Timing (0.50)
HW	□ **Take Test 4***	□ **Take Test 4***	□ **Take Test 4***	□ **Take Test 4***
39/40	□ Correct Test 4[†] (0.50)	□ Correct Test 4[†] (0.50)	□ Correct Test 4[†] (0.50)	□ Correct Test 4[†] (0.50)

*/† See first page of Schedule

WHERE'S THE WRITING SCHEDULE?

The optional Writing Test is covered by our companion tutorial: *The Ultimate ACT Tutorial: Writing*. If you are planning to take the Writing Test, please purchase this tutorial. This book contains detailed programs to help you write great essays in no time.

TAKING THE PRACTICE TESTS

Practice tests are found in *The Official ACT Prep Guide*. Each test is really five tests in one: English, Math, Reading, Science, and Writing (optional); the tests will always be in this order.

/ Make sure to time yourself when you take these tests.

Use the following schedule:
- **English Test: 45 minutes**
- **Math Test: 60 minutes**
  —10-minute break—
- **Reading Test: 35 minutes**
- **Science Test: 35 minutes**
  —10-minute break—
- **Writing Test (optional): 40 minutes (new time)**

You should leave yourself about **4 hours** to take all five tests (or a little over 3 hours for just the first four tests). Because you'll be completing a significant amount of ACT homework as you work your way through the tutorial, you may decide to take some practice tests (English, Math, Reading, Science, and Writing) separately, rather than completing all five tests in one sitting. **You should still *always* time yourself, and never take a break in the middle of a test.**

/ To closely simulate the actual test-taking experience, take at least the last ACT test of your chosen program in *one sitting* and use the full amount of time available for each individual test. This will help you prepare for the actual test day when you may spend nearly 4 hours completing the test.

Show all work in the ACT book. For practice, cut out and use the answer sheets and lined essay pages provided for each test by the ACT. **Do not look back to the tutorial while taking the practice tests.**

GRADING THE PRACTICE TESTS

To grade a practice test you must find a *raw score*, which is just the sum of all the questions you get correct on a given test, and then convert the raw score to a *scaled score* (between 1 and 36) using conversion charts in *The Official ACT Prep Guide*. Details on how to do this are found at the back of the ACT book, after the last test. Make sure to grade your tests carefully so you can chart your progress as you work your way through this tutorial.

CORRECTING THE PRACTICE TESTS

After you've taken and graded a test, the next step is to correct it. Learning from your mistakes is one of the most important ways to improve your scores. But it's important to correct your tests in the right way and at the right time.

USE OUR TECHNIQUES

The key to correcting missed questions is to use the techniques taught in this tutorial. Tackling a problem that you missed while using the same approach that you used the first time doesn't usually make a lot of sense. Rather, try to determine which technique applies to a missed problem, review that technique as necessary, and try the problem again. But how do you know what techniques to use? This is something you'll cover as you work through the curriculum, but if, for a particular problem, you're not sure about what technique to use, we strongly recommend that you turn to the Techniques chapter at the end of this tutorial. Techniques, and often hints, for every single question in the official ACT book are included.

! **Use the Techniques chapter at the end of this tutorial while correcting practice tests.**

WHEN TO CORRECT? AND WHICH QUESTIONS?

Obviously, you don't want to correct questions until you've covered the techniques that apply to those questions. Thus, pay close attention to the Tutoring Schedules (previous pages). These schedules will tell you when to correct specific questions as you finish relevant chapters in the tutorial.

Since questions of different types are scattered throughout each practice test, you'll have to refer to the Techniques chapter at the end of this tutorial to know which ones to correct. For each test, the questions are categorized by type and/or chapter. For example, when it's time to correct *Arithmetic* questions for a Math Test, go to the appropriate test, and look at the list of *Arithmetic* questions for that test. Similarly, when it's time to correct *Extended Reasoning* questions for a Reading test, find the list of *Extended Reasoning* questions for the appropriate test. You'll see more details on correcting practice tests later.

GUESSING ON THE ACT

You do not lose points for guessing on the ACT. This means that when you're done with each individual test, you should have filled in a bubble for every question, even if you had to guess. For this reason, you need to create a strategy for answering the questions. You have two options:

1. **Skip questions:** As you work your way through a test, skip a question that gives you trouble (and leave the corresponding answer blank on your answer sheet). Circle the problem number, either in your *test booklet* or on your *answer sheet*, so you can easily find it later (if you circle the number on your answer sheet, you'll have to erase before finishing the test, but of course these circles are easier to spot). But here's the catch: you must diligently watch the clock so that, worst-case scenario, you have about 30 seconds at the end of the test to guess on any questions that you skipped. Of course, you will hopefully have more time than that so you can go back and actually *look* at some of these questions, but *at the very least* you need to scribble in your favorite letters before you run out of time.

2. **Guess as you go:** If you're not sure about a problem when you get to it, take a guess, fill in the answer on your answer sheet, and move on. Again, circle the question number. If you have time at the end of the test, quickly flip through your test booklet and revisit any of the questions you guessed on. The advantage of this technique is that you don't have to worry about guessing at the end of the test if you run out of time (because you've been filling in answers all along). The disadvantage is that, if you do have time to go back to some of these questions, you might spend a little extra time erasing each guessed answer that you decide to change.

We recommend the first option above, but both are fine. Decide which one you prefer, and stick with it. You might experiment on the practice tests in the ACT book to see which strategy you're more comfortable with. Just make sure you have a plan in place before you take the real ACT.

TIMING STRATEGIES

Because the criteria for ordering the questions varies on each type of test, timing strategies will also vary. For example, when you complete the questions on the English Test (questions that are *not* arranged in order of difficulty), a good goal is to get to the end of the test—the last question may be the easiest one on the test. On the other hand, when you complete the questions on the Math Test (questions that generally *are* arranged in order of difficulty), it is important to spend time on the questions that you can answer correctly, even if that means guessing on some of the harder questions at the end of the test.

SILENT STOPWATCH

The timing strategies below require you to use a stopwatch. Your stopwatch should not beep, and it must be a *wrist* watch. Check out: www.silentstopwatch.com. Make sure you practice with your watch so you are comfortable using it before you take a real ACT.

DEADLINES

Deadlines will help you avoid falling behind as you take the English, Reading, and Science Tests (there are no deadlines for the Math Test—a timing plan will be discussed in the Math Introduction). These deadlines give you an idea of when you need to finish up one passage (English and Reading) or group of questions (Science) and move on to the next passage or group of questions. This way, you won't fall behind as you're working your way through the test. We'll use a "running clock": start the test at "time 00:00." The first deadline will occur when you should finish Passage I and move on to Passage II. The next deadline is for Passage II (move on to Passage III). And so on. Deadlines for each test will be discussed below.

Note that deadlines should be used *in addition* to watching the overall time. A good proctor should tell you when the test will be finished and will give you warnings as you near "time's up."

As you practice using the following deadlines, feel free to use a cheat sheet. Eventually, however, you should have the deadlines memorized (they are based on only two numbers: 9 and 8.5). We recommend making flashcards for each test. Drill yourself frequently so there's no hesitation on "game day."

ENGLISH DEADLINES

The English Test is **45-minutes** long, and there are **5 passages**. Thus, you should plan to spend no more than **9 minutes per passage** (9 + 9 + 9 + 9 + 9 = 45 minutes).

English Deadlines

Start Test	**0 minutes**
Finish Passage I	**9 minutes**
Finish Passage II	**18 minutes**
Finish Passage III	**27 minutes**
Finish Passage IV	**36 minutes**
Finish Passage V	**<45 minutes***

*You should never leave questions blank when you're done with the test. At the end of the test, with the last 30 seconds or so, quickly guess on any unanswered questions.

READING DEADLINES

The Reading Test is **35 minutes** long. You only have **8 minutes and 45 seconds** per passage. To be safe, let's round this down to **8:30**. Here are the deadlines:

Reading Deadlines: Step 3	
Start Test	00:00 min:sec
Finish Passage I	08:30
Finish Passage II	17:00
Finish Passage III	25:30
Finish Passage IV	34:00+*

*You can fall up to a minute behind for this timing plan.

SCIENCE DEADLINES

Like the Reading Test, the Science Test comprises 40 questions in **35 minutes**. Because the number of passages of each type (Data Representation, Research Summaries, Conflicting VIewpoints) and the number of questions per passage often vary, the deadlines will not be based on *passages* (as with the English and Reading tests) but on *sets of questions*, specifically, **four sets of 10 questions** (40 questions total). Here are the deadlines:

Science Deadlines	
Start Test	00:00 (min:sec)
Finish Question 10	8:30
Finish Question 20	17:00
Finish Question 30	25:30
Finish Question 40	34:00+*

*You can fall up to a minute behind.

GETTING FASTER

Not all students will be able to answer every question and meet the deadlines above. You will get faster as you learn techniques and complete practice problems, but even if you're not able to get to every question, you still must be able to follow the deadlines. The trick is to skip the harder questions. This way, if you do run out of time for a passage or section, the questions you did not get to were probably harder ones. You're in control of which questions you choose to answer—not the ACT.

/ If you can't meet the deadlines, skip harder questions.

WHICH QUESTIONS DO I SKIP?

In the Introduction for each test, we'll cover the types of questions to consider skipping. Identifying the harder questions takes practice. Hopefully, over time, you'll get the hang of recognizing, and perhaps skipping, these questions.

■

The above material is an overview of our timing strategies. Review the Timing sections in the Introduction of each part of the tutorial for more details. Make sure you practice the timing strategies whenever you complete practice passages or practice tests (other than the first diagnostic test). Eventually, you should be ready to put them to work for you when you take the real ACT.

EXTENDED TIME (× 1.5)

For most students with "accommodations," extended time on the ACT adds roughly 50% more time to take the test. According to the ACT (at the time of this writing): "Approved examinees taking the ACT have up to 5 hours total to work on all four multiple-choice tests at their own pace. Approved examinees taking the ACT with writing have up to 6 hours to complete all five tests. Both options include time for breaks between tests."

Here are some important assumptions:

- Students may NOT go back to a section (English, Math, Reading, Science, and Writing) once that section is completed. When a student is done with a section, she will let the proctor know (probably by raising a hand), and move on to the next section.
- Students must manage the timing of individual sections on their own. The proctor will not announce the ends of sections.
- Students can take breaks between sections only.

THE PLAN

Here are the times we recommend. **You must memorize these**:

- English: **65 minutes**
- Math: **90 minutes**
- Reading: **60 minutes**
- Science: **60 minutes**
- Writing (essay): **60 minutes**

BREAKS

We recommend you take **5-minute breaks** between English/Math, Reading/Science, and Science/Writing, and a **10-minute break** between Math/Reading. These breaks are important; it's a long test.

TOTAL TIME

Make a note of the time you *start* the ACT; this way you can easily calculate when time is up (5 or 6 hours later). But remember, your primary focus is on *section* times (below).

ENGLISH DEADLINES

You have **13 minutes** per passage.

English Deadlines (13:00/passage)	
Start Test	00:00 min:sec
Finish Passage I	13:00
Finish Passage II	26:00
Finish Passage III	39:00
Finish Passage IV	52:00
Finish Passage V	65:00

READING DEADLINES

You have **15 minutes** per passage.

Reading Deadlines (15:00/passage)	
Start Test	00:00 min:sec
Finish Passage I	15:00
Finish Passage II	30:00
Finish Passage III	45:00
Finish Passage IV	60:00

Actual *reading* time per passage should be between 4 and 6 minutes. Check your reading times occasionally to make sure you're not reading too slowly (or too quickly).

SCIENCE DEADLINES

As stated above, because the number of passages of each type (Data Representation, Research Summaries, Conflicting Viewpoints) and the number of questions per passage are inconsistent, the deadlines will not be based on *passages* (as with the English and Reading sections) but on *sets of questions*, specifically: **four sets of 10 questions** (40 questions total). The Reading Test is also based on four sets of 10 questions, but while the Reading deadlines coincide with actual *passages*, the challenge of the Science Test is that your deadlines will usually *not* coincide with the ends of passages.

Science Deadlines
(15 minutes for every 10 questions)

Start Test	00:00 min:sec
Finish Question 10	**15:00**
Finish Question 20	**30:00**
Finish Question 30	**45:00**
Finish Question 40	**60:00**

When practicing individual passages, use the times below:

Times per passage (for practice only)	
5-question passage (usually Data Representation)	**7:30 (min:sec)**
6-question passage (usually Research Summaries)	**9:00**
7-question passage (usually Conflicting VIewpoints)	**10:30**

ADJUSTMENTS TO THE TIMING PLAN

The timing plan above reflects the fact that most students find it relatively easy to finish the English section on time, and most students find it relatively difficult to finish the Reading and Science sections on time. If you know that you are particularly strong (i.e. fast) on one subtest, but struggle on another one, try adjusting the times and deadlines accordingly. Just make sure you calculate carefully so you don't end up going over the 5-hour (or 6-hour) time limit.

PROCESS OF ELIMINATION

A *process of elimination* is an important, all-around strategy on the ACT. This means physically crossing off the letter in your test booklet when you're "very sure" that an answer choice is wrong. A process of elimination will not only help you focus on the answer choices that may be correct (by eliminating the ones that are *not* correct), but this process will also sometimes lead you to the correct answer simply by removing the three or four (depending on the section) *incorrect* answers. You will undoubtedly identify the correct answer immediately on some questions, without having to scrutinize the other answer choices. This is great. But oftentimes you should aggressively eliminate answer choices to help zero in on correct answers.

FLASHCARDS

There are many opportunities throughout this tutorial to create flashcards. Many of the important and more specific items that should be memorized are indicated with a flashcard symbol:

There are different ways to create flashcards, but, in general, there should be some form of a question on the front of the card and the answer to that question on the back. Create flashcards for any information that you are worried you may forget before taking the test. And, of course, don't forget to study them frequently.

COLLEGE COUNSELING

This tutorial is *not* intended to replace your college counselor. It has only one goal: **to help you achieve the highest score possible on the ACT**. Many students have questions such as:

- How do I sign up for the ACT?
- What do my ACT scores mean?
- To what colleges should I apply?
- Do I even have to take the ACT?
- What about the SAT?

There are a number of places where you can find helpful information:

- The ACT website (www.actstudent.org/) can answer a number of your questions about signing up for the test and what your scores mean.
- Get the free *Preparing for the ACT* booklet, either from your school or from the ACT website. (There's an extra practice ACT here, too!)
- Your school's college guidance counselor should be able to help you make difficult decisions regarding school selections and what tests you need to take.
- Many students seek the advice of private college counselors in their areas.
- You can contact colleges directly to discuss their expectations and requirements, or just review their websites—usually a great source of information.
- Buy or check out a book that specializes in college selection and enrollment.

THE FIRST ASSIGNMENT

OK—it's time to get started. Before completing any of the lessons in this tutorial, we recommend that you take a practice test in the ACT book. This will give you an idea of your starting score and will perhaps allow you to create a sensible program that focuses on your weaknesses. As you make your way through the tutorial and cover relevant topics, you will frequently go back and make corrections to this practice test.

Note the symbol to the left below. We'll use this symbol throughout the tutorial for all practice test assignments.

 All Programs: Take Test 1 in *The Official ACT Prep Guide*. Review "Taking Practice Tests" in this introduction.

PART 1

ENGLISH

I ENGLISH INTRODUCTION

The English section is divided into six chapters:

I.   Introduction

II. Grammar

III. Usage/Mechanics

IV. Rhetorical Skills

V.   Timing

TYPES OF QUESTIONS

All questions on the English Test are multiple choice, with four answer choices. The questions fall into one of two general categories:

1. Usage/Mechanics (approximately 50* questions covering punctuation, basic grammar, and sentence structure)

2. Rhetorical Skills (approximately 25* questions covering writing strategy, organization, and style)

Since you will be taking practice ACTs before these questions are discussed in the tutorial, read the test instructions carefully to understand how to answer these questions.

*These estimates are based on our own system of classification.

TEST LAYOUT

The English Test includes:

- Five passages, each with 15 questions

- A total of 75 multiple-choice questions

- A total test time of 45 minutes

A GENERAL APPROACH

You might want to take a moment now to open up the ACT book and see what these questions look like. Read the directions (this should be the only time you have to do this).

ANSWER QUESTIONS *WHILE* YOU READ THE PASSAGES

Unlike the ACT Reading or Science Tests, where all of the questions for a passage *follow* the passage, nearly all of the questions on the English Test show up *next* to the passage. You can, and *should*, answer them while you're reading the passage.

EXCEPTIONS

Be aware. Sometimes you have to read *beyond* the point where a question shows up before you can answer the question. We'll get more into this later (see Interrelated Questions in the Usage/Mechanics chapter and Main Ideas in the Rhetorical Skills chapter). There aren't many of these, so in general, answer questions aggressively as you read through the passage. This is the best way to maximize your time on the test.

TIMING

Most students find the English Test easier to finish in time than the other tests on the ACT (Math, Reading, and Science). If after taking a few tests you find that you have no trouble finishing the test, you can skip this section.

Many students, however, should have a plan in place to ensure getting to every question on the test. Even students who don't have timing concerns may appreciate the peace of mind of knowing that they're on track while taking the test. Thus, using the timing plan below can be helpful for most students, even those who consistently finish the test in time. You might skim over the following pages, but we'll come back to this section once we've covered Usage/Mechanics questions (Chapter III). (You can skip to Technique Identification now.)

■

The questions on the English Test are generally *not* arranged in order of difficulty. In addition, the last of the five passages may be just as easy as the first passage. **Thus, it is important to get through all five passages.** (This does *not* necessarily mean that you'll spend time answering every question—you may have to guess on some, as we'll explain shortly.)

The test is **45-minutes** long, and there are **5 passages**. Thus, you should plan to spend no more than **9 minutes per passage** (9 + 9 + 9 + 9 + 9 = 45 minutes).

DEADLINES

As discussed in the Introduction to this tutorial, we'll use *deadlines* to help you avoid falling behind as you take the test. Deadlines give you an idea of when you need to finish up one passage and move on to the next. We'll use a "running clock": start the test at "time 00:00" (don't forget to get a silent stopwatch for the actual test, as discussed in the Introduction).The first deadline occurs when you should finish Passage I and move on to Passage II. The next deadline is for Passage II (move on to Passage III). And so on.

As stated above, you will have **9 minutes** per passage. Here are the deadlines:

English Deadlines

Start Test	**0 minutes**
Finish Passage I	**9 minutes**
Finish Passage II	**18 minutes**
Finish Passage III	**27 minutes**
Finish Passage IV	**36 minutes**
Finish Passage V	**<45 minutes***

*You should never leave questions blank when you're done with the test. At the end of the test, with the last 30 seconds or so, quickly guess on any unanswered questions.

HOW TO GET FASTER (SKIPPING QUESTIONS)

Because it is important to get through all five passages, you might have to skip questions to stick to the 9-minute deadlines. Remember, there are two general types of questions on the test: Usage/Mechanics and Rhetorical Skills. On average, Rhetorical Skills questions are harder than Usage/Mechanics ones, so the Rhetorical Skills questions are usually the ones to skip (especially if you're following the **20-hour program**, in which you probably won't get to the Rhetorical Skills chapter).

Also, if you struggle on Vocabulary and Idiom questions (Usage/Mechanics), learn how to identify these types of questions, and consider skipping them. They tend to be harder—not to mention, less "tutorable"—than other types of Usage/Mechanics questions.

So, to summarize, if you need to pick up the pace, consider skipping the following questions:

- **Rhetorical Skills questions**
- **Vocabulary and Idiom questions** (Usage/Mechanics)

Of course, you should strive to eventually tackle nearly every question on the test, but the above questions are good ones to skip, at least at first.

TIMING PRACTICE

You will frequently work on a single passage as you make your way through this tutorial. Unless stated otherwise, for a single passage your timing goal is **9 minutes**.

TECHNIQUE IDENTIFICATION

Often, there are clues that will help you figure out what technique is being tested by a specific question. Throughout the tutorial, look for the magnifying glass for information about identifying techniques:

II
GRAMMAR

This chapter covers the most important part of the English Test: *grammar*. These grammar topics will also help you in your writing, so keep them in mind as you prepare for the ACT's Writing Test (the essay).

1. VERB TENSE

The tense of a verb describes *when* a verb "happens." If events occur at the same time, the verb tenses must be the same. If events occur at different times, the verb tenses should reflect the order of these events.

VERB-TENSE TERMINOLOGY

Verb – The part of speech that expresses existence, action, or occurrence in a sentence.

TENSE

While there are many different tenses, it is helpful to be familiar with the five most important verb tenses found on the ACT. Since you will not be tested on their official names (such as *past perfect*), we will refer to them by the *times* that they occur, as shown on the time-line below:

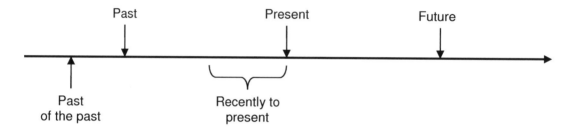

First, let's look at the easy ones. You are probably comfortable with these already.

Present: Today, I *study* with my tutor for the ACT.

Past: Yesterday, I *studied* for several hours for the ACT.

Future: Tomorrow, I *will study* several more hours for the ACT.

Now, for the harder ones—from now on, we'll call these the *"other" verb tenses*:

Past of the past: This tense always uses the word ***had***. For example:

Before Aimee took the ACT last year, she *had studied* for several months. (The studying took place *before* Aimee took the ACT; hence, the *past of the past*).

Recently to present: This tense uses the word **has** for *he*, *she*, *it*, or any *singular* thing performing the action and **have** for *I*, *we*, *they*, *you*, or any *plural* thing performing the action.

I *have studied* for the ACT for what seems like an eternity. (This has been going on for a while, and it sounds like it still is.)

TO SUMMARIZE

Past-of-the-past tense → use the word **had**
Recently-to-present tense → use the word **has** or **have**

TO BE

The verb *to be* is an irregular verb. Most of its forms don't even resemble the word itself. Luckily, your ear will probably pick up on correct and incorrect uses. You are probably already comfortable with the following:

Yesterday, I *was* sick.
Today, I *am* feeling great.
They *were* the best in the class last year, but now they *are* struggling.
She has *been* here for hours.

-ING WORDS

! Words in the *-ing* form can be used to express continuous action. **However, a word in the *-ing* form—on its own—does not function as a verb.** For example:

Incorrect: John *running* to the store.

Doesn't sound good, right? To correctly use an *-ing* word as part of a verb phrase, you must use a *to be* verb. The following are some examples:

Past: Yesterday, we *were emptying* out the cupboard.
Present: Today, John *is running* to the store while we finish the work.
Recently-to-present: John *has been working* as a handyman this summer.
Past-of-the-past: John *had been working* two jobs before he had enough money to buy the bike.

IRREGULAR VERBS

Irregular verbs may behave in unpredictable ways. For example:

present: Today, I *lie* on my bed.

past: Last night, I *lay* on my bed.

past of the past: Before I woke up this morning, I had *lain* on my bed.

recently to present: I have *lain* on my bed all morning.

As you can see, things can get a little tricky. The good news, however, is that the ACT does not put too much emphasis on these irregular verbs. But they *do* occasionally show up, so if your ear tells you that the form of a verb sounds "funny," you may have found one of these irregular verb errors.

VERB TENSE ON THE ACT

Verb tense questions on the ACT almost always ask you to recognize the tense set somewhere else in the passage—usually in the previous sentence or earlier in the sentence in question—and match the underlined verb to the previous verb. In the following problems, make sure you focus on the verbs that are not underlined (and are thus correct).

 To identify verb tense questions, look for questions with answer choices that contain the same verbs in different tenses—for example *look, looked, has looked, will look*, etc.

VERB TENSE LESSON PROBLEMS

Built at the turn of the century, the mansion <u>displaying</u> some of the oldest styles of
₁
architecture seen in the region today.

1. **A.** NO CHANGE
    B. will have displayed
    C. displayed
    D. displays

The scientists were sure they had uncovered an ancient human skeleton, but they <u>had not been sure</u> of its origin.
₂

2. **F.** NO CHANGE
    G. are not sure
    H. will not have been sure
    J. were not sure

Continued →

Since last night, Paul <u>worked</u> on his history

₃

paper, and he will probably still be working on

it until tonight.

3. **A.** NO CHANGE
    B. works
    C. will work
    D. has been working

Patrick learned to swim before he could walk,

competed in his first swimming contest before

he started kindergarten, and <u>winning</u> his first

₄

race when he was five years old.

4. **F.** NO CHANGE
    G. won
    H. wins
    J. will win

Taking the time up front to properly plan the

project will ensure success. Jumping right in

with no planning, however, <u>leads</u> to failure.

₅

5. **A.** NO CHANGE
    B. will have lead
    C. lead
    D. will lead

Early in the morning, the majestic sun peeks

over the distant hillside. Long shadows

<u>stretched</u> out over the yellow fields.

₁

1. **A.** NO CHANGE
    B. stretch
    C. will stretch
    D. stretching

Before I finish my research paper, I <u>have read</u>

₂

three books on the subject.

2. **F.** NO CHANGE
    G. will have read
    H. read
    J. had read

The teacher looked back fondly on the days

when students <u>come</u> to class free of cell phone

₃

distractions.

3. **A.** NO CHANGE
    B. came
    C. will have come
    D. could have come

Continued →

Before the rocket was launched, Ken <u>written</u>
₄
dozens of articles about its expected path.

4. **F.** NO CHANGE
   G. had written
   H. had wrote
   J. will write

Cobwebs fell from the ceiling of the haunted
mansion as Jason carefully <u>crept</u> inside.
₅

5. **A.** NO CHANGE
   B. will creep
   C. creeps
   D. has crept

2. SUBJECT-VERB AGREEMENT

Subjects must always agree with their respective verbs in number. In other words, if the subject is *singular* then the verb must be *singular*, and if the subject is *plural* then the verb must be *plural*.

There are two challenges to this topic. The first one is identifying the subject and its verb in the sentence. The second one is deciding whether the subject is singular or plural.

SUBJECT-VERB-AGREEMENT TERMINOLOGY

Subject – consists of a noun, noun phrase, or noun substitute which often refers to the person, place, or thing performing the action or being in the state expressed by the rest of the sentence.

Preposition – A word that locates things in *time, place,* or *movement.* } See examples below.
Prepositional Phrase – A preposition followed by a noun or pronoun. }

Modifying Phrase – We'll get more into modifying phrases later. For now, you should know that a modifying phrase is part of a sentence that can be removed without greatly altering the grammatical correctness of the sentence. A modifying phrase is separated from the rest of the sentence with commas. This makes it easy to spot.

PREPOSITIONS

Since removing *prepositional phrases* will help you find subjects and verbs, first let's look at a lesson on prepositions. If a word sounds correct in *either one* (not necessarily both) of the following sentences, the word is probably a preposition. Memorize these sentences.

The professor walked _____ the desk. (good for *place* or *movement*: ex. *into*)
The professor talked _____ the class. (good for *time* prepositions: ex. *after*)

Here are some examples of prepositions. Try them out in one or both of the sentences above.

about	beside	in front of	through
across	between	into	throughout
after	by	like	to
against	concerning	next to	toward
around	during	**of***	under
at	except	off	until
before	for	on	upon
behind	in	past	without
beneath			

*The word "of" is probably the most common preposition.

IDENTIFYING THE SUBJECT AND THE VERB

BAREBONES SENTENCES

The ACT loves to trick you by putting prepositional phrases or modifying phrases between the subject and its verb, but the subject is never part of these phrases. So:

/ **Get rid of prepositional and modifying phrases when looking for the subject of a sentence.**

After these phrases are removed, you will be left with the "barebones sentence." For example:

> The number of calories recommended for the average person by the Food and Drug Administration, according to a report last year, depend on the age and size of the individual.

First, remove the modifying phrase: "according to a report last year." Notice the commas on either side of the phrase. Next, remove the prepositional phrases (prepositions are in bold below). You should be left with the following sentence. The subject (and verb) become much easier to see.

> The number **of** ~~calories~~ recommended **for** ~~the average person~~ **by** ~~the Food and Drug Administration~~, ~~according~~ **to** ~~a report last year~~, depend **on** ~~the age and size~~ **of** ~~the individual~~.

> The number recommended depend.

The subject is *number* and the verb is *depend*. (Note: "recommended" is an adjective. It is describing the noun "number." The "number" certainly did not recommend anything.) Since *number* is singular and *depend* is plural, the subject and verb do not agree (more on the number of a verb soon). The correct sentence should read:

> The *number* of calories recommended for the average person by the Food and Drug Administration, according to a report last year, *depends* on the age and size of the individual.

VERBS BEFORE SUBJECTS

Sometimes, the verb comes *before* the subject. When you spot a verb, ask yourself what or who is "performing" the verb, and be prepared to look beyond the verb in the sentence. Look for the word "there," especially at the beginning of a sentence:

There remain questions about the cause of the fire.

Remain is the verb and *questions* is the subject.

Never before has Bill been so successful.

Has is the verb and *Bill* is the subject.

IDENTIFYING THE NUMBER OF THE VERB

Verbs behave in strange ways, as we've already seen in the previous section. In general, the rules that define the number of a verb are the opposite of those for nouns. When a verb is singular, it generally has an *s* at the end:

He eats by himself.

When a verb is plural, it generally does not have an *s* at the end.

They eat together.

If you're ever in doubt, just try out the verb in question with *it* or *they*, and trust your ear.

IDENTIFYING THE NUMBER OF THE SUBJECT

A NOSE SUBJECTS

Some commonly missed subjects can be remembered using the acronym: *A NOSE.* **These are almost always *singular* in number:**

- **A** anybody, anyone
- **N** nobody, no one, neither, none
- **O** one
- **S** somebody, someone
- **E** everybody, everyone, either, each, every

COLLECTIVE NOUNS

Collective nouns are almost always *singular* on the ACT, even though they may seem plural. If you can add an *s* to a collective noun to make it plural (for example: *group* → *groups*), then you know that without the *s*, it is singular:

number	audience	team	city, state, or country
amount	group	company or corporation	staff or department

SUBJECTS WITH *AND* OR *OR*

Make sure you are comfortable with the following rules for *and* and *or*:

AND

Linking two subjects with *and* creates a *plural* subject. For example:

> **Elizabeth *and* Jasmine** are going to drink coffee. (*plural*)

OR

Linking two subjects with *or* makes the linked subject *singular* if the word closest to the verb is singular and *plural* if the word closest to the verb is plural. For example:

> Elizabeth or **Jasmine** *is* going to pay for the coffee. (*singular*)
>
> Andy *or* **the girls** *are* going to the museum. (*plural*)
>
> The girls or **Andy** *is* going to the museum. (*singular*)
>
> There *is* **one can** of soup *or* bagels in the pantry. (*singular*)
>
> There *are* **bagels** or one can of soup in the pantry. (*plural*)

■

The following steps outline the method for working with subject-verb agreement errors:

1. Identify the subject and its verb. Find the "barebones sentence," if necessary.
2. Determine the number of the subject (singular or plural).
3. Make sure the number of the verb matches the number of the subject.

 Subject-Verb Agreement questions will usually have answer choices that have the same verb in singular and plural forms (ex: *take* and *takes*, or *has taken* and *have taken*).

SUBJECT-VERB AGREEMENT LESSON PROBLEMS

Each member of the group of scholars <u>has</u>
₁
taken a number of courses at the university.

1. **A.** NO CHANGE
    B. have
    C. are going to have
    D. having

Ryan or Mike, no matter what you may have
heard, <u>are going to be at</u> the dance.
₂

2. **F.** NO CHANGE
    G. have been going to
    H. is going to be at
    J. have been at

The team of representatives, many from as far
away as China and India, <u>is assembled</u> in the
₃
banquet room.

3. **A.** NO CHANGE
    B. have assembled
    C. are assembled
    D. are in assembly

One of the students <u>is going to the city finals for</u>
₄
<u>his or her</u> success in the spelling bee.
₄

4. **F.** NO CHANGE
    G. are going to the city finals for his or her
    H. is going to the city finals for their
    J. have gone to the city finals for their

I counted numerous boats at the docks, but
there <u>was not</u> as many boats as the year before.
₅

5. **A.** NO CHANGE
    B. were not
    C. will not have been
    D. is not

Either football or basketball <u>are my favorite</u>
₁
<u>sport</u>.
₁

1. **A.** NO CHANGE
    B. are my favorite sports
    C. have been my favorite sport
    D. is my favorite sport

Continued →

Everyone on the team, even the goalies, <u>have been</u> in great shape.
2

2. **F.** NO CHANGE
   G. are
   H. is
   J. are going to be

The audience, mostly made up of rich businessmen and politicians, <u>are paying</u> top-dollar for events like this.
3

3. **A.** NO CHANGE
   B. pay
   C. pays
   D. are payers for

Every nut, bolt, and tool <u>were</u> stolen from the tool shed.
4

4. **F.** NO CHANGE
   G. was
   H. are
   J. have been

The feeling I got after listening to the lecture about the city's traffic jams <u>were that</u> nothing is going to be done about them anytime soon.
5

5. **A.** NO CHANGE
   B. is that
   C. was that
   D. are that

3. PRONOUNS

PRONOUN TERMINOLOGY

Pronoun – A word that generally stands for or refers to a noun or nouns whose identity is made clear earlier in the text.

PRONOUN CASE

CASES OF PRONOUNS

The two general *cases* of pronouns are *subject* pronouns and *object* pronouns. Subject pronouns perform the actions in the sentence. Object pronouns are the recipients of the actions. If you are ever unsure of the case of a pronoun, plug the pronoun into a simple *performer-recipient* sentence and trust your ear, for example:

<u>He</u> threw the ball to <u>her</u>.

He is performing the action and *her* is receiving the action. Thus, *he* is a subject pronoun and *her* is an object pronoun.

Subject pronouns		Object pronouns
I	→	*me*
he	→	*him*
she	→	*her*
they	→	*them*
we	→	*us*
it	→	*it*
who	→	*whom*
you	→	*you*

The following rules will help you choose the correct case for a pronoun.

PRONOUNS AND PREPOSITIONS

! **Use *object* pronouns when the pronoun shows up in a phrase with a preposition:**

...between *you* and *me*...

...to Sherry and *her*...

...among *us* students...

...from *him* and *her*...

A PRONOUN LINKED WITH A NOUN

When a pronoun is side-by-side with a noun (*we* seniors, *us* students), **eliminate the noun to determine which type of pronoun to use.** For example:

(*We, Us*) seniors decided to take the day off.

We is the correct pronoun since *us* is clearly incorrect when *seniors* is removed.

The award was presented to (*we, us*) students.

Us is the correct pronoun since *we* is clearly incorrect when *students* is removed.

This approach can also help you when a pronoun is part of a linked subject or object. For example:

Toby and me decided to take the day off.

Remove the noun (*Toby*) and you will "hear" the error in the sentence.

Me decided to take the day off.

The pronoun should be in the subject case. The correct sentence reads:

Toby and *I* decided to take the day off.

WHO VERSUS *WHOM*

Recall that *who* is the subject pronoun and *whom* is the object pronoun. For example:

My mom, *who* has the day off, is going to the store.
With *whom* are you speaking?
I am speaking to the telephone repair man, about *whom* I'm sure you've heard a lot.

THAT VERSUS *WHICH*

While *who* or *whom* refers to people, as described above, *that* and *which* are pronouns that refer to groups or things. There is often confusion about whether to use *that* or *which*. There are distinct differences between the two.

That is used as a pronoun to introduce essential information that you absolutely need to understand what particular thing is being referred to. For example:

Heather likes bananas *that* are still green.

Out of all the types of bananas in the world, Heather likes the particular ones that are still green. Since the information *are still green* is essential to understand what kind of bananas Heather likes, use *that*. In addition, since this information could not be removed without greatly altering the sentence, do not use a comma.

Which is used as a pronoun to introduce nonessential, added information, which may be helpful but is not totally necessary to understand what particular thing is being referred to. For example:

Heather likes bananas, which are high in potassium.

The fact that bananas are high in potassium is added information that isn't essential to understand what kind of bananas Heather likes (since all bananas are high in potassium). **Which** is usually preceded by a comma because it introduces information that could be removed without drastically changing the desired meaning of the sentence.

■

 To identify pronoun case errors, look for questions with answer choices that have the same pronouns in different cases. (ex: *he* and *him*)

PRONOUN AGREEMENT

NUMBER AGREEMENT

In a sentence, the pronoun must agree in number with the noun or nouns it is replacing.

Everyone who plays an instrument knows *they* must practice for hours everyday to master the craft.

This sentence sounds fine, right? But it is incorrect. The pronoun *they* is referring to the noun *everyone*, the subject of the sentence, which is singular. Therefore, *they* should be replaced with a singular pronoun.

Everyone who plays an instrument knows *he or she* must practice for hours everyday to master the craft.

PRONOUN AGREEMENT

If pronouns are referring to the same thing in a sentence, make sure they are the same pronoun type. Watch out for illogical changes to the pronouns as a sentence develops.

When *one* prepares for a concert, *you* should visualize a standing ovation at the end.

Both pronouns should be *one* or *you*, such as:

When *one* prepares for a concert, *one* should visualize a standing ovation at the end.

————

The following steps will help you work with pronoun-agreement errors:
1. Identify the pronoun in the sentence.
2. Identify the noun that the pronoun is referring to. Usually the noun will precede the pronoun in the sentence.
3. Make sure the pronoun and the noun agree in number.

 To identify pronoun agreement errors, look for questions with answer choices that contain plural *and* singular pronouns.

PRONOUN AMBIGUITY

Pronouns must clearly refer to the noun or nouns they replace. For example:

The early marching music of New Orleans was probably the earliest form of jazz, and *they* used musical elements from both the African and European continents.

In the sentence, *they* is an ambiguous pronoun because there are no groups mentioned in the sentence to which *they* logically refers. The sentence could be corrected by either adding a group of people to the first part of the sentence or replacing *they* appropriately:

The *musicians* of early marching music in New Orleans were probably playing the earliest form of jazz, and *they* used musical elements from both the African and European continents.

OR

The early marching music of New Orleans was probably the earliest form of jazz, and *the musicians* used musical elements from both the African and European continents.

Another ambiguous pronoun problem occurs when it is unclear what noun is being referred to in the sentence. For example:

Thomas told Jason that *he* was responsible for studying the origins of jazz for their report on American music.

It may sound strange, but for the sentence to be totally clear and unambiguous, it should read:

Thomas told Jason that *Jason* (or *Thomas*) was responsible for studying the origins of jazz for their report on American music.

THEY

The pronoun *they* is commonly used when some form of *experts* is intended; this is also ambiguous:

They say that jazz was originally a combination of African and European musical elements.

The correct sentence should read:

Musical historians say that jazz was originally a combination of African and European musical elements.

IT

The pronoun *it* is also used frequently in ambiguous ways. For example:

The musicians combined African musical traditions with the use of classical European instruments, and *it* started a whole new style of music.

To what exactly is *it* referring? The pronoun *it* is ambiguous. Here's an improved version of the sentence:

The musicians combined African musical traditions with the use of classical European instruments, and a whole new style of music was born.

If the pronoun *it* clearly refers to the singular subject of the sentence or another singular noun in the sentence, its use is probably correct. The following examples are correct:

The *music* of early New Orleans had strong rhythmic characteristics because *it* was played in parades, marches, and other processions.

Many contemporary musicians study *jazz* because *it* is the foundation of American music.

 To identify pronoun ambiguity errors, look for answer choices that include simple pronouns (such as *they*, *it*, *these*, *them*, etc.), and at least one answer choice that provides additional (clarifying) information (compare *this* to *this movement* above).

■

PRONOUN LESSON PROBLEMS

I will play the song for Dorothy and <u>he</u>.
₁

1. **A.** NO CHANGE
   B. him
   C. himself
   D. he, who listens

The speaker, about <u>whomever</u> we had been
₂
talking for weeks, spoke with grace and
eloquence.

2. **F.** NO CHANGE
   G. who
   H. whom
   J. OMIT the underlined portion

The after school programs have given the
students something to do with <u>everyone's</u> free
₃
time.

3. **A.** NO CHANGE
   B. their
   C. his or her
   D. one's

Nobody I know who has gone to the water park
thinks <u>they</u> will go again.
₄

4. **F.** NO CHANGE
   G. he or she
   H. he or she, by themselves,
   J. all of them

Continued →

The company was given financial support until
<u>they pulled</u> out of debt.
₅

5. **A.** NO CHANGE
   B. they pulled themselves
   C. it pulled itself
   D. the staff pulled themselves

<u>We</u> seniors are proud to be graduates of such a
₁
fine school.

1. **A.** NO CHANGE
   B. We,
   C. We, the
   D. Us

Waiting for over an hour, we wondered what
<u>had happened to she</u> and Daniel.
₂

2. **F.** NO CHANGE
   G. had happened to her
   H. happened to she
   J. happens to her

Anyone starting ninth grade knows that <u>they</u>
₃
<u>were</u> thrown from the frying pan into the fire.
₃

3. **A.** NO CHANGE
   B. they have been
   C. they will be
   D. he or she has been

When you stand near the conductor, <u>anyone</u>
₄
must be careful not to get hit by his baton.

4. **F.** NO CHANGE
   G. you
   H. one
   J. the audience members

The Polish accordion tradition known as *polka*
has a recognizable rhythmic pattern because of
<u>their</u> consistent use of a triplet meter.
₅

5. **A.** NO CHANGE
   B. the pattern's
   C. their pattern's
   D. the tradition's pattern's

4. PARALLELISM

When you are expressing two or more series of ideas or actions, they should be *parallel* in form. In other words, they should be constructed in the same way. For example:

An excellent employee is open to new ideas, responsive to company needs, and he complies with the company rules of business.

Notice the three phrases that describe the employee:
1. ...open to new ideas... (*adjective-preposition-object*)
2. ...responsive to company needs... (*adjective-preposition-object*)
3. ...he complies with the company rules of business. (*pronoun-verb-preposition-object*)

The first two phrases are similar. In each, an *adjective* ("open" and "responsive") is followed by a *preposition* ("to" in both cases) is followed by an *object* ("new ideas" and "company needs"). In the third phrase, the structure is different. A *pronoun* is followed by a *verb* is followed by a *preposition* is followed by an *object* ("the company rules of business"). The sentence is not parallel in construction.

To correct the sentence, replace "he complies" with the appropriate adjective ("compliant") to match the first two phrases. The words "compliant with" are parallel to "open to" and "responsive to," and the correct sentence reads:

An excellent employee is *open to* new ideas, *responsive to* company needs, and *compliant with* the company rules of business.

> On the ACT, parallelism questions often test the parallelism of *verbs*, so watch out for changing verb forms. Also, look for the following:
> 1. A series of two or more actions or items
> 2. Lists, especially when there are distracting phrases thrown in between the items
> 3. Comparisons (because they always include at least two items)

PARALLELISM LESSON PROBLEMS

Ted would prefer <u>to watch grass grow to</u> finishing his homework.

1. **A.** NO CHANGE
   B. watching grass grow to finishing
   C. to watch grass grow than finishing
   D. watching grass grow than to finish, on time,

While Nick hides in the basement, Louie <u>is looking</u> in the attic.

2. **F.** NO CHANGE
   G. has looked
   H. looks
   J. looked

For most great artists, creative freedom is more important than <u>financially comfortable</u>.

3. **A.** NO CHANGE
   B. being financially comfortable
   C. financial comfort
   D. having a comfortable finance

The coach preaches the idea that all of his players, no matter their current skills, can learn the intricacies of the game and <u>they can become</u> great athletes.

1. **A.** NO CHANGE
   B. become
   C. so they can become
   D. becoming

Jess <u>likes taking</u> the bus more than driving her car because she can read, sleep, or talk to interesting new people.

2. **F.** NO CHANGE
   G. likes to have taken
   H. liked to take
   J. likes to take

For most great artists, <u>being creatively free</u> is more important than being financially comfortable.

3. **A.** NO CHANGE
   B. creative freedom
   C. having the freedom to create
   D. freedom to create

■

Before taking the following quiz, study Sections 1–4. If you're working with a tutor, you will take the quiz during the next lesson. If you're working on your own, take the quiz after reviewing, and do *not* look back to the lessons. After grading, review any topics you struggled on. The quiz is untimed.

GRAMMAR QUIZ 1 (SECTIONS 1–4)

Played in a 1989 chess tournament in Belgrade, the longest game in history <u>ends</u> in a 269-move draw.
₁

1. **A.** NO CHANGE
   B. had ended
   C. will have ended
   D. ended

We wanted to give the package to <u>she</u> and
₂
Marcus, but they had already left town.

2. **F.** NO CHANGE
   G. her
   H. herself
   J. hers

Everyone on the bus, even the shy and uncomfortable freshmen, <u>were laughing and</u>
₃
<u>singing</u> all the way to the museum.
₃

3. **A.** NO CHANGE
   B. laugh and sing
   C. have laughed and sang
   D. was laughing and singing

He reads actively, but when he has to talk in front of a group, he <u>spoke</u> like someone
₄
unfamiliar with the standard rules of grammar.

4. **F.** NO CHANGE
   G. speaks
   H. had spoken
   J. has spoken

<u>Enjoying</u> time with family and friends is more
₅
important than working all day and night.

5. **A.** NO CHANGE
   B. The enjoyment of
   C. To enjoy
   D. Taking enjoyment from

Quiz 1 continued →

The country was largely ignored until <u>they decided</u> to build long-range weapons.
6

6. **F.** NO CHANGE
   G. they had decided
   H. it was decided
   J. it decided

The number of times that I have had to reprimand my employees for wasting time playing on their computers <u>approach</u> the hundreds.
7

7. **A.** NO CHANGE
   B. have approached
   C. will have been approaching
   D. is approaching

He was not only kind to his own children but also <u>showed kindness</u> to the children of others.
8

8. **F.** NO CHANGE
   G. kind
   H. kindly
   J. had kindness

5. PUNCTUATION

The most important aspect of punctuation on the ACT is the correct use of commas and, to a lesser degree, semicolons. The use of apostrophes will be discussed in the Apostrophes & Confused Words section.

Most comma problems on the ACT (over 80%) involve the use of a comma when one is *not* needed. So let's learn about the *correct* uses of commas—once you are familiar with these correct uses, you'll be ready to identify the *unnecessary* uses found on the ACT. First, let's cover some basic terminology. You do not have to memorize any of these terms; they merely aid in teaching the material.

SENTENCE BUILDING BLOCKS

Sentences are generally made up of up to three distinct parts: *independent clauses, dependent clauses,* and *phrases.*

> **Clause** – a sequence of words that contains a subject and its verb
>
> **Independent clause** – a clause that can stand on its own and make sense
>
> **Dependent clause** – a clause that cannot stand on its own because it *depends* on the rest of the sentence to make sense

Let's look at an example to illustrate these parts.

> As he looked up at the blimp, William tripped on the curb.

In the example above, *William tripped on the curb* is the *independent clause*, and *As he looked up at the blimp* is the *dependent clause.*

> **Phrase** – a sequence of two or more words that does not contain a subject and a finite (non-*ing*) verb. We can refer to any group of words that is not a clause as a *phrase.*

By changing the first part of the sentence slightly, we can turn the dependent clause into a *phrase.* The *-ing* form of a verb is a common way to do this.

> Looking up at the blimp, William tripped on the curb.

Because there is no subject in the first part of the sentence, *Looking up at the blimp* is a phrase, modifying *William.*

Sentences must have at least one independent clause. Good writers will add different combinations of dependent clauses and phrases to these independent clauses to make interesting-sounding sentences.

COMMAS

SEPARATING DEPENDENT CLAUSES FROM INDEPENDENT CLAUSES

Commas must be used to separate a dependent clause from a following independent clause of a sentence. For example:

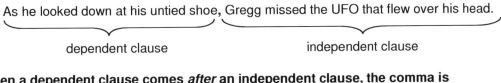

As he looked down at his untied shoe, Gregg missed the UFO that flew over his head.

           dependent clause   independent clause

When a dependent clause comes *after* an independent clause, the comma is unnecessary. Notice that there is no need to *pause* between the clauses in this situation, which is a good reminder that the comma is not needed. For example:

Gregg missed the UFO flying over his head as he looked down at his untied shoe.

        independent clause   dependent clause

OR

Gregg missed the UFO because he was looking down at his untied shoe.

     independent clause   dependent clause

SEPARATING MODIFYING PHRASES FROM INDEPENDENT CLAUSES

Commas must be used to separate modifying phrases from the independent clause of a sentence. This topic was introduced in the Subject-Verb lesson.

Looking down at his untied shoe, Gregg missed the UFO that flew over his head.

      modifying phrase   independent clause

If a modifying phrase shows up in the middle of a clause, there should usually be commas on either side of the phrase. This correctly suggests that the phrase could be removed and the sentence would still make sense. Try this in the following example:

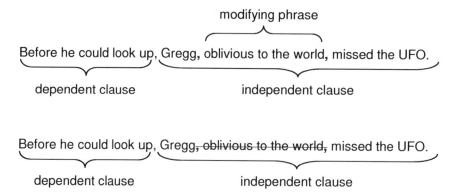

THE ONE-COMMA RULE

You might have two, or even more, commas between the subject and the verb of a sentence, as seen above ("Gregg" is the subject and "missed" is the verb), but you will never have exactly *one* comma between the subject and the verb. This rule will allow you to eliminate many answer choices on punctuation questions:

/ **There will never be <u>exactly one</u> comma between a subject and a verb.**

Incorrect: Gregg oblivious to the world, missed the UFO.
Incorrect: Gregg, oblivious to the world missed the UFO.
Correct: Gregg, oblivious to the world, missed the UFO.

SEPARATING TWO INDEPENDENT CLAUSES

Some sentences will have two independent clauses separated by a conjunction, such as *and*, *or*, or *but* (more on conjunctions later). **A comma must come before the conjunction**, as shown in the following example:

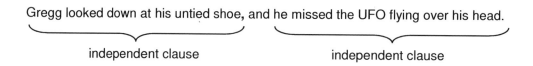

ONE INDEPENDENT CLAUSE WITH TWO ACTIONS

Make sure there are indeed two distinct independent clauses. The following example does not need a comma because the sentence has only one independent clause containing two actions.

Gregg looked down at his untied shoe and missed the UFO flying over his head.

ADJECTIVES

COMMAS BETWEEN ADJECTIVES

Sometimes, a noun will be modified by more than one adjective:

Gregg watched the *bright spinning* UFO.

An easy way to determine whether you should use a comma between adjectives is to see if the word *and* sounds correct between them. If so, you should add the comma:

Gregg watched the bright *and* spinning UFO.

This sounds fine, so the correct sentence should include a comma:

Gregg watched the bright**,** spinning UFO.

Here's another example:

Gregg plans to describe what he's seen in a serious 5,000-word essay.

Since we wouldn't say "serious *and* 5,000-word essay," the correct sentence, as shown, should not have a comma.

NOUNS AS ADJECTIVES

Some students might identify a noun at the beginning of a sentence as the subject of the sentence, when in fact it functions as an adjective, modifying the actual subject. In the example below, the commas suggest that "teacher" is the subject and that "Mr. Fermi" is a modifying phrase (two commas) and could be deleted:

Astronomy teacher, Mr. Fermi, looks forward to reading Gregg's essay.

But remove "Mr. Fermi" and listen to the new sentence:

Astronomy teacher, ~~Mr. Fermi,~~ looks forward to reading Gregg's essay.

Clearly, "Mr. Fermi" cannot be removed. He is the subject of the sentence, and "Astronomy teacher" functions as an adjectival phrase. The correct sentence has no commas:

Astronomy teacher Mr. Fermi looks forward to reading Gregg's essay.

A REMINDER

/ Always test comma-bound phrases by removing them from the sentence. If the new sentence still makes sense, the commas are probably fine. If not, the commas are incorrect.

LISTS

You probably already know that commas are used to separate items in a list:

Gregg will bring a camera, binoculars, a notebook, and a pencil to the park.

The comma before the *and* is optional, but the ACT will typically include it. Make sure you don't add a needless comma after the last item ("a pencil"):

Gregg will bring a camera, binoculars, a notebook, and a pencil, to the park. [remove the comma after "pencil"]

PAUSING

While you read a punctuation question on the ACT, briefly *pause* when you come to a comma. Listen carefully (in your head, of course) for any awkwardness. This approach will help you identify most of the punctuation errors on the test. As stated earlier, the ACT often places commas in places where pauses are unneeded or sound awkward. As you read the following examples, make sure you pause at the commas:

Gregg, looked down at his untied shoe and missed the UFO flying over his head.
Gregg looked down, at his untied shoe and missed the UFO flying over his head.
Gregg looked down at his untied shoe and missed the UFO flying, over his head.

Are the pauses necessary? Do you hear any awkwardness? Try reading without the pauses and see how the sentences sound. In all three examples, the commas are unnecessary.

THE "WHEN IN DOUBT" COMMA RULE

The ACT often places commas in places where they are unneeded. Here's a little rhyme:

/ When in doubt, keep the comma out.

We talked about *pausing* when you see a comma while reading. But you should also do the opposite and try *not* pausing when a no-comma answer is an option. If you don't "hear" a problem, then the no-comma answer is probably correct. For example, should we place a comma after *as* in the example below? (Make sure you read without pausing at this point.)

no pause!

There are important steps one should take before buying a new car, such as reviewing safety ratings, considering resale values, and looking into published reliability reports.

We're not saying the sentence sounds terrible if you *do* pause after *as*, but if the sentence sounds OK *without* pausing, take your chances with the no-comma choice. *When in doubt, keep the comma out.* Indeed, no comma is needed after *as* above.

OTHER PUNCTUATION

SEMICOLONS

Semicolons (;) are similar to periods; the sentences that they separate, however, must be closely related. **Semicolons are used to separate complete sentences**. The following example illustrates the correct use of a semicolon:

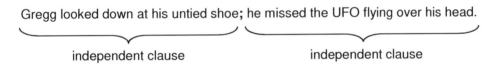

Gregg looked down at his untied shoe; he missed the UFO flying over his head.

independent clause   independent clause

Sometimes semicolons separate items in a list, when those items already contain commas, but this use is uncommon on the ACT.

COLONS

Colons (:) are used to indicate that what follows is an elaboration, summation, or list of what precedes. For example:

Gregg made a list of what he should have ready for the next time a UFO appears: a camera, binoculars, a notebook, and a pencil.

When Gregg told his friends that there had been a UFO sighting, you could describe their reaction in a word: incredulous.

! **Colons generally show up after *independent clauses***, as in the examples above, but some students assume they work before any list. For example:

Incorrect: The list Gregg made for the next time a UFO appears included: a camera, binoculars, a notebook, and a pencil.

Correct: The list Gregg made for the next time a UFO appears included four items: a camera, binoculars, a notebook, and a pencil.
OR
Correct: The list Gregg made for the next time a UFO appears included a camera, binoculars, a notebook, and a pencil.

LONG DASHES

Long dashes (—), also called *em dashes*, are used to note an abrupt break or pause in a sentence or to begin and end a separate phrase or clause. You could think of them as "big" commas. Unless the break is clearly unneeded—you should use the pause idea discussed earlier—it's hard to get dashes wrong.

Gregg decided he would study UFOs for the rest of his life—that he might need to eventually make a living someday did not concern him.

! **Long dashes come in pairs when they separate a phrase or clause from the rest of a sentence:**

His parents—his mom studied botany and his dad was an electrical engineer—both hoped that Gregg's interest was just a passing phase.

■

To identify punctuation errors, look for questions with answer choices that contain changes in punctuation, particularly a variety of comma placements. Watch out for problems that correct one comma error but introduce another.

PUNCTUATION LESSON PROBLEMS

<u>After spending, several years trying to grow a garden</u> Linda decided she'd rather just buy her produce from the store.
1

1. **A.** NO CHANGE
   B. After spending several years trying to grow a garden,
   C. After spending, several years trying to grow a garden,
   D. After spending several years trying to grow a garden

Continued →

Daniel not a large man by any means somehow
seems to dominate our basketball games.

2. F. NO CHANGE
   G. Daniel, not a large man by any means
   H. Daniel not a large man by any means,
   J. Daniel, not a large man by any means,

You should watch the road but you should also
occasionally, check your mirrors.

3. A. NO CHANGE
   B. road; but you should also occasionally,
   C. road, but you should also occasionally
   D. road, but you should also occasionally,

She skated with amazing skill, and finesse as
though she had wings on her back.

4. F. NO CHANGE
   G. skill, and finesse,
   H. skill and finesse;
   J. skill and finesse

The weather may seem nice now. In just a few
weeks, however, the ground will be covered
with snow.

5. A. NO CHANGE
   B. weeks, however the ground
   C. weeks however, the ground,
   D. weeks however the ground

Tommy, friendly as always offered to assist the
confused tourist.

1. A. NO CHANGE
   B. Tommy, friendly as always,
   C. Tommy friendly as always,
   D. Tommy friendly as always

Continued →

<u>Skipping through the sprinklers and rolling</u>
₂
<u>through the grass,</u> Katie became a wet and
₂
grassy mess.

2. **F.** NO CHANGE
   G. Skipping through the sprinklers and rolling through the grass
   H. Skipping through the sprinklers, and rolling through the grass
   J. Skipping through the sprinklers, and rolling through the grass,

Even though many <u>voters apparently unaware</u>
₃
<u>of the country's many problems,</u> are happy with
₃
the incumbent, I feel that we are ready for a
new leader.

3. **A.** NO CHANGE
   B. voters, apparently unaware of the country's many problems,
   C. voters, apparently unaware of the country's many problems
   D. voters apparently unaware of the country's many problems

George rocked the <u>boat many</u> people fell out.
₄

4. **F.** NO CHANGE
   G. boat, many
   H. boat; many
   J. boat in that many

Pete's <u>Bistro, the busiest and noisiest</u> restaurant
₅
on the street, caters to a motley crew of tourists
and locals.

5. **A.** NO CHANGE
   B. Bistro, the busiest, and noisiest
   C. Bistro, the busiest, and noisiest,
   D. Bistro, the busiest and noisiest,

<u>Astronaut, Scott Kelly now</u> officially holds the
₆
record for the longest consecutive time in space
by an American.

6. **F.** NO CHANGE
   G. Astronaut Scott Kelly now
   H. Astronaut, Scott Kelly, now
   J. Astronaut: Scott Kelly now,

Some educators think that computer
coding—the mysterious language that makes
our computers and phones <u>work</u> should be
₇
taught to students starting in elementary
school.

7. **A.** NO CHANGE
   B. work,
   C. work—
   D. work:

6. FRAGMENTS

Several types of fragments show up on the ACT. You can identify them by looking for the specific parts described below.

DEPENDENT CLAUSE

First, let's define the word *conjunction*:

Conjunction – A word that links the parts of a sentence together.

There are several different types of conjunctions (we'll learn about others soon). One kind, called a **subordinate conjunction** (don't worry about memorizing the name), turns an independent clause into a dependent clause when placed in front of the independent clause. Remember that a dependent clause, on its own, is not a complete sentence—it's a fragment.

after	even though	though
although	if	unless
as	if only	until
as if	in order that	when
as long as	now that	whenever
as though	once	where
because	rather than	whereas
before	since	wherever
even if	so that	while

When you spot one of these words at the beginning of a sentence, look out for a fragment. For example:

Fragment: *As* the forest fire burned, bellowing smoke into the air.

The sentence lacks an independent clause. Note that if the word "As" were removed, the sentence would be an independent clause.

-*ING* WORD USED AS A VERB

As taught in the Verb Tense lesson, a word in the *-ing* form—on its own—does not function as a verb. When the subject of a sentence lacks a verb, the sentence is a fragment. For example:

Fragment: The firefighters, many from hundreds of miles away, *preparing* to fight the fire.

The subject "firefighters" lacks a verb. You could fix this sentence by adding "are" or "were" in front of "preparing."

PRONOUN PHRASE

Watch out for phrases that begin with pronouns such as *that*, *which*, *who*, or *whom*. Especially watch out for *that*; the others are easier to identify because they will usually be preceded by a comma. The following are all fragments because the subjects ("fire," "fire," and "residents") lack verbs:

> Fragment: The fire *that* burned over 1,000 acres last summer.
> Fragment: The forest fire, *which* was likely started when someone threw a cigarette from his car.
> Fragment: The residents, *who* lived in the small mountain town all their lives.

"THAT" CLAUSE

Sometimes the word *that* indicates a clause within a clause. This so-called *"that" clause* must have its own subject and verb. For example:

> Fragment: The newspaper reporter said *that* residents returning to their homes.

The subject of the "that" clause ("residents") lacks a verb.

While less common, *question* words such as *why*, *where*, *who*, *what*, *how*, etc. can also create their own clauses, so watch out for them.

MODIFYING PHRASE

The ACT will often use long modifying phrases to disguise fragments. Try removing modifying phrases to find the barebones sentence.

> Fragment: The fire captain, one of the most experienced firefighters in the county and not surprisingly the first on the scene.

The subject "captain" lacks a verb.

SEMICOLON

Watch out for fragments when two clauses are separated by a semicolon. As taught in the Punctuation section, a semicolon (like a period) separates two *independent clauses*.

Fragment: Jerry is a veteran firefighter; having worked his way up to captain.

Fragment: Many unpredictable factors must be considered when fighting a fire; changes in the weather and the direction and velocity of the wind perhaps the most significant.

The second phrase in each of the previous examples is a fragment. Both semicolons should be commas.

The second clause in each of the previous examples is a fragment.

■

A fragment usually contains one of the following:

1. Dependent clause (look for a subordinate conjunction)
2. -*ING* word used as a verb
3. Pronoun phrase
4. "That" clause
5. Modifying phrase
6. Semicolon

FRAGMENTS LESSON PROBLEMS

Bertrand Russell's *The Problems of Philosophy,* often one of the first books assigned in introductory Philosophy courses because of its ability to make the abstruse comprehendible.

1. **A.** NO CHANGE
   B. *The Problems of Philosophy,* is often
   C. *The Problems of Philosophy* is often
   D. *The Problems of Philosophy,* often being

After the committee released its findings on the widespread use of cell phones, scientists warned that there may be a link between cell-phone use and brain tumors.

2. **F.** NO CHANGE
   G. The committee released
   H. The committee releasing
   J. After the committee releasing

Continued →

Although better known as a movie star, Austrian actress <u>Hedy Lamarr, who</u> became a pioneer in the field of wireless communications following her emigration to the United States.

3. **A.** NO CHANGE
   B. Hedy Lamarr
   C. Hedy Lamarr who
   D. Hedy Lamarr; who

When choosing a health insurance <u>company; choose</u> carefully.

4. **F.** NO CHANGE
   G. company. Choose
   H. company, choose
   J. company, and you should choose

The <u>sculptor, carefully shaping</u> with his hands, transformed clay into art.

5. **A.** NO CHANGE
   B. sculptor carefully shaping
   C. sculptor carefully shaped
   D. sculptor, who carefully shaping

Jerry said that climbing <u>trees, an activity not</u> for everyone because of its inherent risks.

1. **A.** NO CHANGE
   B. trees is not an activity
   C. trees, an activity that is not
   D. trees, not an activity

Most <u>people showing</u> little concern for agriculture and farming, even though these fields were keys to the rise of human civilization.

2. **F.** NO CHANGE
   G. people show
   H. people, who show
   J. people, showing

The so-called wind car, possibly the first automobile, which used a machine similar to a windmill to drive gears, which in turn drove the <u>wheels, designed</u> by da Vigevano in 1335.

3. **A.** NO CHANGE
   B. wheels, was designed
   C. wheels; it was designed
   D. wheels. The car was designed

Continued →

When turning right, make sure
                4

to look over your right shoulder for

pedestrians and bikers.

Most of the overnight campers know that the
                        5

ghost stories being told to scare them from
     5

leaving their bunks in the middle of the night.

4. **F.** NO CHANGE
   G. right; make
   H. right; you should make
   J. right; it is a good idea to make

5. **A.** NO CHANGE
   B. that the ghost stories are being
   C. that the ghost stories, which are being
   D. that the ghost stories

7. RUN-ONS

FANBOYS CONJUNCTIONS

Most run-on errors on the ACT involve a *compound sentence*, which is just two independent clauses linked with a conjunction called a FANBOYS, or *coordinating*, conjunction (once again, you don't have to memorize the official name). These are the seven FANBOYS conjunctions:

for, and, nor, but, or, yet, so

To help remember these conjunctions, use the acronym **FANBOYS**: **F**or-**A**nd-**N**or-**B**ut-**O**r-**Y**et-**S**o. You might also notice that each conjunction is either two or three letters long. (Many other conjunctions are longer.)

/ **The FANBOYS conjunctions, listed above, are the only conjunctions that can link two independent clauses. As explained in the Punctuation section, when they link independent clauses, they should be preceded with a comma.** For example:

In his books and essays, Thoreau challenged the traditional ideas of society**, and** he was thus both criticized and praised by his readers.

RUN-ONS ON THE ACT

From the Punctuation section, we know that two independent clauses must be separated by (1) a comma *and* a FANBOYS conjunction or (2) a semicolon—otherwise, the sentence is a run-on. On the ACT, there are three common types of run-on sentences related to this rule:

COMMA BUT NO CONJUNCTION

The first one, called a *comma splice*, involves two independent clauses separated by a comma but lacking a conjunction. For example:

Yoshio thought that his printer was broken**,** it simply was out of ink.

independent clause   independent clause

To correct this run-on, simply add an appropriate conjunction:

Yoshio thought that his printer was broken, *but* it simply was out of ink.

CONJUNCTION BUT NO COMMA

The second type of run-on also has two independent clauses. This one correctly includes a conjunction but is lacking a comma before the conjunction. For example:

Yoshio thought that his printer was broken and this was because the page came out white.

        independent clause   independent clause

Since the second part of the sentence is an independent clause, a comma must come before the conjunction. The correct sentence should read:

Yoshio thought that his printer was broken, and this was because the page came out white.

A more eloquent and succinct way to correct the error is to turn the second clause into a dependent clause or modifying phrase. The ACT may correct run-ons in this way:

Yoshio thought that his printer was broken because the page came out white.
OR
Because the page came out white, Yoshio thought that his printer was broken.

NO COMMA, NO CONJUNCTION

Some compound sentences lack the comma *and* the FANBOYS conjunction. For example:

The page came out white Yoshio, thus, thought that his printer was broken.

You can add a comma and an appropriate FANBOYS conjunction—such as "and" or "so"—after the word "white," or just add a semicolon:

The page came out white; Yoshio, thus, thought that his printer was broken.

NON-*FANBOYS* TRANSITION WORDS

Watch out for transition words between independent clauses that are *not* FANBOYS conjunctions. These sentences may sound fine but are often considered run-ons. For example:

I practiced for hours while I taped myself, *then* I listened back to see how I sounded.

This sentence is a run-on. Use a FANBOYS conjunction, such as *and*, to correct the error. A good test is to notice that the word *then* could be moved around within the sentence (a FANBOYS conjunction is generally "stuck" between the clauses):

I practiced for hours while I taped myself, *and then* I listened back to see how I sounded.
I practiced for hours while I taped myself, *and* I *then* listened back to see how I sounded.
I practiced for hours while I taped myself, *and* I listened back *then* to see how I sounded.

The following table lists some other transition words commonly used (incorrectly) to link independent clauses. This list will hopefully give you an idea of what to look for:

even so	in fact	on the other hand
furthermore	in other words	similarly
however	moreover	therefore
in addition	nevertheless	thus

Note that most of these words should be bound with commas. For example:

Some think this video game is easy; *however,* you will discover that it is quite hard.
OR
Some think this video game is easy; you will discover, *however,* that it is quite hard.

■

> To identify run-on errors, look for questions with answer choices that contain various ways to connect independent clauses, including commas, conjunctions, periods, and semicolons.

RUN-ONS LESSON PROBLEMS

Most people rarely get to see the <u>sunrise they</u> are asleep that early in the morning.
[1]

1. **A.** NO CHANGE
    B. sunrise and they
    C. sunrise because they
    D. sunrise, and because they

Continued →

Kevin had run slowly at first, he then
₂
accelerated quickly to avoid the pursuing
tacklers, who, to the delight of the crowd, fell
harmlessly at Kevin's feet.

2. **F.** NO CHANGE
   G. Kevin had run slowly at first; he
   H. While Kevin had run slowly at first;
   he
   J. Kevin had run slowly at first he

Many health experts agree that young people
are not active <u>enough, this</u> inactivity is likely a
₃
result of the temptations of such sedentary
activities as watching television or working on
the internet.

3. **A.** NO CHANGE
   B. enough this
   C. enough. This
   D. enough and this

Many people now watch more shows on their
computers than on actual <u>televisions, and I</u>
₄
<u>wonder</u> if the end of the television is near.
₄

4. Which of following alternatives to the
   underlined portion would NOT be
   acceptable?

   F. televisions, leading me to wonder
   G. televisions I wonder
   H. televisions. I wonder
   J. televisions, which makes me
   wonder

At the end of the last day of school, the
students <u>celebrated; however,</u> the teachers,
₅
with stacks of ungraded tests on their desks,
had much work ahead.

5. **A.** NO CHANGE
   B. celebrated, however,
   C. celebrated, however
   D. celebrated however

Playing a sport and learning an instrument offer good analogies for effective <u>studying, because</u>
₁
these activities involve considerable practice to master, one can see the obvious benefits of hard work and persistence.

1. **A.** NO CHANGE
   B. studying because
   C. studying; because
   D. studying, and this is because

The book was written without regard to punctuation or <u>paragraphs this unconformity</u>
₂
made it difficult to understand.

2. **F.** NO CHANGE
   G. paragraphs, this unconformity
   H. paragraphs, an unconformity that
   J. paragraphs and this unconformity

He spoke with his <u>hands, but his voice</u> was
₃
silent.

3. **A.** NO CHANGE
   B. hands but his voice
   C. hands, his voice
   D. hands his voice

He worked tirelessly to finish the experiment on the health benefits of soy <u>beans because the</u>
₄
<u>health conference was</u> only a few weeks away.
₄

4. **F.** NO CHANGE
   G. beans, the health conference was
   H. beans, the health conference being
   J. beans. The health conference being

The book *Dune*, by Frank Herbert, is the world's best-selling science fiction novel and has won both the Nebula and Hugo <u>Awards, in other words,</u> it's a sci-fi classic.
₅

5. **A.** NO CHANGE
   B. Awards, in other words
   C. Awards, in other words;
   D. Awards; in other words,

8. MISPLACED WORDS

MOVING WORDS TO AVOID AMBIGUITY

Sometimes the order of the words in a sentence creates an ambiguity. Look at the following example:

There was a scratch on the new wood table right in the center.

This sentence literally suggests that the wood table is "in the center." Likely, this is not the intended meaning. Move the related words together in the sentence to remove the error, as in the corrected version below:

There was a scratch *right in the center* of the new wood table.

Here is another example:

The ice cream competition will be the largest ever with ice-cream samples from over 100 contestants kept in a large freezer.

Our hearts go out to those poor contestants in the freezer. The following sentences remove the ambiguity:

The ice cream competition will be the largest ever with over 100 contestants. The ice-cream samples will be kept in a large freezer.

MOVING WORDS TO AVOID AWKWARDNESS

Sometimes the order of the words just plain sounds wrong:

Computer Aided Design offers at the same time opportunities to be artistic and technical.

Perhaps the meaning is clear, but the sentence doesn't sound great, does it? The following corrects the awkwardness:

Computer Aided Design offers opportunities to be artistic and technical *at the same time*.

IMPROPER MODIFIERS

As we've seen in the previous sections, dependent clauses and phrases can act as modifiers for a noun or nouns in the sentence. On the ACT, *improper modifiers* (sometimes called *danglers*), which are usually at the beginning of a sentence, appear to modify an illogical noun because of this noun's closeness to the modifying phrase. **You should generally make sure that the noun meant to be modified is as close as possible to a leading modifying phrase.** For example:

   With power and skill, the volleyball was spiked over the net by Jill.

The modifying phrase in this sentence is *With power and skill.* It is obviously meant to modify *Jill*, but it seems to modify *the volleyball.* The sentence's intended meaning may be obvious, but the sentence should be corrected to read:

   With power and skill, Jill spiked the volleyball over the net.

Sometimes modifying phrases show up at the ends of sentences. These are usually correct, even though the noun they modify is at the beginning. Here are two examples:

   Jill spiked the volleyball over the net *with power and skill.*
   Jill spiked the volleyball over the net, *hitting it with all her strength.*

Again, these are both correct.

■

There are two ways to identify misplaced words questions:

1. Look for questions with answer choices that give you the option to move the underlined portion to another part of the sentence.
2. Look for questions with answer choices that rewrite a large portion of the sentence, often an entire clause. As you might imagine, words or phrases are repositioned in these answer choices.

APPROACH TO MISPLACED WORDS QUESTIONS

Even though you may use the answer choices to *identify* a misplaced word problem (as described above), try to answer these misplaced words questions without scrutinizing the answer choices right away. Just use the passage. This *aggressive* approach will often help you because the answer choices on Misplaced Words questions can be wordy and confusing.

MISPLACED WORDS LESSON PROBLEMS

You can use this phone card to call your sister and tell her about the expensive dinner you had <u>for less than a dollar</u>.
₁

1. The best placement for the underlined portion would be:

   A. where it is now.
   B. after the word *sister.*
   C. after the word *about.*
   D. after the word *dinner.*

Corporations are more <u>likely to hire college</u>
₂
<u>graduates with advanced degrees than smaller</u>
₂
<u>companies</u>.
₂

2. F. NO CHANGE
   G. likely to hire, as opposed to smaller companies, college graduates with advanced degrees
   H. likely to hire than smaller companies college graduates with advanced degrees
   J. likely than smaller companies to hire college graduates with advanced degrees

After sneaking out the window to play games with his friends, <u>his parents were the last people</u>
₃
<u>Sean expected to run into at the arcade</u>.
₃

3. A. NO CHANGE
   B. Sean least expected to run into his parents at the arcade
   C. running into his parents was the last thing Sean expected at the arcade
   D. his parents, at the arcade, were the last people Sean expected to run into

After sleeping through the entire semester, <u>a shock was receiving the A to Chrissie</u>.
₄

4. F. NO CHANGE
   G. receiving an A was a shock to Chrissie
   H. Chrissie was shocked that she received an A
   J. Chrissie's A was a shock to her

The writer discussed the negative impact of graffiti <u>in the last chapter of his book.</u>
₁

1. The best placement for the underlined portion would be:
   A. where it is now.
   B. after the word *discussed.*
   C. after the word *negative.*
   D. at the beginning of the sentence (capitalizing *in*, ending the underlined portion with a comma, and making the *T* in *The* lowercase).

After hearing the CD of the live performance, <u>our disappointment in missing the show was</u> ₂ <u>unbearable.</u>
₂

2. F. NO CHANGE
   G. our disappointment in having missed the show was unbearable
   H. we were, because of having missed the show, unbearably disappointed
   J. we were unbearably disappointed about missing the show

The new navigation <u>system, when a button is</u> ₃ <u>pressed, will speak directions to the driver, on</u> ₃ <u>the steering wheel.</u>
₃

3. A. NO CHANGE
   B. system will speak directions, when a button is pressed on the steering wheel to the driver
   C. system will speak directions to the driver when a button is pressed on the steering wheel
   D. system, will speak directions to the driver, when a button is pressed on the steering wheel

With strength and endurance not found among any of the other <u>competitors, Greg Lemond's</u> ₄ <u>victory was yet again.</u>
₄

4. F. NO CHANGE
   G. competitors, Greg Lemond rode to victory yet again
   H. competitors, to victory yet again Greg Lemond rode
   J. competitors as Greg Lemond rode to victory yet again

■

Before taking the following quiz, study Sections 5–8. If you're working with a tutor, you will take the quiz during the next lesson. If you're working on your own, take the quiz after reviewing, and do *not* look back to the lessons. After grading, review any topics you struggled on. The quiz is untimed.

GRAMMAR QUIZ 2 (SECTIONS 5–8)

One reason to keep your house <u>clean, is that</u> a
₁
tidy environment leads to a relaxed mind.

1. **A.** NO CHANGE
    B. clean is: that
    C. clean is, that,
    D. clean is that

When you <u>eat too much ice cream, as the child</u>
₂
<u>learned the hard way</u>, you might get a
₂
stomachache.

2. **F.** NO CHANGE
    G. eat too much, as the child learned the hard way, ice cream
    H. eat too much ice cream, as learned the hard way by the child
    J. eat, as the child learned the hard way, too much ice cream

<u>Now that you understand</u> the basics of
₃
electricity, particularly the dangers involved when you are working with bare wires.

3. **A.** NO CHANGE
    B. Now you understand
    C. Now that you have an understanding of
    D. Now you understand that

Considered an expert in her field, the <u>doctor's</u>
₄
<u>research papers</u> were widely read and studied.
₄

4. **F.** NO CHANGE
    G. doctor wrote research papers that
    H. doctor's papers of research
    J. research papers of the doctor

I walked <u>slowly, away from the bear</u> as though
₅
there was nothing out of the ordinary.

5. **A.** NO CHANGE
    B. slowly away, from the bear,
    C. slowly, away from the bear,
    D. slowly away from the bear

Quiz 2 continued →

One of the best ways to keep your house <u>tidy,</u>
<u>donating,</u> which not only minimizes your "stuff"
but also is good for your community.

The storm hit last <u>night, and the</u> electricity was
out for over eight hours.

The lawyer <u>working tirelessly to</u> give her client
a decent chance in court, even though the
evidence strongly suggests guilt.

He thought the math class would be <u>easy, then</u>
his class started working on limits.

The <u>owner or, as he likes to call himself, the</u>
<u>boss,</u> of the business rules with an iron fist.

6. **F.** NO CHANGE
   G. tidy, which is donating
   H. tidy, by donating
   J. tidy is by donating

7. Which of the following alternatives to the underlined portion would NOT be acceptable?

   A. night; the
   B. night and the
   C. night—the
   D. night. The

8. **F.** NO CHANGE
   G. works tirelessly to
   H. had been working with tirelessness to
   J. tirelessly work and

9. **A.** NO CHANGE
   B. easy then
   C. easy but then
   D. easy, but then

10. **F.** NO CHANGE
    G. owner, or, as he likes to call himself, the boss,
    H. owner, or as he likes to call himself the boss
    J. owner or as he likes to call himself the boss,

9. REDUNDANCIES

The ACT likes to make sure that you're paying attention by testing *redundancies*. A redundancy involves saying the same thing twice, thus using more words than necessary. The ACT typically tests this by using words that mean about the same thing.

> That school's water polo team is favored to repeat and duplicate its championship of last year.

Of course, to *repeat* and to *duplicate* mean about the same thing. Eliminate one of them to correct the sentence

> That school's water polo team is favored to *repeat* its championship of last year.

Here's another example that tests the meaning of a word.

> If you start your report the day before it is due, your teachers will think you are a procrastinator who is always waiting until the last minute to begin working on something.

What is a procrastinator? A procrastinator is one who is always waiting until the last minute to begin working on something. The last part of the sentence is redundant and should be eliminated.

> If you start your report the day before it is due, your teachers will think you are a procrastinator.

 To identify redundancy questions, look for obvious redundancies in the answer choices (e.g. "repeat and duplicate"). You might also look for answer choices that all *seem* grammatically correct, with one choice that deletes part of the sentence.

SHORT ANSWERS

! **The correct answer on redundancy questions will almost always be the shortest one (since any redundancy is removed).**

This is an important tip because, as stated above, redundancies questions often have considerable variation in answer choice lengths. Note: Some redundancies questions include an "OMIT the underlined portion" answer choice. This choice, which shortens the passage more than the others, is usually the correct one.

REDUNDANCIES LESSON PROBLEMS

The company is able to stay on top of the tech world because of its emphasis on <u>new</u> innovations.
₁

1. **A.** NO CHANGE
   B. the newness of its
   C. new and current
   D. OMIT the underlined portion.

The judge was forced to <u>free the man and let him go</u> after the judge determined that the evidence had been tampered with.
₂

2. **F.** NO CHANGE
   G. free the man
   H. let the now free man go
   J. free and liberate the man

The tree <u>swayed and moved back and forth</u> in the strong wind.
₃

3. **A.** NO CHANGE
   B. swayed
   C. swayed back
   D. swayed back and forth

Because the conference room is flooded, we'll have to have the community meeting <u>later, at a future date</u>.
₄

4. **F.** NO CHANGE
   G. later, in a while
   H. at a future date
   J. at a later, future date

You have to score at least 90 points <u>or more</u> on the company's written test to be considered for the job.
₁

1. **A.** NO CHANGE
   B. but no less than that
   C. and no less than that
   D. OMIT the underlined portion.

In the last sentence of the book, the author <u>concluded by hinting</u> that everything had been a dream.
₂

2. **F.** NO CHANGE
   G. concluded and hinted
   H. finished writing by hinting
   J. hinted

Continued →

Diego Maradona is without question one of the
<u>fastest and nimblest</u> players soccer has ever
    3
known.

Before Sir Edmund Hillary conquered Mount
Everest in 1953, many agreed that its steep and
treacherous slopes <u>were insurmountable and</u>
                                        4
<u>would never be climbed</u>.
             4

3. **A.** NO CHANGE
    B. fastest, quickest, and nimblest
    C. fastest, nimble and agile
    D. fastest

4. **F.** NO CHANGE
    G. were insurmountably unclimbable
    H. were insurmountable
    J. could not be mounted by climbing

10. APOSTROPHES & CONFUSED WORDS

Sometimes students confuse words that have similar *appearance* or *sound*. For example, you may come across words such as *principal* and *principle* (a *principal* works at your school—he's your "pal" (get it?); a *principle* is a rule or standard). As we'll discuss in the Comparisons lesson, *then* and *than* are also often confused. In a comparison, use *than* (Kyle is happier *than* Maddie). There are hundreds of other confused words, but luckily most of the confused words tested on the ACT have to do with the more manageable subject of apostrophes (').
Apostrophes have two general uses:

1. To indicate that letters have been removed from a word—this is called a *contraction*. For example, *they're* is a contraction of *they are* (note the missing *a*).
2. To show possession. For example, this is *Kathleen's* book. (The book belongs to Kathleen.)

APOSTROPHES USED FOR CONTRACTIONS

The most commonly-tested contractions are the ones that sound like other words. For example,

This is there cooler, so please put it over they're. Their going to be here soon.

If you read the sentence out loud, it sounds fine. But do you see the three errors? The following words may sound alike, but they have different uses: *their* should be used as a possessive for they; *there* should be used to indicate a place; and *they're* should be a contraction for *they are*. The following corrects the sentence:

This is *their* cooler, so please put it over *there*. *They're* going to be here soon.

Here are a few other commonly-confused words involving contractions:

your/you're
The word *your* is used as a possessive for *you* (This is *your* book). The word *you're* is a contraction of *you* and *are* (*You're* going to have to study hard to raise your score).

its/it's/its'

This one can be tricky. The word *its* is a possessive of *it* (*Its* windows are dirty). The word *it's* is a contraction of *it* and *is* (*It's* a lovely day to clean the windows). Finally, *its'* is not a word; it is always incorrect.

There are dozens of other contractions that might show up, but they typically fall into one of two categories. Either the apostrophe replaces the *o* in *not* (*can't = can not, wouldn't = would not*) or the apostrophe replaces the beginning of a *to-be verb* (*I'm = I am, he'd = he would, you'll = you will*). Note that the contraction of *will not* is *won't*, an unexpected change in spelling.

APOSTROPHES USED FOR POSSESSIVES

Apostrophes are often used to indicate that something or someone *possesses* something else. For example:

This is Jeff's car. (The car belongs to Jeff.)

There are three general rules to remember when turning a noun into a possessive:

1. If the word is singular, add *'s*. (Most grammarians, including the ACT test writers, require the *'s* even if the word already ends with an *s*; see the second example below.):
    Jeff → Jeff's car
    moss → the moss's growth
2. If the word is plural and ends with an *s*, add an apostrophe to the end of the word:
    girls → the girls' room
    the Smiths → the Smiths' house
3. If the word is plural and does *not* end with an *s*, add *'s* to the end of the word:
    children → the children's hospital (not *childrens'*)
    men → the men's room (not *mens'*)

PRONOUN POSSESSIVES

As you've already seen (*their, your, its*), pronouns can be used as possessives. **These words do *not* use apostrophes, even if they end with an *s*.** The following are some examples:

your = possessive of *you*
their = possessive of *they*
my = possessive of *I*
his = possessive of *he*
its = possessive of *it*
whose = possessive of *who*

The pronoun possessive may change if it comes at the end of a phrase. Trust your ear:

The bike is *yours*, but the skateboard is *mine*.

APPROACH TO APOSTROPHES ON THE ACT

The ACT often mixes contractions and possessives on the same question, so the first step is to decide which is appropriate. Here's a good test: **first check for a contraction.** If, after expanding the word, the sentence sounds correct, then the contraction is correct. For example:

The day's beautiful at this time—don't you think?

Expand the contraction, and you have:

The *day is* beautiful at this time—don't you think?

This sounds fine. The word is a contraction and the apostrophe is used correctly. Here's another example:

My *friend's* are going to be here soon. → My *friend is* are going to be here soon.

Clearly this is incorrect. Either the word *friend's* is a possessive or (as is the case here) the apostrophe should be removed.

■

To identify **apostrophe errors**, look for answer choices that contain variations in apostrophes for the same word (*aardvark's, aardvarks'*). Also, look for possessive pronouns and pronoun contractions (e.g. *your, you're, yours*).

To identify **confused words** errors, look for answer choices with words that look similar (e.g. *principle, principal*).

APOSTROPHES & CONFUSED WORDS LESSON PROBLEMS

The <u>ancient shells shape</u> tells scientists much
₁
about the shape of the organism that inhabited
it.

1. **A.** NO CHANGE
   B. ancient shells' shape
   C. ancient shell's shape
   D. ancient's shell's shape

Nicholson Baker's first book, *The Mezzanine*,
with <u>its</u> copious digressions and footnotes,
₂
influenced many writers to come.

2. **F.** NO CHANGE
   G. it's
   H. its'
   J. their

Poison oak is difficult to identify because <u>its</u>
₃
propensity to imitate the appearance of nearby
plants.

3. **A.** NO CHANGE
   B. of its
   C. it's
   D. of it's

Since the members of the science team will
work along the coast, <u>they're going</u> to
₄
focus their report on beach erosion.

4. **F.** NO CHANGE
   G. their going
   H. theirs is one
   J. there will be

Small print on the labels of containers is more
likely to <u>elude then</u> attract the attention of
₅
consumers.

5. **A.** NO CHANGE
   B. elude than
   C. allude then
   D. allude than

<u>It's in your best interest</u> to keep your hands
₁
inside the vehicle during the tour.

1. **A.** NO CHANGE
   B. Its in your best interest
   C. Its' in your best interest
   D. It's your best interest

Continued →

Only a few of the <u>country's regions</u> are named

2

using the native language.

2. **F.** NO CHANGE
   G. countries' regions'
   H. country's region's
   J. countries regions

<u>Your going</u> to regret staying up late because

3

classes start an hour earlier tomorrow.

3. **A.** NO CHANGE
   B. You will
   C. Your
   D. You're going

<u>Giraffes long necks</u> allow them to reach tree

4

leaves and other foods that most other animals

cannot.

4. **F.** NO CHANGE
   G. Giraffe's long necks
   H. Giraffes' long neck's
   J. Giraffes' long necks

11. IDIOM

Idiom has to do with the manner or style of a language. Idiom rules are less predictable and consistent (and, thus, more difficult to remember) than most of the other grammar rules in this tutorial. The good news is that many of the idiom errors will simply sound wrong to your ear.

PREPOSITIONAL IDIOMS

Most idiom mistakes on the ACT have to do with an incorrect preposition following an adjective or verb. For example:

> We only wanted to look at the paintings; we were *indifferent **of*** the sculpture exhibit.

Idiom dictates that, in general, the preposition *to* (not *of*) should be used after *indifferent*. There is no real way to predict this rule—the choice seems arbitrary. This is why these idiom rules can be difficult. You must either memorize from a long list of rules or (hopefully) rely on your ear. The correct sentence should read:

> We only wanted to look at the paintings; we were *indifferent **to*** the sculpture exhibit.

Here is another common mistake:

> The oil paintings don't look *different **than*** the acrylic ones.

Idiom dictates that the preposition *from* should follow *different*:

> The oil paintings don't look *different **from*** the acrylic ones.

SAME WORD, DIFFERENT PREPOSITIONS

Complicating matters, sometimes the same word can take different prepositions depending on the context. For example:

> We *agreed **to*** go to the museum together, but we could not *agree **on*** how to get there. I hope you *agree **with*** me that walking is out of the question.

Fortunately, most of these rules will sound natural to your ear. For example, you probably would never say: we could not *agree to* how to get there. It just sounds wrong.

LEARNING IDIOM

The best way to learn idioms is by hearing (or reading) correct idioms. Simply put, this is how we all learn to speak correctly. In other words, there's no real trick or shortcut to learning idioms. That's the bad news. The good news is that many students will already "hear" the idiom errors that show up on the test. And for those who struggle with these idiom rules, keep in mind that any one test will probably include only one or two idiom questions—they are not a huge part of the ACT.

■

 To identify prepositional idiom errors, look for questions with answer choices that contain a variety of *prepositions* (e.g., *of, with, over, to,* etc.). If necessary, review prepositions in the Subject-Verb lesson.

If you expect to play in the game, you must <u>abide by</u> the coach's rules.
₁

1. **A.** NO CHANGE
   B. abide to
   C. abide from
   D. be abiding with

The running back <u>crashed through</u> the
₂
opposing tacklers and never looked back.

2. Which of the following alternatives to the underlined portion would NOT be acceptable?

   F. fought for
   G. muscled through
   H. ran around
   J. jumped over

The author, Sir Arthur Conan Doyle, is <u>famous</u>
₃
<u>for</u> his Sherlock Holmes mystery novels.
₃

3. **A.** NO CHANGE
   B. famous in
   C. famous by
   D. famous of

Continued →

After years of struggle, the country of Kosovo is finally <u>independent by</u> Serbia.
₄

4. **F.** NO CHANGE
   G. independent with
   H. independent of
   J. having independence from

When the traveler arrived <u>via</u> her destination,
₅
the first thing she did was buy a tourist map.

5. **A.** NO CHANGE
   B. at
   C. over
   D. with

IDIOM: COMMON MISTAKES

There are hundreds of common idiom mistakes. Again, these rules are generally not as predictable as the other grammar rules in this tutorial. Here is an example:

The reason I can't compete in the track meet today is because I have a sprained ankle.

This sentence may sound OK, but it is actually idiomatically incorrect because *is because* is following *reason*. The sentence would be correct with *that* in place of *is because*:

The *reason* I can't compete in the track meet today is *that* I have a sprained ankle.

There is no universal rule here—just an idiom rule that you may have to memorize.

These errors are hard to predict and are thus potentially difficult to prepare for. But the good news is: they don't show up very often on the ACT. Thus, unless you have a lot of time, you might choose to just read them over—don't worry about making flashcards and memorizing at first. Try the homework at the end of the section. If you struggle, then you should consider spending some time making flash cards and memorizing. If you get most of them correct, your ear is in good shape and you won't have to put significant time into memorizing the rules.

The following lists a number of common idiom mistakes:

a lot → very much

    Incorrect: I like track and field events *a lot*.

    Correct: I like track and field events *very much*.

around → about

Avoid *around* to designate time, distance, or any other quantity.

    Incorrect: The meet starts at *around* noon.

    Correct: The meet starts at *about* noon.

at

    Incorrect: Where is the pole *at* for the pole vault?

    Correct: Where is the pole for the pole vault?

at once

The words "at once" are generally used with the conjunction "and" in the following way: something is "at once (this) *and* (that)."

    Incorrect: The book was *at once* unsophisticated because of its everyday writing and themes, but it's certainly enjoyable because of its interesting characters.

    Correct: The book was *at once* simple-minded because of its everyday writing and themes *and* enjoyable because of its interesting characters.

badly → desperately

    Incorrect: She *badly* wants to win the decathlon.

    Correct: She *desperately* wants to win the decathlon.

because (used after *reason*) **→ that**

    Incorrect: The reason she runs so quickly is *because* she trains hard.

    Correct: The reason she runs so quickly is *that* she trains hard.

being as/being that → because

    Incorrect: *Being that* she trains so hard, she is difficult to beat.

    Correct: *Because* she trains so hard, she is difficult to beat.

bunch → group

Do not use *bunch* when referring to people.

> Incorrect: There is a *bunch* of athletes getting ready for the marathon.

> Correct: There is a *group* of athletes getting ready for the marathon

center around → center on

A center is a single, fixed point and as such cannot move or exist *around* something.

> Incorrect: The news conference *centered around* the Iraq war.

> Correct: The news conference *centered on* the Iraq war.

flunk → fail

> Incorrect: He may be the best at pole vaulting, but he *flunked* his history quiz.

> Correct: He may be the best at pole vaulting, but he *failed* his history quiz.

former/latter

Former and *latter* should only be used when choosing between *two* things.

> Incorrect: After visiting Paris, Madrid, and London, I prefer the *latter*.

> Correct: After visiting Paris, Madrid, and London, I prefer London.

graduate

Graduate should be followed by *from*.

> Incorrect: He will probably win 20 tournaments before he *graduates* high school.

> Correct: He will probably win 20 tournaments before he *graduates from* high school.

in regards to → in regard to

> Incorrect: *In regards to* the javelin throw, I'll stay as far away as possible.

> Correct: *In regard to* the javelin throw, I'll stay as far away as possible.

inside of → in less than

> Incorrect: He ran the mile *inside of* four minutes.

> Correct: He ran the mile *in less than* four minutes.

irregardless → regardless

> Incorrect: *Irregardless* of what he says, it looks dangerous.

> Correct: *Regardless* of what he says, it looks dangerous.

is when/is where → is/occurs when

Incorrect: The shot put *is when* you throw a heavy metal ball called a shot as far as possible.

Correct: The shot put *is* throwing a heavy metal ball called a shot as far as possible.

Incorrect: A false start is *where* you leave before the gun sounds.

Correct: A false start *occurs when* you leave before the gun sounds.

kind of/sort of → somewhat or rather

Incorrect: She was *kind of* disappointed with her javelin throw.

Correct: She was *somewhat* disappointed with her javelin throw.

like/maybe → approximately, perhaps, or about

Incorrect: There were *maybe* one thousand fans in the stands.

Correct: There were *approximately* one thousand fans in the stands.

lots of → many

Incorrect: There are *lots of* athletes on the field.

Correct: There are *many* athletes on the field.

more … and not → more … than

Incorrect: She is known *more* for her jumping *and not* for her running.

Correct: She is known *more* for her jumping *than* for her running.

most → almost

Incorrect: He runs *most* every day of the week.

Correct: He runs *almost* every day of the week.

nor → or (see the Conjunction section)

Incorrect: If she expects to win, she cannot start late *nor* early.

Correct: If she expects to win, she cannot start late *or* early.

of → have

Incorrect: If you *would of* been here with the stopwatch, I *could of* timed myself.

Correct: If you *would have* been here with the stopwatch, I *could have* timed myself.

plenty → very

> Incorrect: You could tell from his long stride that he was *plenty* fast.
>
> Correct: You could tell from his long stride that he was *very* fast.

plus → and

> Incorrect: He has huge arms, *plus* his legs are also strong.
>
> Correct: He has huge arms, *and* his legs are also strong.

reason is/was because (see *because*)

so → very

> Incorrect: It is *so* difficult to jump over hurdles.
>
> Correct: It is *very* difficult to jump over hurdles.

so as to → to

> Incorrect: He uses chalk *so as to* grip the shot more firmly.
>
> Correct: He uses chalk *to* grip the shot more firmly.

try and → try to

> Incorrect: *Try and* see if you can run one lap without collapsing.
>
> Correct: *Try to* see if you can run one lap without collapsing.

use to/suppose to → used to/supposed to

> Incorrect: He *use* to be the fastest sprinter at our school.
>
> Correct: He *used* to be the fastest sprinter at our school.
>
> Incorrect: She was *suppose* to win the decathlon, but she sprained her ankle.
>
> Correct: She was *supposed* to win the decathlon, but she sprained her ankle.

After reading over the common idiom mistakes on the previous pages, try the problems below. Do NOT look back to the lesson while completing the assignment.

The reason for my late arrival is <u>because</u> the
1
train was running behind schedule due to the
demonstration downtown.

1. **A.** NO CHANGE
   B. due to the fact that
   C. that
   D. for the reason of

The grandfather clock was used more for
decoration <u>than</u> for time keeping.
2

2. **F.** NO CHANGE
   G. and not meant
   H. and not
   J. but not

Winning the lottery is a matter of luck,
<u>irregardless of what</u> the fortune teller may say.
3

3. **A.** NO CHANGE
   B. disregarding what
   C. regardless of what
   D. irregardless what

If you had left earlier, you <u>would of been</u> on
4
time.

4. **F.** NO CHANGE
   G. would of being
   H. would have being
   J. would have been

You should not wear a jacket <u>nor</u> long pants on
5
the raft because both will just get soaked.

5. **A.** NO CHANGE
   B. or
   C. but
   D. and also not

■

Before taking the following quiz, study Sections 9–11. If you're working with a tutor, you will take the quiz during the next lesson. If you're working on your own, take the quiz after reviewing, and do not look back to the lessons. After grading, review any topics you struggled on. The quiz is untimed.

GRAMMAR QUIZ 3 (SECTIONS 9–11)

<u>Its hot enough</u> today to fry an egg on the
₁
sidewalk.

1. **A.** NO CHANGE
   B. Its hotter
   C. Its' hot enough
   D. It's hot enough

Karoline Mariechen Meyer broke the world's
record by holding her breath for <u>18 minutes and</u>
₂
<u>33 seconds—nearly 20 minutes</u>.
₂

2. **F.** NO CHANGE
   G. 18 minutes and 33 seconds, or
      nearly 20 minutes
   H. 18 minutes and 33 seconds
   J. less than 20 minutes—18 minutes
      and 33 seconds

As a reader, she <u>has an ability for making</u> even
₃
the most mundane prose come alive.

3. **A.** NO CHANGE
   B. has an ability to make
   C. has an ability of making
   D. has an ability with making

<u>A puppy's first steps</u> occur three to four weeks
₄
after birth, far earlier than a baby's first steps.

4. **F.** NO CHANGE
   G. A puppy's first step's
   H. A puppies' first steps
   J. A puppies first steps

Their aggressive and inappropriate actions
make it clear <u>that theirs</u> little hope of
₅
compromise.

5. **A.** NO CHANGE
   B. that theirs is
   C. that there's
   D. that they're is

Quiz 3 continued →

I was accepted to Harvard, Yale, and Stanford, and because I wanted to stay in California, I chose the latter.
6

6. **F.** NO CHANGE
   G. the last one
   H. the final choice
   J. Stanford

The sight of the movie's star actor on the red carpet excited and invigorated the huge crowd.
7

7. **A.** NO CHANGE
   B. excited the huge crowd
   C. excited the huge and massive crowd
   D. excited the now invigorated, huge crowd

I understood the material when I read the math book but was confused of my teacher's lengthy
8
and boring lectures.

8. **F.** NO CHANGE
   G. had confusion for
   H. was confused by
   J. was confused with

∎

All programs: At this point, skip to the Usage/Mechanics chapter. If you're following the **30-** or **40-hour program**, we'll come back to the Grammar chapter and complete the following sections later. See the Tutoring Schedules in the Introduction for more details.

12. ADJECTIVES & ADVERBS

ADJECTIVES & ADVERBS TERMINOLOGY

Adjective – a word that describes or modifies a person or thing in a sentence (such as *blue*, *old*, *calm*, or *happy*).

Adverb – a word that modifies a verb, adjective, or other adverb in a sentence (such as *quickly*, *happily*, or *stubbornly*). Adverbs describe *how* something happens.

ADJECTIVE AND ADVERB ERRORS

Adjectives only modify *nouns*. On the ACT, adjective and adverb errors occur when an adjective is used incorrectly in place of an adverb, or vice versa. As you read the example below, first identify the adjective or adverb. If you spot an adjective, remember that it must describe a noun. If you can't identify the noun that the adjective should modify, the adjective is incorrect; replace it with an adverb.

I was surprised how quick she walked to the store.

The adjective is "quick." Ask yourself: what is "quick" modifying? Since it's describing "*how…she walked,*" it should be an adverb:

I was surprised how *quickly* she walked to the store.

GOOD VERSUS WELL AND BAD VERSUS BADLY

The words *good* and *bad* are adjectives, and the words *well* and *badly* are adverbs. Following the rules above, if a noun is being modified, use *good* or *bad*, and if a verb is being modified, use *well* or *badly*. For example:

He performed *well* on the test. (*Well* describes how he *performed*.)
He received a *good* score on the test. (*Good* modifies the noun *score*.)

When dealing with any of the five senses, there is an exception to these rules. Use the word *good* or *bad* to modify verbs. For example:

After sketching with a new type of charcoal, the drawing looks *good* (not *well*).
The burnt bread made dinner smell *bad* (not *badly*).

ADJECTIVES & ADVERBS LESSON PROBLEMS

No matter <u>how careful</u> tax returns are checked,
₁
there is always a good chance of mistakes.

1. **A.** NO CHANGE
   B. how much care
   C. the more care
   D. how carefully

Trying to find the source of the rumor, Elijah <u>moved rapid</u> from one group to another.
₂

2. **F.** NO CHANGE
   G. moved rapidly
   H. moved more rapid
   J. moved with rapidness

The speaker once again showed her skills with one of her <u>typical brilliant</u> dissertations.
₁

1. **A.** NO CHANGE
   B. typically brilliant
   C. typically brilliantly
   D. typical, brilliant

She received accolades for doing a <u>really good job</u> on the science project.
₂

2. **F.** NO CHANGE
   G. real good job
   H. a job as well as possible
   J. job that is well

13. COMPARISONS

THE *NUMBER* OF A COMPARISON

The *number* of a comparison refers to the number of items being compared. There are grammatical differences between comparing two things and comparing three or more things.

When comparing **two** things, you will use the *-er* form of an adjective (words such as happi*er* or strong*er*) or the word *more* prior to an adjective (such as *more* beautiful). You will also often use the word *than* for these comparisons, not *then*, a common mistake (see the Apostrophes & Confused Words and Idiom lessons).

Jason is *better than* I am at shooting with his left hand. (two people)

When comparing **three or more** things, you will use the *-est* form of an adjective (happi*est* or strong*est*) or the word *most* prior to an adjective (such as *most* beautiful). For example:

Jason is the *best* player on the team at shooting with his left hand. (three or more people)

DOUBLE COMPARISONS

Make sure to never create a *double comparison* by putting words like *more* or *most* in the same phrase with words in the *-er* or *-est* form. For example, avoid:

more friendlier, most friendliest

TRICKY COMPARISON WORDS

The table below shows some of the tricky comparison words. If you already hear these correctly, don't worry about memorizing them.

adjective	two things	three or more things
good	better	best
well	better	best
bad	worse	worst
little	less	least
much	more	most
many	more	most

The ACT may try to use *more* or *most* when one of the *tricky* comparison words should be used. For example:

Jason's game went from bad to more bad because of his injury.

The words "more bad" are not grammatically correct. They should be replaced with the word *worse*.

Jason's game went from bad to *worse* because of his injury.

These errors are essentially double comparisons, as described above.

■

 To identify comparison errors, look for questions with answer choices that contain the words *more* and *most* or have the same words in the *-er* and *-est* forms.

COMPARISONS LESSON PROBLEMS

An oil candle is both brighter and <u>more longer-burning</u> than a conventional wax candle.
1

1. **A.** NO CHANGE
   B. longer-burning
   C. far more longer-burning
   D. long-burning

On our track team, Evan may have long legs, but he is definitely not the <u>faster of the group</u>.
2

2. **F.** NO CHANGE
   G. fastest of the group
   H. most fastest of the group
   J. group's faster runner

Since he spends all day and night studying, Brian, not surprisingly, is the <u>most intelligent</u> student in the class.
3

3. **A.** NO CHANGE
   B. more intelligent
   C. more than intelligent
   D. more than anyone else, intelligent

Amanda is definitely the more outspoken of the twins.

1. **A.** NO CHANGE
   B. Amanda is definitely the most outspoken of the twins
   C. Of the twins, Amanda is definitely the most outspoken
   D. More than the other of the twins, Amanda is definitely outspoken

When deciding whether to take the high road or the low road, the best choice is often elusive.

2. **F.** NO CHANGE
   G. most best
   H. more better
   J. better

I would be more than happier to take you and your friends to the airport.

3. **A.** NO CHANGE
   B. the most happiest
   C. more than happy
   D. a quality greater than happiest

14. ILLOGICAL COMPARISONS

These types of problems don't show up frequently on the ACT, but the rule is good to know. The saying goes that *you can't compare apples to oranges*. For example:

> The science department's projects are much more interesting than the English department this year.

The sentence is incorrect because the science department's *projects* are being compared to the English *department*. The correct sentence should read:

> The science department's projects are much more interesting than the English department's *projects* this year.

You don't always have to restate the noun being compared, as above. Using an *apostrophe-s* (*'s*) or the word *that* (singular) or *those* (plural) is usually acceptable. (Just make sure the comparisons are *parallel*, as in the examples below.)

> The science department's projects are much more interesting than the English department*'s* this year.

> The projects of the science department are much more interesting than *those* of the English department this year.

■

When you spot a comparison, ask yourself: what items are being compared? You might want to underline the two items. **Always compare "apples to apples."**

 To identify illogical comparison errors, look for questions with underlined comparisons. The answer choices will contain various comparing options; however, looking for the comparison in the passage is probably the best way to identify these types of questions.

ILLOGICAL COMPARISONS LESSON PROBLEMS

Our school's students are much stronger in math and science <u>than the average school</u>.
₁

1. **A.** NO CHANGE
   B. than the average school is in math and science
   C. than the average school's students
   D. than the students at the average school

The history of Hawaii, <u>like other Pacific islands</u>,
₂
is primarily concerned with the ocean.

2. **F.** NO CHANGE
   G. similar to other Pacific islands
   H. like that of other Pacific islands
   J. in comparison to other Pacific islands

A recent study suggests that eating fish twice a week is healthier <u>than eating other meats</u>.
₁

1. **A.** NO CHANGE
   B. than other meats
   C. than other meats twice a week
   D. than other meats are

Daniel's score on this test, after diligent study and practice, is much better than <u>his last test</u>.
₂

2. **F.** NO CHANGE
   G. his score on his last test
   H. the test he took last
   J. that test that he took last

15. GRAMMAR ODDS AND ENDS

The following grammar rules do not often show up on the ACT, but they are good rules to know. If you have time, look them over.

NOUN AGREEMENT

Nouns must agree in number (plural or singular) with the number of the noun or nouns they are referring to. For example:

Dave and Scott are looking for *a girlfriend*.

Obviously, Dave and Scott are not looking for one girlfriend. *Girlfriend* must be plural so it agrees with the plural subject of the sentence. The correct sentence should read:

Dave and Scott are looking for *girlfriends*.

 To identify noun agreement errors, look for questions with answer choices that contain the same common noun in plural and singular forms.

NOUN AGREEMENT LESSON PROBLEMS

Once considered a place to meet people and
<u>   </u>
             1
drink coffee, bookstores are now generally
used just to buy books.

1. **A.** NO CHANGE
    B. Considered then a place
    C. Once it was considered a place
    D. Once considered places

To become <u>a better reader</u>, students are urged
             2
to read everything they can get their hands on,
including newspapers and magazines.

2. **F.** NO CHANGE
    G. better readers
    H. the best reader
    J. a reader better than before

The cookies all come <u>in an individual box</u>, so
₁
you should have no trouble separating the
chocolate chunk ones from the peanut toffee
ones.

1. **A.** NO CHANGE
   B. in a different box
   C. in different boxes
   D. in different and distinct boxes

<u>The vibraphone, melodic and percussive</u>
₂
<u>instruments</u> used mostly in jazz, can be played
₂
with two or four mallets.

2. **F.** NO CHANGE
   G. Vibraphones, a melodic and
   percussive instrument
   H. The vibraphone, at once melodic
   and percussive instruments
   J. The vibraphone, a melodic and
   percussive instrument

PAIRED CONJUNCTIONS

These conjunctions or phrases, which always come in pairs, are also called *correlative*
conjunctions. Make flash cards for the ones you don't know.

both . . . and: Keep this construction concise and simple (with *and*):

> Incorrect: *Both* the lions *and also* the tigers were putting on a show at the zoo.
> Incorrect (usually): *Both* the lions *as well as* the tigers were putting on a show at the zoo.
> Correct: *Both* the lions *and* the tigers were putting on a show at the zoo.

not only . . . but also: Synonyms of *also*, such as *too* or *as well*, are also fine:

> Incorrect (usually): The new electric car is *not only* more efficient than a gasoline-powered
> car *but* much quieter.
> Correct: The new electric car is *not only* more efficient than a gasoline-powered car *but*
> *also* much quieter.
> Correct: The new electric car is *not only* more efficient than a gasoline-powered car *but*
> much quieter, *too* (or: . . . much quieter, *as well*).

not . . . but: Avoid *also* when there is no *only* following *not*:

Incorrect: The movie is *not* light-hearted or trivial *but also* dark and disturbing in the ways it portrays drug-use.

Correct: The movie is *not* light-hearted or trivial *but* dark and disturbing in the ways it portrays drug-use.

either . . . or: Some students "hyper-correct" the *either-or* construction with *nor*:

Incorrect: You can be *either* for him *nor* against him; there is no in between.

Correct: You can be *either* for him *or* against him; there is no in between.

neither . . . nor: The correct use of *nor* is with *neither*:

Incorrect: He is *neither* as large *or* as strong as his father, but he is much faster.

Correct: He is *neither* as large *nor* as strong as his father, but he is much faster.

whether . . . or: Avoid *or not* after *whether* when both options are given:

Incorrect: *Whether or not* you go to a good university *or* straight to the work force is up to you.

Correct: *Whether* you go to a good university *or* straight to the work force is up to you.

Correct: *Whether or not* you go to a good university is up to you.

as . . . as: In a comparison, one *as* should always be followed by a second one:

Incorrect: Amy was not *as* scholastic *compared to* (or *with*) her older sister, but she was much more sociable.

Incorrect (needlessly wordy): Amy was not *as* scholastic *as compared to* (or *with*) her older sister, but she was much more sociable.

Incorrect: Amy was not *as* scholastic *in comparison to* (or *with*) her older sister, but she was much more sociable.

Correct: Amy was not *as* scholastic *as* her older sister, but she was much more sociable.

not so much . . . as: This one is rarely tested, but it's worth memorizing, just in case:

Incorrect: It is *not so much* the sound of the breaking waves *but* the smell of the sea that characterizes my beach house.

Correct: It is *not so much* the sound of the breaking waves *as* the smell of the sea that characterizes my beach house.

so . . . that: This is a common cause-and-effect pair:

Incorrect: It is *so* hot today *and* I'm afraid to go outside.

Correct: It is *so* hot today *that* I'm afraid to go outside.

 To identify paired-conjunction errors, look for the *first* part of each pair in the passage (the second part will often be incorrect or missing altogether).

PAIRED CONJUNCTIONS LESSON PROBLEMS

The new documentary is not only an important educational film <u>and</u> a pleasurable viewing experience.

₁

1. **F.** NO CHANGE
    G. but it is
    H. but also
    J. but

Both the pencil <u>or</u> the pen are mightier than the sword.

₂

2. **A.** NO CHANGE
    B. and
    C. and also
    D. and, too,

After reviewing paired conjunctions, try the problems below. Do NOT look back to the lesson while completing the assignment:

<u>Neither your muddy shoes or</u> your rain soaked jacket will be allowed in this house.

₁

1. **A.** NO CHANGE
    B. Neither your muddy shoes nor
    C. Either your muddy shoes nor
    D. Neither your muddy shoes and also not

Frank, while frightening in his own ways, was not as gruesome or as sinister <u>compared to</u> Drake.

₂

2. **F.** NO CHANGE
    G. as
    H. as compared to
    J. when compared to

I can tell that you are angry not so much by your choice of words <u>but by</u> the tone of your voice.

₃

3. **A.** NO CHANGE
    B. but because of
    C. as by
    D. but from

MORE CONFUSED WORDS

We already saw how words such as *their*, *there*, and *they're* can be confused because of the similar look and sound of the words (see the Apostrophes & Confused Words section). Other words may be confused because of similar *meanings*. For example:

You can only pay here if you have ten items or less.

Believe it or not, this sentence is incorrect. *Less* should be used when referring to things that cannot be counted, like mashed potatoes or water. *Fewer* should be used in place of *less* when the items can be counted:

You can only pay here if you have ten items or *fewer*.

The following words are a few of the most commonly confused:

between/among

Between is usually used for two items or people; *among* is used for more than two.

Just *between* you and me, I don't think the money was distributed properly *among* all the players at the poker table.

each other/one another

Each other refers to two; *one another* refers to more than two.

While the happy couple kissed *each other* in the darkened room, the people still at the party wished *one another* a happy New Year.

fewer/less

Fewer is for things that can be counted; *less* is for things that cannot be counted.

I would like *fewer* peas and *less* mashed potatoes.

into/in

Into refers to the motion of going from outside to inside; *in* means within.

After jumping *into* the lake, you will be *in* over your head.

like/as

Like means: of the same form, appearance, or kind; *as* means: to the same degree or in the same manner. *Like* is not an acceptable substitute for *as*, *as if*, or *as though*. A good rule of thumb is to replace *like* with *as* whenever the sentence still sounds correct. Try circling the correct choices below:

Adam fouls frequently, just (**as** or **like**?) Andrew does.
The dog scratched on the door (**as if** or **like**?) it wanted to come in.
Nick is (**as** or **like**?) his brother in many ways.

(The correct answers are *as*, *as if*, and *like*.)

many/much

Like *fewer* and *less*, *many* is for things that can be counted; *much* is for things that cannot be counted.

I don't have *much* patience left—I don't know how *many* more arguments I can handle.

number/amount

Number is for things that can be counted; *amount* is for things that cannot be counted.

Bill had a *number* of hundred-dollar bills in his wallet—the *amount* of money stolen is just a guess.

 To identify confused words questions, look for questions with answer choices that contain different word options. Of course, you should also look for the specific words listed above.

Try the following homework problems *after* you have reviewed the lesson material. Do NOT look back to the lesson while completing the problems:

The company's surplus was divided evenly <u>between</u> all twenty hardworking employees.

1.
A. NO CHANGE
B. through
C. around
D. among

After Matt <u>walked in the theater</u>, his eyes took several minutes to adjust to the dark.

2.
F. NO CHANGE
G. walked into the theater
H. was walking in the theater
J. walking inside the theater

Spooked by the moonless dark night and the eerily silent alley, we ran <u>like if</u> we were being chased by a mob of zombies.

3.
A. NO CHANGE
B. like
C. as if
D. as

The members of the internet company had been a bit premature in <u>congratulating one another</u> since just a few months later their company was nothing more than unpaid bills and worthless stock.

4.
F. NO CHANGE
G. congratulating each other
H. their congratulating of each other
J. congratulations for one another

VOCABULARY

The ACT may test your vocabulary on the English Test. These questions involve words that have similar meanings, not unlike the Confused Words lesson above. For example,

When the blow fish senses danger, it brings in water to make its entire body proliferate.

The word "proliferate" means: to increase in number. It is not the correct word for this context. You could correct the sentence with words such as *expand*, *enlarge*, *grow*, etc.:

When the blow fish senses danger, it brings in water to make its entire body *expand*.

Because there aren't many vocabulary questions on the ACT, we don't think it's worth memorizing long lists of words for this test. However, we encourage you to work on vocabulary outside of our ACT curriculum. A strong vocabulary will certainly benefit you beyond this one test, and it will certainly help your Reading scores on the ACT.

 To identify vocabulary questions, look for answer choices that contain different words with similar meanings.

Here's a sample question so you know what to look for:

If I <u>lend</u> the book to you, I expect to get it back
₁
by the end of the month.

1. Which of the following alternatives to the underlined portion would be LEAST acceptable in terms of the context of the sentence?

   A. loan
   B. borrow
   C. entrust
   D. deliver

NONSENSE

Some answer choices create a sentence that simply doesn't make sense. Sometimes you'll hear obvious awkwardness as you read the sentence. Other times you'll have to read carefully and think about the intended *meaning* of the sentence to discover the nonsense. Try the following lesson problem:

Studying history is like going back in time and learning <u>from the mistakes of those</u> that came before.
₁

1. Which of the following alternatives to the underlined portion would be LEAST acceptable?

   A. NO CHANGE
   B. about the mistakes of those
   C. from those
   D. DELETE the underlined portion

John Brown made his name in the raid of Harper's Ferry, <u>where he hoped</u> would lead to a rebellion against Southern slave owners.
₁

1. **A.** NO CHANGE
   B. an act that he hoped
   C. a place that he hoped
   D. DELETE the underlined portion

■

30- and 40-hour programs: See the schedules in the introduction to know when you should review all grammar sections (for homework), including Sections 12–15, and take the following quiz.

GRAMMAR QUIZ 4 (SECTIONS 1–15)

Elephants, <u>a surprisingly fast creature, have</u> been known to run forty miles per hour.
₁

1. **A.** NO CHANGE
   B. surprisingly fast creatures, have
   C. a surprisingly fast creature, has
   D. a surprisingly fast creature that has

I almost fell asleep as the raft floated <u>lazy</u> in the still waters.
₂

2. **F.** NO CHANGE
   G. lazily
   H. lazier
   J. laziness

There are <u>not as much</u> people on the beach each year because of the erosion caused by the high surf.
₃

3. **A.** NO CHANGE
   B. lesser
   C. less
   D. fewer

Because she was having such a great time, the little girl <u>was opposed of</u> leaving the theme park early.
₄

4. **F.** NO CHANGE
   G. was opposed from
   H. was opposed to
   J. had opposition for

After analyzing the evidence and writing the research paper about the health risks of living near a cellular tower, researchers knew <u>it would</u> cause an uproar.
₅

5. **A.** NO CHANGE
   B. the results would
   C. they would
   D. this would

Quiz 4 continued →

The <u>MSPCA or Massachusetts</u> Society for the
₆
Prevention of Cruelty to Animals, is a national
and international leader in the protection of
animals.

6. **F.** NO CHANGE
   G. MSPCA Massachusetts
   H. MSPCA—Massachusetts
   J. MSPCA, or Massachusetts

Each of the three witnesses <u>were wary</u> of
₇
testifying against the frightening gang leader.

7. **A.** NO CHANGE
   B. were warily
   C. was wary
   D. have been wary

The Grapes of Wrath, by John Steinbeck, tells
the story of the <u>Joad family's</u> migration west.
₈

8. **F.** NO CHANGE
   G. Joad's family's
   H. Joad families
   J. Joad's families

It is a <u>usual</u> custom at our family gatherings
₉
to toss the ball around a little after dinner, even
though we are usually too full to run.

9. **A.** NO CHANGE
   B. usual and regular
   C. routine
   D. OMIT the underlined portion.

He is ambivalent about his favorite team going
to the finals, both happy about the chance to
win it all <u>but</u> sad about the fact that he can't
₁₀
afford tickets.

10. **F.** NO CHANGE
    G. and
    H. but also
    J. combined with

Because he <u>hit</u> so many game winning shots,
₁₁
he was considered last season's best closer.

11. **A.** NO CHANGE
    B. hits
    C. has been hitting
    D. will hit

Quiz 4 continued →

New high-definition <u>televisions that</u> have
                                12
resolutions far superior to those of the past.

Those <u>citizens which</u> refuse to vote should be
                13
the last to complain about the government.

Last year's company party, which was catered

by the best cook in town, was much better than

<u>this year</u>.
     14

Martin and Sid have similar running styles, but

Sid is definitely <u>the fastest</u> of the two.
                            15

12. **F.** NO CHANGE
    G. televisions
    H. televisions, that
    J. televisions, which

13. **A.** NO CHANGE
    B. citizens, whom
    C. citizens whom
    D. citizens who

14. **F.** NO CHANGE
    G. this year's party
    H. the one of this year
    J. that of this year

15. **A.** NO CHANGE
    B. the faster
    C. fastest
    D. the most faster

III

USAGE/MECHANICS

We have reviewed the grammar rules, and now it's time to look at the kinds of questions on the ACT that test these rules: the Usage/Mechanics questions. These questions make up a majority of the English questions (about two-thirds, or roughly 50 of the 75 questions on the test). This chapter will discuss some general techniques that will help you tackle Usage/Mechanics questions.

IDENTIFYING USAGE/MECHANICS QUESTIONS

 Usage/Mechanics questions are fairly easy to identify. Unlike the Rhetorical Skills questions (to be discussed in Chapter IV), **Usage/Mechanics questions generally lack a written question next to the question number**—the question is *implied*. In other words, you will only see the answer choices. See the examples below.

USAGE/MECHANICS QUESTION:

9. **A.** NO CHANGE
    B. are
    C. is
    D. has been

RHETORICAL SKILLS QUESTION (CHAPTER IV):

10. Given that all of following sentences are true, which one would most effectively conclude the paragraph?

    A. Michael Douglas certainly has been in a lot of movies.
    B. It is no surprise that an actor with this many awards is so highly respected.
    C. Actors come and go, but Michael Douglas is here for the long haul.
    D. Michael Douglas is certainly more than just an actor.

EXCEPTIONS

There are a few Usage/Mechanics questions on each test that have written questions. The two most common ones are:

- "Which of the following alternatives to the underlined portion would NOT be acceptable?" (Look for a grammar error among the answer choices.)
- "The best placement for the underlined portion would be:" (This is likely a Misplaced Words question.)

There are also a few Rhetorical Skills questions on each test that *lack* a written question. The most common of these are *main idea* and *transition* questions, which will be discussed in the Rhetorical Skills chapter.

Again, most of the Usage/Mechanics questions do *not* have written questions, and most of the Rhetorical Skills questions *do* have written questions, but make sure you can identify the few exceptions.

1. AVOID WORDY ANSWER CHOICES

Good writing is usually as concise and clear as possible, with no needless words. Besides being grammatically correct, the correct answers on the English Test are usually the clearest and often the shortest of the answer choices.

> **In fact, the shortest answer choice available is correct far more than half the time. Certainly, if you find yourself in a guessing situation, guess the answer that is the shortest or has the fewest words.**

DON'T FORGET THE NO CHANGE ANSWER CHOICE

The answer choice labeled NO CHANGE (A for odd problems, F for even problems) refers, of course, to the words in the passage. These words won't be reprinted above the other answer choices—making their length hard to compare to the lengths of the other answer choices—so don't forget to look back to the passage. This NO CHANGE answer choice may very well be the shortest answer choice, but you won't know unless you remember to look.

CLOSE ENOUGH TO CALL A TIE

Sometimes the differences in the lengths of the answer choices are subtle—perhaps a couple letters or one word. Don't worry about wordiness for these answer choices. For example, the verb "is" is shorter than the verb "are," but that's obviously not enough of a reason to select "is" as your correct answer. Look for answer choices that have more significant variations in length.

■

T.S. Eliot was awarded the Nobel Prize in Literature in 1948 <u>by the consideration of</u> his
¹
contributions to poetry and playwriting.

1. **A.** NO CHANGE
    B. for
    C. owing to
    D. due to the fact of

2. AVOID -ING WORDS

Words in the *-ing* form often create fragments or other awkwardness. In fact:

! **Answer choices that use words in the *-ing* form are incorrect about 90% of the time.**

As taught in the Verb Tense lesson, it is important to remember that a single word (on its own) in the *-ing* form does not function as an active verb:

Fragment: John *running* to the store. ✗

Correct: John *has been running* to the store. ✓

Be especially wary of the words *being* and *having*, which are almost always wrong. Let's look at an example:

The professor argued that although many universities have excelled at training future scientists, <u>the failure is in their not educating</u> humanities majors in the methods of scientific thought.

1. **A.** NO CHANGE
    B. they have failed to educate
    C. the failure they have is in their not educating
    D. having failed to educate

EXCEPTIONS

GRAMMATICALLY CORRECT USES

The *-ing* form of a word is not *necessarily* incorrect, as seen in some of the grammar lessons. Thus, you should be able to recognize *-ing* words that *are* used correctly. As covered in the Grammar chapter, there are two common grammatically-correct uses of *-ing* words:

1. Recall that an *-ing* verb phrase can be used to express continuous action over a period of time, for example:

    Bob *has been working* at the mini-mart since he was in high school.
    Bob *is* certainly *gaining* the respect of his boss.

2. Modifying phrases often contain *-ing* words, as displayed in the Punctuation section. For example:

Using both hands, Bob has become the fastest bagger in the store.

Having the most experience, Bob is certain to become the store manager before long.

PARALLELISM

If you have to maintain parallel construction with *-ing* words that are not underlined (which means they must be correct), then an *-ing* word will be part of the correct answer.

For many a great artist, <u>being free to innovate</u>
$_2$
<u>is more important</u> than being well paid.
$_2$

2. **F.** NO CHANGE
    G. having freedom of innovation is more important
    H. there is more importance in the freedom to innovate
    J. to have the freedom to innovate is more important

-*ING* IN EVERY ANSWER CHOICE

Obviously, when there is an *-ing* word in every answer choice, one of them must be correct. You should still probably avoid answer choices that have more *-ing* words than the others or ones that contain *being* or *having*.

HARMLESS -*ING* WORDS

-*ING* words that function as simple nouns are usually OK. For example:

When the *going* gets tough, the tough go *fishing*.

There's really no better way to write this sentence. The good news is that when *-ing* words are used as simple nouns, they're usually found in every answer choice.

SUMMARY

Answer choices with *-ing* words are usually incorrect—eliminate them aggressively. Just make sure you understand the few exceptions described above.

3. *NO CHANGE*

The NO CHANGE answer choice (A for odd problems, F for even problems) is the correct answer about as often as each of the other answer choices (about one-fourth of the time). Students have a tendency to find an error in the sentence at all costs, but often the sentence is correct as written. The ACT folks generally won't try to trick you on these—if the sentence sounds good as written, don't be afraid to select NO CHANGE.

<u>Most experts considered</u> Michael Phelps to be
the greatest swimmer ever after he won eight
gold medals in the 2008 Beijing Olympics.

1. **A.** NO CHANGE
    B. Almost all experts considered
    C. Absolutely many experts considered
    D. Experts, but not all, considered

4. AVOID THE PASSIVE VOICE

The passive voice means that the performer of the action in the sentence is *not* the subject of the sentence. For example,

The books were carefully arranged on the shelf by Dan, a self-proclaimed neat-freak.

The subject of this sentence is *books*, but the books are obviously not performing the action of *arranging—Dan* is. This sentence is in the *passive voice.* To rewrite the sentence in the *active voice*, make *Dan* the subject of the sentence:

Dan, a self-proclaimed neat-freak, arranged the books on the shelf.

Look to eliminate answer choices in the passive voice in the following example:

Dan arranged the books on the shelf, he
                                      ___
                                       1
proceeded to proclaim himself a neat-freak.

1. **A.** NO CHANGE
   B. The books, which were arranged on the shelf by Dan, who
   C. The books were first arranged on the shelf by Dan, who then
   D. After arranging the books on the shelf, Dan

5. AVOID NEW MISTAKES

READ TO THE ENDS OF ANSWER CHOICES

Let's say you're reading a passage on the English Test and you identify a grammar error in an underlined portion of a sentence. When you look at the answer choices, you might pick the first one that corrects the error. But make sure you don't end up selecting an answer choice that introduces a *new* error. How do you avoid these careless mistakes? By being careful! Make sure you read the whole answer choice before picking it, or look at the other answer choices to see if any of them also correct the original error.

His article in the school newspaper <u>challenged, the student body to stop</u> blaming teachers and start becoming accountable for the widespread low test scores.

1. **A.** NO CHANGE
    B. challenged the student body, to stop
    C. challenged the student body in stopping
    D. challenged the student body to stop

READ TO THE ENDS OF SENTENCES

Similar mistakes occur when students don't read an entire sentence, especially when the underlined portion shows up early in the sentence. Generally, it's a good idea to get to the end of a sentence before choosing an answer choice.

While some scholars see a correlation between the rise of social media and the decline of printed books, <u>others</u> think that the decline has more to do with increased internet gaming, the reality is that, for whatever reason, people are reading fewer and fewer physical books.

2. **A.** NO CHANGE
    B. and others
    C. however, others
    D. even so, others

6. THINK "TECHNIQUE-LY"

Throughout the Grammar chapter, you saw information about *identifying* techniques. This information was always indicated with a magnifying glass:

It's essential that you consider techniques (think "technique-ly") while answering Usage/Mechanics questions. Knowing what technique is being tested may change how you approach a problem and will help you overcome the tendency to over-trust your ear.

Here's some technique ID practice. Most techniques can be identified by looking at the answer choices. Try matching the following techniques to the answer choices (each is used once): Verb Tense, Subject Verb Agreement, Pronouns (Agreement), Pronouns (Case), Apostrophes & Confused Words, Vocabulary, Idiom, Redundancies, Punctuation.

A. NO CHANGE	**A.** NO CHANGE	**A.** NO CHANGE
B. pledge	**B.** had left	**B.** their position
C. promise	**C.** left	**C.** his or her position
D. vow	**D.** leave	**D.** its position
1. _____	2. _____	3. _____
A. NO CHANGE	**A.** NO CHANGE	**A.** NO CHANGE
B. of	**B.** work tirelessly	**B.** theirs
C. from	**C.** works tirelessly	**C.** their's
D. about	**D.** working tirelessly	**D.** there's
4. _____	5. _____	6. _____
A. NO CHANGE	**A.** NO CHANGE	**A.** NO CHANGE
B. heading and leading	**B.** in the same way, such as	**B.** who
C. heading, and also leading	**C.** in the same way: such as	**C.** whom
D. heading	**D.** in the same way, such as:	**D.** them
7. _____	8. _____	9. _____

7. USAGE/MECHANICS SUMMARY

As stated before, your knowledge of the grammar rules from chapter II is the most important aspect of the Grammar/Usage questions. If you remember the additional guidelines below, you should be comfortable with these questions:

1. Avoid Wordy Answer Choices.
2. Avoid -*ING* Words.
3. The NO CHANGE answer choice (A or F) is correct about as often as the other answer choices.
4. Avoid the Passive Voice.
5. Avoid New Mistakes.
6. Think "Technique-ly."

8. USAGE/MECHANICS PROBLEMS

PRACTICE PROBLEMS

After reviewing the Usage/Mechanics guidelines taught in this chapter, tackle the lesson and homework passages on the following pages. **Important: unlike the passages on a real ACT, these passages only test material taught in the Grammar and Usage/Mechanics chapters; they are for practice only**.

- ☐ Usage/Mechanics Passage I: "The Same Old Story"
- ☐ Usage/Mechanics Passage II: "Alien Invasion"

In addition to these passages, you will eventually tackle practice passages from *The Official ACT Prep Guide*. These will be assigned after you complete the Rhetorical Skills chapter. See the Tutoring Schedules in the main Introduction for more details.

TEST CORRECTIONS

After completing and grading each practice test, you should correct Usage/Mechanics questions that you missed or guessed on. Below are the three steps to correcting practice tests:

1. Turn to the Techniques chapter at the end of this tutorial and, for the appropriate test, circle the Usage/Mechanics questions that you missed or guessed on.
2. Correct the problems in *The Official ACT Prep Guide*. As you correct the problems, go back to the tutorial and review the techniques. The idea is to (1) identify techniques that have given you trouble, (2) go back to the tutorial so you can review and strengthen these techniques, and (3) apply these techniques to the specific problems you struggled on.
3. If you have trouble identifying the best technique to use on a problem, refer to the Techniques chapter at the end of this tutorial. This is an important part of correcting the tests.

USAGE/MECHANICS PRACTICE PASSAGE

The following lesson passage only tests material taught in the Grammar and Usage/Mechanics chapters. The passage begins on the next page.

Usage/Mechanics Passage I

The Same Old Story

George Smith—a <u>leading</u> archaeologist,
[1]
historian, and linguist of his day—did not

actually *find* his greatest <u>discovery, his</u> claim to
[2]
fame was that he *deciphered* it. It was a

Mesopotamian tablet that had been collecting

dust at the British Museum. In 1872, Smith

<u>captured</u> his fame by translating the tablet into
[3]
English. He read his translation before the

Society of Biblical Archaeology, <u>this was</u> for
[4]
an audience that included the Prime Minister

of Britain. In a quiet and steady voice, <u>Smith</u>
[5]
<u>told a story of a great flood,</u> one that had
[5]

remarkable similarities <u>to the one recounted in</u>
[6]
<u>the Bible</u>.
[6]

Continued →

1. **A.** NO CHANGE
    B. dominating
    C. premium
    D. exquisite

2. **F.** NO CHANGE
    G. discovery, and his
    H. discovery, but which his
    J. discovery; his

3. **A.** NO CHANGE
    B. produced
    C. achieved
    D. completed

4. **F.** NO CHANGE
    G. which was
    H. that was
    J. DELETE the underlined portion

5. **A.** NO CHANGE
    B. the story of the great flood was told
    by Smith,
    C. the great flood story, as told by
    Smith,
    D. Smith's story of the great flood was

6. **F.** NO CHANGE
    G. to the Bible.
    H. in comparison with the Bible.
    J. of that recounted in the Bible.

The tablet Smith translated—using his knowledge of <u>Akkadian, the ancient language of Neo-Assyrian empire,</u> was called "The Flood Tablet," but it has since become known as Tablet XI of the Gilgamesh Epic. This epic, composed of tablets and fragments from numerous sources, <u>describes</u> how the gods sent a flood to Earth to destroy the population of humans. One man, named Utnapishtim, <u>whom had</u> been <u>forewarned in advance</u> about the flood, built a ship for himself and his family.

Of course, <u>he, wiser,</u> saved room for plants and animals of every kind. After the flood,

Utnapishtim <u>released</u> the animals and, after some consultation among the gods, settled down on a mountain. Here he and his wife enjoyed immortality.

Continued →

7. **A.** NO CHANGE
   B. Akkadian—the ancient language of Neo-Assyrian empire—
   C. Akkadian, the ancient language of Neo-Assyrian empire—
   D. Akkadian, the ancient language of Neo-Assyrian empire:

8. **F.** NO CHANGE
   G. describe
   H. have described
   J. describing

9. **A.** NO CHANGE
   B. whom has
   C. who has
   D. who had

10. **F.** NO CHANGE
    G. forewarned
    H. forewarned before
    J. forewarned beforehand

11. **A.** NO CHANGE
    B. he, with more wisdom,
    C. he wisely
    D. he, the wisest,

12. **F.** NO CHANGE
    G. releases
    H. has released
    J. had been releasing

The story was <u>familiar: but</u> no one expected
13

to <u>have found</u> it on an ancient stone tablet. One
14

can only imagine George <u>Smiths</u> amazement
15
as he deciphered these words for the first time.

13. **A.** NO CHANGE
    B. familiar, but
    C. familiar, but:
    D. familiar, but,

14. **F.** NO CHANGE
    G. to finding
    H. to had found
    J. to find

15. **A.** NO CHANGE
    B. Smiths's
    C. Smiths'
    D. Smith's

■

The following homework passage only tests material taught in the Grammar and Usage/Mechanics chapters:

Usage/Mechanics Passage II

Alien Invasion!

A few days ago, my science teacher, Mrs. Higgins, brought in a movie. Of course, <u>my classmates and me</u> were expecting the
1

<u>typical, dull, documentary</u> on biology, but this
2
was different. Mrs. Higgins popped in the disc and then, before pressing the play button, held the DVD case up so the class could see the <u>title; *Alien,*</u> by Ridley Scott, the classic 1979
3
science-fiction horror movie. After warning the class that some of us might want to cover our eyes, <u>the scene played</u> in which one of the
4
baby aliens bursts through the chest of its

human <u>host. However,</u> that wasn't the worst
5
part. After she stopped the movie and turned on the lights, she explained that certain wasps—right here on Earth—reproduce in much the same way.

Continued →

1. **A.** NO CHANGE
    B. my classmates and I
    C. us classmates and me
    D. we classmates and I

2. **F.** NO CHANGE
    G. typical dull, documentary
    H. typical, dull documentary
    J. typical, dull documentary,

3. **A.** NO CHANGE
    B. title: *Alien,*
    C. title. *Alien,*
    D. title, *Alien,*

4. **F.** NO CHANGE
    G. the scene was played
    H. she played the scene
    J. played was the scene

5. **A.** NO CHANGE
    B. host however
    C. host, however
    D. host, however,

These wasps are called parasitoid wasps. After the *Alien* scene, Mrs. Higgins showed us a video of one species of these wasps infecting a caterpillar. In an act called "ovipositing," the wasp sneaks up behind the caterpillar and, with a needle-like organ at the wasps' abdomen, stabs the to-be host and injects its eggs.

Eventually, the eggs hatch within the

caterpillar's body. The wasp larvae feeds on the poor caterpillar's insides until the time comes to burst their way out.

    Gruesome? Indeed. But if that's not bad enough, a few of the wasp larvae stay behind in the still-living caterpillar and essentially take over its body. The caterpillar stops eating and becomes a protector for the released larvae, using its body like a tent to protect its ex-hosts and even swung its head from side to side. Finally, the remaining wasps emerge from the caterpillar's body, and the caterpillar dies.

Continued →

6. **F.** NO CHANGE
   G. wasps abdomen, stabs
   H. wasp's abdomen, stabs
   J. wasp's abdomen, stabbing

7 **A.** NO CHANGE
   B. hatched
   C. have hatched
   D. hatching

8 **F.** NO CHANGE
   G. feed
   H. is feeding
   J. will have fed

9. **A.** NO CHANGE
   B. originally
   C. approximately
   D. factually

10. **F.** NO CHANGE
   G. swinging
   H. swings
   J. had swung

You may think that parasitoid wasps are as

bad <u>as a movie monster,</u> but the surprising truth
₁₁

is that they <u>are quite actually</u> useful.
₁₂
Because each species of wasp is specific to

<u>there</u> host, the wasps help in the battle against
₁₃
insect pests. Scientists, in an effort to control

these pests, <u>have in actuality introduced</u>
₁₄
thousands of parasitoid wasps into ecosystems

around the world. These efforts might be good

for <u>farmers, not to mention, horror-movie buffs</u>
₁₅
but I suspect the caterpillars aren't too thrilled.

11. **A.** NO CHANGE
    B. as movie monsters,
    C. as are movie monsters,
    D. compared to movie monsters,

12. **F.** NO CHANGE
    G. were actually quite
    H. are being quite
    J. are actually quite

13. **A.** NO CHANGE
    B. their
    C. it's
    D. its

14 **F.** NO CHANGE
    G. have actually introduced
    H. have actually introducing
    J. actually introducing

15 **A.** NO CHANGE
    B. farmers, not to mention horror-movie buffs,
    C. farmers, not to mention: horror-movie buffs,
    D. farmers not to mention horror-movie buffs,

■

TIMING

All programs: You should now have a pretty good sense of how to approach the English passages. It's time to bring *timing* into the mix. Go back to the English Introduction now to cover the timing plan (page 4).

PRACTICE TEST (all programs): Now is a good time to take **Test 2** in the ACT book (you should have already taken Test 1). Make sure you've reviewed Timing first (see above). Also consider the following:

- For most students, even though we haven't covered the Rhetorical Skills questions, you should still tackle some, if not most, of them. You'll hopefully get some of the easier ones correct.

- If you're following the **20-hour program**, make sure you aggressively search out and answer the Usage/Mechanics questions. The 20-hour program usually doesn't allow enough time to go over Rhetorical Skills questions, but rest assured that most of the questions on the test are Usage/Mechanics. As we said, tackle some of the Rhetorical Skills questions if you have time; you'll hopefully get some of the easier ones correct.

- After you grade your test, correct any missed Usage/Mechanics questions. Also, make sure you go back and correct any missed Rhetorical Skills questions after you complete the Rhetorical Skills chapter.

IV

RHETORICAL SKILLS

The Rhetorical Skills questions focus on writing strategy, main ideas, organization, and style. These questions—which make up about one-third of the English questions (roughly 25 of 75)—tend to be more difficult than the Usage/Mechanics questions discussed in Chapter III. While the grammar techniques from Chapter II may come in handy, Rhetorical Skills questions, for the most part, do *not* rely on grammar knowledge. This chapter will discuss general techniques that will help you tackle Rhetorical Skills questions.

IDENTIFYING RHETORICAL SKILLS QUESTIONS

 Rhetorical Skills questions, unlike Usage/Mechanics questions, generally have a written question next to the question number. In addition, the answer choices tend to be longer than those on Usage/Mechanics questions.

If necessary, go to page 92 to see examples of Usage/Mechanics and Rhetorical Skills questions.

1. MAIN IDEAS

The most important part of Rhetorical Skills questions is recognizing *main ideas*. The main idea is the central point or message of an essay, paragraph, or even a sentence.

MAIN IDEA OF A PARAGRAPH

While you read an essay, think about the main idea of each paragraph. Most paragraphs have a topic sentence (usually the *first* sentence), which can help you identify the paragraph's main idea. But remember, these essays are in need of revision and may lack clear and effective topic sentences. Therefore, you will likely have to look at details within the paragraph as well.

FIND KEYWORDS

You should usually be able to write down the main idea of a paragraph in just a few words. These words—we'll call them *keywords*—will help you when you consider main ideas.

We'll use a sample essay to teach the techniques in this section. Read Paragraph 1 below. Think about keywords while you read (we'll get to the questions soon):

Snooker: Yesterday and Today

[1]

Snooker, a table sport where each opponent uses a cue to hit colored balls into table pockets, has been around for over a hundred years. If you've watched a game of pool or Billiards, then you might be more familiar with Snooker than you think. ⬚1 The game likely originated in India in the late 1800's when British Army officers made variations to traditional Billiards. The word *snooker* was a slang military term for an inexperienced military man. It is claimed that Colonel Sir Neville Chamberlain was playing this new game when his opponent failed to "pot"—or sink—a ball. ⬚2 Chamberlain called his opponent a snooker." The sport soon took this as its name.

What's the first word that comes to mind? (This should be straightforward. Write your first keyword below before moving on.)

First keyword for Paragraph 1 =

_____

Now that you have the first keyword ("Snooker"), let's dig a little deeper. What word best captures *how* the paragraph focuses on Snooker?

Second keyword for Paragraph 1 =

_____

So, based on these two keywords ("Snooker" and "originated"), the main idea of Paragraph 1 must have something to do with the **origin** of **Snooker**.

Now let's get into the types of Main Idea questions. . . .

MAIN IDEA QUESTIONS

There are five kinds of Main Idea questions:
- Additions/Changes
- Deletions
- Topic/Transition Sentences
- Essay
- Purpose

ADDITIONS/CHANGES

These questions ask if the writer should add something to an essay. Usually a sentence will be given in the question, but sometimes you'll be given the option to change a sentence in the essay. In both cases, you must consider the main idea of the relevant part of the essay.

Most Additions/Changes questions have the following wording: "At this point, the writer is considering adding the following true statement . . . Should the writer make this addition here?" Other questions may simply ask which choice provides the most relevant information.

YES/NO QUESTIONS

These questions usually have two "Yes" answers and two "No" answers (should the statement be added or not?). Try answering the yes/no question first, before looking at the rest of the answer choices. This will (hopefully) allow you to eliminate half of the answer choices.

OFF-TOPIC AND REDUNDANT ANSWER CHOICES

Pay close attention to what follows the "Yes" and the "No" in the answer choices. The second parts of the answer choices might force you to rethink your original *yes* or *no* answer. Watch out for information that is off topic, but also look for redundant choices, ones that repeat information already found in the essay (these will be tempting if you're not reading carefully).

! **Don't be afraid to change your yes/no answer if the second parts of both remaining answer choices sound incorrect.**

Now, let's look at Question 1 (note the ☐1 in the passage). The paragraph is copied below:

Snooker: Yesterday and Today

[1]

Snooker, a table sport where each opponent uses a cue to hit colored balls into table pockets, has been around for over a hundred years. If you've watched a game of pool or Billiards, then you might be more familiar with Snooker than you think. ☐1 The game likely originated in India in the late 1800's when British Army officers made variations to traditional Billiards. The word *snooker* was a slang military term for an inexperienced military man. It is claimed that Colonel Sir Neville Chamberlain was playing this new game when his opponent failed to "pot"—or sink—a ball. ☐2 Chamberlain called his opponent a snooker." The sport soon took this as its name.

(EX) 1. At this point, the writer is considering adding the following sentence:

   Billiards involves more colored balls than does Snooker.

   Should the writer make this addition here?

Before we look at the answer choices, let's first decide whether the answer is *yes* or *no*. Review the first paragraph above. Do you think the sentence in question ties into the main idea of the paragraph (circle one below)?

   YES or NO?

Now, let's look at the answer choices. We can eliminate A and B (the two "Yes" choices). Let's focus on C and D. Which answer choice is better? Consider the main idea of the paragraph.

   A. Yes, because it gives the reader a better idea of the differences between Billiards and Snooker.
   B. Yes, because it allows the reader to visualize Billiards.
   C. No, because it doesn't help expand the historical background of Snooker.
   D. No, because this paragraph is discussing table sports in general, not *specific* table sports.

DELETIONS

These questions ask if the writer should delete something from an essay. Usually the question will refer to a sentence, but sometimes you'll be asked about an underlined portion of a sentence. Either way, you must consider the main idea of the relevant part of the essay.

Questions to ask yourself: Is the sentence (or underlined portion) adding appropriate details, or is it adding needless details that don't benefit the essay? Is it adding support or explanation? Providing a transition to a new topic? Presenting a contrast or comparison? Does the sentence stay on topic? Is it redundant?

As with Additions questions, pay attention to the second parts of answer choices. They may force you to reconsider your first inclination (to keep or to delete).

Deletions questions refer to deleting "the previous sentence" or an underlined portion of a sentence. They may ask the following questions:
- Should the sentence be deleted?
- If the sentence were deleted, what would the passage lose?
- The sentence should be deleted because it . . .
- The sentence should NOT be deleted because it . . .

Let's look at Question 2, a Deletions question (note the ☐2 in the paragraph). Again, the paragraph is copied below:

Snooker: Yesterday and Today

[1]

Snooker, a table sport where each opponent uses a cue to hit colored balls into table pockets, has been around for over a hundred years. If you've watched a game of pool or Billiards, then you might be more familiar with Snooker than you think. ☐1 The game likely originated in India in the late 1800's when British Army officers made variations to traditional Billiards. The word *snooker* was a slang military term for an inexperienced military man. It is claimed that Colonel Sir Neville Chamberlain was playing this new game when his opponent failed to "pot"—or sink—a ball. ☐2 Chamberlain called his opponent a snooker." The sport soon took this as its name.

(EX) 2. The writer is considering deleting the following phrase from the preceding sentence:

—or sink—

If the writer were to make this deletion, the essay would primarily lose:

F. an anecdote about the naming of a sport.
G. a brief explanation of a term.
H. an explanation of why a player is unskilled.
J. an important distinction of Snooker.

TOPIC/TRANSITION SENTENCES

A *topic* sentence, which is usually the first sentence of a paragraph, introduces the paragraph's main idea (the *topic*); it may also transition from the previous paragraph. A *transition* sentence leads the reader from one idea to the next, either between paragraphs or within the same paragraph. Both types of sentences are similar in that they act as bridges between ideas in an essay. Once again, analyzing main ideas and looking for keywords will help you solve these questions.

Here are some typical topic/transition-sentence questions:
- "Which choice would most effectively introduce the topic of this paragraph?"
- "Which choice provides the best opening to this paragraph?"
- "Which choice provides the most effective transition to the next paragraph?"
- "Which choice provides the most effective transition to the next sentence?"

Read Paragraph 2 now. When you're done reading, think about main idea keywords for the paragraph. Can you come up with two or three of them?

[2]

The history of Snooker is filled with exciting matches and skilled players. The goal of Snooker is to score more points than the opponent. The game includes 15 red balls, one white ball, or cue ball, and six balls of different colors. Points are scored by potting balls. But the hard part is that the balls must be potted in a predetermined order. If you miss a shot on the desired ball, then your turn is done and the next player takes over. Imagine the challenge of having to hit one specific ball with all of the other balls scattered around. [4]

Keywords for Paragraph 2 =

_____

_____

Hopefully your keywords ("Snooker," "goal," and "challenge") helped you come up with the main idea of Paragraph 2: **how to play** the **challenging** game **Snooker**.

Now, let's look at Question 3. Since the question asks about the first sentence of the paragraph, it's no surprise that it's testing the topic sentence. Make sure to read the question carefully. The question specifies that you must not only focus on Paragraph 2 but also Paragraph 1.

(EX) 3. Which choice would most effectively and appropriately lead the reader from the topic of Paragraph 1 to that of Paragraph 2?

    A. NO CHANGE
    B. Billiards and Snooker are not the only games played with cues and balls.
    C. Snooker may have gotten its name from an unskilled player, but the game is not easy.
    D. Every game must have a means to determine winning from losing.

To answer Question 4, we'll have to read at least the first couple sentences of Paragraph 3:

[3]
Of the many great Snooker players,
Stephen Hendry stands out. Born on January
13, 1969 in Scotland, Hendry became the
youngest player to become a Snooker World
Champion—at the age of 21. . . .

It sounds like the paragraph is going to discuss one of the "great Snooker players," Stephen Hendry.

Now, let's tackle Question 4 (go back to Paragraph 2). Once again, note that the question is asking you to consider the main ideas of Paragraph 2 *and* Paragraph 3:

(EX) 4. Given that all of the following sentences are true, which one, if added here, would offer the best transition from Paragraph 2 to Paragraph 3?

    F. No wonder Snooker players are considered so skilled.
    G. Tournaments are where Snooker players can show their stuff.
    H. So many balls; so little time.
    J. A major advance for Snooker occurred in 1969 when the balls were used to demonstrate color TV.

Now, let's finish reading Paragraph 3. What are the keywords for this paragraph?

[3]

Of the many great Snooker players, Stephen Hendry stands out. Born on January 13, 1969 in Scotland, Hendry became the youngest player to become a Snooker World Champion—at the age of 21. He went on to win six more World Championships, and he was Snooker's number one player for eight consecutive years, between 1990 and 1998. Hendry's skill as a player lead to amazing riches and fame for him, and helped popularize the sport of Snooker around the world. However, you may not have heard of it.
5
5

Keywords for Paragraph 3 =

_____

_____

PASSAGE QUESTIONS

Some essays will have a question that relates to the main idea of the entire passage.

 Look for some mention of the "passage as a whole" or the "entire passage."

The best way to tackle these questions is to think about the main idea of each paragraph. Let's do this with the practice essay:

- Paragraph 1 has to do with the **origin** of **Snooker**.
- Paragraph 2 has to do with **how to play** the **challenging** game of **Snooker**.
- Paragraph 3 has to do with the **Stephen Hendry** and how he helped **popularize** the sport of **Snooker**.

If you were to summarize the essay, you might say that it offers a general overview of the sport of Snooker, from its origins to its current popularity.

TOO BROAD OR TOO NARROW

Watch out for answer choices that are too broad. For example, the main idea of the whole essay has something to do with Snooker, not table sports in general. A choice that only refers to table sports would be incorrect. But also watch out for answer choices that are too narrow. For example, this essay briefly discusses how Snooker is played, but this is not the main idea of the whole essay.

TITLES

The title of the essay will often help you determine its main idea. This essay is titled "Snooker: Yesterday and Today." See if this helps you answer Question 5 below:

 5. Which of the choices would provide an ending most consistent with the essay as a whole?

    A. NO CHANGE
    B. It's hard to imagine that Snooker, a sport with such humble beginnings, could become what it is today.
    C. The possibility of fame is real indeed.
    D. Snooker may be difficult, but that shouldn't stop you from giving it a shot.

PURPOSE QUESTIONS

Purpose questions ask about whether a writer accomplished a particular goal (or purpose) in the essay. Focus on your keywords. As with other main idea questions, make sure the stated goal is not too specific or too broad. You must focus on the entire essay. When the answer is "No," the reason is usually that the goal either covered only one small part of the essay, or was not discussed in the essay in any depth. Also, once again, keep the title of the essay in mind.

Note that the stated goal (in the question) may be worded in a *general sense*. For example, the question might refer to "a particular table game" rather than "Snooker." Don't let the general reference fool you: both options—specific ("Snooker") or general ("particular table game")—are fine.

These questions are easy to spot. You will see the following words: "Suppose the writer's purpose (or goal) had been . . . Would this essay accomplish this purpose?" When a Purpose question shows up, it will be the last question of a passage.

Let's look at Question 6. (Paragraph 3 is copied below.)

[3]

Of the many great Snooker players, Stephen Hendry stands out. Born on January 13, 1969 in Scotland, Hendry became the youngest player to become a Snooker World Champion—at the age of 21. He went on to win six more World Championships, and he was Snooker's number one player for eight consecutive years, between 1990 and 1998. Hendry's skill as a player lead to amazing riches and fame for him, and helped popularize the sport of Snooker around the world. <u>However, you may not have</u>
5
<u>heard of it.</u>
5

| Question 6 asks about the preceding passage as a whole. |

 6. Suppose the writer had chosen to write a brief essay that compares Snooker to other table games. Would this essay successfully fulfill that goal?

First, before you look at the answer choices, does the writer accomplish the goal of comparing Snooker to other table games? Importantly, does this reflect the main idea of the essay?

YES or NO?

ELIMINATE FALSE ANSWER CHOICES

Main Idea questions often have *false* answer choices. Check to see if one of the remaining answer choices is false. Here are the choices:

- **F.** Yes, because the essay discusses pool, Billiards, and Snooker.
- **G.** Yes, because the essay mentions that Snooker is a variation of Billiards.
- **H.** No, because the essay primarily discusses the origins and development of Snooker.
- **J.** No, because the essay fails to mention any other table games.

■

MAIN IDEAS SUMMARY

To summarize, when you tackle main idea questions:

- Look for *keywords* in the essay that capture main ideas.

- Answer yes/no questions before looking (in detail) at the answer choices.

- When adding or deleting information, watch out for answer choices that are *off topic*, or perfectly on topic but *redundant*.

- Make sure a topic sentence reflects the main idea of its paragraph.

- Make sure a transition sentence leads clearly from the main idea of one paragraph or sentence to that of the next one.

- Make sure the answers to Passage and Purpose questions aren't *too broad* or *too narrow*, and remember to check the essay's title.

- Watch out for, and eliminate, false answer choices.

2. *TRANSITIONS*

CONJUNCTIONS AS TRANSITIONS

As we've already learned, conjunctions are words that connect phrases or sentences together. They transition from one thought or idea to another. These conjunctions can be broken into three main types:

CONTRAST TRANSITIONS

although	even so	instead of	rather than
but	however	nevertheless	still
conversely	in contrast	on the contrary	while
despite	in spite of	on the other hand	yet
even though			

SUPPORT TRANSITIONS

additionally	besides	in fact	similarly
also	furthermore	likewise	(colon) **:**
and	in addition	moreover	

CAUSE AND EFFECT TRANSITIONS

accordingly	for	since	therefore
because	hence	so	thus
consequently	in order to	so... that	when... then

To identify transition questions, look for questions with answer choices that contain various transitions, as shown above. Note that transition questions often look like innocent Usage/Mechanics questions, but they *do* require you to go beyond basic grammar and understand main ideas in the passages.

TRANSITIONS AND MAIN IDEAS

To choose a correct transition, you need to recognize the main idea of where you *were* and the main idea of where you're *going*. Whether you're dealing with phrases, sentences, or whole paragraphs, understanding main ideas is the key. Let's look at an example:

IGNORE THE UNDERLINED TRANSITION WORD

! **Don't let the underlined word influence your choice. Remember, it will be wrong 75% of the time. Ignore it, and just focus on the main ideas of the passage.** Here's an example:

<u>Since</u> it may take a long time to
₁
understand all of the intricacies of Snooker, you can enjoy watching the sport today if you just understand the basic rules.

1. **A.** NO CHANGE
    B. Because
    C. When
    D. While

Forget about the underlined word, and just focus on the two parts of the sentence. What kind of transition are you looking for?

Type of transition:

_____

Now, take a look at the answer choices. What's the best answer?

Answer Questions 1 now.

ELIMINATE SYNONYMS

Often, there will be at least two transitions in the answer choices that are synonyms. These are generally incorrect (we obviously can't have more than one correct answer). In the example above, *since*, *because*, and sometimes *when* (as in *when . . . then*) are all cause & effect transitions. Not surprisingly, none of them is correct.

ILLOGICAL CONJUNCTIONS

Conjunctions are often used in *illogical* ways. For example:

You can easily follow the Snooker action *so that* you understand the basic rules.

Do you see the error? *Following the Snooker action* does not allow you to *understand the basic rules*. Rather, *understanding the basic rules* allows you to *follow the Snooker action*. The direction of causation is wrong. Replace *so that* with a logical word, such as *because*, *since*, *now that*, or *if*:

You can easily follow the Snooker action *because* you understand the basic rules.

Here's another example:

I practiced Snooker for hours every day, *and* I still struggled during the match.

The conjunction *and* is not the best choice here. Can you think of a more logical conjunction? The following sentence reflects the desired contrast:

I practiced Snooker for hours every day, *but* I still struggled during the match.

Let's try an ACT example:

Michael drove as fast as he could, <u>and</u> he arrived in plenty of time to see the start of the match.

2. Which of the following alternatives to the underlined portion would NOT be acceptable?

    F. so not surprisingly
    G. and thus
    H. so
    J. but

Do you see the illogical conjunction? What's the best answer?

Answer Questions 2 now.

SOMETIMES, NO TRANSITION IS BEST

Don't assume that you *must* use a transition. If the flow sounds awkward with a transition, or if none of the transitions seems to work, look for the answer choice that does *not* have a transition. For example:

I wanted to learn how to play Snooker. <u>It seemed</u> the best place to start was learning how to break.

3. **A.** NO CHANGE
    B. Nevertheless, it seemed
    C. On the other hand, it seemed
    D. In any case, it seemed

Consider the main idea of each sentence and answer Question 3 now.

SPECIAL SUPPORT TRANSITIONS

Sometimes a transition will be the right type (contrast, support, or cause and effect), but it will not work in the specific context of the essay. There are several support transitions, in particular, that have special uses. Here are a few examples:

First, second...

Stay consistent with numerical transitions. If you don't see a *first*, don't use a *second*. Also, you should usually stay consistent with how the number is expressed: *first, second, third...*, *number one, number two, number three...*, and so on.

For example

For example is a support transition, but make sure there is indeed an example following the transition.

In summary

Make sure what follows "in summary" is an actual summary. There should not be any new information presented.

In addition

Make sure additional information is included and not just an elaboration of the previous topic.

Finally

Make sure *finally* precedes the last of several items. It should, not surprisingly, generally show up near the end of an essay when used correctly.

3. ORGANIZATION

Some questions ask you to change the organization of an essay. You will either add a sentence to the passage or (potentially) move a sentence within a paragraph. You might also be asked to reposition an entire paragraph, but these questions are less common.

Most organization questions on recent ACTs involve *adding* a sentence to the passage. You will see lettered or numbered "placement points" within the passage ([A], [B], etc., or [1], [2], etc.). These points will be referred to in the answer choices. The question will generally be worded as follows: "The writer wants to add the following sentence. . . . This sentence would most logically be placed at: . . ."

You might also see questions that ask you to *move* a sentence within a single paragraph. The sentences will be numbered ([1], [2], etc.), and the question will generally be worded as follows: "For the sake of logic and coherence of this paragraph, Sentence 1 should be placed: . . ."

WHAT TO LOOK FOR (*CLUES*)

We'll discuss specific approaches to the two types of Organization questions (adding and moving) later. For both types, you should look for four possible *clues* in the sentence to be added or moved: main ideas, transitions, pronouns, and the word *the*.

MAIN IDEAS

Once again, as with many techniques in this chapter, focusing on *main ideas* is essential. Consider the main idea of the sentence to be added, and make sure to place it at the point in the passage that focuses on this same idea.

Can you identify the main idea in the following sentence?

A Snooker club provides young players a place to learn and more experienced players a chance to master the game.

In addition to simply being off topic, a sentence can be *too specific* or *too broad* for part of a passage. Below are some examples:

TOO SPECIFIC

Snooker, a table sport where each opponent uses a cue to hit colored balls into table pockets, has been around for over a hundred years. **A Snooker club provides young players a place to learn and more experienced players a chance to master the game.** If you've watched a game of pool or Billiards, then you might be more familiar with Snooker than you think. . . .

This paragraph focuses generally on Snooker, specifically its history and a bit about how it's played. Discussion of a Snooker *club* is too specific (and, thus, off topic).

TOO BROAD

The Red Lion Snooker Club has been around for nearly 100 years. Founded by a successful lawyer named Walter Benning, himself a lover of the game, the club soon became world famous. **A Snooker club provides young players a place to learn and more experienced players a chance to master the game.** . . .

This paragraph focuses on the "Red Lion Snooker Club." The added sentence, which discusses Snooker clubs generally, is too broad.

JUST RIGHT

While fans of Snooker can watch Snooker superstars battle it out on television, the best place to actually *play* the game is at the local club. **A Snooker club provides young players a place to learn and more experienced players a chance to master the game.** Clubs have regular tournaments, group activities for members, and often offer lessons for novices. . . .

TRANSITIONS

Added sentences may also function as *transitions* from one idea to another. Look out for transition words in the sentences (see the Transitions section). Also, if, while reading the passage, you sense that one idea awkwardly jumps to another idea (especially if you see a placement letter or number), you'll likely move a sentence to this point. Do you sense the transition in the following sentence?

Once you've found a good Snooker club close to you, it's time to learn how to play.

PRONOUNS

The clearest clues are often *pronouns*: words such as *he, they, his, their, its, these,* and so on. In the sentence that comes *before* the sentence in question, you'll probably notice the noun or nouns that the pronoun refers to:

[1] The first World Championship was organized by Englishman **Joe Davis**. [2] **His** efforts moved the game from a pastime to a professional sport.

[1] **New companies are becoming Snooker sponsors** all the time, and the game is showing **huge growth** in the Far East and China. [2] **These** are all signs that the future of Snooker is bright.

In both examples above, the clue words "His" and "These" reveal the order of the sentences.

THE

The definite article *the* often suggests that the noun that follows has already been introduced in the essay (and when *the* is not used, the noun that follows is probably being introduced for the first time). For example, consider the differences between the two sentences below:

The tournament was organized among the local Snooker clubs.

A tournament was organized among the local Snooker clubs.

For the first sentence, the tournament must have been introduced earlier, so the sentence must be placed *after* this introduction. The second sentence is introducing the tournament; the tournament should *not* be discussed earlier in the passage. (Note that in both sentences, "*the* local Snooker clubs" must have already been introduced, another possible clue.)

ADDING SENTENCES

As stated above, most Organization questions involve *adding sentences*. You'll usually have to focus on main ideas and transitions for these. Here's the approach:

1. **Circle the letters in the passage**: If you see bracketed letters as you read ([A], [B], etc.), you should probably expect to see an Organization question at the end of the passage. You might circle these letters in the passage so they're easier to find later.

2. **Read for awkwardness**: As you read the passage, if you notice an awkward flow of ideas, such as something being mentioned that should have been more formally or explicitly introduced, you may have already found your answer. Make a note of this—such as an asterisk (✳)—as you read.

3. **Consider clues when placing the sentence**: When you finally get to the added sentence, read the sentence carefully for clues (main ideas, transitions, pronouns, the word *the*). One or more of these clues should help you place the sentence correctly.

MOVING SENTENCES

As stated above, when you *move* a sentence, the paragraph will include sentences preceded by numbers in brackets ([1], [2], etc.). Here are the steps:

1. **Circle the sentence number in question**: When you get to a paragraph with numbered sentences, check to see if an organization question is on the way (typically the last question for that *paragraph*). If so, <u>before</u> reading the paragraph, skip to the organization question, take note of the sentence number in question, and, in the passage, circle the number of the sentence. This way, you'll know which sentence has a questionable placement, and, just as important, you'll know that the other sentences are correct.

2. **Read for awkwardness**: As you read the paragraph, again listen for an awkward flow of ideas. If a sentence sounds misplaced, and if this sentence is *not* the one you circled, then you'll probably move the circled sentence *before* the awkward-sounding sentence. Mark this point in the passage.

3. **Read the sentence in question warily**: Of course, the sentence whose number you circled is probably misplaced (75% of the time), so don't be surprised if it sounds wrong. Use the other sentences to get a feel for the intended flow of ideas within the paragraph. As with adding sentences, consider *clues* as you choose your answer.

■

Below is a question that asks you to potentially move a sentence. Remember, before reading the paragraph, circle the sentence number in question (look ahead at the question):

[1] The Snooker World Championship, the most important event in Snooker, takes place annually in Sheffield, England. [2] It is televised throughout the United Kingdom, Europe, and the Far East. [3] He or she walks away with status, fame, and riches. [4] The prize money is impressive—over $500,000 goes to the winner.

1

Question 1 below focuses on Sentence 3. First look for clue words in Sentence 3:

Clue word(s) for Sentence 3 =

_____

Now, answer the question:

(EX) 1. For the sake of the logic and coherence of this paragraph, Sentence 3 should be placed:

   A. where it is now.
   B. before Sentence 1.
   C. after Sentence 1.
   D. after Sentence 4.

For Question 2, you'll have to consider the flow of the main ideas of the paragraph. You might also look for the word *the* in the added sentence:

Question 2 asks about the preceding paragraph.

2. Upon reviewing this paragraph and realizing that some information has been left out, the writer composes the following sentence:

> The event is held at the Crucible Theater, which seats fewer than 1,000 people, but that doesn't mean there aren't a lot of viewers.

The most logical placement for this sentence would be:

F. before Sentence 1.
G. after Sentence 1.
H. after Sentence 2.
J. after Sentence 3.

CHECK YOUR ANSWERS

With Organization questions, check your answers. Quickly read the part of the essay that you reorganized, making sure that the sentence order sounds sensible and fluid. If you hear obvious awkwardness with your answer, then you should take a look at the other choices.

4. ANSWER THE QUESTION

This lesson may sound obvious, but make sure you carefully read Rhetorical Skills questions. Sometimes, if you read a question too quickly, more than one answer choice seems to work. The ACT sometimes asks very *specific* questions—we call them "Answer the Question" questions. You must read them carefully and answer *exactly* what the question is asking.

 These questions tend to have very specific instructions (such as "giving credit to Snooker players" in the example below). Also, if all of the answer choices would technically sound fine in the passage, carefully reread the question—it may be an "Answer the Question" question. Finally, you may sometimes see the words in the question: "Given that all the following statements are true . . ."

Let's go back to Paragraph 3 from the sample essay at the beginning of the chapter to look at an example.

[3]

Of the many great Snooker players, Stephen Hendry stands out. Born on January 13, 1969 in Scotland, Hendry became the youngest player to become a Snooker World Champion—at the age of 21. He went on to win six more World Championships, and he was Snooker's number one player for eight consecutive years, between 1990 and 1998. Hendry's skill as a player lead to amazing riches and fame for him, and helped popularize the sport of Snooker around the world. It's hard to imagine that Snooker, a sport with such humble beginnings, <u>could become what it is today</u>.

₁

1. Given that all of the choices are true, which one would conclude the essay by giving credit to Snooker players for the popularity of Snooker?

   A. NO CHANGE
   B. could become the international phenomenon it is today.
   C. could become, thanks to competitors like Hendry, what it is today.
   D. could provide such wealth to its champions.

First of all, notice that every answer choice is true. According to the essay, Snooker *is* an "international phenomenon" (B) and *does* "provide such wealth" to its players (D). But look carefully at the question. It asks you to find an answer that credits *Snooker players* for Snooker's popularity. Which one does that?

Answer Question 1 now.

Here's something interesting about these types of questions:

 Answer-the-Question questions can usually be answered without looking back to the essay!

Just make sure you read the question carefully. If you read the question too quickly, choosing the correct answer can be difficult, if not impossible. But if you "answer the question," the problem becomes straightforward. Here's one more Answer-the-Question question. Try answering it without looking at the passage.

2. Given that all of the choices are true, which one provides the most specific information about a break in Snooker?

   F. Unlike pool breaks, Snooker breaks are entirely defensive.
   G. The break in Snooker—also called "breaking off"—can set the tone for an entire game.
   H. When breaking, most players try to hit the "end red" of the triangle just hard enough for the cue ball to hit three cushions and come to rest near what's called the "baulk cushion."
   J. When hitting the cue ball, a player can achieve different spins—including top spin, back spin, and side spin—depending on what part of the ball is struck.

5. STYLE

The last Rhetorical Skills topic to consider is style. Style questions ask you to consider *consistency* of style. For example, if an essay is written as a formal essay, then make sure the answers to questions reflect this formality. Avoid casual language: for example, *awesome* for *excellent*, *blow off* for *ignore*, or *a lot of stuff* for *many items*.

Also, watch out for language that is *too* formal, such as *whilst* for *while*, or *heretofore* for *since then*.

The writing on the English Test is usually relatively formal, but not *too* formal.

 Most Style questions include answer choices that contain *informal* language, but you might occasionally see choices containing words that are *too* formal.

Besides the World Championship, there are a number of other Snooker tournaments held throughout the world. The UK Championship is right behind the World Championship in importance, and The Masters is also <u>a prestigious tournament</u>.
₁

1. Which of the following alternatives to the underlined portion would NOT be acceptable?

    A. a celebrated event
    B. definitely a lot of fun
    C. high on the list of renowned tournaments.
    D. highly-acclaimed

The paragraph above is formally written (as is the entire essay on Snooker). Do any of the answer choices contradict this formality?

Do you see an answer choice that is too informal?

6. RHETORICAL SKILLS SUMMARY

The following summarizes the techniques that will help you tackle Rhetorical Skills questions:

1. Main Ideas

   - Look for keywords in the essay that capture main ideas.

   - Answer Yes or No questions before looking (in detail) at the answer choices.

   - When adding or deleting information, watch out for answer choices that are off topic or redundant.

   - Make sure a topic sentence reflects the main idea of its paragraph.

   - Make sure a transition sentence leads clearly from the main idea of one paragraph or sentence to that of the next one.

   - Make sure the answers to Passage and Purpose questions aren't too broad or too narrow, and remember to check the essay's title.

   - Watch out for, and eliminate, false answer choices.

2. Transitions

   - Learn the three types of transitions.

   - Consider main ideas.

   - Eliminate synonyms

   - Watch out for illogical conjunctions.

   - Sometimes, no transition is best.

   - Make sure the conjunction works in context (special support transitions).

3. Organization

   - Look for clues:

     o Consider the main idea of the sentence to be moved.

     o Look for transition clues in the sentence.

     o Pronouns in the sentence will probably be defined just *before* a point of placement.

     o Look for the word *the* (the definite article). The word following a definite article will almost always be introduced *before* the point of placement.

4. Answer the question: Make sure you can identify questions with *specific instructions* guiding you to the answer.

5. Keep style consistent: Answers should not be too formal or too casual.

7. RHETORICAL SKILLS PROBLEMS

PRACTICE PROBLEMS

After reviewing the lessons on the previous pages, tackle the lesson and homework passages on the following pages. **Important: unlike the passages on a real ACT, the following two passages only test material taught in the Rhetorical Skills chapter**:

- ☐ Usage/Mechanics Passage I: "The Same Old Story"
- ☐ Usage/Mechanics Passage II: "Alien Invasion"

In addition to these passages, you should tackle practice passages from *The Official ACT Prep Guide*:

- • ***The Official ACT Prep Guide:* "Improving Your English Score" chapter***
  - ☐ Passage I
  - ☐ Passage II
  - ☐ Passage III
- • ***The Official ACT Prep Guide*: Test 5***
  - ☐ Passage I
  - ☐ Passage II
  - ☐ Passage III
  - ☐ Passage IV
  - ☐ Passage V

*****Note**: We recommend you time yourself on the above assignments. See the English Introduction for individual-passage time estimates.

■

 PRACTICE TEST (30- and 40-hour programs): Now is a good time to take **Test 3** in the ACT book. We recommend that you review the Timing plan (see the Introduction), especially if you've had trouble finishing past tests; make sure you have a timing plan in place. Also, don't forget to correct any missed questions after you grade the test (see below).

TEST CORRECTIONS

After completing and grading each practice test, you should correct Rhetorical Skills questions that you missed or guessed on. Below are the three steps:

1. Turn to the Techniques chapter at the end of this tutorial and, for the appropriate test, circle the Rhetorical Skills questions that you missed or guessed on.

2. Correct the problems in *The Official ACT Prep Guide*. As you correct the problems, go back to the tutorial and review the techniques. The idea is to (1) identify techniques that have given you trouble, (2) go back to the tutorial so you can review and strengthen these techniques, and (3) apply these techniques to the specific problems you struggled on.

3. If you have trouble identifying the best technique to use on a problem, refer to the Techniques chapter at the end of this tutorial. This is an important part of correcting the tests.

LESSON PRACTICE PASSAGE

The following lesson passage only tests material taught in the Rhetorical Skills chapter. Do not time yourself on this passage. The passage begins on the next page.

Rhetorical Skills Passage I

The Cat Who Lived and Died

[1]

[1] In 1935, three famous physicists (one of them Einstein), published an article that <u>highlighted the nature of something called</u>₁ <u>quantum superposition.</u> [2] The idea was that a quantum system exists as a combination of multiple states, each state corresponding to a different possible outcome. [3] Einstein even called it "spooky." [4] The system would stay in this state until someone or something outside of the system observed it, at which point the system would "collapse" into one of the possible outcomes. [5] Most would agree that it's an <u>impractical</u>₂ idea for something to be in more than one state at once. [A] 3

1. Which choice most effectively introduces the passage?

   A. NO CHANGE
   B. explained the differences between quantum mechanics and general relativity.
   C. discussed the importance of physicists in helping people understand the world.
   D. brought fame and notoriety to its writers.

2. Which choice best emphasizes the strange nature of quantum superposition?

   F. NO CHANGE
   G. inelegant
   H. astounding
   J. elaborate

3. For the sake of logic and coherence, Sentence 3 should be placed:

   A. where it is now.
   B. after Sentence 1.
   C. after Sentence 4.
   D. after Sentence 5.

Continued →

[2]

Which leads us to Schrödinger's cat. [B] Erwin Schrödinger was a Viennese physicist who won the Nobel Prize in Physics in 1933. [4] Schrödinger's cat was not actually a real

one. It was part of his famous thought experiment. The experiment involved putting the following items inside a sealed box: a glass container of poison; a hammer; radioactive material; a Geiger counter, a device used to detect radiation; and, of course, his imaginary cat. To put it simply, the amount of radioactive material was small enough so that there was only a 50/50 chance that the Geiger counter would detect it. If the radiation was detected, the hammer would drop on the glass container, releasing the poison, and killing the cat. Likewise, the cat would live.
₆

Continued →

4. At this point, the writer is considering adding the following true statement:

> Despite being raised in a religious household—his father was Catholic and his mother was Lutheran—Schrodinger was an atheist.

Should the writer make this addition here?

F. Yes, because it supports the fact that Schrödinger was a great physicist.
G. Yes, because it serves as a transition from a description of Schrödinger to a discussion of his experiment.
H. No, because it weakens the focus of the paragraph by discussing a subject unrelated to physics.
J. No, because it interrupts the flow of the sentences by supplying information about Schrödinger rather than his experiment.

5. Which choice best supports the statement made in the previous sentence?

A. NO CHANGE
B. Schrödinger had a real cat, named Milton, that was not part of his experiment.
C. Schrödinger would need more than just a cat for his experiment.
D. Schrödinger's experiment could have used any living creature.

6. F. NO CHANGE
G. On the other hand,
H. Otherwise,
J. However,

[3]

Schrödinger stressed that until someone opened the box, it would be impossible to predict the experiment's outcome. <u>In other words,</u> the system would be in an un-collapsed
7
state: <u>the cat would exist in a superposition of being both alive and dead.</u> Of course, to most
8
people, the idea is ridiculous, and this was exactly Schrödinger's point. While quantum superposition could work on a small scale, for

example with <u>streaking</u> particles such as
9
electrons, on a larger scale the theory was

inherently flawed. |10| A cat cannot be both alive and dead at the same time. [c]

Continued →

7. **A.** NO CHANGE
   B. Nevertheless,
   C. Finally,
   D. In addition,

8. If the writer were to delete the underlined portion (ending the sentences with a period), the paragraph would primarily lose:

   F. a specific explanation of an un-collapsed state.
   G. a criticism of the idea of superposition.
   H. a possible result of a collapsed system.
   J. a reflection of the experiment's unpredictable nature.

9. Which choice best supports the information presented earlier in this sentence?

   A. NO CHANGE
   B. numerous
   C. complex
   D. tiny

10. The writer is considering deleting the previous sentence. Should the sentence be kept or deleted?

   F. Deleted, because it introduces information that is irrelevant at this point in the passage.
   G. Deleted, because it contradicts the sentence that follows.
   H. Kept, because it provides an example of why superposition is flawed on a larger scale.
   J. Kept, because it develops an important point that Schrödinger makes about superposition.

[4]

An interesting solution to this apparent paradox is the many-worlds interpretation. First formulated in 1957, the theory proclaims that

11

even after the box is opened, both a living cat and a dead cat exist, but in two different realities. That is, reality is split into one world where the observer is looking into a box with a live cat, and another world where the observer is looking into a box with a dead cat. For

12

example, it goes without saying that these

12

different outcomes cannot interact with each other. [D] In any case, Schrödinger's thought

Continued →

11. **A.** NO CHANGE
    B. gets it out there
    C. states
    D. shouts out

12. **F.** NO CHANGE
    G. Finally,
    H. Actually,
    J. DELETE the underlined portion and capitalize the first word of the sentence.

experiment is still discussed in physics classes around the world. In that sense at least, one could say that the cat definitely lived. [14]
13   13

13. The writer wants a conclusion that emphasizes the continued popularity of Schrödinger's experiment. Which choice best accomplishes this goal?

   A. NO CHANGE
   B. Many people erroneously assume that Schrödinger agreed with the idea of large-scale superposition.
   C. The ideas of quantum mechanics continue to evolve today.
   D. Whether anyone actually understands his experiment is another question.

14. The writer wants to add the following sentence to the essay:

> Schrödinger wasn't around to comment on this new theory— unless, of course, he did so from some other reality.

The sentence would most logically be placed at:

   F. Point A in Paragraph 1.
   G. Point B in Paragraph 2.
   H. Point C in Paragraph 3.
   J. Point D in Paragraph 4.

Question 15 asks about the preceding passage as a whole.

15. Suppose the writer's main purpose had been to describe the life and work of a famous physicist. Would this essay accomplish that purpose?

   A. Yes, because the essay provides biographical information about Erwin Schrödinger.
   B. Yes, because the essay describes Schrödinger's famous thought experiment.
   C. No, because the essay focuses on quantum superposition.
   D. No, because the essay discusses the work of several scientists.

■

The following HW passage only tests material taught in the Rhetorical Skills chapter. Do not time yourself on this passage.

The passage begins on the next page.

Rhetorical Skills Passage II

A Prickly Subject

[1]

Bad news travels quickly. In 1998 British medical researcher Dr. Andrew Wakefield studied tissue rejection problems using animal models. Wakefield's study focused on a possible—and unexpected—connection between the vaccination of children and the sharp rise in autism diagnoses over the past 20 years. [2] Research suggests that some combination of genetics and environmental factors leads to the disorder, but the recent rise in cases cannot be attributed to genetics alone. [A] Something else must be going on,

and Wakefield wanted to get to the bottom of it.

[2]

[1] Edward Jenner is considered the first to introduce vaccinology in the West, when, in 1796, he developed the first smallpox vaccine. [2] Louis Pasteur's work in the 1800s ushered in vaccines for cholera and anthrax. [3] Per-

Continued →

1. Which choice most effectively leads into information that follows in the paragraph?
   A. NO CHANGE
   B. performed a study that would later be discredited.
   C. conducted a study that shocked the world.
   D. became widely known as an expert of autism.

2. At this point, the writer is considering adding the following true statement:

   > Autism is a disorder that impairs brain development.

   Should the writer make this addition here?
   F. Yes, because it briefly introduces a disorder that is discussed throughout passage.
   G. Yes, because it confirms the need to find an effective vaccine for a serious disorder.
   H. No, because the autism was not a part of Wakefield's study.
   J. No, because it unnecessarily repeats information from earlier in the passage.

3. Which of the following most effectively links the first paragraph with the information that follows?
   A. NO CHANGE
   B. and the world would hear about soon enough.
   C. and Wakefield's study held the key.
   D. and Wakefield thought he found the explanation: vaccinations.

haps the best known vaccine was Jonas Salk's polio vaccine, which, after the vaccine's introduction in the 1950s, helped nearly eradicate the disease. [4] Vaccinations have been around since seventeenth-century Buddhist monks drank snake venom to become immune to snake bites. [5] Vaccines have also helped nearly eliminate measles, mumps, and rubella. |4| [6] <u>Moreover,</u> over
                                          5
the past several years, thanks largely to Wakefield's study, vaccination rates have plummeted, and, unsurprisingly, infection rates of preventable diseases have skyrocketed. |6|

[3]

In his study, Wakefield reported on the onset of autism-like symptoms in several children soon after they received the popular MMR, or Measles, Mumps, and Rubella, vaccine. The paper made no claim of causal connection, but Wakefield, in a press conference before his paper was published,

Continued →

4. At this point, the writer is considering adding the following sentence:

   > Measles is the most serious of the three diseases, sometimes leading to pneumonia, inflammation of the brain, and even death.

   Should the writer make this addition here?

   F. Yes, because it provides a link between the effectiveness of vaccines and the decline in their acceptance.
   G. Yes, because it clarifies the differences in the types of diseases that vaccines are used against.
   H. No, because it fails to explain how vaccines helped eliminate measles, mumps, and rubella.
   J. No, because it provides information that blurs the focus of the paragraph.

5. **A.** NO CHANGE
   B. However,
   C. Also,
   D. Likewise,

6. For the sake of logic and coherence, Sentence 4 should be placed:

   F. where it is now.
   G. before Sentence 1.
   H. after Sentence 1.
   J. after Sentence 2.

expressed <u>confidence in</u> the MMR vaccine. [B]
₇
One doesn't need a degree in sociology to
know that even the slightest hint that something
might harm the health of children will instill fear

in the hearts of parents. <u>Some parents, how-</u>
₈
<u>ever, were skeptical of Wakefield's findings.</u>
₈

[4]

But was the vaccination–autism link real?
[C] After numerous studies of more than 25
million children, researchers concluded that
there was no causal relationship between
vaccines and autism. Wakefield's findings

<u>were just too farfetched</u>. The publisher of the
₉
original paper fully retracted Wakefield's
article in 2010, noting that parts had been

falsified. <u>Nevertheless,</u> Wakefield was taken
₁₀
off the UK medical register and was barred
from practicing medicine.

Continued →

7. Which choice best supports Wakefield's
claim that autism-like symptoms are
related in some way to the MMR
vaccination?
   A. NO CHANGE
   B. disregard for
   C. approval of
   D. concern about

8. Which choice best provides a likely
consequence of the point made in the
previous sentence?
   F. NO CHANGE
   G. Wakefield's ideas spread like
   wildfire around the world, leaving
   millions of children unvaccinated.
   H. Immunologists immediately went to
   work on a new MMR vaccine that
   would not harm children.
   J. Wakefield's paper brought him
   considerable acclaim.

9. Based on the information in the previous
sentence, which of the following offers
the most logical and precise information
about Wakefield's findings?
   A. NO CHANGE
   B. deserved more careful attention.
   C. were true for only a small group of
   children.
   D. simply could not be reproduced.

10. F. NO CHANGE
    G. Likewise,
    H. Conversely,
    J. Consequently,

[5]

People love a good controversy. After the
                            11
article was published, Vaccination rates in
Britain dropped from 92 percent to 73 percent.
In the United States, an estimated 125,000
children did not receive the MMR vaccine.
Childhood diseases that had been nearly

eradicated had reemerged. |12| One 2011
journal article described the vaccine-autism
connection as the most damaging medical
hoax of the past 100 years. [D] And yet, many

apprehensive parents still choose not to vac-
    13

Continued →

11. Which sentence best introduces the
    main topic of this paragraph and
    connects this paragraph with the
    previous paragraph?

    A. NO CHANGE
    B. Wakefield's study isn't the only thing
       people should be worried about.
    C. The fear that Wakefield helped
       cause will dissipate over time as
       new information is released.
    D. Wakefield's claims, however, have
       suffered a slow death.

12. If the writer were to delete the preceding
    sentence, the paragraph would primarily
    lose a statement that:

    F. explains why many parents were
       afraid to have their children
       vaccinated.
    G. illustrates a consequence of the
       decline in vaccination rates.
    H. proves that the vaccine-autism link
       is flawed.
    J. emphasizes the progress made in
       the use of vaccines to eradicate
       diseases.

13. The writer wants to convey parents'
    concerns while avoiding a strongly
    negative tone. Which choice best
    accomplishes this goal?

    A. NO CHANGE
    B. gullible
    C. naïve
    D. ignorant

-cinate their children. The safety of vac-

cinations has been confirmed by scientists,

but parents recognize that scientists are not
                                          14
infallible.
    14

14. Which choice most effectively concludes the sentence and paragraph?
    F. NO CHANGE
    G. and soon enough parents will get the message.
    H. but only time will tell if the benefits of vaccinations outweigh their potential side effects.
    J. but good news, it seems, travels much slower than bad.

Question 15 asks about the preceding passage as a whole.

15. The writer wants to add the following sentence to the essay:

    After the paper was published, researchers scrambled to confirm its claims.

    The sentence would most logically be placed at:

    A. Point A in Paragraph 1.
    B. Point B in Paragraph 3.
    C. Point C in Paragraph 4.
    D. Point D in Paragraph 5.

■

30- and 40-hour programs: At this point, go back to Section 12 in the Grammar Chapter, and complete the remaining lessons. See the Tutoring Schedules in the Introduction for more details.

PART 2

MATH

I
MATH INTRODUCTION AND BASIC CONCEPTS

This chapter will introduce the ACT Math Test, including test layout and timing strategy. It will also cover the use of your calculator and other basic mathematical concepts and terminologies.

1. INTRODUCTION

The Math section is divided into nine chapters:

    I.   Introduction and Basic Concepts

    II.   Arithmetic

    III.   Algebra

    IV.   Advanced Algebra

    V.   Geometry

    VI.   Functions

    VII.   Trigonometry

    VIII.   Math Odds & Ends

The primary purpose of this part of the tutorial is to teach you *how* to use mathematical techniques. However, while knowing *how* to apply these techniques is obviously important, knowing *when* to use the techniques is perhaps just as important. You may be an expert at a particular technique, but if you come across a problem on the ACT and do not *use* this technique, then your mastery of the technique may not help you. For this reason, the tutorial also focuses on *identifying* the correct technique to use on a particular problem. Throughout the tutorial, look for the magnifying glass for information about identifying techniques.

TEST LAYOUT

The Math Test includes:

- 60 multiple-choice questions (5 answer choices each)
- Total test time = 60 minutes

TIMING STRATEGY

Generally speaking, the ACT Math Test gets harder as you go. However, you will likely find several relatively easy questions near the end of the test and several relatively difficult questions near the beginning. (The order-of-difficulty pattern of the ACT is certainly not as clear-cut as that of the SAT.) Use the following strategy:

STEP 1

As you work your way through the test, plan to leave some questions blank—even if some of these questions occur early in the test. (Don't forget to leave the answer choice bubbles blank as well!) Don't get bogged down on problems that you find especially difficult. Just skip them and keep moving. Stay aggressive and try to get to the last question of the test, even if you have to skip many questions to get there. Because the questions *generally* get harder as you go, the further into the test you get, the more questions you'll likely have to skip. Review our approach to skipping questions in the "Guessing on the ACT" section (in the Introduction).

STEP 2

After you get to the end of the test, with whatever time you have left, go back to the questions you left blank, starting from the beginning. If, for a particular question, you have no idea how to tackle it, take a guess and move on to the next one. (Remember, you don't lose points on the ACT, so you should answer every question, even if you have to guess.)

STEP 3

Make sure you leave yourself about 30 seconds at the end of the test to guess on any remaining questions.

As you learn the techniques in this tutorial and get better at identifying problems that use these techniques, you'll get better at choosing which problems to tackle your first time through. Taking real practice tests will definitely help you develop a timing strategy that works for *you*.

QUESTIONS THAT LOOK HARD ARE OFTEN <u>NOT</u> HARD

Don't assume that just because a question looks hard you should skip it. Some of the hardest-looking questions are often the easiest. There are two types of questions that typically scare away students:

1. Questions with lots of words
2. Questions with long formulas

Stay aggressive on these problems. They may not be too difficult, and getting them correct will certainly give you an edge over other students who will likely skip them or guess. It's worth noting, however, that questions with lots of words often take longer to complete than shorter questions, so as you get into the later (and potentially harder) parts of the test, these long, wordy questions may be good ones to skip and come back to if you have time.

2. CALCULATORS

We recommend that you use a calculator on the ACT. Since functions and their graphs are part of the test, a graphing calculator is highly recommended. Most graphing calculators are fine; **calculators with built-in computer algebra systems, however, are not permitted**. (The most common of these is the Texas Instrument TI-89.) For more information about permitted calculators, go to the ACT website (http://www.actstudent.org/faq/answers/calculator.html).

Many students make careless mistakes because they try to solve difficult computations in their heads. Other students, on the other hand, tend to use calculators for all computations, even the easy ones, costing them valuable seconds on the test. **Keep in mind that the ACT does not require the use of a calculator.** If you find that you're using one on every problem, you might be slowing yourself down. Find a good balance. Don't use your calculator for 2 × 1, but if you have a tendency to make careless mistakes, *do* use it for 20 × 100.

Make sure you are comfortable with your calculator. Bring it to all of your tutoring lessons and use it on your homework assignments and practice tests.

 Your calculator can be used to solve problems involving *fractions*, *radicals*, *scientific notation*, and the π symbol.

If you are not comfortable with any of the above numerical forms, just use your calculator to simplify the problem into one of *decimal numbers*. Of course, you will likely have to convert the answer choices to decimals so you can compare them to the answer you found with your calculator. Make sure to stay accurate. Always round decimals to at least four decimal places to the right of the decimal point. For example:

$$\frac{1}{3} \neq 0.3 \Rightarrow \frac{1}{3} = 0.3333 \text{ (close enough)}$$

FRACTIONS AND YOUR CALCULATOR

It will be very helpful to learn how to use the **fraction key** that is found on most calculators. This will allow you to maintain perfect accuracy and check answer choices more quickly (when they are in fraction form). Check your calculator's manual to see how to enter fractions or convert decimals into fractions, or ask a tutor for assistance.

MIXED FRACTIONS

Mixed fractions include a whole number and a fraction, for example:

$$2\frac{3}{4}$$

To enter a mixed fraction into your calculator, think about how you *say* the number:

$$2\frac{3}{4} \equiv \text{"two \textbf{and} three-fourths"}$$

You probably know that the word "and" is used to describe addition ("1 *and* 1 is 2"). So to enter a mixed number into your calculator, use addition:

$$2\frac{3}{4} \rightarrow 2 + \frac{3}{4}$$

ORDER OF OPERATION

Most calculators follow the standard *order of operation* rules. You should be familiar with these rules for tackling more difficult algebra problems. Remember *PEMDAS*: (1) parentheses, (2) exponents, (3) multiplication/division (in order from left to right), and (4) addition/subtraction (in order from left to right).

CALCULATOR LESSON PROBLEMS

Try the following problems using *only* your calculator. The point of these problems is to become comfortable with your calculator. Do not worry about topics such as fractions, scientific notation, and radical simplification. You only need to know how to plug these numbers into your calculator.

1. $-2^2 =$

2. $(-2)^2 =$

3. $\dfrac{317 + 257}{2} =$

4. $254 - 550 \div 25 =$

5. $2 \times (16 - 3)^2 =$

6. $2\frac{3}{4} + 3\frac{3}{8} =$

7. $\frac{3}{4} \times \frac{2}{3} =$

8. $\frac{3}{4} \div \frac{2}{3} =$
    - A. $\frac{1}{2}$
    - B. $\frac{7}{8}$
    - C. 1
    - D. $1\frac{1}{8}$
    - E. $1\frac{3}{8}$

9. $\dfrac{\frac{1}{2} + \frac{2}{3}}{\frac{3}{4} + \frac{4}{5}} =$
    - F. $\frac{70}{93}$
    - G. $1\frac{1}{2}$
    - H. $2\frac{17}{90}$
    - J. $2\frac{16}{45}$
    - K. 3

10. $125{,}000 \times 200{,}000 =$
    - A. $25{,}000$
    - B. $250{,}000$
    - C. 2.5×10^8
    - D. 2.5×10^{10}
    - E. 2.5×10^{12}

11. $\sqrt{108} + \sqrt{48} =$
    - F. $\sqrt{13}$
    - G. $6\sqrt{3}$
    - H. $2\sqrt{39}$
    - J. $\sqrt{156}$
    - K. $10\sqrt{3}$

3. BASIC CONCEPTS

TERMINOLOGY

The following are some commonly misunderstood terms that show up on the ACT:

- **Integer**: positive or negative whole number or zero: ...–3, –2, –1, 0, 1, 2, 3...
- **Zero**: remember, zero is an integer. Zero is also an *even* number, but it is not a *positive* or a *negative* number—think of it as *neutral*.
- **Natural Numbers** – positive integers and (usually) zero. These are sometimes called *counting* numbers. Unless the question says otherwise, assume that zero is one of the natural numbers: 0, 1, 2, 3, 4...
- **Real Number**: Any number that is not *imaginary*. If you don't know what imaginary numbers are (yet), don't worry about it; we'll cover imaginary numbers in the Odds & Ends chapter. At this point, assume *all* numbers are real numbers.
- **Rational Number**: Any number that can be written as an integer or a *fraction* of integers. Examples: -4, $^{21}\!/_{93}$, $^{\sqrt{16}}\!/_{\sqrt{25}}$ (because it equals $^4\!/_5$)
- **Irrational Number**: Any number that can *not* be written as an integer or a fraction of integers. Examples: π, $\sqrt{2}$, $\sqrt{22}$ (any radical that cannot be simplified to a whole number)
- **Factor** (or **divisor**): any of the numbers multiplied together to form a *product*. For example: $2 \times 3 = 6$ ← 2 and 3 are *factors* (or *divisors*) of the *product* 6.
- **Multiples**: the multiples of a number are simply the products of that number and integers. For example: the multiples of 3 are 3, 6, 9, 12, 15, ...
- **Prime number**: number *greater than one* whose only integer factors are one and itself. For example: The number 11 is only divisible by 11 and 1; it is therefore a *prime number*.

ABSOLUTE VALUE

The SAT may test absolute value. Simply put, the absolute value of a number is the positive form of that number. Just get rid of the negative sign, if there is one.

$$|-20| = 20$$
$$|3 - 6| = |-3| = 3$$

Sometimes you'll have to solve for a variable in an equation containing an absolute value. We'll cover this in the Algebra chapter (Basic Algebra).

BASIC OPERATIONS

It may be helpful to memorize the rules below. If you ever forget one of these rules, just make up some numbers and use your calculator:

- even + even or even − even = even
- odd + odd or odd − odd = even
- odd + even or odd − even = odd

- even × even = even
- odd × odd = odd
- odd × even = even

- positive × positive or positive ÷ positive = positive
- negative × negative or negative ÷ negative = positive
- positive × negative or positive ÷ negative = negative

- (positive or negative real number)^2 = positive
- (positive real number)^3 = positive
- (negative real number)^3 = negative

FACTOR TABLE

When you are asked to find the *positive integer factors* (sometimes simply called the *positive factors*) of a number, use a *factor table*.

 Look for the words *positive integer factors (or divisors)* or *positive factors (or divisors)*.

1. Start with 1 in the first column and the original number in the second column of a table.
2. If the original number is even, mentally increase the number in the first column by 1. If the original number is odd, mentally increase the number in the first column by 2 (only odd numbers are divisors of odd numbers).
3. Is the new number a factor of the original number? Hint: you may want to use your calculator. If it is, place it in a new row in column one, and write the quotient (the number displayed on your calculator) in column 2.
4. Repeat steps 2 and 3 until the number in column one exceeds the number in column 2. When done, the numbers in the table will be the positive factors of the original number.

(EX) What are the positive integer factors of 66?

FACTOR TREE

When you are asked to find the *prime factors* of a number, use a *factor tree*. This is different from a factor table, so make sure you read carefully for the mention of *prime* factors.

 Look for the words *prime factors (or prime divisors)*.

1. Write the original number in your work space.

2. Think of a prime number that divides evenly into the original number. Write this prime number and its quotient as *branches* below the original number. Circle or underline the prime number.

3. Repeat step 2 with the quotient branch.

4. When all branches end with prime numbers, those prime numbers are the prime factors of the original number.

(EX) What are the prime factors of 66?

GREATEST COMMON FACTORS

Remember, a *factor* is part of the product of another number. For example, previously we learned that 2 and 3 are factors of 6. Sometimes you may be asked to find the *greatest common factor* (GCF) of two or more numbers. For example, the GCF of 6 and 21 is 3 (the greatest number that is a factor of both 6 and 21). **For these problems: You can usually simply check the answer choices (starting with the greatest number) and use your calculator.**

(EX) What is the greatest common factor of 60, 84, and 120?

    A. 3
    B. 4
    C. 12
    D. 30
    E. 60

Optional [40-hour program only]: On rare occasions the above approach won't work. Here's the official method (but skip this if you're short on time). Follow along with the example:

1. Find the prime factors of all numbers in question.

2. Look for any prime factors that are common to all of the original numbers.

3. Multiply these prime factors together to find the GCF.

(EX) What is the greatest common factor of 52 and 78?

LEAST COMMON MULTIPLES

The *least common multiple* (LCM) is the *smallest* number that is a multiple of a given set of other numbers. For example, the LCM of 6 and 9 is 18 (18 is the smallest multiple of 6 and 9). One trick to finding LCMs is to use trial and error. **Just check multiples of the <u>largest</u> number in the set until you find one that is also a multiple of the other number(s).** The concept is best explained with an example:

(EX) What is the least common multiple of 10 and 14?

You can also often just check the answer choices. Make sure to start with the *smallest* number, as more than one answer will often be a multiple of the numbers in question, but only one will be the *least* common multiple.

Optional [40-hour program only]: For harder LCM problems, or if on a particular problem the methods above are taking too long, use the following method (again, skip this if you're short on time). Make sure to follow along with the example:
1. Find the prime factors of all numbers in question.
2. For each prime factor, count the greatest number of times this factor shows up for any one of the original numbers.
3. *Raise* each prime factor to the power of the greatest number of times the factor shows up, and multiply these values. This might sound confusing, so follow along with the example below.

(EX) What is the least common multiple of 52 and 78?

ADDING AND SUBTRACTING FRACTIONS

Usually, if you're comfortable using your calculator, dealing with fractions is a snap. The one exception involves problems that require you to find a *common denominator* (the *denominator* is the bottom number in a fraction). A *common denominator* is simply a *common multiple* of all the denominators. You'll usually be asked to find the *least* common denominator. Just use one of the methods above for finding the LCM.

BASIC CONCEPTS LESSON PROBLEMS

1. Circle all integers: 203 2.03 π 0 –2 $\frac{2}{3}$ 4.0

2. Circle all rational numbers: $\sqrt{18}$ $\sqrt{9}$ π $\frac{7}{8}$ 1.2 $\frac{1}{3}$

3. What are the prime numbers between 1 and 10?

4. $|4-5|-|5-4| =$

5. $|2(-3)-(-2)(-3)| =$

6. If $|x| = 4$, what are all possible values of x?

7. What are the positive integer factors of 42?

8. What are the prime factors of 42?

9. What is the least common denominator of $\frac{1}{3}$ and $\frac{1}{7}$?

10. What is the least common multiple of 3, 21, and 45?

37. What is the correct ordering of $\dfrac{5}{6}$, $\dfrac{6}{7}$, and $\dfrac{7}{9}$ from least to greatest?

F. $\dfrac{5}{6} < \dfrac{6}{7} < \dfrac{7}{9}$

G. $\dfrac{6}{7} < \dfrac{5}{6} < \dfrac{7}{9}$

H. $\dfrac{6}{7} < \dfrac{7}{9} < \dfrac{5}{6}$

J. $\dfrac{7}{9} < \dfrac{5}{6} < \dfrac{6}{7}$

K. $\dfrac{7}{9} < \dfrac{6}{7} < \dfrac{5}{6}$

41. If $\dfrac{a}{10} - \dfrac{b}{55} = \dfrac{11a - 2b}{x}$ and a, b, and x are all integers greater than 1, then $x = ?$

A. 2
B. 55
C. 100
D. 110
E. 550

45. Which of the following is a rational number?

F. $\sqrt{\dfrac{1}{4}}$

G. $\sqrt{\dfrac{1}{2}}$

H. $\sqrt{2}$

J. $\sqrt{3}$

K. $\sqrt{8}$

46. $\dfrac{1}{\sqrt{2}} + \dfrac{1}{\sqrt{3}} = ?$

A. $\dfrac{1}{\sqrt{6}}$

B. $\dfrac{2}{\sqrt{5}}$

C. $\dfrac{2}{\sqrt{2} + \sqrt{3}}$

D. $\dfrac{\sqrt{2} + \sqrt{3}}{\sqrt{5}}$

E. $\dfrac{\sqrt{2} + \sqrt{3}}{\sqrt{6}}$

Continued →

47. For real numbers p and q, when is the equation $|p+q| = |-p-q|$ true?

    F. Always

    G. Only when $p = q$

    H. Only when $p = q = 0$

    J. Only when $p = 0$ or $q = 0$

    K. Never

50. If $x = ab$, $y = bc$, and $z = ac$, where a, b, and c are prime numbers, which of the following is the least common multiple of x, y and z? **[40-hour program only]**

    A. ab

    B. bc

    C. abc

    D. $(abc)^2$

    E. Cannot be determined from the information given

II

ARITHMETIC

The Arithmetic chapter covers topics and techniques that do not require complicated algebraic or geometric operations. You may have to use some simple algebra, such as solving for a single variable in a simple equation, but more complex algebra will be covered in Chapter III.

1. PERCENT PROBLEMS

PERCENT ↔ DECIMAL

You must be able to quickly convert a number in percent form to a number in decimal form, and vice versa. This will always involve moving the decimal point *two places* to the right or to the left. An easy way to see which way to move the decimal point is to use 50%. You probably already know that 50% is equivalent to one half, or .50, so when you are working on a percent problem and can't remember which way to move the decimal point, just write:

$$50\% \leftrightarrow 0.50$$

You can easily see which way to move the decimal point:

50% → 0.50 for *percent to decimal* - move decimal point two places to the <u>left</u>.
0.50 → 50% for *decimal to percent* - move decimal point two places to the <u>right</u>.

When using your calculator on percent problems, remember that the calculator only "understands" *decimals* and will only give answers as *decimals*. You must convert percent to decimal before entering data into your calculator, and remember to convert decimal answers back to percent, if necessary.

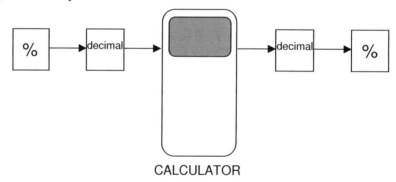

CALCULATOR

Try the following questions (feel free to use your calculator):

1. 4.25 equals what percent?

2. 25% is equivalent to what fraction?

3. 220% is equivalent to what decimal?

4. $\frac{7}{8}$ equals what percent?

5. 0.0013 equals what percent?

OF–IS PERCENT PROBLEMS

Of–Is problems require you to turn percent word problems into mathematical equations. Use the information in the following table.

word	operation
of *as big as*, *as old as*, *as fast as*, etc.	×
is *are*, *was*, *has*, *will be*, *equals*, etc.	=
what, what percent *what number*, *how much*, etc.	variable (*a*, *x*, etc.)

Of/Is problems are percent problems that do not involve *change.* In other words, no time passes and no values or variables change in the problem. **These problems are usually identifiable by the words *of* and *is* in the question.** For harder problems where the *of* or the *is* is not written, try creating an Of/Is sentence in your head.

 20% of 50 =

 15% of what number is 60?

 18 is what percent of 20?

 Bill is 20. Fred is ³⁄₅ as old as Bill. How old is Fred?

Throughout this tutorial, you will notice question numbers that do not follow a consecutive numerical order. These problems use numbers from the ACT to represent the *approximate* level of difficulty for the problem. Remember, as discussed in the introduction, there are **60** questions on the ACT Math Test. **In general, the higher the number, the harder the problem.** See note about problem difficulty on page 153.

OF–IS PERCENT LESSON PROBLEMS

1. 25% of 25% of 32 is ?

    A. ¼
    B. ½
    C. 1
    D. 2
    E. 4

5. During a 10%-Off sale at a store, if a shopper buys an item originally priced at $5.50, by how much is the item discounted?

    F. $0.50
    G. $0.55
    H. $1.50
    J. $4.95
    K. $5.40

25. If 40% of a number is 32, what is 50% of that number?

    A. 16
    B. 40
    C. 50
    D. 80
    E. 100

45. The volume of a cube with edge of length 1 inch is what percent of the volume of a cube with edge of length 2 inches?

    F. $12^{1}/_{2}\%$
    G. 20%
    H. 25%
    J. 40%
    K. 50%

PART-OVER-WHOLE PERCENT PROBLEMS

As the name implies, part over whole percent problems deal with finding a percent *of completeness* by comparing *part* of something to its *whole*.

 Like Of/Is problems, part-over-whole percent problems do not involve change (no time passes, and no values or variables change in the problem). **Look for part of something, and look for its whole.**

(EX) If you have traveled 200 miles of a 1000 mile trip, what percent of the trip have you completed?

Try the following lesson problem:

3. If a 12-ounce can of soda currently contains 8 ounces of soda, how full is the can?

   A. $33^1/_3$%
   B. 50%
   C. $66^2/_3$%
   D. 75%
   E. 80%

24. Before starting a trip from City A to City B, George sets his odometer to 0 miles. After driving for 3 hours, he passes a sign that says that City B is 800 miles away. If his odometer shows 200 miles at this point, what percent of the trip remains?

   A. 20%
   B. 25%
   C. 60%
   D. 75%
   E. 80%

PERCENT INCREASE/DECREASE

These problems deal with increasing or decreasing a value by a given percent. This involves finding a "percent of" something (see the *Of–Is* technique), and then adding or subtracting this value to the original value. Here's an example:

(EX) If a scarf normally costs $18, how much will it cost if the price is reduced 25%?

A SHORTCUT

Some students prefer to tackle these percent increase/decrease problems in one step by finding the *multiplier* for a given percent change. The multiplier can be found by adding the percent change to 100% (for percent increase) or subtracting the percent change from 100% (for percent decrease), and converting the result to a decimal. For example, the multiplier for the example above is:

100% − 25% = 75% = **0.75**

Note that 18 × 0.75 gives you the answer ($13.50) in one step. If you're comfortable finding multipliers, this approach is faster. If you prefer the standard approach, that's fine.

/ NEVER COMBINE PERCENT CHANGES

You must never combine percent changes. For example, you might assume that increasing a number by 20% and then increasing the result by 30% would be the same as increasing the original number by 50%, but this is not the case:

(EX) If the number 10 is increased by 20%, and then the result is increased by 30%, what is the final number?

> Percent increase/decrease problems involve *change*, which obviously means a value or values in the problem change, sometimes over a period of time. The easiest way to identify these problems is to look for a **given percent change—** either a percent increase or a percent decrease.

PERCENT INCREASE/DECREASE LESSON PROBLEMS

6. A store marks up all items 10% of their wholesale cost. In dollars, how much would a radio sell for if its wholesale cost is $200?

    A. 20
    B. 180
    C. 190
    D. 210
    E. 220

32. A book sold for $4.80 after a 20% discount was taken off the list price. What was the list price of the book?

    F. $3.84
    G. $5.00
    H. $5.76
    J. $6.00
    K. $6.50

DIFFERENCE-OVER-ORIGINAL PERCENT PROBLEMS

Difference-over-original percent problems ask for the percent that a value or values have changed. These problems compare some new value to an older or *original* value. The *difference* is simply the new number subtracted from the original number.

As with percent increase/decrease problems, these percent problems involve change, which again means a value or values in the problem change, such as a person's age, a population, or the value of a variable. Usually, there is a passing of time in these problems. The easiest way to identify difference-over-original problems is to see if the question is asking you to find the percent by which something has increased or decreased; in other words, **the question is asking you to find a percent change**.

(EX) A school had 1000 students in 1980. It now has 1200 students. What percent did the school's population change since 1980?

Try the following lesson problem:

34. When Bob started his job, he earned $7 per hour. At the end of 3 years, he earned $28 per hour. By what percent did his hourly rate increase?

    A. 3%
    B. 4%
    C. 25%
    D. 300%
    E. 400%

■

Let's summarize the ways to identify each of the four percent techniques:

Of/Is: Look for the words "of" and "is."
Part-Over-Whole: Look for *part* of something and look for the *whole*.
Percent Increase/Decrease: The question *gives* you a percent change.
Difference-Over-Original: The question *asks you to find* a percent change.

PICK 100

Often, difficult percent problems will involve several percent changes. If no original number is given, it becomes easier to tackle these types of problems by *picking 100* as the original number. Pick 100, and after you've gone through the steps of the problem, compare your final answer to 100. (You can also pick 100 on other types of problems that do not have original numbers given. This will give you a number to work with and a place to start.)

 Look for percent problems that have no original number given. Harder problems may have several percent changes.

Try the following lesson problem. Remember to pick 100 for your starting number (the number of workers in 1990):

53. The number of workers at a company increased 30 percent between 1990 and 2000. Employment increased 40 percent between 2000 and 2009. The employment in 2009 was what percent greater than in 1990?

    A. 30%
    B. 35%
    C. 70%
    D. 80%
    E. 82%

■

7. If $300 is deposited into a savings account that pays 4% interest per year, how much money will be in the account after one year?

    A. $304
    B. $312
    C. $340
    D. $420
    E. $430

9. If it rained 12 days in November and was clear the other 18 days, what percent of the days in November did it rain?

    F. 40%
    G. 50%
    H. $66^2/_3$%
    J. 75%
    K. 80%

Continued →

19. John scored 80 points on test 1 and 92 points on test 2. What was the percent increase?

    A. 8%
    B. 12%
    C. 13%
    D. 15%
    E. 87%

28. At a company, 60 percent of the employees are women. If one-third of the women and one-half of the men drive to work, what percent of the employees do NOT drive to work?

    F. 20%
    G. 40%
    H. 60%
    J. 75%
    K. $83^1/_3$%

55. A positive number p is reduced by 25 percent to produce q. If q is increased by 50 percent to produce r, then r is:

    A. p decreased by 25 percent
    B. p decreased by 12.5 percent
    C. p increased by 12.5 percent
    D. p increased by 25 percent
    E. p increased by 75 percent

60. A machine takes m hours to close 50 boxes. After the machine is upgraded to a new design, it can close 90 boxes in $0.6m$ hours. By what percent did the machine's per-hour production rate increase after the upgrade?

    F. 40%
    G. 80%
    H. 180%
    J. 200%
    K. 300%

2. PROPORTIONS

A *proportion* is two equal *ratios*, or fractions, for example:

$$\frac{2}{3} = \frac{34}{51}$$

In proportion problems, solve unknown values by cross multiplying:

(EX) If $\frac{2}{3} = \frac{62}{x}$, what is the value of *x*?

Proportion problems have at least one *known relationship* between two items. Here are a few examples of *known relationships*:

- 12 socks cost 4 dollars
- 2 ounces of vanilla are needed to make 3 cakes
- 20 miles per gallon

Note that each known relationship includes *two* numbers (no unknowns).

Proportion problems are fairly straightforward to set up. Just use the following method:

1. Identify and underline the known relationship.
2. Write the **units** as a ratio (no numbers yet!). Leave space to the right of the units for the eventual numbers. You can think of this step as similar to setting up a table, with the "headings" (the units) to the left of each row.
3. Now, add the numbers, starting with the known relationship. The units on the top of each ratio must be the same, and the units on the bottom of each ratio must be the same (that's why we only write the units *once*, to the left of the proportion). Of course, use a variable (such as *x*) for the unknown.
4. Solve by cross multiplying.

(EX) If 5 dozen flowers cost $25, how much do 24 flowers cost?

MORE THAN ONE KNOWN RELATIONSHIP

More difficult problems may involve two or more known relationships. Set up a proportion for *each* known relationship. See the following example:

(EX) A florist must purchase 72 flowers to make 6 bouquets. If 8 flowers cost $20, how much
would the florist spend to make 8 bouquets?

LESSON PROBLEMS

12. If Bryan takes 6 minutes to light 15 candles, how many minutes would it take him working at
the same rate to light 35 candles?

   A. 8
   B. 9
   C. 10
   D. 12
   E. 14

27. A bullet train takes 45 minutes to travel 300 kilometers. If it continues at the same rate,
how many hours will it take the train to travel 1600 kilometers?

   F. 3
   G. 4
   H. 5
   J. 6
   K. 8

Continued →

54. A 7-pound bag of apples costs 10 dollars and 5 pounds of apples are needed to make 2 apple pies. What is the dollar cost of apples needed to make 14 apple pies?

    A. 40
    B. 50
    C. 60
    D. 70
    E. 80

3. If cans of soda sell at the rate of 25 every 4 hours, how many cans of soda will be sold in 20 hours?

    A. 125
    B. 100
    C. 80
    D. 50
    E. 5

21. A tree casts a shadow 140 feet long. To determine the height of the tree, Craig stands next to the tree and has someone measure the length of his shadow. If Craig is 6 feet tall and casts a 14-foot shadow, what is the height of the tree?

    F. 12
    G. 36
    H. 60
    J. 132
    K. 140

43. Robot A can assemble 30 computer chips per hour and robot B can assemble 39 computer chips per hour. How many more minutes will it take robot A than robot B to assemble 26 computer chips?

    A. 12
    B. 15
    C. 20
    D. 34
    E. 52

3. RATIOS

BASIC RATIO PROBLEMS

 Basic ratio problems can be recognized by numbers or variables separated by the word *to* or a colon (:), such as 2:3, 2 to 3, *x:y*, or *x* to *y*.

Each ratio symbol—the word "to" or a colon (":")—is equivalent to a *divided-by line*, so ratios can be rewritten as standard fractions. Use the following method for ratio problems:

1. First, get rid of all ratio signs by rewriting the ratios as fractions.
2. Use your calculator and your knowledge of proportions or algebra to solve.

The following examples illustrate basic ratio techniques:

EX What fraction is equivalent to the ratio 3:5 (or 3 to 5)?

EX If the ratio of blue marbles to yellow marbles in a jar is 3:5, and there are 39 blue marbles in the jar, how many yellow marbles are in the jar?

PART-OVER-WHOLE (REVISITED)

Sometimes, the techniques taught in the Percent section come in handy on Ratio problems. Here's an example of the *part-over-whole* technique:

EX What fraction of the marbles in the jar described above are blue?

OF/IS (REVISITED)

Here's an example that tests the *of/is* technique:

 Bob has $200. If he gives $\frac{1}{5}$ of his money to charity, how much does he have left?

RATIO SHARE PROBLEMS

Ratio share problems are different from basic ratio problems, even though their identification is similar.

> Ratio share problems are also recognized by numbers or variables separated by the word *to* or a colon (:), but **they involve splitting some *whole* value or quantity into different *shares*.** Any problem with a ratio containing more than two terms, for example 2:3:4, is *definitely* a ratio share problem.

The method is straightforward and is best explained using the examples below:
1. Add up all the numbers in the ratio.
2. Remember, these problems typically involve some *whole* value (of dollars, eggs, students, etc.) that will be divided into shares. Divide this given whole value by the sum of the ratio numbers (from Step 1). This will give you the value of each "part."
3. To find each share, multiply the value from Step 2 (the "part") by the appropriate number in the original ratio.

 If two friends split $700 dollars in a ratio of 3:4, how much does each friend get?

 If three friends split $700 dollars in a ratio of 3:4:7, how much does each friend get?

(EX) A high school play is made up entirely of sophomores, juniors, and seniors. If the ratio of sophomores, juniors, and seniors in the play is 1:3:2, respectively, each of the following could be the number of students in the play EXCEPT

A. 12
B. 15
C. 18
D. 24
E. 30

RATIOS LESSON PROBLEMS

14. If the ratio of x to y is 1 to 6, then the ratio of $15x$ to y is

A. $\dfrac{5}{18}$

B. $\dfrac{5}{6}$

C. $\dfrac{5}{2}$

D. 3

E. $\dfrac{15}{2}$

23. Prize money for the top three finishers in a golf tournament is divided up in a ratio of 10:4:1. If the total prize money for the three top golfers is $75,000, how much does the first place golfer receive?

F. $5,000
G. $20,000
H. $50,000
J. $67,500
K. $70,000

8. The ratio of *n* to 9 is equal to the ratio of 33 to 198. What is the value of *n*?

   A. $\dfrac{2}{3}$

   B. 1

   C. $1\frac{1}{2}$

   D. 3

   E. 54

35. Apple juice, grape juice, and orange juice are mixed by volume in the ratio of 5:4:1, respectively, to produce fruit punch. In order to make 10 gallons of punch, how many gallons of orange juice are needed?

   F. $\dfrac{1}{2}$

   G. 1

   H. 3

   J. 4

   K. 5

46. A basket contains only red and green apples. If there are 20 apples in the basket, which of the following could NOT be the ratio of red to green apples?

   A. $\dfrac{1}{2}$

   B. $\dfrac{1}{3}$

   C. $\dfrac{2}{3}$

   D. $\dfrac{1}{9}$

   E. $\dfrac{3}{2}$

4. AVERAGES, MEDIANS, & MODES

TERMINOLOGY

Average or **arithmetic mean** – the sum of a set of values divided by the number of values in the set.

Median – the middle number in a set of increasing values. If the set has an even number of values, average the two middle numbers. **Don't forget the values must be in order before you can find the median.**

Mode – the value or values in a set of numbers that occur(s) the most frequently.

 Average problems are easy to identify because you only need to look for the words *average*, *median*, or *mode*. Note: Some *rate* problems also have the word *average*, but these problems use another technique that we will discuss in the next section.

1. What is the median of the following numbers?

   2, 6, 0, 10, –5

2. What is the median and mode of the following numbers?

   2, 6, 0, 10, –5, 10

The table below shows the hourly wages for 11 workers at a small company. Two workers make $9 per hour, two workers make $10 per hour, and so on.

Hourly wage (in $)	# of workers
9	2
10	2
12	1
13	2
14	4

3. What is the average of the 5 wages?

4. What is the median of the 5 wages?

5. What is the average hourly wage of the 11 workers? (Hint: write all 11 workers' wages in a list.)

6. What is the median hourly wage of the 11 workers?

7. What is the mode of the workers' wages?

30. Spencer measures the noon temperature once a day for a week and records the following values: 62°, 70°, 80°, 72°, 72°, 65°, x°. If the median temperature for the seven days is 70°, then x could be any of the following EXCEPT

    A. 59
    B. 66
    C. 67
    D. 70
    E. 73

ANS → $A \times N = S$

The *ANS*wer to average problems can usually be found using *ANS*. This technique will help make harder average problems much easier, but it is also simple enough to use on easier problems. We know that the average (A) is the sum (S) of a set of values divided by the number (N) of values in the set:

$$A = \frac{S}{N}$$

By multiplying both sides by N, we can create the simple equation:

$A \times N = S$

Average x Number of items in set = Sum of the items in the set

Use the following technique for *ANS* problems:

1. Write $A \times N = S$ at the top of your workspace and work in the columns below each letter.
2. Read the problem carefully, and plug values into the *ANS* table. Make sure to keep *averages* under the A column, *numbers in set* under the N column, and *sums* under the S column. Remember, the S column is for the added sum of the items in the set.
3. Anytime two entries in a row are known, calculate to find the missing entry.

(EX) The average of five numbers is –10. What is the sum of these numbers?

HARDER *ANS* PROBLEMS

Harder *ANS* problems typically deal with more than one group of numbers (each group with its own average). This will require you to use multiple rows in an *ANS* table (each group of numbers with its own row). You will also probably use a "Total Row" beneath the other rows. Here's the method:

1. Write *ANS* and plug values into the *ANS* table, as described before. Each group of numbers will get its own row. **Leave any unknowns blank.**

2. Remember, anytime two entries in a row are known, calculate or use algebra to find the missing entry.

3. We'll call the third row the "Total Row." The Total Row is the sums (or sometimes the differences) of the numbers in the *N* and *S* columns. Look for verbal clues to determine whether you should add or subtract the *N* and *S* columns. Whatever operation you perform on one of these columns, you will also perform on the other column. For example, if you add the *N* column, you will also add the *S* column.

   NOTE: The entries in the *A* column should never be added or subtracted into the Total Row. These *A* entries are only used to calculate missing information in their respective rows.

4. You should now have enough information to answer the question.

(EX) If the average age of 500 students at school A is 14 and the average age of 300 students at school B is 18, what is the average age of all the students at the two schools?

A. 14
B. 14.5
C. 15
D. 15.5
E. 16

AVERAGES, MEDIANS, & MODES LESSON PROBLEMS

10. If the average of x, y, and z is 20 and the average of p and q is 25, then which of the following is the value of $x + y + z + p + q = ?$

   A. 22
   B. 22.5
   C. 45
   D. 60
   E. 110

22. An average of 14 people use a park's tennis courts each weekday and an average of 42 people use the courts each weekend day. What is the average daily use of the courts over the entire week?

   F. 20
   G. 22
   H. 25
   J. 26
   K. 27

50. If the average of six numbers is –2 and the average of four of the numbers is 2, what is the average of the other two numbers?

   A. –10
   B. –2
   C. $-\frac{2}{5}$
   D. 0
   E. $\frac{2}{5}$

24. Samara takes a logic test five times and scores 12, 10, x, 20, and 27 points. If the average of her five scores is 18, what is the median of the five scores?

    A. 10
    B. 15
    C. 18
    D. 20
    E. 21

32. A 20-year-old bank gave away an average of 152 toasters a year for the first 15 years of its existence. For the past five years, the bank did not give away any toasters. What was the average number of toasters given away per year over the bank's entire 20 years?

    F. 76
    G. 98
    H. 114
    J. 120
    K. 152

5. RATES, TIMES, & DISTANCES

RTD → R × T = D

You must be familiar with the following equation:

$$R \times T = D$$

Rate or speed $\left(\dfrac{\text{distance}}{\text{time}} \right)$ × Time = Distance

Rate problems usually deal with some sort of travel over time and distance, such as: driving a car, flying an airplane, etc. However, any problem that deals with accomplishing something (not exclusively travel) over a period of time can be an *RTD* problem. For example, a problem dealing with *pages read per hour* or *machines made per day* could be an *RTD* problem. Note that the *D* column in these examples would be used for whatever is being accomplished over time (*pages read*, *machines made*).

 RTD problems will mention something that is accomplished over a period of *time*, usually travel. Look for key words like *rate*, *speed*, *pace*, or *velocity*, or look for any mention of *per time*, such as *per hour* or *per minute*. You will also notice the word *average*, but don't use *ANS* on *RTD* problems.

RTD problems are solved very similarly to *ANS* problems:

1. Write *RTD* and plug values into the *RTD* table, as we did with the *ANS* tables in the previous section. Leave any unknowns blank. Since *RTD* questions involve units (such as miles and hours), you might write the appropriate unit above each letter of the table. (Of course, make sure your inputs match the written units.)

2. Just as with *ANS* tables, anytime two entries in a row are known, calculate or use algebra to find the missing entry.

3. The Total Row for *RTD* problems (when needed) is typically the sums of the numbers in the *T* and *D* columns.

    NOTE: The entries in the *R* column (which are actually averages) should never be added or subtracted into the Total Row. These *R* entries are only used to calculate missing information in their respective rows.

4. You should now have enough information to answer the question.

(EX) Kyle travels ⅔ of a 6-mile trip by bicycle, and the bicycle portion takes 15 minutes. What is the average speed, in miles per hour, of the bicycle portion of the trip?

A. 8
B. 12
C. 16
D. 20
E. 24

RATES LESSON PROBLEMS

13. A car travels 48 miles in 45 minutes. What is the car's average speed in miles per hour?

A. 52
B. 56
C. 60
D. 64
E. 68

50. Erica rides a bicycle from her home to her work 24 miles away at an average speed of 12 miles per hour. She returns home along the same route at an average speed of 8 miles per hour. What was Erica's average speed in miles per hour for the entire trip?

F. 9.2
G. 9.6
H. 9.8
J. 10.0
K. 10.5

26. A helicopter flies 360 miles in 3 hours. If it continues at this rate, how many hours will it take the helicopter to travel 800 miles?

A. $2^2/_9$
B. $3^2/_3$
C. $4^2/_9$
D. $5^7/_9$
E. $6^2/_3$

Continued →

45. Hilary and Vivian begin a 5-mile walk at the same time. When Hilary finishes the walk, Vivian is half a mile behind. If Hilary walked the 5 miles in 75 minutes, what was Vivian's average speed in miles per hour for the portion of the walk that she has completed?

    F. 3.0
    G. 3.2
    H. 3.4
    J. 3.6
    K. 3.8

6. EXPONENTS

RULES FOR EXPONENTS

 These problems involve an *exponent* (raised number) or a *root* ($\sqrt{}$).

Memorize the following exponential rules:

MULTIPLYING WHEN BASES ARE THE SAME

Remember, the bases must be the same.

$$a^m \times a^n = a^{m+n}$$
(EX) $p^2 \times p^3 =$

DIVIDING WHEN BASES ARE THE SAME

$$a^m \div a^n = a^{m-n}$$
(EX) $\dfrac{p^3}{p^2} =$

RAISING POWERS TO POWERS

Don't confuse this rule with the first rule above.

$$(a^m)^n = a^{mn}$$
(EX) $(p^2)^3 =$

DISTRIBUTING EXPONENTS

Don't forget to distribute the outside exponent to *number* terms within the parentheses.

$$(ab)^m = a^m \times b^m$$
(EX) $(2p^2q^3)^2 =$

NEGATIVE EXPONENTS

Write answers with positive exponents:

$$a^{-m} = \frac{1}{a^m}$$

(EX) $\dfrac{p^2}{p^3} =$

(EX) $\dfrac{p^{22}}{p^{30}} =$

THE ZERO EXPONENT

$$a^0 = 1$$

(EX) $(2x^2y^3)^0 =$

ROOTS AND FRACTIONAL EXPONENTS

Convert all roots to fractional exponents. The rules above also apply to these fractional exponents. Get comfortable plugging these into your calculator (use parentheses carefully).

$$\sqrt{a} = a^{\frac{1}{2}}$$

(EX) $\sqrt[3]{64} =$

$$\sqrt[n]{a} = a^{\frac{1}{n}}$$

(EX) If $\sqrt[3]{p^2} = p^x$, $x =$

$$\sqrt[n]{a^m} = a^{\frac{m}{n}}$$

(EX) $\sqrt[7]{2{,}187} =$

COMPARE APPLES TO APPLES

Sometimes, you will be asked to compare the exponents of expressions with different bases, but that's like comparing apples and oranges. **The trick is to make the bases the same so you can easily compare the exponents** (compare apples to apples).

(EX) Which real number for x satisfies $2^x = 4^4$?

  A. 2
  B. 4
  C. 6
  D. 8
  E. 10

COMMON MISTAKES

Watch out for these common mistakes. For practice, see if you can correctly simplify each one, or write "n/a" if the expression cannot be simplified:

	simplify?			simplify?
(EX) $(2pq)^2 \neq 2p^2q^2$		4.	$\sqrt{p^2+q^2} \neq p+q$	
1. $p^2+p^3 \neq p^5$		5.	$p^2p^3 \neq p^6$	
2. $(p+q)^2 \neq p^2+q^2$		6.	$\dfrac{p^2}{p^3} \neq p^{\frac{2}{3}}$	
3. $p^{-2} \neq -p^2$		7.	$2p^{-2} \neq \dfrac{1}{2p^2}$	

EXPONENTS LESSON PROBLEMS

1. $x^2 x^7 =$

2. $\dfrac{x^5}{x^2} =$

3. $(x^4)^5 =$

4. $(5xy)^2 =$

5. $4^{\frac{3}{2}} =$

6. $\dfrac{(3x^2y)^3}{3x^5y^4} =$

28. If $(2^t)^t = 2^{20}$ and $t > 0$, what is the value of t?

   A. $\sqrt{10}$
   B. $2\sqrt{5}$
   C. 10
   D. $4\sqrt{5}$
   E. 20

32. $(-2xy^3)^2(3x^3y) = ?$

   F. $-12x^6y^6$
   G. $-12x^5y^6$
   H. $-6x^5y^7$
   J. $12x^6y^6$
   K. $12x^5y^7$

Continued →

37. For all real numbers x and y, which of the following expressions is equivalent to $x^{\frac{1}{2}}y^{\frac{2}{3}}$?

   A. $\sqrt{xy^3}$

   B. $\sqrt{x^2y^3}$

   C. $\sqrt[6]{x^3y^4}$

   D. $\sqrt[6]{x^2y^3}$

   E. $\sqrt[6]{x^{12}y^{18}}$

42. $3^{n+1} \cdot 3^2 = $?

   F. 3^{2n+2}

   G. 3^{n+3}

   H. 9^{2n+2}

   J. 9^{n+3}

   K. 27^{n+1}

51. If $9^x = \sqrt[3]{81}$, then what is the value of x?

   A. $\dfrac{1}{3}$

   B. $\dfrac{1}{2}$

   C. $\dfrac{2}{3}$

   D. 2

   E. 3

7. TABLES & GRAPHS

Tables and graphs can have many different forms. There are two general steps to tackling these kinds of problems:

1. Carefully study and understand the table or graph *before* trying to answer the question.
2. Watch the problem number. A higher-numbered question may have a trap, so be careful.

Try the following lesson problems:

17. According to the graph below, Company X showed the greatest change in net income between which two consecutive years?

NET INCOME FOR COMPANY X, 1995–2000

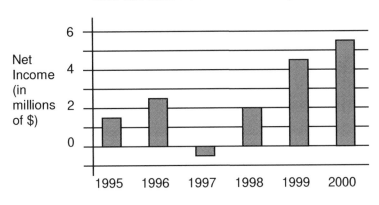

    A. 1995 and 1996
    B. 1996 and 1997
    C. 1997 and 1998
    D. 1998 and 1999
    E. 1999 and 2000

42. How many <u>hours</u> will it take to clean all 40 streets in City A listed in the table below?

STREET CLEANING IN CITY A	
Number of Streets	Cleaning Time per Street
7	20 minutes
8	40 minutes
10	80 minutes
15	100 minutes

    F. 4
    G. 44
    H. 46
    J. 240
    K. 2,760

17. The circle graph below represents all income for a sports stadium in 1999. If the stadium made $15,000 in beverage sales, what was the total dollar income of the stadium in 1999?

INCOME FOR STADIUM *A* IN 1999

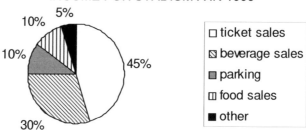

A. 19,500
B. 45,000
C. 50,000
D. 55,000
E. 60,000

28. Chris lives 6 miles from school. On a particular day, he walked for 2 miles, stopped for 5 minutes to talk with some friends, and then ran the rest of the way to school. Which of the following graphs could correctly represent his journey to school on this day?

F.

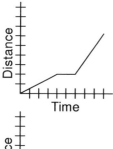

H.

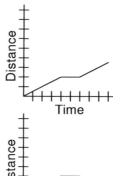

K.

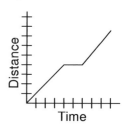

G.

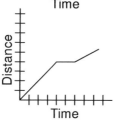

J.

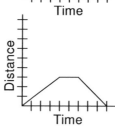

Use the following information to answer questions 39–42.

Wallace's Brick Company sells three different styles of bricks. The prices and number of bricks per pallet are given in the table below. The price is the amount a customer pays for one pallet of the indicated style.

Style of brick	Number of bricks per pallet	Price per pallet
A	75	$75.00
B	50	$80.00
C	30	$90.00

39. Which of the following is the price per brick for a Style B brick?

    A. $1.00
    B. $1.50
    C. $1.60
    D. $2.00
    E. $3.00

40. For a special sale, Wallace's Brick Company offers customers a 5% discount off the total price for any style of brick when at least 5 pallets are purchased. If a customer buys 8 pallets of Style C bricks, what is the price per pallet of these bricks?

    F. $85.00
    G. $85.50
    H. $95.00
    J. $680.00
    K. $684.00

41. If Conrad bought an equal number of Style A, B and C bricks, what is the minimum number of bricks of each style that he could have bought? (Note: customers may not purchase individual bricks at Wallace's Brick Company.)

    A. 5
    B. 75
    C. 100
    D. 125
    E. 150

Continued →

(Question 42 below is based on the previous multi-question set.)

42. Each month, Wallace's Brick Company must pay a fixed cost for each style of brick it manufactures, plus a constant production cost per brick. If the monthly fixed cost for Style A bricks is $75.00, and the production cost per Style A brick is $0.50, how much profit does the company make if it sells 40 pallets of Style A bricks in one month? (Note: Wallace's Brick Company does not offer any discounts this month.)

   F. $1,375
   G. $1,425
   H. $1,500
   J. $1,575
   K. $3,000

---

49. Volts Electric Car Company manufactures only compact and family cars, both of which are available as either all-electric or hybrid. On the basis of the information in the table below, how many family, all-electric cars will the company produce in 2011?

VOLTS ELECTRIC CAR COMPANY'S
SALES FOR 2011

	All-electric	Hybrid	Total
Compact	a	b	
Family		c	
Total			d

   A. $a + b - c$
   B. $d - (a + b)$
   C. $d - (a - b - c)$
   D. $d + (a - b - c)$
   E. $d - a - b - c$

8. PROBABILITY

BASIC PROBABILITY

Probability is a way of describing the mathematical likelihood of a particular event occurring. It is usually written as a fraction and is always a number between 0 and 1 ($0 \leq P \leq 1$). Memorize the following equation:

$$\text{Probability } (P) = \frac{\textbf{Outcomes giving a desired result}}{\textbf{Total possible outcomes}}$$

> Probability problems will include one of the following words: *probability*, *likelihood*, *chance*, or *odds*.

(EX) If a fair die is rolled one time, what is the probability of rolling a 6?

(EX) If a fair die is rolled one time, what is the probability of rolling an even number?

(EX) If a fair die is rolled one time, what is the probability of rolling a prime number?

Try the following lesson problem:

6. A box contains 30 marbles. If the chance of drawing a red marble from the bag is ⅔, how many marbles in the bag are <u>not</u> red?

    A. 5
    B. 10
    C. 15
    D. 20
    E. 25

PROBABILITY OF MULTIPLE EVENTS

 These problems will ask you to find the probability of multiple events occurring together when the probability of each individual event can be found.

The following method can be used to find the probability of multiple events:

1. Find the probability of each event. **Important: Make sure to consider how the occurrence of one event may affect the probability of another event.**

2. *Multiply* the probabilities to find the probability of multiple events occurring together.

(EX) If the probability of winning a game of bingo is $\frac{1}{25}$, what is the probability of winning two games of bingo in a row?

A. $\frac{1}{625}$

B. $\frac{1}{125}$

C. $\frac{1}{50}$

D. $\frac{1}{25}$

E. $\frac{2}{25}$

PROBABILITY AND TABLES

The ACT often tests probability with tables of data. The main challenge with these questions is blocking out all the information that you won't use in your calculations. You usually need to focus on selected members of a subgroup. Here are the steps (follow along with the example):

1. First, identify the *subgroup* that is being asked about. Look for clues such as "of the students who play at least one sport" or "if a person with at least 5 years' experience is chosen at random." This information will give you your <u>denominator</u>.

2. Next, identify the *target group*, that is, the group you're asked to find the probability of. Remember, the target group will only include members that are *also* in the subgroup. The number of members in the target group will be your <u>numerator</u>.

3. Finally, the ratio of the target group to the subgroup is your answer. You may have to reduce your ratio on some problems.

Results of an Entrance Exam

	Passed the entrance exam	Did not pass the entrance exam
Used Smarty Pants Tutoring Company	20	5
Used Easy Does It Tutoring Company	22	28

The table above shows the results of 75 students who took an entrance exam for a private school. If one of the students who passed the exam is chosen at random, what is the probability that the student used Easy Does It Tutoring Company?

A. $\dfrac{20}{42}$

B. $\dfrac{22}{42}$

C. $\dfrac{22}{75}$

D. $\dfrac{22}{50}$

E. $\dfrac{50}{75}$

Try the following lesson problem:

19.

Results of Adults in Weight Loss Programs

	Lost Weight	Gained Weight	Total
Diet program	187	13	200
Exercise program	102	98	200
Total	289	111	400

The table above shows the results of a research study designed to investigate the weight loss effectiveness of dieting and exercise. A random sample of 400 adults participated in either the diet program or the exercise program for a month. At the end of the month, each adult's weight was compared to his or her weight at the beginning of the program. If an adult gained weight, what is the probability that the adult was in the exercise program?

A. $\dfrac{1}{2}$

B. $\dfrac{98}{111}$

C. $\dfrac{13}{98}$

D. $\dfrac{111}{400}$

E. $\dfrac{111}{200}$

PROBABILITY DISTRIBUTION TABLES

Sometimes probabilities will be presented in a *probability distribution table*. This is a table that displays the probability of each of a number of different events. For example, the following table shows the probability of winning certain prizes in a lottery:

Prize	Probability
$100	0.01
$50	0.05
$5	0.10
$0	0.84

 These problems will include a table similar to the one above (look for two columns, with the second column labeled "Probability"). You'll also see the words "probability distribution" in the question.

SUM OF THE PROBABILITIES

The sum of probabilities in a distribution table will equal 1 (0.01 + 0.05 + 0.10 + 0.84 = 1.0). This means that the only possible outcomes are those listed in the first column; in other words, if you play the lottery, you'll receive one of the listed "prizes."

PROBABILITY OF MULTIPLE EVENTS

When a question asks for the probability of multiple events, simply add the probabilities of the individual events.

(EX) Based on the probability distribution given in the table below, what is the probability that Aimee will win at least $5 if she buys one ticket?

Prize	Probability
$100	0.01
$50	0.05
$5	0.10
$0	0.84

A. 0.06
B. 0.15
C. 0.16
D. 0.70
E. 0.94

EXPECTED VALUE

Most of these probability-distribution-table problems ask you to find the *expected value*. The expected value is the theoretical mean outcome we would expect for infinitely many trials. In other words, if we bought millions of lottery tickets, how much would we win, on average, each time we played? Clearly the number will be low, since the probability of winning $0 is so high, but we would expect to occasionally win some of the real prizes. The method is simple for finding the expected value. Follow along with the example that follows.

1. Multiply the value of each event (Column 1) by its probability (Column 2).
2. Add these products. The result is the expected value.

(EX) Based on the probability distribution given in the table below, what is the expected value for a prize if Aimee buys one lottery ticket?

Prize	Probability
$100	0.01
$50	0.05
$5	0.10
$0	0.84

    A. $0.00
    B. $0.84
    C. $3.00
    D. $4.00
    E. $38.75

Be careful: The trapdoor answer for these expected-value problems is the event with the greatest probability. Of course, you'll never actually win exactly $4 with one ticket (you'll more likely win $0), but expected-value problems are interested in the average result after *infinitely many trials*. Answer choice A above is incorrect. Don't fall for the trap.

/ **The expected value will typically NOT be the value of the event with the greatest probability.**

■

2. A bag contains 5 green marbles, 6 blue marbles, and 7 yellow marbles. If a marble is selected at random from the bag, what is the probability that the marble selected will be blue?

    A. $\frac{5}{18}$
    B. $\frac{1}{3}$
    C. $\frac{7}{18}$
    D. $\frac{1}{2}$
    E. $\frac{6}{7}$

40.

Number of Sports Played per Student

	None	1 to 2	3 or more	Total
School A	86	110	4	200
School B	166	409	125	700
Total	252	519	129	900

The table above displays the number of sports played by students at two schools. School A is a rural school with an enrollment of 200 students. School B is an urban school with an enrollment of 700 students. If a student is chosen at random who plays at least one sport, what is the probability that the student attends School B?

A. $\dfrac{534}{700}$

B. $\dfrac{534}{900}$

C. $\dfrac{115}{648}$

D. $\dfrac{534}{648}$

E. $\dfrac{700}{900}$

48. Wallace counts the number of people in line at Wallace's Pet Supply every minute for a day. Based on the probability distribution given below, what is the expected value of the number of people in line at any one time?

Number of people in line	Probability
0	0.10
1	0.10
2	0.20
3	0.30
4	0.10
5	0.20
6	0.00

A. 2.6
B. 2.8
C. 3.0
D. 3.2
E. 3.5

Continued →

57. In a game, 100 cards are labeled 1 to 100. A player draws 2 cards at random, without returning the first card. If both cards have the same tens digit, the player is a winner. If the first card Grant draws is a 12, what is the probability that he will be a winner on the next draw?

   A. $\dfrac{1}{9}$

   B. $\dfrac{1}{10}$

   C. $\dfrac{1}{11}$

   D. $\dfrac{1}{99}$

   E. $\dfrac{1}{110}$

9. ARITHMETIC WORD PROBLEMS

As you may have noticed, most problems on the ACT are *word* problems (they all contain words), but some problems have more words than others. Arithmetic word problems, which can take several different forms, usually involve basic calculations. You'll likely have to use your calculator. (Word problems that involve *algebra*, where you'll have to solve for unknowns (variables), will be discussed in the next chapter.)

As you tackle arithmetic word problems, read carefully, and keep track of the information. It's often a good idea to write down and label information as you read the question. Also, keep in mind that these problems are usually not as difficult as they look. Let's look at an example:

(EX) 10. A museum parking lot charges $3.00 for the first hour and $1.25 for each additional hour after the first, or any portion thereof. If Tom has only a $20 bill, how much change should he expect if he parked for 4½ hours?

    A. $8.00
    B. $8.25
    C. $10.00
    D. $12.00
    E. $12.63

12. A rental car company owns 45 small cars and 25 large cars. There are 3 small cars and 7 large cars that are currently being repaired and are out of commission. If the company rents 80% of its available cars, how many cars does it rent?

    A. 22
    B. 42
    C. 48
    D. 56
    E. 60

10. ARITHMETIC PROBLEMS

PRACTICE PROBLEMS

The worksheets on the following pages test techniques taught in this chapter. For additional practice, we'll use problems from Test 5 in *The Official ACT Prep Guide*.

- ☐ Arithmetic Worksheet 1
- ☐ Arithmetic Worksheet 2
- ☐ **The Official ACT Prep Guide: Test 5**: Only tackle questions related to *this chapter*. For a list of these relevant questions, see the Techniques chapter at the end of this tutorial (first page of "Techniques: Test 5").

As stated before, here are some important notes about completing practice problems:

- **Use techniques**: It is very important to look back to the lessons in this chapter and review the techniques *while completing these problems*. Try to determine which technique relates to each problem and apply the methods taught in the tutorial.
- **No timing**: Do *not* time yourself. The problems are provided to give you an opportunity to practice, and hopefully master, the techniques in this tutorial before you use them on real ACTs in a timed setting.
- **Scheduling**: You should space the above assignments out over the course of your studies. See the Tutoring Schedules section in the Introduction for more details.

TEST CORRECTIONS

After each practice test is graded, you should correct questions related to this chapter that you missed or guessed on. See "Correcting Practice Tests" in the Introduction for more details. Here are the three steps to correcting practice tests:

1. Turn to the Techniques chapter at the end of this tutorial and circle the Arithmetic questions that you missed or guessed on for the test you are correcting.
2. Correct the problems in *The Official ACT Prep Guide*. As you correct the problems, go back to the tutorial and review the techniques. The idea is to (1) identify techniques that have given you trouble, (2) go back to the tutorial so you can review and strengthen these techniques, and (3) apply these techniques to the specific problems on which you struggled.
3. If you have trouble identifying the best technique to use for a problem, refer to the Techniques chapter. This is an important part of correcting the tests.

ARITHMETIC WORKSHEET 1

6. In a table, Luther recorded the number of minutes he watched television over the course of a week during his summer vacation, as shown below. What was the mean number of minutes he watched television per day for this week?

Day	Mon.	Tues.	Wed.	Thurs.	Fri.	Sat.	Sun.
Minutes	20	120	100	0	140	240	360

    A. 100
    B. 120
    C. 140
    D. 163 ⅓
    E. 180

7. The ratio of two numbers is 4:5. If one of the numbers is 80, what is a possible value of the other number?

    F. 64
    G. 74
    H. 84
    J. 94
    K. 104

17. If 20% of x equals 1, what is 50% of x?

    A. 0.5
    B. 1
    C. 1.5
    D. 2
    E. 2.5

Continued →

18. The mayoral election results for the 54,000 voting residents of Vonnegut City are shown below. If the information in the table were converted into a circle (or pie) graph, then what would be the measure of the central angle of the sector for the candidate named Pilgrim?

Candidate	Number of voters
Pilgrim	20,400
Rumfoord	17,100
Trout	10,500
Hoover	5,280
Hoenikker	720

    F. 130°
    G. 132°
    H. 134°
    J. 136°
    K. 224°

24. Two trains leave a station at the same time on two sets of straight parallel tracks. Train A heads east at an average speed of 50 kilometers per hour. Train B heads west at an average speed of 70 kilometers per hour. How many minutes after the trains leave the station will they be 30 kilometers apart?

    A. 60
    B. 45
    C. 30
    D. 20
    E. 15

Continued →

25. If, for all x, $\left(x^{3a-1}\right)^2 = \left(x^4\right)^{\frac{1}{2}}$, then $a = ?$

    F. $\dfrac{1}{3}$

    G. $\dfrac{1}{2}$

    H. $\dfrac{2}{3}$

    J. $\dfrac{3}{4}$

    K. 2

26. A new car loses 20% of its value after a year of ownership. Which of the following gives the value, after one year, of a car that cost $20,000 new?

    A. 20,000 − 20

    B. 20,000(0.20)

    C. 20,000 − 20,000(0.02)

    D. 20,000 − 20,000(0.20)

    E. 20,000 − 20,000(20)

35.

Gender	Movie Grade		Total
	Thumbs up	Thumbs down	
Male	22	5	27
Female	7	11	18
Total	29	16	45

The table above shows the opinions given by 45 audience members for a recent movie. If a member is selected at random, what is the probability that the member will be either a male who liked the movie ("Thumbs up") or a female who did <u>not</u> like the movie ("Thumbs down")?

    A. $\dfrac{11}{45}$

    B. $\dfrac{11}{15}$

    C. $\dfrac{22}{29}$

    D. $\dfrac{4}{5}$

    E. $\dfrac{29}{45}$

Continued →

44. The distance the earth travels around the sun in a year is about 5.80×10^8 miles. Approximately how many miles does the earth travel in the 30-day month of November (assume 365 days in one year)?

    F. $(30)(365)(5.80 \times 10^8)$

    G. $\dfrac{(30)(5.80 \times 10^8)}{365}$

    H. $\dfrac{(365)(5.80 \times 10^8)}{30}$

    J. $\dfrac{5.80 \times 10^8}{(30)(365)}$

    K. $\dfrac{365}{(30)(5.80 \times 10^8)}$

47. Rachel needs to average 80.0 points on 5 equally weighted gymnastics tests if she hopes to be invited to an upcoming tournament. If she has taken 4 of the tests, and her average score is 75.5, how many points must she score on the 5th test to get invited to the tournament?

    A. 92
    B. 94
    C. 96
    D. 98
    E. 100

48. A kitchen drawer is filled with forks, spoons, and knives. The probability that a spoon is selected at random is $\frac{1}{2}$, and the probability that a knife is selected at random is $\frac{1}{6}$. If all of the forks are removed from the drawer, what is the probability of selecting a knife at random?

    A. $\frac{1}{6}$

    B. $\frac{1}{4}$

    C. $\frac{1}{3}$

    D. $\frac{1}{2}$

    E. $\frac{3}{4}$

Continued →

49. A machine creates metallic arms with length x centimeters. A quality control specialist measures the length of 1,000 arms and creates the distribution table below. What is the expected value, rounded to the nearest hundredth of a centimeter, of the length of one metallic arm?

Length, x, in inches	Probability
1.8	0.02
1.9	0.13
2.0	0.81
2.1	0.04
2.2	0.00

A. 1.97
B. 1.98
C. 1.99
D. 2.00
E. 2.01

52. At Wright High School, 80% of the students of the graduating class plan to go to four-year universities. Of the remaining graduating class members, 90% plan to go to community colleges. What percent of the graduating class do NOT plan to go to a four-year university or a community college?

A. 1%
B. 2%
C. 10%
D. 20%
E. 98%

59. A scientist measures the lengths of the back legs of lizards from two different islands. She measures 200 lizards from Island A and 250 lizards from Island B. If the average back-leg length of the lizards from Island A is 5 centimeters and the average back-leg length of the lizards from Island B is 4 centimeters, to the nearest tenth of a centimeter, what is the average back-leg length of all 450 lizards?

F. 4.3
G. 4.4
H. 4.5
J. 4.6
K. 4.7

ARITHMETIC WORKSHEET 2

7. If a player plays one game on a slot machine, the probability that she will win is 0.01. What is the probability that she will NOT win if she plays one game?

   F. 0.01
   G. 0.09
   H. 0.19
   J. 0.90
   K. 0.99

8. The product of $(3x^2y^3)(4x^5y^4)$ is equivalent to:

   A. $7x^7y^7$
   B. $12x^7y^7$
   C. $7x^{10}y^{12}$
   D. $12x^{10}y^{12}$
   E. $12xy^7$

9. The average of 24 numbers is −2. If each of the numbers is increased by 2, what is the average of the 24 new numbers?

   F. −1.0
   G. −0.5
   H. 0.0
   J. 0.5
   K. 1.5

15. The distance from Town A to Town B is 20 miles, the distance from Town B to Town C is 15 miles, and the distance from Town C to Town D is 5 miles. An automobile starts at Town A, travels through Towns B and C, and stops at Town D. If the total time for the trip is 1 hour, what is the automobile's average speed, in miles per hour?

   A. 20
   B. 30
   C. 40
   D. 50
   E. 60

22. Pedro copied a map of the world onto a square sheet of paper with a side of 11 inches. He measures the distance from Los Angeles to the Panama Canal as 2 inches. If he enlarges the map so it fits on a square poster board that has a side of 40 inches, what is the new distance, to the nearest inch, between Los Angeles and the Panama Canal?

   F. 7
   G. 8
   H. 9
   J. 10
   K. 11

Continued →

216 • ARITHMETIC

23. The recipe for rice pilaf calls for 2 parts vegetable broth to 3 parts rice to 4 parts water. If you want to make 8 cups of rice pilaf, how many cups of vegetable broth will you need?

A. $\dfrac{8}{9}$

B. $1\dfrac{7}{9}$

C. $2\dfrac{2}{3}$

D. $3\dfrac{5}{9}$

E. 16

28. The graph below shows the number of books sold at Read-A-Lot's 5 bookstores. According to the graph, what was the average number of books sold per bookstore for Read-A-Lot?

Store	Books sold
Hemingway City	
Faulkner Town	
Twain Falls	
Steinbeck Rowe	
Hawthorne Park	

= 5,000 books

F. 5,000
G. 7,500
H. 10,000
J. 17,500
K. 50,000

29. The number 0.2 is 1,000 times as large as what number?

A. 0.0002
B. 0.002
C. 0.02
D. 200
E. 2,000

Continued →

33. The table below shows the number of three point shots hit by Team A in each of its 25 games during a tournament. What is the average number of three-point shots hit by Team A per game?

Total number of 3-point shots in a game	Number of games with this total
0	1
1	0
2	2
3	4
4	8
5	2
6	5
7	2
8	1

F. 3.6
G. 3.8
H. 4.0
J. 4.2
K. 4.4

38.

Number of Cats or Dogs per Household in Two Regions

	None	1	2 or more	Total
Households in Region A	52	35	13	100
Households in Region B	17	38	45	100
Total	69	73	58	200

The table above displays the number of cats or dogs in each of 200 households. Region A is an urban area, and Region B is a rural area. If a household is chosen at random from those that have at least one cat or dog, what is the probability that the household is in an urban area?

A. $\dfrac{13}{58}$

B. $\dfrac{48}{131}$

C. $\dfrac{83}{131}$

D. $\dfrac{48}{200}$

E. $\dfrac{100}{200}$

Continued →

49. In the real numbers, what is the solution of the equation $8^a = 4^{2a+1}$?

    A. -8
    B. -6
    C. -4
    D. -2
    E. 0

55. A bag contains exactly 7 blue marbles. If there are 21 marbles in the bag, what is the probability that the first three marbles drawn at random will be blue if the marbles are not replaced after they are drawn?

    F. $\frac{1}{3}$

    G. $\frac{1}{9}$

    H. $\frac{1}{27}$

    J. $\frac{1}{38}$

    K. $\frac{1}{46}$

58. Marc is trying to increase his weight for an upcoming wrestling match. After each training session, Marc's weight increases 2%. If Marc has two training sessions, by what percent does his weight increase?

    A. 2.02%
    B. 4%
    C. 4.04%
    D. 8%
    E. 8.08%

III

ALGEBRA

This is the most important chapter in the Math section of the tutorial, not only because algebra is such an important part of the ACT, but also because a number of *tricks* (called *The Pick Tricks*) will be taught that will allow supposedly difficult, high-numbered problems to be solved with relative ease.

1. BASIC ALGEBRA

EQUALITIES

If you've come this far, you probably already have a grasp of the basic algebraic operations that allow you to solve simple equalities. If not, the Working with Variables lesson on page 224 might help you get started, or find a good Algebra 1 book and review. For problems 1–10, solve for a:

1. $3a = -54$

2. $10a - 4 = 6$

3. $4 - 5a = 14$

4. $3a + 6 = 4\frac{1}{2}a$

5. $3a - 4 = 2a + 2$

6. $2(a - 6) = -4$

7. $\frac{2}{3}(9 - a) = \frac{1}{2}a - 8$

8. $\dfrac{1}{a+2} = \dfrac{3}{5}$

9. $\dfrac{1}{2a+2} = \dfrac{3}{a+11}$

10. $a = b - 2$ and $b = 2a$, solve for a

INEQUALITIES

If you can solve equalities like the ones on the previous page, then solving *inequalities* shouldn't be a problem. Just treat the inequality sign ($<, >, \leq, \geq$) as if it were an equal sign, but you must remember one important rule:

When multiplying or dividing both sides of an inequality by a negative number, the inequality sign changes direction. For example:

$$-2a \geq 14 \;\rightarrow\; \frac{-2a}{-2} \leq \frac{14}{-2} \;\rightarrow\; a \leq -7$$

inequality sign changes direction

Solve for *a*:

1. $4a < 120$

2. $-\frac{1}{2}a + 6 \leq 8$

SOLVING EXPONENTIAL EQUATIONS

To solve for a squared variable (such as x^2), use the method below. Look at the following example as you read each step:

1. Get the squared variable alone on one side of the equal sign.
2. Take the square root of each side of the equation.
3. **Add a plus or minus sign (±).** This is the most common mistake on these problems. You should generally expect *two* answers when you solve for a squared variable.

(EX) If $x^2 = 121$, what is a possible value of $x + 11$?

- **A.** 0
- **B.** 11
- **C.** 21
- **D.** 133
- **E.** 242

SOLVING EQUATIONS WITH RADICALS

Radicals were introduced in the Exponents lesson. There are two steps for solving equations with radicals:

1. Isolate the radical expression so it is alone on one side of the equal sign.
2. Square both sides.
3. Always check your answers when working with radicals. Sometimes you will get an "extraneous solution," one that is actually *not* a solution to the equation. (Hint: This may occur when you have variables inside *and* outside the radical sign.)

(EX) If $2\sqrt{a} = 12$, then $a =$

Solve for *a*:

1. $2\sqrt{a} - 5 = 11$

2. $2\sqrt{a-5} = 8$

SOLVING ABSOLUTE VALUE EQUATIONS

Absolute value was introduced in the Basic Concepts chapter. There are two steps for solving absolute value equations:

1. Isolate the absolute value expression on one side of the equal sign.
2. Set whatever is inside the absolute value bars equal to ± whatever is outside the bars. This should give you two new equations.
3. Solve each equation separately. As with radicals, check your answers. Sometimes you will get an extraneous solution.

(EX) If $|x + 5| - 3 = 0$, then $x =$

WORKING WITH VARIABLES

Some ACT problems will ask you to perform operations on variables. You should be comfortable with the following three rules:

- **Distributive property**: $a(b + c) = ab + ac$
- **Combine like terms**, for example: $2x^2 + 5x^2 = 7x^2$
- **Canceling terms**, for example: $\dfrac{8ab}{4b} = \dfrac{2 \cdot 4ab}{4b} = 2a$

Caution: You can only cancel terms that are *factors* of the whole top and the whole bottom of a fraction. In other words, if a term is part of an addition or subtraction expression, you can *not* cancel it. This is a very common mistake. For example:

$$\frac{8 + ab}{4b} \neq \frac{2 \cdot 4 + ab}{4b}$$

Try the following lesson problem:

4. $m^2 - 22m + 11 - 12m^2 + 11m$ is equivalent to:

   A. 11
   B. $-22m^6 + 11$
   C. $-22m^2 + 11$
   D. $-11m^2 - 11m + 11$
   E. $-11m^2 + 11m + 11$

BASIC ALGEBRA HOMEWORK

2. What is the value of the expression $a \cdot \sqrt{a} \cdot \sqrt{a+3}$ for $a = 1$?

   A. 6
   B. 5
   C. 4
   D. 3
   E. 2

8. If $50(4x) = 200$, then $4x =$

   F. $\dfrac{1}{4}$

   G. 1

   H. 2

   J. 4

   K. 50

Continued →

14. For what value of x is $p = 2$ a solution to the equation $x - 3 = px - 1$?

    A. −6
    B. −3
    C. −2
    D. 0
    E. 3

20. If $a = x + y$ and $b = x - y$, which of the following equals $(a + b) - (a - b)$?

    F. $2x$
    G. $2y$
    H. $2x - 2y$
    J. $2y - 2x$
    K. $x - y$

2. ALGEBRAIC WORD PROBLEMS

We talked about arithmetic word problems in the previous chapter. What we call *algebraic* word problems are ones that require one of the following:

1. Plugging numbers into a given equation.
2. Coming up with your own equation or equations.

Of course, you will likely have to use some of the algebraic techniques from the previous lesson to get a final answer.

GIVEN EQUATIONS

Sometimes the equation you need is conveniently given in the problem. You will usually simply plug numbers into the equation. These problems may look difficult (because they are wordy or have difficult-looking equations), but they tend to be easier than they look. Try the following problem:

30. The surface area, S, of a sphere is determined by the formula $S = 4\pi r^2$, where r is the radius of the sphere. What is the surface area, in square inches, of a sphere with diameter 6 inches long?
    A. 24π
    B. 36π
    C. 48π
    D. 60π
    E. 144π

If you thought the problem above was fairly straightforward, great! Notice that it's a number 30 (out of 60). Stay aggressive on these problems, especially the wordier ones, and you'll gain valuable points on problems that other students tend to skip or guess on.

CREATE YOUR OWN EQUATION(S)

Some questions *do* require you to make up your own equations and sometimes your own variables for these equations. The following table will help:

Word	Operation
product, of, multiplied, times	$\times$
sum of, more than, older than, farther than, greater than, added	$+$
difference, less than, younger than, fewer, subtracted	$-$
quotient, per, for, divided	$\div$
square	x^2
cube	x^3

32. When the square of the product of x and 4 is subtracted from the square of the difference of x and 4, the result is 0. Which of the following equations will allow you to solve for x?

  A. $(x - 4)^2 - (4x)^2 = 0$
  B. $(x - 4)^2 - 4x^2 = 0$
  C. $(4x)^2 - (x - 4)^2 = 0$
  D. $4x^2 - (x - 4)^2 = 0$
  E. $4x^2 - (x - 4) = 0$

A COMMON EXPRESSION

Perhaps the most common operation found in algebraic word problems is a simple product of two variables. We'll explain with an easy example:

If each javelin weighs p pounds, we could write the total weight of j javelins using the expression jp. In other words, the number of javelins times the weight of each javelin will give you the total weight of all javelins. Easy enough, right?

As you can see, it's just a simple product, but it's something the ACT tests again and again. Try the following lesson problem:

2. To rent scuba gear, a customer must pay a flat fee of $25 plus d dollars for each hour h that the gear is rented. Which of the following expressions correctly models the amount a customer would pay for renting scuba gear for h hours?

  A. $25 + dh$
  B. $25d + h$
  C. $25 + d + h$
  D. $25dh$
  E. $25d + 25h$

A COMMON ALGEBRAIC WORD PROBLEM

You will likely come across a two-unknown/two-equation algebraic word problem similar to the one below. The example below covers the steps:

 Look for questions that have two unknowns, and two "situations" involving these unknowns. Often, these will include one for the total number of items, and one for a total cost or income.

(EX) 40. The Bakerville Library held a charity event. Tickets for library members cost $5, and tickets for nonmembers cost $15. If an amount of $2,500 was collected from the 200 guests who paid admission, how many guests were members?

A. 15
B. 25
C. 50
D. 75
E. 150

A COUPLE TRICKY EQUATIONS

Students frequently make mistakes on the following two types of word problems. We'll use examples to teach them:

(EX) In a parking lot, let c be the number of cars and t be the number of trucks. If there are 50 more cars than trucks, which of the following displays the relationship between c and t?

A. $c = 50 - t$
B. $50 - c = t$
C. $c = t + 50$
D. $c + 50 = t$
E. $c = 50t$

EX In a parking lot, let c be the number of cars and t be the number of trucks. If there are three times as many cars as trucks, which of the following displays the relationship between c and t?

A. $3c = t$

B. $c = 3t$

C. $ct = 3$

D. $ct = \dfrac{1}{3}$

E. $c = 3 + t$

INEQUALITY WORD PROBLEMS

Not all word problems deal with *equations*. Some will include *inequalities*. Look for the keywords below to recognize these problems.

> Most of these problems will have *less than* or *greater than* signs in the answer choices ($<$, $>$, $\leq$, $\geq$). You can also look for words such as these:
> - maximum or greatest possible
> - minimum or least possible
> - at least
> - at most
> - up to
> - greater than
> - less than

24. A company plans to sell 100 containers of hand sanitizer for p dollars each. If the company's total cost for each container is $1.50, what is the lowest price p the company can charge for each container if it wants to make at least $200 in profit?

A. $2.00

B. $2.50

C. $3.00

D. $3.50

E. $4.00

■

8. George will be paid $150 to write an article for a magazine, plus 1% of the profits made by the magazine for the issue in which George's article is published. Let *p* be the profit for the issue, in dollars. Which of the following expressions gives George's total pay, in dollars, for his article?

    A. $1.5p$
    B. $1.5 + 0.01p$
    C. $150 + 0.01p$
    D. $150 + 0.1p$
    E. $150 + p$

11. You have been hired to make sales calls for a small company. For each day of calling, you make $50 plus a fixed amount for each call you make. Currently you earn $140 per day for making 60 calls. If you increased the number of calls per day by 20, what would be your new daily earnings?

    A. $170
    B. $165
    C. $160
    D. $155
    E. $150

17. Four times a number is four more than two times the number. What is the number?

    F. -2
    G. 0
    H. 2
    J. 4
    K. 8

36. Paul is going to make and sell lemonade for his summer job. He estimates that it will cost $0.50 for all ingredients for each cup of lemonade, including the cost of the cup itself. In addition, Paul incurs an upfront payment of $40 for all other supplies, including a pitcher, a table, and a sign. Assume that there are no other expenses. If Paul decides to sell each cup of lemonade for $1.50, which of the following equations represents his profit, *P*, in dollars, if he sells *x* cups of lemonade?

    A. $P = x - 40$
    B. $P = -x + 40$
    C. $P = 1.50x - 40$
    D. $P = 1.50x - 20$
    E. $P = 39x$

Continued →

56. Nick purchased a box that contained red, blue, and yellow straws. There were ⅓ as many red straws as there were blue straws. If ⅓ of the straws were blue and 20 of the straws were yellow, how many straws were in the box?

   A. 12
   B. 24
   C. 36
   D. 48
   E. 60

3. THE PICK TRICKS

The two most important techniques in this tutorial are called *Pick Numbers* and *Pick Answers*—collectively called the *Pick Tricks*. These techniques make problems easier, often by eliminating difficult algebra. In addition, the Pick Tricks may allow you to solve a problem that would otherwise require a specific mathematical approach that you are not familiar with.

> *!* **How important are the Pick Tricks? On average, nearly 1 out of every 3 problems on the ACT Math Test can be solved using a Pick Trick!**

That doesn't mean you'll have to use the Pick Tricks on 20 problems per test. Most problems that can be solved with Pick Tricks can also be solved using more traditional mathematical approaches. However, you should learn these techniques. Because the Pick Tricks make problems *easier*, they will benefit all levels of students. And the Pick Tricks are tools that can get you out of jams. The next several pages will ensure that you are comfortable using these tools.

PICK NUMBERS

The Pick Numbers technique allows variables (or unknowns) to be replaced with actual numbers that you pick. There are four types of Pick Numbers problems:

- Type 1: Variables in the answer choices
- Type 2: Variables in the question only
- Type 3: No variables
- Type 4: Guess and check

We'll discuss each one on the following pages.

PICK NUMBERS TYPE 1: VARIABLES IN THE ANSWER CHOICES

The first type of Pick Trick is the easiest to identify and the most straightforward and systematic to solve. Simply look for problems with **variable *expressions* in the answer choices**, for example:

    A. $x - 3$
    B. $x - 2$
    C. $x - 1$
    D. x
    E. $x + 1$

Note: For most problems with equal signs (=) or inequalities (<,>...) in the answer choices, this technique will not work. Make sure the answer choices are variable *expressions* (not equations or inequalities).

The following is a step-by-step method for solving these types of problems:

1. **Pick numbers for variables found in the answer choices.** The numbers 0 and 1 are usually not good choices. If there is more than one variable, pick *different* numbers for each variable. Write your picked numbers somewhere close to the answer choices—you will have to plug them in later. Draw a *box* around the numbers so they are easy to keep track of.

2. **Answer the question using an appropriate technique.** Remember, the variables should now be read as the numbers you picked in step 1, thereby simplifying the problem. Once you've solved the problem, *circle* or *underline* the answer.

3. **Plug your picked numbers into *each* of the answer choices.** You must plug in the number values that you picked in step 1. Cross out any answer choices that don't match your circled or underlined answer from step 2. **YOU MUST CHECK EVERY ANSWER CHOICE!** If only one answer equals your circled answer from step 2, you're done. Occasionally, more than one answer choice works, and you will have to go back to step 1 and pick new numbers to complete the elimination process. Once an answer choice has been eliminated, you do not have to check it again.

(EX) If a pen costs p cents, how many pens can be purchased for $4.00?

    A. $4p$

    B. $400p$

    C. $p/4$

    D. $4/p$

    E. $400/p$

Try the following lesson problems:

33. The expression $(a + b + 1)(a - b)$ is equivalent to: ?

   A. $a^2 - b^2$
   B. $a^2 - b^2 - b$
   C. $a^2 - b^2 + b$
   D. $a^2 + a - b^2 - b$
   E. $a^2 + a - b^2 + b$

42. If m and n are consecutive even integers and $m > n > 0$, how many integers are greater than $m + n$ and less than $m \times n$?

   F. 1
   G. 2
   H. $m - n$
   J. $n^2 - 3$
   K. $m^2 - n^2$

A note on Pick Numbers (type 1) identification:

As mentioned on the previous page, you should look for variable *expressions* in the answer choices (no equations or inequalities), but if every answer choice begins with the same variable and an equal sign (see example below), then you can still use Pick Numbers (type 1):

   A. $y = x - 3$
   B. $y = x - 2$
   C. $y = x - 1$
   D. $y = x$
   E. $y = x + 1$

Since the "$y =$" could have been the last words in the question, we can look at the answer choices as just variable expressions ($x - 3$, $x - 2$, etc.). In other words, pick a number for x, and follow the steps described above.

PICK NUMBERS TYPE 2: VARIABLES IN THE QUESTION ONLY

 These problems have **variables in the question** and **no variables in the answer choices**. This means the answer choices are actual numbers.

Picking numbers for some or all of the variables in the question may lead you to the correct answer. You must read the question carefully to avoid picking numbers that break the specific rules of the problem. **You will usually <u>not</u> pick numbers for *every* variable.** Use the following method:

1. Start with the easiest equation or expression in the problem and pick a number for *one* of the variables.
2. Solve for as many other variables as possible.
3. If necessary, pick numbers for additional variables (that could not be solved in step 2) until you have enough information to solve the problem.

Remember to read the problem carefully. To avoid picking numbers for too many variables, make sure all of the specific rules for the problem are being followed.

(EX) If $a(b - c) = 6$ and $ab = 12$, what is the value of ac?

    A. −6
    B. 2
    C. 3
    D. 4
    E. 6

Try the following lesson problem:

50. If $\dfrac{a}{b} = \dfrac{2}{3}$ and $\dfrac{b}{c} = \dfrac{2}{5}$, then $\dfrac{a}{c} = ?$

    A. $\frac{4}{15}$
    B. $\frac{3}{10}$
    C. $\frac{2}{5}$
    D. $\frac{2}{3}$
    E. $\frac{5}{3}$

PICK NUMBERS TYPE 3: NO VARIABLES

Picking numbers when there are no variables allows you to create an example problem with your own numbers. This will give you a place to start and something to work with. The number 100 is sometimes a convenient number to pick, as we've already seen in some of the percent problems in chapter II.

> These problems feel "open ended" because they usually do not give actual values or quantities, such as a population, the size of a square (see below), etc. Usually these problems do not include variables.

(EX) Last week, Bill scored 10 fewer points than Fred in a game, and today, Bill scored 2 more points than Fred. Which of the following must be true about Bill's point total for the two games compared to Fred's?

A. Bill scored 1/5 of what Fred scored
B. Bill scored 5 times of what Fred scored
C. Bill scored 8 points more than Fred
D. Bill scored 8 points fewer than Fred
E. Bill scored 12 points fewer than Fred

Try the following lesson problem:

31. When the perimeter of a square doubles, then the square's area increases by what percent?

A. 50%
B. 100%
C. 200%
D. 300%
E. 400%

PICK NUMBERS TYPE 4: GUESS AND CHECK

Sometimes when you Pick Numbers (type 2), something doesn't work. For example, if you pick a number and end up with 2 = 3, you know something's wrong. Or perhaps you know the answer is supposed to be an integer and you keep getting fractions. You may have to *guess* numbers and *check* to see if you're getting closer to the correct answer. Use the following general method:

1. Pick a number or numbers for variables, as with the Pick Numbers (type 2) technique. You will usually *not* pick numbers for every variable. This is your *guess*.

2. *Check* to see if your picked number or numbers lead you to the correct answer. **Always keep track of your results. You need to make sure that, when you pick new numbers, you're getting closer to the correct answer. You will often want to use a table to keep track of your picked numbers and their results.**

3. Continue picking numbers until you find the correct answer. Sometimes you might have to pick decimals, fractions, or negative numbers (not all problems on the ACT deal only with positive integers).

> This technique works on many types of difficult, high-numbered problems. Often, they involve one or more equations that you cannot easily solve.

(EX) If $xy = 91$ and $x + y = 20$, then $x^2y + xy^2 = ?$

   A. 111
   B. 1,820
   C. 1,919
   D. 2,000
   E. 2,091

Try the following lesson problem:

50. If $7x + 3y = 29$, where x and y are positive integers, what is the value of $x + y$?

   A. 3
   B. 7
   C. 8
   D. 10
   E. 17

PICK ANSWERS

If the answer choices are actual numbers, you may be able to *pick answers* to make the problem easier to solve. This tip is especially useful on harder problems or problems that have you stumped. Essentially, this technique allows you to solve a problem by picking answers and *working backwards*.

Before picking answers, you must identify the *barebones question*. This is the question in its simplest form and describes exactly what the problem is asking. Barebones questions are usually very simple, such as: "...what is the value of *x*?" or "...what was the price of the book?"

 These problems generally have **numbers as answer choices** (no variables). **Usually, the barebones question is very simple and involves at most one variable.** If you are ever stuck on a high-numbered problem, consider picking answers.

The method is as follows:

1. **Identify and underline the barebones question**, as described above.
2. **Answer this question by picking one of the answer choices.** Since the answers are often in ascending order, you should usually start with the middle answer choice (C or H). This may allow you to eliminate answers more quickly. If some answer choices appear easier to check than others, however, you can check these first.
3. **Look at the rest of the question to see if the answer you picked makes sense.** Essentially, you are creating an *if-then* question: *If* the answer to the barebones question is C (for example), *then* are the parameters of the problem possible? **Once you find the answer that works, stop—you do *not* have to check all the answers for picking answer problems.**

(EX) If Ed and Lorena divide a deck of 52 cards so that Lorena has 8 fewer cards than Ed, how many cards does Lorena receive?

A. 18
B. 22
C. 26
D. 30
E. 34

Try the following lesson problems:

29. Ryan had *d* dollars when he took Amy on a date. He spent one-fourth of his money on flowers and two-thirds of his <u>remaining</u> money on dinner. If he only spent money for flowers and dinner, and he is left with 35 dollars at the end of the night, what is the value of *d*?

    A. 70
    B. 140
    C. 160
    D. 180
    E. 210

41. Raymond has 8 buckets and 22 rocks. Each bucket can hold at most 5 rocks. What is the greatest possible number of buckets that can contain 5 rocks if NONE of the buckets are empty?

    F. 0
    G. 1
    H. 2
    J. 3
    K. 4

MORE PICK NUMBERS

You can often pick numbers on problems that have *ranges* of possible values—either in the question or in the answer choices—such as inequalities, tables, or graphs (especially graphs with shaded regions).

 As described above, these questions usually have *ranges* of values, such as inequalities, either in the question or in the answer choices.

WHERE TO START?

There are two possible starting places when using this technique:

1. **The question**: When it's easier to pick a number or numbers that satisfy the information given in the *question*, start with the question, and then check your picked number(s) in the answer choices.
2. **The answer choices**: Sometimes you'll find that it's easier to pick numbers for the *answer choices* and then check your picked number(s) in the question.

STARTING WITH THE QUESTION

When you can easily pick a number that satisfies the *question*, use the following technique (follow along with the example):

1. Pick a number or numbers that satisfy the question.
2. Eliminate answer choices that do NOT include this number.
3. Continue picking numbers until you have eliminated all three incorrect answers. (Note: If necessary, you may have to pick a number that does NOT satisfy the question, in which case you will eliminate answer choices that DO include the number.)

(EX) On a roller coaster ride at an amusement park, riders must be greater than 4 feet tall but less than 6 feet tall. If x represents the allowable height of a rider, in feet, which of the following represents all of the possible values of x?

A. $|x+6| < 4$
B. $|x-6| = 4$
C. $|x-5| < 1$
D. $|x-5| > 1$
E. $|x-5| = 1$

Try the following problem by picking numbers:

39. Which of the following equations gives the relationship between t and d in the table below?

t	1	2	3	4
d	1	3	6	10

A. $d = t + (t - 1)$

B. $d = \dfrac{t(t + 1)}{2}$

C. $d = \dfrac{t + 1}{2}$

D. $d = 2t$

E. $d = 2t + 1$

STARTING WITH THE ANSWER CHOICES

When picking numbers that satisfy the question is difficult, start with the *answer choices*. Here's the technique (follow along with the example):

1. Pick a number that works for at least one answer choice. But be careful: the number you pick should not work for *all* of the choices:

    ! **The number you pick should be true for *at least one* of the choices, but *not all* of them.**

2. Check your picked number in the question and eliminate answer choices. Once again, eliminating answer choices is the key. If the number you picked *works* in the question, eliminate answer choices that do *not* contain that number. If the number you picked *fails* in the question, eliminate answer choices that *do* contain that number.

3. Repeat the steps until you have eliminated three of the answer choices.

(EX) If $\dfrac{x - 5}{2}$ is an integer, then x must be: ?

A. a negative integer
B. a positive integer
C. a multiple of 5
D. an even integer
E. an odd integer

Try the following lesson problem:

57. If $x \geq 0$, which of the following is the solution set of $\left| x^2 - 10 \right| \leq 6$?

    A. $0 \leq x \leq 2$

    B. $0 \leq x \leq 4$

    C. $1 \leq x \leq 4$

    D. $2 \leq x \leq 4$

    E. $2 \leq x \leq 8$

∎

PICK TRICK HOMEWORK

Use at least one of the Pick Tricks on each of the following problems. Yes, you may know how to solve some of these problems using more traditional techniques, but remember that the goal of this section is to get comfortable with the *Pick Tricks*, so you can use them—when you choose to—on the ACT.

21. Six people visit Anna's blog every x seconds. At this rate, how many people will visit her blog in y minutes?

    A. $10xy$

    B. $10x/y$

    C. $10y/x$

    D. $360x/y$

    E. $360y/x$

23. If $a = b$, $c = d$, and $e = f$, which of the following equations must be true?

    F. $a + b = e + f$
    G. $a + c = d + e$
    H. $a + d = a + f$
    J. $a + d = b + c$
    K. $a + c = b - d$

Continued →

31. If m and n are positive integers, what is the least value of m for which $\dfrac{2m}{11} = n^2$?

    A. 1
    B. 2
    C. 11
    D. 22
    E. 44

34. If $3^x = 8$, then $3^{2x} = ?$

    F. 4
    G. 16
    H. 24
    J. 40
    K. 64

35. Anna, Tanya, and Stephanie decide to split the buried treasure that they find so that Anna receives $\dfrac{3}{5}$ of the treasure, Tanya receives $\dfrac{1}{3}$ of the treasure, and Stephanie receives the rest. What is the ratio of Anna's share to Tanya's share to Stephanie's share?

    A. 15:5:3
    B. 9:5:1
    C. 9:3:1
    D. 5:3:1
    E. 3:2:1

37. Max can sweep his patio in x minutes. What fraction of the task remains if he sweeps his patio steadily for y minutes, where $y < x$?

    F. $\dfrac{x+y}{y}$

    G. $\dfrac{x+y}{x}$

    H. $\dfrac{x+y}{x-y}$

    J. $\dfrac{x-y}{x}$

    K. $\dfrac{x-y}{y}$

Continued →

38. Which of the following is the solution set for the inequality below?

$$|x+2| > 6$$

    A. $x < -6$ or $x > 6$
    B. $x < -8$ or $x > 4$
    C. $x < 4$ or $x > 8$
    D. $x < -4$ or $x > 4$
    E. $x < -4$ or $x > 8$

42. Joshua is ½ as old as Keith and ¼ as old as Sean. If the average of all three ages is 21, how old is Keith now?

    F. 3
    G. 9
    H. 12
    J. 18
    K. 36

43. A business is owned by 3 men and 1 woman, each of whom has an equal share. If one of the men sells $\frac{1}{3}$ of his share to the woman, and another man keeps $\frac{1}{3}$ of his shares and sells the rest to the woman, what fraction of the business will the woman own?

    A. $\frac{5}{12}$
    B. $\frac{1}{2}$
    C. $\frac{3}{4}$
    D. $\frac{11}{12}$
    E. $1\frac{1}{4}$

48. Which of the following defines the solution set for the the system of inequalities below?

$$-2x + 3 > -1$$
$$2x - 3 > -7$$

    F. $x > -2$
    G. $x < 2$
    H. $-4 < x < 4$
    J. $-2 < x < 2$
    K. $-2 < x < 4$

Continued →

51. Jody played a video game three times and improved his score by the same percent each time. If he scored 600 points the first time and 864 points the third time, what was the percent change after each game?

A. 13.2%
B. 20%
C. 22%
D. 26.4%
E. 44%

56. For every dollar that a software company raises the price of a computer program, it sells 1,000 fewer programs. The company normally sells 5,000 programs a day at a cost of $75.50 per program. If the company raises the price d dollars, which of the following expressions represents the number of programs sold per day?

F. $75.50 - d$
G. $5,000(75.50 - d)$
H. $5,000 - 1,000(75.50 - d)$
J. $5,000 - 1,000d$
K. $75.50(5,000 - 1,000d)$

4. ALGEBRA PROBLEMS

PRACTICE PROBLEMS

The worksheets on the following pages test techniques taught in this chapter. For additional practice, we'll use problems from Test 5 in *The Official ACT Prep Guide*.

    ☐   Algebra Worksheet 1

    ☐   Algebra Worksheet 2

    ☐   Algebra Worksheet 3

    ☐   ***The Official ACT Prep Guide*: Test 5**: Only tackle questions related to *this chapter*. For a list of these relevant questions, see the Techniques chapter at the end of this tutorial (first page of "Techniques: Test 5").

Reminders:

- **Use techniques**: These assignments are "open book." Go back to the tutorial as often as you need to, and use techniques aggressively.

- **No timing**: Do *not* time yourself on these assignments.

- **Scheduling**: See the Tutoring Schedules section in the Introduction for more details on scheduling.

TEST CORRECTIONS

After each practice test is graded, you should correct questions related to this chapter that you missed or guessed on. See "Correcting Practice Tests" in the Introduction for more details.

! Note: If you're following the **20- or 30-hour program**, you should also try correcting Advanced Algebra questions. Hint: use the Pick Tricks aggressively.

Here are the steps:

1. Turn to the Techniques chapter at the end of this tutorial and circle the Algebra questions that you missed or guessed on for the test you are correcting.

2. Correct the problems in *The Official ACT Prep Guide*. As you correct the problems, go back to the tutorial and review the techniques. The idea is to (1) identify techniques that have given you trouble, (2) go back to the tutorial so you can review and strengthen these techniques, and (3) apply these techniques to the specific problems on which you struggled.

3. If you have trouble identifying the best technique to use for a problem, refer to the Techniques chapter. This is an important part of correcting the tests.

ALGEBRA WORKSHEET 1

4. For what value of *x* is the equation $3(2x - 4) = 2x - 16$?

    A. 0
    B. −1
    C. −3
    D. −4
    E. −18

5. The total cost to hire a web service company is $50.00 for each day plus 75¢ for each customer click on a keyword. What is the total cost to hire this company for 30 days if a total of 2,500 keywords are clicked?

    A. $(50)(30) + $(0.75)(2,500)
    B. $(50)(30) + $(75)(2,500)
    C. $(50)(2,500) + $(0.75)(30)
    D. $(50)(2,500) + $(75)(2,500)
    E. $(50)(30)(2,500)(0.75)

10. If *a*, *b*, and *c* are all nonzero real numbers and $a + b = c$, which of the following equations is always true?

    F. $a = b - c$
    G. $a = b + c$
    H. $a = -(c - b)$
    J. $-a = c - b$
    K. $-a = b - c$

12. If *x* is a positive real number and $\dfrac{3}{x} \leq \dfrac{1}{3}$, what is the smallest possible value of *x* ?

    A. $\dfrac{1}{9}$

    B. $\dfrac{1}{3}$

    C. 1

    D. 3

    E. 9

Continued →

15. What binomial must be subtracted from $2x^2 + 7x - 14$ so that the difference is $x^2 - 14$?

   F. $x^2 - 14x$
   G. $x^2 + 7$
   H. $x^2 - 7$
   J. $x^2 + 7x$
   K. $x^2 - 7x$

24. Which of the following is equivalent to $a(a + a) - a(a + a - 1)$?

   A. $-a$
   B. $-4a^2 + a$
   C. $-4a^2 - a$
   D. $-2a^2 - a$
   E. a

30. The formula used to calculate the current value of an investment is $A = P(1 + r)^n$, where A is the current value, P is the investment amount, r is the rate of interest for 1 compounding period, and n is the number of compounding periods that have passed. Which of the following, to the nearest dollar, is the value after 10 years of a $5,000 investment at a 6% annual interest compounded yearly?

   A. $\$\dfrac{(1.06)^{10}}{5,000}$

   B. $\$\dfrac{5,000}{(1.06)^{10}}$

   C. $\$\dfrac{5,000}{(1.06)(10)}$

   D. $\$5,000(1.06)^{10}$
   E. $\$5,000(1.6)^{10}$

36. Which of the following is equivalent to the identity $-3x + 6 < -6x$?

   F. $x < -\frac{2}{3}$
   G. $x < 2$
   H. $x > 2$
   J. $x < -2$
   K. $x > -2$

Continued →

41. A circle in the standard (x,y) coordinate plane has center $(0,2)$ and radius 2 units. Which of the following equations represents the circle?

A. $x^2 + (y - 2)^2 = 2$
B. $x^2 + (y + 2)^2 = 2$
C. $x^2 - (y - 2)^2 = 4$
D. $x^2 + (y - 2)^2 = 4$
E. $x^2 + (y + 2)^2 = 4$

42. For all $x > 4$, $\dfrac{x^2 - 4x}{x^2 + 4x - 32} = ?$

F. $\dfrac{-x}{x + 8}$

G. $\dfrac{x}{x + 8}$

H. $\dfrac{-1}{x + 8}$

J. $\dfrac{-1}{32}$

K. $\dfrac{1}{32}$

ALGEBRA WORKSHEET 2

14. Which of the following is equivalent to $\dfrac{x+x}{x}$?

    A. 2
    B. x
    C. $2x$
    D. x^2
    E. $2x^2$

29. At a fair, red tickets are good for rides and blue tickets are good for carnival games. Red tickets cost r dollars and blue tickets cost b dollars. The difference between the cost of 5 red tickets and 10 blue tickets is $15. Which of the following equations could be used to find possible costs for the two types of tickets?

    F. $r-b=15$
    G. $\dfrac{5r}{10b}=15$
    H. $|5r+10b|=15$
    J. $|5r-10b|=15$
    K. $|10r-5b|=15$

32. A boat sits in still water off the coast of an island with two lighthouses. The light from the first lighthouse is visible every 21 seconds and the light from the second lighthouse is visible every 60 seconds. If the captain of the boat sees the lights from both lighthouses at the same time, how many seconds will pass before he again sees the lights at the same time?

    F. 120
    G. 210
    H. 420
    J. 840
    K. 1,260

33. If $\sqrt{x-3}-3=3$, then $x=$?

    A. 3
    B. 7
    C. 36
    D. 39
    E. 42

Continued →

45. A rectangle is twice as long as it is wide. If all sides are tripled, then the area of the new rectangle is how many times greater than the area of the original rectangle?

   F. 3
   G. 6
   H. 9
   J. 12
   K. 15

47. A bowling alley charges three different prices per game, one price for children, one price for adults, and one price for seniors. On Friday night, visitors paid for exactly 200 games. If there were 60 more adult games played than senior games and 40 more senior games played than child games, how many adult games were played?

   A. 20
   B. 60
   C. 100
   D. 120
   E. 150

54. Which of the following inequalities is represented by the graph below?

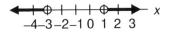

$$-4\;-3\;-2\;-1\;0\;1\;2\;3$$

   A. $|x + 3| > 1$
   B. $|x + 1| < 3$
   C. $|x + 1| > 3$
   D. $|x + 1| > 2$
   E. $|x + 1| < 2$

Continued →

55. Patrick's basketball team has won 8 of its first 16 games. What is the minimum number of additional games his team must play to raise its win percentage to 80%?

  A. 4
  B. 8
  C. 16
  D. 24
  E. 40

58. Let x be a positive 2-digit number with a tens digit a and units digit b. If y is the 2-digit number formed by reversing the digits of x, which of the following is equal to $x + y$?

  F. $11|a - b|$
  G. $11|b - a|$
  H. $a + b$
  J. $11(a + b)$
  K. $121(a + b)$

59. For all real numbers x and y, if the sum of 10 and x is y, which of the following expressions represents the product of 10 and x in terms of y?

  A. $10y$
  B. $10y + 100$
  C. $10y - 100$
  D. $y + 100$
  E. $y - 100$

ALGEBRA WORKSHEET 3

8. If $q = -10$, then $-q^2 + q - 100 = $?

   A. -210
   B. -200
   C. -190
   D. 110
   E. 210

9. The five consecutive integers below add up to 115.

$$x - 3, \ x - 2, \ x - 1, \ x, \ x + 1$$

   What is the value of x?

   F. 21
   G. 22
   H. 23
   J. 24
   K. 25

24. A car rental company charges $25.00 per day to rent a car plus 25¢ per mile driven. Which of the following expressions represents the cost to drive a rented car m miles per day for d days?

   A. $\$25.00(d + m)$
   B. $\$25.00d(1 + m)$
   C. $\$25.00d + \$0.25m$
   D. $\$25.00d + \$0.25md$
   E. $\$25.00d + \$0.25(m + d)$

32. If two numbers are both divisible by 3, which of the following numbers must be a factor of the product of the two numbers?

   F. 6
   G. 9
   H. 12
   J. 15
   K. 18

Continued →

35. If $x - y = -8$, then $\sqrt{2y - 2x} = ?$

    F. $2\sqrt{2}$

    G. $4\sqrt{2}$

    H. 4

    J. 8

    K. 16

38. If $a^2 - b^2 = 16$ and $a^2 + b = 28$, then what is a possible value of a?

    A. 3

    B. 4

    C. 5

    D. 6

    E. 7

53. Which of the following is the graph in the standard (x,y) coordinate plane of the points that satisfy the inequality $|x| \geq 10$?

A.

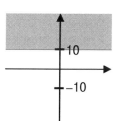

D.

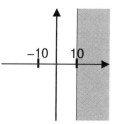

B.

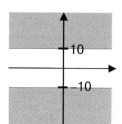

E.

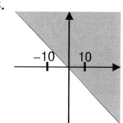

C.

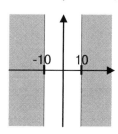

Continued →

57. If $\dfrac{a}{a^2+1} + \dfrac{1}{a^2+1} = \dfrac{5}{b}$ for integers a and b and $a > 1$, what is a possible value of b?

   A. 2
   B. 4
   C. 5
   D. 17
   E. 85

59. There are 270 questions on a high-school entrance exam. To achieve a maximum scaled score of 100, the school scales the exam so that a student's score equals $\frac{1}{3}C + 10$, where C is the number of correct answers. If a student can take the exam twice, how many additional questions must a student answer correctly on the second exam in order to raise her initial score by 20 points?

   A. 30
   B. 45
   C. 60
   D. 75
   E. 90

IV
ADVANCED ALGEBRA

The topics covered in this chapter include factoring and working with polynomials. Many of these problems can be solved using the Pick Tricks (see Chapter III), but often the algebraic approaches taught in this chapter are faster and/or easier. You will learn techniques that will help on some of the ACT's harder algebra questions.

SKIP THIS CHAPTER?

If you're following the **20- or 30-hour program**, you should skip this chapter and go to the Geometry chapter (see the Tutoring Schedules in the Introduction). If you're comfortable with the material in the Algebra chapter (Chapter III), you'll be in good shape for most algebra-based questions on the test. And, as stated above, the Pick Tricks will often allow you to solve Advanced Algebra questions. In fact, for students who don't get to this chapter in our regular programs, we'll assign Advanced Algebra questions and corrections to be completed with regular Algebra questions (again, see Chapter III). But for students with time, the material in this chapter is important.

1. SYSTEMS OF EQUATIONS AND INEQUALITIES

SYSTEMS OF EQUATIONS

Speaking graphically, the "solution" of two equations is the point (or points) where the graphs of these equations *intersect*. Rather than finding this point graphically, you should typically find it *algebraically*. We briefly discussed the "substitution method" in the Basic Algebra lesson (Chapter III). However, most of the systems of equations questions on the ACT are easier to solve using the *elimination method*:

THE ELIMINATION METHOD

Use the elimination method to solve *linear equations*, which have the form $ax + by = c$, where a, b, and c are numbers, called *coefficients*:

Coefficient – a number or constant that multiplies a variable (for example, in the expression $2x$, the coefficient is 2).

Use the following method:

1. Stack the equations (one above the other) with variables aligned.
2. If necessary, multiply one or both of the equations by a constant (or constants) so that one of the variables has the same coefficient in each equation.
3. Add or subtract the equations to eliminate this variable.
4. Solve for the remaining variable using algebra.
5. Plug this value into one of the original equations to find the other variable.

Solve for x and y:

(EX) $x + 2y = 8$ and $x - 2y = -4$

1. $2x + 2y = 8$ and $3x - 2y = 2$

2. $100x + y = 25$ and $200x + y = 45$

3. $5x - 5y = -10$ and $2x + 3y = 16$

SYSTEMS OF LINEAR INEQUALITIES

On the ACT, these questions usually give you a system of linear inequalities and ask you to identify the graph in the answer choices, although occasionally you'll be given the graph and asked to identify the system of inequalities.

Here's the method for graphing a system of inequalities. Follow along with the example on the following page:

1. Ignoring the inequalities, graph the lines as if they were equations.
2. For each line, *lightly* shade the side that satisfies the inequality. There are two ways to do this:
   a. An easy way is to simply test a point. The origin—(0, 0)—is usually a good test, assuming the line doesn't go through this point. If the point you test works, shade this side of the line. Otherwise, shade the other side. Remember to shade *lightly* at this point.
   b. You could also remember that if $y >$ (or $\geq$) something, you'll shade *above* the line. If $y <$ (or $\leq$) something, you'll shade *below* the line.
3. Finally, shade the region that includes *all* of the lightly shaded regions from step 2.

(EX) Graph the solution of the system of inequalities below:

$$y \leq 3x + 6$$
$$y \leq -x + 6$$
$$y \geq 0$$

On actual ACT problems, it's unlikely that you'll actually have to graph inequalities. More often, you'll need to *identify* the correct graph for a given system of inequalities. Other problems may give you the graph and ask you to identify the correct system of inequalities. In either case, your knowledge of graphing, as taught above, will get you to the correct answer. Here's a lesson problem:

51. Which of the following graphs best represents the system of inequalities below?

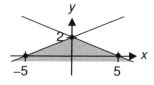

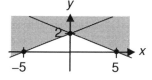

A.

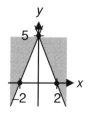

B.

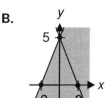

C.

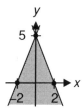

D.

E.

SOLID LINES AND DOTTED LINES

The questions above involved "greater than or equal to" (≥) or "less than or equal to" (≤) signs. The lines for these questions are represented with *solid lines* (as shown above). If, however, the inequalities involve "greater than" (>) or "less than" (<) signs, use *dotted lines*.

50. Which of the following inequalities is graphed below in the (x, y) coordinate plane?

A. $y > 3$
B. $y \geq 3$
C. $y > 2$
D. $y \geq 2$
E. $y < 2$

23. If $2x - 2y = 12$ and $x + 3y = -6$, what is the value of y?

    A. -3
    B. -1
    C. 1
    D. 3
    E. 6

37. Let $3x + 4y = 2$ and $5x + 6y = 2$, what is the value of $x + y$?

    A. -2
    B. -1
    C. 0
    D. 1
    E. 2

50. Which of the following inequalities is graphed below in the (x, y) coordinate plane?

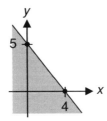

    A. $y \le -\dfrac{5}{4}x$

    B. $y \ge -\dfrac{5}{4}x$

    C. $y \le -\dfrac{5}{4}x + 5$

    D. $y \ge -\dfrac{5}{4}x + 5$

    E. $y \le -\dfrac{4}{5}x + 5$

Continued →

55. Which of the following graphs best represents the system of inequalities below?

$$y \geq \frac{1}{2}x$$
$$y \leq x$$
$$2 \leq x \leq 4$$

A.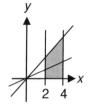

D.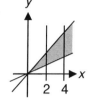

B.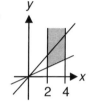

E.

C.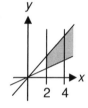

2. FACTORING

There are only three types of *factoring* you need to be familiar with for the ACT:

1. Common factors
2. Factoring quadratics
3. Difference of two squares

COMMON FACTORS

First, some terminology:

Term – a product of numbers and/or variables, such as $4x$ or $\frac{1}{2}x^2$

Expression – one or more terms added or subtracted together, such as $4x + \frac{1}{2}x^2$

If you are solving a difficult equation, always check to see if you can pull a common factor out of every term of an expression. This may sound complicated, but the method is actually fairly straightforward and is best displayed with examples:

Factor the following expressions:

(EX) $\frac{1}{2}x^2 + 4x =$

1. $20q^2 - 40q =$

(EX) $12a^3b - 6a^2b^2 =$

2. $2x^2y + 3xy^2 =$

 Look for difficult equations that have common factors in every term on one side of the equal sign.

SOLVING EQUATIONS BY FACTORING

Factoring will often help you solve an otherwise difficult equation. First, remember that whenever the product of two expressions equals zero, either the first expression equals zero or the second expression equals zero (or they both do). This is called the *Zero Product Theorem*:

If $a \cdot b = 0$, then $a = 0$ or $b = 0$

For example, if $x(\frac{1}{2}x + 4) = 0$, then $x = 0$ or $(\frac{1}{2}x + 4) = 0$. If you solve the second equation for x, you'll get $x = -8$. So the solutions are: $x = 0$ or $x = -8$.

The following method is useful on many *common factor* problems:

1. For most of these problems, add or subtract terms so that one expression equals zero (all terms on one side of the equal sign).

2. Factor out common factors.

3. Set each new expression equal to zero and solve (as explained by the Zero Product Theorem). These solutions are sometimes called "zeros" because the original expression equals zero when any of the solutions are plugged in.

(EX) If $x^2 + 9x = 0$, then what is the <u>sum</u> of the possible values of x?

    A. -9
    B. -3
    C. 0
    D. 3
    E. 9

Try the following lesson problem:

29. If $x^2 = 4x$, which of the following is a possible value of $x - 4$?

    A. -4
    B. -2
    C. 2
    D. 4
    E. 8

FACTORING QUADRATICS

 Quadratics usually take the form $ax^2 + bx + c = 0$, where a, b, and c are numbers. In general, on the ACT, a will equal 1, which is fortunate because it makes solving the quadratic much easier.

If you are unfamiliar with factoring quadratics, read over the following method carefully:

1. Set the quadratic equal to zero with the *x-squared term* (x^2) first and the *number term* (no *x*) last.

2. Find two numbers that *multiply* to the number term. If necessary, use a *factor table* to find the pairs of factors (see Basic Mathematical Concepts), but don't forget about negative numbers, as well.

3. The factor pair from step 2 that *adds* to the coefficient of the *x term* is the correct pair.

4. Write the quadratic in a factored form (see example).

5. Solve for *x* using the Zero Product Theorem.

(EX) Factor $x^2 - 7x + 10 = 0$ and solve for *x*.

Factor the following quadratics and solve for *x*.

1. $x^2 + 5x = -6$

2. $x^2 - 12x + 12 = -8$

3. $x^2 + 4x = 21$

4. $x^2 + 22x - 23 = 0$

THE QUADRATIC FORMULA

On rare occasion a question may show up that requires you to use the *quadratic formula*. This formula allows you to find the solutions of a quadratic equation of the form $ax^2 + bx + c = 0$. We recommend you memorize the formula:

$$\boxed{\begin{array}{c} FLASH \\ CARDS \end{array}} \quad x = \frac{-b \pm \sqrt{b^2 - 4ac}}{2a}$$

The expression within the square root ($b^2 - 4ac$, called the *discriminant*) offers some useful information:

- If $b^2 > 4ac$, then the quadratic equation has 2 *real* solutions (since you'll be taking the square root of a positive number).
- If $b^2 = 4ac$, then the quadratic equation has 1 real solution ($b^2 - 4ac = 0$).
- If $b^2 < 4ac$, then the quadratic equation has 2 *imaginary* solutions (since you'll be taking the square root of a negative number—we'll cover imaginary numbers in the Odds & Ends chapter).

SPECIAL QUADRATIC EQUATIONS

There are three special quadratic equations that may be tested on the ACT. They're worth memorizing. You can FOIL to confirm each one:

$$\boxed{\begin{array}{c} FLASH \\ CARDS \end{array}}$$

1. $(x + y)(x - y) = x^2 - y^2$

2. $(x + y)^2 = x^2 + 2xy + y^2$

3. $(x - y)^2 = x^2 - 2xy + y^2$

 To identify these problems, look for any of the elements of the three equations: $(x + y)$, $(x - y)$, $(x + y)^2$, $(x - y)^2$, $x^2 + 2xy + y^2$, $x^2 - 2xy + y^2$, $2xy$, etc.

Use the following method to tackle these problems (follow along with the example):

1. **Identify which of the three quadratic equations above is being tested.** Look for clues; for example, if you see the expressions $(x + y)$ and $(x - y)$, you know that the first equation above is being tested.
2. **Write the appropriate equation as it appears above.** Enter no numbers at this point.
3. **Beneath the equation, write all given numerical values.**
4. You should be able to solve for the variable, term, or expression in question.

(EX) If $m - n = 5$ and $m + n = 7$, then $m^2 - n^2 =$

    A. 12
    B. 25
    C. 35
    D. 49
    E. 74

Try the following lesson problem:

44. If $a + b = 5$ and $2ab = 5$, then $a^2 + b^2 =$

    A. 0
    B. 5
    C. 10
    D. 20
    E. 25

DIFFERENCE OF TWO SQUARES

A *square* is just a number or variable (or term) that has been squared. Some examples of squares are: 16 (square of 4), x^2 (square of x), and $36y^4$ (square of $6y^2$). Expressions that are a *difference* (subtraction) of two squares can be factored using the following formula (see Equation 1 of the special quadratics above):

$$a^2 - b^2 = (a + b)(a - b)$$

 To identify these problems, look for an expression that is a difference of squared items. Note that these squared items can be numbers, variables, terms, or

(EX) If $(x - 4)^2 - (4x)^2 = 0$, what is the <u>product</u> of the possible values for x?

    A. $-\dfrac{7}{15}$

    B. $-\dfrac{8}{15}$

    C. $-\dfrac{11}{15}$

    D. $-\dfrac{16}{15}$

    E. $-\dfrac{17}{15}$

FACTORS AND ROOTS

As discussed earlier (Zero Product Theorem), when an equation is factored, each part can be used to find a zero, or *root*, of the equation. For example, the polynomial $f(x) = x^3 + 6x^2 - x - 30$ factors as follows (trust us):

$$f(x) = (x - 2)(x + 3)(x + 5).$$

If we set the function equal to zero and use the Zero Product Theorem, we find the roots 2, –3, and –5. In the Graphs of Functions lesson (Chapter VI), we'll learn that these values are the actual points where a function crosses the *x*-axis (see below):

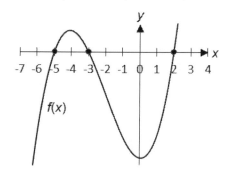

Here's a lesson problem that tests factors and roots:

11. If the polynomial $ax^3 + bx^2 + cx + d$, where a, b, c, and d are constants, has roots –1, 0, and 2, which of the following could be the factored form of the polynomial?

   A. $x(x + 1)(x - 2)$
   B. $x(x - 1)(x + 2)$
   C. $(x + 1)(x - 2)$
   D. $(x - 1)(x + 2)$
   E. $-x(x + 2)$

FACTORING HOMEWORK

1. For practice, use *FOIL* to derive the three special quadratic equations taught in this section:

Continued →

15. Which of the following has both $x = 3$ and $x = -4$ as solutions?

    A. $(x - 3)(x + 4) = 0$
    B. $(x + 3)(x - 4) = 0$
    C. $(x - 3)(x - 4) = 0$
    D. $x + 3 = x - 4$
    E. $x - 3 = x + 4$

42. For all $x \neq -7$, which of the following expressions is equal to $\dfrac{x^2 - x - 56}{x + 7} - (x + 8)$?

    A. -16

    B. 0

    C. $x^2 - 64$

    D. $x^2 - x - 65$

    E. $\dfrac{x^2 - 2x - 64}{x + 7}$

46. If $a^2 - ka + 6 = (a - 3)(a - 2)$, then $k = $?

    F. 1
    G. 3
    H. 5
    J. 6
    K. 7

Continued →

52. If $a^2 + b^2 = 18$ and $a - b = -6$, then which of the following is a in terms of b?

A. $\dfrac{-9}{b}$

B. $\dfrac{-6}{b}$

C. $\dfrac{-3}{b}$

D. $\dfrac{6}{b}$

E. $\dfrac{9}{b}$

53. Which of the following is a quadratic equation that has $\dfrac{1}{3}$ as its only solution?

A. $9x^2 - 6x + 1 = 0$
B. $9x^2 + 6x + 1 = 0$
C. $9x^2 - 9x + 2 = 0$
D. $9x^2 + 1 = 0$
E. $9x^2 - 1 = 0$

3. *WORKING WITH POLYNOMIALS*

A *polynomial* is the sum of a one or more terms of the form ax^n, where a is a coefficient and n is a whole number. Here are some examples of polynomials:

- -5
- $-5x$
- $-5x^2 + 4x - 3$

This section covers problems that involve adding, subtracting or multiplying polynomials, as described above.

DEGREE OF A POLYNOMIAL

The *degree* of a polynomial is the greatest power (exponent) of any term of the polynomial:

- The degree of $-5x$ is 1.
- The degree of $-5x^2 + 4x - 3$ is 2.

COMPARING POLYNOMIALS

When two polynomials are equal, the coefficients of variables having the same exponent will also be equal. This is best explained with an example. Follow the steps below:

1. First simplify both sides of the equation so that the polynomials are arranged in decreasing powers for x.
2. Now, compare coefficients. To put it algebraically, if $ax^n = bx^n$, then $a = b$.

(EX) If $x(2x^2 + 3x) = ax^3 + bx^2 + cx + d$, where a, b, c, and d are constants, what is the value of b?

- A. 6
- B. 3
- C. 2
- D. 1
- E. 0

OPERATIONS WITH POLYNOMIALS

ADDITION/SUBTRACTION

Adding and subtracting polynomials is just a matter of combining like terms. For example, $2x^2 + 3x^2 = 5x^2$. Go back to the Basic Algebra section if you need to review this topic.

MULTIPLICATION

You're probably already comfortable using *FOIL*. It's an important part of working with quadratics (see the last section). To *FOIL*, multiple *First* terms, *Outer* terms, *Inner* terms, and *Last* terms, and then add these products. For example:

$$(x + y)^2 = (x + y)(x + y) = x^2 + xy + xy + y^2 = x^2 + 2xy + y^2$$

You won't always multiply two *binomials*, as above, but the process is similar:

1. Multiply the first term of the first polynomial by every term of the second polynomial.
2. Multiply the second term of the first polynomial by every term of the second polynomial. And so on . . .
3. Add up the resulting products (combine like terms).

Try the lesson problem below:

9. Which of the following is equivalent to $(2x - 1)(x^2 + 2x - 3)$?

    A. $x^2 + 4x - 4$
    B. $2x^2 + 4x + 3$
    C. $2x^3 + 4x^2 - 6x + 3$
    D. $2x^3 + 3x^2 - 8x + 3$
    E. $2x^3 + 3x^2 - 8x - 3$

6. The expression $(3x - 2)(x + 7)$ is equivalent to which of the following expressions?

    A. $3x^2 - 14$
    B. $3x^2 + 5$
    C. $3x^2 + 23x - 14$
    D. $3x^2 + 19x - 14$
    E. $3x^2 + 19x + 14$

8. Which of the following is equivalent to the expression below?

$$(x^2y + 3x) - (2x^2y - 3y)$$

    A. $-x^2y + 3x + 3y$
    B. $-x^2y + 6x$
    C. $-x^2y + x - y$
    D. $-3x^2y + 3xy$
    E. $-3x^2y + 3x + 3y$

38. If $3a^2 + ka - 10 = (3a - 2)(a + 5)$, then $k = $?

    A. 3
    B. 10
    C. 13
    D. 17
    E. 21

49. What binomial must be subtracted from $2x^2 + 7x - 14$ so that the difference is $x^2 - 14$?

    A. $x^2 + 7$
    B. $x^2 - 7$
    C. $x^2 + 7x$
    D. $x^2 - 7x$
    E. $x^2 + 14x$

4. ADVANCED ALGEBRA PROBLEMS

PRACTICE PROBLEMS

The worksheets on the following pages test techniques taught in this chapter. For additional practice, we'll use problems from Test 5 in *The Official ACT Prep Guide*.

- ☐ Advanced Algebra Worksheet 1
- ☐ Advanced Algebra Worksheet 2
- ☐ ***The Official ACT Prep Guide***: **Test 5**: Only tackle questions related to *this chapter*. For a list of these relevant questions, see the Techniques chapter at the end of this tutorial (first page of "Techniques: Test 5").

Reminders:

- **Use techniques**: These assignments are "open book." Go back to the tutorial as often as you need to, and use techniques aggressively.
- **No timing**: Do *not* time yourself on these assignments.
- **Scheduling**: See the Tutoring Schedules section in the Introduction for more details on scheduling.

TEST CORRECTIONS

After each practice test is graded, you should correct questions related to this chapter that you missed or guessed on. See "Correcting Practice Tests" in the Introduction for more details. Here are the three steps to correcting practice tests:

1. Turn to the Techniques chapter at the end of this tutorial and circle the Advanced Algebra questions that you missed or guessed on for the test you are correcting.
2. Correct the problems in *The Official ACT Prep Guide*. As you correct the problems, go back to the tutorial and review the techniques. The idea is to (1) identify techniques that have given you trouble, (2) go back to the tutorial so you can review and strengthen these techniques, and (3) apply these techniques to the specific problems on which you struggled.
3. If you have trouble identifying the best technique to use for a problem, refer to the Techniques chapter. This is an important part of correcting the tests.

ADVANCED ALGEBRA WORKSHEET 1

12. Which of the following expressions is equal to $(2x^2 + 3x + 4) - (-x^2 - 2x + 3)$ for all real values of x ?

   A. $3x^2 + x + 7$
   B. $3x^2 + 5x + 1$
   C. $x^2 + x + 7$
   D. $x^2 + 5x + 1$
   E. $-2x^2 - 6x + 12$

20. If $x^3 + x^2 = 0$, which of the following is the <u>sum</u> of the possible values of x?

   F. -3
   G. -2
   H. -1
   J. 0
   K. 1

24. The system of equations below has 1 solution (x, y). What is the value of x ?

$$6x + 2y = 8$$
$$3x - 3y = -8$$

   A. 1

   B. $\dfrac{1}{3}$

   C. $\dfrac{2}{3}$

   D. $1\dfrac{1}{3}$

   E. 3

25. If $(m - n)^2 = 4$ and $2mn = 16$, what is the value of $m^2 + n^2$?

   F. -12
   G. 12
   H. 20
   J. 44
   K. 64

Continued →

26. Which of the following gives all the solutions of $x^2 - 2x = 35$?

    A. −5 and 7
    B. −7 and 5
    C. −2 and 0
    D. 0 and 2
    E. 0 only

39. Which of the following expressions is equal to $(2x^2 + 3) \cdot (4x^2 - 5x)$?

    A. $6x^2 - 5x + 3$
    B. $6x^4 - 2x$
    C. $8x^4 - 15x$
    D. $8x^4 - 10x^3 - 12x^2 + 15x$
    E. $8x^4 - 10x^3 + 12x^2 - 15x$

44. Which of the following expressions is the greatest monomial factor of $85x^2y^3 - 51x^3y^2$?

    A. x^2y^2
    B. $17x^3y^3$
    C. $17x^2y^2$
    D. $255x^3y^3$
    E. $255x^2y^2$

48. If $4a^2 - 25b^2 = 0$, what is the <u>sum</u> of the possible values of a in terms of b?

    F. $-\tfrac{5}{2}b$

    G. $-\tfrac{2}{5}b$

    H. 0

    J. $\tfrac{2}{5}b$

    K. $\tfrac{5}{2}b$

Continued →

54. A company wants to buy phones for its employees. Employee executives will get smart phones at a cost of $250 each and regular employees will get flip phones at a cost of $50 each. If the company spends $4,000 on a total 40 phones, and every employee gets a phone, how many more regular employees than executives work at the company?

F. 20
G. 25
H. 30
J. 35
K. 40

55. Which of the following graphs best represents the system of inequalities below?

$$y \geq -2x + 3$$
$$y \geq 2x + 3$$
$$y \geq 0$$

A.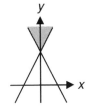

D.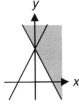

B.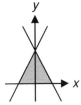

E.

C.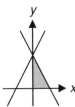

ADVANCED ALGEBRA WORKSHEET 2

10. What is the sum of $0.2x^2 + 2x - 0.5$ and $0.3x^2 - 0.2x + 1.8$ for all x ?

    A. $0.06x^2 + 0.4x + 0.9$
    B. $0.06x^2 - 0.4x - 0.9$
    C. $0.6x^2 + 0.4x + 0.9$
    D. $0.5x^2 + 1.8x - 1.3$
    E. $0.5x^2 + 1.8x + 1.3$

27. Which of the expressions below is a factor of the polynomial $x^3 + x^2 + x$?

    I. x
    II. $x + 1$
    III. $x^2 + 1$

    A. I only
    B. I and II only
    C. I and III only
    D. II only
    E. I, II, and III

30. If (x, y) is the solution of the system of equations below, what is $x + y$?

$$10x = 2$$
$$5x + 15y = -2$$

    A. 0

    B. $\dfrac{1}{5}$

    C. $\dfrac{2}{5}$

    D. $\dfrac{4}{5}$

    E. 5

31. If $a - b = 4$ and $a^2 + b^2 = 26$, what is the value of ab?

    A. -10
    B. -5
    C. 1
    D. 5
    E. 25

Continued →

32. In the equation $px^2 - qx - r = 0$, p, q, and r are integers. For which of the following will there be more than one real number solution for the equation?

A. $q^2 + 4pr > 0$
B. $q^2 - 4pr > 0$
C. $p^2 + 4qr > 0$
D. $p^2 - 4qr > 0$
E. $r^2 - 4pq > 0$

40. For all $x \neq 3$, which of the following expressions is equal to $\dfrac{x^2 - x - 6}{x - 3} + x^2 - x - 2$?

A. x^2
B. $x^2 - 2x$
C. $x^2 - 2x - 4$
D. $x^2 - x - 4$
E. $x^2 - x - 5$

42. Which of the following expressions is a factor of $(xy)^4 - (xy)^2$?

A. $xy^2 - xy$
B. $xy^2 + xy$
C. $xy^2 - 1$
D. $xy - 1$
E. xy^2

42. The product of the expressions $2x^3 + 3x^2 - 6x + 12$ and $7x^2 - 6x + 11$ is given by the expression $ax^5 + bx^4 + cx^3 + dx^2 + ex + f$, where a, b, c, d, e, and f are real numbers. Which of the following is equal to a ?

A. 5
B. 9
C. 14
D. 21
E. 23

Continued →

47. When graphed in the standard (x,y) coordinate plane, the lines $2x - 2y = 30$ and $x - 5y = 7$ intersect at what point?

    F. (16, 2)
    G. (2, 16)
    H. (17, 2)
    J. (2, 17)
    K. (30, 7)

50. Which of the following system of inequalities is graphed below in the (x, y) coordinate plane?

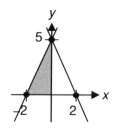

A. $y \geq -\dfrac{5}{2}x + 5$

$y \leq \dfrac{5}{2}x + 5$

$y \leq 0$

$x \geq 0$

B. $y \leq -\dfrac{5}{2}x + 5$

$y \leq \dfrac{5}{2}x + 5$

$y \geq 0$

$x \geq 0$

C. $y \geq -\dfrac{5}{2}x + 5$

$y \leq \dfrac{5}{2}x + 5$

$y \geq 0$

$x \geq 0$

D. $y \geq -\dfrac{5}{2}x + 5$

$y \geq \dfrac{5}{2}x + 5$

$y \geq 0$

$x \leq 0$

E. $y \leq -\dfrac{5}{2}x + 5$

$y \leq \dfrac{5}{2}x + 5$

$y \geq 0$

$x \leq 0$

Continued →

60. Pam rode her bike to work in the morning at an average speed of 10 miles per hour. After work, she discovered that she had a flat tire, so she walked home along the same route at an average speed of 2 miles per hour. If Pam spent a total of 3 hours commuting to and from work, what was the total distance in miles that Pam traveled to and from work?

    F. 2
    G. 3
    H. 5
    J. 10
    K. 12

V
GEOMETRY

This chapter will cover all relevant geometry topics. Preparing for geometry problems is a matter of familiarizing yourself with the geometry formulas and rules that are tested on the ACT and completing practice problems.

1. *GEOMETRY INTRODUCTION*

NO REFERENCE INFORMATION

The ACT (unlike the SAT) does *not* provide geometry reference information. You need to memorize the formulas that are discussed in the following sections. For any formulas you don't know, make flash cards.

GEOMETRY FIGURES

While the ACT says that figures are NOT necessarily drawn to scale, we have found that the figures are *almost always* drawn perfectly to scale. Feel free to use the figures to check the likelihood of your answers or to make educated guesses.

MEASURE THE DRAWING

DISTANCES

Here's a great trick that you can use if you're ever stuck on a difficult or time-consuming problem that gives at least one distance (see the following example):

1. Use the edge of your answer sheet, starting at a corner, to mark a distance given in the drawing. If the distance is relatively long, divide the distance into smaller parts (hint: you can find half the distance by folding the given distance in half).
2. Your answer sheet is now a ruler. Use it to measure the distance in question.

ⒺⓍ In the figure below, $AB = 5$. If the perimeter of the rectangle is 10 less than twice the square of AB, what is the *area* of the rectangle?

A. 2
B. 25
C. 50
D. 70
E. 75

Caution: This approach works best when there is only <u>one</u> answer choice close to your measured value. (If there was an answer choice of 74 or 76 in the example above, we would be less confident of our answer.)

ANGLES

You can also "measure the drawing" by estimating angles. Hopefully you can (roughly) recognize 30°, 45°, 60°, and 90° angles. (You can always use the corner of your answer sheet to see 90°. If you're really fancy, you can fold any corner exactly in half, and now you have a 45° angle—but don't crease your answer sheet.) See if you can solve the following problem by "measuring the angle":

55. In the figure below, D, E, and F are the midpoints of the sides of $\triangle ABC$. If the measure of $\angle BAC$ is 20°, and the measure of $\angle ABC$ is 45°, what is the measure of $\angle EFD$?

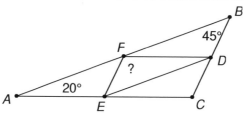

- **A.** 15°
- **B.** 75°
- **C.** 95°
- **D.** 115°
- **E.** 145°

Try "measuring the drawing" for the following problem:

57. Triangle $\triangle ABC$ is shown in the figure below. Which of the following is the length of $\overline{BC}$?

(Note: For a triangle with sides of length a, b, and c and opposite angles $\angle A$, $\angle B$, and $\angle C$, respectively, the law of sines states $\frac{\sin\angle A}{a} = \frac{\sin\angle B}{b} = \frac{\sin\angle C}{c}$ and the law of cosines states $c^2 = a^2 + b^2 - 2ab\cos\angle C$.)

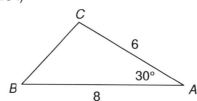

- **A.** $6\sin 30°$
- **B.** $\dfrac{\sin 30°}{6}$
- **C.** $\sqrt{6^2 + 8^2}$
- **D.** $\sqrt{8^2 - 6^2}$
- **E.** $\sqrt{6^2 + 8^2 - 2(6)(8)\cos 30°}$

2. AREA & PERIMETER

Memorize the following formulas. Make flash cards if necessary.

AREA OF A RECTANGLE

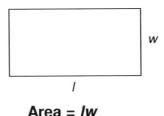

Area = _lw_

AREA OF A TRIANGLE

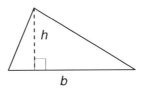

$$A = \frac{1}{2}bh$$

Finding the area of a triangle can be difficult. The base, _b_, can be _any_ side of the triangle, not just the lowest and, oftentimes, horizontal side. The height is defined as the _perpendicular distance_ from the corner _opposite the base_ to the _line containing the base_. The following method will help you find the height of a triangle relative to a given base:

1. **Identify the base.** Note that the base is a _line segment_.

2. **Identify the corner opposite this base.** This is the corner that is _not_ an endpoint of the base's line segment.

3. **With your pencil starting on this corner, draw a perpendicular line to the line containing the base.** Sometimes, the height line will intersect the actual base, as in the first example below. Other times, you may have to extend the base's line segment because the height falls _outside_ the triangle, as in the second example below. Note that this does not change the length of the base, which is bound by the endpoints of the triangle.

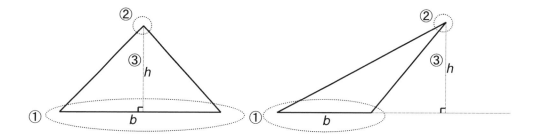

In each drawing below, sketch the height relative to the given base. Note that the bases are different from above.

1.

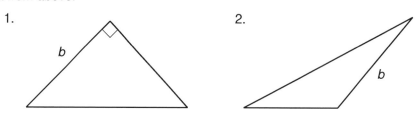

2.

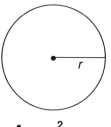

AREA & CIRCUMFERENCE OF A CIRCLE

$$A = \pi r^2$$
Circumference $= 2\pi r$

We call the "perimeter" of a circle its *circumference*. If you're worried about remembering which formula is which above, it might help to know that measures of area have "square" units (for example, the size of a house is measured in *square* feet). Thus, the formula for area is the one with the r^2.

AREA OF A PARALLELOGRAM

A *parallelogram* is a four-sided shape (a *quadrilateral*) that has *parallel* and *congruent* (equal-length) opposite sides.

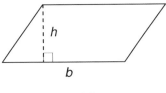

$$A = bh$$

AREA OF A TRAPEZOID

A *trapezoid* is a quadrilateral that has *two* parallel sides.

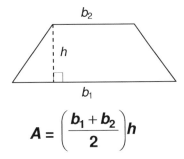

$$A = \left(\frac{b_1 + b_2}{2} \right) h$$

PERIMETER

The *perimeter* of a shape is the sum of the measures of each side.

SHADED REGION PROBLEMS

There are two ways to solve shaded region area problems:

1. **Area Cutting**: Cut the shaded region into simpler shapes whose areas you can find, and add up these areas:

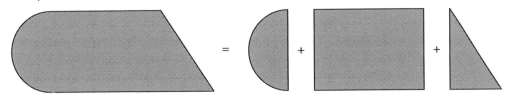

2. **Area Subtracting:** Subtract the areas of known shapes from the total area of the entire figure so that you're left with the shaded area.

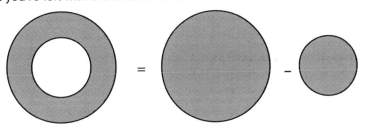

AREA FITTING PROBLEMS

You may be asked to find the the number of small two-dimensional shapes (such as tiles) that can fit onto a larger shape (such as a floor).

 Area fitting problems will ask how many shapes can fit onto or within a larger shape.

The method for area fitting problems is straightforward:

1. Find the areas of the large shape and the small shape.
2. Divide the large area by the small area.

Number of *small areas* that will fit into the *larger area* = $\dfrac{\textbf{Large Area}}{\textbf{Small Area}}$

(EX) How many 24 inch × 24 inch square tiles are needed to cover the 20 foot × 30 foot floor shown below?

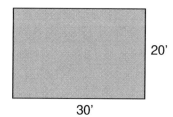

20'

30'

A. 50
B. 100
C. 150
D. 200
E. 600

SIDE-ANGLE-SIDE AREA FORMULA FOR A TRIANGLE

The ACT may test the *side-angle-side* (SAS) formula for finding the area of a triangle. As the name says, you can use this formula when you can find two sides and the included angle of a triangle. You'll see a little trigonometry here ($\sin \theta$). Sine (abbreviated sin) is a trig function, and θ is the angle. For now, you don't really need to know more than that; we'll cover trigonometry in detail in a later chapter. Here's the formula:

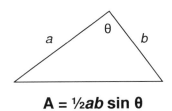

$$A = \tfrac{1}{2}ab \sin \theta$$

> Look for a triangle area problem where you're given two sides and the included angle (SAS). You'll also probably see the SAS formula given in the question, but if not, look for sin θ (and perhaps other trig functions) in the answer choices.

AREA & PERIMETER LESSON PROBLEMS

5. The figure below is composed of square *ACDF* and equilateral triangles △*ABC* and △*DEF*. The length of *AF* is 5 inches. What is the perimeter, in inches, of *ABCDEF*?

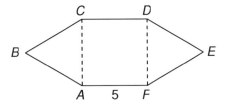

  A. 20
  B. 25
  C. 30
  D. 35
  E. 40

7. If the rectangle below has a perimeter of 20, what is the area of the rectangle?

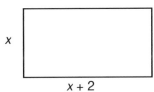

  F. 16
  G. 24
  H. 36
  J. 40
  K. 49

Continued →

25. A parallelogram, with dimensions in inches, is shown in the diagram below. What is the area, in square inches, of the parallelogram?

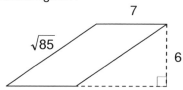

A. $42\sqrt{85}$

B. $7\sqrt{85}$

C. $6\sqrt{85}$

D. 42

E. 21

40. The figure below is made up of a square with side of length 8 and two semicircles with diameters of length 3. What is the area of the shaded region?

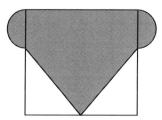

F. $24 + \frac{9}{4}\pi$

G. $24 + \frac{9}{2}\pi$

H. $44 + \frac{9}{4}\pi$

J. $44 + 9\pi$

K. $64 + 9\pi$

Continued →

48. The eight equal semicircles below are placed so that they exactly cover the sides of the square. If the perimeter of the square is 32, what is the area of one of the semicircles?

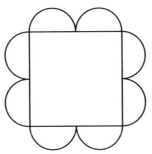

A. 2π
B. 4π
C. 8π
D. 16π
E. 32π

10. In the figure below, the large square is divided into two smaller squares and two rectangles (shaded). If the perimeters of the two smaller squares are 8 and 24, respectively, what is the sum of the perimeters of the two shaded rectangles?

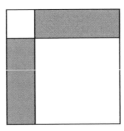

A. 12
B. 16
C. 24
D. 32
E. 36

Continued →

29. The equilateral triangle below is formed by connecting the centers of three tangent circles. If the perimeter of the triangle is 12, what is the sum of the circumferences of the three circles?

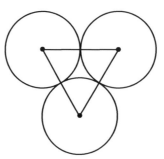

   F. 4π
   G. 8π
   H. 12π
   J. 18π
   K. 24π

Note: the problem above uses the word "**tangent**," which means *touching at exactly one point.* Notice that each circle above touches each of the other circles at exactly one point. The circles are, thus, *tangent* to one another.

43. Square *ABCD* has side of length 8. The width of the border between squares *ABCD* and *EFGH* is 2. What is the area of the shaded region?

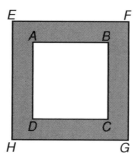

   A. 36
   B. 40
   C. 48
   D. 80
   E. 100

Continued →

46. In the figure below, O is the center of the circle of diameter 12. What is the area of △AOB ?

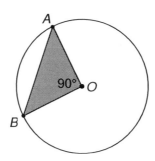

F. 36
G. 18
H. 15
J. 12
K. 6

52. In the figure below, points A, B, C, D, E, and F are equally spaced on line segment AF. If the sum of the areas of the three circles is 18π, what is the radius of the smaller circle?

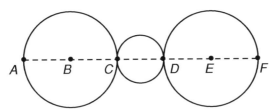

A. 1
B. $\sqrt{2}$
C. 2
D. $2\sqrt{2}$
E. 3

53. The area of circle O is x square inches, and the circumference of circle O is y inches. If x = y, what is the radius of the circle?

F. 1
G. 2
H. 3
J. 4
K. 5

Continued →

52. In triangle △ABD shown below, point C lies on side AD, and the measure of angle A is θ. In terms of x, y, and θ, what is the area of triangle △BCD?

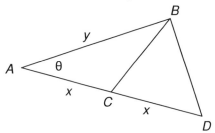

(Note: The area of any triangle with sides of length a, b, and c opposite angles of measure A, B, and C, respectively, is given by ½ab sin C.)

A. $\dfrac{xy}{2}$

B. xy

C. $\dfrac{xy \sin \theta}{2}$

D. $xy \sin \theta$

E. $2xy \sin \theta$

58. In the figure below, ABCD is a rectangle inscribed in the semicircle with center O. If AD = 5 and the semicircle has an area of 84.5π, what is the length of segment AB?

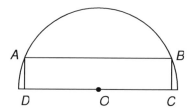

A. 12
B. 13
C. 24
D. 26
E. 28

3. TRIANGLES

In addition to finding the area of a triangle, as discussed in the previous section, there are a number of other topics related to triangles:

TYPES OF TRIANGLES

Isosceles triangles have two equal sides (and two equal angles).

Equilateral triangles have three equal sides (and three equal angles, each measuring **60°**).

RIGHT TRIANGLES

PYTHAGOREAN THEOREM

Memorize the *Pythagorean Theorem*. Make sure the *c* side is the *hypotenuse*, which is the longest side and always opposite the right angle.

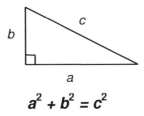

$$a^2 + b^2 = c^2$$

 You can use the Pythagorean Theorem with *right* triangles when you know *two* of the three sides.

SPECIAL RIGHT TRIANGLES

30-60-90 AND 45-45-90 TRIANGLES

Memorize the relationships for the two special right triangles, the *isosceles-right* (*45°-45°-90°*) and *30°-60°-90°* triangles.

 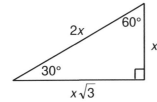 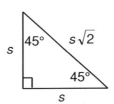

Never assume a triangle is a special right triangle. You must confirm that the angles are 30-60-90 or 45-45-90, or that the ratio of the sides are $1:2:\sqrt{3}$ (for the 30-60-90 triangle) or $1:1:\sqrt{2}$ (for the 45-45-90 triangle).

Remember that all isosceles-right triangles are 45-45-90 triangles.

PYTHAGOREAN TRIPLES: 3-4-5 AND 5-12-13 TRIANGLES

These right triangles with integer sides show up frequently. You can save time if you have them memorized. You might also see multiples of these sides, such as 6-8-10.

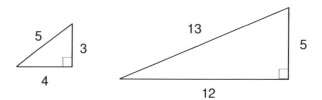

SIMILAR TRIANGLES

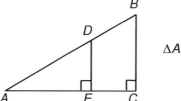

$\triangle ABC$ is similar to $\triangle ADE$

Similar triangles can be identified because they have equal angles. There are two relationships to remember:

1. **The ratio of any two sides of one triangle is equal to that of any two *related* sides of a similar triangle.** For example, in the triangle above:

$$\frac{AB}{AC} = \frac{AD}{AE}$$

Try the number 1 below, based on the triangles above:

1. $\dfrac{DE}{AE} =$

2. **The ratio of *equivalent* sides of similar triangles remains constant.**

$$\frac{AD}{AB} = \frac{AE}{AC} = \frac{DE}{BC} = k \text{ , where } k \text{ is some constant.}$$

To identify similar triangle problems, look for triangles that have equal angles. Usually, on the ACT, triangles that *appear* similar are indeed similar, but if you can, try to identify angles.

ANGLE-SIDE RELATIONSHIPS

In any triangle, the largest angle is opposite the longest side; the smallest angle is opposite the shortest side; and so on. Similarly, if two angles are equal, then their opposite sides are equal.

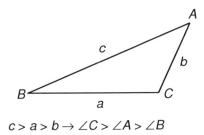

$$c > a > b \rightarrow \angle C > \angle A > \angle B$$

THIRD SIDE RULE

In any triangle, the sum of the two shortest sides must be greater than the longest side.

If a, b, and c are the lengths of sides of a triangle and $a \le b \le c$, then:

FLASH
CARDS $a + b > c$

To illustrate the point, imagine sticks of different lengths. In the first example below, where the sum of the two shortest sides is *larger* than the third side, a triangle can obviously be constructed. In the second example, where the sum of the two shortest sides is *smaller* than the third side, the triangle is incomplete. You may want to make a flash card to remember this rule.

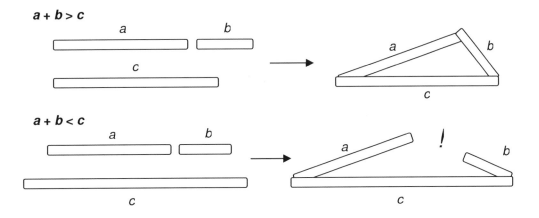

CONGRUENT TRIANGLES

Occasionally, a problem may require you to recognize *congruent triangles*. Two congruent triangles have the exact same size and shape. If you've covered congruent triangles in school, then the following rules should be a review. If you haven't covered congruent triangles, you might skip the following rules—rest assured that these types of problems are not common on the ACT.

RULES FOR CONGRUENT TRIANGLES

- **Side-Side-Side (SSS):** If all sides of one triangle are congruent to those of another triangle, then the triangles are congruent.
- **Side-Angle-Side (SAS):** If two sides and the included angle of one triangle are congruent to those of another triangle, then the triangles are congruent.
- **Angle-Side-Angle (ASA):** If two angles and the included side of one triangle are congruent to those of another triangle, then the triangles are congruent.
- **Angle-Angle-Side (AAS):** If two angles and the adjacent side of one triangle are congruent to those of another triangle, then the triangles are congruent.
- **Hypotenuse-Leg (HL):** For right triangles, if the hypotenuse and one leg of one right triangle are congruent to those of another right triangle, then the triangles are congruent.

TRIANGLE PROBLEMS WITH NO TRIANGLES

Many geometry problems on the ACT are triangle problems even though there is no triangle given. Remember that drawing a triangle, usually a right triangle, can often help you solve a problem. Question 58 in the previous section is a good example of this. We will see many more of these types of problems.

TRIANGLE LESSON PROBLEMS

In the following triangles, find the lengths of all sides. You do *not* need to simplify you answers.

(Note: If short on time, the eight questions below can be completed for homework.)

1.
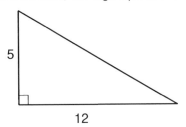

5.
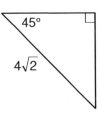

2.
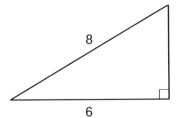

6.
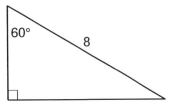

3.
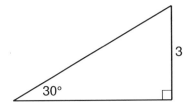

7.
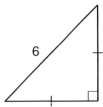

4.
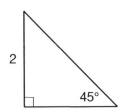

8.
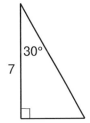

8. In the right triangle shown below, which of the following statements is true about side AB?

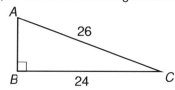

    A. $AB = 26 - 24$
    B. $AB = 26^2 - 24^2$
    C. $AB^2 = 26^2 + 24^2$
    D. $AB^2 = 24^2 - 26^2$
    E. $AB^2 = 26^2 - 24^2$

20. If the area of the triangle below is 54, what is the length of the hypotenuse?

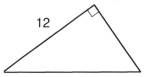

    F. 9
    G. 13
    H. 15
    J. 18
    K. 21

29. If the area of a square is 50, how long is the longest straight line that can be drawn between any two points of the square?

    A. 5
    B. $5\sqrt{2}$
    C. 10
    D. 25
    E. $25\sqrt{2}$

41. If an equilateral triangle with a perimeter of 6 is inscribed in a rectangle, as shown in the figure below, what is the area of the rectangle?

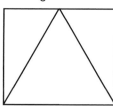

    F. $\sqrt{3}$
    G. 3
    H. $2\sqrt{3}$
    J. 4
    K. $3\sqrt{3}$

17. Given the equilateral triangle below, what is the value of x?

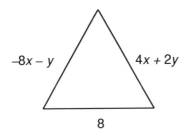

   A. -2
   B. -1
   C. 0
   D. 1
   E. 2

40. In the figure below, AB and DE are each perpendicular to AE. If $AB = 2$, $DE = 4$, and $CD = 10$, what is the length of AE?

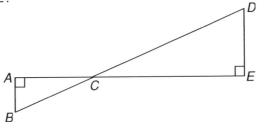

   F. $\sqrt{21}$
   G. $2\sqrt{21}$
   H. 5
   J. $3\sqrt{21}$
   K. 15

Continued →

44. What is the <u>perimeter</u> of the figure shown below?

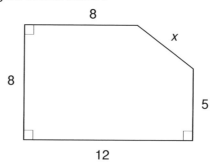

A. 33
B. 36
C. 38
D. 40
E. 42

45. In $\triangle ABC$ below, $AB > AC$. Which of the following must be true?

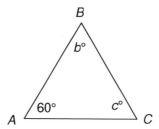

F. $BC > AB$
G. $BC = AB$
H. $b = c$
J. $c = 70$
K. $b < 60$

48. A triangle has sides of lengths 4 and 5. If the third side is an integer, what is the shortest possible length for this side?

A. 1
B. 2
C. 3
D. 5
E. 8

4. ANGLES

Let's see what you know. Fill in the missing information below. If you have trouble with any of these, check the answers online.

LINE

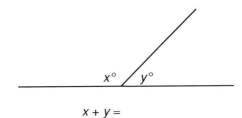

$$x + y =$$

TRIANGLE

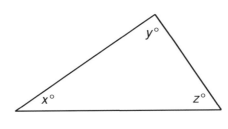

$$x + y + z =$$

CIRCLE

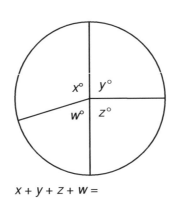

$$x + y + z + w =$$

RIGHT ANGLE

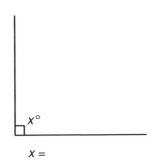

$$x =$$

VERTICAL ANGLES

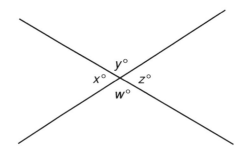

If x = 50°, then:

$z =$

$y =$

$w =$

PARALLEL LINES

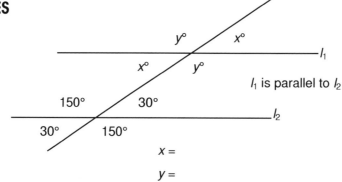

l_1 is parallel to l_2

$x =$

$y =$

"same-side interior": $x + 150° = y + 30° =$

LINE TANGENT TO A CIRCLE

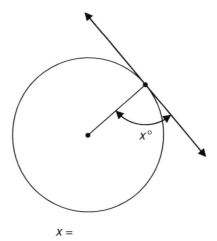

$x =$

ANGLE INSCRIBED IN A CIRCLE

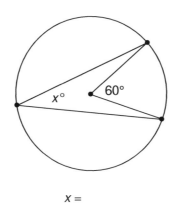

$x =$

Note that there are many (infinite) ways to draw inscribed angles, each intersecting the same arc (in this case, arc $\overset{\frown}{AB}$):

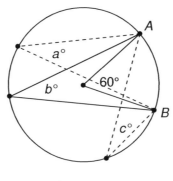

$a = b = c =$

SUM OF INTERIOR ANGLES

The sum *S* of the measures of the interior angles of a polygon of *n* sides can be found using the following equation: $S = (n - 2)180°$. If you already have this memorized, great. If not, to avoid having to memorize anything, we recommend using the following simple method for finding this sum:

1. Start at one vertex (corner) of the polygon.
2. From this one vertex, draw straight lines to all other (non-adjacent) vertices.
3. Count the number of triangles and multiply by 180°.

QUADRILATERAL

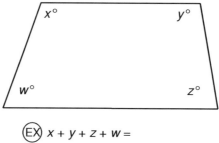

(EX) $x + y + z + w =$

OTHER POLYGONS

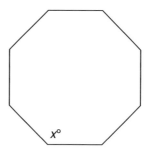

1. What is the sum of the interior angles of the polygon above?

2. If the above polygon is a *regular polygon* (all sides and angles are equal), what is the value of *x*?

COMPLEMENTARY/SUPPLEMENTARY ANGLES

Memorize these terms:

- If two angles add up to 90°, they are called *complementary* angles.
- If two angles add up to 180°, they are called *supplementary* angles.

ANGLE BISECTOR

As the name implies, an *angle bisector* is a line that divides an angle into two equal angles.

Segment *BD* is the angle bisector of ∠*ABC*, below:

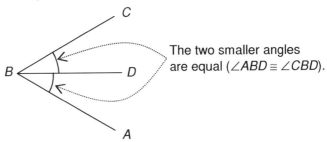

The two smaller angles are equal (∠*ABD* ≅ ∠*CBD*).

THE ISOSCELES TRAPEZOID

An *isosceles trapezoid* has two congruent, non-parallel sides (just like an isosceles triangle) and two sets of equal base angles (in the diagram below, *AB* = *CD*, m∠*BAD* = m∠*CDA*, and m∠*ABC* = m∠*DCB*). The ACT likes isosceles trapezoid problems, so you should memorize the properties below:

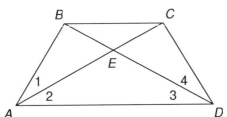

- m∠1 = m∠4 and m∠2 = m∠3
- △*AED* and △*BEC* are both **isosceles triangles**; they are also **similar** to each other.
- △*ABE* and △*DCE* are **congruent**.

If you ever forget any of these properties for an isosceles trapezoid, remember that the figures are generally drawn to scale on the ACT. Most of the above properties are visually apparent, so trust your eyes.

ANGLES LESSON PROBLEMS

3. In the figure below, what is the value of *x*?

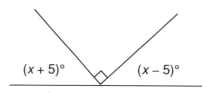

    A. 0
    B. 30
    C. 45
    D. 60
    E. 90

32. If lines *m* and *n* are parallel in the figure below, *a* + *g* must equal which of the following?

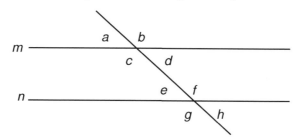

    A. $a + d$
    B. $3e$
    C. $b + 2h - d$
    D. $c + 2e - g$
    E. $d + 2h + 60°$

48. In triangle *PQR* below, what is the value of *y* in terms of *x*?

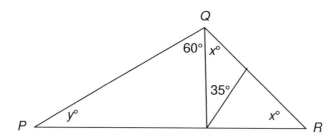

    F. x
    G. $2x$
    H. $100 - 2x$
    J. $120 - 2x$
    K. $140 - 2x$

Continued →

50. In the figure below, what is the value of $a + b + c + d + 2e$?

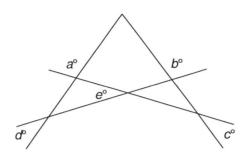

F. 90
G. 180
H. 360
J. 450
K. 540

7. In the right triangle below, what is the value of x?

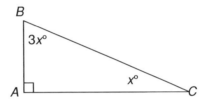

A. $22\frac{1}{2}$

B. 30

C. 45

D. $67\frac{1}{2}$

E. 90

Continued →

28. In the figure below, what is the value of *y*?

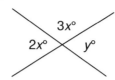

    F. 36
    G. 45
    H. 60
    J. 72
    K. 80

50. In the figure below, lines *l* and *m* are parallel. What is *y* in terms of *x*?

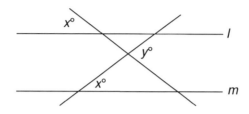

    F. *x*
    G. ¾ *x*
    H. 2*x*
    J. 180 − *x*
    K. 180 − 2*x*

Continued →

51. In the figure below, points *A*, *B*, *C*, and *D* are on circle *O*. Which of the following statements must be true?

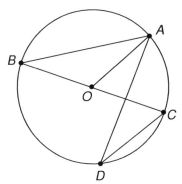

   I. $m\angle ABC = m\angle ADC$
   II. $m\angle ABC + m\angle ADC = m\angle AOC$
   III. $m\angle ADC = m\angle DAO$

   A. I only
   B. II only
   C. I and II only
   D. I and III only
   E. I, II, and III

52. Pentagon *ABCDE* below has equal angles and equal sides. If *O* is the center of the pentagon, what is the degree measure of $\angle AOB$ (not drawn)?

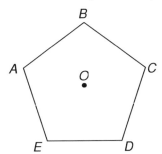

   A. 45°
   B. 60°
   C. 72°
   D. 108°
   E. 540°

5. COORDINATES

The coordinate plane consists of two perpendicular axes called the *x-axis* and the *y-axis*. The *x-axis* is horizontal and the *y-axis* is vertical.

POINTS

The most common mistake on simple coordinate problems is to confuse the *x-* and *y-*coordinates of *points*. **Remember, the *x-coordinate* is always the *first* coordinate of a point, and the *y-coordinate* is always the *second* coordinate of a point.** Identify the coordinates of the following points:

1. $A =$
2. $B =$
3. $C =$
4. $D =$
5. $E =$

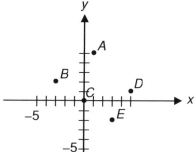

HORIZONTAL AND VERTICAL DISTANCES

The coordinate plane allows you to easily find horizontal and vertical distances between points, just by knowing the points' *x-* and *y-coordinates*.

1. **To find the *horizontal* distance between two points, find the *positive difference* between the points' *x-coordinates*.** In other words, *subtract* the x-coordinates and take the *absolute value* of the result.

2. **To find the *vertical* distance between two points, find the *positive difference* between the points' *y-coordinates*.** In other words, *subtract* the y-coordinates and take the *absolute value* of the result.

Try the following lesson problem:

17. On the standard (x,y) coordinate plane shown below, Matt wants to draw a rectangle (not shown) that has two of its vertices at points (3,9) and (−1,3). If two sides of the rectangle are parallel to the x-axis, what is the perimeter of the rectangle?

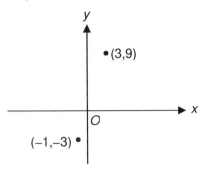

A. 8
B. $4\sqrt{10}$
C. 16
D. 32
E. 48

SLANTED DISTANCES BETWEEN POINTS

If you need to find the straight-line distance between two points that do *not* lie on a vertical or horizontal line, you have two options:

1. THE PYTHAGOREAN THEOREM REVISITED

If you draw a right triangle, with the hypotenuse connecting the two points in question, you can use the Pythagorean Theorem to find the distance between the points, as shown below:

(EX) In the standard (x,y) coordinate plane, what is the distance between the points (−1,−1) and (2,3)?

A. $\sqrt{7}$
B. 3
C. 4
D. 5
E. 25

2. THE DISTANCE FORMULA

The other option is the *distance formula*. The distance between two points with coordinates (x_1,y_1) and (x_2,y_2) is:

$$\boxed{\text{FLASH CARDS}} \quad d = \sqrt{(x_1 - x_2)^2 + (y_1 - y_2)^2}$$

For the example above, $d = \sqrt{(-1-2)^2 + (-1-3)^2} = \sqrt{9+16} = \sqrt{25} = 5$, which agrees with our answer using the Pythagorean Theorem approach. (You might be interested to know that the distance formula actually derives from the Pythagorean Theorem. The calculations are the same. It's not surprising that you'll get the same answer using either approach.)

■

For finding slanted distances between points, we recommend the first approach (using the Pythagorean Theorem) because you don't have to memorize a new formula and there are fewer chances of careless calculator mistakes. However, both approaches work.

MIDPOINT

You may have to find the coordinates of the *midpoint* between two points. The formula is straightforward. The *x-coordinate* of the midpoint is the average of the *x-coordinates* of the two endpoints. Similarly, the *y-coordinate* of the midpoint is the average of the *y-coordinates* of the two endpoints:

$$\boxed{\text{FLASH CARDS}} \quad \text{Midpoint} = \left(\frac{x_1 + x_2}{2}, \frac{y_1 + y_2}{2} \right)$$

COORDINATE PLANE MODELING

Some problems will require you to set up a two-dimensional problem using a coordinate plane. Once you have the problem drawn onto a coordinate plane, you should be able to use the previous rules to answer the question. For example:

$\widehat{EX}$ An architect places an overlay of the standard (x,y) coordinate plane on the blueprint of a house to find the length of a diagonal pathway. If one end of the pathway lies at (0,0) and the other end lies at (6,2), what is the unit length of the pathway?

- A. $\sqrt{8}$
- B. 6
- C. $\sqrt{40}$
- D. 8
- E. 10

■

COORDINATES LESSON PROBLEMS

5. In the standard (x,y) coordinate plane below, both circles are centered at point O and $OA =$ AB. If the coordinates of A are (0,–6), what are the coordinates of C?

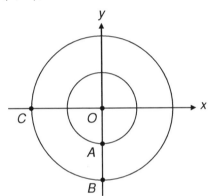

- A. (–6,0)
- B. (–12,0)
- C. (0,–12)
- D. (0,–6)
- E. (0,12)

17. In the standard (x,y) coordinate plane, what are the coordinates of the midpoint of a line segment with endpoints at (–2,–6) and (2,5)?

- F. (0,–11)
- G. (0,–5.5)
- H. (0,–0.5)
- J. (0,–1)
- K. (–1,0)

11. In the standard (x,y) coordinate plane below, $\triangle ABC$ is an isosceles right triangle. Which of the following are the coordinates of point A?

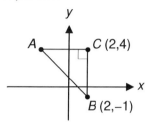

   A. $(4,-3.5)$
   B. $(4,-3)$
   C. $(-2,4)$
   D. $(-2.5,4)$
   E. $(-3,4)$

39. Point A has coordinates $(-2,-3)$ and point B has coordinates $(6,9)$. If point C is the midpoint of $\overline{AB}$ and D is the midpoint of $\overline{AC}$, then what are the coordinates of point D?

   F. $(-4,-6)$
   G. $(-2,-3)$
   H. $(2,-3)$
   J. $(-2,3)$
   K. $(0,0)$

59. In the standard (x,y) coordinate plane, what is the area of the triangle shown below?

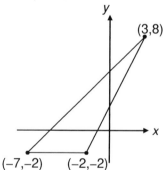

   A. 10
   B. 15
   C. 25
   D. 50
   E. 100

6. *LINES*

There are several different types of problems that deal with lines. First, let's look at some general definitions:

TERMINOLOGY

LINE

A *line* is perfectly straight and extends infinitely in both directions. Line *AB* can be notated as $\overleftrightarrow{AB}$:

LINE SEGMENT

A *line segment* is a section of a line, having two endpoints. Segment *AB* can be notated as $\overline{AB}$:

RAY

A *ray* has one endpoint and extends infinitely in one direction. Ray *AB* can be notated as $\overrightarrow{AB}$:

ONE-DIMENSIONAL LINE PROBLEMS

One-dimensional line problems include *number line* problems and *line segment* problems. You won't have to worry about vertical distances or slanted lines with these problems—the lines will generally be *horizontal*, like the *x-axis* of a standard coordinate plane.

 One-dimensional line problems tend to deal with horizontal lines (no vertical or slanted lines).

NUMBER LINES

Number line problems usually have tick marks. The tick marks may *not* always be a distance of *1* apart, but the marks will be equally spaced. Number lines generally increase to the right. As taught in the Coordinates section, to find the distance between two points, find the *positive difference* between them. In other words, *subtract* the endpoints and find the *absolute value* of the result.

Try the following lesson problem:

6. The marks on the number line below are equally spaced. What is the distance between points *A* and *B*?

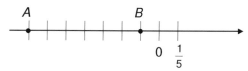

A. $\dfrac{1}{5}$

B. $\dfrac{4}{5}$

C. 1

D. $\dfrac{6}{5}$

E. 6

LINE SEGMETRS

On some number line problems, there won't be any tick marks. These problems tend to deal with *line segments*. The Pick Tricks often prove useful on these types of problems.

(EX) On line segment *AB*, if point *C* lies one third of the distance from *A* to *B* and point *D* is the midpoint of *AC*, what is $\dfrac{DB}{AB}$?

A. $\dfrac{1}{3}$

B. $\dfrac{1}{2}$

C. $\dfrac{2}{3}$

D. $\dfrac{3}{4}$

E. $\dfrac{5}{6}$

Try the following one-dimensional line problem:

48. The antennas for two radio stations lie 250 miles apart on a straight highway. The radio signal for station A can be received within a radius of 200 miles in all directions from its antenna, and the radio signal for station B can be received within a radius of 100 miles in all directions from its antenna. For how many miles along the highway can the radio signals of *both* stations be received?

   A. 50
   B. 75
   C. 100
   D. 125
   E. 150

SLOPE OF A LINE

Memorize the formula for the slope of a line in a coordinate plane:

$$\boxed{\begin{matrix} FLASH \\ CARDS \end{matrix}} \quad m = \frac{y_1 - y_2}{x_1 - x_2} \begin{matrix} \leftarrow (rise) \\ \leftarrow (run) \end{matrix}$$

Make sure the difference of the *y-coordinates* (the "rise") is in the *numerator* and the difference of the *x-coordinates* (the "run") is in the *denominator*. The order of the points does not matter as long as the order in the numerator is the same as that in the denominator.

SOME IMPORTANT CHARACTERISTICS OF SLOPE

- Lines with a *positive* slope angle up to the right, and lines with a *negative* slope angle up to the left:

- Vertical lines have an *undefined* slope, and horizontal lines have a slope of *zero*:

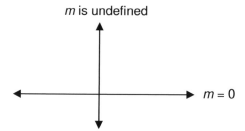

- The greater the absolute value of the slope, the steeper the line:

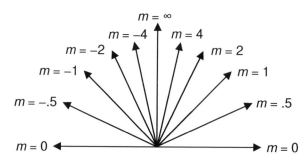

USING SLOPE TO FIND UNKNOWN COORDINATES

 These problems will ask you to solve for an unknown *coordinate* of a point on a line. If there are two missing coordinates, you should pick a number for one of the coordinates, and then follow the method below.

Use the method below. An example follows.

1. **Find the slope of the line.** If the line appears to go through the origin, then point (0,0) can be used as one of the points on the line.
2. **Use the equation for slope with one of the known points and the point with the missing coordinate.** Set the equation equal to the slope found in step 1.
3. **Use algebra to find the missing coordinate.**

(EX) In the standard (x,y) coordinate plane below, the three points lie on the same line. What is the value of b?

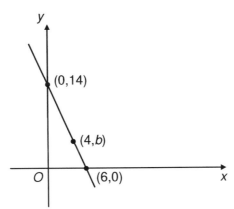

A. 3¾
B. 4
C. 4¼
D. 4⅓
E. 4⅔

SLOPE OF PARALLEL AND PERPENDICULAR LINES

For the following examples, the slope of line a is m_a, and the slope of line b is m_b.

When two lines are parallel, their slopes are *equal*:

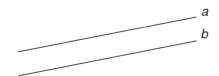

FLASH
CARDS

Line a is parallel to line b.

$$m_a = m_b$$

When two lines are perpendicular, use the following formula:

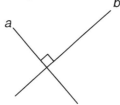

FLASH
CARDS

$$m_a = -\frac{1}{m_b} \quad \text{(or vice versa)}$$

■

Try the following slope lesson problem:

17. The standard (x,y) coordinate plane has four quadrants, as labeled below. If a line has one point in Quadrant II and another point in Quadrant IV, which of the following gives the possible values of the slope of the line? (Note: the points do not lie on the *x-axis* or *y-axis*.)

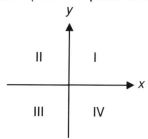

A. Any negative real number
B. 0
C. Any positive real number
D. No real numbers
E. Cannot be determined from the information given

EQUATION OF A LINE

THE SLOPE-INTERCEPT EQUATION

The most common equation of a line found on the ACT is called the *slope-intercept* equation. This equation is convenient because, at a glance, it gives you the *slope* of the line and the place where the line crosses the *y-axis* of the coordinate plane (called the *y-intercept*).

FLASH CARDS

$y = mx + b$

Slope-intercept equation of a line

In the equation above, *m* is the slope, *b* is the *y-intercept*, and *x* and *y* are the variables. The variables x and y are the coordinates of points on the line—for example, if you know an *x-coordinate* of a point, you could use the equation to find the *y-coordinate*.

OTHER LINEAR EQUATIONS → THE SLOPE-INTERCEPT FORM

If the equation for a line is not in the slope-intercept form, use basic number operations to rearrange the equation so that y is alone on the left side of the equal sign. See the following example:

(EX) What is the *y-intercept* of the line defined by the equation $(y + 2) = 2(x - 1)$?

FINDING THE SLOPE-INTERCEPT EQUATION

When you are given the *y-intercept* and the slope of a line, finding the slope-intercept equation is straightforward. Just plug values for m and b into the slope-intercept equation above.

You can also find the slope-intercept equation when you are given:

1. **A point on the line and the slope of the line**

OR

2. **Two points on the line**

Use the following method:

1. Identify or calculate the slope of the line (m).
2. Plug the x and y values of a given point and the slope (m) from step 1 into the slope-intercept equation.
3. Solve for b.
4. Rewrite the equation with x and y as variables: $y = mx + b$.

(EX) What is the slope-intercept equation of the line that goes through the point (2,0) and has a slope of 3?

THE LINE $y = x$

This line shows up frequently. The slope of the line is 1 and the *y-intercept* is 0. The equation ($y = x$) makes clear that for each point on the line, the *x-coordinate* equals the *y-coordinate* (for example: (1,1), (−20,−20), etc.). Note that the line makes a 45° angle with the *x-axis* (assuming the *x* and *y* scales are the same, as they usually are). See the following figure:

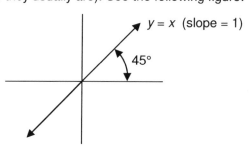

WHERE'S THE x? WHERE'S THE y?

Equations that involve only the *x* variable are vertical lines. Equations that involve only the *y* variable are horizontal lines. Write the equations for the following lines:

(EX) Line *A*:

1. Line *B*:

2. Line *C*:

3. Line *D*:

4. Line *E*:

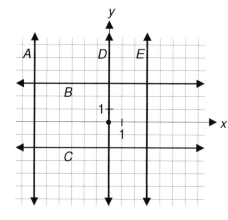

Try the following line equation lesson problems:

10. The point (2, *p*) lies on the line with equation $y - 3 = 2(x - 4)$. What is the value of *p*?

    A. −1
    B. 0
    C. 1
    D. 2
    E. 3

37. In the figure below, if line *l* has a slope of $\frac{3}{2}$, what is the *y-intercept* of *l*?

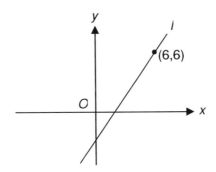

F. −1

G. −$\frac{3}{2}$

H. −2

J. −3

K. −6

INTERSECTING LINES

Equations that define lines are called *linear* equations. When you have two linear equations, the "solution" can be found algebraically using methods taught in the Algebra chapters (substitution or elimination methods). But what does this solution mean? Graphically speaking, the solution (when there is one) is the *point of intersection* of the two lines. For example:

(EX) When graphed in the standard (x,y) coordinate plane, the lines $y = 5$ and $y = 5x - 5$ intersect at what point?

A. (0,5)

B. (0,−5)

C. (1,5)

D. (2,−5)

E. (2,5)

INFINITE SOLUTIONS

When would two lines have an infinite number of solutions?—when the two lines are in fact *the same line*. In other words, if the equations of both lines are simplified to point-intercept forms ($y = mx + b$), the slopes will be the same and the *y-intercepts* will be the same.

- Infinite solutions: **Same slopes, same *y-intercepts***

NO SOLUTIONS

When would two lines have no solutions?—when the two lines are *parallel*. The lines never cross. In other words, if both equations are simplified to point-intercept forms, the slopes will be the same but the *y-intercept*s will be *different*.

- No solutions: **Same slopes, different *y-intercept*s**

You may want to make flash cards to help memorize the rules above.

Try the following lesson problem:

42. For which of the following values of k will the system of equations below have <u>no</u> solutions?

$$y = 2x + 20$$
$$y = kx + 40$$

    A.   −10
    B.   −2
    C.   0
    D.   2
    E.   4

LINES HOMEWORK

4. If R is the midpoint of segment QS below, then $x = ?$

$$\overset{\displaystyle x+3 \qquad\quad y-1}{\underset{\displaystyle Q \qquad\qquad R \qquad\qquad S}{\rule{5cm}{0.4pt}}}$$

    A. $y - 4$
    B. $y - 3$
    C. $y - 2$
    D. $y - 1$
    E. y

Continued →

10. If point *C* is the midpoint of segment *AB* and point *D* is the midpoint of segment *CB*, which of the following is NOT true?

   F. $AC - CD = DB$
   G. $CB < AD$
   H. $AB - CD = AD$
   J. $CB < AC$
   K. $3DB = AD$

32. In the figure below, line *l* passes through the origin. What is the value of $\dfrac{b}{a}$?

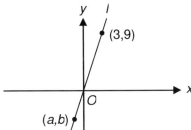

   A. -3
   B. $-\dfrac{1}{3}$
   C. $\dfrac{1}{3}$
   D. $\dfrac{2}{3}$
   E. 3

53. In the standard (*x*,*y*) coordinate plane below, line *b* is perpendicular to line *a*. Which of the following is the equation for line *a*?

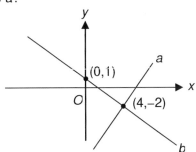

   F. $y = -\dfrac{3}{4}x + 1$
   G. $y = \dfrac{3}{4}x - \dfrac{10}{3}$
   H. $y = -\dfrac{3}{4}x - \dfrac{22}{3}$
   J. $y = \dfrac{4}{3}x - \dfrac{10}{3}$
   K. $y = \dfrac{4}{3}x - \dfrac{22}{3}$

Continued →

56. The marks on the number line below are equally spaced. What is the value of *A*?

A. 3

B. $3\dfrac{1}{5}$

C. $3\dfrac{3}{5}$

D. 4

E. $4\dfrac{1}{5}$

7. MORE CIRCLES

We have already discussed the area and circumference of a circle. We have also looked at the sum of the degrees in a circle (360°). There are a few more topics that have to do with circles.

EQUATION OF A CIRCLE

The equation of a circle in the standard (x, y) coordinate plane is shown below. While most equation-of-circle problems can be solved using the Pick Tricks (for example, see Algebra Worksheet 1, #41), you'll save time by memorizing the equation:

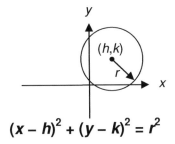

$$y$$
$$(h,k)$$
$$r$$
$$x$$

FLASH CARDS

$$(x - h)^2 + (y - k)^2 = r^2$$

 To identify circle equation problems, make sure you can identify the equation of a circle in its standard form. You'll either see the equation in the question or in the answer choices.

(EX) In the (x,y) coordinate plane, what are the coordinates of the center and the length of the radius of the circle defined by the equation below:

$$(x + 2)^2 + (y + 2)^2 = 25 ?$$

A. center: $(-2, -2)$; radius = 5
B. center: $(-2, -2)$; radius = 25
C. center: $(-2, -2)$; radius = 625
D. center: $(2, 2)$; radius = 5
E. center: $(2, 2)$; radius = 25

OTHER CONIC SECTIONS

In addition to circles, you may be tested on the equations of other *conic sections*, specifically *parabolas* and *ellipses* (*hyperbolas* have not shown up on any recent tests). We'll cover these in the Odds & Ends chapter. Even if you don't get to this section, you can probably use the Pick Tricks, your graphing calculator, or the Measure the Drawing technique to get out of a jam.

SECTORS OF CIRCLES

A *sector* of a circle is like a piece of pizza. Below are the three most common measurements we can use to evaluate the size of a sector:

1. **Angle** – this is the measure of ∠AOB in the figure below. It is sometimes called the "**measure of arc AB**" or the "**central angle**" to arc AB.

2. **Arc length** – this is the actual curved distance from point A to point B along the circle.

3. **Area** – this is the area between line segments AO and BO and arc AB (shaded below).

We can write each of these measurements as a *part over whole* ratio, where the *part* is relating to the sector of the circle and the *whole* is relating to the entire circle. The trick to sector problems is to realize that each of these ratios is *equal*:

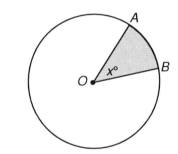

$$\underbrace{\frac{\text{part (sector)}}{\text{whole (circle)}}}_{} \rightarrow \frac{x}{360°} = \frac{\text{length of arc } AB}{\text{circumference of circle}} = \frac{\text{area of sector } AOB}{\text{area of circle}}$$

 Look for circles with sectors, but don't confuse these problems with circle-graphs (pie-graphs), which also have sectors drawn.

The method below should be used for circle sector problems. An example follows.

1. **Identify which *two* of the three measurements of the sector are mentioned in the problem.** Remember, the three measurements are *degrees*, *arc length*, and *area*. Usually, only *two* of them will be tested in a problem.

2. **Set up a proportion problem with the two appropriate ratios above, and solve for the missing information.** Keep in mind that if the radius (or diameter) of the circle is given, then you can calculate the circumference or area of the circle.

(EX) If the area of circle O below is 240 in^2 and the area of sector AOB is 20 in^2, what is the value of x?

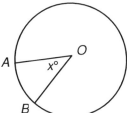

A. 25
B. 30
C. 35
D. 40
E. 45

SECTORS OF CIRCLES: OTHER MEASUREMENTS

We've looked at the *areas*, *arc lengths*, and *angles* of sectors, but there are other ways sectors can be measured, including:

- Minutes (or hours) on a clock (think of the sector formed by the sweep of a hand)
- Volume or weight of a disk
- Any quantity (population, dollars, etc.) on a pie graph

Just remember that the part-over-whole ratios of any two measurements will always equal.

REVOLUTION PROBLEMS

These problems have to do with a rolling circle or wheel. When a circle rolls *one* revolution without slipping, it will travel a distance equal to the *circumference* ($2\pi r$) of the circle. This is a *known relationship* that you must memorize. You will use this known relationship as part of a proportion problem:

$$\frac{\text{revolutions}}{\text{distance (units)}} \rightarrow \frac{1}{2\pi r \text{ (circumference)}} = \frac{\text{total revolutions}}{\text{total distance}}$$

(EX) A wheel with circumference of 10 inches rolls a distance of 40 inches without slipping. How many revolutions did the wheel make?

A. 4
B. 8
C. 10
D. 40
E. 400

GRAPHING A CIRCLE WITH YOUR CALCULATOR

If in general you're comfortable using your graphing calculator, you might want to occasionally graph a circle. Most graphing calculators offer you a "$y =$" graph prompt. But, unlike, say, a parabola, circles are rarely in this form. The trick is to solve for y, and remember, when you solve for a squared variable, you'll get a positive and a negative solution. For example:

$$x^2 + y^2 = 16 \;\to\; y^2 = 16 - x^2 \;\to\; y = \pm\sqrt{16 - x^2}$$

So you'll actually graph *two* equations: $y = \sqrt{16 - x^2}$ and $y = -\sqrt{16 - x^2}$. Hint: Make sure the scale or "zoom" is set to "square." Otherwise, the circle will look like an ellipse. You probably won't ever *have* to graph a circle, but knowing how might come in handy.

MORE CIRCLES LESSON PROBLEMS

32. If the length of arc *AB* in the circle below with center *O* is 5 and angle *AOB* is 120°, what is the circumference of the circle?

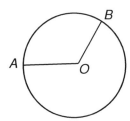

    A. 10
    B. 15
    C. 5π
    D. 10π
    E. 100

41. Which of the following equations represents a circle in the standard (x,y) coordinate plane that has center (3,5) and radius $\sqrt{5}$ units?

    F. $(x - 3)^2 + (y - 5)^2 = 5$
    G. $(x + 3)^2 + (y + 5)^2 = 5$
    H. $(x - 3)^2 + (y - 5)^2 = \sqrt{5}$
    J. $(x + 3)^2 + (y + 5)^2 = \sqrt{5}$
    K. $(x - 3)^2 - (y - 5)^2 = \sqrt{5}$

51. A device measures distance by counting the revolutions of a wheel with a diameter of 6 inches. What is the distance, in feet, if the device measures 1000 revolutions?

    A. 200π
    B. 400π
    C. 500π
    D. 1000π
    E. 6000π

18. Each of the 200 students at George Washington High School voted for his or her favorite American president. The results of the poll are given in the table below.

President	Number of Voters
George Washington	60
Abraham Lincoln	58
Thomas Jefferson	35
Franklin D. Roosevelt	17
Other	30

If the information in the table were converted into a circle graph (pie chart), then the central angle of the sector that voted for George Washington would measure how many degrees?

A. 60°
B. 100°
C. 108°
D. 110°
E. 252°

35. In circle *O* below, *x* = 36. What is the area of sector *AOB*?

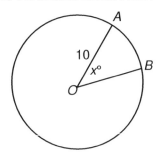

F. 2π
G. 10
H. 20
J. 10π
K. 100π

Continued →

50. Which of the following is an equation of the circle in the standard (x,y) coordinate plane shown below?

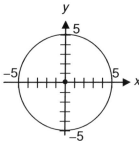

A. $x^2 - y^2 = 25$
B. $x^2 + y^2 = 25$
C. $x^2 + y^2 = 5$
D. $(x + y)^2 = 5$
E. $x + y = 5$

56. Kevin had a bicycle with 30-inch diameter wheels. He decided to replace the front wheel with a 20-inch diameter wheel. If he traveled 300 feet on the modified bicycle, how many more full revolutions did the front wheel make than the back wheel?

F. 19
G. 20
H. 21
J. 22
K. 60

8. SOLIDS & VOLUME

Solids are shapes that occupy three dimensions, such as cubes, cylinders, or rectangular boxes. Most solids problems are *volume* problems that deal with rectangular solids or cubes. Though less common, some problems will require you to know the formula for the volume of a cylinder.

> **Volume** – the amount of space occupied by a solid or a substance.

> **Surface area** – the sum of the areas of all the faces of a solid.

RECTANGULAR SOLIDS

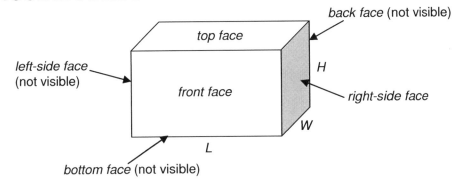

$$V = L \cdot W \cdot H$$

To find surface area, notice that there are 3 different rectangular faces (the 3 faces you can see above), and each one has an opposite rectangular face of the exact same size. For example, the front face (visible above) is the exact same size as the back face (*not* visible above). This can help you find the formula for surface area. Don't memorize this. Just make sure you understand how we found it:

$$SA = 2LH + 2LW + 2WH$$

Try the following lesson problems, based on the rectangular solid below:

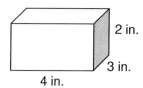

1. What is the area of the front face?

2. What is the area of the top face?

3. What is the area of the right-side face?

4. What is the total surface area of the box?

5. What is the volume of the box?

CUBES

Since all sides of a cube are the same length, the formulas for volume and surface area are simplified:

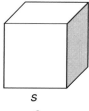

s

$$V = s^3$$
$$SA = 6s^2$$

SURFACE AREA OF CUBE → VOLUME OF CUBE

You might need to find the *volume* of a cube when the *surface area* is given. Consider a cube with a surface area of 600 in^2:

1. What is the area of one face?

2. What is the length of an edge?

3. What is the volume of the cube?

The above example illustrates the following method for finding the volume of a cube when the surface area is given:

1. *Divide* the surface area by 6 to find the area of one face.

2. Take the *square root* of this area to find the length of a side.

3. *Cube* this length to find the volume of the cube.

DIAGONALS OF RECTANGULAR SOLIDS

You may be asked to calculate the length of a rectangular solid's *diagonal*, which is a segment that connects a pair of opposite vertices. The formula is below.

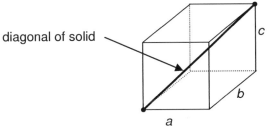

diagonal of solid

$$\boxed{\text{FLASH CARDS}} \quad \textbf{diagonal} = \sqrt{a^2 + b^2 + c^2}$$

Note that a *cube*, where $a = b = c$, uses the same formula.

If you're interested, here's the proof for the general formula:

1. Let e = the diagonal of the bottom face and d = diagonal of the solid.
2. Triangle 1: Use the Pythagorean Theorem to find e: $e = \sqrt{a^2 + b^2}$
3. Triangle 2: Use the Pythagorean Theorem again to find d:
   $d = \sqrt{e^2 + c^2} \;\rightarrow\; e^2 = a^2 + b^2 \;\rightarrow\; d = \sqrt{a^2 + b^2 + c^2}$

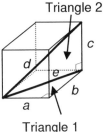

Triangle 2

Triangle 1

VOLUME OF PRISMS

A *prism* is a three-dimensional shape that has the same cross section along its entire length. Prisms have two *bases*, one at each end. Below is a prism with a triangular cross section:

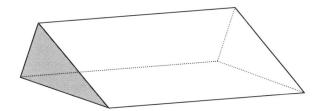

Below is a prism with a circular cross section (a cylinder):

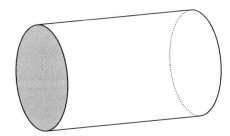

The volume of any prism is:

$$V = \text{Area of base} \times \text{Length of prism}$$

Try the following lesson problem:

47. The figure below shows the elliptical cross section of a 20 foot long storage tank. If the area of the cross section is found to be 18π square feet, what is the volume, in cubic feet, of the tank?

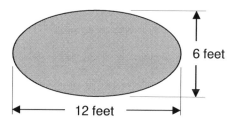

A. 1440
B. 1240
C. 405π
D. 360π
E. 180π

VOLUME FITTING PROBLEMS

Some volume problems will ask you to find the volume or number of small solids that can fit into a larger volume or solid. These problems are similar to *area fitting* problems (see the Area & Perimeter section).

 Volume fitting problems will ask you to find the volume or number of small solids that can fit into a larger volume or solid.

Here's the method:

1. Find the volumes of the large solid and the small solid.
2. Divide the large volume by the small volume.

$$\text{Number of } \textit{small volumes} \text{ that will fit into the } \textit{larger volume} = \frac{\textbf{Large Volume}}{\textbf{Small Volume}}$$

Try the following lesson problem:

48. A cylindrical cup has a radius of 2 inches and a height of 6 inches. A cylindrical water jug has a radius of 10 inches and a height of 12 inches. If the jug is full of water, how many cups of water can be filled before the jug is empty?

    A. 5
    B. 20
    C. 35
    D. 50
    E. 65

■

11. Elisa has two boxes, each with lengths 10 inches, widths 8 inches, and heights 6 inches. If she wants to ship these boxes in a third box with length 20 inches, width 10 inches, and height 8 inches, how much additional space, in cubic inches, will be left in the larger box?

    A. 600
    B. 640
    C. 680
    D. 720
    E. 1120

29. If cube A has an edge of length 2 centimeters and cube B has an edge of length 3 centimeters, what is the ratio of the volume of cube A to the volume of cube B?

    F. 3:2
    G. 8:27
    H. 5:9
    J. 4:9
    K. 2:3

32. A steel worker is going to pour 300 cubic inches of molten steel into the rectangular mold shown below. If the molten steel is spread evenly over the entire base of the mold, what will be the approximate height, in inches, of the molten steel?

6 inches

5 inches

30 inches

    A. 0.5
    B. 1
    C. 2
    D. 4
    E. 6

Continued →

54. Soap cubes, each with a total surface area of 54 square centimeters, are stacked in a cube box. If the box has a volume of 729 cubic centimeters, what is the maximum number of soap cubes that can fit in the box?

 F. 13
 G. 27
 H. 100
 J. 192
 K. 8304

9. *GEOMETRY PROBLEMS*

PRACTICE PROBLEMS

The worksheets on the following pages test techniques taught in this chapter. For additional practice, we'll use problems from Test 5 in *The Official ACT Prep Guide*.

- ☐ Geometry Worksheet 1
- ☐ Geometry Worksheet 2
- ☐ Geometry Worksheet 3
- ☐ Geometry Worksheet 4
- ☐ **The Official ACT Prep Guide: Test 5**: Only tackle questions related to *this chapter*. For a list of these relevant questions, see the Techniques chapter at the end of this tutorial (first page of "Techniques: Test 5").

Reminders:

- **Use techniques**: These assignments are "open book." Go back to the tutorial as often as you need to, and use techniques aggressively.
- **No timing**: Do *not* time yourself on these assignments.
- **Scheduling**: See the Tutoring Schedules section in the Introduction for more details on scheduling.

TEST CORRECTIONS

After each practice test is graded, you should correct questions related to this chapter that you missed or guessed on. See "Correcting Practice Tests" in the Introduction for more details. Here are the three steps to correcting practice tests:

1. Turn to the Techniques chapter at the end of this tutorial and circle the Geometry questions that you missed or guessed on for the test you are correcting.
2. Correct the problems in *The Official ACT Prep Guide*. As you correct the problems, go back to the tutorial and review the techniques. The idea is to (1) identify techniques that have given you trouble, (2) go back to the tutorial so you can review and strengthen these techniques, and (3) apply these techniques to the specific problems on which you struggled.
3. If you have trouble identifying the best technique to use for a problem, refer to the Techniques chapter. This is an important part of correcting the tests.

GEOMETRY WORKSHEET 1

12. In the figure below, *Z* is on line *AB* and *AB* ∥ *XY*. Which of the following is NOT true?

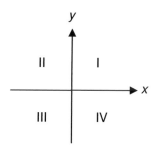

   A. $m\angle 3 = m\angle 4$
   B. $m\angle 3 + m\angle 4 = 90°$
   C. $m\angle 1 = 90°$
   D. $m\angle 2 + m\angle 3 = 90°$
   E. $m\angle 1 + m\angle 2 + m\angle 4 = 180°$

23. The coordinates of point *A* are (p,q), with $p \neq 0$ and $q \neq 0$. If $p = -q$, then *A* must be located in which of the 4 quadrants of the standard (x,y) coordinate plane labeled below?

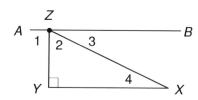

   F. I only
   G. II only
   H. IV only
   J. I or IV only
   K. II or IV only

Continued →

25. You want to build a square garden that will be fenced on all four sides. If you have enough material to build 30 feet of fence, what can be the maximum area, to the nearest square foot, of your garden?

A. 225
B. 128
C. 64
D. 60
E. 56

27. A rope is stretched straight from the top of a 50 foot vertical tower to a point on the ground 120 feet from the base of the tower. Assuming the ground is level, how long, in feet, is the rope?

F. 125
G. 130
H. 135
J. 140
K. 145

31. Which of the following lines has the largest slope?

A. $y = 2x + 2$
B. $y = 2x + 4$
C. $y = 4x + 2$
D. $2y = 4x + 4$
E. $2y = 6x + 2$

44. In right triangle *ABC* below, points *A*, *D*, and *C* are collinear and line segment *BD* bisects ∠*ABC*. If the measure of ∠*ACB* is 35°, as shown, what is the measure of ∠*BDC*?

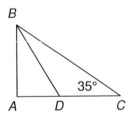

F. 110°
G. 112.5°
H. 115°
J. 117.5°
K. 120°

Continued →

46. In △ABC shown below, $\overline{DE}$ is parallel to $\overline{AC}$. The length of $\overline{AB}$ is 8 inches, the length of $\overline{BC}$ is 9 inches, and the length of $\overline{DE}$ is 4 inches. If points D and E are the midpoints of $\overline{AB}$ and $\overline{BC}$, respectively, which of the following is the length, in inches, of $\overline{AC}$?

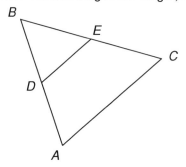

A. 8
B. 8½
C. 9
D. 9½
E. 10

50. As shown below, a clock has a minute hand with a tip that is 6 inches from the center of the clock. To the nearest inch, how far does the tip of the minute hand travel between 12:05 PM and 12:30 PM?

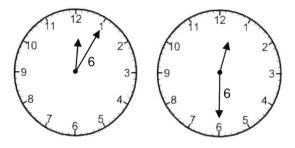

F. 12
G. 13
H. 14
J. 15
K. 16

Continued →

51. The area of trapezoid *ABCD*, shown below, is 108 square inches. If the lengths of the bases are 14 and 22, what is the height, *h*, in inches, of the trapezoid?

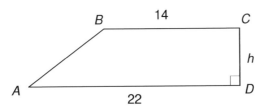

A. 5½
B. 6
C. 6½
D. 7
E. 7½

55. The target below is made up of three circles with the same center. The radius of the small circle is one-third of the radius of the middle circle and one-fifth of the radius of the large circle. If an archer hits the target, what is the probability that he hits the shaded region?

F. $\frac{1}{25}$

G. $\frac{17}{35}$

H. $\frac{3}{5}$

J. $\frac{17}{25}$

K. $\frac{26}{35}$

Continued →

56. Which of the following is an equation of the circle in the standard (x,y) coordinate plane shown below?

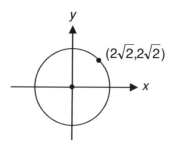

F. $x^2 + y^2 = 16$
G. $x^2 + y^2 = 8$
H. $x^2 + y^2 = 4$
J. $x^2 + y^2 = 4\sqrt{2}$
K. $x^2 + y^2 = 2\sqrt{2}$

 PRACTICE TEST (all programs): Now is a good time to take **Test 2** in the ACT book. (You should have already taken Test 1.) If you have any questions about taking these tests, review "Taking Practice Tests" in this tutorial's Introduction.

GEOMETRY WORKSHEET 2

6. On a number line, if point *A* has coordinate –5 and point *B* has coordinate 3, what is the coordinate of the point that is ¾ of the way from *A* to *B*?

   A. –1
   B. 0
   C. 1
   D. 3
   E. 6

12. In the triangle shown below, what is the sum of *a*, *b*, and *c*?

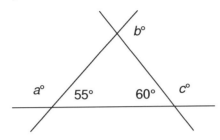

   F. 375
   G. 360
   H. 245
   J. 180
   K. Cannot be
       determined from
       the given
       information

25. In the figure below, Δ*I* is similar to Δ*II*, with lengths given in inches. What is the perimeter of Δ*II*?

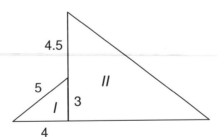

   A. 23.5
   B. 26
   C. 28.5
   D. 30
   E. 36

Continued →

26. In the circle with center O shown below, which of following statements is NOT true?

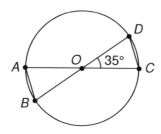

F. AO = DO
G. AB = DC
H. measure of arc ABD = 215°
J. ∠AOD = 145°
K. ∠ABO = 70°

33. The figure below shows square XYZO, with vertices X and Z lying on circle O. If the area of the square is 25 square centimeters, what is the area, in square centimeters, of the circle?

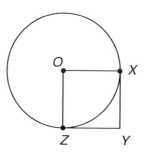

A. 25π
B. 50π
C. 100π
D. 250π
E. 625π

Continued →

41. What is the distance in the standard (x,y) coordinate plane between the points $(-12,-5)$ and $(12,5)$?

F. $\sqrt{13}$

G. $\sqrt{26}$

H. 13

J. 26

K. 34

56. In the standard (x,y) coordinate plane, lines a and b intersect at point $(-2,3)$ and lines a and c intersect at point $(-2,-2)$. Which of the following is an equation for line a?

A. $y = -2x - 6$

B. $y = -2x - 1$

C. $y = -2x + 3$

D. $x = -2$

E. Cannot be determined from the information given

57. Gavin runs a length of rope over a nail in a wall, and attaches the rope to the floor at two locations to create the triangle shown below. One side of the triangle is 50 inches, and the angle between the two sides of the rope at the nail is 85°. In terms of l, the length of the rope, what is the area, in square inches, of the shaded triangle?

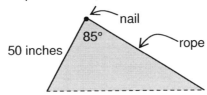

(Note: The area of any triangle with sides of length a, b, and c opposite angles of measure A, B, and C, respectively, is given by ½ab sin C.)

A. l sin 85°

B. $25l$ sin 85°

C. $50l$ sin 85°

D. $50(l - 50)$ sin 85°

E. $25(l - 50)$ sin 85°

Continued →

58. The cross section of a 10 foot long trough used for watering cattle is an equilateral triangle. If the trough is filled with water to a depth of 6 inches, as shown below, what is the volume, in cubic inches, of water in the trough?

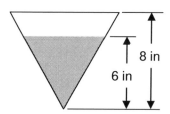

- **F.** $320\sqrt{3}$
- **G.** $360\sqrt{3}$
- **H.** $640\sqrt{3}$
- **J.** $720\sqrt{3}$
- **K.** $1,440\sqrt{3}$

60. In △*ABC* below, the measure of ∠*A* is 45° and the measure ∠*C* is 30°. What is the perimeter of the triangle?

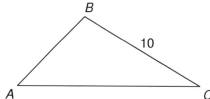

- **A.** $5+5\sqrt{3}$
- **B.** $10+5\sqrt{2}+5\sqrt{3}$
- **C.** $15+5\sqrt{5}$
- **D.** $10+10\sqrt{3}$
- **E.** $15+5\sqrt{2}+5\sqrt{3}$

GEOMETRY WORKSHEET 3

2. Chuck wants to determine the height of a wall. He props a 10-foot long ladder against the wall, so that the top of the ladder meets the top of the wall and the base of the ladder is 2 feet from the base of the wall, as shown below. What is the height, in feet, of the wall?

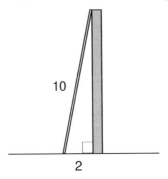

    A. 8
    B. 9
    C. $\sqrt{96}$
    D. $\sqrt{104}$
    E. $\sqrt{112}$

7. In the figure below, $l_1 \parallel l_2$ and $l_3 \parallel l_4$. What is the measure, in degrees, of angle x?

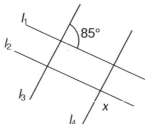

    F. 85
    G. 95
    H. 100
    J. 105
    K. Cannot be determined from the given information

Continued →

25. In hexagon *ABCDEF* below, ∠*A* is given. What is the measure of angles *B* + *C* + *D* + *E* + *F*?

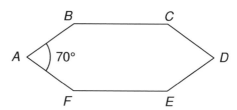

- **A.** 630°
- **B.** 650°
- **C.** 670°
- **D.** 700°
- **E.** 720°

26. In the figure below, vertex *E* of △*ADE* lies on square *ABCD*. What is the ratio of the area of △*ADE* to the area of square *ABCD*?

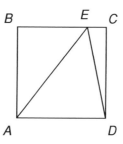

- **A.** 1:2
- **B.** 3:4
- **C.** 1:1
- **D.** 2:1
- **E.** Cannot be determined from the given information

Continued →

352 • GEOMETRY

35. Which of the following could be the equation for the graph of the line shown in the standard (x,y) coordinate plane below?

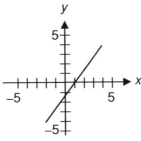

A. $y = -\frac{4}{3}$

B. $y = -\frac{4}{3}x + \frac{4}{3}$

C. $y = -\frac{4}{3}x - \frac{4}{3}$

D. $y = \frac{4}{3}x - \frac{4}{3}$

E. $y = \frac{4}{3}x$

47. The target below is made up of three circles with the same center. The radius of the small circle is one-third of the radius of the middle circle and one-fifth of the radius of the large circle. If the radius of the small circle is 2, what is the area of the shaded region?

F. 36π

G. 64π

H. 68π

J. 72π

K. 100π

Continued →

48. In the circle below, O is the center. Chord $\overline{AB}$ is 8 inches long and line segment $\overline{OC}$ is 3 inches long. What is the circumference of the circle?

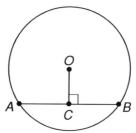

A. 5π
B. 7π
C. 8π
D. 9π
E. 10π

Continued →

52. The circle below is inscribed in a square with sides of length 4 units. What is the perimeter, in units, of the shaded region shown below?

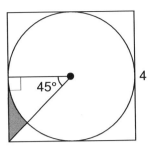

A. $2 + \dfrac{\pi}{2}$

B. $2\sqrt{2} + \dfrac{\pi}{2}$

C. $2\sqrt{3} + \dfrac{\pi}{2}$

D. $4\sqrt{2} + 2\pi$

E. $4\sqrt{3} + 2\pi$

55. In the standard (x,y) coordinate plane, point M with coordinates $(4,1)$ is the midpoint of line segment AB. If B has coordinates (p,q), what are the coordinates of A, in terms of p and q?

F. $(8 + p, 2 + q)$
G. $(8 - p, 2 - q)$
H. $(p - 8, q - 2)$
J. $(4 - p, 1 - q)$
K. $(p - 4, q - 1)$

GEOMETRY WORKSHEET 4

14. A rectangular water tank 4 ft wide, 8 ft long, and 10 ft high is filled to 20% of capacity. How many additional cubic feet of water must be added to the tank so that it is 30% full?

   A. 32
   B. 64
   C. 96
   D. 160
   E. 256

24. The lengths of corresponding sides of two similar right triangles are in the ratio 3 to 4. If the hypotenuse of the larger triangle is 10 centimeters, then how long, in centimeters, is the length of the hypotenuse of the smaller triangle?

   F. 5
   G. $6\frac{2}{3}$
   H. $7\frac{1}{2}$
   J. 10
   K. $13\frac{1}{3}$

27. In the figure below, square ABCD has sides of length 5 inches, and the four right triangles are congruent. What is the area of the shaded region?

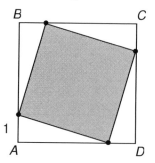

   A. 25
   B. 17
   C. $\sqrt{17}$
   D. 8
   E. 2

Continued →

30. Thomas finds the treasure map shown below. The treasure is buried exactly halfway between points *A* and *B*. If he overlays a standard (*x,y*) coordinate plan onto the map, with the origin at the bottom left corner, he finds that the coordinates of points *A* and *B* are (2, 3) and (8,9), respectively. What are the coordinates of the buried treasure?

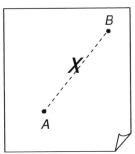

F. (4,5.5)
G. (4,6)
H. (5,5.5)
J. (5,6)
K. (10,12)

44. Trapezoid *PQRS* below is isosceles, with side lengths indicated and diagonals intersecting at *T*. What is the ratio of the length of segment *QT* to the length of segment *PT*?

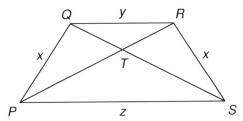

A. $\dfrac{x}{z}$

B. $\dfrac{y}{z}$

C. $\dfrac{y}{x}$

D. $\dfrac{x}{y}$

E. $\dfrac{z}{y}$

Continued →

45. In the figure below, segment *AB* is tangent to circle *C* and has a length of 12. If circle *C* has a radius of 4, what is the area of △*ABC*?

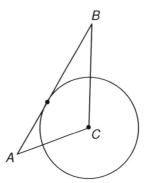

F. 12
G. 18
H. 24
J. 30
K. 36

49. Mary measures the distance around the perimeter of a circular track as 100 feet. What is the area, in square feet, enclosed by the circular track?

A. $\dfrac{10{,}000}{\pi}$

B. $\dfrac{2{,}500}{\pi}$

C. $\dfrac{1{,}000}{\pi}$

D. $\dfrac{50}{\pi}$

E. 100π

50. Points *A*, *B*, and *C* lie on the same line. If the length of *AB* is 6 and the length of *BC* is 3, what are the possible unit lengths for *AC*?

F. 3 only
G. 9 only
H. 3 and 9 only
J. Any number less than 2 or greater than 8
K. Any number greater than 2 or less than 8

Continued →

55. The parallelogram shown below has sides of length *a* and *b*. In terms of *a*, *b*, and θ, what is the area of the parallelogram?

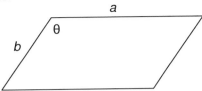

A. *ab*

B. $\frac{1}{2}$ *ab* sin θ

C. *ab* sin θ

D. 2*ab* cos θ

E. 2*ab* sin θ

60. In the figure below, if *OA* has length 2*b*, what is the slope of the segment?

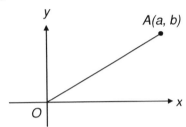

A. $\frac{1}{2}$

B. $\frac{\sqrt{3}}{3}$

C. 1

D. $\sqrt{3}$

E. Cannot be determined from the information given

VI
FUNCTIONS

This chapter will cover all relevant topics related to functions, including their graphs.

1. BASIC FUNCTIONS

It is important to be familiar with basic function notation. A function is typically notated with a letter (often f) and parentheses containing a variable, number, or expression. The letter is the "name" of the function. Whatever is inside the parentheses is the *input* of the function. It may be helpful to think of a function as a *rule* that tells you how to find an *output* for any given input. For example:

$$f(x) = 2x + 3$$

The function above is called "the function f." The variable inside the parentheses, x, represents the input. The rule for this function is: "multiply the input by 2 and then add 3." Several examples are below.

 Look for the function notation, such as $f(x)$, $g(a)$, $P(2)$, etc. When functions are represented graphically, they may only contain the letter of the function without the parentheses (f, g, P, etc). Not surprisingly, the word "function" will also help you identify these problems.

We'll use $f(x) = 2x + 3$ for the following examples:

(EX) $f(2) =$

(EX) $f\left(\dfrac{a-3}{2}\right) =$

(EX) $f(2 + 3) =$

(EX) $f(g(x)) =$

(EX) $f(a) =$

(EX) If $f(x) = -1$, what is the value of x?

Use the following general method for function problems. The steps are illustrated in the example following the method.

1. **Identify the function rule.** It will usually be represented as an equation (as above), but functions can also be represented by graphs or tables. In all cases, the function will give you a *rule* that will allow you to find outputs for given inputs.
2. **Find another expression or equation that contains the function found in step 1.**
3. **Write the problem without the function notation by following the rule of the function.** The trick is to get rid of the function notation so you can solve using basic algebra.
4. Use basic math or algebra to answer the question.

(EX) Let the function g be defined by $g(x) = x + 3$. If $g(m) = 2m$, what is the value of m?

    A. 6
    B. 5
    C. 4
    D. 3
    E. 2

Try the following lesson problems. **Note:** The following problems are part of a *multi-question set*. Typically, for these multi-question sets: **regardless of the number, the first one will usually be easy, but the last one will usually be hard**. Watch out for these problems on the ACT.

Questions 23–25 refer to the following functions f and g.

$$f(n) = n^2$$
$$g(n) = n^2 - n$$

23. $f(6) - f(-6) =$

    A. −6
    B. 0
    C. 6
    D. 36
    E. 72

24. Which of the following is equivalent to $g(m + 1)$?

    F. $f(m) + 1$
    G. $f(m) + 3$
    H. $f(m) + m$
    J. $g(m) + 1$
    K. $g(m) + m$

25. Which of the following is an expression for $f(g(x))$?

    A. $x^4 + 2x^3 + x^2$
    B. $x^4 - 2x^3 + x^2$
    C. $x^4 - 2x^3 - x^2$
    D. $x^4 + x^2$
    E. $x^4 - x^2$

19. For the function $f(x) = -2x^3 - 3x^2 + 4$, what is the value of $f(-2)$?

   A. 8
   B. 4
   C. 0
   D. −12
   E. −24

21. A function h of the variables p and q is defined as $h(p,q) = p^p - q^q$. What is the value of $h(5,4)$?

   F. 1
   G. 9
   H. 399
   J. 2,869
   K. 3,125

51. Let the function g be defined by $g(x) = x + 4$. If $\frac{1}{2}g(\sqrt{a}) = 4$, what is the value of a?

   A. 4
   B. 6
   C. 16
   D. 36
   E. 64

Continued →

55. According to the table below, if $a = g(3)$, what is the value of $h(a)$?

x	g(x)	h(x)
0	3	4
1	1	3
2	2	2
3	0	1

F. 0
G. 1
H. 2
J. 3
K. 4

2. GRAPHS OF FUNCTIONS

GRAPHING BASICS

The function $f(x)$ can be represented graphically on an (x, y) *coordinate plane*. The *x-axis* represents the values of x (the inputs of the function) and the *y-axis* represents the values of $f(x)$ (the outputs of the function). There are several characteristics of these graphs that you should be comfortable with; they will be taught using the following graph of $f(x)$:

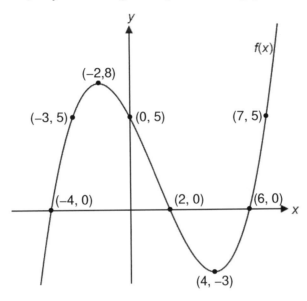

POINTS

Each point on the graph of a function has an *x-coordinate* and a *y-coordinate*. Remember, the *x-coordinates* are the function's *inputs*, and the *y-coordinates* are the function's *outputs*:

$$(x, y) \Leftrightarrow (x, f(x))$$

(EX) 1. $f(-2) =$

(EX) 2. $f(7) =$

(EX) 3.   If $f(x) = 5$, what are the possible values of x?

AXIS INTERCEPTS

The points where a function crosses (or touches) the *x*- and *y*-axes are called *axis intercepts*. The *x-intercept*s are often called *zeros* or *roots* of the function (see "Factors and Roots" in the Factoring lesson [Advanced Algebra chapter]). There may be more than one *x-intercept*. A function, however, will never have more than one *y-intercept*. (You might remember that functions must pass the "vertical-line test": a vertical line can never intersect a function more than once; the *y-axis*, of course, is a vertical line.)

(EX) 4.   What are the roots of $f(x)$?

(EX) 5.   If $x < 0$ and $f(x) = 0$, what is the value of x?

(EX) 6. $f(0) =$

Note: When a function is given, you can find axis intercepts using algebra:
1.   To find the *y*-intercept, let $x = 0$. Solve for y.
2.   To find the *x*-intercept(s), let $y = 0$. Solve for x.

POSITIVE/NEGATIVE

A function is positive when $f(x)$ is greater than zero, and negative when $f(x)$ is less than zero. Remember, when we say "$f(x)$," we're talking about the *outputs* of $f(x)$ (the *y* values).

(EX) 7.   What are the values of x for which $f(x)$ is positive?

(EX) 8.   What are the values of x for which $f(x)$ is negative?

INCREASING/DECREASING

When $f(x)$ slopes up as x increases (in other words, as we move left to right), we say the function is *increasing*. When $f(x)$ slopes down as x increases (again, as we move left to right), we say the function is *decreasing*.

(EX) 9.   What are the values of x for which $f(x)$ is increasing?

(EX) 10.   What are the values of x for which $f(x)$ is decreasing?

MAXIMA/MINIMA

Here are some terms you should be comfortable with:
- **maximum**: the value of a function at a certain point that is greater that the values at all other points in the immediate vicinity (also called the **relative maximum**).
- **minimum**: the value of a function at a certain point that is less that the values at all other points in the immediate vicinity (also called the **relative minimum**).
- **absolute maximum**: the largest value for a given function.
- **absolute minimum**: the smallest value for a given function.

Note that the function at the beginning of this lesson does not have an absolute maximum or an absolute minimum, but the one maximum and one minimum should be easy to spot.

(EX) 11. At which point does $f(x)$ have a relative maximum?

(EX) 12. At which point does $f(x)$ have a relative minimum?

∎

Try the following lesson problems:

40.

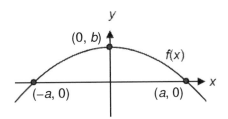

The function f shown above is defined as $f(x) = \dfrac{(x-4)(x+4)}{-8}$. What is the value of b?

A. 2
B. 3
C. 4
D. 6
E. 8

48. What is the *y-intercept* of the quadratic function f given by $f(x) = ax^2 + bx + c$ where a, b, and c are different positive integers?

A. a
B. $a\!/\!c$
C. b
D. $b\!/\!c$
E. c

Continued →

52. Point A lies on the graph of $f(x)$ in the standard (x,y) coordinate plane shown below. If the coordinates of point A are $(a, -4)$, and function f is defined as $f(x) = 2x^{\frac{1}{3}}$, what is the value of a?

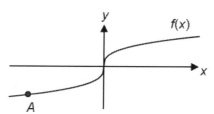

F. −4
G. −7
H. −7.5
J. −8
K. −8.5

EVEN AND ODD FUNCTIONS

An *even function* is one where $f(x) = f(-x)$. Below is an example of an even function. Notice that the right and left sides of the function (on either side of the *y-axis*) are mirror images of each other; in other words, the part of the graph to the right of the *y-axis* is *reflected* across the *y-axis*:

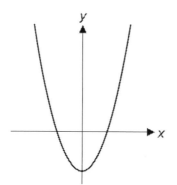 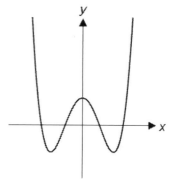

$$f(x) = f(-x)$$

An *odd function* is one where $f(x) = -f(-x)$. Below is an example of an odd function. Notice that the right and left sides of the function (on either side of the y-axis) are *upside-down* mirror images of each other; in other words, the part of the graph to the right of the y-axis is *rotated* *180°* about the origin:

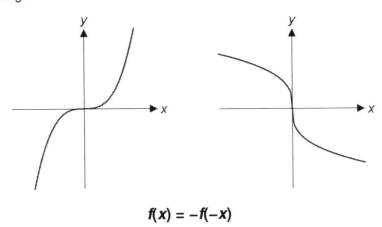

$$f(x) = -f(-x)$$

Try the following lesson problem:

50. The graph of $f(x) = 4\sin(0.5x)$ in the standard (x,y) coordinate plane is shown below. Which of the following is true?

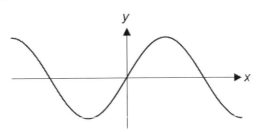

   A. $f(x)$ is an even function
   B. $f(x)$ is an odd function
   C. $f(x)$ is neither even nor odd
   D. $f(x)$ is symmetrical about the *x-axis*
   E. $f(x)$ is symmetrical about the *y-axis*

GRAPHING CALCULATOR

If you have a graphing calculator, make sure you are comfortable using its graphing features. If you don't have a graphing calculator, don't worry—no problems on the ACT *require* you to graph functions. When the specific algebraic function is not given, your calculator's graphing features will generally *not* help you. But if the function *is* given, don't be shy. (Note: make sure to review the calculator guidelines on the ACT website. See the Calculators lesson in Chapter I.)

28.

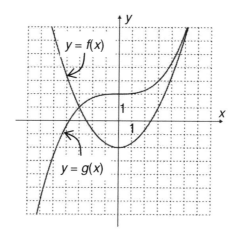

Graphs of functions f and g are shown in the (x, y) coordinate plane above. For which of the following values of x does $f(x) - g(x) = 0$

A. −4
B. −3
C. −2
D. 0
E. 2

35. Based on the graph of the function f below, what are the values of x for which $f(x)$ is negative?

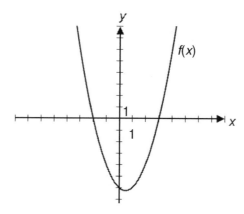

A. $-6 < x < 0$
B. $-\frac{7}{2} \leq x < -2$
C. $-\frac{7}{2} \leq x < -2$ or $3 < x \leq \frac{9}{2}$
D. $-2 < x < 3$
E. $-2 < x < 0$

Continued →

54. *ABCD* is a rectangle with one side on the *x-axis* and point *A* on the graph of *f(x)*, as shown in the figure below. If $f(x) = \sqrt{x} + 2$, what is the area of *ABCD*?

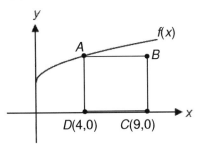

F. 10
G. 18
H. $6\sqrt{10}$
J. 20
K. $10\sqrt{6}$

Continued →

58. The graph of $f(x)$ is shown below. Which of the following is the graph of $|f(x)|$?

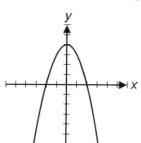

A.

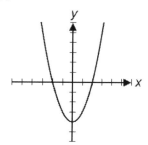

D.

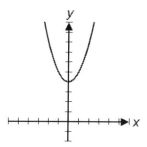

B.

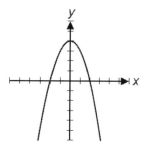

E.

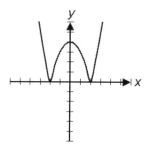

C.

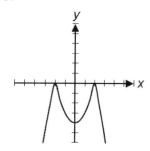

■

30- and 40-hour programs: Jump to the end of this chapter and complete Functions Worksheet 1 and relevant test corrections for Tests 1 and 2. Then move on to the Trigonometry chapter. If you're in the **40-hour program**, you'll finish the Functions chapter later (see the Tutoring Schedules in the Introduction).

3. MORE GRAPHS OF FUNCTIONS

This section will cover a few more topics relating to graphs of functions, including end behavior, domain & range, asymptotes, symmetry, and transformations.

END BEHAVIOR

End behavior of a polynomial function refers to the behavior of a function as x approaches positive and negative infinity ($\pm\infty$). Of course, we can look at the graph and easily see the end behavior, but you might have to consider end behavior based on a polynomial (without the benefit of a graph). Here are a few rules you should know:

When the degree of a polynomial is *even* and the leading coefficient is *positive*: • $x \to \infty$, $f(x) \to \infty$ • $x \to -\infty$, $f(x) \to \infty$	 $f(x) = x^2$
When the degree of a polynomial is *even* and the leading coefficient is *negative*: • $x \to \infty$, $f(x) \to -\infty$ • $x \to -\infty$, $f(x) \to -\infty$	 $f(x) = -x^2$
When the degree of a polynomial is *odd* and the leading coefficient is *positive*: • $x \to \infty$, $f(x) \to \infty$ • $x \to -\infty$, $f(x) \to -\infty$	 $f(x) = x^3$
When the degree of a polynomial is *odd* and the leading coefficient is *negative*: • $x \to \infty$, $f(x) \to -\infty$ • $x \to -\infty$, $f(x) \to \infty$	 $f(x) = -x^3$

Try the following lesson problem:

21.

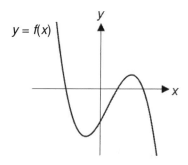

The graph of the function f is shown in the (x, y) coordinate plane above. If a, b, c, and d are positive integers, $f(x)$ could equal which of the following polynomials?

A. $ax^2 + bx - c$
B. $-ax^2 + bx - c$
C. $-ax^3 + bx^2 + cx - d$
D. $ax^3 + bx^2 + cx - d$
E. $ax^4 + bx^3 + cx^2 - dx$

DOMAIN & RANGE

DOMAIN

The *domain* of a function $f(x)$ is the set of *inputs* that may be put into a function without violating any laws of math. In other words, the domain is all allowable values of x.

 These problems may mention the word *domain*. They may also ask for the values of x for which $f(x)$ is a real number, or, alternatively, they may ask for the values of x for which $f(x)$ is "undefined."

There are two rules used for finding the domain of a function:

1. **The denominator of a fraction cannot equal zero.**

2. **It is impossible to take the square root (or any *even* root) of a negative number.**

The following rules are used to find the domain of a function:

1. **If there is a variable in the denominator of a fraction, set the entire denominator *not-equal* (≠) to zero.** Solve for the variable. Any values of the variable that make the denominator zero are *not* part of the function's domain.

(EX) What is the domain of $f(x) = \dfrac{25}{x - 25}$?

2. **If there is a variable under an <u>even</u> root ($\sqrt{}$, $\sqrt[4]{}$, $\sqrt[6]{}$, etc.), set the entire expression under the root *greater than or equal* ($\geq$) to zero.** Solve for the variable. These values are the domain of the function. (Note: if the root is *odd*, then negative numbers are allowed.)

(EX) What is the domain of $f(x) = \sqrt{x - 25}$?

3. **If there is a variable under an even root that is in the denominator of a fraction, set the entire expression under the root *greater than* ($>$) zero.** Solve for the variable. These values are the domain of the function.

(EX) What is the domain of $f(x) = \dfrac{25}{\sqrt{x - 25}}$?

Try the following lesson problem:

27. For the function f, defined below, what are the values of x for which $f(x)$ is a real number?

$$f(x) = \frac{5}{\sqrt{x + 4}}$$

   A. $x = -4$
   B. $x = 0$
   C. $x \geq -4$
   D. $x \geq 0$
   E. $x > -4$

RANGE

The *range* of a function $f(x)$ is the set of values that can be *produced* by the function. In other words, the range is all possible values of $f(x)$, the *outputs* of the function. These outputs are the y values in the (x,y) coordinate plane. Range questions are not very common on the ACT, and the method for finding range is not as straightforward as that of domain. You should, however, be able to recognize the range of a function by looking at the function's graph. Don't forget, you may use your graphing calculator if the function is given.

Try the following lesson problem:

42. The graph of the function $f(x) = \dfrac{-1}{x-1} + 2$ is shown below. Which of the following could be the range of the function f?

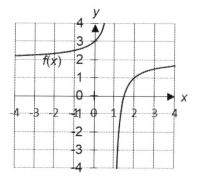

A. $\{y \mid y \neq 1\}$
B. $\{y \mid y \neq 2\}$
C. $\{y \mid y \neq 3\}$
D. $\{x \mid x \neq 1\}$
E. $\{x \mid x \neq 2\}$

ASYMPTOTES

An asymptote is a straight line that is approached by a function. The function will never reach the line (in any finite distance). Asymptotes show up when we have *rational expressions*, which are expressions of the form $\dfrac{p(x)}{q(x)}$, where p and q are polynomial functions. There are two kinds of asymptotes:

VERTICAL ASYMPTOTES

Vertical asymptotes are usually found at the zeros of the denominator, $q(x)$, of a *simplified* rational expression (in other words, at the places where the function $\dfrac{p(x)}{q(x)}$ is undefined).

Note: Make sure you factor and simplify the rational expression *before* finding vertical asymptotes. Sometimes factors can be canceled, in which case any corresponding zeros will *not* be vertical asymptotes (they are called "holes").

HORIZONTAL ASYMPTOTES

A function approaches a *horizontal asymptote* (when there is one) as x approaches $\pm\infty$. Here are the rules (review *degrees* in the Working with Polynomials section, if necessary):

- If the degree of $p(x)$ is less than the degree of $q(x)$, then the horizontal asymptote is $y = 0$.

  For example: $\dfrac{p(x)}{q(x)} = \dfrac{5x^2 - 6x + 7}{4x^3 - 6x + 7}$ → $(2 < 3)$ → horizontal asymptote: $y = 0$

- If the degree of $p(x)$ is equal to the degree of $q(x)$, then the horizontal asymptote is the leading coefficient of $p(x)$ divided by the leading coefficient of $q(x)$.

  For example: $\dfrac{p(x)}{q(x)} = \dfrac{5x^2 - 6x + 7}{4x^2 - 6x + 7}$ → $(2 = 2)$ → horizontal asymptote: $y = \dfrac{5}{4}$

- If the degree of $p(x)$ is greater than the degree of $q(x)$, then there is no horizontal asymptote.

  For example: $\dfrac{p(x)}{q(x)} = \dfrac{5x^3 - 6x + 7}{4x^2 - 6x + 7}$ → $(3 > 2)$ → no horizontal asymptote

SYMMETRY

When a function is symmetrical across an axis or a line, it appears to have a mirror image reflected across that axis or line. The quadratic function is a common function that is symmetrical across some vertical line. In the figure below, the line of symmetry is $x = 2$.

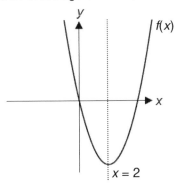

45. The figure above shows a quadratic function f. The vertex of f is $(2, -4)$. If two points (not shown) on f are $(-2, 12)$ and $(a, 12)$ and $a > 0$, what is the value for a?

    A. 12
    B. 6
    C. 4
    D. 2
    E. 0

TRANSFORMATIONS

Some questions may ask you to identify the effects of a *transformation* on the graph of a function. There are several types of transformations, including movements (translations), reflections, stretches, contractions, and rotations.

REFLECTIONS

As mentioned in the previous section, a *reflection* creates a mirror image of a shape across a line (called the *line of reflection*). For example, $\triangle A'B'C'$ is the reflection of $\triangle ABC$ across line *l* below:

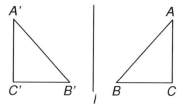

ROTATIONS

A *rotation* spins a shape around some given point. Rotation problems tend to use degrees to tell you how much to spin the shape. For example, point *A'* below is a 90° clockwise rotation of point *A* around the point (0,0):

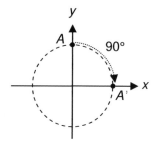

ALGEBRAIC TRANSFORMATIONS

Sometimes, instead of *visually* transforming a graph, as in the examples above, you may have to transform a graph by making changes to the function's *algebraic expression*. If you've covered this in school, the following offers a good review of the material. If you have not yet covered this, you might want to skip this part of the lesson. These algebraic transformations are not common on the ACT.

TRANSFORMATION RULES FOR MOVING (OR TRANSLATING) A FUNCTION

- $f(x) + a$ → moves graph UP a units
- $f(x) - a$ → moves graph DOWN a units
- $f(x + a)$ → moves graph to the LEFT a units
- $f(x - a)$ → moves graph to the RIGHT a units

TRANSFORMATION RULES FOR REFLECTING A FUNCTION

- $-f(x)$ → reflects graph across *x-axis*
- $f(-x)$ → reflects graph across *y-axis*

TRANSFORMATION RULES FOR STRETCHING/CONTRACTING A FUNCTION

- $af(x)$, where $a > 1$ → STRETCHES the graph vertically
- $af(x)$, where $0 < a < 1$ → CONTRACTS the graph vertically
- $f(ax)$, where $a > 1$ → CONTRACTS the graph horizontally
- $f(ax)$, where $0 < a < 1$ → STRETCHES the graph horizontally

Transformation questions involve the *movement* (or *translation*), *reflection*, *rotation*, *stretch*, or *contraction* of a graph of a function. *Algebraic* transformations ask about the change in the graph of a function when that function is algebraically changed in some way.

Try the following lesson problem:

58. The graph of $f(x)$ is shown below. Which of the following could be the graph of $-f(x-1)$?

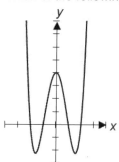

A.

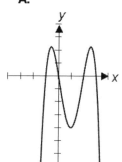

C.

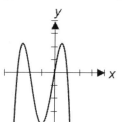

E.

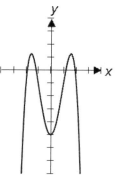

B.

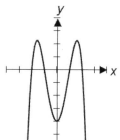

D.

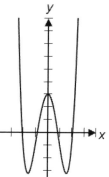

■

14. In the standard (x,y) coordinate plane, $\triangle ABC$ has vertices $(-2,-2)$, $(-1,4)$, and $(2,3)$.

Suppose $\triangle ABC$ is transposed 1 unit to the right and 2 units up to form $\triangle A'B'C'$. Which of the following shows the coordinates for the vertices of $\triangle A'B'C'$?

   A. $(0,-1)$, $(0,6)$, $(4,5)$
   B. $(0,-1)$, $(1,5)$, $(4,5)$
   C. $(-1,0)$, $(1,6)$, $(3,1)$
   D. $(-1,0)$, $(0,6)$, $(3,5)$
   E. $(-1,0)$, $(1,6)$, $(3,5)$

34. Which of the following could be the graph of $f(x) = ax^6 + bx^3 + cx + 2$, where a, b, and c are negative integers?

A.
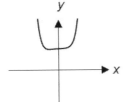

D.
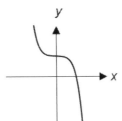

B.
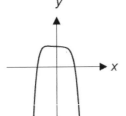

E.
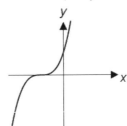

C.
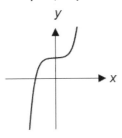

Continued →

42. What is the domain of the function f, defined below?

$$f(x) = (x+2)^{\frac{1}{4}}$$

   A. All real numbers
   B. $x \geq -2$
   C. $x \geq 0$
   D. $x \geq \frac{1}{4}$
   E. $x \geq 2$

60. The figures below show the graphs of f and g. The function f is defined by $f(x) = x^2 + 2x + 3$. The function g is defined by $g(x) = f(x + h) + k$, where h and k are constants. What is the value of $h - k$?

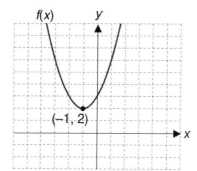 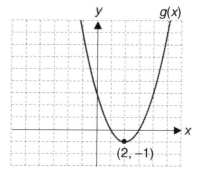

   F. -6
   G. -3
   H. 0
   J. 3
   K. 6

4. FUNCTIONS AS MODELS

Functions are often used to *model* real life situations. These problems are very similar to some of the problems we've already seen in the Algebraic Word Problems section. They often look difficult because they are wordy and may contain complicated-sounding formulas, but they are usually much easier than the look. Typically, you'll only have to plug in a few values to find your answer.

Be aggressive on Functions as Models questions. They usually turn out to be easier than they look.

 These questions provide a function or formula that models some real life situation. The functions may appear complicated, and the questions are often wordy.

(EX) The position, p, of a rolling bowling ball on a bowling alley is given by the function $p(t) = vt$, where v is the initial velocity of the ball, in feet per second, t is time, in seconds, and p is the distance, in feet, from the start of the alley where the ball is thrown. If a bowling alley is 63 feet long and a bowling ball is rolled at an initial velocity of 10½ feet per second, how long, in seconds, will it take for the bowling ball to reach the pins?

A. 5
B. 6
C. 7
D. 8
E. 9

Try the following lesson problem:

34. Dennis deposited $1000 into a savings account that paid 2% interest per year. The amount of money in the account n years from the original deposit is given by the function M, where

$$M(n) = 1000\left(\tfrac{51}{50}\right)^n.$$

Approximately how much money will be in the account, in dollars, after 10 years?

A. 1002
B. 1200
C. 1219
D. 1220
E. 10,200

24. If the profit, in dollars, of a small company is given by the function P, where $P(x) = 100\sqrt{x}$, and x is the number of products sold, how many products must the company sell to make a profit of \$10,000?

   A. 10
   B. 1,000
   C. 1×10^4
   D. 1×10^6
   E. 1×10^8

36. The volume, V, of a cone is determined by the formula $V = \dfrac{1}{3}Bh$, where B is the area of the base of the cone and h is the height of the cone. What is the volume, in cubic centimeters, of a cone with a base area of 60 square centimeters and a height of 10 centimeters?

   F. 200
   G. 300
   H. 400
   J. 500
   K. 600

5. *FUNCTIONS PROBLEMS*

PRACTICE PROBLEMS

The worksheets on the following pages test techniques taught in this chapter. For additional practice, we'll use problems from Test 5 in *The Official ACT Prep Guide*.

- ☐ Functions Worksheet 1 (Sections 1 and 2)
- ☐ Functions Worksheet 2 (All Sections)
- ☐ ***The Official ACT Prep Guide*: Test 5**: Only tackle questions related to *this chapter*. For a list of these relevant questions, see the Techniques chapter at the end of this tutorial (first page of "Techniques: Test 5").

Reminders:

- **Use techniques**: These assignments are "open book." Go back to the tutorial as often as you need to, and use techniques aggressively.
- **No timing**: Do *not* time yourself on these assignments.
- **Scheduling**: See the Tutoring Schedules section in the Introduction for more details on scheduling.

TEST CORRECTIONS

After each practice test is graded, you should correct questions related to this chapter that you missed or guessed on. See "Correcting Practice Tests" in the Introduction for more details. Here are the three steps to correcting practice tests:

1. Turn to the Techniques chapter at the end of this tutorial and circle the Functions questions that you missed or guessed on for the test you are correcting.
2. Correct the problems in *The Official ACT Prep Guide*. As you correct the problems, go back to the tutorial and review the techniques. The idea is to (1) identify techniques that have given you trouble, (2) go back to the tutorial so you can review and strengthen these techniques, and (3) apply these techniques to the specific problems on which you struggled.
3. If you have trouble identifying the best technique to use for a problem, refer to the Techniques chapter. This is an important part of correcting the tests.

FUNCTIONS WORKSHEET 1 (SECTIONS 1 AND 2)

4. Let the function f be defined as $f(x) = 3x^2 - 15x$. What is the value of $f(5)$?

   A. -75
   B. -25
   C. -15
   D. 0
   E. 75

14. If $f(x) = 2x^2 + x$ and $g(x) = 5x$, what is the value of $f(2) \times g(2)$?

   F. 1
   G. 10
   H. 20
   J. 100
   K. 1,000

20. The graph of $f(x)$ is shown on a standard (x,y) coordinate plane below. Which of the following is NOT a zero of $f(x)$?

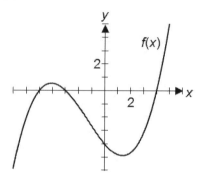

   A. -5
   B. -4
   C. -3
   D. 4
   E. All of the above are zeroes of $f(x)$

22. A function f is defined as $f(x,y,z) = \dfrac{x^y}{y^z}$. What is $f(2,4,3)$?

   A. $\dfrac{1}{4}$

   B. $\dfrac{1}{2}$

   C. 4

   D. 16

   E. 32

Continued →

32. If $f(x) = 2x + 5$ and $g(x) = x^2$, what is the value of $g[f(x)]$?

    A. $4x^2 + 25$
    B. $4x^2 + 20x + 25$
    C. $2x^2 + 20x + 25$
    D. $2x^2 + 10x + 5$
    E. $2x^2 + 5$

36. Let the function f be defined by $f(x) = \left| x^2 - 6 \right|$. When $f(x) = 5$, what is one possible value of

    $x - 6$?

    F. -25
    G. -7
    H. -6
    J. -1
    K. 0

55. If $f(x) = ax^{\frac{1}{3}}$ and point A lies on the graph of $f(x)$ below, what is the value of a?

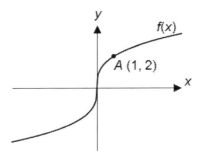

    A. $\dfrac{1}{3}$

    B. $\dfrac{1}{2}$

    C. 2

    D. 4

    E. 6

Continued →

57. Which of the following functions in standard (x,y) coordinate planes is an even function?

F.   **H.**   **K.**

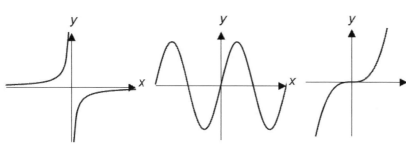

G.   **J.**

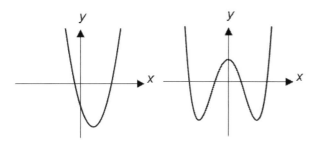

FUNCTIONS WORKSHEET 2 (ALL SECTIONS)

12. Point *P* lies in the standard (x,y) coordinate plane and has coordinates (2,2). Suppose point *P* is translated 4 units to the left, then translated 4 units down, and then reflected across the *y-axis*, forming point *P'*. What are the coordinates of *P'*?

   A. (2,2)
   B. (2,–2)
   C. (–2,2)
   D. (–2,–2)
   E. (0,–4)

16. The graph of $f(x)$ in the standard (x,y) coordinate plane is shown below. For what value or values of *x*, if any, is $f(x) = 4$?

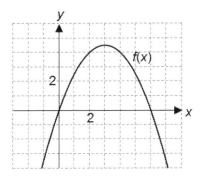

   A. 0 and 6 only
   B. 2 only
   C. 4 only
   D. 2 and 4 only
   E. No real values

19. For which value or values of *x* is the expression $\dfrac{(x-4)}{(x+3)(x-2)}$ undefined?

   F. 4 only
   G. –3 only
   H. –3 and 2 only
   J. 3 and –2 only
   K. –3, 2, and 4

Continued →

34. To study population growth, a biologist released 70 frogs on an island. The population, p, of frogs on the island is given by the function $p(t) = 300t^{\frac{3}{4}} + 70$, where t is the number of days after the frogs were released. According to this function, how many frogs will be on the island after 1 year (1 year = 365 days)?

F. $300(1)^{\frac{3}{4}} + 70$

G. $300^{\frac{3}{4}} + 70$

H. $300(365)^{\frac{3}{4}} + 70$

J. $365^{\frac{3}{4}} + 70$

K. $(300 \cdot 365)^{\frac{3}{4}} + 70$

43. For a certain pipe, the velocity, v, of water flow is given by the formula $v = 50\sqrt{\dfrac{h^2 d}{1 + 71d}}$ where h is the head length coefficient of the pipe and d is the diameter of the pipe. What is the velocity, in feet per second, of water flow for a 1 foot diameter pipe of this type if the head length coefficient is 12 feet per second?

A. 30
B. 40
C. 50
D. $50\sqrt{2}$
E. $50\sqrt{5}$

44. The graph of $f(x)$ in the standard (x,y) coordinate plane is shown below. For what real values of x, if any, is $f(x) < 0$?

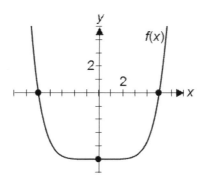

A. $-5 < x < 5$
B. $x > -1$
C. $x < -1$
D. $x < -5$ or $x > 5$
E. No real values

Continued →

45. The graphs of $f(x)$ and $nf(x)$ are shown in the standard (x,y) coordinate plane below, where n is a constant. What is a possible value of n?

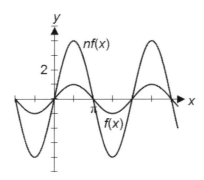

F. -4

G. -1

H. 0

J. $\dfrac{1}{4}$

K. 4

46. The graph of $y = \dfrac{x-7}{x+7}$ in the standard (x,y) coordinate plane has a vertical asymptote with equation $x = ?$

A. 7

B. 1

C. $\dfrac{-3}{4}$

D. -1

E. -7

47. If $f(x) = 2x^2$, then what is the value of $\dfrac{f(x+h) - f(x)}{h}$?

F. $4x + 2h$

G. $2x + 4h$

H. $4x^2 + 2h$

J. $2x^2 + 2h$

K. $2x^2 + 4h$

Continued →

52. In the standard (x,y) coordinate plane, the equation of line l is $y = -3x - 4$. If line m is the reflection of line l across the y-axis, what is the equation of line m?

    A. $y = -3x + 4$
    B. $y = 3x + 4$
    C. $y = 3x - 4$
    D. $y = \frac{3}{4}x - 4$
    E. $y = \frac{3}{4}x + 4$

58. In the figure below, $ABCD$ is a square centered on the y-axis. If points B and C lie on the graph $y = ax^4$ where a is a constant, what is the value of a?

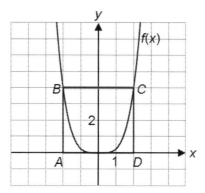

    F. 4
    G. 2
    H. 1
    J. $\dfrac{1}{2}$
    K. $\dfrac{1}{4}$

VII
TRIGONOMETRY

This chapter covers what you need to know about trigonometry (we'll call it "trig" for short). If you haven't covered trig yet in school, then you might just go over Section 1: Basic Trigonometry. This section covers about half of the trig you'll see on the ACT. If you're looking to maximize your score, or if you've covered trig in school and feel pretty comfortable with it, then tackle the whole chapter.

1. BASIC TRIGONOMETRY

Basic trigonometry, or *trig*, is the study of the relations between the angles and the sides of *right triangles*. Look at the triangle below:

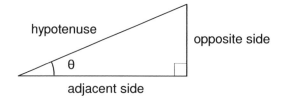

In a right triangle, each trig function of an angle is a ratio of 2 of the sides of the triangle. Notice that relative to each angle (such as the angle θ—pronounced "THEY-tuh"—in the figure above), there is an *opposite* side, an *adjacent* side, and the *hypotenuse*. Note that the hypotenuse is always the longest side of the triangle and is always opposite the right angle. **Don't confuse the hypotenuse with one of the other sides.** Let's get started with an important word:

SOHCAHTOA

Memorize this acronym. It will help you remember the basic trig functions:

SOH: The **Sine** (*sin* for short) of an angle is the ratio of the **Opposite** side to the **Hypotenuse**:

$$\sin\theta = \frac{\text{opposite}}{\text{hypotenuse}} = \frac{O}{H}$$

CAH: The **Cosine** (*cos* for short) of an angle is the ratio of the **Adjacent** side to the **Hypotenuse**:

$$\cos\theta = \frac{\text{adjacent}}{\text{hypotenuse}} = \frac{A}{H}$$

TOA: The **Tangent** (*tan* for short) of an angle is the ratio of the **Opposite** side to the **Adjacent** side:

$$\tan\theta = \frac{\text{opposite}}{\text{adjacent}} = \frac{O}{A}$$

NO NEED FOR A CALCULATOR

You can use your calculator to find the values of trig functions (look for the SIN, COS, and TAN keys), but you'll never actually *have* to use it. The ACT does not require the use of a calculator. If you know how to use your calculator with trig, great—but if you don't, don't worry about it.

(EX) In the right triangle below, what is the value of cos θ?

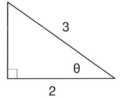

A. $\dfrac{2}{3}$

B. $\dfrac{3}{2}$

C. $\dfrac{\sqrt{5}}{3}$

D. $\dfrac{\sqrt{5}}{2}$

E. $\sqrt{5}$

FINDING MISSING INFORMATION

The power of trig is that it allows us to find the missing sides of any right triangle when we know just *one* of the sides. In the past, we could only do this with the two special right triangles (30-60-90 and 45-45-90). So trig is an important tool. Let's put it to work:

(EX) Side *BC* of △*ABC* below is 10 inches long. If the sin of ∠*A* is $\frac{5}{13}$, how long, in inches, is the hypotenuse of the triangle?

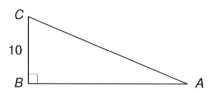

A. 12
B. 13
C. 24
D. 26
E. 28

THE SPECIAL RIGHT TRIANGLES, REVISITED

Remember these?

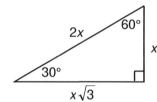
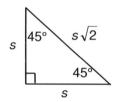

Sometimes, you will be asked for the trig functions of the special angles: 30°, 45°, and 60°. If you have the two special right triangles memorized, you can quickly find these trig values. First, let $x = s = 1$, above, so you have the following triangles:

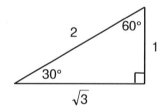
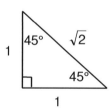

Now, just by looking at these triangles, you can find the trig functions of important angles. Try filling in the information in the following table.

	30°	45°	60°
sin			
cos			
tan			

Note: Unless you're comfortable working with radicals, some of these functions can be tricky. It's probably not that important to stay in radical form. Just use decimals if you'd like. If you do want to stay in radical form, that's great—it might save time when you look at answer choices. Below is how you would find sin 45°, for example:

$$\sin 45° = \frac{O}{A} = \frac{1}{\sqrt{2}} = \frac{1}{\sqrt{2}}\frac{\sqrt{2}}{\sqrt{2}} = \frac{\sqrt{2}}{2}$$

As you can see, it can get a little tricky. You can either memorize the values, or just use decimals.

■

BASIC TRIGONOMETRY LESSON PROBLEMS

43. What is the value of tan θ in the triangle shown below?

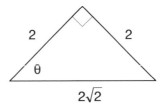

A. $2 + 2\sqrt{2}$

B. 2

C. $\sqrt{2}$

D. 1

E. $\dfrac{1}{\sqrt{2}}$

58. Henry wants to measure the length of the pond shown below. If the length of leg *YZ* of △*XYZ* is 50 feet and the measure of ∠*X* is 20°, which of following expresses the length of the pond?

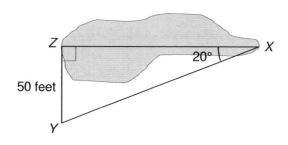

F. $\dfrac{50}{\sin 20°}$

G. $\dfrac{50}{\cos 20°}$

H. $\dfrac{50}{\tan 20°}$

J. $50 \sin 20°$

K. $50 \tan 20°$

30. In the right triangle pictured below, *x*, *y*, and *z* are the lengths of its sides, as shown. What is the value of cos θ?

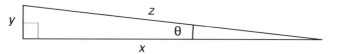

A. $\dfrac{x}{y}$

B. $\dfrac{y}{x}$

C. $\dfrac{x}{z}$

D. $\dfrac{y}{z}$

E. $\dfrac{z}{y}$

60. Right triangle *ABC* is shown below. Which of the following is equal to sin α − cos β?

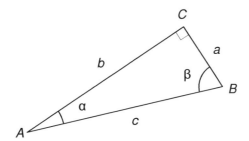

F. 0

G. 1

H. $\dfrac{a-b}{c}$

J. $\dfrac{a-c}{b}$

K. $\dfrac{a}{c} - \dfrac{a}{b}$

2. TRIG & THE UNIT CIRCLE

We can analyze trig functions for the angles of right triangles, but what if we're dealing with angles that wouldn't fit into a right triangle? For example, what's the cosine of 120°? This angle could not be part of a right triangle—it's too big—but it *does* have a cosine. That's where the unit circle comes in.

THE UNIT CIRCLE

THE FOUR QUADRANTS

The unit circle has a radius equal to 1 and is centered at the origin of a standard (x,y) coordinate plane. The x- and y-axes divide the circle into four quadrants, labeled I, II, III, and IV below.

! **Notice that the top right quadrant is I, and the subsequent quadrants are numbered *counterclockwise*.**

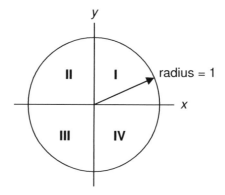

ANGLES

The circle is used to display the measures of angles. Like the quadrants, the angles are measured *counterclockwise* from the positive side of the *x-axis*. The example below shows the angle 120°. The line where the angle ends is called the *terminal side* of the angle:

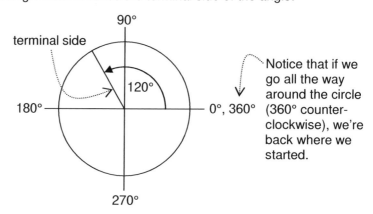

REFERENCE TRIANGLE

If you draw a *vertical* line to the *x-axis* from the end of the angle's terminal side, you create what is called a *reference triangle*. This is a right triangle. Remember, the unit circle has a radius of 1, so the hypotenuse of this right triangle is 1. **Make sure you always draw a *vertical* line to the *x-axis*.**

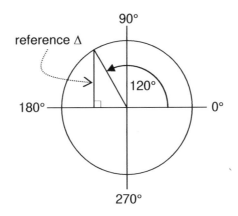

REFERENCE ANGLE

Let's enlarge the triangle. Can you calculate the measure of the angle between the *x-axis* and the terminal side? This is an important angle. It's called the *reference angle*.

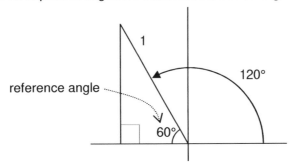

The reason for looking at these reference triangles and reference angles is that they allow us to find trig functions of larger angles. Remember our original question? What's the cosine of 120°? We couldn't figure that out because 120° isn't part of a right triangle, but the reference angle for 120°, which we found to be 60°, *is* part of a right triangle. So:

$$\overset{?}{\cos 120° = \cos 60°}$$

Not quite. We have to think about one more thing:

THE QUADRANTS AND THE TRIG FUNCTIONS

Reference angles and triangles will give us the *absolute value* of a trig function, but we need to know whether the trig function is positive or negative. That's where the four quadrants and the initialism *ASTC* come in to play:

Starting in Quadrant I and moving counterclockwise (as usual), we write *ASTC*. There are several ways to memorize this initialism. The most popular is "All Students Take Calculus." Feel free to think of your own. Just remember to move in a *counterclockwise* direction from Quadrant I.

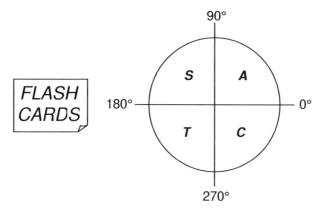

Each letter tells us something important about the trig functions in that letter's quadrant:

- ***A***: All trig functions are positive in Quadrant I.
- ***S***: Sine only is positive in Quadrant II.
- ***T***: Tangent only is positive in Quadrant III.
- ***C***: Cosine only is positive in Quadrant IV.

USING THE UNIT CIRCLE TO FIND TRIG FUNCTIONS: SUMMARY

Finally, we can answer the original question. What is the cosine of 120°? The reference angle tells us that the absolute value of cos 120° is equal to cos 60°. But we're in Quadrant II, so cosine must be *negative*. So we have:

$$\cos 120° = -\cos 60°$$

If you remember the special right triangles, you can find that $\cos 60° = \dfrac{1}{2}$, so:

$$\cos 120° = -\cos 60° = -\dfrac{1}{2}, \text{ and we're done!}$$

Here's a summary of the method:

1. Draw the angle in question on a unit circle.
2. Draw the reference triangle and identify the reference angle.
3. Consider the sign of the trig function (positive or negative) by using the *ASTC* initialism.
4. Find the trig function of the reference angle, and apply the correct sign from step 3.

> There are a few ways you can identify these trig problems. Some problems will have a drawing of a unit circle. Otherwise, look for a reference to one of the quadrants—such as the degree inequality shown in the example below—or look for large angles (> 90°) that wouldn't fit into a right triangle.

Here's how the ACT will typically test trig and the unit circle:

(EX) If $180° \leq x \leq 270°$ and $\sin x = -\dfrac{4}{5}$, then $\cos x = ?$

A. $-\dfrac{3}{5}$

B. $-\dfrac{4}{5}$

C. $-\dfrac{3}{4}$

D. $\dfrac{3}{5}$

E. $\dfrac{3}{4}$

COORDINATES

An interesting thing about the points along the unit circle is that they can tell you the sine and cosine of an angle. **Each *x-coordinate* is the *cosine* of the related angle, and each *y-coordinate* is the *sine* of the related angle.**

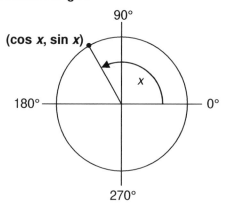

FOUR IMPORTANT POINTS

The most useful reason for memorizing the relationship above (cos *x*, sin *x*) is that you can find the trig functions for angles that don't have reference triangles, namely (0°, 90°, 180°, and 270°):

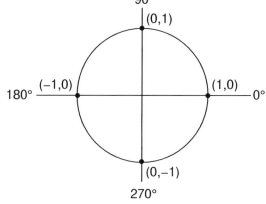

$$\cos 0° = 1, \sin 0° = 0$$
$$\cos 90° = 0, \sin 90° = 1$$
$$\cos 180° = -1, \sin 180° = 0$$
$$\cos 270° = 0, \sin 270° = -1$$

You shouldn't have to memorize these values. Just use the unit circle, and remember that cos *x* is the *x-coordinate* and sin *x* is the *y-coordinate*.

DEGREES AND RADIANS

Up until now, we've only worked with degrees when measuring an angle. Sometimes, the ACT will use alternate units of measurement called *radians*. Radians may look and sound complicated, but if you memorize the following proportion, you can always switch back and forth.

$$\boxed{\textit{FLASH} \atop \textit{CARDS}} \quad \frac{\text{degrees}}{\text{radians}} \frac{180°}{\pi} = \frac{?}{?}$$

Let's use this proportion to find a few important radian measures:

(EX) What is the radian measure of 90°?

1. What is the radian measure of 180°?

2. What is the radian measure of 270°?

3. What is the radian measure of 360°?

THE UNIT CIRCLE, WITH RADIANS

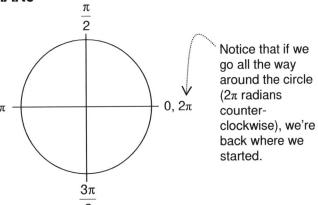

Notice that if we go all the way around the circle (2π radians counterclockwise), we're back where we started.

TRIG AND YOUR CALCULATOR

While you won't ever *have* to use your calculator to find values of trig functions, that doesn't mean it won't come in handy. Here are a couple things to watch out for when you use your calculator on a trig question:

DEGREES/RADIANS

Most calculators have separate modes for *radians* and *degrees*. Make sure you have your calculator set correctly. If you're in radian mode and you type in degrees, your answer will be incorrect (and vice versa).

POWERS OF TRIG FUNCTIONS

You have to be careful when you raise a trig function to a power. For example, how do we square the sin x? Math books will usually notate $(\sin x)^2$ as $\sin^2 x$. This makes clear that the entire function is squared, not just the variable (x). For most calculators, you can type either: $(\sin (x))^2$ or $\sin (x)^2$. Just make sure you don't type $\sin (x^2)$; this will not give the correct answer (unless of course you're looking for the sine of x^2).

■

UNIT CIRCLE LESSON PROBLEMS

51. If tan $x \approx 0.577$, which of the following could be true about x?

   A. $90° \leq x \leq 135°$
   B. $135° \leq x \leq 180°$
   C. $180° \leq x \leq 225°$
   D. $270° \leq x \leq 315°$
   E. $315° \leq x \leq 360°$

57. If $\sin \theta = -\dfrac{5}{13}$, and $\dfrac{3\pi}{2} \leq \theta \leq 2\pi$, then $\tan \theta = $?

   F. $\dfrac{12}{13}$

   G. $-\dfrac{13}{12}$

   H. $-\dfrac{12}{5}$

   J. $-\dfrac{12}{13}$

   K. $-\dfrac{5}{12}$

49. If $\cos x = a$, where $\dfrac{\pi}{2} \leq x \leq \pi$, then what is $\sin x$?

  A. $\dfrac{1}{a}$

  B. $-\dfrac{1}{a}$

  C. $-a$

  D. $\dfrac{1}{\sqrt{1-a^2}}$

  E. $\sqrt{1-a^2}$

54. If $\cos 30° = \dfrac{\sqrt{3}}{2}$, what is $\cos 330°$?

  F. 1

  G. $\dfrac{\sqrt{3}}{2}$

  H. $\dfrac{1}{2}$

  J. $-\dfrac{1}{2}$

  K. $-\dfrac{\sqrt{3}}{2}$

■

30- and 40-hour programs: Jump to the end of this chapter and complete Trigonometry Worksheet 1 and relevant test corrections for Tests 1 and 2. Then move on to the Odds & Ends chapter. If you're in the **40-hour program**, you'll finish the Trigonometry chapter later (see the Tutoring Schedules in the Introduction).

3. GRAPHS OF SINE & COSINE

You may have noticed that we've used the word *function* to refer to sine, cosine, and tangent. They are, indeed, functions, and like other functions, they can be graphed on a standard (x,y) coordinate plane. Our inputs, x, are the measure of angles (in degrees or radians). Our outputs, y, are the values of the trig function for those angles. It's a safe bet that you'll only have to worry about sine and cosine graphs on the ACT. Here's what they look like:

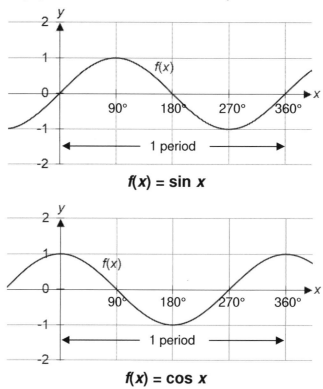

$$f(x) = \sin x$$

$$f(x) = \cos x$$

If you ever forget which graph is which, just type sin 0 (or cos 0) into your calculator to see which one goes through (0,0). Also, note that the graphs above are the graphs of points as you go around the *unit circle*. For example, the unit circle shows us that at $\theta = 180°$, $\cos \theta = -1$. You can see this point on the second graph above. This is an important connection to make.

The ACT is *not* going to expect you to memorize much about these graphs, but you should understand some of their basic features.

PERIOD

Trig functions are called *periodic functions* because they keep repeating. Notice that when the graph reaches 360°, it looks the same as it did at 0°. (If you think about the unit circle, which also begins repeating at 360°, this may not surprise you.) The *period* is the x distance that the function travels before it begins repeating again, as shown in the graphs above. For the standard functions of both sine and cosine:

$$\text{period} = 360° \text{ (or } 2\pi)$$

PERIOD FOR OTHER TRIG FUNCTIONS

On recent ACTs, we've seen a couple period questions for tangent functions (tan θ) and "reciprocal" trig functions—cosecant (csc θ), secant (sec θ), and cotangent (cot θ) (we'll cover these functions in the Trigonometry Odds & Ends section). Instead of going over the graphs of these other functions, just remember, again, that the period is the x distance that the function travels before it begins repeating. You should be able to identify the period of any function just by looking at its graph.

AMPLITUDE

The amplitude is the measure of the vertical distance from the *midline*, or *neutral axis* (often the x-axis), to the function's highest (or lowest) point. Look back to the graphs. For both sin x and cos x, the function never goes higher than 1 (or lower than –1). For the standard functions of both sine and cosine:

$$\text{amplitude} = 1$$

The graph below displays the amplitude and period for a general sine or cosine function:

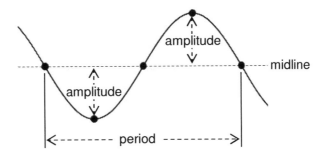

RADIANS

In the graphs above, the units for the *x-axis* are *degrees*. More typically, graphs of trig functions will use *radians*, as shown below. If necessary, review degree to radian conversions in the Basic Trigonometry section.

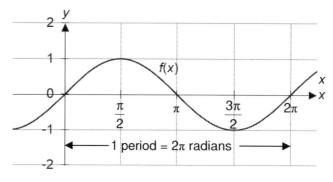

$$f(x) = \sin x$$

IMPORTANT POINTS

Notice some of the important points on the two graphs:

- $\sin 0 = \sin 2\pi = 0$, $\cos 0 = \cos 2\pi = 1$
- $\sin \dfrac{\pi}{2} = 1$, $\cos \dfrac{\pi}{2} = 0$
- $\sin \pi = 0$, $\cos \pi = -1$
- $\sin \dfrac{3\pi}{2} = -1$, $\cos \dfrac{3\pi}{2} = 0$

TRANSFORMATIONS

The ACT may ask you to *transform* a trig function. All of the transformation rules that you learned in Chapter VI apply to trig functions. For example, if you multiply a trig function by a positive number greater than 1, as with $f(x) = 4\sin x$, the trig function will *stretch* vertically by a factor of that number (multiply by 4). Similarly, if you multiply the *x* part of the function by a number greater than 1, as with $f(x) = \sin 4x$, the function (and its period) will *contract* horizontally by a factor of that number (divide by 4). You might want to review the transformations in the More Graphs of Functions section.

Try the following lesson problems:

45. What is the period of the function $f(x) = 4\sin(3x)$?

  A. $\dfrac{\pi}{4}$

  B. $\dfrac{\pi}{3}$

  C. $\dfrac{2\pi}{3}$

  D. 3π

  E. 2π

54. Which of the following displays the graph $y = 2 \sin x$?

  A.

  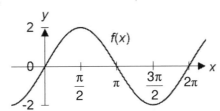

  D.

  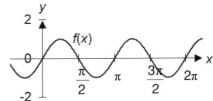

  B.

  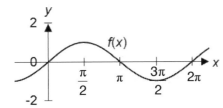

  E.

  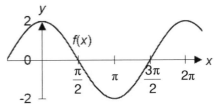

  C.

  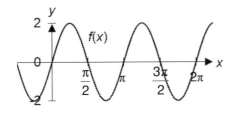

44. The graph of $y = \tan\left(\dfrac{x}{2}\right)$ is shown in the standard (x, y) coordinate plan below. What is the period of $\tan\left(\dfrac{x}{2}\right)$?

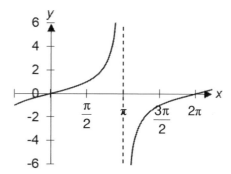

A. $\dfrac{1}{2}$

B. $\dfrac{\pi}{2}$

C. 2

D. π

E. 2π

57. The following figure shows the graph of $y = \cos bx$, where b is a constant and the period of the function is equal to $\dfrac{2\pi}{b}$. What is the value of b?

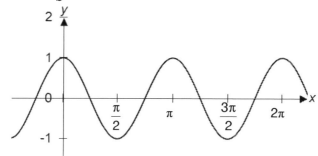

A. $\dfrac{1}{2}$

B. 2

C. π

D. 2π

E. 4π

4. THE LAWS OF SINES & COSINES

So far, trigonometry works great with *right* triangles, but in the real world not all triangles are right. That's where the Law of Sines and the Law of Cosines come in.

THE LAW OF SINES

Notice that the letter we use for each side is the lowercase version of the angle opposite that side. This is standard notation. Here's the Law of Sines:

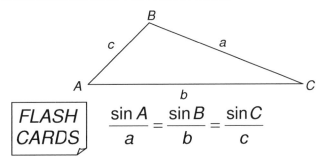

FLASH CARDS

$$\frac{\sin A}{a} = \frac{\sin B}{b} = \frac{\sin C}{c}$$

 First of all, these problems deal with **non-right triangles**. The ACT will probably make it easy to recognize Law of Sines problems. They'll probably even mention the "Law of Sines." In general, the Law of Sines can be used when you know either 2 sides and 1 opposite angle (SSA) or 2 angles and 1 opposite side (SAA).

You probably agree that the Law of Sines is fairly easy to memorize. Here's how it works:

(EX) In △ABC below, which of the following expresses the length of side AB?

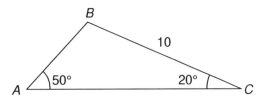

A. $\dfrac{10\sin 110°}{\sin 50°}$

B. $\dfrac{10\sin 110°}{\sin 20°}$

C. $\dfrac{10\sin 20°}{\sin 110°}$

D. $\dfrac{10\sin 20°}{\sin 50°}$

E. $\dfrac{10\sin 50°}{\sin 20°}$

THE LAW OF COSINES

The Law of Cosines is a little more complicated:

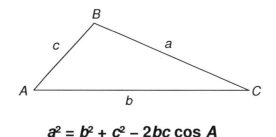

$$a^2 = b^2 + c^2 - 2bc \cos A$$

Notice a few things about this equation. The side on the left (*a*) will always match the angle on the right (*A*). The other two sides (*b* and *c*) form the rest of the right side of the equation. We only gave you one of the equations (the one for side *a*). The other two (for sides *b* and *c*) follow the same form. Here's the good news. **If the ACT tests the Law of Cosines, they will give you the equation!** So don't memorize it; just make sure you're comfortable using it. Here's an example:

(EX) In △*ABC* below, which of the following expressions gives the length of side *AC*? (Note: The Law of Cosines states that for any triangle with vertices *A*, *B*, and *C* and the sides opposite those vertices with lengths *a*, *b*, and *c*, respectively, $c^2 = a^2 + b^2 - 2ab \cos C$.)

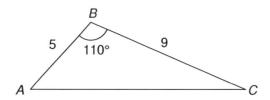

A. $\sqrt{16 \cos 110°}$

B. $\sqrt{106 \cos 110°}$

C. $\sqrt{14 - 90 \cos 110°}$

D. $\sqrt{106 - 90 \cos 110°}$

E. $\sqrt{106 - 45 \cos 110°}$

Again, these problems deal with **non-right triangles**. As you can see, the ACT will give you the Law of Cosines equation, so you'll know when you're working on a Law of Cosines problem. In general, the Law of Cosines can be used when you know either 2 sides and the included angle (SAS) or all 3 sides (SSS)—hint: think of a "SASsy SSSnake."

Try the following lesson problem:

47. Triangle *ABC* has sides of unit length 19, 20, and 21, as shown below. Which of the following equations could be used to find the measure of angle *B* of the triangle? (Note: The Law of Cosines states that for any triangle with vertices *A*, *B*, and *C* and the sides opposite those vertices with lengths *a*, *b*, and *c*, respectively, $c^2 = a^2 + b^2 - 2ab \cos C$.)

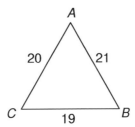

A. $\cos B = \dfrac{19^2 - 20^2 - 21^2}{-2(20)(21)}$

B. $\cos B = \dfrac{20^2 - 19^2 - 21^2}{-2(19)(21)}$

C. $\cos B = \dfrac{21^2 - 19^2 - 20^2}{-2(19)(20)}$

D. $\cos B = 19^2 - 20^2 - 21^2 - 2(20)(21)$

E. $\cos B = 20^2 - 19^2 - 21^2 - 2(19)(21)$

45. In △ABC below, which of the following expressions gives the length of side AC? (Note: The Law of Sines states that, for any triangle, the ratios of the sines of the interior angles to the lengths of the sides opposite those angles are equal.)

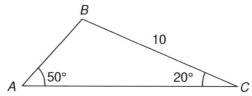

A. $\dfrac{10\sin 110°}{\sin 20°}$

B. $\dfrac{10\sin 110°}{\sin 50°}$

C. $\dfrac{10\sin 110°}{\sin 70°}$

D. $\dfrac{10\sin 20°}{\sin 50°}$

E. $\dfrac{10\sin 50°}{\sin 20°}$

Continued →

54. The radar screen below displays two approaching airplanes. Airplane A is 10 nautical miles from the control tower and bearing 45°, and airplane B is 15 nautical miles from the control tower and bearing 195°. Which of the following expressions would give the straight line distance, in nautical miles, between the 2 airplanes? (Note: The Law of Cosines states that for any triangle with vertices A, B, and C and the sides opposite those vertices with lengths a, b, and c, respectively, $c^2 = a^2 + b^2 - 2ab \cos C$.)

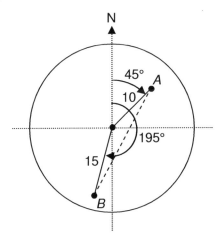

A. $\sqrt{15^2 + 10^2 - 2(15)(10)\cos 15°}$

B. $\sqrt{15^2 + 10^2 - 2(15)(10)\cos 45°}$

C. $\sqrt{15^2 + 10^2 - 2(15)(10)\cos 150°}$

D. $\sqrt{15^2 + 10^2 - 2(15)(10)\cos 195°}$

E. $\sqrt{15^2 + 10^2 - 2(15)(10)\cos 240°}$

5. TRIGONOMETRY ODDS & ENDS

INVERSE TRIG FUNCTIONS

Thus far, trig functions have been expressed as a function of *angles*. Angles are the inputs of the functions, and we get out numbers, which we know are ratios of sides of a triangle. For example, in the triangle below, $\sin \theta = \dfrac{O}{H}$.

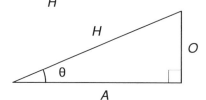

But what if we know the *sides* and want to find the *angle*? That's where we use inverse trig functions, which are notated with a raised −1. Below is the inverse function for sine:

$$\boldsymbol{\theta = \sin^{-1}\left(\dfrac{O}{H}\right)}$$

It's a good idea to be able to put $\sin^{-1}\left(\dfrac{O}{H}\right)$ into words: "The $\sin^{-1}\left(\dfrac{O}{H}\right)$ is the angle whose sine

is $\dfrac{O}{H}$." **The important thing to realize is that an inverse trig function gives you an angle.**

(Note: unlike regular exponent problems, $\sin^{-1} x \neq \dfrac{1}{\sin x}$.) Let's try an example:

(EX) For △ABC below, which of the following expressions gives the value of measure of ∠A?

A. $\sin^{-1}\left(\dfrac{3}{5}\right)$

B. $\sin^{-1}\left(\dfrac{4}{5}\right)$

C. $\cos^{-1}\left(\dfrac{3}{5}\right)$

D. $\cos^{-1}\left(\dfrac{3}{4}\right)$

E. $\tan^{-1}\left(\dfrac{4}{3}\right)$

If you're ever asked to find an angle using trigonometry, or if you see the raised –1 next to a standard trig function, then you know you're dealing with an inverse trig problem.

THE OTHER TRIG FUNCTIONS

You may come across 3 other trig functions: cosecant (csc), secant (sec), and cotangent (cot).

Each one is simply the inverse of one of the other trig functions that we've already seen.

$$\csc x = \frac{1}{\sin x}$$

FLASH CARDS

$$\sec x = \frac{1}{\cos x}$$

$$\cot x = \frac{1}{\tan x}$$

Questions involving the other trig functions are not common, but if you're looking for the maximum score possible, memorize the names and equations above.

TRIG PROPERTIES

There are only two trig properties that you should memorize for the ACT.

FLASH CARDS

$$\tan x = \frac{\sin x}{\cos x}$$

$$\sin^2 x + \cos^2 x = 1$$

These trig properties questions tend to look more *algebraic* and less *geometric* than other kinds of trig questions. Notice that there is no triangle in the example below.

(EX) Which of the following is equivalent to (tan x)(cos x) ?

　A. csc x
　B. sec x
　C. cot x
　D. sin x
　E. cos x

GIVEN FORMULAS

Some ACT problems will give you a trig formula. These formulas may look complicated, but typically you'll just have to plug in some numbers. Like other ACT problems that give you formulas, be aggressive. Many students are scared off by these problems, but you should find them easier than they look.

Try the following lesson problem:

48. In $\triangle ABC$ below, line segment AD is the angle bisector for $\angle A$. Which of the following gives the sin α ?

(Note: $\sin^2\left(\dfrac{x}{2}\right) = \dfrac{1}{2}(1 - \cos x)$, for all x.)

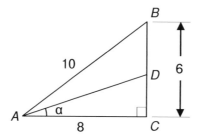

A. $\sqrt{\dfrac{1}{2}\left(1 - \dfrac{3}{4}\right)}$

B. $\sqrt{\dfrac{1}{2}\left(1 - \dfrac{3}{5}\right)}$

C. $\sqrt{\dfrac{1}{2}\left(1 - \dfrac{4}{5}\right)}$

D. $\sqrt{\dfrac{1}{2}\left(1 + \dfrac{3}{5}\right)}$

E. $\sqrt{\dfrac{1}{2}\left(1 + \dfrac{4}{5}\right)}$

■

TRIGONOMETRY ODDS & ENDS HOMEWORK

45. Right triangle ABC is shown below, with lengths in centimeters. Which of the following expressions is the length, in centimeters, of the hypotenuse of the triangle?

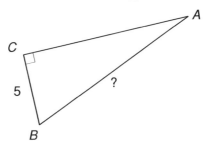

    A. 5 tan A
    B. 5 sin A
    C. 5 csc A
    D. 5 cos A
    E. 5 sec A

51. Which of the following is equivalent to the expression $(1 - \sin x)(1 + \sin x)$?

    F. $\cos^2 x$
    G. $\sin^2 x$
    H. 1
    J. $\cos x$
    K. $\sin x$

Continued →

59. A line connects vertices A and C of Quadrilateral $ABCD$, below, forming two right triangles.

Which of the following gives the degree measure of $\angle A$?

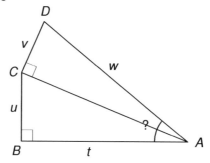

A. $\sin^{-1}\left(\dfrac{u}{t}\right) + \cos^{-1}\left(\dfrac{v}{w}\right)$

B. $\tan^{-1}\left(\dfrac{u}{t}\right) + \cos^{-1}\left(\dfrac{v}{w}\right)$

C. $\tan^{-1}\left(\dfrac{u}{t}\right) + \sin^{-1}\left(\dfrac{v}{w}\right)$

D. $\sin^{-1}\left(\dfrac{u}{t}\right) + \cos^{-1}\left(\dfrac{v}{w}\right)$

E. $\tan^{-1}\left(\dfrac{u}{t}\right) + \tan^{-1}\left(\dfrac{v}{w}\right)$

6. *TRIGONOMETRY PROBLEMS*

PRACTICE PROBLEMS

The worksheets on the following pages test techniques taught in this chapter. For additional practice, we'll use problems from Test 5 in *The Official ACT Prep Guide*.

- ☐ Trigonometry Worksheet 1 (Sections 1 and 2)
- ☐ Trigonometry Worksheet 2 (All Sections)
- ☐ ***The Official ACT Prep Guide*: Test 5**: Only tackle questions related to *this chapter*. For a list of these relevant questions, see the Techniques chapter at the end of this tutorial (first page of "Techniques: Test 5").

Reminders:

- **Use techniques**: These assignments are "open book." Go back to the tutorial as often as you need to, and use techniques aggressively.
- **No timing**: Do *not* time yourself on these assignments.
- **Scheduling**: See the Tutoring Schedules section in the Introduction for more details on scheduling.

TEST CORRECTIONS

After each practice test is graded, you should correct questions related to this chapter that you missed or guessed on. See "Correcting Practice Tests" in the Introduction for more details. Here are the three steps to correcting practice tests:

1. Turn to the Techniques chapter at the end of this tutorial and circle the Trigonometry questions that you missed or guessed on for the test you are correcting.
2. Correct the problems in *The Official ACT Prep Guide*. As you correct the problems, go back to the tutorial and review the techniques. The idea is to (1) identify techniques that have given you trouble, (2) go back to the tutorial so you can review and strengthen these techniques, and (3) apply these techniques to the specific problems on which you struggled.
3. If you have trouble identifying the best technique to use for a problem, refer to the Techniques chapter. This is an important part of correcting the tests.

TRIGONOMETRY WORKSHEET 1 (SECTIONS 1 AND 2)

23. In right triangle △ABC below, which of the following is equal to sin A?

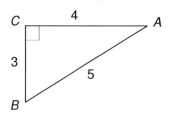

A. sin B
B. cos B
C. tan B
D. cos A
E. tan A

35. A line through the origin and point (5, 4) creates an angle of θ with the positive x-axis, as shown in the standard (x, y) coordinate plane below. What is the value of tan θ ?

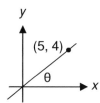

A. $\dfrac{4}{\sqrt{41}}$

B. $\dfrac{5}{\sqrt{41}}$

C. $\dfrac{\sqrt{41}}{5}$

D. $\dfrac{4}{5}$

E. $\dfrac{5}{4}$

Continued →

43. A vertical structure casts a shadow at an angle of 40° from the ground, as shown below. If the shadow ends 30 feet from the edge of the structure, how high, in feet, is the structure?

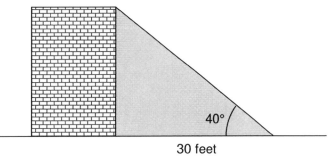

30 feet

    A. 30 sin 40°

    B. 30 tan 40°

    C. 30 cos 40°

    D. $\dfrac{30}{\sin 40°}$

    E. $\dfrac{30}{\tan 40°}$

45. Quadrilateral *ABCD* is shown in the figure below, with sides given in inches. What is sin *C* ?

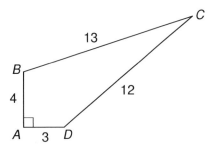

    A. $\dfrac{5}{13}$

    B. $\dfrac{5}{12}$

    C. $\dfrac{4}{13}$

    D. $\dfrac{4}{12}$

    E. $\dfrac{3}{4}$

Continued →

50. An observer at Point A measured the angle of elevation of a plane above Point B to be 25°. If the observer was 7,000 feet from Point B when she made the angle measurement, how high, in feet, was the plane?

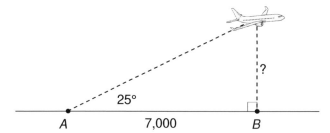

A. 7,000 cos 25°

B. 7,000 tan 25°

C. $\dfrac{7,000}{\sin 25°}$

D. $\dfrac{7,000}{\cos 25°}$

E. $\dfrac{7,000}{\tan 25°}$

55. If $0° \le \theta \le 90°$ and $\tan \theta = 2$, then $\sin \theta = ?$

F. -2

G. $\dfrac{1}{2}$

H. $\dfrac{\sqrt{5}}{2}$

J. $\sqrt{5}$

K. $\dfrac{2}{\sqrt{5}}$

TRIGONOMETRY WORKSHEET 2 (ALL SECTIONS)

38. For right triangle △ABC below, what is the cos ∠B?

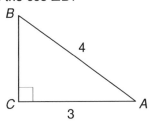

A. $\dfrac{3}{4}$

B. $\dfrac{4}{3}$

C. $\dfrac{4}{\sqrt{7}}$

D. $\dfrac{\sqrt{7}}{4}$

E. $\dfrac{\sqrt{7}}{3}$

45. The lengths of right triangle △ABC are shown below. What is the secant of ∠A in terms of a, b, and c?

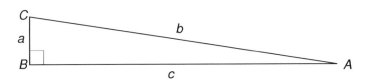

F. $\dfrac{c}{b}$

G. $\dfrac{b}{c}$

H. $\dfrac{a}{b}$

J. $\dfrac{b}{a}$

K. $\dfrac{c}{a}$

Continued →

47. In △ABC, shown below, the length of side BC is 6 units, the length of side AC is 15 units, and sin γ = 0.8. What is the area, in square units, of △ABC?

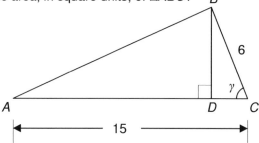

F. 80
G. 75
H. 72
J. 40
K. 36

56. If $\pi \le \alpha \le \dfrac{3\pi}{2}$ and $\sin \alpha = -\dfrac{\sqrt{3}}{2}$, then $\tan \alpha = ?$

A. $2\sqrt{3}$

B. $\sqrt{3}$

C. $\dfrac{\sqrt{3}}{2}$

D. $-\dfrac{\sqrt{3}}{2}$

E. $-\sqrt{3}$

Continued →

57. Which of the following equations is represented by the graph below?

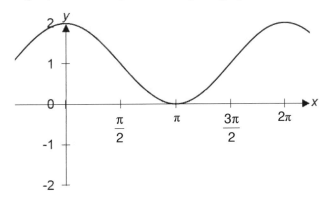

A. $y = 2 \sin x$
B. $y = 2 \cos x$
C. $y = \sin x + 1$
D. $y = \cos x + 1$
E. $y = \cos 2x + 1$

58. In $\triangle ABC$ below, line segment CD is the angle bisector of $\angle ACB$, and point D lies on side AB. In terms of a, b, and θ, what is the area of $\triangle ABC$?

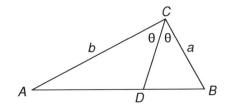

(Note: $\sin 2\theta = 2 \sin \theta \cos \theta$, and the area of any triangle with sides of length a, b, and c and opposite angles of measure A, B, and C, respectively, is given by $\frac{1}{2}ab \sin C$.)

A. $ab \sin \theta \cos \theta$

B. $\frac{1}{2} ab \sin \theta \cos \theta$

C. $\frac{1}{2} ab \sin \theta$

D. $ab \sin \theta$

E. $ab \cos \theta$

Continued →

59. If cos 40° = x and sin 40° = y, what is cos 80° given that cos (2θ) = cos² θ − sin² θ?

   F. $x^2 - y^2$
   G. $x^2 + y^2$
   H. $y^2 - x^2$
   J. $x - y$
   K. $x + y$

60. A manufacturing firm creates a steel triangular plate that fits into a triangular housing, as shown below. If the vertices are labeled A, B, and C, and the lengths of the sides of the triangular plate are 5 inches, 6 inches, and 7 inches, which of the following expressions gives the measure of the recess angle ($\angle A$)? (Note: The Law of Cosines states that for any triangle with vertices A, B, and C and the sides opposite those vertices with lengths a, b, and c, respectively, $c^2 = a^2 + b^2 - 2ab \cos C$.)

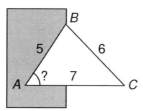

   A. $\cos^{-1}\left(\dfrac{1}{5}\right)$

   B. $\cos^{-1}\left(\dfrac{19}{35}\right)$

   C. $\cos^{-1}\left(\dfrac{5}{7}\right)$

   D. $\cos^{-1}\left(-\dfrac{1}{5}\right)$

   E. $\cos^{-1}\left(-\dfrac{11}{7}\right)$

VIII
MATH ODDS & ENDS

This chapter covers a number of topics that occasionally show up on the ACT. The lessons are arranged roughly in order of importance. Some of these topics are relatively difficult, and you might want to cover them only if you've studied them in school. It's difficult to predict what topics will be tested on any one ACT, but you can be sure that at least some of these "odds & ends" will show up on every test.

1. PRINCIPLE OF COUNTING

The *principle of counting* allows you to figure out the number of different ways multiple **independent** events can occur together. When events are *independent*, the occurrence of one event does not affect the occurrence of another event. When one event can happen in *m* ways and a second event can happen in *n* ways, the total ways in which the two events can happen can be found by the expression: **m × n**. If there are more than two events, simply multiply the number of ways that any additional events can occur.

> Counting problems will have **multiple events that are independent of each other**, as described above. The problems will ask you to find the number of ways that these events can occur together.

(EX) Mike has 5 dress shirts and 3 ties. How many different shirt-tie combinations are possible?

A. 8
B. 14
C. 15
D. 16
E. 17

Try the following lesson problem:

14. Luigi's Pizzeria is offering a 1-topping special. Each pizza can be ordered with 1 of 2 types of bread, 1 of 2 types of sauce, 1 of 3 types of cheese, and 1 of 8 toppings. How many types of 1-topping pizzas can you order?

A. 96
B. 94
C. 92
D. 15
E. 4

18. Company employees are given a two-digit ID code, *AB*, where *A* represents the 1st digit and *B* represents the 2nd digit. If $1 \leq A \leq 6$ and $1 \leq B \leq 6$, how many different codes are possible?

A. 12
B. 15
C. 25
D. 30
E. 36

2. PERMUTATIONS & COMBINATIONS

PERMUTATIONS

A *permutation* is an arrangement of items in a **definite order**. Some examples where the order of the items matters include:

- A phone number (555-1234 is different from 555-4321—same numbers, different order)
- A code or password (think about the importance of the order of your inputs when you type in a password)
- A word ("TAR" is different from "RAT")

 Permutation problems ask for the number of possible arrangements of items or events where **order matters**.

There are a few ways to tackle permutation problems (including using the $_nP_r$ function on your calculator), but we think the following method is the easiest approach to solving these problems, especially if you're learning about permutations and combinations for the first time, or if the other methods haven't "stuck." Follow along with the example problem.

1. Draw underlines representing each position you have to fill.
2. From left to right, write the number of items available for each position. **Note that items put into previous positions may not be available for a new position.**
3. Multiply the numbers to find the number of permutations.

(EX) How many 4-letter arrangements can be made from the letters in the word MATH?

(Assume each letter can only be used once.)

A. 4
B. 16
C. 20
D. 24
E. 256

(EX) How many 4-letter arrangements can be made from the letters in the word NUMBER?

(Assume each letter can only be used once.)

A. 24
B. 30
C. 256
D. 360
E. 1296

FACTORIAL

The answers to permutation and combination problems will usually NOT be represented with large numbers, as above. Rather, the ACT will use something called a *factorial* (!). This operation involves finding the product of a series of integers counting from a specified number down to 1. For example:

$$\text{"six factorial"} = 6! = 6 \times 5 \times 4 \times 3 \times 2 \times 1 = 720$$

When the answer choices are written with factorials, you have two options:

1. Use your calculator to turn the answer choices into regular numbers. (Check your calculator's manual, or look online, if you're not sure where the factorial function is found.)

OR

2. Put your answer into factorial form. If you're comfortable with factorials, this is the faster approach. Here are the steps:

    a. Expand the numerator to make it a factorial.

    b. Divide by the appropriate factorial so that you cancel the numbers added in Step a.

    For example, here's the solution to the second example above (note the answer choices have changed):

A. $4!$

B. 4^4

C. $\dfrac{6!}{4!}$

D. $\dfrac{6!}{(6-4)!}$

E. $6!$

PERMUTATIONS WITH IDENTICAL ITEMS

When some of the items are identical, you must add the following steps to the permutation method:

1. For each item that is identical, count the number of repetitions.
2. Divide your usual permutation solution by the *factorial* of each number found above.

(EX) How many distinct 4-letter arrangements can be made from the letters in the word HEEDED?

   A. 4!

   B. 6!

   C. $\dfrac{6!}{(3!)(6-4)!}$

   D. $\dfrac{4!}{(3!)(6-4)!}$

   E. $\dfrac{6!}{(3!)(2!)(6-4)!}$

■

Try the following permutations lesson problem:

50. How many different ways may 6 books be arranged on a book shelf?

   A. $6 \cdot 5$

   B. 6^2

   C. 6!

   D. $6! \cdot 4!$

   E. 6^6

COMBINATIONS

Combinations are different from permutations because the order of the items does *not* matter. Some examples include:

- The members of a team (typically, the *order* of the players makes no difference)
- The members of a group (as above, the important thing is *who* is in the group, not the order of the members)
- Items found in or on something (for example, think about different combinations of pens in a drawer—the order of the pens does not matter)

> Combination problems ask for the number of possible arrangements of items or events where **order does not matter**.

Again, there's more than one way to solve combination problems (including using the $_nC_r$ function on your calculator), but we'll use a method similar to that for permutation problems, with one extra step, involving a factorial:

1. Draw underlines representing each position you have to fill.
2. From left to right, write the number of items available for each position. This will be the numerator. As with permutations, remember that an item put into a previous position may not be available for a new position.
3. Divide the numerator by the *factorial of the number of positions to be filled*. This will give you the number of combinations of the items.

 How many 4-person teams can be made from a roster of 10 players?

A. $\dfrac{10!}{(4!)(10-4)!}$

B. $\dfrac{10!}{(10-4)!}$

C. $\dfrac{10!}{4!}$

D. $10!$

E. 10^4

Try the following combinations lesson problem:

56. A pizza parlor offers 8 possible toppings for its pizzas. If a pizza must have three different toppings, how many different kinds of pizza can be made?

A. $\dfrac{8!}{(3!)(8-3)!}$

B. $\dfrac{8!}{(8-3)!}$

C. $\dfrac{8!}{3!}$

D. $8!$

E. $3!$

USING PERMUTATIONS AND COMBINATIONS WITH THE PRINCIPLE OF COUNTING

 These problems deal with finding permutations or combinations when there is **more than one** independent group of items.

Use the following method:

1. Find the number of permutations and/or combinations for each independent group.

2. Using the Principle of Counting (see the previous section), multiply the values you calculated in step 1.

(EX) A security code has 4 digits. If the first 2 digits must be letters from the set {A, B, C, D, E, G, H}, and the second two digits must each be a different positive even integer less than 10, how many 4-digit codes are possible?

A. 24
B. 256
C. 504
D. 588
E. 784

■

51. Employees at a small company are given a two-digit ID code, *AB*, where *A* represents the first digit and *B* represents the second digit. If $1 \le A \le 6$ and $1 \le B \le 6$, how many different ID codes are possible?

   A. $6 \cdot 2$

   B. $\dfrac{6!}{2!(6-2)!}$

   C. $\dfrac{6!}{(6-2)!}$

   D. $6!$

   E. 6^2

53. How many ways can a family of 5 be arranged in a 5-seat car if the father drives the car?

   A. 1

   B. 5

   C. 12

   D. 24

   E. 120

59. There are 4 juniors and 5 seniors on a debate team. If the teacher must choose 2 juniors and 3 seniors to compete, how many ways may this 5-person team be assembled?

   A. $\dfrac{4!}{(2!)(4-2)!}$

   B. $\dfrac{5!}{(3!)(5-3)!}$

   C. $\dfrac{9!}{(5!)(9-5)!}$

   D. $\left(\dfrac{4!}{(2!)(4-2)!}\right)\left(\dfrac{5!}{(3!)(5-3)!}\right)$

   E. $\left(\dfrac{5!}{(2!)(5-2)!}\right)\left(\dfrac{4!}{(3!)(4-3)!}\right)$

3. COMPLEX NUMBERS

IMAGINARY NUMBERS (*i*)

Try finding $\sqrt{-25}$ using your calculator. You'll get an error message (unless your calculator is smarter than most). There is no *real number* solution to $\sqrt{-25}$, but there *is* what is called an *imaginary* solution, which uses the variable *i* to refer to $\sqrt{-1}$. First, make sure you are comfortable with the following property of radicals:

$$\sqrt{ab} = \sqrt{a}\sqrt{b}$$

Using this property, we can write:

$$\sqrt{-25} = \sqrt{25(-1)} = \sqrt{25}\sqrt{-1} = 5i$$

That's all *i* is—just a way for us to refer to the square roots of negative numbers.

WORKING WITH *i*

Notice what happens when we take some simple powers of *i*:

$i^1 = i$

$i^2 = \left(\sqrt{-1}\right)^2 = -1$

$i^3 = i^2 \cdot i = (-1)(i) = -i$

$i^4 = i^2 \cdot i^2 = (-1)(-1) = 1$

If we go on to find i^5, you'll see that the pattern begins to repeat:

$i^5 = i \cdot i^4 = i \cdot 1 = i$

This is an important pattern to memorize: {*i*, −1, −*i*, 1, *i*, −1, −*i*, 1...}. It allows us to find *i* to the power of large numbers, using the following rules:

1. If the power is divisible by 4, *i* to that power is 1.
2. If the power is NOT divisible by 4, find the nearest power that IS divisible by 4, and count up or down to the power in question.

Look at the following example:

(EX) What is the value of i^{45}?

    A. −1
    B. 0
    C. 1
    D. −*i*
    E. *i*

ALGEBRA WITH *i*

Nearly all of the ACT problems that involve *i* have to do with basic algebraic operations. When you're solving equations with *i*, you can pretend that *i* is just like any other variable, but with one exception: **You must remember the power rules for *i*.** For example, if you get an i^2, you have to remember to turn it into -1. Simplify the following expressions:

1. $3i + 7i =$

2. $(3i)(7i) =$

3. $\dfrac{24i^5}{12i} =$

4. $(2 + i)(3 - i) =$

5. $(x - i)(2x + 2i) =$

> These problems will obviously include the variable *i*. The ACT tends to be nice enough to tell you that $i^2 = -1$, so look for that, too.

27. For $i^2 = -1$, what is the value of $2i^4 + 2i^2$?
    - **A.** 4
    - **B.** 3
    - **C.** 2
    - **D.** 1
    - **E.** 0

i AND YOUR CALCULATOR

Many newer calculators have an *i* key (usually a "second" function for an existing key). Look around on your keyboard for an italicized *i*. If you have one, by all means, use it. Not only is this approach often faster than the algebraic methods above, but you can rely on your calculator to get the question correct. If your calculator does *not* have an *i* key, don't worry. Just make sure you're comfortable with the rules above.

COMPLEX NUMBERS

A complex number is the sum (or difference) of a real number and an imaginary number. If *a* and *b* are real numbers, a complex number takes the form:

$$a + bi$$

An example of a complex number is $3 + 5i$. The real number part is 3; the imaginary part is $5i$.

You should be able to convert an expression into a complex number, which, remember, has the form $a + bi$. You can use the algebra rules, as described before.

(EX) Which of the following is equivalent to $\dfrac{6 + 9i}{3}$?

    A. −1
    B. 2 + 3*i*
    C. 2 + 9*i*
    D. 9 + 12*i*
    E. 18 + 9*i*

i IN THE DENOMINATOR

Problems that require you to simplify a fraction with *i* in the denominator are rarely found on the ACT, but in case one shows up, there are two tricks:

1. If *i* (or a term including *i, such as 3i*) is alone in the denominator, multiply the numerator and denominator by *i*. This will give you an i^2 in the denominator (and thus, because i^2 = −1, the *i* goes away). Now you can put the number in complex form, as in the example above.

2. If the denominator is a complex number, multiply the numerator and denominator by the *complex conjugate* of the complex number. The complex conjugate of a complex number is simply the complex number with the *i* term multiplied by −1. For example: 2 − 3*i* is the conjugate of 2 + 3*i*. Multiplying by a complex conjugate gets rid of the imaginary number when you FOIL the two expressions. Look at the example below:

(EX) Which of following is equivalent to $\dfrac{20}{6 + 2i}$?

    A. 1 + *i*
    B. 1 − *i*
    C. 2 − *i*
    D. 3 − *i*
    E. 4 − *i*

THE COMPLEX PLANE

If you're comfortable with the (*x,y*) coordinate plane, you should be fine with the *complex plane*. The *real* part of the complex number is graphed on the *horizontal axis* of the complex plane, and the *imaginary* part is graphed on the *vertical axis*. The complex number 3 + 5*i* is graphed below:

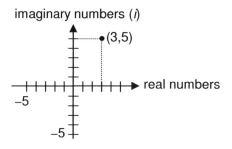

THE ABSOLUTE VALUE OF A COMPLEX NUMBER

If you can graph a complex number on the complex plane, and if you remember the Pythagorean Theorem, you should have no problem finding the *absolute value* of a complex number. Think of the absolute value as the "distance from the complex number to zero." (This is actually the same way we thought about absolute values in Chapter I.) Draw a line from the complex number "point" to the origin ("0") and find the length of the line. See the following example:

(EX) $|2 + 3i| = ?$

    A. $\sqrt{5}$
    B. $\sqrt{6}$
    C. $\sqrt{10}$
    D. $2\sqrt{3}$
    E. $\sqrt{13}$

■

46. For $i^2 = -1$, $(3 - 5i)^2 =$

    A. $-16 - 30i$
    B. -16
    C. $9 + 25i$
    D. $9 - 25i$
    E. $9 - 30i$

58. For $i^2 = -1$, which of the following is equivalent to $\dfrac{5}{2 + i}$?

    F. $10 - i$
    G. $5 - i$
    H. $4 - i$
    J. $3 - i$
    K. $2 - i$

60. Five complex numbers are graphed in the complex plane below. Which of the complex numbers has the greatest absolute value?

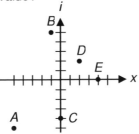

    A. A
    B. B
    C. C
    D. D
    E. E

4. LOGARITHMS

The following rules should cover any logarithm problems that you may see.

DEFINITION OF LOGARITHM

Logarithms (or logs) are just tools that allow us to solve exponential equations. The basic definition is:

FLASH CARDS $\log_a x = y \leftrightarrow a^y = x$

The way you say this is: "the log of base *a* of *x* is *y*." Notice how the two equations compare:

$$\log_a x = y \leftrightarrow a^y = x$$

Perhaps the easiest thing to remember is that the "base," which is the lowered "*a*" following the word "log," is also the base in the exponential part of the equation.

Here's how you may be asked to use this equation:

(EX) Which of the following values of *x* satisfies $\log_x 27 = 3$?

    A. 3
    B. 6
    C. 9
    D. 12
    E. 13.5

LOGARITHMIC PROPERTIES

The three following properties allow you to simplify logarithmic equations. Use flashcards to memorize them:

FLASH CARDS

THE PRODUCT RULE

$$\log_x (ab) = \log_x a + \log_x b$$

THE QUOTIENT RULE

$$\log_x \left(\frac{a}{b} \right) = \log_x a - \log_x b$$

THE POWER RULE

$$\log_x a^b = b \log_x a$$

(EX) What is the value of the $\log_2 (AB)$ if $\log_2 A = 5$ and the $\log_2 B = 6$?

    A. 10
    B. 11
    C. 12
    D. 30
    E. 60

Try the following lesson problem:

51. If $\log_p a = q$, then $\log_p a^3 = ?$

    A. $3q$
    B. $9q$
    C. q^3
    D. $3q^3$
    E. $9q^3$

LOG$_{10}$

When a log has a base of 10, you can write it without the base—the 10 is implied.

$$\log_{10} x = \log x$$

THE BASE-CHANGE RULE

This rule will probably only come in handy if you want to type logs into your calculator (something you would never *have* to do on the ACT, but something you might *choose* to do if you're stuck on a problem). Notice the "LOG" key on your calculator. Your calculator accepts logs that have a base of 10. So if you wanted to calculate, say, $\log_2 32$, you could use the base-change rule:

$$\log_a b = \frac{\log b}{\log a}$$

Notice that the number on top goes to the numerator and the base number goes to the denominator. This is what you might visually expect.

Here's how you could use your calculator to find $\log_2 32$:

$$\log_2 32 = \frac{\log 32}{\log 2} = 5$$

∎

LOGARITHMS HOMEWORK

31. What is the value of $\log_4 64$?

    A. 1
    B. 2
    C. 3
    D. 16
    E. 24

34. Which of the following values of x satisfies $\log_{2x} 4 = 2$?

    F. 16
    G. 8
    H. 4
    J. 2
    K. 1

58. If $\log_a 10 = A$ and $\log_a 5 = B$, then $\log_a 2 = $?

    A. $\dfrac{A}{B}$
    B. $A + B$
    C. $A - B$
    D. $2A - 4B$
    E. AB

5. *PATTERNS*

Pattern problems deal with sequences of numbers or other items. These problems can take several different forms.

 Number pattern problems will either give you a long list of numbers or other items, or give you enough information to create a long list on your own. You may see the words *sequence* or *pattern*.

SHORT PATTERNS

Many pattern problems deal with a short sequence of numbers or items, often less than 20. There will usually be instructions that tell you how to find each number in the sequence. If you can find a pattern, great. This will generally help you solve the problem quickly. But if you can't find a pattern, follow the instructions and simply *count* to the term you're looking for. These problems usually don't take as long as you may expect. Here are some examples:

2. In the sequence below, each term after the first is obtained by finding the sum of <u>all</u> terms preceding the given term. If the pattern continues indefinitely, 256 will be which term of the sequence?

   1, 1, 2, 4, 8, 16, 32, …

   A. 7th
   B. 8th
   C. 9th
   D. 10th
   E. 11th

12. Each triangle in the pattern below is surrounded by 3 congruent rectangles. How many of these rectangles will there be if the pattern is repeated until there are 7 triangles?

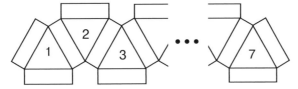

   F. 15
   G. 17
   H. 19
   J. 21
   K. 23

LONG PATTERNS

Long pattern problems will typically take too long to figure out "by hand." You need to find a pattern. Often, the best way to do this is to look at the results of the first three or four items given, and see if you can figure out an equation. This is best explained with an example:

 Each triangle in the pattern below is surrounded by 3 congruent rectangles. How many of these rectangles will there be if the pattern is repeated until there are 31 triangles?

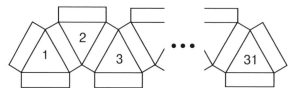

 A. 63
 B. 65
 C. 67
 D. 91
 E. 93

REPEATING PATTERNS

Some long pattern problems have a *group* of numbers (or items) that repeats.

> Look for a group of numbers or items that repeats. Some examples: 1, 2, 3, 1, 2, 3... and ♠, ♣, ♥, ♦, ♠, ♣, ♥, ♦... Repeating decimal problems (such as 1.234 234 234...) often test this technique.

Use the method below with the following example problem:

1. Write out enough numbers or items so you can identify the group that is being repeated.
2. Count the number of items in the group. This is your repeating pattern.
3. If the *term-number* whose value you are being asked to find is divisible by the number of items in the pattern, then the term is equal to the *last item* in the pattern.
4. If the term-number whose value you are being asked to find is *not* divisible by the number of items in the pattern, then find a nearby term-number that *is* divisible, and count up or down to the term you're looking for.

100, 150, 200, 100, 150, 200, ...

(EX) How many numbers are repeated in the pattern above?

What is the 3rd term in the pattern?

What is the 6th term in the pattern?

What is the 30th term in the pattern?

What is the 32nd term in the pattern?

What is the 133rd term in the pattern?

Try the following lesson problem:

26. In the pattern below, the numbers –2, –1, 0, 1, 2 repeat as shown.

   –2, –1, 0, 1, 2, –2, –1, 0, 1, 2, ...

   What is the 45th term in the pattern?

   A. –2
   B. –1
   C. 0
   D. 1
   E. 2

SPECIAL SEQUENCES

ARITHMETIC SEQUENCES

Arithmetic sequences are formed by taking a starting value and *adding* the same value over and over again. For example:

   2, 8, 14, 20, 26, ... The starting value is 2, and the number added each time is 6. (2 + 6 = 8, 8 + 6 = 14, and so on)

We can refer to terms in the sequence using a_n, where the n represents the nth term in the sequence. In the example above, a_1 is the first term in the sequence (2), a_2 is the second term in the sequence (8), and so on. The number that is added each time, in this case 6, is called the *difference* and is represented by the variable d. There is no great trick for these problems, so memorize the formula for an arithmetic sequence:

FLASH
CARDS

$$a_n = a_1 + (n - 1)d$$

37. The nth term of a sequence is defined as $2 + (n - 1)2$. The 500th term is how much greater than the 499th term?

    F. 1
    G. 2
    H. 4
    J. 6
    K. 8

GEOMETRIC SEQUENCES

Geometric sequences are similar to arithmetic sequences except they are formed by taking a starting value and *multiplying* the same value over and over again. The following are examples:

- 2, 8, 32, 128, ... The starting value is 2, and the number multiplied each time is 4. $(2 \times 4 = 8, 8 \times 4 = 32,$ and so on)

- 2, 1, $\frac{1}{2}$, $\frac{1}{4}$, ... The starting value is 2, and the number multiplied each time is $\frac{1}{2}$.

- 2, –8, 32, –128, ...The starting value is 2, and the number multiplied each time is –4.

The number multiplied each time, called the *ratio*, is represented by the constant r. Memorize the formula for a geometric sequence:

 FLASH CARDS
                                 $a_n = a_1 r^{n-1}$

44. The nth term of a sequence is defined as $4 \times (\frac{1}{2})^{n-1}$. What is the average of the 2nd, 3rd, and 4th terms in this sequence?

    A. $\frac{7}{12}$
    B. $\frac{7}{6}$
    C. $\frac{7}{3}$
    D. $\frac{7}{2}$
    E. 2

RECURSIVE SEQUENCES

Some sequences define a term (such as a_n) based on *previous* terms (one term before a_n is a_{n-1}, two terms before a_n is a_{n-2}, and so on). These are called *recursive sequences*. If you're comfortable with the notation for arithmetic and geometric sequences, these problems shouldn't offer any special challenges. Here's a lesson problem:

30. A sequence is defined by the equation $a_n = a_{n-2} - a_{n-1}$. If the first 4 terms of the sequence are given in the table below, what is the 5th term in the sequence?

a_1	a_2	a_3	a_4	a_5
10	5	5	0	?

A. −5
B. 0
C. 5
D. 10
E. 15

SERIES PROBLEMS

A *series* is the *sum* of the terms of a sequence.

> Any problem that involves the *sum* of the terms in an arithmetic or geometric sequence is a series problem. Or, of course, look for the word "series."

For most ACT series problems, you don't *have* to use a formula. Just add the terms, if there aren't too many, using your calculator, or look for clues in the answer choices. For example:

(EX) In an arithmetic series, each term is x more than the preceding term. If the first term of an arithmetic series is 5, the last term is 200, and the sum is 615, what are the first three terms of the series?

F. 5, 10, 20
G. 5, 20, 35
H. 5, 25, 45
J. 5, 25, 125
K. 5, 102.5, 200

ARITHMETIC SERIES

While there is usually a way to solve series questions without using formulas, knowing the formula for an arithmetic series of n terms (S_n) occasionally comes in handy:

 FLASH CARDS

$$S_n = n\left(\frac{a_1 + a_n}{2}\right)$$

(EX) Doug wants to build a structure by starting with one block, and adding one more block to each new row, so that each successive row of blocks has 1 more block than the level above it. If Doug wants to build a structure with 30 rows, how many blocks will he need?

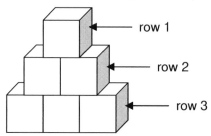

row 1

row 2

row 3

A. 30
B. 60
C. 240
D. 405
E. 465

GEOMETRIC SERIES

You probably won't see a *geometric* series problem, and if you do, it's unlikely you'd have to have any formulas memorized. Just make sure you understand the basic concept, that is, a geometric series is the sum of the terms in a geometric sequence.

(HW)

5. In the sequence below, each term after the first term is $\frac{1}{5}$ of the term preceding it. What is the fifth term of this sequence?

150, 30, 6 . . .

A. −6
B. 0
C. $\frac{6}{25}$
D. 1
E. $\frac{6}{5}$

Continued →

21. A number is a "perfect cube" if it is the cube of a positive integer. How many integers less than or equal to 1,000 are perfect cubes?

    F. 10
    G. 15
    H. 20
    J. 25
    K. 30

41. What is the 6th term of the geometric sequence $49\frac{1}{2}, 16\frac{1}{2}, 5\frac{1}{2}, \ldots$?

    A. $\dfrac{11}{162}$

    B. $\dfrac{11}{54}$

    C. $\dfrac{11}{18}$

    D. $1\frac{5}{6}$

    E. $4\frac{5}{6}$

45. The fraction $\dfrac{9}{7}$ is equivalent to the repeating decimal $1.\overline{285714}$. What is the 100th digit to the right of the decimal point?

    F. 1
    G. 2
    H. 4
    J. 5
    K. 7

52. What is the 17th term of the arithmetic sequence in which the 5th term is 6 and the 9th term is 13?

    F. 20
    G. 27
    H. 29
    J. 34
    K. 39

Continued →

58. The sum of the first n terms of an arithmetic series with first term a and nth term b is given by:

$$S_n = n\left(\frac{a+b}{2}\right)$$

If the common difference of the series is 3 and the sum of the first 7 terms is 49, what is the first term in the series?

A. −7
B. −2
C. 2
D. 7
E. 14

60. The sum of the first 50 positive integers is 1,275. What is the sum of the first 100 positive integers?

F. 2,550
G. 3,775
H. 5,050
J. 6,250
K. 6,275

6. MATRICES

Matrices problems generally take one of two forms. They either provide you information in a word problem, just as *tables* do, or they test *matrix operations*.

MATRICES AS TABLES

Matrices may look difficult, especially if you haven't spent much time working with them in school, but most matrices problems are really just table problems. Once you understand how the information is displayed, you can find your answer. Let's look at an example.

(EX) At a track meet, 10 points are awarded for a 1st place finish, 5 points are awarded for a 2nd place finish, and 2 points are awarded for a 3rd place finish. The matrices below show the number of 1st, 2nd, and 3rd place finishes for two schools: Richmond and Oakville. How many more points did Richmond score than Oakville in the track meet?

$$\text{Richmond} \begin{matrix} \text{1st} & \text{2nd} & \text{3rd} \\ [4 & 5 & 2] \end{matrix} \quad \text{Oakville} \begin{matrix} \text{1st} & \text{2nd} & \text{3rd} \\ [3 & 6 & 4] \end{matrix}$$

- **A.** 1
- **B.** 2
- **C.** 3
- **D.** 4
- **E.** 5

Try the following lesson problem:

15. The Manatee Shirt Store sells four styles of a particular shirt (A, B, C, and D). The matrices below display the numbers of each style of shirt sold last month and the cost of each style of shirt. What was the total dollar amount that the store charged for these shirts last month?

$$\begin{matrix} \text{A} & \text{B} & \text{C} & \text{D} \\ [10 & 15 & 5 & 20] \end{matrix} \qquad \begin{matrix} & \text{Cost} \\ \text{A} & \$5.00 \\ \text{B} & \$10.00 \\ \text{C} & \$7.50 \\ \text{D} & \$12.50 \end{matrix}$$

- **A.** $477.50
- **B.** $480.00
- **C.** $482.50
- **D.** $485.00
- **E.** $487.50

MATRIX OPERATIONS

Sometimes you might have to add, subtract, or multiply matrices. Unlike the previous matrices problems, these *matrix operations* problems are usually *not* word problems.

ADDING AND SUBTRACTING MATRICES

You can only add or subtract matrices that are the same size. The process is straightforward. Simply add or subtract elements in the same position of each matrix. For example:

$$\begin{bmatrix} 5 & -2 \\ 3 & 6 \end{bmatrix} + \begin{bmatrix} 3 & 6 \\ -4 & 4 \end{bmatrix} = \begin{bmatrix} 5+3 & -2+6 \\ 3+(-4) & 6+4 \end{bmatrix} = \begin{bmatrix} 8 & 4 \\ -1 & 10 \end{bmatrix}$$

MULTIPLYING A MATRIX BY A NUMBER

This operation is also straightforward. Simply multiply each element in the matrix by the number in front. For example:

$$5 \begin{bmatrix} 3 & -3 \\ 2 & 1 \end{bmatrix} = \begin{bmatrix} 5 \cdot 3 & 5 \cdot (-3) \\ 5 \cdot 2 & 5 \cdot 1 \end{bmatrix} = \begin{bmatrix} 15 & -15 \\ 10 & 5 \end{bmatrix}$$

MULTIPLYING MATRICES

Now that the easier stuff is out of the way, let's look at multiplying matrices. First, let's refer to the size of a matrix as $m \times n$, where m is the number of rows and n is the number of columns. Don't forget: the number that comes first refers to the number of *rows*.

There are two rules that you should know before we get into actually multiplying matrices:

Rule 1: To multiply two matrices, the number of *columns* in the first matrix must equal the number of *rows* in the second matrix. For example, we can multiply matrices A and B below:

$$A_{1 \times 2} = \begin{bmatrix} -1 & 2 \end{bmatrix} \qquad B_{2 \times 4} = \begin{bmatrix} 3 & 0 & -1 & 3 \\ -2 & 1 & 2 & 0 \end{bmatrix}$$

$$2 = 2$$

Rule 2: The product of two matrices will result in a matrix with the same number of rows as the first matrix and the same number of columns as the second matrix.

$$A_{1 \times 2} \times B_{2 \times 4} = C_{1 \times 4} = \begin{bmatrix} ? & ? & ? & ? \end{bmatrix}$$

So how do we actually multiply matrices? Most graphing calculators can perform matrix multiplication; you may want to learn how to do this; check your calculator's manual. If you don't have a graphing calculator, use the following method. Follow along with the example below:

1. Circle each row in the first matrix and circle each column in the second matrix (see the example below). Note that each row of the first matrix and each column of the second matrix must have the same number of elements (in this case, 2)—see rule 1 above.

2. Draw a blank matrix with the same number of rows as the first matrix and the same number of columns as the second matrix (see rule 2 above). This will become the final product matrix.

3. To find the first element in row 1 of the product matrix, multiply each element in row 1 of the first matrix by each related element of column 1 of the second matrix, and add these products together. This sounds confusing, but it's not that hard. See step 3 in the example below.

4. To find the second element in row 1 of the product matrix, multiply each element in row 1 of the first matrix by each related element of column 2 of the second matrix, and add these products together. Repeat these steps until you have constructed the product matrix.

(EX) What is the matrix product $\begin{bmatrix} -1 & 2 \end{bmatrix} \begin{bmatrix} 3 & 0 & -1 & 3 \\ -2 & 1 & 2 & 0 \end{bmatrix}$?

A. $\begin{bmatrix} -7 & 2 & 5 & -3 \end{bmatrix}$

B. $\begin{bmatrix} -3 & 0 & 1 & -3 \end{bmatrix}$

C. $\begin{bmatrix} -3 & 0 & 1 & -3 \\ -4 & 2 & 4 & 0 \end{bmatrix}$

D. $-\begin{bmatrix} 6 & 0 & -2 & 6 \\ -4 & 2 & 4 & 0 \end{bmatrix}$

E. -3

Try the following lesson problem:

47. What is the matrix product of $\begin{bmatrix} 1 & 2 \\ 3 & 4 \end{bmatrix} \cdot \begin{bmatrix} -1 & -2 \\ -3 & -4 \end{bmatrix}$?

    A. $\begin{bmatrix} 0 & 0 \\ 0 & 0 \end{bmatrix}$

    B. $\begin{bmatrix} -7 & -10 \\ -15 & -22 \end{bmatrix}$

    C. $\begin{bmatrix} 10 & -10 \end{bmatrix}$

    D. $\begin{bmatrix} -7 & -10 & -15 & -22 \end{bmatrix}$

    E. 0

DETERMINANT OF A MATRIX

The *determinant* of a matrix is sometimes used to help solve linear equations, but the ACT only seems to test the basic calculation, as defined below. (Note: the ACT typically uses "square brackets," as shown below, but most math books use simple vertical bars.)

$$\begin{bmatrix} a & b \\ c & d \end{bmatrix} = ad - bc$$

The easiest way to remember this is to think in *diagonals*. First find the product of the diagonal from *upper left to lower right*; then *subtract* from that the product of the diagonal from *upper right to lower left*:

Here's a lesson problem:

47. For what value of *t* does the determinant of the matrix $\begin{bmatrix} 1 & 2 \\ t & 4 \end{bmatrix}$ equal 8?

    A. −8
    B. −4
    C. −2
    D. 1
    E. 2

10. $3\begin{bmatrix} 2 & -3 \\ -1 & 0 \end{bmatrix} - 2\begin{bmatrix} 2 & -6 \\ -3 & -2 \end{bmatrix} = ?$

A. $\begin{bmatrix} 2 & -9 \\ -4 & -2 \end{bmatrix}$

B. $\begin{bmatrix} 10 & -21 \\ -9 & -4 \end{bmatrix}$

C. $\begin{bmatrix} 2 & -3 \\ 3 & 0 \end{bmatrix}$

D. $\begin{bmatrix} 2 & 3 \\ -9 & 4 \end{bmatrix}$

E. $\begin{bmatrix} 2 & 3 \\ 3 & 4 \end{bmatrix}$

34. Sell-U-Phone Company makes three types of phones (X, Y, and Z). The matrix below shows the number of phones of each type manufactured last week at two Sell-U-Phone factories (A and B).

$$\begin{array}{c} \quad X \quad\ \ Y \quad\ \ Z \\ \begin{array}{c} A \\ B \end{array}\begin{bmatrix} 500 & 300 & 160 \\ 600 & 0 & 900 \end{bmatrix} \end{array}$$

If a manufactured phone cannot be sold, it is called a "failure." Quality control at Sell-U-Phone provides estimates of the failure rate for each type of phone, as shown in the matrix below.

$$\begin{array}{c} \begin{array}{c} X \\ Y \\ Z \end{array}\begin{bmatrix} 0.02 \\ 0.01 \\ 0.05 \end{bmatrix} \end{array}$$

Based on the matrices, what is the estimate for the total number of failures at both factories last week?

A. 72
B. 74
C. 76
D. 78
E. 80

Continued →

56. $\begin{bmatrix} 2 & -3 \\ -1 & 0 \end{bmatrix} \cdot \begin{bmatrix} -3 \\ 1 \end{bmatrix} = ?$

   A. $\begin{bmatrix} -9 \\ 3 \end{bmatrix}$

   B. $\begin{bmatrix} -3 \\ 3 \end{bmatrix}$

   C. $\begin{bmatrix} -6 & 9 \\ -1 & 0 \end{bmatrix}$

   D. $\begin{bmatrix} 2 & 9 \\ -1 & 0 \end{bmatrix}$

   E. $\begin{bmatrix} -1 & -6 \\ 0 & 1 \end{bmatrix}$

60. The determinant of the matrix $\begin{bmatrix} a & b \\ b & a \end{bmatrix}$ is 6. If $a + b = 3$, what is the value of $a - b$?

   A. 6
   B. 3
   C. 2
   D. 1
   E. Cannot be
      determined from the
      given information

   ■

30- and 40-hour programs: Jump to the end of this chapter and complete Odds & Ends Worksheet 1. If you're in the **40-hour program**, you'll finish this chapter later (see the Tutoring Schedules in the Introduction).

7. PARABOLAS & ELLIPSES

PARABOLAS

Most of the questions that test parabolas on the ACT can be solved using techniques from previous chapters, such as Graphs of Functions or Factoring. But it's possible you'll see a parabola question that requires interpreting a parabolic *equation*. We'll cover the three common forms below.

QUADRATIC FORM

The quadratic form of a parabola was introduced in the Factoring lesson (Chapter III):

$$y = ax^2 + bx + c$$

The letters a, b, and c are coefficients. When graphed, a quadratic equation is called a *parabola*. Below is the graph of $y = x^2 - 6x + 5$:

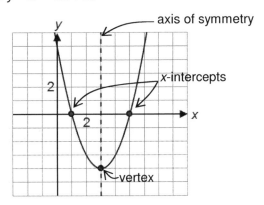

The quadratic form can, at a glance, tell us the direction that the parabola opens:

- If $a > 0$, the parabola opens *up*—see the example above.
- If $a < 0$, the parabola opens *down*.

The quadratic form allows for easy input into the quadratic formula (see Factoring in Chapter III). We can also determine the number of x-intercepts (0, 1, or 2) by calculating the *discriminant* ($b^2 - 4ac$), as discussed in the Factoring section. Here's a review:

- If $b^2 > 4ac$, then the quadratic equation has 2 *real* solutions (since you'll be taking the square root of a positive number). These solutions are represented graphically as x-intercepts.
- If $b^2 = 4ac$ ($b^2 - 4ac = 0$), then the quadratic equation has 1 real solution/x-intercept.
- If $b^2 < 4ac$, then the quadratic equation has 2 *imaginary* solutions (since you'll be taking the square root of a negative number). There are no x-intercepts. The parabola either opens up above the x-axis or opens down below the x-axis.

Finally, the quadratic form can tell us the *x*-coordinate of the vertex:

$$\boxed{\text{FLASH CARDS}} \quad x_v = -\frac{b}{2a}$$

To find the *y*-intercept of the vertex, plug x_v into the original equation and solve for *y*. Here's a lesson problem:

52. The equation $y = -x^2 - 2x + 3$ represents a parabola in the (x, y) coordinate plane. Which of the following are the coordinates of the maximum value of the parabola?

    A. $(-1, 3)$
    B. $(-1, 4)$
    C. $(-1, 6)$
    D. $(1, 0)$
    E. $(1, 2)$

x-INTERCEPT FORM

When a quadratic equation is factored, it takes the following form:

$$y = a(x - p)(x - q)$$

In the equation, *a*, *p*, and *q* are real numbers (often integers). This is called the *x-intercept* form because, at a glance, you can see the *x*-intercepts: $x = p$ and $x = q$. We've covered this form in the Factoring lesson.

VERTEX FORM

We know that the *vertex* of a parabola is the minimum point of an upward opening parabola, or the maximum point of a downward opening parabola. The vertex form is:

$$y = a(x - h)^2 + k$$

In the equation, *a*, *h*, and *k* are real numbers (again, often integers). When an equation is in this form, the vertex is at the point (h, k). The *line of symmetry* will always be the vertical line $x = h$.

Note that the equation above is simply a *transformation* of a parabola with vertex at $(0, 0)$ ($y = ax^2$). The new parabola will move *h* units to the right and *k* units up. Review Transformations in the More Graphs of Functions section (Chapter VI). Here's a lesson problem:

41. The function *f* below is defined as $f(x) = x^2$. If $g(x)$ is the translation of $f(x)$ 1 unit to the left and 3 units down, with vertex shown below, which of the following defines the function g?

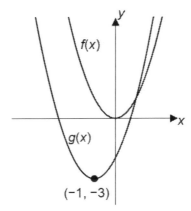

A. $g(x) = (x - 1)^2 - 3$
B. $g(x) = (x + 1)^2 - 3$
C. $g(x) = (x + 1)^2 + 3$
D. $g(x) = (x - 3)^2 + 1$
E. $g(x) = (x + 3)^2 - 1$

ELLIPSES

Ellipses (to put it simply) look like ovals (although technically a circle is a special ellipse). You should memorize the two standard equations of an ellipse:

When an ellipse is longer in the x direction, the equation is $\dfrac{x^2}{a^2} + \dfrac{y^2}{b^2} = 1$ (where $a > b$).

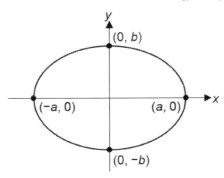

Ellipses have two axes, a major axis (the longer one) and a minor axis (the shorter one):

- The *major axis* (along the *x*-axis) has a length of 2*a*.

- The *minor axis* (along the *y*-axis) has a length of 2*b*.

When an ellipse is longer in the y direction, the equation is $\dfrac{x^2}{b^2}+\dfrac{y^2}{a^2}=1$ (again, $a > b$).

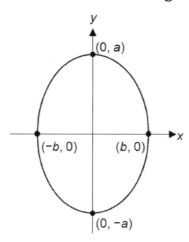

Axes:

- The *major axis* (along the y-axis) has a length of $2a$.
- The *minor axis* (along the x-axis) has a length of $2b$.

ELLIPSES: TRANSFORMATIONS

As with other functions, ellipses can be *transformed*, or moved, algebraically. Here's the equation for an ellipse with major axis in the x direction:

$$\frac{(x-h)^2}{a^2}+\frac{(y-k)^2}{b^2}=1$$

The ellipse, including its center, will move h units to the right and k units up. Review Transformations in the More Graphs of Functions lesson (Chapter VI) if necessary. You might also review More Circles (Chapter V).

GRAPHING AN ELLIPSE WITH YOUR CALCULATOR

Similar to the approach for graphing circles with your calculator, you can graph an ellipse by solving for y, and graphing *two* equations. If the equation is complicated, you probably won't have time to do this. But for easier ellipse equations (centered at the origin), or if you have time at the end of a test, graphing an ellipse might get you out of a jam. Below is a simple example. Review the More Circles lesson ("Graphing a Circle with Your Calculator") for more details:

$$\frac{x^2}{4}+\frac{y^2}{9}=1 \ \rightarrow \ \frac{y^2}{9}=1-\frac{x^2}{4} \ \rightarrow \ y^2=9\left(1-\frac{x^2}{4}\right) \ \rightarrow \ y=\pm\sqrt{9\left(1-\frac{x^2}{4}\right)}$$

Let's try a lesson problem:

50. Which of the following is the equation of the ellipse shown in the standard (x, y) coordinate plane below?

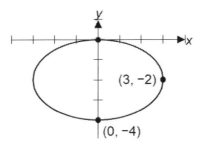

(3, −2)

(0, −4)

A. $\dfrac{x^2}{3} + \dfrac{(y+2)^2}{2} = 1$

B. $\dfrac{x^2}{6} + \dfrac{(y+2)^2}{4} = 1$

C. $\dfrac{x^2}{9} + \dfrac{(y+2)^2}{4} = 1$

D. $\dfrac{(x+2)^2}{9} + \dfrac{y^2}{4} = 1$

E. $\dfrac{(x+2)^2}{4} + \dfrac{y^2}{9} = 1$

(HW)

45. The parabola in the standard (x, y) coordinate plane below has a vertex at point $(4, 0)$, as shown. Which of the following could be the equation of the parabola?

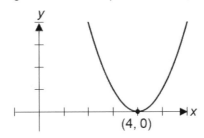

(4, 0)

A. $y = x - 4$
B. $y = x^2 - 4$
C. $y = (x - 4)^2$
D. $y = (x + 4)^2$
E. $y = 2(x - 4)$

49. In the standard (x, y) coordinate plane below, line l intersects the parabola at the parabola's vertex. If the parabola is defined by the equation $y = 4x^2 + 12x + 14$, and if line l goes through point $(0, 0)$, which of the following is the slope of line l ?

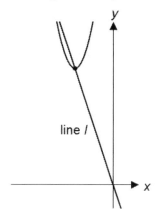

   line l

  A. −4

  B. $-\dfrac{10}{3}$

  C. −3

  D. $-\dfrac{8}{3}$

  E. −2

Continued →

58. The ellipse below is graphed in the standard (x, y) coordinate and centered at $(0, 0)$. If point Q lies on the ellipse, as shown below, what is the value of the coordinate q?

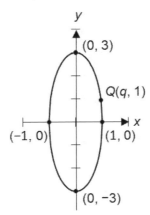

A. $\sqrt{\dfrac{1}{9}}$

B. $\sqrt{\dfrac{7}{9}}$

C. $\sqrt{\dfrac{8}{9}}$

D. 1

E. $\sqrt{8}$

8. VECTORS

A *vector* is defined as a quantity possessing both magnitude and direction and is graphically represented by an arrow (usually on an (*x*, *y*) coordinate plane). The length of the arrow is the vector's *magnitude*. The direction of the arrow indicates (obviously) the *direction* of the vector. Vectors can be labeled either with an arrow over the endpoints, in the order of the vector's direction ($\overrightarrow{AB}$), or as a lowercase, bold letter (**a**):

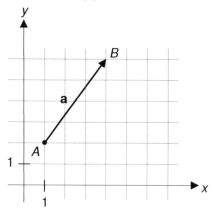

VECTOR NOTATION

Each vector has an *x* component (how far the vector stretches in the *x* direction) and a *y* component (how far it stretches in the *y* direction). In the example above, the *x* component is 3, and the *y component* is 4.

- **Unit vector notation**: 3**i** + 4**j**. Just put the *x component* in front of a bold **i**, and the *y component* in front of a bold **j**. (In case you're wondering, **i** and **j** are called *unit vectors*—they stretch 1 unit in the *x* and *y* directions, respectively.)
- **Component notation**: ⟨3, 4⟩. This is probably the easier notation. We'll use this one for the rest of this lesson, but make sure you're comfortable with the unit vector notation above, in case it shows up on a problem.

MULTIPLYING A VECTOR BY A SCALAR

If a vector is multiplied by a number (often called a *scalar* when talking about vectors), the vector's magnitude will change; in other words, it will get longer or shorter. Multiplying by a *negative* number will reverse the vector's direction. The math is straightforward. We'll continue using the vector **a**: $\langle 3, 4 \rangle$:

$2\mathbf{a} = 2\langle 3, 4 \rangle = = \langle 2 \cdot 3, 2 \cdot 4 \rangle = \langle 6, 8 \rangle$ → The vector stretches by a factor of 2 (see below).

$-\mathbf{a} = -\langle 3, 4 \rangle = \langle -3, -4 \rangle$ → The vector reverses direction (see below).

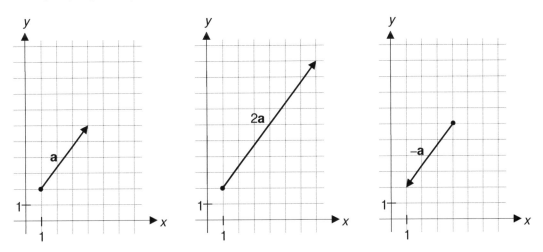

Note that a vector's *placement* in the (x, y) coordinate plane is *not* important. We are only concerned with a vector's *direction* and *length*. Assuming a vector is drawn with the correct length and direction, it can be placed anywhere on the (x, y) coordinate plane.

ADDING VECTORS

To add two vectors graphically, we place the starting point of the second vector on the end point (arrowhead) of the first vector. The sum of the two vectors is the resulting vector that stretches from the starting point of the first vector to the end of the second vector. This is easier to show than explain. If $\mathbf{a} = \langle 3, 4 \rangle$ and $\mathbf{b} = \langle 2, -3 \rangle$, then the vector $\mathbf{a} + \mathbf{b}$ is shown below:

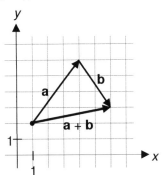

Generally, when adding (or subtracting) vectors you'll want to work *algebraically*, not geometrically. Just add the *x components* and *y components* (similar to combining like terms):

$$\mathbf{a} + \mathbf{b} = \langle 3, 4 \rangle + \langle 2, -3 \rangle = \langle 3 + 2, 4 + (-3) \rangle = \langle 5, 1 \rangle \rightarrow \text{Check the } \mathbf{a} + \mathbf{b} \text{ vector above. } \checkmark$$

(EX) The component forms of **a** and **b** are given by $\mathbf{a} = \langle 3, 4 \rangle$ and $\mathbf{b} = \langle 2, -3 \rangle$. If $\mathbf{d} = 2\mathbf{a} - 2\mathbf{b}$, what is the value of **d**?

- **A.** $\langle 2, 8 \rangle$
- **B.** $\langle 2, 14 \rangle$
- **C.** $\langle 2, 16 \rangle$
- **D.** $\langle 5, 1 \rangle$
- **E.** $\langle 5, 16 \rangle$

MAGNITUDE AND DIRECTION

We'll use the $\langle 3, 4 \rangle$ vector below to cover magnitude and direction:

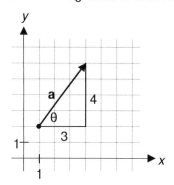

MAGNITUDE

If you're asked to find a vector's magnitude (length)—notated |a| (or sometimes ||a||)—use the Pythagorean theorem:

$$\text{Magnitude of } \mathbf{a}: \quad |\mathbf{a}| = \sqrt{3^2 + 4^2} = \sqrt{25} = 5$$

DIRECTION

If you're asked to find the direction, or angle (θ), of a vector, you'll have to use inverse trigonometry: Since $\tan \theta = \dfrac{4}{3}$, we can write:

$$\text{Direction of } \mathbf{a}: \quad \theta = \tan^{-1}\left(\frac{4}{3}\right)$$

(The answer will likely be left in this form.)

■

Try the following vectors lesson problem:

55. The component forms of vectors **x** and **y** are given by **x** = $\langle a, -2a \rangle$ and **y** = $\langle -b, b \rangle$, where a and b are integers. If **x** − **y** = $\langle 2, 1 \rangle$, what is the value of a?

    A. −3
    B. 0
    C. 1
    D. 2
    E. 5

(HW)

49. The component forms of vectors **a** and **b** are given by **a** = $\langle 2, 3 \rangle$ and **b** = $\langle 4, 5 \rangle$. If vector **d** = 4**a** − 2**b**, which of the following is the component form of **d**?

    A. $\langle -2, -2 \rangle$
    B. $\langle 0, 2 \rangle$
    C. $\langle 2, 4 \rangle$
    D. $\langle 4, 7 \rangle$
    E. $\langle 16, 22 \rangle$

56. Vectors **a** and **b** are shown in the standard (x, y) coordinate plane below. Which of the following is the unit vector notation of the vector **a** + **b** ?

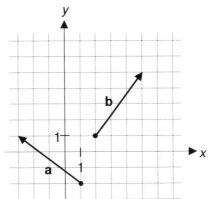

    A. $-\mathbf{i} + 7\mathbf{j}$
    B. $6\mathbf{j}$
    C. $6\mathbf{i}$
    D. $7\mathbf{i} - \mathbf{j}$
    E. $7\mathbf{i} + 7\mathbf{j}$

9. DIRECT & INVERSE VARIATION

You should memorize two simple equations for *direct* and *inverse variation* problems.

DIRECT VARIATION

If two positive numbers are *directly proportional*, then as one number increases (or decreases) the other number also increases (or decreases). To help remember the following equation, notice that **d**irect variation and **d**ivision start with the same letter—the equation for direct variation shows that the **d**ivision of two numbers y/x will always equal a constant number k:

$$\frac{y}{x} = k$$

 These problems usually mention the words *directly proportional*, but could also say: *x* and *y* are *in direct variation*, *x* and *y* are *in proportion*, or *x varies directly with y*.

INVERSE VARIATION

If two positive numbers are *inversely proportional*, then as one number increases the other number does the opposite—it decreases, or if one number decreases the other number increases. The equation for inverse variation shows that the *product* of two numbers *xy* will always equal a constant number k:

$$xy = k$$

 These problems usually mention the words *inversely proportional*, but could also say *x varies indirectly with y*.

SOLVING VARIATION PROBLEMS

To solve these problems, you will usually be given initial values for *x* and *y*.

1. Using the correct equation above with the given values of *x* and *y*, solve for *k*.
2. Once you know the value for *k*, you can solve for *y* (for any given value of *x*) or solve for *x* (for any given value of *y*).

(EX) If y is directly proportional to x and $y = -5$ when $x = 5$, what is the value of y when $x = 15$?

    A. 15
    B. 5
    C. 0
    D. −5
    E. −15

Try the following lesson problem:

6. If x varies indirectly with y and $x = 20$ when $y = 2$, what is the value of y when $x = -2$?

    A. −40
    B. −20
    C. $-\frac{1}{5}$
    D. 10
    E. 20

26. If x varies indirectly with y^2 and $x = 200$ when $y = 2$, what is the value of y when $x = 8$?

    F. 50
    G. 40
    H. 30
    J. 20
    K. 10

38. If x is directly proportional to y and $x = \frac{1}{2}$ when $y = 4$, what is the value of $\frac{y}{x}$ when $y = 2 \times 10^8$?

    A. 2
    B. 8
    C. 2×10^8
    D. 4×10^8
    E. 8×10^8

Continued →

51. The cost to use Sound Ideas Studios varies directly with the square root of the time the studio is used. If a band pays $60 for 36 minutes of studio time, how much would 15 hours of studio time cost?

   F. $1,500
   G. $640
   H. $300
   J. $144
   K. $12

10. SETS & GROUPS

SETS

A *set* is a collection of items. These items are called *elements* or *members* of the set. A set is usually represented by brackets, for example:

set A = {1, 3, 4, 5, 7, 8, 9}
set B = {2, 4, 6, 8, 10}

VENN DIAGRAMS

You may be asked to find the *intersection* or the *union* of two or more sets. It may be helpful to look at sets as circles and the members of the sets as numbers inside the circles. These are called Venn diagrams.

Intersection – the common elements of the sets. The intersection of sets A and B above is {4, 8} since 4 and 8 are members in *both* sets:

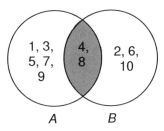

Union – consists of the elements that are in either set *or* in both sets (in other words—all the elements). The union of sets A and B above is {1, 2, 3, 4, 5, 6, 7, 8, 9, 10} since these 10 numbers are in either set (1, 2, 3, 5, 6, 7, 9, and 10) or in both sets (4 and 8):

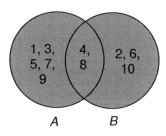

VENN DIAGRAMS: *NUMBERS* OF ELEMENTS

The Venn diagrams above display the actual elements of each region. For example, the intersection of sets *A* and *B* is made up of the numbers 4 and 8. Venn diagrams can also display the *number* of elements in each region. The Venn diagram for sets *A* and *B* is shown below:

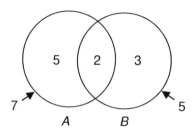

Make sure you are clear that each number represents the *number* of elements in that region. For example, there are 5 elements unique to set *A*, and 2 elements in set *A and* set *B* (the intersection). Thus, the total number of elements in set A is 7 (written outside the circle).

■

 To identify set problems, look for elements surrounded by brackets, such as {1, 2, 3}, or look for Venn diagrams.

Try the following lesson problem:

7. Sets *M* and *N* are shown below. How many numbers are in the intersection of sets *M* and *N*?

       set *M* = {all prime numbers less than 10}
       set *N* = {all odd numbers less than 10}

  A. 1
  B. 2
  C. 3
  D. 4
  E. 5

GROUPS

When you are asked to find the number of members of a particular group, you're probably dealing with a *groups* problem. Let's use a Venn diagram to visualize a typical group problem:

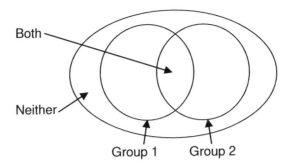

In the Venn diagram above, we have two groups that intersect (the intersection is labeled "Both"). Notice that we also have a region where members are not part of either group ("Neither"). You can create a simple equation from this Venn diagram:

 Total = Members of Group 1 + Members of Group 2 + Neither – Both

Why did we subtract members in "Both" groups? Because when we counted Group 1 and Group 2, we ended up counting members in both groups twice, so subtract them once.

For groups problems, you can usually use either the equation above or a Venn diagram. If you ever see a problem with more than two groups, use a Venn diagram.

 These problems will usually involve two groups (generally of people). They ask about the number of members in *one*, *both*, or *none* of the groups.

(EX) If at a school of 200 students, 75 students take Spanish and 25 students take Latin. 10 of the students who take Latin also take Spanish, how many students are not taking Spanish or Latin?

A. 80
B. 90
C. 100
D. 110
E. 120

Try the following lesson problem:

52. At a school of 90 students, all of the students take Spanish, Latin, or both. If 75 students take Spanish and 25 students take Latin, how many students take Spanish or Latin but <u>not</u> both?

    A. 10
    B. 70
    C. 80
    D. 90
    E. 100

SETS AND GROUPS HOMEWORK

31. The figure below is a Venn diagram for sets X, Y, and Z. The number in each region indicates how many elements are in that region. If there are 20 elements common to sets X and Y, what is the value of a?

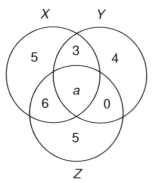

    A. 2
    B. 5
    C. 11
    D. 17
    E. 20

Continued →

52. Of the 120 international students at a camp, 90 spoke Spanish and 40 spoke French. What is the least possible number of campers that could speak both Spanish and French?

   F. 0
   G. 10
   H. 40
   J. 50
   K. 80

58. Hot Rod Auto Body's employees perform the three basic tasks of auto body repair: body work, sanding, and painting. All employees can perform at least one of these tasks, and some can perform more than one. Using the information in the table below, how many people are employed at Hot Rod Auto Body?

Number of workers	Task(s)
5	body work
7	sanding
7	painting
2	both body work and sanding but not painting
0	both body work and painting but not sanding
1	both sanding and painting but not body work
1	body work, sanding, and painting

   A. 14
   B. 16
   C. 18
   D. 19
   E. 23

11. GREATEST & LEAST POSSIBLE VALUES

Some problems may ask you to find the *greatest possible value* (GPV) or *least possible value* (LPV) of a number or group of numbers.

 Look for the words *greatest* (or *maximum*, *biggest*, etc.) *possible value* or *least* (or *minimum*, *smallest*, etc.) *possible value*.

Be familiar with the following rules:

GREATEST AND LEAST VALUES

Students often forget that if a variable is negative (for example: $-x$), then the *greater* the value of x, the *lesser* the value of $-x$. Alternatively, the *lesser* the value of x, the *greater* the value of $-x$. Look at the following example:

(EX) If $-2 \le x \le 3$, what is the maximum value of $-2x$?

    A. −6
    B. 0
    C. 2
    D. 4
    E. 6

GPV OF NUMBERS MULTIPLIED TOGETHER

Some problems ask you to find the GPV of a *product* of two numbers. These problems typically give you the *sum* of the numbers. The GPV of two numbers multiplied together will occur when the values of the two numbers are *equal or as close to each other as possible*. Look at the following example:

(EX) If the sum of two positive integers is 12, what is the greatest possible value of the product of the two integers?

    A. 12
    B. 32
    C. 35
    D. 36
    E. 144

LPV OF NUMBERS MULTIPLIED TOGETHER

You might also see a problem that gives you the *difference* of two numbers and asks for the LPV of the *product* of the numbers. The LPV will occur when:

1. One value is negative and one value is positive (to get a negative product).
2. The *absolute* values of the two numbers are equal or as close to each other as possible.

For example:

(EX) What is the least possible value for the product of 2 integers that differ by 7?

- **A.** −49
- **B.** −12
- **C.** −10
- **D.** 0
- **E.** 10

LESSON PROBLEMS

42. The sum of three positive integers is 40. If one of the integers is 11, what is the greatest possible value of the product of the other two integers?

- **A.** 29
- **B.** 200
- **C.** 210
- **D.** 225
- **E.** 400

50. If x is a member of the set $\{-2, 0, 2\}$ and y is a member of the set $\{-3, -1, 1, 3\}$, what is the greatest possible value of $x - y$?

- **F.** 5
- **G.** 4
- **H.** 3
- **J.** 2
- **K.** 1

54. If $0 \leq x \leq 3$ and $-3 \leq y \leq 0$, what is the maximum value of $|2y - x|$?

    A. 12
    B. 9
    C. 6
    D. 3
    E. 0

60. If x and y are real numbers and $x - y = 10$, what is the smallest possible value for xy?

    F. −25
    G. −21
    H. 0
    J. 1
    K. 11

12. MATH ODDS & ENDS PROBLEMS

PRACTICE PROBLEMS

The worksheets on the following pages test techniques taught in this chapter. For additional practice, we'll use problems from Test 5 in *The Official ACT Prep Guide*.

- ☐ Odds & Ends Worksheet 1 (Sections 1–6)
- ☐ Odds & Ends Worksheet 2 (Sections 7–11)
- ☐ **The Official ACT Prep Guide: Test 5**: Only tackle questions related to *this chapter*. For a list of these relevant questions, see the Techniques chapter at the end of this tutorial (first page of "Techniques: Test 5").

Reminders:

- **Use techniques**: These assignments are "open book." Go back to the tutorial as often as you need to, and use techniques aggressively.
- **No timing**: Do *not* time yourself on these assignments.
- **Scheduling**: See the Tutoring Schedules section in the Introduction for more details on scheduling.

TEST CORRECTIONS

After each practice test is graded, you should correct questions related to this chapter that you missed or guessed on. See "Correcting Practice Tests" in the Introduction for more details. Here are the three steps to correcting practice tests:

1. Turn to the Techniques chapter at the end of this tutorial and circle the Odds & Ends questions that you missed or guessed on for the test you are correcting.
2. Correct the problems in *The Official ACT Prep Guide*. As you correct the problems, go back to the tutorial and review the techniques. The idea is to (1) identify techniques that have given you trouble, (2) go back to the tutorial so you can review and strengthen these techniques, and (3) apply these techniques to the specific problems on which you struggled.
3. If you have trouble identifying the best technique to use for a problem, refer to the Techniques chapter. This is an important part of correcting the tests.

MATH ODDS & ENDS WORKSHEET (SECTIONS 1–6)

28. Floyd starts at City A. He must pick up a package at City B and deliver the package to City C. If there are 7 possible routes between City A and City B and 8 possible routes between City B and City C, how many routes are possible for Floyd to travel from City A to City B to City C?

   F. 15
   G. 48
   H. 52
   J. 56
   K. 150

30. Which of the following values of a satisfies $\log_a 1{,}000 = 3$?

   A. 1
   B. 10
   C. 100
   D. 1,000
   E. 10,000

39. For $i^2 = -1$, what is the value of $(4 + i)(-3 - i)$?

   F. $-7 - 7i$
   G. $-11 - 7i$
   H. $-11 - i$
   J. $-12 - 7i$
   K. $-12 - 8i$

45. What is the matrix product $\begin{bmatrix} x & y & z \end{bmatrix} \cdot \begin{bmatrix} 1 \\ 2 \\ 3 \end{bmatrix}$?

   F. $\begin{bmatrix} 6x + 6y + 6z \end{bmatrix}$
   G. $\begin{bmatrix} 3x + 2y + z \end{bmatrix}$
   H. $\begin{bmatrix} x + 2y + 3z \end{bmatrix}$
   J. $\begin{bmatrix} x \\ 2y \\ 3z \end{bmatrix}$
   K. $\begin{bmatrix} 6x \\ 6y \\ 6z \end{bmatrix}$

50. The first and second terms in an arithmetic sequence are p and $p + q$, in that order. What is the 1000th term of the sequence?

   F. $999(p + q)$
   G. $1{,}000(p + q)$
   H. $p + 998q$
   J. $p + 999q$
   K. $p + 1{,}000q$

Continued →

53. Greg decides to collect bottle caps each day during a family vacation. On his first day, he collects 10 bottle caps. His goal is to collect 1 more bottle cap on each successive day than he collected the day before. If Greg meets, but does not exceed, his goal, and if the vacation lasts 24 days, how many bottle caps in all will Greg collect?

    F. 483
    G. 484
    H. 516
    J. 517
    K. 518

55. How many distinct permutations can be made from the letters in TEXT ?

    A. $2!$

    B. $4!$

    C. $\dfrac{4!}{2!}$

    D. 4^2

    E. 4^4

57. If today is Friday, what day of the week will it be in 100 days?

    A. Sunday
    B. Monday
    C. Tuesday
    D. Wednesday
    E. Thursday

58. Which of the following values of x satisfies $\log_5 125^2 = 2x$?

    A. 3
    B. 5
    C. 6
    D. 15
    E. 25

Continued →

59. Four newspaper reporters are each to be assigned one of four assignments. Two of the assignments are in Mexico, one is in Canada, and one is in England. If Amy and Ryan are two of the four reporters, what is the probability that they will both be assigned the jobs in Mexico?

A. $\frac{1}{16}$

B. $\frac{1}{12}$

C. $\frac{1}{6}$

D. $\frac{1}{4}$

E. $\frac{1}{2}$

60. The sum of the first n terms of a geometric series with first term a and common ratio $r \neq 1$ is given by $\frac{a(r^n - 1)}{r - 1}$. The sum of a given geometric series is −1,100, there are 5 terms in the series, and the common ratio is −2. What is the second term of the series?

F. −100
G. 0
H. 1
J. 100
K. 200

PRACTICE TEST (30- and 40-hour programs): Now is a good time to take **Test 3** in the ACT book. (You should have already taken Tests 1 and 2.) If you have any questions about taking these tests, review "Taking Practice Tests" in this tutorial's Introduction.

MATH ODDS & ENDS WORKSHEET (SECTIONS 7–11)

20. Given that $a \geq 5$ and $a + b \leq 10$, what is the greatest possible value of b ?

    A. -5
    B. 0
    C. 5
    D. 10
    E. 50

22. The annual membership fee at a country club varies indirectly with the number of years that you have been a member, up to the point where membership is free. If you pay $4,000 for your 2nd year of membership, how much will you pay for your 10th year of membership?

    A. $400
    B. $700
    C. $800
    D. $2,000
    E. $20,000

38. At a car repair shop, 10 of the cars have mechanical problems and 16 of the cars have electrical problems. If there are 20 cars at the shop and all of the cars have either mechanical problems, electrical problems, or both, how many cars have both mechanical and electrical problems?

    A. 6
    B. 8
    C. 16
    D. 20
    E. 26

40. If k is a constant and x, y, and z are positive real number variables, in which of the following equations does x vary directly with the square of y and inversely with the cube of z ?

    A. $x = \dfrac{ky^2}{z^3}$

    B. $x = \dfrac{kz^3}{y^2}$

    C. $x = \dfrac{ky^3}{z^2}$

    D. $x = \dfrac{ky^2}{z^2}$

    E. $x = ky^2 z^3$

Continued →

42. Given that $x \geq 5$ and $x - y \leq 10$, what is the LEAST possible value of y ?

   A. −5
   B. 0
   C. 5
   D. 10
   E. 50

43. The parabola below is in the standard (x, y) coordinate plane. Which of the following systems of inequalities defines the shaded region bound by the parabola and the x-axis?

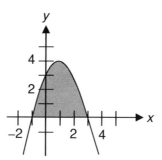

   A. $y < 0$
   $y > x^2 - 2x - 3$

   B. $y < 0$
   $y < -x^2 + 2x + 3$

   C. $y > 0$
   $y < x^2 - 2x - 3$

   D. $y > 0$
   $y < -x^2 + 2x + 3$

   E. $y > 0$
   $y > -x^2 + 2x + 3$

Continued →

57. Vectors **a**, **b**, **c**, **d**, and **e** are shown in the standard (x, y) coordinate plane below. Which of the following vector operations would result in a vector with a magnitude of 0 units?

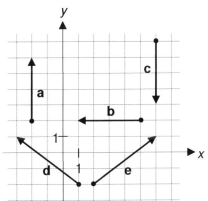

A. **a** + **b**
B. **a** + **c**
C. **b** + **c**
D. **a** − **c**
E. **d** + **e**

58. The figure below is an ellipse in the standard (x, y) coordinate plane. If the ellipse is rotated 90° about the origin $(0, 0)$, which of the following equations defines the resulting ellipse?

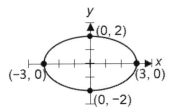

A. $\dfrac{x^2}{9} + \dfrac{y^2}{4} = 1$

B. $\dfrac{x^2}{6} + \dfrac{y^2}{4} = 1$

C. $\dfrac{x^2}{4} + \dfrac{y^2}{9} = 1$

D. $\dfrac{x^2}{4} + \dfrac{y^2}{6} = 1$

E. $\dfrac{x^2}{2} + \dfrac{y^2}{3} = 1$

Continued →

60. If x and y are real numbers and $x - y = 10$, what is the smallest possible value for xy?

    A. −25
    B. −21
    C. 0
    D. 1
    E. 11

PART 3

READING

I
READING INTRODUCTION

The Reading section is divided into five chapters:

I. Introduction

II. Reading Strategies

III. Question Types

IV. Practice

TYPES OF QUESTIONS

The questions on the Reading Test are multiple-choice, with four answer choices each.

TEST LAYOUT

The Reading Test includes:

- 40 questions
- 4 passages (10 questions each)
- A total test time of 35 minutes

TYPES OF PASSAGES

The test includes three long passages and one "double passage" (two shorter passages with one set of (10) questions). The passages will typically be of the following types and in the following order:

- Prose Fiction (from a novel or short story)
- Social Science (including biography, history, political science, etc.)
- Humanities (including art, film, music, etc.)
- Natural Science (including chemistry, geology, technology, etc.)

More details about these passages are found at the end of this section (homework).

DOUBLE PASSAGES

The ACT now includes one *double passage* on every test. These passages ask the usual ten questions, but they include *two* passages. Not surprisingly, the passages will be related in some way, often even written by the same author. The ten questions will be divided into three sets: one set for Passage A, one set for Passage B, and one set for both passages. Tackle these double passages in the following order:

1. Read Passage A and answer the questions related to this passage only.
2. Read Passage B and answer the questions related to this passage only.
3. Finally, move on to the questions for both passages.

This approach turns double passages into, essentially, two short passages, each with a few questions, followed by what we call Comparison Questions, which we'll discuss in detail later.

! **Always tackle double passages one passage at a time.**

TIMING

All programs: Skip this Timing section for now. We'll be coming back to it once we've covered a couple question types in Chapter III.

Most students agree that one of the most difficult parts of the Reading Test is the minimal time allotted to complete it. Remember, the Reading Test is NOT arranged in order of difficulty. Thus, it is essential that you get to the *last* question of the *last* passage. On the Math test, running out of time is sometimes OK, because the questions at the end are usually difficult. But on the Reading Test , you must strive to get your eyeballs on every question.

The test is **35 minutes** long. If your goal is to get to every passage and answer every question, you only have **8 minutes and 45 seconds** per passage. So it's important to develop a timing approach to the Reading Test that maximizes your score.

DEADLINES

As discussed in the Introduction to this tutorial, we'll use *deadlines* to help you avoid falling behind as you take the test. They give you an idea of when you need to finish up one passage and move on to the next. We'll use a "running clock": start the test at "time 00:00" (don't forget to get a silent stopwatch for the actual test, as discussed in the Introduction). The first deadline will occur when you should finish Passage I and move on to Passage II. The next deadline is for Passage II (move on to Passage III). And so on.

As stated above, you will have 8 minutes and 45 seconds per passage. To be safe, let's round this down to **8:30**. Will each passage take you the exact same time? Probably not. Harder passages will take longer than easier ones. Your times will probably vary, but the 8:30 number should give you a general idea of how long to take for each passage, and you'll have a minute of cushion, in case you start to fall behind. Here are the deadlines:

Reading Deadlines: Step 3	
Start Test	00:00 min:sec
Finish Passage I	08:30
Finish Passage II	17:00
Finish Passage III	25:30
Finish Passage IV	34:00*

*You can fall up to a minute behind for this timing plan.

READING TIMES

You should expect to *read* each passage (before you look at the answer choices) in **3 to 4 minutes**. Why the range? Because you'll likely find some passages easier (and faster) to read than others. Just make sure you don't spend *more* than 4 minutes reading a passage.

MOVING FASTER THAN THE DEADLINES

Remember that these times are all *deadlines*—you don't *have* to take this long. If you move faster than these times, great. Don't slow down! You might need the extra time for one of the later passages. The deadlines just ensure that you don't fall behind.

ANSWER EASIER QUESTIONS FIRST

Here's a very important rule:

/ You can answer the questions in any order you'd like!

On your first pass through a passage's questions, you should skip the harder questions, and tackle the easier ones. Thus, if you run out of time and need to move on to the next passage, you've answered the easiest questions. Of course, if you have time after you finish the easier questions, go back and answer skipped questions (the more questions you skip on your first pass, the more time you will hopefully have to go back). Below are the types of questions to consider skipping on your first pass (we'll cover these soon):

- **Extended Reasoning and Purpose questions**: Look for keywords in the question such as "it is reasonable to infer" or "in order to." These questions are often more difficult than other types and should thus be skipped if time is an issue.

- **EXCEPT/NOT questions**: These questions aren't necessarily harder than other types, but they often take longer to answer. Consider skipping them, but if you have time, come back to them before moving to the next passage, especially if the identifiers (to be discussed soon) are good.
- **Paragraph questions**: If a question asks about a whole paragraph, especially a long paragraph, it might be a good question to skip. Rereading an entire paragraph takes time.
- **Poor identifiers**: If a question and its answer choices lack good identifiers, consider skipping the question. Students often spend too much time looking for information in the passage, even if the question sounds easy. Additionally, you might find what you're looking for as you answer other questions.

You should also skip any questions that seem difficult to you or test a part of the passage that you found confusing. Again, the idea is to answer the easier questions first, and answer the harder questions only if you have time. Don't feel bad about skipping questions, especially on harder passages. Answer the questions in the order that works best for you.

SKIMMING (OPTIONAL)

Skimming is not recommended for most students. The goal is to actually *read* the passages, as you'll learn on the following pages. Improving your actual reading times is something that will happen naturally from practice (and you'll be doing plenty of practice in this tutorial). Make sure you push yourself while you're reading. Make your markups (identifiers, etc.) quickly, and don't let your mind wander. Hopefully, over time, your reading speed will increase (your goal is 3–4 minutes per passage).

But what if you've been practicing for a while and you just can't get your reading times fast enough to get through the whole test? You might try *skimming*. Here's how to do it:

1. If the first paragraph is short (less than about 10 lines), read it. Otherwise, just read the first couple sentences and skim the rest of the paragraph.
2. **While skimming, look for and circle identifiers.** You may find this challenging at first, since you're not actually *reading*, but with practice you'll hopefully be able to spot many, if not most, of the good identifiers.
3. Read the first sentence or two of each paragraph, and then *skim* the rest of the paragraph. **Keep circling identifiers.**
4. If the last paragraph is short (less than about 10 lines), read it. Otherwise, just read the first couple sentences, skim the middle sentences, and then read the last sentence or two. The last couple sentences of a passage are often important.

SKIMMING TIME

With practice, you should be able to get through the passage in **less than 2 minutes**. If you have trouble staying under 2 minutes, try skimming more; you might have to sacrifice reading some of the topic sentences. Circle your identifiers quickly, and keep moving. Make sure you don't get held up anywhere in the passage.

ANSWERING THE QUESTIONS

The whole point of this approach is to give you more time for the questions. You'll likely have to skip some of the harder Main Idea, Extended Reasoning, and Purpose questions, or questions with poor identifiers, but hopefully the extra time will allow you to get through all four passages and answer most of the easier questions. Experiment with this approach and see if your scores increase.

TIMING PRACTICE

You'll frequently work on a single practice passage as you make your way through this tutorial. For single passages, your goal is **8 minutes and 45 seconds** (remember, we round down to 8:30 for the deadlines).

■

For homework, read over the following information about passage types, style, and rhetorical devices:

PASSAGE TYPES (AN OVERVIEW)

There are some specific features of each type of passage (Prose, Social Science, Humanities, and Natural Science) that you should be familiar with:

PROSE FICTION

Some students find these passages more difficult to understand because they are often written in a stylized language. Furthermore, things are not always as they seem. Be on the lookout for literary tools such as *sarcasm*, *satire*, *metaphor*, and *irony* as you read fiction passages. These are ways that an author may say one thing but mean something else:

- **sarcasm:** a form of irony in which apparent praise conceals another, scornful meaning.
- **satire:** the use of witty and sometime humorous language to convey insults or scorn.

- **metaphor:** a figure of speech in which a word or phrase literally denoting one kind of object or idea is used in place of another to suggest a likeness or analogy between them (as in *drowning in money*).
- **irony:** a technique of indicating, as through character or plot development, an intention or attitude opposite to that which is actually or ostensibly stated.

Tones and emotions are particularly important in Prose Fiction passages. How does the author feel about the characters? How do the characters feel about the other characters in the passage? How do these emotions create mood in the passage?

SOCIAL SCIENCE

These passages are typically a result of gathered research. Be prepared to see dates, events, and names of people, places, and concepts. Things can get confusing, so make sure to keep track of the specific details. As discussed in the next chapter, you'll do a lot of marking up on the Social Science passages.

HUMANITIES

Humanities passages, unlike Prose Fiction passages, are *non*-fictional. They tend to be written in a straightforward prose. As in Prose Fiction passages, the author's tone is important. How does the author feel about the topic? How does the author feel about the people in the passage? Can you predict the author's likely response to some hypothetical situation or event?

NATURAL SCIENCE

These passages are often difficult to read because of technical-sounding language and concepts. You will very likely read about some scientific topic with which you are not familiar. And you can expect to see unfamiliar words. But don't worry about it! Stay aggressive. Because the questions are often based on concrete details in the passage, they are usually easier than those of other types of passages. You might find the reading a challenge, but that doesn't mean the questions will be—and you score points answering *questions*, not reading passages.

STYLE AND RHETORICAL DEVICES

The tests in the *The Official ACT Prep Guide* may include questions that test *style* or *rhetorical devices* (metaphors, irony, sensory details, etc.). We've found that more recent tests do *not* frequently test these topics, so we decided not to cover these types of questions in detail. However, you might want to review some of these terms, just in case you see a question or two on a real test. Here are the most common topics tested:

- **imagery:** Refers to words that trigger mental pictures (images) in the reader's mind of any of the five senses. "They arrive at dawn in their geography of hats. A dark field of figures, stalks in motion, bending towards the docklands." —Colum McCann

- **irony:** A technique of indicating, as through character or plot development, an intention or attitude opposite to that which is actually or ostensibly stated. Guy Montag, the protagonist of Ray Bradbury's *Fahrenheit 451*, a man who starts fires, is ironically called a "fireman." Irony also may describe an outcome contrary to what might have been expected, such as a traffic cop losing his job because of unpaid parking tickets.

- **metaphor:** A statement where one thing is something else, when in fact, literally, it is not. "Thus a mind that is free from passion is a very citadel." —Marcus Aurelius

- **personification:** The attribution of human characteristics to animals or inanimate objects. "Only the champion daisy trees were serene. After all, they were part of a rain forest already two thousand years old and scheduled for eternity, so they ignored the men and continued to rock the diamondbacks that slept in their arms. It took the river to persuade them that indeed the world was altered." —Toni Morrison

- **simile:** A figure of speech in which two unlike things are compared. A simile displays an *alikeness* between two things, using the words "like" or "as." "Elderly American ladies leaning on their canes listed toward me like towers of Pisa." —Vladimir Nabokov

II
READING STRATEGIES

The act of actually *reading* the passages is, of course, one of the most important parts of the test. In this chapter we'll give you some tips on what to do while you're reading the passage. Your skill as a reader—and of course your ability to find correct answers—will improve by following these tips.

1. THE PASSAGE

READ THE INTRODUCTION (IF THERE IS ONE)

Each passage will include some brief text preceding the main body of the passage. Some important parts of these sections should be read before moving on:

- Confirm the passage type (Prose Fiction, Social Science, Humanities, Natural Science).
- Read the title of the book/article from which the passage is excerpted. This may give you a clue about the passage's main idea (especially on Social Science, Humanities, and Natural Science passages).
- Some passages may have a short sentence or two following the copyright information. This introductory information will assist you in understanding the context of the passage, so read it carefully.

READ THE PASSAGE

After reading the introduction, read the passage—and when we say read, we mean *read*. For most students, we do not recommend skimming.

! Do *not* read the questions first. Here's why:

1. Reading the passage is the best way to understand its *main idea* and *tone*. (More on main idea and tone soon.)
2. Most questions do *not* provide line numbers, so it is difficult to know where to look for information if you haven't read the passage.
3. The questions are generally *not* arranged in the order of the passage, again making it difficult to find information unless you've just read the passage.

EXCEPTIONS

Students who have ongoing difficulty finishing the Reading Test may try *skimming* the passages. This gives students more time to answer the questions. Also, if a student is running out of time at the end of the test, going straight to the questions of the last passage might make sense. We will discuss both strategies in the Timing chapter (Chapter III).

WHAT TO DO WHILE YOU'RE READING

As you read, you should plan to mark up the passage. This will help you identify main ideas and tone and quickly find information when you start answering questions.

LOOK FOR TONE WORDS

Tone words are words that convey *feeling*, sometimes positive and sometimes negative. Some examples of tone words are: *stubborn*, *envious*, *irritated*, *pleased*, and *groundbreaking*. Tone words help you identify the attitude of the author or a character in the passage.

Darkly underline tone words as you read.

CONTRAST SIGNALS

A great way to determine the author's tone is to look for *contrast signals*. Contrast signals are words that signal a change in the flow of a sentence. Examples:

although	even so	instead of	rather than
but	however	nevertheless	still
despite	in contrast	on the contrary	yet
even though	in spite of	on the other hand	

What's the big deal with contrast signals? The information that comes *after* contrast signals is often something the author feels is important. For example, would you say the following sentence is more positive or more negative?

> The candidate's poll numbers have been slipping, but she performed well in yesterday's debate.

The fact that the candidate performed well in the debate, which follows the contrast signal ("but"), suggests that the author is feeling somewhat positive about her chances. Sure, the candidate's poll numbers have been slipping, *but* perhaps things are about to change.

How about this sentence—more positive or more negative?

> The candidate performed well in yesterday's debate, but her poll numbers have been slipping.

Now things sound gloomier. Maybe the candidate's performance in the debate isn't making much of a difference. The voters don't seem to care.

While the words are the same in both sentences, those that follow the contrast signal make a big difference in the sentence's overall tone.

Draw a **box** around contrast signals as you read.

Let's try an example. Darkly underline tone words and draw a box around contrast signals in the following paragraph, and then try the example question:

> . . . The result of this diligent attention to detail may be well and good, but even the most accomplished editor has the tendency to lose the forest for the trees, as the saying goes. Yes, of course one must take care, cross his *t*'s and dot his *i*'s. Let us not forget, however, *why* we do this—to bring about art from a tangle of letters and words.

(EX) According to the passage, the author expresses which of the following attitudes?

- **A.** Many editors today have become lax about crossing *t*'s and dotting *i*'s.
- **B.** Editors must do more than simply concern themselves with the details of writing.
- **C.** Editors must learn that creating artistic work is the sole domain of the writer.
- **D.** The best editors excel at looking at details and identifying mistakes in writing.

FOCUS ON THE EASY STUFF

Don't worry about the hard stuff. Focus on the easy stuff. Every test will likely offer even the best readers with some challenging reading. The trick is to focus on the parts of these harder passages that you *do* understand. Don't get discouraged. Don't give up. Even if you finish a passage and only understood half of it (or less), that's better than giving up entirely.

Underline the easy stuff while you read, particularly on harder passages. Search out clear statements that help you understand the passage.

Underline *the easy stuff* in the following paragraph, and then try the example question:

> One must wield his mighty sword against the manifest bureaucracy surrounding him, the sweeping malfeasance of our day. Do not bridle. Do not defer. But no shining shank or cutlass will do. No. Rather, put your pen to paper, and write, with anger, yes, and with resolve. Write.

(EX) One of the main points that the author seeks to make in the passage is that:

A. when writing fails, one must turn to violent activism.
B. the best writers hold their emotions in check when writing.
C. the pen is mightier than the sword.
D. any means of action is better than doing nothing when faced with injustice.

CIRCLE IDENTIFIERS

Knowing where to look for information while you answer questions is probably the most important part of the Reading Test. As we said before, questions are typically out-of-order and usually do not have line numbers. You must use *clues* in the question (and sometimes the answer choices) to know where to find information in the passage. Since there is not enough time to skim the passage for every question, you must look for and **circle** *identifiers* while you read the passage. These will be words, almost always *nouns*, that stand out for a particular part of the passage. The following guidelines will help you find identifiers:

- **Proper Nouns**: The best identifiers are proper nouns, such as the name of a city, organization, book, movie, or person (just circle last names). These words will be *capitalized*.
- **Titles**: Identifiers may be the specific title or designation of a concepts or idea, such as *evolution* or *intelligent design*. These identifiers are often *not* capitalized.
- **Common Nouns**: Identifiers can also be common nouns, such as *truck* or *wallpaper*. You should circle common nouns that effectively relate to one small part of the passage (such as a single paragraph), especially if the passage doesn't have many proper nouns. You'll frequently circle common nouns on the Prose Fiction passages, which often lack many proper nouns.

Some words are *not* good identifiers, or should not be *circled* as identifiers:

- Do not circle **numbers** or **dates**. These are great identifiers, but they're fairly easy to spot without being circled.
- Do not circle words that aren't good identifiers. As discussed earlier, you might *underline* important words (such as tone words and "easy stuff"), but don't *circle* these words. **Save circles for identifiers only.**
- Do not circle words that show up too frequently, perhaps more than three or four times in a passage. For example, the word *airplane* is likely <u>not</u> a good identifier for a passage on *airplanes* because the word is probably used throughout the passage. Similarly, *George Washington* is <u>not</u> a good identifier for a passage that focuses on *George Washington*.

Circle identifiers as you read the passage.

Circle identifiers in the following paragraph:

> The discovery of penicillin is popularly attributed to the Scottish scientist Alexander Fleming in 1928, but its use was reported far earlier. The use of blue mold from bread (presumably penicillin) as folk medicine to treat suppurating wounds dates back to Europe's Middle Ages. Much later, in 1875, the first published reference appears in the Royal Society publication by John Tyndall. An 1897 paper by Ernest Duchesne documented the potential positive side effects of penicillin. Between 1915 and 1927, Costa Rican doctor Picado Twight studied the inhibitory actions of penicillin in his home country, and eventually reported these to the world at the Paris Academy of Sciences. This all suggests that perhaps it is the *development* of penicillin as a medicine, not its *discovery*, that is Fleming's great achievement.

OVER-CIRCLING?

Many students assume that if they circle too many words, they will have trouble finding relevant information for a given question. Of course, you don't want to circle words that are not good identifiers (rarely, for example, should you circle a non-noun), but every paragraph should have at least a few identifiers circled, especially words that have something to do *specifically* with that paragraph. You will be surprised how much this technique will help you quickly find information.

MAIN IDEAS

Passages often have one question that directly asks about the passage's main idea, so it's a good idea to consider the main idea while you read. If you identify a sentence or two that you believe may reflect the main idea—anything that you think is particularly important—put an asterisk (★) in the margin to the left of the sentence. This may help you find important information when you get to a main idea question.

FIRST AND LAST PARAGRAPHS

To identify main ideas, pay close attention to the first and especially the last paragraphs. (If the paragraphs are long, focus on the first couple sentences of the first paragraph and the last couple sentences of the last paragraph.) Often, just reading a few sentences will give you a good sense of the passage's main idea.

> Indicate potential main ideas with an asterisk (★) in the margin.

■

Below is a summary of what to mark up while you read a passage:

- Darkly underline tone words
- Box contrast signals
- Underline the easy stuff (especially main ideas)
- Circle identifiers
- Indicate main ideas with an asterisk

/ **Always remember that the most important of these markups is <u>circling identifiers</u>.**

You will have plenty of opportunities to practice these markups on the following pages and on homework passages.

2. CONTEXT

ANSWER QUESTIONS USING <u>CONTEXT</u>

Context – the parts before or after a statement that can influence its meaning.

Answering questions using context is analogous to figuring out the meaning of an unknown word by using the context of the sentence in which the word is found. You must answer questions *contextually*, using the information in the passage. This simple-sounding rule is perhaps the most important one found in this tutorial:

 Make sure your answer to any question is clearly stated or supported by context.

ANSWER QUESTIONS <u>BEFORE</u> LOOKING AT THE ANSWER CHOICES

This is one of the best ways to answer questions contextually. This approach will force you to use the information in the passage to find your answer, and it will eliminate the temptation of picking answer choices that sound correct *out* of context.

> Always answer the question before looking at the answer choices when the question provides:
> 1. **Line numbers**
> 2. **Identifiers**

THE EXCEPTION: BROAD OR GENERAL QUESTIONS

When the question is broad or if it covers a large part of the passage (such as a main idea question), you will have to look at the answer choices first and *then* use the context of the passage. See the following figure:

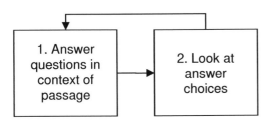

Questions with line numbers or identifiers

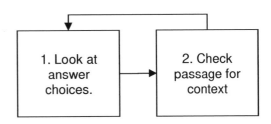

Broad questions and most main idea questions

Remember, regardless of whether you look at the answer choices before or after answering the question, you will still answer *all* questions using the context of the passage.

USE BRACKETS TO KEEP TRACK OF WHAT TO REREAD

If the question gives line numbers, draw a *bracket* to the left of the passage to keep track of what to reread. (This is faster than underlining and won't interfere with the underlines you may have already drawn.)

But keep in mind: you should be prepared to read several lines above and/or below the given line numbers to find your answer. If the specified lines are near the beginning of a paragraph, go back and start reading from the paragraph's first sentence. If the lines are near the end of a paragraph, you might read to the end of that paragraph. In short:

/ The correct answer is often <u>not</u> found in the lines specified in the question.

3. ANSWERING THE QUESTIONS

READ THE QUESTIONS CAREFULLY

There are three main reasons why it is important to carefully read a given question before trying to answer it:

1. Often one or two answer choices are absolutely true according to the *passage* yet don't properly answer the *question*.

2. The question will often give clues (identifiers) that will help you know where to look in the passage to find your answer. (Of course, sometimes the question will give line numbers.)

3. Words in the question may help identify its *type* (as listed below). Different types of questions will be answered in different ways.

TYPES OF QUESTIONS

The ACT uses several different types of questions on the Reading Test . The list below is roughly in order of most common to least:

- Direct
- Extended Reasoning
- Purpose
- Main Idea
- Comparison
- Tone
- Words in Context (WIC)

We'll get into each of these question types in the next chapter.

ANSWER CHOICES

ELIMINATING ANSWER CHOICES

Eliminating answer choices that you know are incorrect, particularly when you don't spot the correct answer right away, is an essential technique on the Reading Test . We call this "Process of Elimination" (POE). Usually, anywhere from one to three answer choices can be eliminated using context. The following elimination methods, listed roughly in order of importance, will be covered in the next chapter:

- Not Mentioned
- Tone
- Eye Catchers
- False
- Too Strong
- Every Word Counts

When we introduce an elimination method, you'll see the following symbol:

CAMOUFLAGED ANSWER CHOICES

The ACT likes to *camouflage* the correct answers with words that are different from, and often more *difficult* than, the words used in the passage. For lack of understanding, students are often tempted to eliminate these answer choices.

! **Just because the words in an answer choice are different from those in the passage, don't assume the answer choice is wrong. It may be *camouflaged*.**

III

QUESTION TYPES

This chapter will get into the different types of questions that show up on the test. Different types of questions should be approached in different ways. Understanding and practicing these different strategies is one of the keys to success on the Reading Test. We'll also cover methods for eliminating answer choices in this chapter.

1. DIRECT QUESTIONS

Now it's time to answer some questions. We'll use the abridged passages on the following pages to introduce each type of question. We'll also cover the methods for eliminating answer choices. **Note that real ACT passages will be longer, and will have 10 questions each.** We'll see plenty of these in the homework assignments and practice tests.

Remember that we'll be using *context* as we answer the questions, often by answering questions *before* we look at the answer choices (review the Context section if necessary).

Don't forget to mark up these passages while you read them:

- **Circle identifiers** ← most important!
- Darkly underline tone words
- Box contrast signals
- Underline the easy stuff (especially main ideas)
- Indicate main ideas with an asterisk

DIRECT QUESTIONS

Direct questions ask you to find information that is *explicitly stated* in the text. This doesn't mean these questions will necessarily be easy—the context may be difficult to understand, or the answer choices may be camouflaged—but these questions are usually easier than those that require you to *infer* something from the passage, such as Extended Reasoning questions (to be discussed soon).

 Direct questions are probably easier to identify by *default*. Most of the other question types have clear keywords, for example words such as "main purpose" (Main Idea question) or "implies" (Extended Reasoning question). If a question does not seem to fit into another category, it's probably a Direct question.

Read the following passage. Make sure to mark it up, as described above. . . .

NATURAL SCIENCE: This passage is adapted from *The World of Trees* by Hugh Johnson (©2010).

Darwin could have been more specific. Not of all landscapes, but of most, he could have said: "trees form the chief embellishment." Of all plants they are the most prominent and the most permanent, the ones that set the scene and dictate the atmosphere. Trees define the character of a landscape, proclaim its climate, divulge
5 the properties of its soil—even confirm the preoccupation of its people.

I wrote the first edition of this book 37 years ago, in the excitement of discovering for the first time the beauty and diversity there is in trees, and dismay at seeing the principal and biggest trees around me suddenly dying. In 1973 Dutch elm disease had just arrived. Within five years it had destroyed the landscape where I had come to live,
10 in the east of England.

I remember a before-and-after sequence of two photographs in *Time* magazine. Before: main street in some New England town; all harmony; comely cream clapboard dappled with light from the crowns of an avenue of tremendous elms. After: the elms gone; comeliness has become nakedness. What was all proportion and peace is
15 desolate.

It was partly in impotent protest that I started this book. What, I asked, can we do and what should we plant to restore the serenity we had lost? Over time the question has answered itself: in East Anglia oaks, ashes, and willows now fill many of the spaces and delineate the devastated skyline. But as soon as I started to investigate, to visit
20 botanical gardens and get lost in forests, above all simply to look around me with an inquiring mind, I discovered a variety of beauty and meaning I had never suspected.

First, make sure you marked up the passage appropriately.

Did you circle identifiers? Proper nouns, such as "Darwin," "Dutch elm disease," and "England," are the most obvious identifiers, but you might have also circled common nouns such as "climate" (line 4), "soil" (line 5), "photographs" (line 11), and so on.

Did you underline tone words? Some examples include "excitement" (line 6), "beauty" (lines 7 and 21), "dismay" (line 7), and "devastated" (line 19) (there are several others).

Did you draw a box around the important contrast signal ("But") in line 19?

Start getting into the habit of quickly and efficiently marking up passages as you read. Make sure you practice this now, so that it becomes second nature when you start taking practice tests.

DIRECT QUESTIONS WITH WORD-FOR-WORD ANSWERS

The answers to some Direct questions are word-for-word taken from the passage. The challenge to these is entirely in finding the information in the passage. Many students agree that these are the easiest questions on the test (assuming they find the correct context). Here's an example:

(EX) 1. According to the passage, following the destruction caused by Dutch elm disease after 1973, East Anglia oaks, ashes, and willows:

Here's where we get to put our identifiers to work. Hopefully you have "East Anglia oaks, ashes, and willows" circled. These are the kinds of nouns that are important identifiers. You might be able to skim a short passage like this one for these words, but with longer passages (like the ones on the ACT), you'll need to look for these circled identifiers. Go back to the passage and try answering the question (don't look at the answer choices yet).

Do you see the answer?

    A. were similarly and devastatingly affected by the disease.
    B. now fill many of the spaces and delineate the devastated skyline.
    C. will hopefully help counter the effects of future tree diseases.
    D. were a source of serenity that is now lost.

Before moving on to the next question, let's introduce an elimination technique:

⊘ ELIMINATE ANSWER CHOICES THAT ARE FALSE

The ACT sometimes includes answer choices that are just plain *false*. Of course, make sure to eliminate these answer choices. Do you see any answer choices for the question above that are false?

Here's another question. With this one, try using identifiers in the *answer choices* to find context.

(EX) 2. The author of the passage characterizes trees as:
- **A.** better suited for embellishment than other plants.
- **B.** the most prominent and the most permanent of all plants.
- **C.** easier to categorize than other plants because of their distinguishing features.
- **D.** Darwin's primary focus in his study of landscapes and vegetation.

Let's introduce some more elimination techniques:

⊘ ELIMINATE ANSWER CHOICES THAT ARE *NOT MENTIONED*

This is probably the most commonly used elimination technique. Especially look for **specific references** in the answer choices that are not mentioned in the passage (answer choices that are vague or broad are more difficult to eliminate using this technique).

Look back to Question 2 above. Do you see an answer choice that can be eliminated using the Not Mentioned technique?

⊘ WATCH OUT FOR EYE CATCHERS

Eye catchers are words or phrases that come directly from the passage but are not part of the correct answer. Students tend to be attracted to answer choices with eye catchers because they recognize these words or phrases from the passage. Before you select an answer choice with an eye catcher, be absolutely sure it answers the question correctly. (When we get into "camouflaged" answers—correct answers that are *not* written with the exact words of the passage—eye catchers will be even more tempting. We'll get to these soon.)

Go back to Question 2. Do you see any eye catchers in the incorrect answer choices?

DIRECT QUESTIONS WITH CAMOUFLAGED ANSWERS

As stated above, the correct answers will not always use the words from the passage. They may be *camouflaged*. If the camouflaged answer is clear, then you'll hopefully be able to connect it to the context of the passage. If the camouflaged answer is confusing, you might have to use a process of elimination (POE). Let's try one of these questions now:

(EX) 3. In discussing the importance of trees in the first paragraph (lines 1–5), the author mentions that all of the following are true EXCEPT:

First of all, note that this question requires you to look for an answer choice that is *false*. These EXCEPT/NOT questions typically involve going back to the passage and eliminating answer choices that are *true*. We recommend you write a "not true" sign (Ⓣ) next to the answer choices so you don't forget to eliminate *true* answer choices. Let's try that now with the answer choices below:

A. trees live longer than other plants.
B. trees characterize the general appearance of the land.
C. trees alter the soil properties of the land.
D. trees can verify the likely occupations of a region's inhabitants.

Here's another Direct question:

(EX) 4.   The aspect of trees that the author finds most impressive is their:

The challenge to this question is finding the appropriate context in the passage (note that the question does not offer a good identifier). But do you remember the contrast signal that you boxed in line 19 ("But")? What follows is often important. Try to answer the question using this context (don't look at the answer choices yet).

Can you identify the answer that best reflects this statement?

    A. resilience
    B. mystery
    C. size
    D. diversity

As stated earlier, direct questions are not necessarily easy. If the context is difficult, the question might be difficult:

(EX) 5.   According to the passage, when the author started writing his book, he was:

Once again, try to answer the question, using context, before you look at the answer choices.

If you're comfortable with the vocabulary here, the answer is straightforward. Otherwise, the answer may be difficult to find. Can you spot it?

    A. concerned that his book will not find a large readership.
    B. doubtful of his ability to effect real change with his writing.
    C. confident that his book will answer the questions related to the destruction of trees.
    D. encouraged by changes that he sees in botanical gardens and forests.

■

On the following passage, focus especially on identifying and answering the Direct questions. You will see other types of questions as well. We recommend you come back to any of these (missed) questions after covering their relevant lessons on the following pages. Here are some reminders:

- **Don't time yourself with this passage**. We'll worry about timing soon.
- Don't forget to mark up the passage appropriately. **Especially look for identifiers.**
- Try answering most questions, using context, *before* looking at the answer choices.
- Look for opportunities to eliminate incorrect answer choices, especially those that mention something specific that is not found in the passage.
- Watch out for eye catchers.

Passage I

PROSE FICTION: This passage is adapted from the short story "American History" by Judith Ortiz-Cofer (©1992 by Judith Ortiz-Cofer).

There was only one source of beauty and light for me my ninth grade year. The only thing I had anticipated at the start of the semester. That was seeing Eugene. In
5 August, Eugene and his family had moved into the only house on the block that had a yard and trees. I could see his place from my bedroom window in El Building. In fact, if I sat on the fire escape I was literally sus-
10 pended above Eugene's backyard. It was my favorite spot to read my library books in the summer. Until that August the house had been occupied by an old couple. Over the years I had become part of their family,
15 without their knowing it, of course. I had a view of their kitchen and their backyard, and though I could not hear what they said, I knew when they were arguing, when one of them was sick, and many other things. I
20 knew all this by watching them at mealtimes. I could see their kitchen table, the sink, and the stove. During good times, he sat at the table and read his newspapers while she fixed the meals. If they ar-
25 gued, he would leave and the old woman would sit and stare at nothing for a long time. When one of them was sick, the other would come and get things from the kitchen and carry them out on a tray. The old man
30 had died in June. The house had stood empty for weeks. I had had to resist the temptation to climb down into the yard and water the flowers the old lady had taken such good care of.

35 By the time Eugene's family moved in, the yard was a tangled mass of weeds. The father had spent several days mowing, and when he finished, from where I sat, I didn't see the red, yellow, and purple clusters that
40 meant flowers to me. I didn't see this family sit down at the kitchen table together. It was just the mother, a redheaded tall woman who wore a white uniform; the fa-ther was gone before I got up in the morn-
45 ing and was never there at dinner time. I only saw him on weekends when they sometimes sat on lawn-chairs under the oak tree, each hidden behind a section of the newspaper; and there was Eugene. He
50 was tall and blond, and he wore glasses. I liked him right away because he sat at the kitchen table and read books for hours.

That summer, before we had even spoken one word to each other, I kept him com-
55 pany on my fire escape.

Once school started I looked for him in all my classes, but P.S.13 was a huge place and it took me days and many dis-creet questions to discover Eugene. After
60 much maneuvering I managed "to run into him" in the hallway where his locker was—on the other side of the building from mine—and in study hall at the library where he first seemed to notice me, but did not
65 speak; and finally, on the way home after school one day when I decided to approach him directly, though my stomach was doing somersaults.

I was ready for rejection, snobbery, the
70 worst. But when I came up to him and blurted out: "You're Eugene. Right?" He smiled, pushed his glasses up on his nose, and nodded. I saw then that he was blush-ing deeply. Eugene liked me, but he was
75 shy. I did most of the talking that day. He nodded and smiled a lot. In the weeks that followed, we walked home together. He would linger at the corner of El Building for a few minutes then walk down to his house.

80 I did not tell Eugene that I could see inside his kitchen from my bedroom. I felt dishonest, but I liked my secret sharing of his evenings, especially now that I knew what he was reading since we chose our
85 books together at the school library.

I also knew my mother was unhappy in Paterson, New Jersey, but my father had a good job at the blue-jeans factory in Pas-saic and soon, he kept assuring us, we
90 would be moving to our own house there. I had learned to listen to my parents' dreams, which were spoken in Spanish, as fairy tales, like the stories about life in Puerto Rico before I was born. I had been
95 to the island once as a little girl. We had not been back there since then, though my parents talked constantly about buying a house on the beach someday, retiring on the island—that was a common topic
100 among the residents of El Building. As for me, I was going to go to college and be-come a teacher.

But after meeting Eugene I began to think of the present more than of the future.
105 What I wanted now was to enter that house

I had watched for so many years. I wanted to see the other rooms where the old people had lived, and where the boy spent his time. Most of all, I wanted to sit at the 110 kitchen table with Eugene like two adults, like the old man and his wife had done, maybe drink some coffee and talk about books.

1. Based on the passage, which of the following statements best describes the overall attitudes of the narrator and Eugene at the time of their first meeting?
   A. Eugene is interested but embarrassed, while the narrator is direct but nervous.
   B. Eugene is disinterested and snobbish, while the narrator is eager and optimistic.
   C. Eugene is attentive but shy, while the narrator is confident but reserved.
   D. Eugene is talkative and direct, while the narrator is brave but apprehensive.

2. According to the passage, when the narrator spoke to Eugene for the first time:
   F. Eugene had been unaware of the narrator.
   G. Eugene and the narrator had spent time together on the fire escape.
   H. Eugene had noticed but never spoken to the narrator.
   J. Eugene was not interested in having a relationship with the narrator.

3. According to the passage, the narrator describes the "old couple" as:
   A. often arguing and distant with each other.
   B. typical examples of the immigrant experience in America.
   C. possible models for her own relationship with Eugene.
   D. eager to have the narrator become part of their family.

4. Which of the following questions can NOT be answered using information given in the passage?
   F. Has the narrator ever walked around in her neighbor's (the old couple's/Eugene's) house?
   G. What activity do the narrator and Eugene both enjoy?
   H. What makes the old couple's house different from the other houses on the block?
   J. Other than teaching, what careers is the narrator interested in pursuing?

5. The narrator compares her father's desire to move to a new house to:
   A. a romantic attraction.
   B. a fairy tale.
   C. an impossible dream.
   D. a career-oriented desire.

6. Which of the following statements about Eugene's father is best supported by the passage?
   F. He is largely absent from the rest of the family.
   G. He does not live at the house but visits on weekends.
   H. He is focused on his career in America but is eager to return to his homeland.
   J. He feels mutual hostility toward Eugene and Eugene's mother.

Continued →

7. The main function of the last two paragraphs (lines 86–113) is to:
    A. provide background information about the narrator's family in order to highlight the narrator's own unique and changing perspective.
    B. give information about the narrator's family in order to contrast the narrator's and Eugene's parents.
    C. describe the narrator's family in order to show how the narrator's friendship with Eugene affected the other members of her family.
    D. portray the desires and dreams of the narrator's parents in order to show how her parents' hopes changed over time.

8. The narrator's words, "I began to think of the present more than of the future" (lines 103–104), most likely mean that her friendship with Eugene led her to:
    F. shift some of her focus away from education and career plans and to the developing relationship.
    G. consider her own career interests rather than those her parents thought most important.
    H. delay her plans of visiting Puerto Rico in favor of continuing to prepare for college and her future career.
    J. want to spend time with him rather than helping her parents prepare to visit Puerto Rico.

9. According to the passage, which of the following does NOT describe one of the narrator's feelings about her "secret" (line 82) viewings of Eugene?
    A. The narrator is concerned that Eugene will discover her secret arrangement.
    B. The narrator feels dishonest about not telling Eugene that she can see him.
    C. The narrator is happier now that she knows what books Eugene reads.
    D. The narrator is happy to share time with Eugene, even if he is not aware that she can see him.

10. It can reasonably be inferred that the phrase " 'to run into him' " (lines 60–61) is in quotes because:
    F. the narrator felt lucky to meet Eugene in a part of the school away from her locker.
    G. the words are not to be taken literally.
    H. the narrator's intention all along was to meet Eugene.
    J. the narrator had not expected to meet Eugene.

2. *EXTENDED REASONING QUESTIONS*

Extended Reasoning questions require you to go *beyond* the text to find the answers. This doesn't mean that you'll be making things up—you still must use context:

! **Even when you must "extend your reasoning" beyond the text, the answers, as always, must be supported by the passage.**

MINIMIZE YOUR "EXTENDED REASONING"

The challenge to Extended Reasoning questions usually depends on how far your reasoning must be extended. In other words, how clearly does the passage support the correct answer? How much do you have to "read into it"? A good rule of thumb:

! **Go with the answer choice that requires the least amount of extended reasoning.**

Also, don't be surprised if some questions that sound like Extended Reasoning questions (because of keywords in the question such as *implies* or *suggests*) are actually Direct questions, with clear and explicit supportive context. Don't make questions harder than they need to be. If an answer choice is clearly supported by context, go for it.

Extended Reasoning questions usually include one of the following words:
- infer (as in: "it can logically be inferred" or "it is reasonable to infer")
- most (as in: "most likely," "most strongly," or "most nearly means")
- suggests
- apparently
- seems
- implies

Below are some very short "passages" and examples that will help you get the feel for these types of questions:

Writing my first screenplay was not something I considered trying alone. Late at night, when my characters fell flat, I'd read a few words of *Casablanca*. When my action felt forced, I'd read from *Jaws*. When I needed mystery, just a few lines from *Chinatown* would do. And dialogue? I'd turn to my old worn and dog-eared copy of *Annie Hall*.

(EX) 1.   Which of the following statements is most likely true according to the passage?

   A. The narrator collaborated with other writers while writing his screenplay.
   B. There is wide acceptance among screenwriters about which screenplays are the most influential.
   C. The narrator frequently found inspiration from other screenplays.
   D. The narrator based different scenes of his first screenplay on similar scenes from other well-known screenplays.

"Harry," said Basil Hallward, looking him straight in the face, "every portrait that is painted with feeling is a portrait of the artist, not the sitter. The sitter is merely the accident, the occasion. It is not he who is revealed by the painter; it is rather the painter who, on the coloured canvas, reveals himself." (Oscar Wilde, *The Picture of Dorian Gray*)

(EX) 2.   Which choice best describes the statements of Hallward in the passage?

   A. The best painters are more interested in self-portraits than in portraits of other sitters.
   B. The painter's character is revealed in the painting, regardless of the subject.
   C. Painters consciously use their subjects to reveal their own appearances.
   D. Painters must carefully look for sitters who reflect their own beliefs.

To go into solitude, a man needs to retire as much from his chamber as from society. I am not solitary whilst I read and write, though nobody is with me. (Ralph Waldo Emerson, "Nature")

(EX) 3.   What does the author imply about "solitude"?

   A. Only when one is completely alone does one experience solitude.
   B. People often feel solitude even among company.
   C. To find solitude, one must leave familiar comforts.
   D. The type of books people read can determine their level of solitude.

I crossed into the Eastern time zone and then over the Blue River, which was a brown creek. Blue, Green, Red: yes—yet who ever heard of a Brown River? For some reason, the farther west the river and the scarcer the water, the more honest the names become: Stinking Water Branch, Dead Horse Fork, Cutthroat Gulch, Damnation Creek. (William Least Heat Moon, *Blue Highways*)

(EX) 4. Based on the information in the passage, it can reasonably be inferred that some people:

    A. name a place before they have actually seen it.
    B. use names to discourage people from visiting certain places.
    C. become more honest as they move farther west.
    D. consider the name of a place more important than the place itself.

The difficult question below tests the first paragraph of the passage from the previous section:

Darwin could have been more specific. Not of all landscapes, but of most, he could have said: "trees form the chief embellishment." Of all plants they are the most prominent and the most permanent, the ones that set the scene and dictate the atmosphere. Trees define the character of a landscape, proclaim its climate, divulge the properties of its soil— even confirm the preoccupation of its people.

(EX) 5. In the context of the passage, Darwin most likely stated that:

    A. plants are more important than trees in determining the character of a landscape.
    B. plants are the most conspicuous features of a landscape.
    C. plants and trees are only one of many types of organisms found on Earth.
    D. the classification of some plants can be difficult for scientists.

Now let's try a longer passage. As usual, mark up the passage while you read. . . .

SOCIAL SCIENCE: This passage is adapted from Daphne Bavelier and C. Shawn Green, "The Brain Boosting Power of Video Games." ©2016 Scientific American.

The stereotype of the avid player of Call of Duty and other action games is of someone who is impulsive and easily distracted. Our studies contradict this outdated preconception. Much of our research has focused on how action games affect a player's attention—the mental processes that lead to finding relevant information in
5   one's environment. Studies of attention have been carried out ever since psychology emerged as a social science in the 19th century. Call of Duty and Medal of Honor have now become tools in research facilities because of their ability to enhance attention. A player must shift between a state of mental focus while monitoring the game scene for potential enemies, switching purposely between what psychologists call focused and
10   distributed attention.
The show a true cause-and-effect relation, scientists recruit a group of individuals who rarely play video games, and this larger group is randomly split into two. One group plays an action game, whereas a control group immerses itself in a social game or another non-action game. Groups trained on action games show consistently larger
15   gains in cognition than control groups.

Now, let's try some questions. . . .

(EX) 1. It can reasonably be inferred from the passage that before psychology emerged as a social science in the 19th century, the study of attention was:

The question has pretty good identifiers ("psychology," "social science," "19th century"), and the context is fairly clear. What can you say about the idea of attention before psychology emerged as a social science?

Do you see the answer?

    A. accomplished as its own field of scientific inquiry.
    B. considered an unworthy occupation by most scientists.
    C. not formerly or widely carried out.
    D. not linked to the playing of games.

(EX) 2. The games "Call of Duty and Medal of Honor" (line 6) most likely refer to:

Once again, consider context before looking at the answer choices. What do these games refer to?

Do you see the answer?

    A. action games that can enhance cognition in those who play them.
    B. action games that are mostly played by people who are impulsive or easily distracted.
    C. tools designed to facilitate learning by requiring players to frequently shift their attentions.
    D. tools that scientists use to identify people with enhanced attention.

(EX) 3. The passage suggests that the best participants in studies involving attention and games are those who:

There isn't much in the way of identifiers in the question, but do you remember where the passage gets into an actual experiment? What does the passage say about the participants of this experiment?

Do you see the answer?

    A. are impulsive or easily distracted.
    B. show large gains in cognition when playing action games.
    C. have minimal experience playing action games.
    D. prefer social games to action games.

One more question for this passage:

(EX) 4. Based on the experiment described in the second paragraph (lines 11–15), it is reasonable to conclude that:

As usual, think about context before looking at the answer choices. What can you conclude from the information in this last paragraph?

Can you find the correct answer?

    A. action games and other non-action games influence players in similar ways.
    B. people who play action games can find relevant information more effectively than those who play other kinds of games.
    C. most intelligent people prefer playing action games to social games or other non-action games.
    D. those who choose to play action games are more likely to be avid players because of likely gains in cognition.

                    ■

On the following passage, focus especially on identifying and answering the Direct and Extended Reasoning questions. Once again, you will see other types of questions, which you should review (especially the misses) after covering relevant upcoming sections. Here are some reminders:

- Once again, don't worry about timing yet. Focus on marking up the passage effectively (especially circling identifiers).
- Make sure you can identify the Direct and Extended Reasoning questions (review the magnifying glass information in the previous two sections).
- Try answering most questions, even Extended Reasoning questions, using context, *before* looking at the answer choices.

Passage II

PROSE FICTION: This passage is adapted from *The Antelope Wife* by (©1998 Louise Erdrich).

My mother sewed my birth cord, with dry sage and sweet grass, into a turtle holder of soft white buckskin. She beaded that little turtle using precious old cobalts
5 and yellows and Cheyenne pinks and greens in a careful design. I remember every detail of it, me, because the turtle hung near my crib, then off my belt, and was my very first play toy. I was supposed
10 to have it on me all my life, bury it with me on reservation land, but one day I came in from playing and my indis was gone. I thought nothing of it, at first and for many years, but slowly over time the absence . . .
15 it will tell. I began to wander from home, first in my thoughts, then my feet took after, so at last at the age of eighteen, I walked the road that led from the front of our place to the wider spaces and then the country
20 beyond that, where that one road widened into two lanes, then four, then six, past the farms and service islands, into the dead wall of the suburbs and still past that, finally, into the city's bloody heart.

25 My name is Cally Roy. Ozhawash-kwamashkodeykway is what the spirits call me. All my life so far I've wondered about the meaning of my spirit name but nobody's told it, seen it, got ahold of my his-
30 tory flying past. Mama has asked, she has offered tobacco, even blankets, but my grandmas Mrs. Zosie Roy and Mary Shawano only nod at her, vague and shrewd-eyed, holding their tongues as they
35 let their eyes wander. In a panic, once she knew I was setting out, not staying home, Mama tried to call up my grandmas and ask if I could live at their apartment in the city. But once they get down to the city, it
40 turns out they never stop moving. They are out, and out again. Impossible to track down. It's true, they are extremely busy women.

So my mom sends me to Frank.

45 Frank Shawano. Famous Indian bakery chef. My Mama's eternal darling, the man she loves too much to live with.

I'm weary and dirty and sore when I get to Frank's bakery shop, but right away,
50 walking in and the bell dinging with a cheerful alertness, I smell those good bak-ery smells of yeasty bread and airy sugar. Behind the counter, lemony light falls on Frank. He is big, strong, pale brown like a
55 loaf of light rye left to rise underneath a towel. His voice is muffled and weak, like it is squeezed out of the clogged end of a pastry tube. He greets me with gentle pleasure and shakes his hair out of the thin
60 dark ponytail that he binds up in a net.

"Just as I'm closing." His smile is very quiet. He cleans his hands on a towel and beckons me into the back of the bakery shop, between swinging steel doors. I re-
65 member him as a funny man, teasing and playing hand games and rolling his eyes at us, making his pink sugar-cookie dogs bark and elephants trumpet. But now he is serious, and frowns slightly as I follow him up
70 the back stairs and into the big top-floor apartment with the creaky floors, the groaning pipes, odd windows that view the yard of junk and floating trees. My little back room, no bigger than a closet, over-
75 looks this space. Gazing down, through the pretty fronds of oval leaves, I can see an old brown car seat below, a spool table, spring lawn chairs, a string of Christmas lights.

80 I'm so beat, though, I just want to crawl into my corner and sleep.

"Not too small, this place?" He sounds anxious.

I shake my head. The room seems
85 safe, the mattress on the floor, the blankets, the shelves for my things, and the somehow familiar view below.

"Call your mom?" Frank gives orders in the form of a question. He acts all pur-
90 poseful, as though he is going back downstairs to close up the store, but as I dial the number on the kitchen wall phone he lingers. He can't drag himself away from the magnetic field of my mother's voice, muf-
95 fled, far off, but on the other end of the receiver. He stands in the doorway with that same towel he brought from downstairs, folding and refolding it in his hands.

"Mama," I say, and her voice on the
100 phone suddenly hurts. I want to curl next to her and be a small girl again. My body feels too big, electric, like a Frankenstein body enclosing a tiny child's soul.

We laugh at some corny joke and
105 Frank darts a glance at me, then stares at
his feet and frowns. Reading between my
Mama's pauses on the phone, I know she
is hoping I'll miss the real land, and her,
come back and resume my brilliant future
110 at the tribal college. In spite of how I want
to curl up in my city corner, I picture everything back home. On the wall of my room
up north, there hangs a bundle of sage and
Grandma Roy's singing drum. On the op-
115 posite wall, I taped up a poster of dogs,

photos of Jimi Hendrix and the Indigo Girls,
this boyfriend I had once and don't have
anymore, bears, and Indigenous, my favorite band, another of a rainbow and buffalo
120 trudging underneath. Ever since I was little,
I slept with a worn bear and a new brown
dog with wiry blondish hair and a red felt
tongue. And my real dog, too, curled at my
feet sometimes, if Mama didn't catch us. I
125 never liked dolls. I made good scores in
math. I get to missing my room and my dog
and I lose track of Mama's voice.

1. The main conflict in the passage could
   best be expressed as:
   A. the tension between Frank and
      Mama.
   B. the bitterness expressed between
      the narrator and her mother.
   C. the narrator's desire to break her
      ties with her direct family.
   D. the narrator's struggle to connect
      her past to her future.

2. Which of the following best describes
   the narrator's decision to leave home?
   F. It was made suddenly, after the
      narrator lost her indis.
   G. It was a decision that all members
      of the reservation eventually have
      to make.
   H. It began as just a thought and
      eventually led to physical journey.
   J. It was one the narrator made as a
      small child.

3. It can reasonably be inferred from the
   passage that Frank "darts a glance" at
   the narrator, and "then stares at his
   feet and frowns" (lines 105–106)
   because he:
   A. desires an intimate connection with
      the narrator's mother.
   B. is concerned that the narrator's
      positive connection with her mother
      will induce her to return home.
   C. is anxious to go back downstairs to
      close up the store.
   D. nostalgically recollects his own life
      as a boy on the reservation.

4. It can reasonably be inferred from the
   passage that Mama's voice "suddenly
   hurts" (line 100) because the narrator:
   F. is angry that her mother wants her
      to return home.
   G. is unhappy because of her own
      physical appearance.
   H. is torn between her yearning to be
      a young girl again and her desire to
      live on her own.
   J. wants to return home but must
      obey her mother's wishes that she
      stay with Frank.

5. Which of the following is NOT listed in
   the passage as a characteristic of the
   narrator's indis?
   A. It symbolizes the narrator's desire
      to leave her reservation land.
   B. It contains colorful beads.
   C. It is intended to serve the narrator
      for her entire life.
   D. It is partially made from the
      narrator's birth chord.

6. As described in the passage, which of
   the following might best reflect any
   positive feelings the narrator has about
   leaving home:
   F. Mama's voice
   G. Grandma Roy's singing drum
   H. Frank's bakery shop
   J. The narrator's posters and photos

Continued →

7. The narrator implies that because she lost her indis, she:
   A. clung more desperately to her family.
   B. eventually left her home.
   C. had to remember every detail of it.
   D. developed animosity toward her family.

8. It can reasonably be inferred from the passage that the narrator's mother and Frank:
   F. are old friends who have grown distant over time.
   G. disagree over the narrator's choice of where to live.
   H. desire each other but cannot live together.
   J. were once married and now jointly care for the narrator.

9. According to the passage, when the narrator's mother finds out that the narrator is leaving home, the mother:
   A. anxiously begins making plans for the narrator.
   B. reluctantly gives in to the narrator's decision to make her own choices.
   C. discourages the narrator to leave by requiring her to live with her grandmas.
   D. happily accepts the narrator's decision because the mother can now reconnect with Frank.

10. Which of the following best describes the way the eleventh paragraph (lines 99–103) functions in the passage?
    F. It suggests a change in attitude of the narrator's mother regarding the narrator's desire to leave home.
    G. It foreshadows the narrator's eventual return to the reservation.
    H. It reveals the narrator's lack of interest in returning to her home.
    J. It reveals the narrator's ambivalence about leaving home.

TIMING

All programs: You should now have a pretty good sense of how to approach the Reading passages, including what to mark up as you read. It's time to bring *timing* into the mix. Go back to the Reading Introduction now to review the timing plan (page 493).

Since the homework assignments usually focus on one passage at a time, the magic number is always **8 minutes and 45 seconds** (we round down for the deadlines). From now on, start timing the homework passages.

Of course, on a real test, when your time is up, your time is up. But for these homework passages—whether you're working on your own or with a tutor—go ahead and answer any questions that you didn't get to in the allotted time. It's good practice. Just make a clear mark—we recommend an "OT" (for overtime)—next to any problems that you didn't answer in time, especially if you're working with a tutor:

! **Write "OT" next to problems that you answer *after* your time is up.**

The following passage primarily tests Direct and Extended Reasoning questions. To keep track of your timing, fill in the blanks at the end of the passage and the end of the questions (you can stop the clock to fill them in).

Timing Passage

SOCIAL SCIENCE: This passage is adapted from volume 2 of Blanche Wiesen Cook's biography *Eleanor Roosevelt* (©1999 by blanche Wiesen Cook)

Eleanor Roosevelt [ER] is the most controversial First Lady in United States history. Her journey to greatness, her voyage out beyond the confines of good wife
5 and devoted mother, involved determination and amazing courage. It also involved one of history's most unique partnerships. Franklin Delano Roosevelt [FDR] admired his wife, appreciated her strengths, and
10 depended on her integrity.

However, ER and FDR had different priorities, occasionally competing goals, and often disagreed. In the White House they ran two distinct and separate courts.

15 By 1933 [her first year as First Lady], ER was an accomplished woman who had achieved several of her life's goals. With her partners, ER was a businesswoman who co-owned the Val-Kill crafts factory, a
20 political leader who edited and copublished the Women's Democratic News, and an educator who co-owned and taught at a New York school for girls.

As First Lady, Eleanor Roosevelt did
25 things that had never been done before. She upset race traditions, championed a New Deal for women, and on certain issues actually ran a parallel administration. On housing and the creation of model commu-
30 nities, for example, ER made decisions and engineered policy.

At the center of a network of influential women who ran the Women's Committee of the Democratic Party led by Molly
35 Dewson, ER worked closely with the women who had dominated the nation's social reform struggles for decades. With FDR's election, the goals of the great progressive pioneers, Jane Addams, Florence
40 Kelley, and Lillian Wald, were at last at the forefront of the country's agenda. ER's mentors since 1903, they had battled on the margins of national politics since the 1880s for public health, universal educa-
45 tion, community centers, sanitation programs, and government responsibility for the welfare of the nation's poor and neglected people.

Now their views were brought directly
50 into the White House. ER lobbied for them personally with her new administrative allies, in countless auditoriums, as a radio broadcaster, and in monthly, weekly, and, by 1936, daily columns. Called "Eleanor
55 Everywhere," she was interested in everyone.

Every life was sacred and worthy, to be improved by education, employment, health care, and affordable housing. Her
60 goal was simple, a life of dignity and decency for all. She was uninterested in complex theories, and demanded action for betterment. She feared violent revolution, but was not afraid of socialism—and she
65 courted radicals.

As fascism and communism triumphed in Europe and Asia, ER and FDR were certain that there was a middle way, what ER called an American "revolution without
70 bloodshed." Her abiding conviction, however, was that nothing good would happen to promote the people's interest unless the people themselves organized to demand government responses. A people's move-
75 ment required active citizen participation, and ER's self-appointed task was to agitate and inspire community action, encourage united democratic movements for change.

Between 1933 and 1938, while the De-
80 pression raged and the New Deal unfolded, ER worked with the popular front. She called for alliances of activists to fight poverty and racism at home, and to oppose isolationism internationally.

85 Active with the women's peace movement, ER spoke regularly at meetings of the Women's International League for Peace and Freedom, and the Conference on the Cause and Cure of War. She de-
90 parted, however, from pacifist and isolationist positions and encouraged military preparedness, collective security, and ever-widening alliances.

Between 1933 and 1938 ER published
95 countless articles and six books. She wrote in part for herself, to clear her mind and focus her thoughts. But she also wrote to disagree with her husband. From that time to this, no other First Lady has actually
100 rushed for her pen to jab her husband's public decisions. But ER did so routinely, including in her 1938 essay This Troubled

World, which was a point-by-point rejection of FDR's major international decisions.

105   To contemplate ER's life of example and responsibility is to forestall gloom. She understood, above all, that politics is not an isolated individualist adventure. She sought alliances, created community, worked with 110 movements for justice and peace. Against great odds, and under terrific pressure, she refused to withdraw from controversy. She brought her network of agitators and activists into the White House, and never con- 115 sidered a political setback a permanent defeat. She enjoyed the game, and weathered the abuse.

Reading Time: _____

---

1. According to the passage, ER changed from a pacifist and isolationist to one who:
   A. supported military strength and multi-national cooperation.
   B. encouraged war to fight fascism and communism in Europe.
   C. encouraged military build up to help the United States avoid foreign entanglements.
   D. fought openly with socialists and radicals.

2. According to the passage, as First Lady, ER was the first to accomplish all of the following EXCEPT:
   F. the reversals of assumptions about race.
   G. the development of a New Deal for women.
   H. the organization of a parallel administration.
   J. the editing and co-publishing of a newspaper for women.

3. According to the last paragraph, the author would likely agree with which of the following statements about ER's vision and ideals?
   A. ER only tackled political issues when she knew that she could successfully influence their outcomes.
   B. ER worked with agitators and activists to bring about justice and peace.
   C. ER took on presidential responsibilities so she could determine White House policy.
   D. ER considered herself a role model who could single-handedly bring about change.

4. To improve the social issues discussed in lines 58–59, ER would likely encourage:
   F. direct and focused action.
   G. the development of complex theories that went to the root causes of the problems.
   H. violent and unequivocal revolution.
   J. government repeal of existing laws.

5. According to the passage, ER believed that people should:
   A. work separately to bring about progressive policies in the government.
   B. form a relationship with the government as modeled by the White House.
   C. work together to demand government change.
   D. communicate with the government through radio broadcasts and other formal channels.

6. As portrayed in the passage, ER could best be described as:
   F. outwardly controversial but quietly compromising.
   G. politically courageous and socially involved.
   H. morally sound and deeply conservative.
   J. fearlessly driven but reservedly moderate.

Continued →

7. Which of the following best describes FDR's feelings toward ER?
   A. He fought bitterly with her and rejected her ideas outright.
   B. He admired her as a wife and supported her as a writer.
   C. He admired her influence but disagreed with many of her policies.
   D. He depended on her integrity and supported her social movements.

8. According to the passage, the women who "battled on the margins of national politics since the 1880s" (lines 42–44) moved to the forefront of the nation's agenda after FDR's election because:
   F. FDR's social policies closely mirrored those of the women.
   G. the women could now organize groups that would agitate and inspire community action.
   H. issues such as public health, universal education, and community centers were ones that concerned the women for decades.
   J. ER had direct influence on White House policy and action.

9. It can reasonably be inferred from the passage that the New Deal was a response to:
   A. the Depression.
   B. the triumph of fascism and communism in Europe and Asia.
   C. international isolation.
   D. racism.

10. The statement "no other First Lady has actually rushed for her pen to jab her husband's public decisions" (lines 99–101) most nearly means:
    F. ER used her writing to openly reject FDR's policies.
    G. ER used her writing to illuminate the positive points of FDR's public decisions.
    H. ER hoped to privately change FDR's ideas and convictions.
    J. ER wrote down her disagreements with FDR because she could not confront him directly.

Total Time: _____

Questions answered (in time): _____/10

■

TEST CORRECTIONS

Let's go back to Test 1 (which you should have already completed) in *The Official ACT Prep Guide* and correct any **Direct** and **Extended Reasoning** questions that you missed. There are three steps to correcting the Reading practice tests:

1. Turn to the Techniques chapter at the end of this tutorial and circle relevant questions that you missed or guessed on for the test you are correcting.

2. Correct the problems in *The Official ACT Prep Guide*. As you correct the problems, go back to the tutorial and review appropriate question types, as necessary. Make sure you are using context to answer the questions. You are encouraged to reread passages that you may have forgotten.

3. If you have trouble finding context for a question, or identifying the question type, see the Techniques chapter.

3. PURPOSE QUESTIONS

Purpose questions ask *why* an author makes a particular decision with his or her writing. Some Purpose questions are clearly supported by the text (similar to Direct questions), but most will require you to go beyond the text (similar to Extended Reasoning questions). Put yourself in the author's shoes (or, perhaps, a character's shoes). What is the author's central point or claim? What is the author trying to accomplish? It's important to consider authorial *intent* as you tackle Purpose questions.

To identify Purpose questions, look for the words "purpose," "aim," or "function" in the question. In addition, look for the phrases below. Note that all of these include the word "to"; it's a small word, but it will usually help you identify Purpose questions.
- . . . primarily **to**
- . . . serves **to**
- . . . in order **to**
- . . . **to** suggest that

TYPES OF PURPOSE QUESTIONS

DETAILS

Most Purpose questions ask about details within the passage. The question will usually refer to a word, phrase, or sentence. Line numbers will often be given in the question.

PARAGRAPHS

Some Purpose questions are concerned with the role of a paragraph in the passage, or the relationship between different paragraphs. These questions can usually be answered by looking at the first sentence or two of the paragraph in question. Of course, it is helpful to be comfortable with details within the paragraph, but usually the answer can be found early in the paragraph:

! **To solve most Purpose questions relating to a paragraph, read the first couple sentences of the paragraph in question.**

PASSAGE

Some Purpose questions ask about the purpose of the entire passage. The ACT usually puts these questions *first* for a given passage. They are similar to Main Idea questions (next section).

As with Extended Reasoning questions, we'll use some very short "passages" and examples to help you get the feel for Purpose questions:

First ascertain the facts, said the positivists, then draw your conclusions from them. In Great Britain, this view of history fitted in perfectly with the empiricist tradition which was the dominant strain in British philosophy from Locke to Bertrand Russell. (Edward Hallett Carr, *What is History?*)

(EX) 1. The author refers to "Locke" and "Bertrand Russel" in order to:

    A. highlight the differences between British philosophers and positivists.
    B. indicate his own philosophical influences concerning the empiricist tradition.
    C. support the idea that conclusions should always be drawn from facts.
    D. emphasize the enduring appeal of a certain way of interpreting history.

It is not the philosopher's job to investigate particular moral issues, such as the issue of whether (or when) abortion is justified. Philosophers are not ministers or guidance counselors, it is said, and philosophers have no greater expertise in these matters than anyone else. This attitude, however, has recently begun to lose its influence. More and more work is now being done in which the techniques of philosophical analysis are used in the treatment of substantive issues. (adapted from James Rachels, *Moral Problems*)

(EX) 2. The author includes the words "it is said" in line 3 to indicate that:

    A. the role of philosophers in society is generally understood to not include the analysis of particular moral issues.
    B. some people confuse the roles of philosophers with those of ministers and guidance counselors.
    C. the views of some people regarding the role of philosophers may be different from the author's own views.
    D. the job of being a philosopher is more similar to other jobs than some people realize.

Until now, only a handful of American cities and states have experimented with voucher programs. Around 500,000 of the country's 56 million schoolchildren use voucher-type programs to attend private or parochial schools. The results have been spotty. In the 1990s studies of small voucher programs in New York City, Washington, D.C., and Dayton, Ohio, found no demonstrable academic improvement among children using vouchers and high rates of churn—many students who used vouchers dropped out or transferred schools, making evaluation impossible. (Peg Tyre, "A Matter of Choice," *Scientific American*)

(EX) 3. The most likely purpose of the clause following the dash in line 6 ("many . . . schools") is to:

    A. acknowledge a fault in the research.
    B. clarify an abstract concept.
    C. explain a term.
    D. support a hypothesis.

PURPOSE QUESTIONS FOR PARAGRAPHS

Many Purpose questions ask about a paragraph or even the entire passage. We'll discuss Purpose questions for the whole passage in the Main Idea lesson (coming soon). Purpose questions for paragraphs require you to have a sense of the main idea of the paragraph. Once again, consider the author's intent. What role does a paragraph serve in the larger essay? Here's an example, based on the paragraph above (of course, you can answer this one without reading the rest of the passage):

(EX) 4. The main purpose of the paragraph is to make the claim that "voucher-type programs":

    A. have been largely overrated by their proponents.
    B. are difficult to study but probably ineffective in raising academic achievement.
    C. are definitely counterproductive to efforts for improving education.
    D. are growing in popularity despite the lack of sufficient evidence of their efficacy.

There are two simple yet deeply rooted structures that form the foundation of special relativity. One concerns properties of light; we shall discuss this more fully in the next section. The other is more abstract. It is concerned not with any specific physical law but rather with *all* physical laws, and is known as the *principle of relativity*. The principle of relativity rests on a simple fact: Whenever we discuss speed or velocity, we must specify precisely who or what is doing the measuring. (adapted from Brian Greene, *The Elegant Universe*)

. . .

(EX) 5. The paragraph above serves mainly to:

A. discuss the similarities of the two elements that make up special relativity.
B. outline the properties that form the foundation of special relativity.
C. contrast special relativity with the principle of relativity.
D. introduce one of the structures that form the foundation of special relativity.

■

Read the following passage. As usual, don't forget to mark it up (especially with identifiers).

> **NATURAL SCIENCE**: This passage is adapted from *A Brief History of Time* by Stephen W. Hawking (©1988).

A well-known scientist (some say it was Bertrand Russell) once gave a public lecture on astronomy. He described how the earth orbits around the sun and how the sun, in turn, orbits around the center of a vast collection of stars called our galaxy. At the end of the lecture, a little old lady at the back of the room got up and said: "What

5   you have told us is rubbish. The world is really a flat plate supported on the back of a giant tortoise." The scientist gave a superior smile before replying, "What is the tortoise standing on?" "You're very clever, young man, very clever," said the old lady. "But it's turtles all the way down!"

Most people would find the picture of our universe as an infinite tower of tortoises

10 rather ridiculous, but why do we think we know better? What do we know about the universe, and how do we know it? Where did the universe come from, and where is it going? Did the universe have a beginning, and if so, what happened *before* then? What is the nature of time? Will it ever come to an end? Can we go back in time? Recent breakthroughs in physics, made possible in part by fantastic new technologies, suggest

15 answers to some of these longstanding questions. Someday these answers may seem as obvious to us as the earth orbiting the sun – or perhaps as ridiculous as a tower of tortoises. Only time (whatever that may be) will tell.

Let's take a moment and make sure you're marking up the passage effectively:

- **Tone words** (darkly underlined): well-known (line 1), rubbish (line 5), superior smile (line 6), ridiculous (lines 10 and 16)
- **Contrast signals** (boxed): But (line 7), but (line 10)
- **Identifiers** (circled): Russell, lecture, astronomy, earth, sun, galaxy, old lady, tortoise, time, breakthroughs, physics, technologies

Hopefully you had most of the above words marked accordingly. If not, you might want to go back and review the Passage section in Chapter II.

Now, on to the questions . . .

Here's a Purpose question (make sure you recognize how you could have identified it as such—note the "to" in the question):

(EX) 1.   The author refers to the scientist's superior smile primarily to suggest that:

Consider the author's reasons for mentioning the scientist's "superior smile" (line 6). What quality of the scientist is the author trying to convey? Make sure to use context.

Can you find the correct answer?

> **A.** the scientist believes he has cleverly found a flaw in the lady's theory.
> **B.** the scientist considers the woman's ideas counterintuitive to real scientific discourse.
> **C.** the scientist is genuinely interested in the woman's claim.
> **D.** the scientist's social standing is much higher than the woman's.

Here's another Purpose question. Again, note the "to" in the question:

(EX) 2. The author most likely mentions the "infinite tower of tortoises" (line 9) in order to:

As usual, let's explore context before looking at the answer choices. Make sure to consider the text that follows the quote in the question, and look out for contrast signals (such as *but*).

Can you find the answer?

   F. reveal a false impression of the nature of the universe.
   G. examine recent changes in humans' knowledge of the cosmos.
   H. display the humorous notions of some non-scientists about astronomy.
   J. emphasize how little about the universe we actually know.

(EX) 3. The author's use of the phrase "(whatever that may be)" (line 17) in reference to time most nearly serves to emphasize which of the following points?

As usual, explore context before looking at the answer choices. Why does the author include this parenthetical comment?

Can you spot the answer that is best supported by context?

- **A.** Time is a complex concept best understood by scientists.
- **B.** The answers to the author's questions will inevitably be answered.
- **C.** Scientists do not know how long it will take to answer the questions mentioned by the author.
- **D.** The nature of time is not clearly understood by scientists.

Here's a Purpose question that focuses on the function of *paragraphs*:

(EX) 4. Which of the following statements best describes the way the two paragraphs function in the passage?

You might take a quick glance at the answer choices (below). Note that they are double answer choices. The question asks about the role of each paragraph. Generally speaking, how would you describe each paragraph? Consider main ideas.

Purpose questions sometimes have broad answer choices. Which one do you think best describes the organization of the passage?

    A. The first paragraph provides a humorous anecdote and the second paragraph introduces a subject.
    B. The first paragraph recounts a personal story and the second paragraph provides a general overview of a subject.
    C. The first paragraph describes a contentious conversation and the second paragraph details resulting actions.
    D. The first paragraph gives a historical overview of a topic and the second paragraph summarizes the topic's current state.

⊘ EVERY WORD COUNTS

The ACT will sometimes include an answer choice that is close to *perfect*, except for just one or two words. Don't fall for this trap. Every word counts! Do you see an answer choice above that is perhaps one word away from correct?

Let's try one more Purpose question for the previous passage:

(EX) 5. The main purpose of the second paragraph (lines 9–17) is to present:

Take a quick glance at the answer choices. You can see that the question is asking about the general construction of the second paragraph. Think about how you might describe the second paragraph. Don't forget to eliminate double answers one part at a time:

- **F.** a scientific study and its ramifications.
- **G.** a statement followed by ironic questions.
- **H.** questions followed by speculation.
- **J.** questions followed by possible answers.

■

Don't forget to time yourself on these homework passages (you have **8 minutes and 45 seconds**). Remember, try to answer the easier questions first (review the timing plan in the Reading introduction, if necessary). Put "OT" next to any questions you answer after running out of time.

Passage III

SOCIAL SCIENCE: This passage is adapted from Morton Hunt's *The Story of Psychology* (©1993 by Morton Hunt). In the passage, the term *maturation* refers to the process of growth and development, and the term *perceptual ability* refers to the capacity to recognize something through the senses (sight, smell, touch, etc.).

Much maturation research is concerned with physical skills and physical attributes, and adds little to our knowledge of the growth of the mind. But research on
5 the development of perceptual abilities begins to provide solid factual answers to the ancient central question of psychology: How much is due to nature and him much to nurture (or, in developmental terms, to
10 maturation and to learning)?

The work has been focused on early infancy, when perceptual abilities evolve rapidly: its aim is to discover when each new ability first appears, the assumption
15 being that at its first appearance, the new ability arises not from learning but from maturation of the optic nervous structures and especially of that part of the brain cortex where visual signals are received and
20 interpreted.

Much has been learned by simply watching infants. What, exactly, do very young infants see? Since we cannot ask them what they see, how can we find out?

25 In 1961, the psychologist Robert Fantz devised an ingenious method of doing so. He designed a stand in which, on the bottom level, the baby lies on her back, looking up. A few feet above is a display area
30 where the experimenter puts two large cards, each containing a design—a white circle, a yellow circle, a bull's-eye, a simple sketch of a face. The researcher, peering down through a tiny peephole, can watch
35 the movement of the baby's eyes and time how long they are directed at one or the other of each pair of patterns. Fantz found that at two months babies looked twice as long at a bull's-eye as at a circle of solid
40 color, and twice as long at a sketch of a face as at a bull's-eye. Evidently, even a two-month-old can distinguish major differences and direct her gaze toward what she finds more interesting.

45 Using this technique, developmental psychologists have learned a great deal about what infants see and when they begin to see it. In the first week infants distinguish light and dark patterns; during the
50 first month they begin to track slowly moving objects; by the second month they begin to have depth perception, coordinate the movement of the eyes, and differentiate among hues and levels of brightness; by
55 three months they can glance from one object to another, and can distinguish among family members; by four months they focus at varying distances, make increasingly fine distinctions, and begin to
60 recognize the meaning of what they see (they look longer at a normal sketch of a face than at one in which the features have been scrambled); and from four to seven months they achieve stereopsis, recognize
65 that a shape held at different angles is still the same shape, and gain near-adult ability to focus at varying distances.

Exactly how maturation and experience interact in the brain tissues to produce such
70 developmental changes is becoming clear from neuroscience research. Microscopic examination of the brains of infants shows that as the brain triples in size during the first two years of life, a profusion of den-
75 drites (branches) grow from its neurons and make contact with one another.

By the time a human is twelve, the brain has an estimated hundred trillion synapses (connections between nerve
80 cells). Those connections are the wiring plan that establishes the brain's capabilities. Some of the synaptic connections are made automatically by chemical guidance, but others are made by the stimulus of ex-
85 perience during the period of rapid dendrite growth. Lacking such stimulus, the dendrites wither away without forming the needed synapses. Mice reared in the dark develop fewer dendritic spines and synap-
90 tic connections in the visual cortex than mice reared in the light, and even when exposed to light never attain normal vision.

Why should nature have done that? Why should perceptual development he
95 possible only at a critical period and not later? It does not make evolutionary sense for the organism to be permanently impaired in sensory performance just because it fails to have the proper experi-
100 ences at specific times in its development. But some brain researchers say that there is an offsetting advantage: the essential

experiences are almost always available at the right time, and they fine-tune the brain
105 structure so as to provide far more specific perceptual powers than could result from genetic control of synapse formations.

With that, the vague old terms nature and nurture take on precise new meaning.
110 Now, after so many centuries of speculation, we catch the first glimpse of how mind is constructed out of matter by experience.

1. The main purpose of the passage could best be described as an effort to:
   A. describe the accelerated pace of learning for infants between four and seven months of life.
   B. raise questions about whether organisms deprived of important life experiences develop normal perceptual abilities.
   C. explain the interaction between nature and experience in the development of perceptual abilities.
   D. discount the importance of research concerned with physical skills and attributes in expanding our knowledge of the growth of the mind.

2. The parenthetical comment in lines 61–63 most likely serves to:
   F. explain a difficult term.
   G. question a controversial opinion.
   H. describe the reasoning behind a claim.
   J. add distinct but unrelated information.

3. According to the passage, synaptic connections are formed:
   A. primarily from automatic chemical instructions.
   B. rapidly throughout a human's lifetime.
   C. from a combination of chemical and experiential influence.
   D. entirely from the stimulus of experience.

4. According to some brain researchers, sensory development from experience has an "offsetting advantage" (line 102) because:
   F. most organisms fail to have the proper experiences at the right time.
   G. perceptual abilities that arise from experience are more specific than those that could arise from natural physical changes in the brain.
   H. brain structures of organisms develop similarly regardless of the organisms' sensory experiences.
   J. most essential experiences occur after the physical structure of the brain has developed.

5. The main function of the fourth paragraph (lines 25–44) in relation to the fifth paragraph (lines 45–67) is to:
   A. explain the method for determining what infants see.
   B. introduce psychologist Robert Fantz as a major contributor to the nature versus nurture debate.
   C. confirm that by two months old, an infant can distinguish major differences in the appearance of objects.
   D. display the development of an infants' vision.

6. It is reasonable to infer from the passage that one-month-old babies can perform which of the following actions?
   F. Notice the difference between a pale yellow rattle and a bright yellow rattle.
   G. Recognize siblings as individuals.
   H. Look from their mother's face to their father's face and back to their mother again.
   J. Follow a slow-moving butterfly from a mobile hanging above their bed.

Continued →

7. According to the passage, research on the development of perceptual abilities has been focused on early infancy because:
   A. perceptual abilities evolve more quickly for infants than for children or adults.
   B. infants lack physical skills and physical attributes.
   C. scientists assume that infants learn more quickly than children or adults.
   D. perceptual abilities of infants are easier to measure than those of children or adults.

8. The author uses the term "nurture" (line 9) to refer to:
   F. the development of perceptual abilities due to the physical growth of the brain.
   G. the development of perceptual abilities that are learned.
   H. a controversial topic that is largely discounted by today's scientists.
   J. physical skills and physical attributes of infants.

9. The main function of the sixth paragraph (lines 68–76) in relation to the passage as a whole is most likely to:
   A. shift the discussion from nurture to nature as the driving force behind the perceptual development of infants.
   B. shift the discussion from the outward nature of perceptive ability in infants to the inward physical development of the brain.
   C. conclude the author's discussion of perceptive development in infants so he can focus on older children.
   D. provide evidence to support the findings in the fifth paragraph.

10. Based on the passage, which of the following statements best supports the claim that experience plays an important role in perceptual development?
    F. By the time a human is twelve, the brain has an estimated hundred trillion synapses.
    G. Mice reared in the dark develop fewer dendritic spines than mice reared in the light.
    H. A human's brain triples in size during the first two years of life.
    J. Some of the synaptic connections are made automatically by chemical guidance.

■

TEST CORRECTIONS

Go back to Test 1 (which you should have already completed) in *The Official ACT Prep Guide* and correct any **Purpose** questions that you missed or guessed on. Review the three steps to correcting Reading tests on page 536.

4. MAIN IDEA QUESTIONS

Main Idea questions ask about central ideas of the text. For example:

- What is the passage about?
- How would you summarize the passage?
- What is the principle argument expressed in the passage?
- What is the passage's point of view?
- How is the passage organized?

When you recognize a Main Idea question, watch out for answer choices that are absolutely *true*, according to the passage, but don't reflect the passage's main idea. Often, two or more answer choices will be supported by context, but only one will best capture the passage's main idea.

Main Idea questions usually include phrases such as:
- main idea
- main point
- central idea
- point of view of the passage
- organization of the passage

PURPOSE QUESTIONS AND MAIN IDEA QUESTIONS

Purpose questions (see Section 3) are often similar to Main Idea questions. Both questions typically require you to understand the author's main point and grasp the larger ideas of a passage. The difference is that Purpose questions specifically ask you about *why* an author makes a certain literary, narrative, or structural decision. Main Idea questions more generally ask about *what's going on*.

MAIN IDEA QUESTIONS FOR *PART* OF A PASSAGE

Main Idea questions don't always focus on the entire passage. They may ask about just a *section* of a passage, such as a paragraph or even a single sentence. As usual, we will focus on context for these questions.

Read the following passage. Don't forget to mark up the passage while you read:

SOCIAL SCIENCE: This passage is adapted from the book *Chasing the Scream* by Johann Hari (©2015 by Bloomsbury Publishing).

I had been taught how to respond—by my government, and by my culture—when you find yourself in this situation. It is with a war. We all know the script: it is etched onto your subconscious, like the correct direction to look when you cross the street. Treat drug users and addicts as criminals. Repress them. Shame them. Coerce them
5   into stopping. This is the prevailing view in almost every country in the world. For years, I had been publicly arguing against this strategy. I wrote newspaper articles and appeared on television to argue that punishing and shaming drug users only makes them worse—and creates a blizzard of other problems for the society. I argued instead for a second strategy—legalize drugs stage by stage, and use the money we currently
10   spend on punishing addicts to fund compassionate care instead.

But as I stared at these people I loved through my own drugged glaze, a small part of me wondered if I really meant what I had been saying. The voices in my mind were like a howling drill sergeant in an old Vietnam War movie, shrieking abuse at the recruits. You are an idiot to do this. This is shameful. You are a fool for not stopping.
15   Somebody should prevent you. You should be punished.

So even as I criticized the drug war with my words, I was often waging it in my head. I can't say I was evenly divided—my rational mind always favored reform—but this internal conflict wouldn't stop.

Let's try a Main Idea question for *part* of the passage:

(EX) 1.   Which of the following best expresses the main idea of the first paragraph (lines 1–10)?

You probably don't want to take the time to read the whole paragraph again, but go back and give it a skim. Did you note any of its most important points (with underlines or asterisks)? It's always a good idea to have some idea of what you're looking for before you check the answer choices:

   A.   The criminalization of drug use helps addicts eventually stop using drugs.
   B.   No single approach to dealing with drug use works for all people.
   C.   Government and culture often determine how one feels about solving social problems.
   D.   The prevailing approaches to dealing with drug use create more problems than they solve.

MAIN IDEA QUESTIONS FOR THE WHOLE PASSAGE

Often, after reading a passage, you will have a feel for the passage's main idea. You may have also indicated some of the passage's main ideas with an asterisk (✱) in the margin, as described earlier in the Passage section.

FIRST AND LAST PARAGRAPHS

If you're not sure about a passage's main idea, remember to focus on the first and especially the last paragraphs. If the paragraphs are long, focus on the first couple sentences of the first paragraph and the last couple sentences of the last paragraph:

> **To quickly find a passage's main idea, look at the *first* and (more importantly) the *last* paragraphs.**

NOT TOO BROAD, AND NOT TOO NARROW

Main-Idea-of-Passage questions often have answer choices that are too broad or too narrow:

- **Too Broad**: These answer choices will usually fail to mention the specific person or topic discussed in the passage.
- **Too Narrow**: These answer choices will usually only reflect *part* of the passage.

Here's a Main Idea question for the whole passage:

(EX) 2. The main idea of the passage is that:

You might quickly skim the last paragraph. Keep its main points in mind as you look at the answer choices:

- **A.** the act of using drugs must be criticized with words, even as activists show compassion for drug users.
- **B.** punishing drug users has never been effective in the fight against drug abuse.
- **C.** drug use should immediately be legalized so that money can be used on care rather than criminalization.
- **D.** treating drug users as criminals is embedded in our culture but is not the best approach for solving the problems of drug abuse.

⊘ ELIMINATE ANSWER CHOICES THAT ARE TOO STRONG

Answer choices that are too strong may take one of two forms:

EXTREME WORDS

The first type uses extreme words such as *always*, *only*, *never*, *without exception*, *completely*, or *perfectly*. These answer choices are usually incorrect.

EXAGGERATIONS

The second type uses words that go *too far* in describing someone or something. An author may be *disappointed* but not *devastated*. She may be *upset* but not *furious*. She may be *surprised* but not *shocked*. Watch out for answer choices that seem to overly exaggerate the attitude of an author or character in a passage—the ACT may be trying to trick you.

Look back to the previous answer choices. Do you see one that is Too Strong?

Here's one more Main Idea question. Note how the answer choices reflect the passage's organization (something often tested on Main Idea questions):

(EX) 3. Which choice best summarizes the passage?

   A. An advocate for changes in drug-abuse laws first introduces his position on the issue and then acknowledges his own internal ambivalence.
   B. A defender of drug use first gives an overview of the issue and then makes clear his personal opinion.
   C. A recovering drug user first introduces the topic of drug abuse and then recounts his own experiences.
   D. A social scientist evenhandedly discusses the ways in which drug users can be treated.

Here's one more short passage that we'll use to introduce Main Idea questions:

HUMANITIES: This passage is adapted from Simon Winchester, *The Professor and the Madman*. ©2005 by HarperCollins Publishers.

At the railway station a polished landau and a liveried coachman were waiting, and with James Murray aboard they clip-clopped back through the lanes of rural Berkshire. After twenty minutes or so the carriage turned up a long drive lined with tall poplars, drawing up eventually outside a huge and rather forbidding red-brick mansion. A
5 solemn servant showed the lexicographer upstairs, and into a book-lined study, where behind an immense mahogany desk stood a man of undoubted importance. Dr. Murray bowed gravely, and launched into the brief speech of greeting that he had so long rehearsed:

"A very good afternoon to you, sir. I am Dr. James Murray of the London
10 Philological Society, and Editor of the Oxford English Dictionary. It is indeed an honor and a pleasure to at long last make your acquaintance—for you must be, kind sir, my most assiduous helpmeet, Dr. W.C. Minor?"

There was a brief pause, a momentary air of mutual embarrassment. A clock ticked loudly. There were muffled footsteps in the hall. A distant clank of keys. And
15 then the man behind the desk cleared his throat, and he spoke:

"I regret, kind sir, that I am not. It is not at all as you suppose. I am in fact the Governor of the Broadmoor Criminal Lunatic Asylum. Dr. Minor is most certainly here. But he is an inmate. He has been a patient here for more than twenty years. He is our longest-staying resident."

Here's a Main Idea question:

(EX) 1. Which of the following best describes the interaction between Mr. Murray and the Governor of the asylum?

    A. They are embarrassed to be meeting after such a long time.
    B. They are pleased to finally be meeting each other.
    C. They speak to each other with polite formality.
    D. They speak to each other courteously but suspiciously.

Here's another main idea question for the whole passage:

(EX) 2.   Which choice best summarizes the events in the passage?

Think about the passage's main idea as you tackle this question. Don't forget to focus on the last paragraph. Here are the answer choices:

- **A.** Two strangers meet in embarrassing circumstances.
- **B.** One man discovers the true identity of another man.
- **C.** Two adversaries discuss the possibility of reconciliation.
- **D.** One man humorously recounts a case of mistaken identity.

BROAD ANSWER CHOICES

Did you notice that the answer choices for this question were *broad*? You might have expected to see something about "Dr. James Murray" or "Dr. W.C. Minor," but instead the answer choices mention such vagaries as "two strangers" and "a man." Most ACT questions have specific answer choices, but don't be surprised to see some with answer choices that are broad.

BACK TO THE DRAWING BOARD

Sometimes, especially as you begin getting comfortable answering questions using context, your contextual answer does not lead you to the correct answer. Don't be afraid to go *back to the drawing board*: return to the passage and reconsider the context, or attempt POE. The point is, as you may have seen with the question above, you may not always spot the correct answer on your first try.

Also, if you're eliminating answer choices, don't go with the the fourth (remaining) answer choice simply because you've eliminated the other three. Read all answer choices carefully when using POE.

Here's a Main Idea question that focuses on organization:

(EX) 3. Which of the following descriptions best reflects the way the passage is organized?

A. It focuses first on one man's travels and then on another man's mental state.
B. It describes a meeting of two men, first as cordial and then as contentious.
C. It depicts a man meeting first a stranger and then an old acquaintance.
D. It recounts a man's physical journey, followed by his journey of discovery.

The following question reviews a past question type:

(EX) 4. According to the passage, Dr. Murray views Dr. W.C. Minor as a:

A. psychotic inmate.
B. important leader.
C. helpful associate.
D. solemn rival.

■

Now might be a good time to review the techniques you've learned so far.

- Make sure you're effectively marking up the passage while you read, especially by circling **identifiers** (see the Passage section in Chapter II).

- Make sure you're using **context** while answering the questions (see the Context section in Chapter II). **Are you answering most questions *before* looking at the answer choices?**

- Review the question types and elimination techniques that we've covered so far. You'll approach different types of questions in different ways, so make sure you can identify each type (review the magnifying glass information).

- Review timing (see Timing in the Reading introduction). Are you strategically skipping some of the questions so you can get your eyeballs on all of them? Are you getting faster? Don't forget, you have **8 minutes and 45 seconds** to answer all 10 questions. You might want to record your reading and total times for each passage so you can monitor your progress.

NATURAL SCIENCE: This passage is adapted from *Fire in America: A Cultural History of Wildland and Rural Fire* by Stephen J. Pyne (©1982 by Princeton University Press).

Lightning affects electrical equilibrium on the earth. Air is a poor conductor, but some electricity constantly leaks to the atmosphere, creating an electrical potential.
5 Electricity moves back according to the gradient [change in potential with distance]. During a thunderstorm, the gradient becomes very steep, and the electrical potential discharges as lightning. The discharge
10 may move between any oppositely charged regions—from cloud to earth, from earth to cloud, or from cloud to cloud. It was calculated as early as 1887 that the earth would lose almost all its charge in less than an
15 hour unless the supply were replenished; that is, on a global scale, lightning will discharge to the earth every hour a quantity of electricity equal to the earth's entire charge. Thunderstorms are thus an electromag-
20 netic as well as a thermodynamic necessity. It has been reckoned chat the earth experiences some 1,800 storms per hour, or 44,000 per day. Collectively, these storms produce 100 cloud-to-ground dis-
25 charges per second, or better than 8 million per day globally. And these estimates are probably low. The total energy in lightning bolts varies greatly, but about 250 kilowatt hours of electricity are packed into each
30 stroke. Almost 75 percent of this total energy is lost to heat during discharge.

Two types of discharge patrons are commonly identified: the cold stroke, whose main return [ground-to-cloud] stroke
35 is of intense current but of short duration, and the hot stroke, invoking lesser currents of longer duration. Cold lightning, with its high voltage, generally has mechanical or explosive effects; hot lightning is more apt
40 to start fires. Studies in the Northern Rockies suggest that about one stroke in 25 has the electrical characteristics needed to start a fire. Whether it does or not depends strongly on the object it strikes, the
45 fuel properties of the object, and the local weather. Ignition requires both heat and kindling. Lightning supplies the one with its current and occasionally finds the other among the fine fuels of rotten wood, nee-
50 dles. grass, or dustlike debris blown from a

tree by the explosive shock of the bolt itself.

The consequences of lightning are complex. Any natural force of this magni-
55 tude will influence the biological no less than the geophysical environment, and the secondary effects of lightning are significant to life. Lightning helps to fix atmospheric nitrogen into a form that rain can
60 bring to earth. In areas of heavy thunderstorm activity, lightning can function as a major predator on trees, either through direct injury or by physiological damage. In the ponderosa pine forests of Arizona, for
65 example, one forester has estimated that lightning mortality runs between 0.7 and 1.0 percent per year. Other researchers have placed mortality as high as 25–33 percent. For southern pines, the figure may
70 he even steeper. A study in Arkansas calculated that 70 percent of mortality, by volume, was due to lightning. These figures describe only direct injury, primarily the mechanical destruction of branches and
75 bole; the other major causes of mortality— insects, wind, and mistletoe—are likely secondary effects brought about in trees weakened by lightning. All of these effects, in turn, may be camouflaged by fire in-
80 duced by lightning.

The process of "electrocution" is increasingly recognized. Lightning scorch areas of between 0.25 and 25 acres have been identified. Nor is the process limited
85 to trees: it has been documented for grasses, tomatoes, potatoes, cabbages, tea, and other crops. Long attributed to inscrutable "die-offs" or to infestation by insects or diseases (often a secondary ef-
90 fect), such sites are now recognized worldwide as a product of physiological trauma caused by lightning.

The most spectacular product of lightning is fire. Except in tropical rain forests
95 and on ice-mantled land masses, lightning fire has occurred in every terrestrial environment on the globe, contributing to a natural mosaic of vegetation types. Even in tropical landscapes lightning bombardment
100 by itself may frequently be severe enough to produce a mosaic pattern similar to that resulting from lightning lire. Lightning fires have ignited desert grasslands, tundra, chaparral, swamplands, marshes, grass-

105 lands, and, of course, forests. Though the intensity and frequency of these fires vary by region, their existence is undeniable.

1. Which of the following best describes the overall structure of the passage?
   A. An analysis of the specific features of lightning is followed by a more general discussion of the types of lightning.
   B. A discussion of the specific features of lightning is discussed first globally and then locally.
   C. A discussion of the characteristics of lightning is followed by an analysis of the effects of lightning.
   D. A discussion of the damaging effects of lightning is followed by a discussion of the causes of lightning.

2. According to the passage, which of the following would likely NOT be considered a secondary effect of lightning?
   F. A tree weakened by lightning falls during a wind storm.
   G. The branches of a large tree are damaged after being struck by lightning.
   H. A tree in a scorch area succumbs to insect infestation.
   J. A tree is killed in a forest fire started by a direct lightning strike.

3. The *process of "electrocution"* in line 81 could best be described as:
   A. limited to trees.
   B. infestation by insects.
   C. a secondary effect of lightning.
   D. a product of physiological trauma caused by lightning.

4. As it is described in the first paragraph, which of the following is NOT true about thunderstorms?
   F. They produce 100 cloud-to-ground discharges per second.
   G. They occur at a rate of over 8 million per day.
   H. They produce lightning bolts with various levels of energy.
   J. Nearly 75% of the lightning energy they produce is lost to heat.

5. One of the most important points of the third paragraph (lines 53–80) is that:
   A. researchers in Arizona and Arkansas measure tree mortality by volume.
   B. rates of tree mortality only capture one aspect of lightning-related damage.
   C. pine trees are more susceptible to lightning-related damage than other kinds of trees.
   D. pine tree forests experience fewer lightning strikes than other types of habitats.

6. According to the passage, electrical potential discharges as lightning when:
   F. two charged regions move very close together.
   G. the change in electrical potential across a distance is great.
   H. an electrical potential is suddenly reversed.
   J. the earth is properly charged.

7. It can reasonably be inferred from the third paragraph (lines 53–80) that if lightning did not fix atmospheric nitrogen, then:
   A. nitrogen would be left in the atmosphere due to lack of rain fall.
   B. less nitrogen would fall to the earth surface.
   C. less electrical current would be conducted by the air.
   D. fewer lightning bolts would strike the earth.

8. According to the passage, which of the following best describes the differences between the two types of lightning discharge patterns?
   F. One has greater currents and longer durations.
   G. One has lesser currents but longer durations.
   H. One has longer duration and higher voltage.
   J. One has intense current that is more likely to start fires.

Continued →

9. It can reasonably be inferred from the passage that tropical landscapes:
   A. are susceptible to lightning fires that produce mosaic patterns.
   B. have climates that prevent lightning fires.
   C. display mosaic patterns even when lightning is not present.
   D. are the only type of terrestrial environment that is not susceptible to lightning fires.

10. The author states that thunderstorms are an "electromagnetic as well as a thermodynamic necessity" (lines 19–21) because:
   F. they replenish the earth's electrical charge.
   G. they produce more than 8 million discharges per day.
   H. most of the energy associated with thunderstorms is lost to heat.
   J. most pine forests would die off without the beneficial effects of lightning strikes.

■

TEST CORRECTIONS

Go back to Test 1 in *The Official ACT Prep Guide* and correct any **Main Idea** questions that you missed or guessed on. Review the three steps to correcting Reading tests on page 536.

5. COMPARISON QUESTIONS

Comparison questions ask you to compare two short passages. Usually these questions focus on *contrasts*, but some questions ask you to find *similarities* in two otherwise different opinions. We covered a general approach to double passages in the Reading Introduction. Here's a review:

DOUBLE PASSAGES: ORDER

Double passages will be followed by 10 questions divided into 3 sets: one set for Passage A, one set for Passage B, and one set for both passages. For these double passages, go in the following order:

1. Read Passage A and answer the questions for this passage only.
2. Read Passage B and answer the questions for this passage only.
3. Finally, move on to the questions for both passages (where you'll see the Comparison questions).

! **Do not read Passage B until you have answered the questions for Passage A.**

FOCUS ON THE CORRECT PASSAGE

When you get to the Comparison questions, the first step is to underline (in the question) which passage to focus on. You will likely see information from *both* passages in the answer choices, so be careful. For example, in the question below, which passage should you focus on?

> In the response to the claims made in lines 2–3 of Passage A, the author of Passage B would most likely assert that . . .

Hopefully you underlined *Passage B*. Yes, of course you must consider the "claims" made in Passage A, but you should focus on the *opinion* of the Passage-B author.

Note: Some double passages include two passages written by the same author. You should still make sure to focus on the correct passage.

Comparison questions (which show up on double passages) mention *both* passages (and, often, the authors of the passages) in the question. For example:

- Unlike Passage A, Passage B . . .
- The author of Passage A would most likely respond to the author of Passage B . . .
- Which statement characterizes the differences between the authors of Passage A and Passage B . . .
- Both passages . . .

While typically, as explained above, you will read one passage and then answer questions for that one passage, before moving on to the next passage, the questions that follow Passage VII below are Comparison questions, so go ahead and read *both* passages now. (Pretend that you already answered the questions related to each passage individually.)

Passage VII

SOCIAL SCIENCE: Passage A is adapted from *Violence in the Black Imagination: Essays and Documents* by Ronald T. Takaki (©1972). Passage B is adapted from the biography *Frederick Douglass* by Jon Sterngass (©2009).

Passage A

Violence against the oppressor was a question Frederick Douglass faced with profound ambivalence. Committed to Garrisonian abolitionism during the 1840's, Douglass sincerely hoped the abolitionist movement could successfully appeal to men's sense of right and emancipation could be achieved nonviolently. As a moral suasionist,
5 Douglass denounced Henry Highland Garnet's bold address to the slaves advocating a war to the knife against the slaveholding class. "There was," Douglass protested, "too much physical force both in the address and remarks of Garnet." But at the same time Douglass believed slave violence against the master class could have crucial psychological and political meaning for the wretched, for the oppressed. The
10 ambivalence Douglass felt toward violence was very personal: It was deeply rooted in his years of childhood and early manhood, in his relationships with gentlewomen like his slaveholding mistress Sophia Auld, and in his racial ties to both white and black.

Passage B

Douglass had never been a real pacifist, even when he followed Garrison. Douglass took pride in having fought Edward Covey. He doubted the effectiveness of
15 Garrison's tactic of "moral persuasion" as a weapon for slaves. Douglass' arguments against violence were usually practical: The white masters had the guns, and the black slaves who fought against them would be killed. He wrote, "I never see much use in fighting, unless there is a reasonable probability of whipping somebody."

Let's try some Comparison questions for the passage above:

(EX) 1. Both authors would likely agree that Frederick Douglass:

This question is broad, so let's look at the answer choices. Since you're looking for an answer that is true for both passages, eliminate answer choices that are true for only one of the passages.

 A. fought for emancipation using William Lloyd Garrison's tactic of "moral persuasion."
 B. considered violence a viable tool for emancipation in some instances.
 C. always thought that emancipation could be achieved nonviolently.
 D. was steadfast in his ideas about violence and emancipation.

Try the following Comparison question. Underline the author (or passage) that you should focus on:

EX 2. In response to the claim made in line 13 of Passage B, the author of Passage A would most likely assert that:

The answer will reflect the opinions of the author of Passage A, but first go back to Passage B and make sure you understand the claim made in line 13. How would the author of Passage A respond to this claim?

Now look at the answer choices. Do you see one that expresses the main idea of Passage A?

    F. Douglass's views on violence were complex and multifaceted.
    G. Garrison and Douglass both considered violence a last resort in the battle for emancipation.
    H. Douglass always disagreed with Garrison's views as an abolitionist.
    J. Douglass dismissed violence as an ineffective means to achieve an end.

Here's another Comparison question:

(EX) 3. Which of the following aspects of Frederick Douglass is addressed in Passage A but <u>not</u> in Passage B?

The answer to this question will reflect the context of Passage A (again, don't forget to focus on the correct passage when answering these Comparison questions). The question is broad, so here are the answer choices. Eliminate answer choices that are either addressed in Passage B or not addressed in either passage:

    A. Douglass's opinions about Garrison's principles of abolition
    B. Douglass's reasons for his stance against violence
    C. Douglass's race
    D. The specific steps that Douglass felt should be taken before violence was acceptable

Here's one more Comparison question:

(EX) 4. Which statement best characterizes the different ways in which the authors of Passage A and Passage B approach Frederick Douglass and his ideas?

We have another broad question, so look at the answer choices. Note that they are double answers, so eliminate answer choices one part at a time:

  F. The first speculates on the origin of Douglass's ideas, while the second examines their results.
  G. The first alludes to those who influenced Douglass, while the second presents Douglass's ideas as uniquely his own.
  H. The first stresses the evolution of Douglass's ideas, while the second examines his background as an abolitionist.
  J. The first emphasizes the ambiguity of Douglass's ideas, while the second focuses on their explicitness.

■

On the following homework passage, don't forget to approach it one passage at a time:

1. Read Passage A and answer the questions for this passage only.
2. Read Passage B and answer the questions for this passage only.
3. Finally, move on to the questions for both passages (where you'll see the Comparison questions).

Time = 8:45.

Passage V

SOCIAL SCIENCE: Passage A is adapted from Garett Jones, *Hive Mind* (©2016 by Stanford University Press). Passage B is adapted from Stephanie Solomon, *Stakeholders or Experts?* (©2009 by Palgrave Macmillan). An *epistocracy* is a system of government in which the votes of citizens with a particular knowledge or ability are given more weight than the votes of other citizens.

Passage A by Garett Jones

Yale's Dan Kahan and his coauthors gave people two kinds of tables to read. One group saw a table providing data about gun violence, and another group saw
5 data on skin rashes. The researchers asked respondents whether the data in the table backed the theories that (in the first case) gun control laws reduce violence and (in the second case) a particular cream
10 helped cure the rash.

Here's the trick: the data were all made up. As part of the experiment, Kahan asked people what political party they belonged to and how partisan they were. Also, there
15 were two sets of gun data given out randomly to different participants, one of which made it look like gun control cut crime rates while the other made it look like gun control raised crime rates; they did the same
20 scrambling with the rash data. The test subjects also took a short IQ-type test, a test of numerical skill. What did Kahan and coauthors find? Perhaps naturally, they found that Democrats were more likely to
25 say the gun data supported gun control regardless of which data they were given and Republicans fell victim to the opposite bias. As the saying goes, where you stand depends on where you sit. But Kahan's
30 study went further. He checked to see whether people who did well on the IQ-type test were more likely to get at the truth in both the skin rash case and the gun control case. And, no surprise, people who were
35 better at math were usually more likely to get to the truth.

That's not the end of the story, though. In the gun control case, greater numeracy predicted greater disagreement between
40 Democrats and Republicans. So if the data said that gun control worked, high-scoring Republicans were only a little more likely than low-scoring Republicans to read the table correctly, but high-scoring Democrats
45 were much more likely than low-scoring Democrats to realize that the news favored their team. The lesson: the well-informed disagree more than the poorly informed. More math skill means more knowledge,
50 and more knowledge might mean more disagreement, not more harmony.

But there's another lesson to draw from Kahan's study: overall, people with higher IQ type scores were more likely to read the
55 graph correctly, even when it was news they didn't want to see. And when it was news they wanted to see, the high scorers in both parties were likely to get the right answer. So overall, people with higher IQ-
60 type scores were more likely to get to the objective truth in studies at Yale, and perhaps they get closer to the objective truth in the real world as well. Yes, you're more likely to see the light if it's light you want to
65 see. But you're also more likely to see the light if you do better on a cognitive skill test.

Passage B by Stephanie Solomon

There are many reasons to desire that our political systems are democracies and not epistocracies. The social organization
70 in a democracy is organized around the principle that the procedure ought to be fair in that each citizen gets one voice and one vote. Famously, John Stuart Mill argued for a hybrid democratic/epistocratic system of
75 weighted voting, where more votes are given to the better educated. He based this assertion on the somewhat intuitive, if politically incorrect, notion that superior wisdom justifies superior political authority. He
80 also argued that giving more votes to the educated minority is the only way to prevent political decisions from consistently reflecting the unreasoned views of the majority, who by their sheer numbers would
85 not be required to convince anyone of their views.

The argument against a political epistocracy is that the educated portion of a population may correspond to a popula-
90 tion that also has features that make it less worthy to rule, such as race, class, or gender biases, and that there is no systematic way to prevent this. Another, more obvious problem with an epistocracy is that many

95 political decisions regard beliefs about priorities of life, such as what should be taught in schools, or whether health care should be universally accessible. In the domain of science, questions of which re-
100 search questions to prioritize and fund and how to disseminate and apply research findings in society also reflect social priorities and values that are indeterminable by specialist expertise. It is unclear how spe-
105 cialized training in a specific area, either within science or outside of it, has any direct bearing on the right one has to determine these issues.

Questions 1–4 ask about Passage A.

1. The central claim of Passage A is that compared to people with lower IQs, people with higher IQs:
   A. rarely make mistakes in interpreting information.
   B. tend to agree with one another, regardless of their political beliefs.
   C. are more likely to find objective truth in the real world.
   D. are incapable of speaking for the majority of the population.

2. As it is used in line 38, the word *numeracy* specifically refers to the:
   A. number of participants in a study.
   B. tendency to read data in a way that supports one's own opinions.
   C. disagreement between members of different political parties.
   D. ability on a test of numerical skill.

3. The author refers to the saying in lines 28–29 ("where . . . sit") in order to:
   A. show that peoples' beliefs are profoundly impacted by exposure to new information.
   B. illustrate that peoples' beliefs are often at odds with their actions.
   C. signal that biases in data have no effect on how people identify the truth.
   D. emphasize that peoples' beliefs are usually hard to influence.

4. Based on Passage A, the author implies which of the following about the "IQ-type test" discussed in the first paragraph?
   A. An IQ-type test is not necessarily a good measure of a person's intelligence.
   B. The test subjects' IQ-type test scores were dependent on their political views.
   C. A good IQ-type test should measure a person's proficiency in math.
   D. The IQ-type test directly measured the test taker's ability to determine what is true and what is fiction.

Questions 5–7 ask about Passage B.

5. In the first paragraph of Passage B (lines 67–86), the author considers the views of John Stuart Mill as:
   A. unfamiliar but worthy of further study among political scientists.
   B. apparently logical but objectionable upon closer examination.
   C. flawed but ultimately desirable if enacted as a hybrid democratic/epistocratic system.
   D. effective in preventing political decisions from always reflecting the uneducated minority.

Continued →

6. The author of Passage B mentions schools and health care primarily to:
   A. emphasize the need for unanimity when making decisions about typical social issues.
   B. provide examples of issues that should not be determined by well-educated experts alone.
   C. highlight the need for scientific expertise when making decisions about universal issues.
   D. support the claim that people must become better educated to more effectively make political decisions.

7. The author of Passage B claims that in the domain of science, specialist expertise:
   A. can help apply scientific findings to real-world problems.
   B. may offer solutions to problems in epistocracies associated with race, class, and gender biases.
   C. should not determine policies related to the application of research findings in society.
   D. should be utilized to make political decisions about priorities of life.

Questions 8–10 ask about both passages.

8. Which choice best describes the relationship of the two passages?
   A. Passage B offers an alternate solution to the problems of democracies discussed in Passage A.
   B. Passage B challenges the primary deduction made in Passage A.
   C. Passage B expands on one of the main points made in Passage A.
   D. Passage B questions the accuracy of the evidence discussed in Passage A.

9. The author of Passage B would most likely respond to the claims made about people with high IQs in lines 59–63, Passage A, by claiming that high IQ:
   A. does not properly measure race, class, or gender biases.
   B. is impossible to measure objectively.
   C. fails to determine the special experts in a society.
   D. is not a good criterion for determining who gets to vote on political issues.

10. John Stuart Mill and the author of Passage A would most likely agree that:
   A. people who are better at math are are more likely to be better informed voters.
   B. superior wisdom is not necessarily a guarantee of superior political authority.
   C. people with high IQ-type scores are more likely to get to the objective truth of an issue.
   D. the only way political decisions can be made fairly is if an educated minority is given more voting weight.

TEST CORRECTIONS

Go back to Test 1 in *The Official ACT Prep Guide* and correct any **Comparison** questions that you missed or guessed on. Review the three steps to correcting Reading tests on page 536.

■

 PRACTICE TEST (all programs): After you complete and review the homework passage above, and complete any assigned corrections (see the Tutoring Schedules), take **Test 2** (in *The Official ACT Prep Guide*). Don't forget to correct any missed questions after you grade the test. Note: This test marks the end of the **20-hour program.**

6. TONE QUESTIONS

Tone is defined as a quality, feeling, or attitude expressed by a person, usually in speaking or in writing. Tone questions typically refer to the author of a passage, but they may also ask about characters in a passage, particularly those in prose fiction passages.

Tone questions often contain the following words:
- tone
- attitude
- characterized as

Also, be on the lookout for *tone words* in the answer choices. As described in the Passage section, tone words are words that convey positive or negative *feelings*.

⊘ ELIMINATE ANSWER CHOICES THAT CONTRADICT TONE

Since the answer-choice vocabulary is sometimes challenging on Tone questions, you might not spot the correct answer right away, but hopefully you can eliminate incorrect answers. Often one or more answer choices can be eliminated simply because they contradict tone (usually the author's tone).

Make sure to look for, and darkly underline, tone words (see the Passage section) as you read the following passage. In addition to tone words, you should continue to mark up the passage as usual, including circling identifiers.

PROSE FICTION: This passage is adapted from *Cold Mountain* by Charles Frazier (©1998).

At the first gesture of morning, flies began stirring. Inman's eyes and the long wound at his neck drew them, and the sound of their wings and the touch of their feet were soon more potent than a yardful of roosters in rousing a man to wake. So he came to yet one more day in the hospital ward. He flapped the flies away with his hands

5   and looked across the foot of his bed to an open triple-hung window. Ordinarily he could see to the red road and the oak tree and the low brick wall. And beyond them to a sweep of fields and flat piney woods that stretched to the western horizon. The view was a long one for the flatlands, the hospital having been built on the only swell within eyeshot. But it was too early yet for a vista. The window might as well have been

10 painted grey.

Had it not been too dim, Inman would have read to pass the time until breakfast, for the book he was reading had the effect of settling his mind. But he had burned up the last of his own candles reading to bring sleep the night before, and lamp oil was too scarce to be striking the hospital's lights for mere diversion. So he rose and dressed

15 and sat in a ladderback chair, putting the gloomy room of beds and their broken occupants behind him. He flapped again at the flies and looked out the window at the first smear of foggy dawn and waited for the world to begin shaping up outside.

The window was tall as a door, and he had imagined many times that it would open onto some other place and let him walk through and be there.

Let's try some questions that test tone:

(EX) 1.   That passage indicates that the hospital staff would most likely view the act of reading as:

The word "view" in the question tells us that this is probably a Tone question. You might also glance at the answer choices below. Let's first try answering the question using context.

Here are the answer choices:

> **A.** an insignificant distraction.
> **B.** an enriching endeavor.
> **C.** a calming amusement.
> **D.** a harmful procrastination.

Continued →

(EX) 2. Inman's attitude toward the other occupants (line 16) in the hospital ward is best described as one of:

We know this is a Tone question because of the word "attitude." Again, let's first try answering the question using context.

Here are the answer choices:

    A. dread.
    B. ambivalence.
    C. detachment.
    D. arrogance.

(EX) 3. In the last paragraph (lines 18–19), Inman's tone is best described as:

First, consider context.

Now let's look at the answer choices. If the answer choice vocabulary is difficult for you, try POE:

    A. introspective.
    B. wistful.
    C. resolute.
    D. resigned.

Continued →

Here's one more passage that we'll use to cover Tone questions. Note how on nonfiction passages (this is a social science one) Tone questions focus more on the *author*. Don't forget to underline tone words while you read:

> **SOCIAL SCIENCE**: This passage is adapted from *Four Arguments for the Elimination of Television* by Jerry Mander (©1978).

> The first really shocking burst of figures appeared in newspapers in the early 1970s.
>   It was reported that in the generation since 1945, 99 percent of the homes in the country had acquired at least one television set. On an average evening, more than 80
> 5 million people would be watching television. Thirty million of these would be watching the same program. In special instances, 100 million people would be watching the same program at the same time.
>   The average household had the set going more than six hours a day. If there was a child, the average was more than eight hours. The average person was watching for
> 10 nearly four hours daily. And so, allowing eight hours for sleep and eight hours for work, roughly half of the adult nonsleeping, nonworking time was spent watching television. Considering that these were average figures, they meant that half of the people in this country were watching television even more than that.
>   As these numbers sank in, I realized that there had been a strange change in the
> 15 way people received information, and even more in the way they were experiencing and understanding the world. In one generation, out of hundreds of thousands in human evolution, America had become the first culture to have substituted secondary, mediated versions of experience for direct experience of the world. Interpretations and representations of the world were being accepted as experience, and the difference
> 20 between the two was obscure to most of us.

Let's try a tone question for the previous passage:

(EX) 1.   Over the course of the author's research into television, the author apparently had a shift in feeling from:

Note the keyword "feeling" in the question (hence, it's a Tone question). How does the author feel at the beginning of the passage? How does the author's tone change in the last paragraph ("As these numbers sank in . . .")? Go back to the passage, and make sure to look for tone words.

Do you see the correct answer below? Watch out for answer choices that are too strong (something commonly found on Tone questions):

   A. amazement to concern.
   B. surprise to curiosity.
   C. complacency to despair.
   D. apprehension to contentment.

⊘ ELIMINATE DOUBLE ANSWER CHOICES ONE PART AT A TIME

When each answer choice includes two parts (as in the example above), try eliminating one part at a time. If you can eliminate any *half* of an answer choice (particularly the *easier* half), you can eliminate the whole thing.

In the example above, you can quickly eliminate B and D by looking at the second part of each answer choice, and if you're comfortable with the Too Strong elimination technique, you can also eliminate C by looking at the second part. You didn't actually have to worry about the first words of the answer choices at all!

Here's another Tone question:

(EX) 2. The author would most likely characterize the way people were "experiencing and understanding the world" (lines 15–16) as:

Go back to the passage. How would you describe the author's tone in this paragraph? Do you see any other context that might come in handy?

Once again, the answers are "double answers":

    F. rapidly-changing and long-lasting.
    G. expected and disastrous.
    H. sudden and unfortunate.
    J. familiar and welcome.

Let's try one more Tone question:

(EX) 3.   Regarding a culture's direct experience of the world, the author expresses which of the following attitudes?

If you circled "direct experience" as an identifier, you will see that the context is found in the last paragraph. Otherwise, you hopefully have a sense of where this topic was discussed in the passage. What is the author's tone toward "direct experience of the world" (line 18)?

Note that the answer-choice vocabulary may not be easy for you. As we said earlier, vocabulary can be one of the main challenges of Tone questions. If you don't spot the correct answer, use POE:

    A. Sorrow
    B. Indifference
    C. Resentment
    D. Esteem

■

(**HW**)

The homework passage begins on the next page. The time, as usual, is 8:45, but remember that when you take a full test, we'll round down to 8:30 for the deadlines.

Passage VI

PROSE FICTION: This passage is adapted from the short story "Araby" by James Joyce, originally published in 1905.

North Richmond Street, being blind, was a quiet street except at the hour when the Christian Brothers' School set the boys free. An uninhabited house of two stories
5 stood at the blind end, detached from its neighbors in a square ground. The other houses of the street, conscious of decent lives within them, gazed at one another with brown imperturbable faces.

10 The former tenant of our house, a priest, had died in the back drawing-room. Air, musty from having been long enclosed, hung in all the rooms, and the waste room behind the kitchen was littered with old
15 useless papers. Among these I found a few paper-covered books, the pages of which were curled and damp: *The Abbot*, by Walter Scott, *The Devout Communicant*, and *The Memoirs of Vidocq*. I liked the last
20 best because its leaves were yellow. The wild garden behind the house contained a central apple-tree and a few straggling bushes, under one of which I found the late tenant's rusty bicycle-pump. He had been a
25 very charitable priest; in his will he had left all his money to institutions and the furniture of his house to his sister.

When the short days of winter came, dusk fell before we had well eaten our din-
30 ners. When we met in the street the houses had grown somber. The space of sky above us was the color of ever-changing violet and towards it the lamps of the street lifted their feeble lanterns. The cold air
35 stung us and we played till our bodies glowed. Our shouts echoed in the silent street. The career of our play brought us through the dark muddy lanes behind the houses, where we ran the gauntlet of the
40 rough tribes from the cottages, to the back doors of the dark dripping gardens where odors arose from the ashpits, to the dark odorous stables where a coachman smoothed and combed the horse or shook
45 music from the buckled harness. When we returned to the street, light from the kitchen windows had filled the areas. If my uncle was seen turning the corner, we hid in the shadow until we had seen him safely
50 housed. Or if Mangan's sister came out on

the doorstep to call her brother in to his tea, we watched her from our shadow peer up and down the street. We waited to see whether she would remain or go in and, if
55 she remained, we left our shadow and walked up to Mangan's steps resignedly. She was waiting for us, her figure defined by the light from the half-opened door. Her brother always teased her before he
60 obeyed, and I stood by the railings looking at her. Her dress swung as she moved her body, and the soft rope of her hair tossed from side to side.

Every morning I lay on the floor in the
65 front parlor watching her door. The blind was pulled down to within an inch of the sash so that I could not be seen. When she came out on the doorstep my heart leaped. I ran to the hall, seized my books and fol-
70 lowed her. I kept her brown figure always in my eye and, when we came near the point at which our ways diverged, I quickened my pace and passed her. This happened morning after morning. I had never spoken
75 to her, except for a few casual words, and yet her name was like a summons to all my foolish blood.

Her image accompanied me even in places the most hostile to romance. On
80 Saturday evenings when my aunt went marketing I had to go to carry some of the parcels. We walked through the flaring streets, jostled by drunken men and bargaining women, amid the curses of labour-
85 ers, the shrill litanies of shop-boys who stood on guard by the barrels of pigs' cheeks, the nasal chanting of street-singers, who sang a *come-all-you* about O'Donovan Rossa, or a ballad about the
90 troubles in our native land. These noises converged in a single sensation of life for me: I imagined that I bore my chalice safely through a throng of foes. Her name sprang to my lips at moments in strange prayers
95 and praises which I myself did not understand. My eyes were often full of tears (I could not tell why) and at times a flood from my heart seemed to pour itself out into my bosom. I thought little of the future. I did not
100 know whether I would ever speak to her or not or, if I spoke to her, how I could tell her of my confused adoration. But my body was like a harp and her words and ges-

tures were like fingers running upon the
105 wires.

1. The author of the passage suggests which of the following about the "other houses" (lines 6–7)?
   A. They are uninhabited during the days.
   B. They appear similar to the uninhabited house at the blind end.
   C. They architecturally clash with one another.
   D. They reflect the demeanor of their occupants.

2. When Mangan's sister first appeared on the doorstep each morning, the narrator:
   A. continued observing her secretly from the window.
   B. kept her figure always in sight.
   C. ran to her so that he could accompany her to the place where their paths diverged.
   D. ran to the hall, seized his books, and followed her.

3. The narrator views the priest described in the second paragraph (lines 10–27) as:
   A. kindly.
   B. altruistic.
   C. neighborly.
   D. sociable.

4. As presented in the passage, the narrator and his companions are best described as
   A. unruly and somber.
   B. rebellious and foolish.
   C. secretive and infatuated.
   D. boisterous and collaborative.

5. Mangan's attitude toward his sister could best be described as:
   A. outwardly disobedient.
   B. reluctantly obedient.
   C. quietly affectionate.
   D. good-naturedly mocking.

6. The narrator portrays going marketing with his aunt as:
   A. conducive for considering his affections for Mangan's sister.
   B. desirable because the setting distracts him from thoughts of romance.
   C. dangerous because of the behavior of drunken men and bargaining women.
   D. inhospitable for contemplating his feelings for Mangan's sister.

7. The sentence in lines 61–63 ("Her dress . . . side") mainly serves to
   A. contrast the narrator's image of Mangan's sister from that of Mangan himself.
   B. emphasize the narrators dislike of Mangan's sister's authoritarian nature.
   C. show the difficulty of seeing Mangan's sister clearly in the shadows.
   D. present a description of Mangan's sister as viewed by the characters in the story.

8. When the narrator followed Mangan's sister, he sought to
   A. follow her to her destination.
   B. speak to her before their paths separated.
   C. call to her so he could reveal his feelings for her.
   D. keep her in view but avoid conversing with her.

9. Which choice best describes the narrator's characterization of Mangan's sister?
   A. Appealing but condescending
   B. Beautiful but foolish
   C. Desirable but unattainable
   D. Silent but stern

Continued →

10. The narrator indicates that when passing among the figures at the market, his thoughts of the future:
    A. foreshadowed metaphorically his eventual meeting with Mangan's sister.
    B. were diminished in comparison with his feelings of the present.
    C. became a place of refuge to escape the present unrest of the market.
    D. focused entirely on his anticipation of meeting Mangan's sister.

■

TEST CORRECTIONS

Go back to Test 1 in *The Official ACT Prep Guide* and correct any **Tone** questions that you missed or guessed on. Review the three steps to correcting Reading tests on page 536.

7. WORDS IN CONTEXT QUESTIONS

Words in Context (WIC) questions ask you to define a word or short phrase using context. There are two steps to these problems:

1. **Define the original word.** Read the sentence from the passage that contains the word or phrase in question, and define the word or phrase **using context**. Even if you know (or think you know) what the word means, use *context*, not the dictionary in your head.

   Make sure to use context as you define the word. These questions usually deal with words that have several meanings, and the correct answer is almost *never* the most common of these definitions (so you must use context).

2. **Choose an answer and check.** Choose the answer that is closest to your definition. Substitute your answer for the original word, and read the original sentence. The correct answer should sound correct.

If you don't spot the correct answer, or if the context is difficult and you have trouble defining the word before looking at the answer choices, consider the following:

- **Awkwardness**: Try plugging the answer choices into the passage (in place of the word in question). When you read the passage with the answer choices plugged in, incorrect answer choices will often sound awkward or obviously wrong.

- **Tone**: If you know the word is, for example, *negative*, eliminate any words that sound *positive*.

- **Difficult Answer Choices**: It's OK to pick a difficult word as your answer, even if you don't know what the word means. POE is encouraged on WIC questions. If you know the other words don't work perfectly, go with the remaining answer choice.

- **Word Familiarity**: If you're familiar with the word in question, consider possible definitions, especially if the context is difficult. This can help if you've narrowed it down to a couple answer choices that both seem to work.

 Words in Context questions will ask what a word or phrase "means" or "most nearly means." (Don't confuse these questions with ones that ask what a word "most nearly *refers to*.")

We'll use the following passage for some WIC questions. Many students find this one challenging. Just get through it, make your markups, and look for "the easy stuff."

HUMANITIES: This passage is adapted from *Modernism and Melancholy* by Sanja Bahun (©2014 by Oxford University Press).

If writing is to be re-envisioned as the ethically most appropriate way to engage with a catastrophic historical moment, the question of representation, of what is written and how it is read, gains preeminence. The essential property of great art, Virginia Woolf claims in her essay "A Sketch of the Past," is the art's capacity to evoke a hidden
5   pattern, a pattern that unites us all and that is itself ingrained in particular works of art.
But what are the means and modes appropriate to representation of a history which, to its traversers at least, looks like "a criss-cross of lines making no pattern"? To disregard reality in favor of a false harmony conflicts with the humanly and progressively informed understanding of life and art that Woolf advances. So her last novel shapes
10 itself into a performance of what Freud deemed a particularly poetic form of melancholia—"anticipatory grief;" an impulse to foretaste mourning, melancholically to probe an impending historical catastrophe.

Let's try some Words in Context questions:

(EX) 1.   As it is used in line 1, the words *engage with* most nearly means:

Remember, define the word or phrase using context *before* looking at the answer choices. This is the most important strategy with WIC questions.

Here are the answer choices. Remember to use process of elimination (POE) if necessary. Try plugging the answer choices into the passage:

    A. attract.
    B. secure.
    C. hold fast to.
    D. occupy oneself with.

Continued →

As stated above, always consider context *before* looking at the answer choices. If necessary, cover the answer choices below with a sheet of paper until you've defined the words using context (but eventually, before you take a real test, you'll have to get into the habit of ignoring the answer choices):

(EX) 2. As it is used in line 2, the word *moment* most nearly means:

    A. instant.
    B. definite period.
    C. present time.
    D. consequence.

(EX) 3. As it is used in line 3, the word *property* most nearly means:

    A. quality.
    B. possession.
    C. goods.
    D. domain.

On the following WIC question, remember to answer double answer choices one part at a time:

(EX) 4. As it is used in line 6, the words *means and modes* most nearly means:

    A. methods and forms.
    B. certainties and behaviors.
    C. averages and conditions.
    D. capabilities and types.

Continued →

Here's one more WIC question for this passage:

(EX) 5. As it is used in line 9, the word *advances* most nearly means:
   A. brings into consideration.
   B. travels forward.
   C. improves.
   D. increases.

■

The homework passage begins on the next page (time = 8:45).

HUMANITIES: This passage is adapted from the essay "Faith and Work" by Scott Russell Sanders (©1995 by Scott Russell Sanders).

The difference between a machine and a tool—between a bread-maker and a bread pan—is that a tool extends human skills, a machine replaces them. When the
5 freedom and craft have been squeezed out of work it becomes toil, without mystery or meaning, and that is why many people hate their jobs. You can measure the drudgery of a job by the number of layers of supervi-
10 sion required to keep the wheels spinning or the cash registers ringing. Toil drains us; but good work may renew us, by giving expression to our powers.

A generation or two ago it would have
15 seemed less strange to relish hard work. My grandparents might smile at the laziness of Tom Sawyer, who fooled others into doing his chores, but they would remind you that Tom was a child. Grown-ups
20 do their own chores, unless they are idlers, good-for-nothings, ne'er-do-wells. Grownups look after their own needs, provide for their families, help their neighbors, do something useful. So my grandparents
25 taught by word and example. Any job worth doing is worth doing right, they used to say. To try sliding by with the least effort, my grandparents believed, was to be guilty of a sin called sloth.

30 I knew this cluster of values by experience long before I heard it referred to as the work ethic, a phrase that has lost its edge from tumbling over the lips of too many cynical bosses and politicians. What-
35 ever happened to the work ethic? laments the manager who wishes to squeeze more profit from his employees. Whatever happened to the work ethic? groans the official who wants to shrink the welfare rolls. As I
40 understand it, a regard for the necessity and virtue of work has nothing to do with productivity or taxes, and everything to do with fulfilling one's humanity. As I have seen it embodied in the lives not only of
45 grandparents but of parents and neighbors and friends, this ethic arises from a belief that the creation is a sacred gift, and that by working we express our gratitude and celebrate our powers. To honor that gift, we
50 should live simply, honestly, conservingly, saving money and patching clothes and fixing what breaks, sharing what we have.

Those values are under assault every minute of the day in a consumer econ-
55 omy—from advertising, from the glittering goodies in stores, from the luxurious imagery of television, magazines, and films, and from a philosophy that views the universe not as a gift to be honored but as a
60 warehouse to be ransacked. If money is meaning, if winning the lottery or beating the stock market defines success, if the goal of life is easy sensation, then why lift a finger so long as you can force someone or
65 something else to do it for you?

I can think of many reasons to lift a finger, among them the delight in exercising skill, in sharing labor with companions, in planning a task and carrying it through, in
70 bringing some benefit to the world. But the chief reason for relishing work is that it allows us to practice our faith, whatever that faith may be. The Buddha advised his followers to seek right livelihood, to provide
75 for their needs in a modest and responsible manner, with respect for other creatures, in harmony with the way of things. We show our understanding of the way of things by the quality of our work, whether or not we
80 have heard the Buddha's teachings. The old theological debate as to whether salvation is to be gained by works or by faith begins from a false dichotomy. Faith concerns our sense of what is real, what is
85 valuable, what is holy; work is how we act out that faith.

The Shakers condensed their faith into the maxim "Hands to work, hearts to God." Anyone who has looked at their furniture or
90 buildings can sense the clarity of their vision. "One feels that for the Shaker craftsmen," Thomas Merton observed, "love of God and love of truth in one's own work came to the same thing, and that work itself
95 was a prayer, a communion with the inmost spiritual reality of things and so with God." Mother Ann Lee, who launched the Shaker movement, counseled her followers to "Do all your work as if you had a thousand
100 years to live, and as you would if you knew you must die tomorrow."

If the purpose of life is not to acquire but to inquire, to seek understanding, to discover all we can about ourselves and
105 the universe, to commune with the source of things, then we should care less about

what we earn—money, prestige, salvation—and more about what we learn. In
light of all we have to learn, the difference
110 between dying tomorrow and a hundred
years from tomorrow is not very great.

1. It can reasonably be inferred from the
   passage that the author's grandparents
   "might smile at the laziness of Tom
   Sawyer" (lines 16–17) because:
   A. they know that there is a time for
      play and a time for work.
   B. later in life, Tom Sawyer helped his
      family and neighbors and did much
      that was useful.
   C. they recognize that young people
      are not yet expected to understand
      the importance of hard work.
   D. they consider Tom Sawyer a
      humorous case of someone who
      taught by word and example.

2. As it is used in line 43, the word
   humanity most nearly means:
   F. obligation to care for one's elders.
   G. right to maximize one's
      productivity.
   H. desire to accomplish as much as
      possible in the shortest time.
   J. obligation to live simply, honestly,
      and conservingly.

3. In the last paragraph, the author
   emphasizes the distinction between
   which of the following terms?
   A. acquiring and inquiring
   B. inquiring and learning
   C. money and salvation
   D. tomorrow and a hundred years
      from tomorrow

4. As it is used in line 13, the term *powers*
   most nearly refers to the:
   F. ability to persevere in a physically
      difficult job.
   G. knowledge to differentiate between
      work that drains and work that
      renews.
   H. responsibility needed to perform a
      job without supervision.
   J. skill required for some kinds of
      work.

5. The author suggests that many people
   do not like their jobs because:
   A. new machines make their work
      more complicated.
   B. there are many layers of
      supervision.
   C. their jobs are rigidly controlled.
   D. they are forced to use tools that
      could easily be replaced with
      machines.

6. According to the passage, which of the
   following describes the essential
   difference between a bread-maker and
   a bread pan?
   F. The bread pan was used by
      previous generations while the
      bread maker is used today.
   G. The bread-maker came on the
      market in recent years while the
      bread pan has been around for
      much longer.
   H. The bread-maker is more
      complicated than a bread pan.
   J. The bread-maker diminishes the
      human role in performing a task
      while the bread pan extends the
      human role.

7. The "false dichotomy" described in line
   83 could best be described as a:
   A. failure to recognize the differences
      in two distinct ideas.
   B. use of two different ideas to
      answer a question that can only be
      answered with one of them.
   C. dissociation of two ideas that are
      actually closely related.
   D. combination of two different ideas
      to explain a concept.

Continued →

8. The phrase "work ethic" (line 32) is described in the passage as:
   - **F.** something the author understood conceptually before he heard the term used.
   - **G.** a phrase whose meaning is more powerful now than ever before.
   - **H.** something bosses, politicians, managers, and officials might strive for.
   - **J.** a phrase that is no longer used in a world where profit is more important than hard work.

9. The author indicates that the most important reason for appreciating hard work is that it:
   - **A.** gives the worker pleasure in exercising a skill.
   - **B.** benefits the world.
   - **C.** allows people to practice their faith.
   - **D.** usually leads to financial security.

10. As it is used in line 3, the word *extends* most nearly means:
    - **F.** enlarges the scope of.
    - **G.** increases the length of.
    - **H.** prolongs the time of.
    - **J.** stretches out.

■

TEST CORRECTIONS

Go back to Test 1 in *The Official ACT Prep Guide* and correct any **Words in Context** questions that you missed or guessed on. Review the three steps to correcting Reading tests on page 536.

8. DIFFICULT PASSAGES

Many ACTs will include at least one especially difficult passage. As you work on these passages, we remind you to:

FOCUS ON THE EASY STUFF

! **If the passage is hard to understand or phrases or whole sentences confuse you, focus on the parts you *do* understand.**

Don't get discouraged. Read through the passage, diligently circle your identifiers, and focus on the easy stuff. Many of the questions, perhaps most of them, will focus on the parts of the passage that you *do* understand.

STAY OPEN-MINDED

This is an important tip, especially on difficult passages. As you know by now, for most questions we recommend you try answering the question using context *before* looking at the answer choices. But what happens if you go back to the passage and simply don't understand the relevant context? You shouldn't necessarily give up on the question. Start looking at the answer choices, and stay *open-minded*. If an answer choice is supported by context, even if it answers the question in a way you hadn't anticipated, it is probably the correct answer.

Many students will find the following passage difficult. Remember, just get through it. Circle identifiers and focus on the easy stuff.

SOCIAL SCIENCE: This passage is adapted from the biography *Beyond the Hundredth Meridian* by Wallace Stegner (©1992)

The tourist and the nature lover occupied a good large corner of Clarence Edward Dutton. He never quite made up his mind whether he was literary traveler or sober scientific analyst: the temptations were essentially equal. He escaped his dilemma by being both, and in his reports a rich and embroidered nineteenth-century traveler's
5 prose flows around bastions of geological fact as some of the lava coulees on the Uinkaret flow around gables of sedimentary strata. The literary tendency is progressive; it is apparent in *The Geology of the High Plateaus of Utah* (1880) and dominant in *The Tertiary History of the Grand Canyon* (1882). With hardly an apology, Dutton forsook the "sever ascetic style" of science when he came to deal with the Grand Canyon. The
10 Grand Canyon was beyond the reach of superlatives, it compelled effusion of a kind. The result is a scientific monograph of great geological importance which contains whole chapters as ebullient as the writing of John Muir, and deviates constantly into speculations so far from geological that they sound more like Ruskin than Lyell.

By now you are hopefully getting comfortable identifying question types. You should also have a sense of when to look back to the passage for context *before* looking at the answer choices, and when not to. For the following questions, the answer choices will immediately follow the questions (which of course is how the questions look on the ACT). Just remember that for most questions, you should look for context *before* looking at the answer choices. Don't let the placement of the answer choices tempt you to peek.

(EX) 1.   The primary purpose of the passage is to:

    A. point out the differences in two works of scientific writing.
    B. caution against combining literary and scientific writing styles.
    C. discuss the dualistic nature of a scientist's writing.
    D. examine the background and success of a scientist.

This is a Main Idea question. If you grasped the main idea while you were reading, you probably identified the correct answer. If not, then read through the answer choices and decide which one is best supported by the passage. As stated at the beginning of this section, you may have to be open-minded while reading the answer choices (especially if you weren't comfortable with the context).

(EX) 2. As it is used in line 2, the word *sober* most nearly means:

  F. grave.
  G. not intoxicated.
  H. quiet.
  J. dispassionate.

(EX) 3. The language in lines 3–6 ("He escaped . . . strata") is particularly notable for its:

  A. humorous allusions.
  B. noted understatement.
  C. abstract language.
  D. metaphorical prose.

(EX) 4. The author presents Dutton's decision to write in a literary manner between 1880 and 1882 as something that:

F. expanded markedly.
G. became apparent for the first time.
H. grew inconsistently.
J. had wide-ranging influence.

(EX) 5. The author's attitude toward Dutton's writing about the Grand Canyon is best described as one of:

A. condescension.
B. indifference.
C. ambiguity.
D. understanding.

6. The author most likely mentions Muir and Ruskin in order to:

    F. give examples of writers who influenced the work of Dutton.
    G. compare Dutton to scientists known more for their informative scientific writing.
    H. argue that Dutton's writing is more like that of literary writers than science writers.
    J. provide well-known authors whose styles of writing are similar to that of Dutton.

■

The homework passage begins on the next page (time = 8:45). Many students find this passage difficult. Your goal is to get through it quickly, mark it up efficiently (especially with identifiers), and underline "the easy stuff" when you find it. Make sure you give yourself plenty of time to answer the questions. The passage may be difficult, but that doesn't mean all of the questions will be difficult too. Remember to tackle the easier questions first. Work confidently on these difficult passages.

Passage VIII

SOCIAL SCIENCE: This passage is adapted from the essay "Learning from Pop" by Denise Scott Brown (©1984 by Harper and Row). Pop art is an American art movement from the 1950s and 1960s in which everyday objects of American life were used as subject matter.

Las Vegas, Los Angeles, Levittown, the swinging singles on the Westheimer Strip, golf resorts, boating communities, Co-op City, the residential backgrounds to soap
5 operas, TV commercials and mass mag ads, billboards, and Route 66 are sources for a changing architectural sensibility. New sources are sought when the old forms go stale and the way out is not clear; then a
10 Classical heritage, an art movement, or industrial engineers' and primitives' "architecture without architects" may help to sweep out the flowery remains of the old revolution as practiced by its originators'
15 conservative descendants. In America in the sixties an extra ingredient was added to this recipe for artistic change: social revolution. Urban renewal, supplier of work for architects for two decades and the major
20 locus of the soft remains of the Modern movement, was not merely artistically stale, it was socially harmful. The urgency of the social situation, and the social critique of urban renewal of the architect as server of
25 the rich narrow spectrum of the population have been as important as the Pop artists in steering us toward the existing American city and its builders. If high-style architects are not producing what people want or
30 need, who is, and what can we learn from them?

Sensitivity to needs is a first reason for going to the existing city. Once there, the first lesson for architects is the pluralism of
35 need. No builder-developer in his right mind would announce: I am building for Man. He is building for a market, for a group of people defined by income range, age, family composition, and life style.
40 Levittowns, Leisureworlds, Georgian-styled town houses grow from someone's estimation of the needs of the groups who will be their markets. The city can be seen as the built artifacts of a set of subcultures. At the
45 moment, those subcultures which willingly resort to architects are few.

Of course learning from what's there is subject to the caveats and limitations of all behaviorisitic analysis—one is surveying
50 behavior which is constrained, it is not what people might do in other conditions. The poor do not willingly live in tenements and maybe the middle classes don't willingly live in Levittowns; perhaps the Georgian-
55 styling is less pertinent to the townhouse resident than is the rent. In times of housing shortage this is a particularly forceful argument against architectural behaviorism since people can't vote against a particular
60 offering by staying away if there is no alternative. To counteract this danger one must search for comparison environments where for some reason the constraints do not hold. There are environments which sug-
65 gest what economically constrained group's taste might be if they were less constrained. They are the nouveau rich environments: Hollywood for a former era, Las Vegas for today, and homes of film
70 stars, sportsmen and other groups where upward mobility may resemble vertical takeoff, yet where maintenance of previous value systems is encouraged.

Another source is physical back-
75 grounds in the mass media, movies, soap operas, pickle and furniture ads. Here the aim is not to sell houses but something else, and the background represents someone's (Madison Avenue's?) idea of
80 what pickle buyers or soap opera watchers want in a house. Now the Madison Avenue observer's view may be as biased as the architect's, and it should be studied in the light of what it is trying to sell—must pickle
85 architecture look homey like my house or elegant like yours if it is to sell me pickles? But at least it's another bias, an alternative to the architectural navel contemplation we do so often for research, i.e., ask: What did
90 Le Corbusier do? Both Madison Avenue and the builder, although they can tell us little of the needs of the poor, cover a broader range of the population and pass a stiffer market test than does the architect in
95 urban renewal or public housing, and if we learn no more from these sources than that architecture must differ for different groups, that is a great deal. But an alternative to both is to examine what people do to
100 buildings—in Levittowns, Society Hills, gray areas and slums—once they are in them.

Here costs and availability are less constraining forces since the enterprise is smaller. Also, changes tend often to be

105 symbolic rather than structural, and aspirations can perhaps be more easily inferred from symbols than from structures.

Attention to built sources for information on need does not imply that asking

110 people what they want is not extremely necessary as well. This is an important topic, as is the relation between the two types of survey, asking and looking; but it is not the subject of this enquiry, which is on

115 what can be learned from the artifacts of pop culture.

1. As used in line 37, *market* most nearly refers to:
   A. a place where food is sold.
   B. people with similar social and economic interests.
   C. a field of trade or business.
   D. a group of architects with similar tastes.

2. According to the author, which of the following is a reason for why "behavioristic analysis" (line 49) is of limited value?
   A. When people have multiple options, their decisions become random.
   B. Most groups would prefer to live in parts of a city they cannot afford.
   C. A group of people should not be analyzed using its individual members.
   D. People's behavior is often limited by their circumstances.

3. The author's use of the words "vertical takeoff" (lines 71–72) mainly serves to:
   A. illustrate the close connection between social mobility and value systems.
   B. emphasize the rapid change in some people's economic status.
   C. highlight the recent transformations of some cities.
   D. provide a contrast to the gradual nature of environmental change.

4. As presented in the passage, Le Corbusier is best described as:
   A. an architect noted for his elegant designs.
   B. an architect who offers an alternative viewpoint to traditional architectural theory.
   C. an architect whose work other architects frequently turn to while researching.
   D. an architect who paid little attention to the social needs of his clients.

5. The author states that no builder-developer admits to "building for Man" (lines 36–37) in order to emphasize that:
   A. architects build for subgroups within the greater population.
   B. some builder-developers use terms that are now considered antiquated.
   C. architects must find ways to design buildings that appeal to most people.
   D. builder-developers usually keep their methodologies secret.

6. One central claim of the fourth paragraph (lines 74–107) is that architects should:
   A. create physical backgrounds rather than entire houses.
   B. focus less on building houses and more on selling them.
   C. consider traditional solutions to design considerations.
   D. study how people alter the places in which they live.

Continued →

7. According to the author, the perspective of the typical Madison Avenue observer is presented as:
   A. more focused on selling houses than on designing them.
   B. an alternative to the perspective of the typical architect.
   C. one that reveals the shifting tastes in architecture.
   D. concerned with both the rich and the poor.

8. The main purpose of the fifth paragraph (lines 108–116) is to:
   A. shift the essay to a new subject of inquiry.
   B. emphasize the relation between two types of survey.
   C. summarize the points made elsewhere in the passage.
   D. qualify the author's belief in the importance of a particular source of information.

9. As used in line 94, *stiffer* most nearly means:
   A. more solid
   B. more stringent
   C. more formal
   D. more extreme

10. It can reasonably be inferred from the passage that "Levittowns, Leisureworlds, [and] Georgian-styled town houses" (lines 40–41) are examples of:
    A. places of leisure and escape from cities.
    B. styles of architecture which make up most cities.
    C. places frequently desired by the rich.
    D. places each inhabited by a different type of subgroup.

■

TEST CORRECTIONS

Go back to Test 2 in *The Official ACT Prep Guide* and correct **all questions** that you missed or guessed on. Review the three steps to correcting Reading tests on page 536.

■

30- and 40-hour programs: The next section (Practice) describes additional practice assignments and includes an extra practice passage. Review the Tutoring Schedules in the Introduction to know when to complete these assignments. The Schedules also will tell you when to take Test 3 and (for 40-hour only) Test 4.

9. PRACTICE

For additional practice, we'll use Test 5 in *The Official ACT Prep Guide*. There is also an additional practice passage on the following pages to be completed for homework. See the Tutoring Schedules section in the Introduction for more on when to tackle these passages for different programs:

- ***The Official ACT Prep Guide:* Test 5***
    - ☐ Passage I
    - ☐ Passage II
    - ☐ Passage III
    - ☐ Passage IV
- ☐ Passage IX (end of this section)*

*Make sure to time yourself for these passages. See the Reading Introduction to review times for individual passages.

READ

Perhaps the best way to raise your Reading Test scores is to read as much as possible. Read material that is hard to understand at first. Choose a variety of reading materials, such as novels, newspapers, and even poetry. While the previous techniques are certainly helpful and will begin to compensate for less-than-great reading skills, no instruction can completely take the place of a solid reading background. For this reason, *reading* is a significant part of improving your Reading scores.

The homework passage begins on the next page (time = 8:45). This is the last passage in this tutorial. By now you should be comfortable with the basic strategies:

- Make sure you're effectively marking up the passage while you read, especially with **identifiers** (see the Passage section in Chapter II).

- Make sure you're using **context** while answering the questions (see the Context section in Chapter II). **Try answering most questions *before* looking at the answer choices.**

- Make sure you can identify each of the different question types (review the magnifying glass information for each type).

- Are you able to at least look at every question, even if you have to strategically skip some of the (harder) questions on your first pass? By now, you should have a pretty good rhythm to tackling these passages. If necessary, review timing (see Timing in the Reading introduction).

Passage IX

NATURAL SCIENCE: This passage is adapted from "Publish and Punish: Science's Snowball Effect" by Jon Van (©1997 by the Chicago Tribune Company).

It's a scientific finding so fundamental that it certainly will make the history books and maybe snag a Nobel Prize if it pans
5 out, but the notion that cosmic snowballs are constantly pelting Earth is something Louis Frank just as soon would have ducked.

Frank is the University of Iowa physicist whose research led him to declare more
10 than a decade ago that Earth is being bombarded by hundreds of house-sized comets day after day that rain water on our planet and are the reason we have oceans. That weather report caused the widely re-
15 spected scientist to acquire a certain reputation among his colleagues as a bit unstable, an otherwise estimable fellow whose hard work may have pushed him over the edge.

20 Frank and his associate, John Sigwarth, probably went a way toward salvaging their reputations when they presented new evidence that leaves little doubt Earth is indeed being bombarded by
25 *something* in a manner consistent with Frank's small-comet theory. Rather than gloating or anticipating glory, Frank seemed relieved that part of a long ordeal was ending. "I knew we'd be in for it when
30 we first put forth the small-comet theory," Frank conceded, "but I was naive about just how bad it would be. We were outvoted by about 10,000 to 1 by our colleagues. I thought it would have been more like 1,000
35 to 1."

To the non-scientist this may seem a bit strange. After all, the point of science is to discover information and insights about how nature works. Shouldn't every scientist
40 be eager to overturn existing ideas and replace them with his or her own? In theory, that is the case, but in practice, scientists are almost as loath to embrace radically new ideas as the rest of us.

45 "Being a scientist puts you into a constant schizophrenic existence," contends Richard Zare, chairman of the National Science Board. "You have to believe and yet question beliefs at the same time. If you
50 are a complete cynic and believe nothing,

you do nothing and get nowhere, but if you believe too much, you fool yourself."

It was in the early 1980s when the small-comet theory started to haunt Frank
55 and Sigwarth, who was Frank's graduate student studying charged particles called plasmas, which erupt from the sun and cause the aurora borealis (northern lights). As they analyzed photos of the electrical
60 phenomena that accompany sunspots, they noted dark specks appearing in several images from NASA's Dynamics Explorer I satellite. They assumed these were caused by static in the transmission.

65 After a while their curiosity about the dark spots grew into a preoccupation, then bordered on obsession. Try as they did, the scientists couldn't find any plausible explanation of the pattern of dark spots that ap-
70 peared on their images. The notion that the equipment was picking up small amounts of water entering Earth's upper atmosphere kept presenting itself as the most likely answer.

75 Based on their images, the Iowa scientists estimated 20 comets an hour—each about 30 feet or so across and carrying 100 tons of water—were bombarding the Earth. At that rate, they would produce water va-
80 por that would add about an inch of water to the planet every 10,000 years, Frank concluded. That may not seem like much, but when talking about a planet billions of years old, it adds up.

85 Such intimate interaction between Earth and space suggests a fundamentally different picture of human evolution—which depends on water—than is commonly presented by scientists. Frank had great diffi-
90 culty getting his ideas into a physics journal 11 years ago and was almost hooted from the room when he presented his theory at scientific meetings. Despite the derision, colleagues continued to respect Frank's
95 mainstream work on electrically charged particles in space and the imaging cameras he designed that were taken aboard recent NASA spacecraft to explore Earth's polar regions.

100 Unbeknown to most, in addition to gathering information on the northern lights, Frank and Sigwarth designed the equipment to be able to snatch better views

of any small comets the spacecraft might
105 happen upon. It was those images from the latest flights that caused even harsh critics of the small-comet theory to concede that some water-bearing objects appear to be entering Earth's atmosphere with regularity.

110 To be sure, it has not been proved that they are comets, let alone that they have anything to do with the oceans. But Frank's evidence opens the matter up to study. Had he been a researcher of lesser stand-
115 ing, his theory probably would have died long ago.

1. One of the main points of the passage is that:
   A. without water from small comets entering the atmosphere, the earth would have dried up long ago.
   B. important scientific discoveries rarely come from research into unrelated subjects.
   C. the scientific community has a tendency to reject radical new scientific ideas.
   D. the small-comet theory is now embraced by most physicists.

2. According to the passage, which of the following best describes Frank's reaction to the "new evidence" (line 23)?
   F. He was not surprised that his theory was finally embraced.
   G. He was happy to put a difficult ordeal behind him.
   H. He openly celebrated the success of his theory.
   J. He immediately went to work on a new, equally-radical theory.

3. It can reasonably be inferred from the passage that Frank had trouble publishing his small-comet theory in physics journals because:
   A. Frank's colleagues typically viewed him as an unstable scientist.
   B. the small-comet theory challenged a commonly-held idea of human evolution.
   C. Frank had not looked into other possible reasons for the patterns of dark spots on the satellite images.
   D. scientists had always believed that the earth's water supply was in some way replenished from space.

4. In order to emphasize the significance of the amount of water vapor produced by the comets, the author states that one must consider the:
   F. number of comets bombarding the earth per hour.
   G. size of each comet.
   H. amount of time that the comets have been bombarding the earth.
   J. amount of water carried by each comet.

5. According to the passage, the idea of the small-comet theory originated during research originally intended to study:
   A. the electrical nature of sunspots.
   B. the source of water entering the earth's atmosphere.
   C. transmission static in the Dynamics Explorer 1 satellite.
   D. dark specks in satellite images.

6. According to the passage, Richard Zare would most likely describe a scientist as one who:
   F. must strictly adhere to the theories of past scientists.
   G. cannot possibly accomplish research because of dueling notions of scientific discovery.
   H. must steadfastly believe in his or her own theories in order to challenge resistance from scientific peers.
   J. searches for but must diligently question new ideas.

Continued →

7. According to the passage, Frank and Sigwarth suggested that the dark spots on the satellite images were water because:
   A. this was the most logical explanation for the existence of the earth's oceans.
   B. they could find no other likely explanation for the spots.
   C. their study of sunspots suggested a high likelihood of water in comets.
   D. the chemical makeup of the spots suggested the existence of water.

8. According to the passage, Frank's research on small comets has:
   F. proven that small, water-bearing comets enter the earth's atmosphere with regularity.
   G. encouraged scientists to study the small-comet theory.
   H. discouraged future scientists from tackling controversial subjects.
   J. proven that the earth's oceans are a direct result of water-bearing comets entering the earth's atmosphere.

9. According to the tenth paragraph (lines 100–109), scientists began to accept Frank's ideas in part because:
   A. the small-comet theory explained the existence of water in our atmosphere better than any other theory.
   B. new images allowed the small comets to be seen more clearly.
   C. the images of small comets were taken from space rather than from land.
   D. new views of small comets unequivocally confirmed the small-comet theory.

10. The author most likely regards the choice of the word *ducked* in line 7 as:
    F. an amusing play on words.
    G. a scholarly word in keeping with the formal mood of the passage.
    H. a word that reflects the technical language of scientific papers.
    J. a word to be taken literally.

10. SOLUTIONS

Answers, solutions, and elimination techniques for all passages in this tutorial are found below.

PASSAGE I: SOLUTIONS

1. Tone: Eugene "smiled" (lines 72, 76), was "blushing deeply" (lines 73–74), is "shy" (line 75), and "liked me" (line 74). He seems interested in the narrator but is embarrassed. The narrator "blurted out" (line 71), so she is direct, but her "stomach was doing somersaults" (lines 67–68), so she is also nervous. The answer is **A**. Remember that you can eliminate double answers one part at a time.
   Eliminate:
   B. False—Eugene is not "disinterested" and "snobbish." Notice the contrast signal "But" (line 70).
   C. False—the narrator is not "reserved;" she "blurted out" her greeting and did most of the talking.
   D. False—Eugene is not talkative; the narrator says: "I did most of the talking that day. He nodded and smiled a lot" (lines 75–76).

2. Direct: The narrator states that in the library, "he first seemed to notice me, but did not speak" (lines 64–65). Soon after, the narrator "decided to approach him directly" (lines 66–67). The answer is **H**.
   Eliminate:
   F. False—see above.
   G. False—when the narrator says: "I kept him company on my fire escape" (lines 54–55), she means that she *watched* him from the fire escape. They were not physically together. Remember, the words in prose passages are often not to be taken literally (see Prose Fiction in the Reading Introduction).
   J. This is not mentioned, and it's probably false: "He smiled" (lines 71–72).

3. Direct: The challenge to this problem is finding the information in the passage. Most of the discussion of the "old couple" is in Paragraph 1. However, the correct answer is not found in this paragraph. Look at the last paragraph: "…I wanted to sit at the kitchen table with Eugene like two adults, like the old man and his wife had done…" (lines 109–111). This supports **C**.
   Eliminate:
   A. The word "often" makes this answer choice too strong. The author mentions that they argue but does not mention how often. Do not assume things.
   B. There is no mention that the old man and woman are immigrants.
   D. False—the narrator "had become part of their family, without their knowing it" (lines 14–15). The old couple was not familiar with the narrator, and would thus not be eager to have her become part of the family.

4. Direct: Eliminate answer choices by finding answers in the passage to each question. Only **J** cannot be eliminated.
   Eliminate:
   F. The narrator has never been into the house: "I wanted to see the other rooms where the old people had lived, and where the boy spent his time" (lines 106–109).
   G. Books are mentioned in lines 52 and 85.
   H. The house's uniqueness is discussed in lines 6–7.

5. Direct: The father's desire to move to a new house is discussed in lines 87–90. The next line compares the parents' "dreams" (we can infer that these dreams include the new house) to "fairy tales." The best answer (a direct hit), is **B**.

Eliminate:

    A. ~~False~~—the narrator, not her parents, may have a "romantic attraction."

    ~~C.~~ Eye Catcher: "dream." The use of the word "impossible" makes this answer too strong. The father's "good job" (line 88) certainly makes a move to Passaic, if we interpret the dream as that, seem possible.

    ~~D.~~ False—the parents' dreams are more focused on *place* ("Passaic," "Puerto Rico") than career.

6.   Direct: The narrator says: "...the father was gone before I got up in the morning and was never there at dinner time" (lines 43–45). Even on weekends, when the narrator did see the father, he (like his wife) was "hidden behind a section of the newspaper" (lines 48–49). The best answer is **F**.

    Eliminate:

    ~~G.~~ False—the father was gone before the narrator got up in the morning, implying the father *does* live in the house.

    ~~H.~~ There is no mention that the father is eager to return to his homeland. Don't confuse the father with the residents of El Building.

    ~~J.~~ The father may be distant, but "hostility" is too strong and is not supported by the passage.

7.   Purpose: This Purpose question asks about the function of paragraphs. Let's get a feel for what these paragraphs are about. Notice the contrast signal "But" at the beginning of the last paragraph. What follows is probably important: "But after meeting Eugene I began to think of the present more than of the future." The narrator's aspirations have changed. Only **A** touches on this change. The fact that her perspective is "unique" is supported by the sentence beginning: "As for me…" (line 100).

    Eliminate:

    ~~B.~~ False—the parents of Eugene and the narrator are never contrasted.

    ~~C.~~ There is no mention of how the narrator affects her parents in any way.

    ~~D.~~ False—it's the narrator's, not her parents', hopes that have changed.

8.   Extended Reasoning: This is a potential direct hit. First, the narrator says: "I was going to go to college and become a teacher" (lines 101–102). Then she says: "But after meeting Eugene I began to think of the present more than of the future" (lines 103–104). She then talks about her maturing relationship with Eugene. **F** is the perfect answer. Hopefully you don't have to eliminate answer choices on this one.

9.   Tone: Review Paragraph 5. Only **A** is not supported by the passage.

    Eliminate:

    ~~B.~~ "I felt dishonest . . ." (lines 81–82)

    ~~C.~~ "I liked my secret sharing… especially now that I knew what he was reading . . ." (lines 82–84)

    ~~D.~~ "I liked my secret sharing . . ." (line 82)

10. Extended Reasoning: The narrator says that she met Eugene after "much maneuvering" (line 60). She did not really "run into him," which implies a chance or random meeting—her meeting was *intentional*. The quotes humorously make light of the narrator's choice of words. The best answer is **H**. Watch out for G, which is true, but doesn't answer the question.

    Eliminate:

    ~~F.~~ False—the narrator planned to meet Eugene; the meeting wasn't "lucky."

    ~~G.~~ True enough—the words "to run into him" are not to be taken literally—however, the words are not in quotes for this reason. The better answer is H.

    ~~J.~~ False—see F.

PASSAGE II: SOLUTIONS

1. Main Idea: This is similar to a main idea question. To determine the "main conflict" you must have a general understanding of the whole passage. While the passage clearly discusses a conflict of place (home versus away), as best exemplified by the sentence: "In spite of how I want to curl up in my city corner, I picture everything back home" (lines 110–112), the conflict is also rooted in past versus future: Past: "I've wondered about the meaning of my spirit name" (lines 27–28); "I want to… be a small girl again" (lines 100–101). Future: "I began to wander from home" (line 15); "my city corner" (line 111). The best answer is **D**.
   Eliminate:
   A. There may be tension between Frank and Mama, but this is not the main conflict of the passage, a passage that primarily reflects the experiences of the narrator.
   B. The narrator's mother is not happy about the narrator's leaving home, but "bitterness" is too strong a word.
   C. False—the narrator wants to leave home but does not want to "break her ties" with her family, as evidenced by the phone call to Mama soon after arriving at Frank's shop.

2. Direct: After the narrator lost her indis, she "thought nothing of it, at first and for many years, but slowly over time the absence… it will tell. I began to wander from home, first in my thoughts, then my feet took after…" (lines 12–16). The answer is **H**.
   Eliminate:
   F. False
   G. There is no mention in the passage that all members have to make this decision. In fact, the implication is that members are supposed to be buried on the reservation land (line 8).
   J. False—the narrator leaves "at the age of eighteen" (line 17).

3. Extended Reasoning: Frank "can't drag himself away from the magnetic field" of the narrator's mother's voice (lines 93–94). We know the mother loves frank "too much" (line 47). It seems Frank has similar feelings toward the mother. The best answer is **A**. Note that this answer explains much of Frank's behavior: "he lingers" and he is "folding and refolding" the towel (lines 92–93, 98).
   Eliminate:
   B. There is no mention that Frank is concerned about the narrator returning home.
   C. Watch out for eye catchers. Closing up the store is discussed in lines 90–91 but is off topic here.
   D. There is no mention of Frank's time as a boy on the reservation.

4. Extended Reasoning: Go back to the passage and read carefully. The narrator states: "I want to curl next to her and be a small girl again" (lines 100–101). The best answer is **H**.
   Eliminate:
   F. False—the narrator is not "angry." Nor does she feel negatively about a return home, as is apparent in the quote above.
   G. This may be true, in a sense—"My body feels too big…" (lines 101–102)—but the main point is the narrator's wish to reconnect with her past and her home. G is not the best answer choice.
   J. False—the mother wants the narrator to "come back" (line 109), not stay with Frank.

5. Direct: Eliminate answer choices that are mentioned in the passage (remember, you're looking for the one that is NOT mentioned). Only **A** is not mentioned. As discussed in lines 1–11, the indis symbolizes a life-long connection to the reservation, not a desire to leave it.
   Eliminate:
   B. True—lines 3–6
   C. True—lines 9–10
   D. True—lines 1–3

6. Tone: Notice the positive tone words that the narrator uses when she arrives at Frank's shop (see lines 48–60): "cheerful," "good bakery smells," "lemony light," "He greets me with gentle pleasure." These words suggest that the narrator is (at least temporarily) happy to be at this new place, away from the reservation. The answer is **H**. All of the other answer choices have to do with the narrator's longing to return home.

7. Extended Reasoning: If you got Question 2 correct, you'll probably get this one, too. Review lines 12–24, which describe how, after the narrator lost her indis, she eventually decided to leave her home. The answer is **B**.
    Eliminate:
    A. False—she decides to leave her mother, so she definitely didn't cling to her family.
    C. There is no mention that she had to remember every detail of the indis after losing it.
    D. False—she decides to leave her mother, but the word "animosity" is too strong and is disproved by the information in the last two paragraphs.

8. Extended Reasoning: Review the explanation to Question 3. Both Frank and the narrator's mother have feelings for each other. Frank is described as "the man [the narrator's mother] loves too much to live with" (lines 46–47). The best answer is **H**.
    Eliminate:
    F. Frank and the mother are probably old friends, but it is unlikely they have grown "distant" (too strong a word). Not only do they have strong feelings for each other, but also Frank is the first non-family member the mother contacts regarding the narrator's leaving home. This does not suggest a distant relationship.
    G. Frank's opinion about where the narrator should live is not discussed.
    J. There is no mention that Frank and the mother were once married.

9. Direct: The passage states: "In a panic, once she knew I was setting out, not staying home, Mama tried to call up my grandmas and ask if I could live at their apartment in the city" (lines 35–39). The best answer is **A**.
    Eliminate:
    B. False—while Mama *does* allow the narrator to leave, she apparently does not want the narrator to make all of her own choices.
    C. False—Mama let's the narrator leave *and* would like her to live with her grandmas.
    D. False—Frank was not Mama's first choice, so this answer choice is unlikely. In addition, evidence suggests that Mama was not happy about the narrator leaving home; read the last paragraph.

10. Purpose: Review the explanations to Questions 4 and 6. This eleventh paragraph shifts the focus from the narrator's contentment in the bakery shop to her longing to revisit her past ("I want to…be a small girl again"). The best answer is **J**.
    Eliminate:
    F. False—the mother continues to want the narrator to return home. There is no change in the mother's attitude.
    G. False—in the time covered by the passage, the narrator does not return to the reservation.
    H. False—the narrator is clearly interested in returning home: "I want to curl next to her…" (lines 100–101).

TIMING PASSAGE: SOLUTIONS

1. Direct: The passage states: "She departed, however, from pacifist and isolationist positions and encouraged military preparedness, collective security, and ever-widening alliances" (lines 89–93). The answer is **A**.
    Eliminate:
    B. There is no mention that she encouraged "war," just "military preparedness" and "security." The words "fascism and communism" are good examples of eye catchers (line 66).

C. False—"ever-widening alliances" signals a shift from isolationism and toward involvement with foreign countries.

D. False—ER "was not afraid of socialism—and she courted radicals" (lines 64–65). Once again, don't get fooled by eye catchers.

2. Direct: Read the fourth paragraph ("As First Lady, [ER] did things that had never been done before…"). Eliminate true answer choices. The correct answer is **J**. There is no question that ER edited and co-published a newspaper for women (see lines 20–21), but there is no mention that she was the *first* to do this.

3. Extended Reasoning: The last paragraph emphasizes two aspects of ER: (1) she was not an "isolated individualist"—in other words, she worked with others—and (2) "she refused to withdraw from controversy" or "defeat." You may have more luck eliminating answer choices for this question. The best answer is **B**.
Eliminate:
A. False—ER tackled issues "[a]gainst great odds" and was not always successful in her endeavors.
C. This is not mentioned; being active politically, questioning the president, and even running a "parallel administration" (line 28) are not the same as taking on presidential responsibilities.
D. False—the key word here is "single-handedly." ER did *not* work alone but sought "alliances" and "community."

4. Extended Reasoning: ER "demanded action" (line 62). The answer is **F**.
Eliminate:
G. False—"She was uninterested in complex theories" (lines 61–62).
H. False—"She feared violent revolution" (line 63).
J. This answer choice is not mentioned.

5. Direct: "Her abiding conviction, however, was that nothing good would happen to promote the people's interest unless the people themselves organized to demand government responses. A people's movement required active citizen participation…" (lines 70–75). The best answer is **C**.
Eliminate:
A. False—ER stresses "active citizen participation."
B. There is no mention of a relationship "modeled by the White House."
D. There is no mention of "radio broadcasts…" in the part of the passage dealing with the relationship between people and government (Paragraph 8). Don't be fooled by eye catchers.

6. Extended Reasoning: This is a broad question and one that requires a good general idea of how ER is portrayed. Remember, eliminate double answer one part at a time. If you don't see the right answer, a process of elimination will help. ER was politically courageous: "Against great odds, and under terrific pressure, she refused to withdraw from controversy" (lines 110–112). ER's social involvement is discussed throughout the passage, especially in Paragraphs 4–7. The best answer is **G**.
Eliminate:
F. There is no mention that ER is "quietly compromising."
H. False—ER is not "deeply conservative." She actively, and radically, seeks change.
J. False—ER is not "reservedly moderate." See H.

7. Tone: Make sure to read the question carefully. We are looking for FDR's feelings toward ER (not the other way around). FDR "admired his wife, appreciated her strengths, and depended on her integrity" (lines 8–10). We also know that FDR and his wife "often disagreed" (line 13) on many issues. The best answer is **C**.
Eliminate:
A. This answer is too strong. There is no mention that they "fought bitterly."

B. There is no mention that FDR supported ER's writing; in fact, it's quite likely that he did *not*, considering that ER "wrote to disagree with her husband" (lines 97–98).

D. This is a classic eye catcher. Yes, he "depended on her integrity" (line 10), but he very likely disagreed with many of her social movements.

8. Extended Reasoning: The answer is nearly direct: After FDR was elected, "Now [the women's] views were brought directly into the White House" (lines 49–50). Only **J** ties into this direct connection to the White House, thanks to ER.
   Eliminate:
   F. False—FDR's policies were often different from ER's and the women's.
   G. False—the passage implies that the women had been organizing groups for action long before FDR was elected.
   H. This is true but does not answer the question. Remember to read questions carefully.

9. Extended Reasoning: Hopefully, your identifiers are helping you find information quickly. "New Deal" is a good identifier. "Between 1933 and 1938, while the Depression raged and the New Deal unfolded..." (lines 79–80). The best answer, the only one with any support from the passage, is **A**. If the Depression is raging, it's not a stretch to assume that the New Deal is a response to this. All of the other answers are eye catchers (see line 66 for B ("fascism and communism"), line 84 for C (international "isolationism"), and line 83 for D ("racism")).

10. Extended Reasoning: ER "wrote to disagree with her husband" (lines 9798). The best answer is **F**.
    Eliminate:
    G. False
    H. False—her writings were not private; they were "published" (line 94).
    J. There is no mention that ER could not confront FDR directly.

PASSAGE III: SOLUTIONS

1. Purpose: You may have found this passage difficult. On difficult passages, focus on the specific detail questions first. Since this is a main idea question, it's not a bad one to skip (at least at first) until you've answered the other questions. The main purpose of the passage is glimpsed in the first paragraph where the author asks: "How much [of the development of perceptual abilities] is due to nature and how much to nurture . . . ?" (lines 8–9). The author states that a combination of nurture and nature play a role in development: "Some of the synaptic connections are made automatically by chemical guidance [nature], but others are made by the stimulus of experience [nurture/learning]" (lines 82–85). And finally, the author confirms the role of experience (nurture): "...we catch the first glimpse of how mind is constructed out of matter by experience" (lines 111–112). The best answer is **C**.
   Eliminate:
   A. This is not the main focus of the entire passage. On main idea questions, remember to avoid answer choices that are true but don't reflect the main idea of the whole passage.
   B. Similar to A, this is not the main focus of the passage.
   D. The author suggests this answer choice is true in Paragraph 1 ("Much maturation research is concerned with physical skills and physical attributes, and adds little to our knowledge of the growth of the mind"), but again this answer choice does not reflect the purpose of the passage.

2. Purpose: The author claims that four-month olds "begin to recognize the meaning of what they see" (lines 59–60). The parenthetical comment, which immediately follows the statement, explains the reasoning behind the claim: since infants "look longer" at a normal face than one with scrambled features, infants must (according to the author) "recognize the meaning" of what they see. The best answer is **H**.
   Eliminate:

F. False—there is no "difficult term."

G. False—the parenthetical comment does not question anything.

J. False—the information is certainly related.

3. Direct: Hopefully your identifiers ("synaptic connections") helped you zero in on the right part of the passage. The passage states: "Some of the synaptic connections are made automatically by chemical guidance, but others are made by the stimulus of experience" (lines 82–85). This is also ties into the main point of the passage. The best answer is **C**. Eliminate:

   A. There is no mention that the connections are formed "primarily" from chemical guidance, or "instructions."

   B. False—the passage implies that synaptic connections occur rapidly during infancy and young age, "during the period of rapid dendrite growth" (lines 85–86).

   D. False—see the quoted sentence in the explanation above.

4. Direct: The passage states that essential experiences "fine-tune the brain structure so as to provide far more specific perceptual powers than could result from genetic control of synapse formations" (lines 104–107). The key word is "specific." The answer is **G**. Note the camouflage: "genetic control of synapse formation" is replaced with "natural physical changes in the brain." Both refer to changes in the brain *not* based on experience. Eliminate:

   F. False—"the essential experiences are almost always available at the right time" (lines 102–104).

   H. Evidence in the passage suggests this answer choice is false (see Question 3 and Paragraph 7), but in any case, it does not answer the question.

   J. False—the author stresses that experiences help determine the physical structure of the brain. Again, review Question 3 and Paragraph 7.

5. Purpose: The fourth paragraph answers the question asked in the third paragraph: "Since we cannot ask [infants] what they see, how can we find out?" Once we understand the *method* for determining what infants see, we are prepared for a specific look at *what* infants see, in the fifth paragraph. The answer is **A**. Eliminate:

   B. Watch out for the eye catcher. There is no mention that Robert Fantz is a major contributor to the nature versus nurture debate.

   C. This is not the main point of the paragraph.

   D. False—the fifth, not the fourth, paragraph discusses this development.

6. Extended Reasoning: Even though the answer choices are not specifically mentioned in the passage, diligently use the context in the passage to find your answer. One-month-old babies "begin to track slowly moving objects" (lines 50–51). The best answer is **J**. Eliminate:

   F. The "levels of brightness" are perceived by the second month.

   G. Recognizing "family members" occurs by three months.

   H. See G.

7. Direct: Hopefully your identifiers led you to the second paragraph: "The work has been focused on early infancy, when perceptual abilities evolve rapidly." This is a potential direct hit. The answer is **A**. Eliminate:

   B. This is not mentioned in the passage.

   C. False—scientists assume that new abilities in infants arise "not from learning but from maturation of the optic nervous structures..." (lines 16–17).

   D. False—the effects are *not* easier to measure for infants, as discussed in Paragraphs 3 and 4.

8. Purpose: The author elaborates on the term *nurture* in the first paragraph, explaining that "in developmental terms," it is synonymous with "learning" (lines 9–10). The answer is **G**. Eliminate:
   F. False—*nurture* has to do with *experience* and *learning*, not specifically the natural physical growth of the brain.
   H. False—if you understand the similarities of *nurture*, *learning*, and *experience*, then the last sentence of the passage makes clear that nurture is *not* discounted by today's scientists.
   J. This is an eye catcher (first sentence). It does not refer specifically to the term *nurture*.

9. Purpose: The fifth paragraph discussed the apparent perceptual developments of infants. The sixth paragraph begins to discuss how the brain physically changes to produce these developmental changes (see the first sentence of Paragraph 6, lines 68–71). The best answer is **B**. Eliminate:
   A. False—there is no evidence to suggest a shift from nurture to nature.
   C. False—the author continues to discuss infants (line 72) and does not focus on older children specifically (even though one is *mentioned* in line 77).
   D. False—no evidence is given to support the findings in the fifth paragraph, which are taken to be true.

10. Extended Reasoning: Which answer choice suggests that experience affects perceptual development? In **G**, the *experiences* of mice living in the dark affect their ability to see: they "never attain normal vision" (line 92). Eliminate:
    F. These synapses may be (and likely are) partially a result of experiences, but G is certainly the stronger answer choice.
    H. This is a physical change, one not clearly based on experience.
    J. This answer choice refers to synaptic connections that are *not* created by experience (note the "but" in line 84).

PASSAGE IV: SOLUTIONS

1. Main Idea: Read the first sentences of each of the first three paragraphs: "Lightning affects electrical equilibrium on the earth" (first paragraph), "Two types of discharge patterns are commonly identified…" (second paragraph), and "The consequences of lightning are complex" (third paragraph). The passage first discusses lightning in technical terms and then discusses the effects ("consequences") of lightning. The answer is **C**. Eliminate:
   A. False—the second part of the passage discusses the *effects*, not the "types," of lightning,
   B. False—the "specific features" of lightning are discussed in the first part of the passage. The second part of the passage discusses local ("Arizona," "Arkansas") *effects*, not "features," of lightning.
   D. False—the "damaging effects" of lightning are discussed in the second half of the passage; the "causes" are discussed in the first part.

2. Extended Reasoning: The passage defines "direct injury" as "primarily the mechanical destruction of branches and bole" (lines 73–75). Examples given of secondary effects include: "insects, wind, and mistletoe" (line 76) as well as "fire" (line 79). The answer is **G**.

3. Extended Reasoning: If you read lines 90–92 ("such sites . . . lightning"), you'll see that this is a potential direct hit. Keep in mind that answers may be camouflaged, but often the answers use the same words as the passage, as we see in **D**. Eliminate:
   A. False—"Nor is the process limited to trees" (lines 84–85)

B. False—lines 87–92 suggests that "electrocution" sites are no longer attributed to infestation by insects (although they were in the past).

C. False—*insect infestation* or *diseases* may be a "secondary effect" (lines 89–90), but the passage contrasts these conditions with "electrocution" (the implication is, thus, that "electrocution" is a primary effect).

4. Direct: Eliminate answers that are true. This can be a tricky one. If you read carefully, you'll see that thunderstorms produce 8 million *discharges* per day. The thunderstorms themselves do not occur 8 million times per day. Watch out for this kind of ACT trickery on what otherwise seems like a straightforward question. The answer is **G**.
   Eliminate:
   F. 100 cloud-to-ground discharges per second: lines 24–25
   H. lightning bolts with various levels of energy: lines 27–28
   J. 75% of the lightning energy is lost to heat: lines 30–31

5. Main Idea: This is similar to a main idea question ("most important points"). Because it is broad, as main idea questions usually are, you'll probably have to look at the answer choices before trying to answer the question. If necessary, eliminate incorrect answer choices. First notice that the mortality rates given in lines 66–72 describe only "direct injury" (line 73) (not secondary effects). The passage states: "the other major causes of mortality—insects, wind, and mistletoe—are likely secondary effects…" (lines 75–77). This information should lead you to **B**.
   Eliminate:
   A. This is not an important point of the paragraph. On main idea questions, remember to watch out for true answer choices that don't reflect main points of the passage.
   C. This is not mentioned in the passage.
   D. Again, this is not mentioned in the passage.

6. Direct: Hopefully, your identifiers ("electrical potential") led you to the first paragraph: "electricity moves back according to the gradient [change in potential with distance]. During a thunderstorm, the gradient becomes very steep…" (lines 5–8). The answer, **G**, is camouflaged ("gradient" = "change in electrical potential" and "steep" = "great").
   Eliminate:
   F. This is not mentioned in the passage. The only thing the passage states is that oppositely-charged regions must have a steep gradient.
   H. There is no mention of a *reversal* of electrical potential in the passage.
   J. False—the passage suggests that one possible cause of lightning is the fact that the earth is *not* properly charged (lines 9–15).

7. Extended Reasoning: The passage states: "Lightning helps to fix atmospheric nitrogen into a form that rain can bring to earth" (lines 58–60). Answer choice **B** is a direct hit.
   Eliminate:
   A. There is no mention of a lack of rain fall. Make sure to read this answer choice carefully—the first part is correct.
   C. This is not mentioned in the passage.
   D. This, too, is not mentioned.

8. Direct: The words "discharge patterns" hopefully lead you to the second paragraph. Take note of the characteristics of the two types: (1) cold stroke—"intense current but of short duration" (line 35), "has mechanical or explosive effects" (lines 38–39), and (2) hot stroke—"lesser currents of longer duration" (lines 36–37), "more apt to start fires (lines 39–40). From this information, you can see that **G** describes the hot stroke. All of the other answer choices include an element from each of the two types of discharge patterns.

9. Extended Reasoning: The passage states: "Except in tropical rain forests and on ice-mantled land masses, lightning fire has occurred . . ." (lines 94–96). In other words,

lightning fires do not occur in tropical landscapes (probably because of climate). The answer is **B**.
Eliminate:
A. ~~False~~—see above.
~~C.~~ False—the mosaic patterns are caused by "lightning bombardment" (line 99).
~~D.~~ False—"ice-mantled land masses" are also not susceptible to lightning fires (see solution above).

10. Direct: Go back to the passage. The word "thus" (line 19) suggests that the answer to the question will be found before the given quote. Lines 12–18 explain that lightning replenishes the earth's electrical charge. The answer is **F**.
Eliminate:
~~F.~~ This is true but doesn't answer the question.
~~H.~~ Again, a true answer choice, but it doesn't answer the question.
~~J.~~ Off topic for this part of the passage.

PASSAGE V: SOLUTIONS

1. Main Idea: Unsurprisingly, the last paragraph of Passage A announces the author's main claim: "So overall, people with higher IQ-type scores were more likely to get to the objective truth in studies at Yale, and perhaps they get closer to the objective truth in the real world as well" (lines 59–63). The best answer is **C**.
Eliminate:
~~A.~~ Not Mentioned: Lines 40–47 suggest that people with high IQs might still make mistakes. Additionally, this choice is probably Too Strong.
~~B.~~ False: See line 47–48.
~~D.~~ Not Mentioned

2. Direct: The best evidence is found in lines 49–51: "More math skill means more knowledge, and more knowledge might mean more disagreement, not more harmony." The word "numeracy" is referring to the "short IQ-type test, a test of numerical skill" (lines 21–22). The answer is **D**.
Eliminate:
~~A.~~ Not Mentioned: number of participants.

3. Purpose: The author refers to the saying in order to support the point made in lines 24–28: "Democrats were more likely to say the gun data supported gun control regardless of which data they were given and Republicans fell victim to the opposite bias." In other words, peoples' ideas are usually rigid. The best answer is **D**.
Eliminate:
~~A.~~ False: see above.
~~B.~~ No mention of people's actions.
~~C.~~ Eye Catcher: "truth" (lines 32 and 36). This choice is also probably Too Strong.

4. Extended Reasoning: The answer is found in two places: a "test of numerical skill" (line 22) and "people who were better at math" (lines 34–35). By stating that the "IQ-type test" primarily measures math, the author implies that math is a good measure of IQ. The answer is **C**.
Eliminate:
~~B.~~ Eye Catcher: "political views" (line 13, etc.)
~~D.~~ Eye Catcher: "truth" (line 32 and 36). IQ may be a good measure of one's ability to determine what is true (People who did better on the IQ test "were usually more likely to get to the truth" (lines 35–36)), but the test itself, according to the passage, did not *directly* measure this, at least not beyond the realm of numbers and math.

5. Direct: If you understand that Mill argued for some form of an epistocracy, and the author of Passage B clearly argues *against* this form of government (see the first sentence of

Paragraph 2), the answer is apparent (**B**). You might also note the context: Mill's views are "somewhat intuitive, if politically incorrect" (lines 77–78).
Eliminate:

A̶.̶ False: "Famously" (line 73). Mill's views are clearly not "unfamiliar."

C̶.̶ Eye Catcher: "a hybrid democratic/epistocratic system" (line 74)

D̶.̶ Eye Catcher: see lines 79–84; this choice reflects the view of Mill's, not the author's.

6. Purpose: We have to connect the dots on this one. First, schools and healthcare are issues having to do with "beliefs about priorities of life" (lines 95–96). That these decisions must be made politically is an "obvious problem" (lines 93–94) with an epistocracy. And we know an epistocracy gives greater weight to the "educated portion of a population" (lines 88–89 and the introduction of the passages). In sum, the author clearly implies that issues such as school curricula and universal healthcare should not be determined by an educated elite. The best answer is **B**.
Eliminate:

A̶.̶ Not Mentioned: "unanimity"

C̶.̶ False: This is counter to the author's views.

D̶.̶ Not Mentioned

7. Direct: The passage states "In the domain of science, questions of which research questions to prioritize and fund and how to *disseminate and apply research findings* in society also reflect social priorities and values that are indeterminable by specialist expertise" (lines 98–104, emphasis added). Answer choice **C** reflects the emphasized part of the quote above.
Eliminate:

B̶.̶ Eye-catchers: "race, class, and gender biases" (lines 91–92)

D̶.̶ False: This is counter to the author's views.

8. Comparison: Consider the main idea of each passage. The author of Passage A suggests (in so many words) that those with higher education might make better political decisions. The author of Passage B argues that those with higher education should *not* have greater voting strength. The best answer is **B**.
Eliminate:

A̶.̶ False: Passage B does not discuss any "problems of democracies."

D̶.̶ False: Passage B may question the views or deductions of Passage A but not the accuracy of the evidence.

9. Comparison: Focus on Passage B. The author claims, in the last sentence: "It is unclear how specialized training in a specific area, either within science or outside of it, has any direct bearing on the right one has to determine these [political] issues." This clearly supports answer choice **D**.
Eliminate:

A̶.̶ Eye Catcher: "race, class, or gender biases" (lines 91–92)

B̶.̶ Not Mentioned

C̶.̶ Not Mentioned / Eye Catcher: "specialist expertise" (line 104)

10. Comparison: Both the author of Passage A and John Stuart Mill (first paragraph of Passage B) likely agree that "the better educated" (line 76) might make better political decisions: "superior wisdom justifies superior political authority" (lines 78–79). The best answer is **C**. People with higher IQ-type scores getting "closer to the objective truth in the real world" (lines 62–63) is probably analogous to these same people making good political decisions. Be careful of choice A: While this choice might be true, Mill makes no mention of "math." As always, go with the choice that requires less extended reasoning.
Eliminate:

A̶.̶ See above.

B̶.̶ False: Both Mill and the author of Passage A would disagree with this choice.

D. Not Mentioned: The author of Passage A and Mill seem more concerned with issues of effectiveness and appropriateness of voting policies, not fairness (more likely a concern of the author of Passage B). In any case, this choice is probably Too Strong ("the only way").

PASSAGE VI: SOLUTIONS

1. Extended Reasoning: We know the residents lived "decent lives," and we might extend our reasoning to say that this is reflected in the houses' "imperturbable" faces. Imperturbable means incapable of being upset or agitated. The best answer is **D**. Feel free to use POE if you didn't spot the right answer.
   Eliminate:
   A. Eye Catcher: "uninhabited" (line 4)
   B. Not Mentioned / False: The other houses are juxtaposed against the uninhabited house ("detached from"), so it's unlikely that they appear similar.
   C. Not Mentioned

2. Direct: The context is clear: "When she came out on the doorstep my heart leaped. I ran to the hall, seized my books and followed her" (lines 67–70). The best answer is **D**. Note that the answer uses the exact words from the passage; it is *not* camouflaged. Watch out for eye catchers in the other answer choices. Also, watch out for A: The narrator *had* been observing her from the window, but only until she first appeared.

3. Tone: The only answer choice directly supported by context is **B**: "He had been a very charitable priest . . ." (lines 24–25). The other answer choices *may* be true, but are not directly supported by the passage: one can be altruistic, or charitable, without being kindly, neighborly, or sociable.

4. Tone: The passage provides evidence for the first part of each answer choice, so focus on the second parts. The only choice supported by the passage is **D**. The narrator and his companions are boisterous ("Our shouts echoed in the silent street. The career [swift course] of our play . . ." [line 36, etc.]) and collaborative, or working together ("we played" [line 35], "our play" [line 37], "we hid" [line 48]).
   Eliminate:
   A. Eye Catcher: "somber" (line 31)
   B. Eye Catcher: "foolish" (line 77)
   C. Not Mentioned: "infatuated"—as far as we know, only the narrator is infatuated (foolishly passionate).

5. Tone: Mangan does ultimately obey his sister: "he obeyed" (lines 59–60), but he does so "resignedly," only after waiting to see if she would give up and go in (lines 53–56), and he teases her before obeying (lines 59–60). This supports choice **B**.
   Eliminate:
   A. False: See lines 59–60 ("he obeyed").
   C. False: "teases" does not suggest affection.
   D. Every Word Counts: "mocking" might work ("teasing"), but there is no mention that he mocked his sister "good-naturedly."

6. Tone: The tone is revealed at the beginning of this last paragraph: the narrator describes the scene as "hostile to romance." The best answer is **D**. Be careful of A: True, the narrator manages to consider Mangan's sister, but this is *despite* his surrounding, not *because* of them.
   Eliminate:
   B. False: One (including the narrator) would think the setting is distracting, but the narrator still clearly thinks about "romance"; the setting does not actually distract him from his thoughts.

7. Purpose: Mangan views his sister with some negativity: he "always teased her" (line 59). The narrator, in contrast, seemed infatuated with her: for example, "my heart leaped" (line 68). The best answer is **A**. If you don't spot the correct answer, try POE:
Eliminate:
~~B.~~ False: See solution above.
~~C.~~ Not Mentioned
~~D.~~ False: The description is clearly as viewed by the *narrator*, not the other characters: "*I* stood by the railing looking at her" (lines 60–61, emphasis added).

8. Direct: The context is clear: "I kept her brown figure always in my eye" (lines 70–71), and "I had never spoken to her" (lines 74–75). The best answer is **D**.
Eliminate:
~~A.~~ False: "our ways diverged" (line 72).
~~B.~~ False: See above.
~~C.~~ False: See above.

9. Tone: The narrator's intense focus on Mangan's sister, and the fact that his "heart leaped" for her (line 68) allows us to infer that he finds her appealing, beautiful, and desirable. So we must look at the second parts of the answer choices. The main clue is in the last sentence of the fourth paragraph: by referring to his "foolish blood" (line 77), we can guess that he finds her unattainable. The best answer is **C**.
Eliminate:
~~A.~~ Not Mentioned: "condescending"
~~B.~~ Eye Catcher: "foolish" (line 77)

10. Direct: If you can find the correct context ("future" may have been an identifier), this one is straightforward. The narrator says: "I thought little of the future" (line 99). He seems to focus more on his *present* feelings ("My eyes were full of tears," "my heart seemed to pour itself out into my bosom," "my body was like a harp . . ."). The best answer is **B**.
Eliminate:
~~D.~~ False: The word "anticipation" in the answer choice suggests a focus on the future, an idea contradicted in the passage.

PASSAGE VII: SOLUTIONS

1. Extended Reasoning: This is a potential direct hit. The passage states that the grandparents "would remind you that Tom was a child" (lines 18–19). In other words, his laziness could be explained by his age. The best answer is **C**.
Eliminate:
A. This answer choice is not mentioned in the passage.
B. Again, not mentioned in the passage.
D. False—the grandparents, not Tom Sawyer, "taught by word and example" (line 25). Watch out for eye catchers.

2. Words in Context: In the third paragraph, the passage describes fulfilling ones "humanity" as the belief that "creation is a sacred gift, and that by working we express our gratitude and celebrate our powers." The passage goes on to say: "To honor that gift, we should live simply, honestly, conservingly…" The answer is **J**. Notice that correct answers are not always camouflaged, as we see here—the answer uses words exactly as they are used in the passage.
Eliminate:
~~F.~~ Probably true, but not mentioned in the passage.
~~G.~~ False—the author states "As I understand it, a regard for the… virtue of work has nothing to do with productivity…" (lines 39–42)
~~H.~~ False—see G.

3. Direct: The first sentence of this last paragraph gives it away: "…the purpose of life is not to acquire but to *inquire*." The answer is **A**, a direct hit. Watch out for eye catchers. All of the other answer choices contain words from the passage.

4. Direct: Don't confuse these with standard Words in Context questions. The question asks what a term "refers to," not what it "nearly means." The word "powers" refers to "human skills" (lines 3–4), something that good work will allow a person to express. It is the fact that a good job requires skill that gives it "mystery or meaning" (lines 6–7). The best answer is **J**. Watch out for eye catchers in the incorrect answer choices ("drains," "renews," "supervision").

5. Extended Reasoning: See the first paragraph: "When the freedom and craft have been squeezed out of work it becomes toil…" (lines 4–6). The key word is "freedom." The best answer is **C**.
    Eliminate:
    A. This answer choice is not mentioned in the passage.
    B. False—read the passage carefully. The passage implies that the many "layers of supervision" are a *result* of the drudgery of a job, not the *reason* behind the drudgery. In other words, the work becomes "toil," people hate their jobs, and thus, layers of supervision are needed to keep people working ("keep the wheels spinning" (line 10)).
    D. False—the passage implies that workers are forced to use *machines*, not tools, and this is why the work becomes "toil."

6. Direct: The passage clearly describes the difference: "…a tool extends human skills, a machine replaces them" (lines 3–4). The best answer, which is camouflaged, is **J**.
    Eliminate:
    F. This answer choice is not mentioned in the passage.
    G. Again, not mentioned in the passage.
    H. Once again, not mentioned in the passage.

7. Extended Reasoning: The passage states "work is how we act out that faith" (lines 85–86). The ideas of work and faith are closely related. This idea is also supported by the quote in lines 91–96 ("One feels . . ."). The "false dichotomy" is that these two closely related ideas are considered separate. The answer is **C**.
    Eliminate:
    A. False—the failure is recognizing a difference where there isn't one.
    B. False—the question is answered with both ideas, not one of them.
    D. False—this is not the "false dichotomy." It actually comes close to describing the views of the author—"salvation" is gained by both faith and work, not one or the other; the author would obviously not consider his own views "false."

8. Direct: The passage states: "I knew this cluster of values by experience long before I heard it referred to as the work ethic" (lines 30–32). The answer is **F**.
    Eliminate:
    G. False—the phrase has "lost its edge" (lines 32–33).
    H. False—the phrase is something bosses, etc. *use* (verbally); it is not likely something that these people strive for. The idea of work ethic is *positive*. The author views the bosses, etc. *negatively*. Always remember the author's *tone*.
    J. False—the author thinks the phrase is used too often (lines 32–34).

9. Direct: Perhaps you boxed the contrast signal, "But," in line 70. What follows is probably something the author feels is very important (more important than what came before). Some of the answer choices are reasons for appreciating hard work, but **C** is the most important—*faith* is the "chief reason" (line 71).

10. Words-in-Context: When you defined "extends" in context, you should have come up with something such as *expands*, or perhaps a phrase such as *helps to flourish*. Make sure you

consider that the word is being used figuratively. The human skills are not expanding in *size* but in *scope*. The best answer is **F**. If necessary, plug the answer choices into the passage and eliminate ones that sound awkward or ridiculous. For example, can one increase the length of human skills (choice G)?

PASSAGE VIII: SOLUTIONS

1. Words in Context: The "market" is well defined in the passage: "a group of people defined by income range, age, family composition, and life style" (lines 37–39). The best answer is **B**.
   Eliminate:
   D. Eye Catcher: "architects" (line 36, etc.)

2. Direct: The author states that people's behavior is "constrained, it is not what people might do in other conditions" (lines 50–51). The best answer is **D**. The answer is somewhat camouflaged: "constrained" becomes "limited," and "conditions" becomes "circumstances."

3. Purpose: The author refers to the "nouveau rich" (line 67)—"nouveau" means *newly or recently created*. If you're not comfortable with this word, note the mention of "upward mobility" (line 71). The best answer is **B**.
   Eliminate:
   A. Eye Catcher: "value systems" (line 73)
   C. Eye Catchers: "Hollywood" and "Las Vegas" (lines 68–69)
   D. Eye Catcher: "environments" (lines 62, 64, and 68)

4. Direct: The context might not be easy here, but the answer is fairly explicit. The key phrase is "architectural navel contemplation" (line 88), meaning that architects frequently turn to other architects, notably Le Corbuser, when making decisions. (The navel, or bellybutton, is sometimes used as a metaphor for turning or looking inward). You might also simply note the question architects ask "so often for research": "What did Le Corbusier do?" (lines 89–90). The best answer is **C**.

5. Purpose: The builder-developer builds "for a market, for a group of people defined by income range, age, family composition, and life style" (lines 37–39). Also note the mention of "groups" (line 42) and "subcultures" (line 44). "Man," especially the capitalized version, traditionally (and, yes, somewhat controversially) represents *all* people. The best answer is **A**.
   Eliminate:
   C. False: the passage makes clear that architects must build for subgroups.

6. Main Idea: The answer is found in lines 98–101 (unsurprisingly following a contrast signal—"But"): "But an alternative to both is to examine what people do to buildings . . . once they are in them." The answer is **D**.
   Eliminate:
   A. Eye Catcher: "physical backgrounds" (lines 74–75)
   C. False: The author argues against traditional approaches to design considerations (see lines 87–89).

7. Direct: The perspective of the Madison Avenue observer (that is, advertisers) is presented as "an alternative to the architectural navel contemplation we do so often for research" (lines 87–89). In other words, one can learn "a great deal" (line 98) from studying these non-architecturally focused sources. The best answer is **B**.
   Eliminate:
   A. Not mentioned: Madison Avenue is not represented as buying *or* selling houses, just other products (such as pickles).
   C. Not mentioned: "shifting tastes of architecture"
   D. False: "they can tell us little of the needs of the poor" (lines 91–92)

8. Purpose: In this last paragraph, the author stresses that asking people what they want is "an important topic," but it is not the topic of the essay. Focus on what follows the contrast signal "but" (line 113). By stating that other sources of information are important, the author is *qualifying* the essay's thesis—that information should be gathered from "the artifacts of pop culture"—by acknowledging that other methods are viable as well. The best answer is **D**. Feel free to use POE:
   Eliminate:
   A. False: this paragraph maintains the discussion of the passage (note the title of the original article).
   B. Eye Catcher: "relation between two types of survey" (lines 112–113). Don't fall for this answer; it is a minor point.
   C. False: no summary is presented in this paragraph.

9. Words in Context: The author discusses making a type of "market test" (line 94) more difficult to pass. In other words, the test is more *stringent*. The answer is **B**. Feel free to use POE if you're not comfortable with the word *stringent* (which means rigorously binding or exacting).

10. Extended Reasoning: Consider the main idea of this paragraph: "He [the architect] is building for a market, for a group of people defined by income range, age, family composition, and life style" (lines 37–39). The passage also mentions "groups" and "subcultures" (see Questions 1 and 5). The best answer is **D**.

PASSAGE IX: SOLUTIONS

1. Main Idea: Certainly, an important part of the passage is Louis Frank and his work on the small-comet theory, but the author also discusses the general nature of scientific research. The Frank example is used to illustrate points made in the fourth and fifth paragraphs that "scientists are…loath to embrace radically new ideas…" (lines 43–44). The last sentence of the passage suggests the tenuousness of new scientific ideas: "Had [Frank] been a researcher of lesser standing, his theory probably would have died long ago." The best answer is **C**.
   Eliminate:
   A. This is a minor and, more importantly, unproven point in the passage (lines 13, 75–84, 110–112)
   B. Probably false—the small-comet theory itself came about from research in an unrelated field (see the sixth paragraph (lines 53–64)).
   D. False—"it has not been proved" (line 110).

2. Extended Reasoning: The passage states: "Frank seemed relieved that part of a long ordeal was ending" (lines 27–29). The answer is **G**.
   Eliminate:
   F. False—he was not "anticipating glory" (line 27).
   H. False—he was not "gloating" (line 27).
   J. This is not mentioned in the passage.

3. Extended Reasoning: A physics journal is discussed in line 90. In that paragraph, Frank's research is described as suggesting "a fundamentally different picture of human evolution… than is commonly presented by scientists." The answer is **B**.
   Eliminate:
   A. The word "unstable" is an eye catcher (lines 16–17). It is perhaps partially correct, but it is not the best answer choice.
   C. False—"Try as they did, the scientists couldn't find any plausible explanation…" (lines 67–70).
   D. False—the "intimate interaction between Earth and space" was "fundamentally different" (lines 85–87) from the common views of scientists.

4. Direct: The author states: "That may not seem like much, but when talking about a planet billions of years old, it adds up" (lines 82–84). The answer is **H**. All of the other answer choices are eye catchers. Each one ties into the fact that an inch of water is added every 10,000 years, which "may not seem like much."

5. Direct: Look at the sixth paragraph: "It was in the early 1980s when the small-comet theory started..." (lines 53–54). As stated in this paragraph, Frank and Sigwarth were researching "the electrical phenomena that accompany sunspots." The answer is **A**. This should be a direct hit. Don't let the other answer choices fool you. None of them were subjects of Frank's and Sigwarth's *original* research.

6. Extended Reasoning: Zare says that if a scientists "believe nothing" (line 50), they won't make progress. He also cautions against "too much" (line 52). This idea of *balance* in a scientist's work is reflected in answer choice **J**.
   Eliminate:
   F. False—"You have to . . . question beliefs" (lines 48–49).
   G. Wrong tone—it is unlikely that the chairman of the National Science Board would portray a scientist as one who cannot "accomplish research."
   H. False—Zare warns against believing too much.

7. Direct: Even though Frank and Sigwarth tried to find other explanations, the existence of water was "the most likely answer" (lines 73–74). The answer is **B**.
   Eliminate:
   A. There is no mention in the passage that the existence of the earth's oceans influenced Frank's and Sigwarth's research into the dark spots. It was likely the other way around: the research into the dark spots (and the discovery of the likelihood of water) led Frank and Sigwarth to hypothesize possible sources of the oceans.
   C. False—as far as we know from the passage, the study of sunspots led to the *discovery* of the dark spots, but the research of these topics was otherwise unrelated.
   D. The chemical makeup of the spots is not mentioned in the passage. In addition, if the chemical makeup could be analyzed, there wouldn't be much of a controversy.

8. Direct: This question is broad, so check out the answer choices before searching for context. The passage states: "...Frank's evidence opens the matter up to study" (lines 112–113). The answer is **G**.
   Eliminate:
   F. False—"it has not been proved that they are comets" (lines 110–111). The word "comet" is important here. Don't forget, every word counts.
   H. This is not mentioned in the passage.
   J. False—"it has not been proved... that they have anything to do with the oceans" (lines 110–112).

9. Direct: The images from new equipment designed by Frank and Sigwarth "caused even harsh critics of the small-comet theory to concede that some water-bearing objects appear to be entering Earth's atmosphere with regularity" (lines 106–109). The answer is **B**.
   Eliminate:
   A. There is no mention of this answer choice.
   C. False—the original images were also taken from space (via satellite).
   D. False—as discussed in the last paragraph of the passage, the theory was not proved.

10. This is one of those rare questions that test writing style (see the Reading Introduction). The author writes in a relatively casual manner throughout. Nowhere is this more apparent than in the first paragraph. The word "ducked" humorously reflects the use of the words "cosmic snowballs" (line 4). Get it? The answer is **F**.
    Eliminate:
    G. False—"ducked" is not a scholarly word.

H. The passage is not particularly technical, especially when compared to other Natural Science passages. In any case, the word "ducked" is not a technical word.

J. False—the word is *not* to be taken literally. One assumes that Frank did not physically duck to avoid the controversy.

PART *4*

SCIENCE

I

SCIENCE INTRODUCTION

The Science section is divided into seven chapters:

   I. Introduction

   II. Data Representation

   III. Research Summaries

   IV. Conflicting Viewpoints

TEST LAYOUT / TYPES OF PASSAGES

The questions on the Science Test are multiple choice, with four answer choices each. You will see three types of passages (Data Representation, Research Summaries, and Conflicting Viewpoints).

The Science Test will typically include:

- 2–3 Data Representation passages (12–16 total questions)
- 3 Research Summaries passages (18–22 total questions)
- 1 Conflicting Viewpoints passage (6–8 questions)

DATA REPRESENTATION

These passages present information using tables, graphs, and other diagrams. The questions ask you to interpret the given information.

RESEARCH SUMMARIES

These passages present descriptions of scientific experiments or studies, along with tables and graphs showing the results. Some of the questions will ask you to evaluate the methods used in the experiment. Many of the questions ask you to interpret the results presented in tables and graphs (Data Representation questions).

CONFLICTING VIEWPOINTS

These passages present usually two or more viewpoints on a given topic. The questions test your understanding of the topic and each viewpoint. Some questions will ask you to compare the viewpoints. Conflicting Viewpoints passages tend to have more words and fewer tables and graphs.

TYPES OF QUESTIONS

While being able to identify the three types of *passages*, as described above, is important, we think it's much more important to know what type of *question* you're working on. How you approach a question has more to do with the question itself than with the passage it's testing.

We can *generally* say that Data Representation questions show up on Data Representation passages, Research Summaries questions show up on Research Summaries passages, and Conflicting Viewpoints questions show up on Conflicting Viewpoints passages, but many questions of one type show up on passages of another type.

Like the test makers, we will indeed refer to the three types of *passages*. But more important is the type of *question*, regardless of the type of passage it shows up on.

TEST CORRECTIONS (BY QUESTION TYPE, NOT BY PASSAGE TYPE)

When you correct practice tests, focus on *question* types, not passage types. For example, after completing the Data Representation chapter, you'll correct all missed Data Representation *questions*, even if some of these questions showed up on Research Summaries passages. For more details on correcting Science Tests, see this tutorial's Introduction. For problem lists for each test, see the Techniques chapter at the end of this tutorial.

WHAT IF I DON'T KNOW ANY SCIENCE!?

Don't worry. For the most part, this test does *not* directly test science. The information you need is found in the *passages*. The Science Test is similar to the Reading Test in that you must answer questions using *context*, that is, the information given in the passage. In other words, don't worry about what you know (or what you *don't* know) about science. Just worry about the information given on the test.

As stated, the Science and Reading Tests are similar in *approach*, but they are very different in *appearance*. If you've seen a Science Test, then you probably already know the following:

The Science Test looks hard! But here's the good news:

❗ The Science Test is not as hard as it looks. Not even close!

Most of it (well over half) involves interpreting graphs and tables, something you may already be comfortable with from your math classes. Yes, you're going to see some scary-looking figures. Yes, you're going to read about topics you've never heard of. And yes, you're going to come across countless scientific words that you've never seen before. But don't let the unfamiliarity of the material scare you!

You don't actually need to be an expert chemist or physicist to do well on the Science Test. Look past the intimidating material, and you'll realize that the questions don't expect you to be a scientist with a college degree. The sooner you overcome your fear of the test and confidently and aggressively attack each passage, the sooner your score will rise. The following chapters will help you dig beneath the imposing façade of the Science Test.

TIMING

All programs: Skip this Timing section for now. We'll be coming back to it once we've covered several section in the next chapter.

As with the Reading Test, many students find the Science Test difficult to complete in time. Remember, the Science Test questions are NOT arranged in order of difficulty. You must strive to get your eyeballs on every question.

Like the Reading Test, you'll see 40 questions in **35 minutes**. That's less than 1 minute per question. The timing approach below should help you maximize your score.

DEADLINES

As with the English and Reading Tests, we will use *deadlines* to help you avoid falling behind as you take the test. Because the number of passages of each type (Data Representation, Research Summaries, Conflicting Viewpoints) and the number of questions per passage often vary, the deadlines will not be based on *passages* (as with the English and Reading tests) but on sets of *questions*: specifically, **four sets of 10 questions** (40 questions total). (The Reading Test is also based on four sets of 10 questions, but while the Reading deadlines coincide with the ends of actual *passages*, the challenge of the Science Test is that your deadlines will usually *not* coincide with the ends of passages.)

Since the test is 35 minutes long, you have 8 minutes and 45 seconds for each 10-question set. To be safe, let's round this down to **8:30**. Your times will probably vary, but the 8:30 number should give you a general idea of how long to take for each 10-question set, and you'll have a minute of cushion, in case you start to fall behind. Here are the deadlines; make sure to memorize them:

Science Deadlines	
Start Test	00:00 (min:sec)
Finish Question 10	8:30
Finish Question 20	17:00
Finish Question 30	25:30
Finish Question 40	34:00+*

*You can fall up to a minute behind.

ANSWER EASIER QUESTIONS FIRST

We'll repeat the same rule we introduced for the Reading Test:

/ You can answer the questions in any order you'd like!

As we said, the Science Test can be very difficult to finish in time. If you find that you fall behind, or if you make a number of mistakes because you're rushing through the passages too quickly, you won't be able to tackle every question, at least not right away. The trick is too skip the harder questions on your first pass. Below are the questions to consider skipping:

- **Research Summaries method questions**: These are questions that don't test graphs or tables. Luckily, many of the questions on Research Summaries passages *do* test graphs or tables (just like Data Representation questions), but each Research Summaries passage will have a few questions that ask about the experimental *method*. These questions tend to be more difficult than basic table/graph questions and might be worth skipping.

- **Long questions**: Just because a question is long does not necessarily mean it will be hard, but these questions, not surprisingly, tend to take more time to answer than other questions. Consider skipping them.

- **Questions with new information**: As we'll discuss in the Data Representation section, some questions will provide information that is not found in the passage. These questions are often more difficult, not to mention longer, than other questions.

- **Conflicting Viewpoints questions**: Many students find the Conflicting Viewpoints passage the most difficult passage on the test. We don't recommend skipping it entirely, but skipping some of its harder questions might help you either get ahead (if the passage shows up early in the test) or make up time (if the passage shows up later).

Besides the questions above, any question that has you stumped or seems to be testing a part of the passage you found difficult can be skipped. Needless to say, you'll probably answer more questions on easier passages than on harder passages.

And of course, you can (and should) go back to a skipped question if you find yourself ahead of a deadline.

TIMING YOURSELF ON INDIVIDUAL PASSAGES

As you practice individual passages, you'll start to get a feel for how many questions you should probably plan to skip. The table below gives you time estimates, based on the number of questions per passage:

Times per passage (for practice only)	
5-question passage	4:15 (min:sec)
6-question passage	5:15
7-question passage	6:00

These time estimates are just that: *estimates*. Some passages will certainly take longer than others, but these times should help you practice. If you have to skip a number of questions at first as you start practicing, that's OK. Just push yourself to move as quickly as you can, and with practice, your speeds should increase.

SKIMMING TIMES

DATA REPRESENTATION

You will skim, *not* read, Data Representation passages before you start answering the questions. Depending on the passage, this should take you anywhere from **30 seconds to at most 1 minute**. Remember, you just want to get a general idea of the information presented in these passages, so get to the questions as quickly as you can.

RESEARCH SUMMARIES

As with Data Representation passages, you'll quickly skim Research Summaries passages. We've found that the *total* time to skim the passage ranges from **1 to 1.5 minutes**.

HARDER PASSAGES

As you work through practice tests, you'll probably find one or two passages per test that seem *much harder* than the others (in fact, we often see *exactly one* really hard passage on each test). This awareness will hopefully encourage you to battle through on the harder passages— take comfort in knowing that easier passages are probably right around the corner. Make sure you watch your times carefully so you don't spend too much time on the hard passages.

You'll probably want to skip more questions on these harder passages. Remember, you're always trying to maximize your score, so tackle the questions that you have the best chance of getting correct. These questions usually show up on passages that you find easier.

II

DATA REPRESENTATION

Most of this chapter discusses the analysis of graphs and other diagrams, which happens to be the most important part of the Science Test. Once you finish this chapter, you'll be ready to tackle well over half of the questions on the test.

1. *DATA REPRESENTATION INTRO*

As stated before, Data Representation passages present information using tables, graphs, and other diagrams. The questions ask you to interpret the given information.

> The following clues should help you identify Data Representation passages:
> - Each passage typically includes **5–7** questions (usually 6).
> - These passages are heavy on figures, especially tables and graphs.
> - Data Representation passages typically do NOT include multiple "studies," "experiments," "activities," etc.
> - Data Representation passages typically do NOT include in-depth descriptions of the actual experiments.

To get a feel for what these passages look like, go ahead and check out some of the Data Representation passages in the ACT book. You should notice the following:

1. A short introduction.
2. One or more graphs, tables, or other diagrams.
3. Usually, each figure has a brief explanation, found either in the introduction or in a separate paragraph preceding the figure.

SKIM THE PASSAGE

You will not have time to read and understand the entire passage. (We'll talk more about timing in Chapter V.) You should, however, expect to *skim* the passage before you start answering the questions. Do not read every word, and do not expect to understand much of the passage, at least not in any depth. You just want to get some idea (perhaps just a *vague* idea) of what the passage is about. Here's what to look for:

1. If the introduction is short, go ahead and read it. Otherwise, skim it.
   - Circle *identifiers*. As taught in the Reading section, identifiers are important words that you may have to locate later, when you start answering questions. These may be words that describe something *specific* in the passage, including the scientific words that the ACT puts in *italics*.
   - Circle any *numbers* in the text. These numbers might show up in a question.
2. As you go through the passage, skim any other paragraphs. Look for and circle identifiers and numbers.

3. The most important step is to get a general idea of how information is presented in the figures (graphs, tables, etc.). In particular, read the *labels* and *units* for each figure. **Most of your "skim time" should be spent looking at figures.**

4. Look for labels (and units) that are *repeated* in separate figures. Circle these labels and, if not too inconvenient, connect them with a line.

We'll talk about how long to take skimming the passage later, when we discuss timing in detail.

VARIABLES

Whether you're looking at a graph or a table, the labels (along the axes of a graph or in the column headings of a table) are *variables*. You must understand the two types of variables:

Independent variable: An *independent variable* is a value that *determines* the value or values of other variables. The person conducting the experiment typically varies, or changes, independent variables to see what effect they have on another variable (the dependent variable). Scientists generally have some *control* over independent variables. Independent variables usually (but not always!) show up on the horizontal axis of a graph (the exception is when the independent variable is a *vertical* measurement, such as with height, altitude, or depth).

Dependent variable: A dependent variable is a value that is *determined by* the value of another variable. The values of dependent variables are typically the *results* of an experiment.

Let's look at a simple example:

The figure below shows the average snow depth, in inches, at a popular California ski resort.

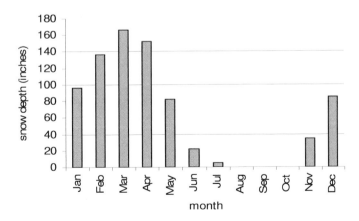

This type of graph is called a *bar graph*. Can you identify the variables? Which one is the independent invariable? Which one is the dependent variable?

Let's look at one more example, more typical of what you'll see on the ACT:

Under the right circumstances, light can be used to free electrons from the surface of a solid. This process is called *photoelectric emission*. A material that can exhibit this phenomenon is said to be *photoemissive*. The electrons that are ejected from the surface are called *photoelectrons*. The kinetic energy of photoelectrons depends on the frequency of the light and the kind of metal. Figure 1 shows how the kinetic energy varies for a range of light frequencies for potassium.

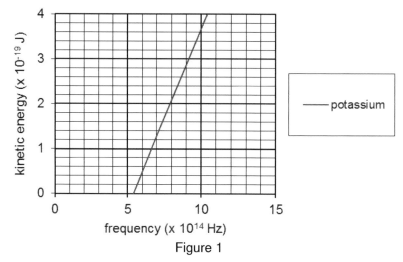

Figure 1

Yes, this may sound complicated. But remember: don't worry about understanding the information in the introduction. Just skim it. Circle some of the key words. The most important thing is to focus on the graph. This is called a *line graph*. Look at the labels and units. Can you identify the independent and dependent variables?

LINE GRAPHS

Since we're on the subject of line graphs, you should be familiar with *linear*, *exponential*, and *parabolic* graphs. We'll see more of these in the coming sections.

Linear graphs display a simple straight line:

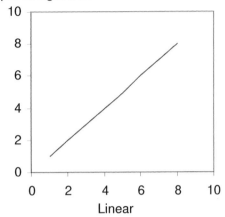

Linear

Exponential graphs display a curve that either gets steeper (as below) or shallower.

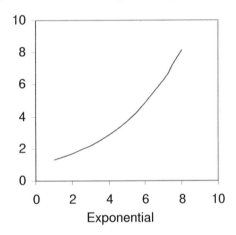

Exponential

Parabolic graphs may open up or down. Notice that these graphs have a minimum point (as below) or a maximum point (if the parabola opens down):

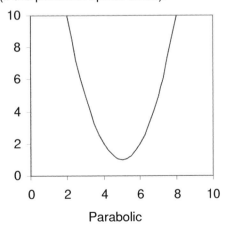

Parabolic

2. GRAPH BASICS

DIRECT QUESTIONS

Most questions on the Science Test directly test the material found in graphs or tables. We'll call these *direct questions*. Let's look at an example, using the previous graph:

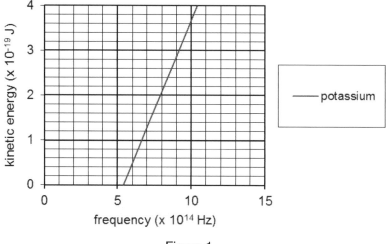

Figure 1

UNDERLINE IMPORTANT PARTS OF THE QUESTION

When you read a question on the Science Test, underline the following information:

- Any figures or tables mentioned in the question (such as "Figure 1" or "Table 2")
- Numbers and, more importantly, the <u>units</u> for these numbers
- Materials (in this example, there is only one—"potassium"—but you'll often see more)
- Words such as *greater*, *lesser*, *increased*, *decreased*, and *not*. Students often make careless mistakes because they misread these words.

(EX) According to Figure 1, the photoelectric kinetic energy for potassium in a light frequency of 10×10^{14} Hz is closest to:

A. 3.0×10^{-19} J.
B. 3.3×10^{-19} J.
C. 3.6×10^{-19} J.
D. 3.9×10^{-19} J.

RESTATE THE QUESTION

Direct questions can get harder by the way they are worded. Sometimes you need to restate the question in a way that makes sense. Look at the following example:

(EX) A student wants to determine if a metal sample is potassium. If she uses a light frequency of 7×10^{14} Hz, what photoelectric kinetic energy should she expect to measure if the metal is potassium?

A. 1.1×10^{-19} J
B. 1.2×10^{-19} J
C. 2.0×10^{-19} J
D. 2.4×10^{-19} J

■

Try the following direct question:

1. Based on the data in Figure 1, at which of the following frequencies of light would potassium emit no photoelectric kinetic energy?

A. 5.4×10^{14} Hz
B. 6.6×10^{14} Hz
C. 7.8×10^{14} Hz
D. 9.0×10^{14} Hz

EXTRAPOLATION

To extrapolate is to estimate a value *outside* the observed or tabulated range. (Interpolation, where you will estimate values *between* known values, is more common on table problems; we will cover this technique later, when we cover tables.) Look at the following example. Note that a new material (titanium) has been introduced in Figure 2:

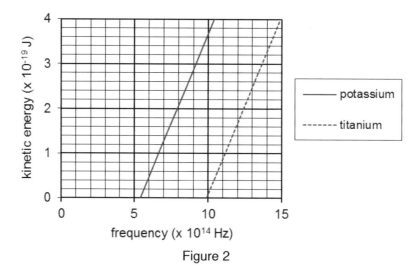

Figure 2

(EX) Based on the information in Figure 2, a sample of titanium exposed to a light with frequency 20×10^{14} Hz will exhibit photoelectric kinetic energy:

- **A.** between 3.0×10^{-19} and 3.5×10^{-19} J.
- **B.** between 3.5×10^{-19} and 4.0×10^{-19} J.
- **C.** between 4.0×10^{-19} and 4.5×10^{-19} J.
- **D.** over 4.5×10^{-19} J.

Try the following lesson problem. Notice that Figure 3 below now shows *three* different metals:

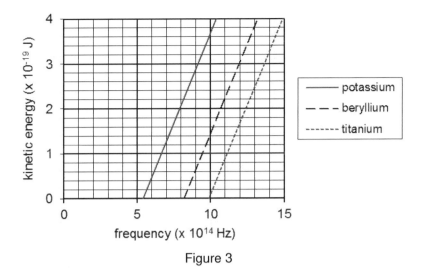

Figure 3

2. A scientist wants to determine whether a sample of metal is potassium, beryllium, or titanium. The scientist exposes the sample to light at a frequency of 12×10^{14} Hz and measures a photoelectric kinetic energy emission of 5.2×10^{-19} J. Based on the information in Figure 3, the sample is most likely:

A. potassium only.
B. beryllium only.
C. titanium only.
D. potassium or beryllium only.

■

Passage I

Binary fission is the process by which a single cell of bacteria divides into two cells. The rate of exponential growth of a bacterial culture is expressed as *generation time*, which is defined as the time required for the bacterial population to double. Table 1 displays a variety of bacteria at optimal growth temperatures and the resulting generation times.

Table 1			
Bacterium	Growth medium	Temperature (°C)	Generation time (min)
Escherichia coli	glucose-salts	37	17
Bacillus megaterium	sucrose-salts	34	25
Streptococcus lactis	milk	37	26
Streptococcus lactis	lactose broth	37	48
Staphylococcus aureus	heart infusion broth	30	29
Lactobacillus acidophilus	milk	35	82
Rhizobium japonicum	mannitol-salts	25	403
Mycobacterium tuberculosis	synthetic	37	862
Treponema pallidum	rabbit testes	31	1980

The *bacterial growth curve* consists of four characteristic phases, as shown in Figure 1.

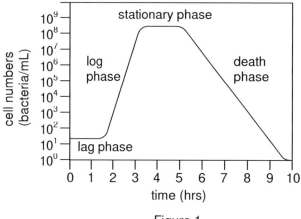

Figure 1

1. Based on the data in Table 1, if *Streptococcus lactis* was placed in a test tube containing a growth medium at 37°C, the generation time would most likely be:

    A. less than 20 min.
    B. between 20 and 25 min.
    C. between 25 and 50 min.
    D. greater than 50 min.

2. The initial population of the bacteria displayed in Figure 1 is closest to:

   F. 1 bacteria/mL.
   G. 10 bacteria/mL.
   H. 20 bacteria/mL.
   J. 100 bacteria/mL.

3. According to Table 1, which of the following combinations of bacteria and growth medium, at 37°C, would take closest to 30 minutes to double its population?

   A. *Escherichia coli* in glucose-salts
   B. *Mycobacterium tuberculosis* in a synthetic medium
   C. *Staphylococcus aureus* in heart infusion broth
   D. *Streptococcus lactis* in milk

4. According to the passage, if the temperatures of the growth mediums had been increased, the generation times for the bacterium in Table 1 would most likely have:

   F. increased, because the temperatures would no longer be optimal.
   G. increased, because temperature and generation times are always directly proportional.
   H. decreased, because temperature and generation times are always inversely proportional.
   J. decreased, because bacteria grow faster in hotter environments.

5. Which of the following hypotheses about bacterial growth is supported by Figure 1?

   A. Bacteria population will return to its initial population at the end of the death phase.
   B. Bacteria population begins to increase immediately after transfer to a new growth medium.
   C. Bacterial cells do not grow in volume or mass immediately after transfer to a new growth medium.
   D. Bacterial fission does not begin immediately after transfer to a new growth medium.

Continued →

6. According to Figure 1, the greatest rate of change in the number of bacteria occurred at what time interval on the bacterial growth curve?

    F. 0 to1 hours
    G. 2 to 3 hours
    H. 5 to 6 hours
    J. 9 to 10 hours

3. *NEW INFORMATION*

Sometimes, a question will add information that is not found in the passage.

 These questions provide *new information* in the question—perhaps a new material or test subject, perhaps a new definition or hypothesis—that is clearly not found in the passage. Sometimes these questions begin with the words "Suppose that . . ."

NEW MATERIALS

Many questions add some new item or material, one that is not found in the passage. Look at the following example:

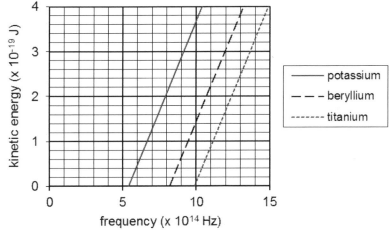

Figure 3

(EX) Suppose that a student tested a sample of magnesium in a light frequency of 10×10^{14} Hz and found that the emitted photoelectric kinetic energy was 2.0×10^{-19} J. Based on Figure 3, which of the following correctly lists the 4 metals by their photoelectric kinetic energy at 10×10^{14} Hz from *least* to *greatest*?

A. titanium, magnesium, beryllium, potassium
B. titanium, beryllium, magnesium, potassium
C. potassium, magnesium, beryllium, titanium
D. potassium, beryllium, titanium, magnesium

NEW DEFINITIONS

Another way the ACT may throw new information into a question is by introducing a new term or formula. Before we look at an example, a quick lesson on *yes or no* questions:

YES OR NO QUESTIONS

Glance at the answer choices for the following question. Two are *Yes's* and two are *No's*. After you read one of these types of questions, first decide whether the answer is *yes* or *no*, and eliminate answer choices accordingly. Then you can focus on only two answer choices. Now, to the question…

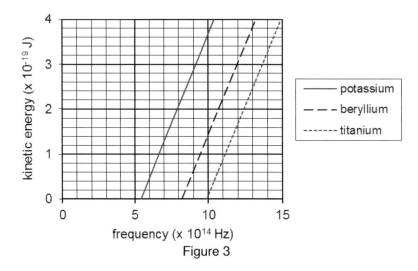

Figure 3

(EX) The slope of a line in the frequency-kinetic energy graph is defined as the ratio of the change in kinetic energy to the corresponding change in frequency. The value of the slope for a given material is called *Planck's Number*. Based on the information in Figure 3, would one be justified in concluding that Planck's Number is constant for potassium, beryllium, and titanium?

A. Yes, because all three lines start at a kinetic energy of 0 J.
B. Yes, because the slopes of all three lines are equal.
C. No, because the frequency ranges of all three lines are different.
D. No, because the information provided is insufficient to determine Planck's Number.

Try the following lesson problem. Figure 3 is reprinted below:

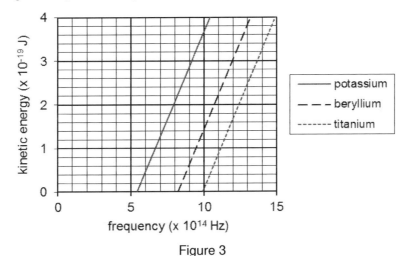

Figure 3

3. A *metal alloy* is a material composed of two or more metals. A student hypothesizes that a metal alloy will have a higher photoelectric kinetic energy emission rate at a given light frequency than the greater of the kinetic energy emission rates of the composite metals tested separately. To test the hypothesis, the student uses a titanium-beryllium sample, exposed to light at a frequency of 11×10^{14} Hz, and measures 1.2×10^{-19} J of emitted kinetic energy. Does the data in Figure 3 support the student's hypothesis?

    A. Yes, because the emitted kinetic energy is greater than the sum of the kinetic energies emitted by each material separately.
    B. Yes, because the emitted kinetic energy is greater than the kinetic energy emitted by titanium separately.
    C. No, because the emitted kinetic energy is less than the kinetic energy emitted by beryllium separately.
    D. No, because the emitted kinetic energy is less than the sum of the kinetic energies emitted by each material separately.

THE SECOND PARTS OF ANSWER CHOICES

Yes/No questions, as described above, are examples of questions that have answer choices each containing *two parts*. The second parts of these answer choices, through process of elimination, can often lead you easily to the correct answer, even when the question is confusing.

We've hidden the passage and the question in the following example, but see if you can guess the correct answer using process of elimination:

A. lower, because the average temperature decreased as the comet approached the sun.
B. lower, because the average temperature increased as the comet approached the sun.
C. higher, because the average temperature decreased as the comet approached the sun.
D. higher, because the average temperature did not change as the comet approached the sun.

You can be pretty sure that temperature will *increase* as a comet approaches the sun. The only sensible answer is **B** (even though we have no idea what the question was actually asking).

Feel free to use the second parts of answer choices to your advantage, especially for questions that sound difficult otherwise.

4. TRENDS

It is important that you recognize *trends* as you analyze data on the ACT. Think about what happens to one variable as another variable changes. As one variable increases, does the other also increase? Does it decrease? Does it stay the same? Does it go up and then down? Down and then up? And so on.

Keep track of trends using arrows (↑ or ↓). For example, we can see in Figure 3 that as frequency increases, kinetic energy also increases, so write: *F*↑ *K*↑ (you can abbreviate however you'd like). Arrows will especially help when you're dealing with more than two variables. Let's try an example. Note the addition of "threshold frequency" below:

The *threshold frequency* of a metal is defined as the maximum frequency of light that emits no photoelectric kinetic energy.

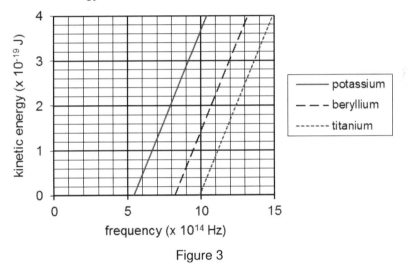

Figure 3

(EX) Figure 3 shows that the photoelectric kinetic energy increases:

   A. more slowly for metals with higher threshold frequencies.
   B. more quickly for metals with higher threshold frequencies.
   C. at the same rate for different metals as frequency decreases.
   D. at the same rate for different metals as frequency increases.

5. MAKE CONNECTIONS

On a single question, you may have to use information from different parts of the passage.

MULTIPLE FIGURES

Most of these connections problems deal with using *multiple figures* (graphs, tables, etc.). If you recall in the introduction, one of the things to look for in multiple figures is *repeated* labels (and units). Make sure to circle these labels and connect them with a line. These connections are the key to questions that require you to look at more than one figure. Let's add a figure to the example on photoelectric emission. Which label is repeated in both figures?

Figure 3 shows how the kinetic energy varies for a range of light frequencies for three types of metals.

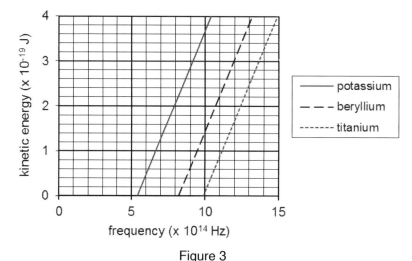

Figure 3

Light is visible if it falls in the *visible frequency spectrum*. Table 1 shows the frequency of six visible colors.

Table 1		
Color	Frequency (x 10^{14} Hz)	Wavelength (nm)
red	4.3–4.8	700–635
orange	4.8–5.1	635–590
yellow	5.1–5.4	590–560
green	5.4–6.1	560–490
blue	6.1–6.7	490–450
violet	6.7–7.5	450–400

Let's look at an example:

(EX) According to Figure 3 and Table 1, photoelectric emission occurs in the visible light spectrum for which of the following metals?

  A. potassium and beryllium
  B. potassium only
  C. beryllium only
  D. titanium only

Sometimes, new figures will be introduced in the questions or the answer choices:

(EX) Based on the information in Figure 3 and the table below, which of the following statements best describes the relationship, if any, between a material's atomic number and its emitted photoelectric kinetic energy at a light frequency of 10×10^{14} Hz?

Material	Atomic number
beryllium	4
potassium	19
titanium	22

  A. As the atomic number increases, the kinetic energy increases.
  B. As the atomic number increases, the kinetic energy decreases.
  C. As the atomic number increases, the kinetic energy does not change.
  D. There is no apparent relationship between a material's atomic number and its emitted photoelectric kinetic energy.

Try the following lesson problem, which uses the same data as the previous examples. The information is reprinted below:

Figure 3 shows how the kinetic energy varies for a range of light frequencies for three types of metals.

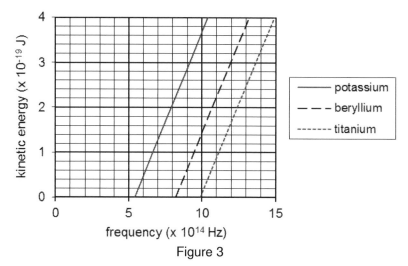

Figure 3

Light is visible if it falls in the *visible frequency spectrum*. Table 1 shows the frequency of six visible colors.

Table 1		
Color	Frequency (x 10^{14} Hz)	Wavelength (nm)
red	4.3–4.8	700–635
orange	4.8–5.1	635–590
yellow	5.1–5.4	590–560
green	5.4–6.1	560–490
blue	6.1–6.7	490–450
violet	6.7–7.5	450–400

4. Based on the data, which of the following best describes the change in emitted kinetic energy as light wavelength increases?

   A. The emitted kinetic energy increases.
   B. The emitted kinetic energy decreases.
   C. The emitted kinetic energy remains constant for a given material.
   D. The information provided is insufficient to determine the relationship between wavelength and kinetic energy.

MAKING CONNECTIONS WITH THE TEXT

Don't forget about the *text*. While most of the questions refer specifically (and entirely) to figures, sometimes you must pull information from the text as well, especially words that are written in italics. If you ever find yourself stuck or believe that the figures don't provide enough information to answer a question, skim the text.

! **When a question uses words or symbols that are not found in a passage's figures or tables, check the passage's *text*.**

These text–figure connections are some of the most important connections you will make on the Science Test .

Passage II

A solid object will either sink or float in a liquid, depending on the relative densities of the object and the liquid. A fraction of a floating object will extend above the surface of the liquid.

Table 1 lists 6 objects and their densities, in grams per cubic centimeter (g/cm^3), at 15°C.

Table 1	
Object	Density (g/cm^3)
Balsa wood	0.12
Cedar wood	0.33
Birch wood	0.55
Ash wood	0.61
Polyethylene	0.92
Polystyrene	0.97

Table 2 lists 4 liquids and their densities, in g/cm^3, at 15°C.

Table 2	
Liquid	Density (g/cm^3)
Ethanol	0.79
Water	0.99
Benzene	1.23
Mercury	13.6

Each object in Table 1 was placed in containers containing the liquids in Table 2, and the fraction of each object extending above the liquid's surface was recorded. The results are shown in Figure 1.

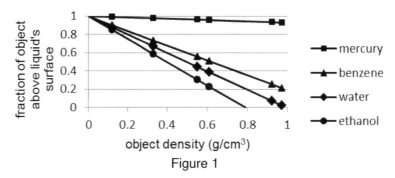

Figure 1

1. According to Figure 1, as object density increased, the fraction of the object that extended above each of the liquid's surface:

   A. decreased only.
   B. increased only.
   C. varied, but with no general trend.
   D. remained the same.

2. According to Table 1 and Figure 1, the fraction of polystyrene extending above the surface of benzene was closest to which of the following values?

   F. 0.1
   G. 0.2
   H. 0.3
   J. 0.4

3. The density of water varies with temperature. A scientist noticed that the fraction of a sample of birch wood extending above the surface of water decreased as the temperature of the water was increased from 15°C to 80°C. Based on the information provided in the the passage, as the temperature of the water increased from 15°C to 80°C, did the density of water increase or decrease?

   A. Decrease, because as the density of water decreases, the fraction of an object extending above the surface increases.
   B. Increase, because as the density of water increases, the fraction of an object extending above the surface decreases.
   C. Decrease, because as the density of water decreases, the fraction of an object extending above the surface also decreases.
   D. Increase, because as the density of water increases, the fraction of an object extending above the surface also increases.

4. According to Table 1 and Figure 1, which object(s) sank when placed in a container of ethanol at 15°C?

   F. balsa wood
   G. polyethylene only
   H. polystyrene only
   J. polyethylene and polystyrene

5. A scientist tests a sample of cedar wood in an unknown liquid at 15°C and finds that the fraction of the wood extending above the surface is 0.8. According to the passage, the density of the unknown liquid was most likely:

   A. less than 0.79 g/cm^3.
   B. between 0.79 g/cm^3 and 1.23 g/cm^3.
   C. between 1.23 g/cm^3 and 13.6 g/cm^3.
   D. greater than 13.6 g/cm^3.

Continued →

6. A scientist measures the weight of 1 L of each of the liquids in Table 2 by placing an empty 1 L container on a scale, setting the scale to 0.0 g, adding the liquid to the container, and then recording the weight. Which of the liquids would have the greatest weight?

    F. Ethanol
    G. Water
    H. Benzene
    J. Mercury

6. TABLES

Of course, graphs aren't the only figures that show up on the test. We've already seen tables in some of the previous examples. Tables can be more difficult to read than graphs because you don't have the advantage of a visual representation. We will cover a number of topics that are commonly associated with tables.

INTERPOLATION

As mentioned earlier, *interpolation* involves estimating values *between* known values. **When interpolating with a table, draw a horizontal line between the values in question.** This will help you avoid making a careless mistake. We'll do this in the following example:

    Atmospheric pressure reflects the average density and thus the weight of the column of air above a given level. The pressure at a point on the earth's surface must be greater than the pressure at any height above it because of differences in the weight of the air. A *pressure gradient* is the vertical difference in pressure between two points.

    Table 1 shows the percent of sea-level density and atmospheric pressure (in kilopascals) at various altitudes.

Table 1		
Altitude ($\times 10^3$ m)	Percent of sea-level density	Atmospheric pressure (kPa)
0	100	101
10	70	65
20	42	38
30	25	22
40	20	13
50	14	10
60	10	7

The following formula gives the *air density* (*d*) in kg/m³ at –40°C for pressure (*P*) in kPa:

$$d = \frac{P}{84.108}$$

Table 1		
Altitude (× 10³ m)	Percent of sea-level density	Atmospheric pressure (kPa)
0	100	101
10	70	65
20	42	38
30	25	22
40	20	13
50	14	10
60	10	7

EX) According to Table 1, the density of air at about what altitude is 50% of the density of air at sea level?

A. 8,000 meters
B. 17,000 meters
C. 30,000 meters
D. 50,000 meters

GRAPHS FROM TABLES

Some problems will ask you to visually interpret the information in a table. There are two ways to tackle these problems:

1. Check values from the table and eliminate answer choices accordingly.
2. Find the differences between adjacent vertical values in a table. This will give you an idea of the general shape of the graph.

(EX) According to the information in Table 1, a plot of atmospheric pressure versus altitude is best represented by which of the following graphs?

A.

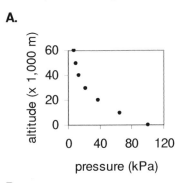

B.

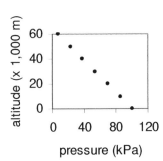

C.

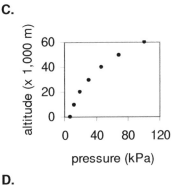

D.

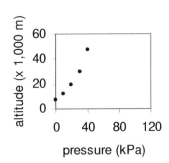

Try the following lesson problem. The information below is the same as that for the previous examples, but now we've added a second table:

Atmospheric pressure reflects the average density and thus the weight of the column of air above a given level. The pressure at a point on the earth's surface must be greater than the pressure at any height above it because of differences in the weight of the air. A *pressure gradient* is the vertical difference in pressure between two points.

Table 1 shows the percent of sea-level density and atmospheric pressure (in kilopascals) at various altitudes.

Table 1		
Altitude ($\times 10^3$ m)	Percent of sea-level density	Atmospheric pressure (kPa)
0	100	101
10	70	65
20	42	38
30	25	22
40	20	13
50	14	10
60	10	7

The following formula gives the *air density* (*d*) in kg/m³ at –40°C for pressure (*P*) in kPa:

$$d = \frac{P}{84.108}$$

The maximum migratory altitude of birds in clear weather is determined primarily by atmospheric pressure. Table 2 shows the maximum migratory altitude of various types of birds.

Table 2	
Bird type	Maximum migratory altitude ($\times 10^3$ m)
Swifts and swallows	0.3
Robins and crows	1.0
Most songbirds	3.4
Ducks and geese	4.9
Eagles, vultures, and hawks	6.7

5. Based on the information provided, the minimum atmospheric air pressure in which vultures can migrate is about:

   A. 77 kPa.
   B. 65 kPa.
   C. 6.7 kPa.
   D. 4.9 kPa.

KEEP IT EASY

Science questions often sound much harder than they are. Consider the previous question. The question tells us what bird to focus on (vultures). From Table 2, we can see that vultures correspond to an attitude of 6.7×10^3 m. Take this information to Table 1 (make connections), and we find a corresponding pressure of about 77 kPa (by interpolation). Without worrying about "maximum altitudes" or "minimum air pressures," we can take our chances on A.

STAY FOCUSED

This is a good time to remind you to *stay focused*. These passages tend to give you a lot of information, most of which you won't use for any one question:

Most information is not used on any one problem!

Look at the lesson problem you just completed. It had nothing to do with air density. So the middle column of Table 1 and the given formula are not used for this question. Put this unneeded information out of your mind and focus on the information you *do* need.

Some information in the passage, in fact, you won't use on *any* of the problems. This is one of the main reasons why you should *skim* the passage instead of reading it. Otherwise, you might spend 5 minutes trying to understand something that's never actually tested:

Some information is not used on *any* problems!

Notice, for example, that a *pressure gradient* was defined in the passage introduction, but this term never came up in any of the questions. Aren't you glad you didn't worry about it too much? Just make sure you circle terms like this, just in case they do show up.

7. CALCULATIONS & MATH

While the Science Test is definitely not a math test, you may be asked to perform some relatively basic mathematical operations. Review the following topics from the Math section of this tutorial (all topics are found in the Arithmetic section):

- Percent
- Proportions
- Ratios
- Averages
- Rates (RTD)
- Tables and Graphs

You should also be prepared to make some calculations. **You are NOT permitted to use a calculator on the Science Test of the ACT, so don't expect any of the calculations to be too difficult.** The following examples are based on the table introduced in the previous section:

Table 1 shows the percent of sea-level density and atmospheric pressure (in kilopascals) at various altitudes.

Table 1		
Altitude ($\times 10^3$ m)	Percent of sea-level density	Atmospheric pressure (kPa)
0	100	101
10	70	65
20	42	38
30	25	22
40	20	13
50	14	10
60	10	7

The following formula gives the *air density* (d) in kg/m³ at –40°C for pressure (P) in kPa:

$$d = \frac{P}{84.108}$$

6. Based on Table 1, the ratio of the atmospheric pressure at sea level to the atmospheric pressure at 50×10^3 meters is closest to which of the following?

   A. 100:1
   B. 10:1
   C. 1:10
   D. 1:50

The following is an example problem that requires *calculations*. See if you can follow along with the solution. Most students find this question challenging:

(EX) Using the information in the passage, which of the following expressions could be used to calculate the density at sea level, in kg/m³, if the temperature at an altitude of 30,000 meters is −40°C?

A. $\dfrac{22}{(84.108)}$

B. $\dfrac{(0.25)(22)}{(84.108)}$

C. $\dfrac{22}{(0.25)(84.108)}$

D. $\dfrac{25}{0.25}$

The previous question was a tough one, so don't worry if you found it difficult. The important thing to remember from this section is that, on the Science Test , you will have to occasionally use your math skills, set up equations, and make some calculations.

8. *COMBINING GRAPHS*

MORE THAN TWO AXIS LABELS

Take a look at the graphs below. Do you see the common label?

Figure 1 shows the average temperature (in degrees Celsius) at various altitudes.

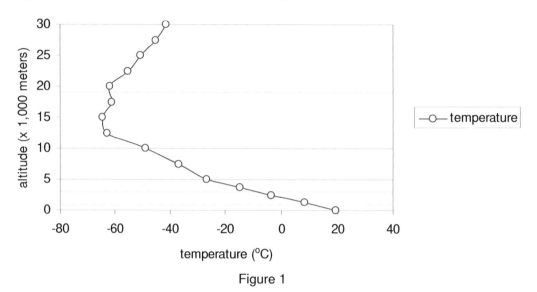

Figure 1

Figure 2 shows the average wind speed (in knots) at various altitudes.

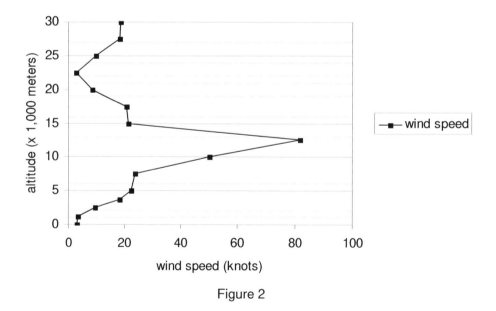

Figure 2

The ACT may combine these two graphs into one, using "altitude" as the common label. Use the information below for the following example:

The *troposphere* is the lowest layer of the atmosphere, ranging in elevation from sea level (0 meters) to a height of 10,000–12,000 meters above sea level.

The figure shows average temperature (in degrees Celsius) and wind speed (in knots) at various altitudes.

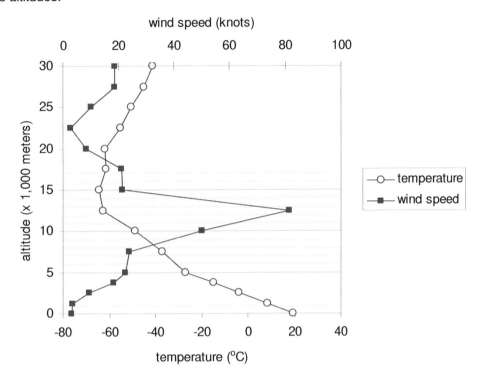

(EX) Based on the information provided, which of the following best describes the behavior of temperature and wind speed within the troposphere?

A. As altitude increases, both temperature and wind speed increase.
B. As altitude increases, both temperature and wind speed decrease.
C. As altitude increases, temperature increases and wind speed decreases.
D. As altitude increases, temperature decreases and wind speed increases.

Try the following problem, based on the previous figure:

7. A scientist wants to estimate the height of a weather balloon. If instruments on the balloon measure a temperature of –62° C and a wind speed of 8 knots, then the balloon's altitude is most likely:

    A. 2,000–4,000 meters above sea level.
    B. 12,000–14,000 meters above sea level.
    C. 19,000–21,000 meters above sea level.
    D. 25,000–27,000 meters above sea level.

Page intentionally left blank.

Passage III

A *bomb calorimeter* is a device used for determining heats of combustion by igniting a sample in oxygen in a sealed vessel submerged in water. Each bomb calorimeter has a constant *heat capacity* (C_{cal}), measured in kilojoules per degree Celsius (KJ/°C). The heat of the reaction (q_r), measured in kilojoules (kJ), is calculated by multiplying the heat capacity of the bomb calorimeter by the change in temperature of the water surrounding the sealed vessel (ΔT):

$$q_r = C_{cal} \times \Delta T$$

Table 1 shows the heat released for various chemical compounds when burned in a bomb calorimeter. Table 2 shows the heat released when different amounts of octane were burned.

Table 1					
Chemical compound	Molecular formula	Mass (g)	ΔT (°C)	Heat released (kJ)	Molar mass (g/mol)
Sucrose	$C_{12}H_{22}O_{12}$	1.0	12.0	18.0	342.2965
Hydrazine	N_2H_4	1.0	13.9	20.9	32.0452
Methanol	CH_3OH	1.0	15.2	22.8	32.0419
Ethanol	C_2H_5OH	1.0	19.7	29.6	46.0684
Benzene	C_6H_6	1.0	28.1	42.2	78.1118
Octane	C_8H_{18}	1.0	31.7	47.6	114.2285

Table 2	
Amount of octane (g)	Heat released (kJ)
0.5	23.8
1.5	71.4
3.0	142.8
6.0	285.6

1. Based on the information in Table 2, the heat released from the burning of 4.0 grams of octane in a bomb calorimeter would be closest to which of the following?

   A. 100 kJ
   B. 200 kJ
   C. 300 kJ
   D. 400 kJ

2. Which of the following graphs best illustrates the relationship between the change in water temperature and the heat released of the chemical compounds listed in Table 1?

F.

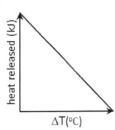

H.

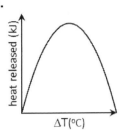

G.

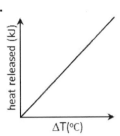

J.

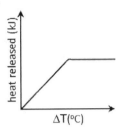

3. Using the results of the burning of 1.0 gram of sucrose in a bomb calorimeter, as shown in Table 1, which of the following could be used to calculate the heat capacity of the bomb calorimeter used in the experiments?

  A. $C_{cal} = 18.0 \text{ kJ} + 12.0°C$
  B. $C_{cal} = 18.0 \text{ kJ} - 12.0°C$
  C. $C_{cal} = 18.0 \text{ kJ} \times 12.0°C$
  D. $C_{cal} = 18.0 \text{ kJ} \div 12.0°C$

4. Based on the information in Tables 1 and 2, if 3.0 grams of methanol had been burned in a bomb calorimeter, the heat released would be closest to:

  F. 23 kJ.
  G. 68 kJ.
  H. 106 kJ.
  J. 143 kJ.

Continued →

5. If a substance with a molar mass of 148.16 g/mol is burned in a bomb calorimeter, the change in temperature would be closest to which of the following?

    A. Less than 28°C
    B. Between 28°C and 32°C
    C. Greater than 32°C
    D. Cannot be determined
    from the given information

6. Which of the following was *not* an independent variable in the experiments performed in the passage?

    F. Chemical compound
    G. Molecular formula
    H. Mass of octane
    J. Change in water
    temperature

■

TIMING

 All programs: Now that we've covered the first several sections of the Data Representation chapter, it's time to consider *timing*. Turn to and read the Timing section in the Introduction (starting on page 627). When you've covered the timing strategies, continue with the next section (Data Representation Odds & Ends).

9. DATA REPRESENTATION ODDS & ENDS

DESCRIPTIONS & HEADINGS

When a passage provides a number of similar figures, especially tables, pay close attention to the written descriptions for each figure, or the headings of each table. Underline any numerical values given, and note how these values may change from figure to figure. These values will likely show up in some of the questions.

In the example passage on the next page, what important part of the headings changes from table to table?

Consider the following reversible reaction:

$$N_2 + 3H_2 \rightleftharpoons 2NH_3$$

At chemical equilibrium, the formation of ammonia gas (NH_3) occurs at the same rate as the formation of nitrogen (N_2) and hydrogen (H_2) gasses.

The *equilibrium constant* is given by the following equation, where brackets represent the concentration (mol/L) of the reactant or product:

$$K_{eq} = \frac{[NH_3]^2}{[N_2][H_2]^3}$$

The tables below show the data collected while varying either temperature or initial reactant concentrations.

Table 1							
Temperature = 360°C							
Trial	Initial [N$_2$] (mol/L)	Initial [H$_2$] (mol/L)	Initial [NH$_3$] (mol/L)	Final [N$_2$] (mol/L)	Final [H$_2$] (mol/L)	Final [NH$_3$] (mol/L)	K$_{eq}$
1	0.50	1.50	0	0.100	0.300	0.800	237.0
2	1.00	3.00	0	0.146	0.438	1.708	237.0
3	1.50	4.50	0	0.182	0.545	2.637	237.0

Table 2							
Temperature = 380°C							
Trial	Initial [N$_2$] (mol/L)	Initial [H$_2$] (mol/L)	Initial [NH$_3$] (mol/L)	Final [N$_2$] (mol/L)	Final [H$_2$] (mol/L)	Final [NH$_3$] (mol/L)	K$_{eq}$
4	0.50	1.50	0	0.104	0.311	0.793	201.4
5	1.00	3.00	0	0.156	0.455	1.697	201.4
6	1.50	4.50	0	0.189	0.566	2.623	201.4

Table 3							
Temperature = 400°C							
Trial	Initial [N$_2$] (mol/L)	Initial [H$_2$] (mol/L)	Initial [NH$_3$] (mol/L)	Final [N$_2$] (mol/L)	Final [H$_2$] (mol/L)	Final [NH$_3$] (mol/L)	K$_{eq}$
7	0.50	1.50	0	0.108	0.325	0.784	165.8
8	1.00	3.00	0	0.159	0.476	1.683	165.8
9	1.50	4.50	0	0.197	0.592	2.605	165.8

(EX) Based on the data in the passage, as temperature increased the value of the equilibrium constant:

    A. decreased only.
    B. increased only.
    C. remained the same.
    D. varied, but with no general trend.

When an equation is given in the passage, there's a good chance you'll be tested on calculations (review the Calculations & Math section if necessary). Try the following lesson problem:

9. A scientist reacted nitrogen and hydrogen to produce ammonia gas in two separate trials, Trial A and Trial B, and found that, compared to Trial A, the final concentration of nitrogen increased in Trial B, but the final concentration of hydrogen and the equilibrium constant did not change. What must be true about the final concentration of ammonia gas in Trial B compared to that in Trial A?

    A. The concentration of NH_3 did not change.
    B. The concentration of NH_3 cannot be determined.
    C. The concentration of NH_3 decreased.
    D. The concentration of NH_3 increased.

LEARN

Sometimes the ACT will ask a question that you cannot answer *directly* from the information given in the passage. The question may require you to *learn* something from the given data. For the following question (which relates to the passage at the beginning of this section), consider what we have learned about equilibrium constants, temperature, and concentrations of the reactants:

10. When hydrogen gas (H_2) reacts with chlorine gas (Cl_2), the following reversible reaction occurs:

$$H_2 + Cl_2 \rightleftharpoons 2HCl$$

When 1.0 mol/L of H_2 reacts with 1.0 mol/L of Cl_2 at 300°C, the equilibrium constant is found to be 4.0×10^{31}. Based on the data in the passage, if 3.0 mol/L of H_2 reacts with 3.0 mol/L of Cl_2 at 300°C, the equilibrium constant will be:

    A. less than 4.0×10^{31}.
    B. 4.0×10^{31}.
    C. 12.0×10^{31}.
    D. greater than 12.0×10^{31}.

RATIOS

Sometimes you must consider the *ratios* of values. Consider a mixture of lemonade. It is not the amount of lemon juice and sugar-water that determines the taste but rather the *ratio* of these ingredients. For example, 1 part lemon juice to 9 parts sugar-water (1:9) will taste the same as 100 parts lemon juice to 900 parts sugar-water (100:900 = 1:9). Any time substances are mixed together, consider the importance of the *ratio* of the composition.

Let's add some new information to the passage at the beginning of this section and try one more lesson problem. We'll consider ratios as we tackle it:

A scientist assumes that a temperature, T_c, exists where the given chemical reaction becomes *irreversible*, as shown below:

$$N_2 + 3H_2 \rightarrow 2NH_3$$

The scientist uses a computer simulator and records the following information:

Table 4							
			Temperature = T_c				
Trial	Initial [N_2] (mol/L)	Initial [H_2] (mol/L)	Initial [NH_3] (mol/L)	Final [N_2] (mol/L)	Final [H_2] (mol/L)	Final [NH_3] (mol/L)	K_{eq}
10	1.00	3.00	0	0	0	2.00	∞
11	1.50	3.00	0	0.50	0	2.00	∞
12	2.00	3.00	0	1.00	0	2.00	∞
13	1.00	3.50	0	0	0.50	2.00	∞
14	1.00	4.00	0	0	1.00	2.00	∞

(EX) Based on Table 4, if a scientist started with 2.0 mol/L of N_2 and 6.0 mol/L of H_2, then the final concentration of H_2 would be closest to:

A. 0 mol/L.
B. 0.50 mol/L.
C. 1.00 mol/L.
D. 3.00 mol/L.

OTHER FIGURES

Not all figures on the ACT are line graphs or tables. Here's an example that incorporates an illustration and a bar graph.

To measure the concentrations of hydrocarbon pollutants near or within the Cook Wetlands, soil samples were taken at four locations, as shown in Figure 1.

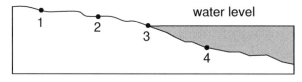

Figure 1

The concentrations of pollutants, measured as parts-per-million by total weight of the sample, are shown in Figure 2.

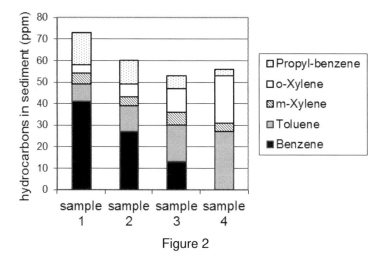

Figure 2

Try the following lesson problems:

11. According to the data, which hydrocarbon pollutant or pollutants showed an increase in concentration as the sample locations decreased in elevation?

   A. Propyl-benzene only
   B. Propyl-benzene and Benzene only
   C. o-Xylene and Toluene only
   D. m-Xylene, o-Xylene, and Toluene only

12. If a fifth sample was taken in water deeper than that of sample 4, based on the data, which of the following hydrocarbon pollutants would most likely NOT be found in concentrations greater than 10 ppm?

F. Benzene only
G. Benzene and Propyl-benzene only
H. Benzene, Propyl-benzene, and m-Xylene only
J. o-Xylene and Toluene only

■

You've now seen a number of different kinds of figures, but you should expect to see other types as you work your way through the practice problems and practice tests found in this tutorial and in the ACT book. Hopefully you're starting to feel prepared to tackle whatever may be thrown your way, no matter how strange or complicated it may look.

■

RESEARCH SUMMARIES AND CONFLICTING VIEWPOINTS

If you're following the **20-hour program**, you probably won't have time to cover the other two types of passages found on the Science Test (Research Summaries and Conflicting Viewpoints), but you should still plan to tackle these problems when you take the test:

- **Research Summaries:** Many of the Research Summaries questions are very similar to Data Representation ones (because they test graphs, tables, and other figures). You may not get to the Research Summaries chapter, but now that you've completed the Data Representation chapter, you should feel comfortable tackling many—if not most—of the Research Summaries questions.

- **Conflicting Viewpoints:** The Conflicting Viewpoints passages tend to be less about tables, graphs, and numbers and more about *reading*, so you can tackle them as you would the passages on the Reading Test. Even though you probably won't have time to cover the Conflicting Viewpoints chapter, you'll hopefully get some of the easier questions correct.

TIMING

You should have covered Timing by now. Make sure to time yourself on all future homework assignments. If necessary, review Timing in the Introduction to see how long you have for each practice passage (based on the number of questions).

Passage IV (6 questions = 5:15 min:sec)

Contaminated water from a coal mine had been detected flowing into the Vesey River. Engineers constructed two artificial marshes to help reduce the amounts of iron and manganese in the water and to reduce the water's acidity (see Figure 1).

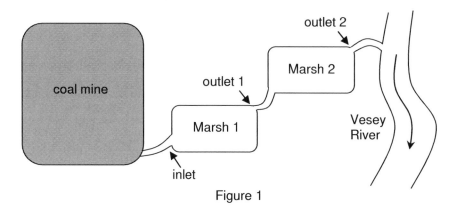

Figure 1

Measurements were taken at the inlet of Marsh 1 (I) and the outlets of both marshes (O1 and O2). Table 1 shows precipitation in centimeters (cm), flow rate in liters per minute (L/min), pH, and the content of iron and manganese in milligrams per liter (mg/L) over 5 days.

Table 1												
Day	Precipitation (cm)	Flow rate (L/min)			pH			Iron (mg/L)			Manganese (mg/L)		
		I	O1	O2	I	O1	O2	I	O1	O2	I	O1	O2
1	0	100	95	90	5.3	6.0	6.4	95	45	5.1	6.4	6.4	6.3
2	3.5	105	300	405	5.3	6.8	7.5	95	60	24.3	6.4	4.2	0.9
3	0.1	130	195	265	5.4	6.4	7.0	85	42	11.2	6.2	5.2	4.1
4	0	145	140	135	5.3	6.1	6.5	80	41	7.4	6.0	5.8	5.8
5	0	130	100	95	5.4	6.0	6.4	90	44	5.5	6.3	6.1	6.0

Table 2 shows the allowed contaminant levels for water. The given pH value is the minimum allowed. The given iron and manganese values are the maximum allowed.

Table 2		
Allowed contaminant levels		
pH	Iron (mg/L)	Manganese (mg/L)
6.0	3.5	2.0

1. According to Tables 1 and 2, which day, if any, was the water leaving Outlet 2 within acceptable contaminant levels?

    A. Day 1
    B. Day 2
    C. Day 3
    D. None of the days

2. Which of the following statements about Outlet 1 and Outlet 2 flow rates is supported by the information in Table 1?

F. The flow rates increased during the heavy rain and returned to their Day 1 values the day after the heavy rain.

G. The flow rates increased during the heavy rain and gradually decreased during the days after the rain.

H. The flow rates increased both the day of the heavy rain and the day after the heavy rain.

J. The flow rates did not change during the heavy rain.

3. Based on Table 1, on average, at which location was the water most contaminated with iron?

A. The inlet of Marsh 1
B. The outlet of Marsh 1
C. The outlet of Marsh 2
D. The Vesey River

4. According to Tables 1 and 2, did the marshes effectively bring pH measurements to within allowable contaminant levels prior to water entering the Vesey River?

F. Yes; the water's acidity was higher than the allowed level at Outlet 2 for all 5 days.

G. No; the water's acidity was higher than the allowed level at Outlet 2 for all 5 days.

H. Yes; the water's acidity was lower than the allowed level at Outlet 2 for all 5 days.

J. No; the water's acidity was lower than the allowed level at Outlet 2 for all 5 days.

5. According to the information in the passage, which of the following actions would best reduce the iron levels in the water that is released into the Vesey River?

A. Removing the first marsh
B. Removing the second marsh
C. Adding a third marsh
D. Increasing the inlet flow rate

Continued →

6. A copper mine utilizes two marshes in an identical arrangement to those shown in Figure 1. Based on the information in the passage, which of the following are likely values for the content of manganese in milligrams per liter (mg/L) on a day of no precipitation?

	Inlet	Outlet 1	Outlet 2
F.	8.5	8.5	8.4
G.	8.5	5.3	2.1
H.	8.5	9.4	10.5
J.	8.5	8.4	0.5

10. DATA REPRESENTATION PROBLEMS

PRACTICE PROBLEMS

The Official ACT Prep Guide offers one Data Representation passage in the "Improving Your Science Score" chapter. For additional practice, we'll use passages from Test 5. See the Tutoring Schedules in the Introduction for more on when to tackle these passages for different programs. Complete these passages *timed* (see the Science Introduction for single-passage timing estimates):

- *The Official ACT Prep Guide*: **"Improving Your Science Score" chapter:**
  - ☐ Passage I
- *The Official ACT Prep Guide*: **Test 5:**
  - ☐ Passage I
  - ☐ Passage III
- Additional Data Representation practice passages (following pages):
  - ☐ Passage I
  - ☐ Passage II
  - ☐ Passage III

 PRACTICE TEST (all programs): Now is a good time to take **Test 2** in the ACT book (you should have already taken Test 1).

Research Summaries and **Conflicting Viewpoints**: Even though we haven't covered Research Summaries and Conflicting Viewpoints passages, plan to tackle them, especially the Research Summaries passages, which contain many Data Representation questions.

Corrections: Don't forget to correct any missed questions after you grade the test (see below).

TEST CORRECTIONS

After each practice test is graded, you should correct questions related to this chapter that you missed or guessed on. See "Correcting Practice Tests" in the Introduction for more details. Here are the three steps to correcting practice tests:

1. Turn to the Techniques section at the end of this tutorial and circle the Data Representation *questions* that you missed or guessed on for the test you are correcting. (Remember, some of these will show up on Research Summaries passages.)

2. Correct the problems in *The Official ACT Prep Guide*. As you correct the problems, go back to the tutorial and review the techniques. The idea is to: (1) identify techniques that have given you trouble, (2) go back to the tutorial so you can review and strengthen these techniques, and (3) apply these techniques to the specific problems on which you struggled.

3. If you have trouble identifying the best technique to use on a problem, or if you need a hint to head you in the right direction, see the Techniques section at the end of this tutorial.

Page intentionally left blank.

DATA REPRESENTATION PASSAGES

Passage I (5 questions = 4:15 min:sec)

Enzymes are proteins that increase the rates of chemical reactions. In enzymatic reactions, molecules called *substrates* are converted into different molecules called *products*. The *relative activity rate* describes the rate by which a reaction increases due to the influence of an enzyme, in terms of 100 arbitrary units. Figures 1–3 show the effects of temperature, Ph, and substrate concentration on the relative activity rate for constant concentrations of Enzymes A and B. Figure 4 shows the effects of enzyme concentrations of Enzymes A and B on the relative activity rate.

The *pH scale* measures how *acidic* or *basic* a substance is. The pH scale ranges from 0 to 14. A pH of 7 is neutral. The lower a pH, the more acidic the substance.

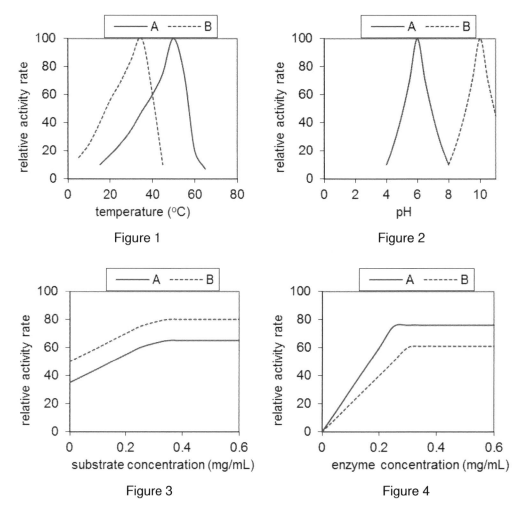

Figure 1

Figure 2

Figure 3

Figure 4

1. According to Figure 1, Enzyme A has the fastest activity rate of reaction at a temperature closest to:

   A. 35°C.
   B. 50°C.
   C. 65°C.
   D. 100°C.

2. Based on the data in Figure 2, which of the following is the best estimate for the relative activity rate for Enzyme B at a pH of 12?

F. 10
G. 30
H. 50
J. 70

3. A scientist claims that the relative activity rates of Enzymes A and B are dependent on the concentration of the substrate at concentrations below 0.3 mg/mL. Does the information in Figure 3 support the scientist's claim?

A. Yes, because the activity rates of Enzymes A and B do not change at concentrations above about 0.3 mg/mL.
B. Yes, because the activity rates of Enzymes A and B increase as concentrations increase below a concentration of about 0.3 mg/mL.
C. No, because the activity rates of Enzymes A and B do not change at concentrations above about 0.3 mg/mL.
D. No, because there is no relationship between the activity rates of Enzymes A and B.

4. The table below shows the relative activity rates for the enzyme Aspergillus at various pH readings.

pH	Relative activity rate
6	11
7	44
8	100
9·	45
10	10

Based on the table and Figure 2, one could conclude that Aspergillus is most effective at a pH that is:

F. more acidic than the most effective pH readings for Enzymes A and B.
G. less acidic than the most effective pH readings for Enzymes A and B.
H. more acidic than the most effective pH reading for Enzyme A only.
J. less acidic than the most effective pH reading for Enzyme A only.

5. According to Figures 1 and 4, which of the following conditions will give the greatest relative activity rate for Enzyme B?

A. 0.5 mg/mL of Enzyme B at 60°C
B. 0.4 mg/mL of Enzyme B at 50°C
C. 0.3 mg/mL of Enzyme B at 35°C
D. 0.2 mg/mL of Enzyme B at 20°C

Passage II (6 questions = 5:15 min:sec)

A chain is released from rest with its lower end touching a scale (see Figure 1). While the chain is falling, its *momentary length* (x) is the length of the chain on the scale pan, and its *momentary weight* is the weight of this momentary length. The scale measures all weights and forces in newtons (N) (a *newton* is the force required to accelerate a 1-kilogram mass at a rate of 1.0 m/sec^2).

Various chains were released from rest and allowed to fall on a scale. The masses, lengths, momentary lengths, momentary weights, and forces are shown in Tables 1–3.

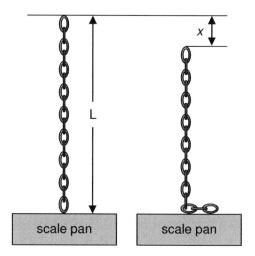

Figure 1

Table 1				
Mass of chain = 0.50 kg				
Trial	L (m)	x (m)	Momentary weight (N)	Force on scale pan (N)
1	1.0	0.2	0.98	2.94
2	1.0	0.4	1.96	5.89
3	1.0	0.6	2.94	8.83
4	1.0	0.8	3.92	11.77

Table 2				
Mass of chain = 0.75 kg				
Trial	L (m)	x (m)	Momentary weight (N)	Force on scale pan (N)
5	1.0	0.2	1.47	4.41
6	1.0	0.4	2.94	8.83
7	1.0	0.6	4.41	13.24
8	1.0	0.8	5.89	17.66

Table 3				
Mass of chain = 1.00 kg				
Trial	L (m)	x (m)	Momentary weight (N)	Force on scale pan (N)
9	0.5	0.1	1.96	5.89
10	1.0	0.2	1.96	5.89
11	1.5	0.5	3.27	9.81
12	2.0	0.5	2.45	7.36

1. A scientist hypothesizes that doubling the mass of a chain while keeping the length and the momentary length of the chain constant will double the force on the scale pan. Which of the following trials best supports this hypothesis?

    A. Trials 1 and 10
    B. Trials 1 and 9
    C. Trials 1 and 2
    D. Trials 9 and 10

2. Based on the information provided in the passage, if a 1.0-meter long chain with a mass of 0.25 kg is dropped onto a scale, the momentary weight on the pan if $x = 0.2$ m would be closest to:

   F. 0.50 N.
   G. 0.75 N.
   H. 1.0 N.
   J. 1.5 N.

3. Based on the information in Table 3 for a 1.00-kg chain, as the momentary weight of the chain on the scale pan increased:

   A. the momentary length of the chain increased.
   B. the momentary length of the chain decreased.
   C. the ratio of the momentary length to the length of the chain increased.
   D. the ratio of the momentary length to the length of the chain decreased.

4. For each trial, after the chain was released, the length of the chain that had not yet come in contact with the scale pan equaled:

   F. $L + x$
   G. $L - x$.
   H. $x - L$.
   J. x.

Continued →

5. According to the data in the passage, which of the following graphs best represents the relationship between a chain's momentary weight and its force on a scale pan?

A.

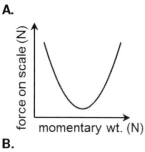

B.

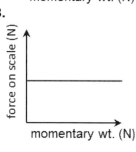

C.

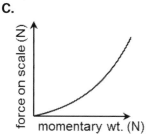

D.

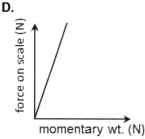

6. The mass of each chain used in the trials was determined by multiplying the mass of one individual link of the chain by the total number of links. Based on the information in the passage, the chain of which trial was composed of the most links?

   F. Trial 8
   G. Trial 9
   H. Trial 12
   J. Cannot be determined from the given information

Page intentionally left blank.

Passage III (7 questions = 6:00 min:sec)

An atom is made up of three primary particles: *protons* and *neutrons*, which are found in the atom's *nucleus*, and *electrons*, which move in orbits (see Figure 1) around the nucleus. Protons are positively charged particles, neutrons are uncharged particles, and electrons are negatively charged particles.

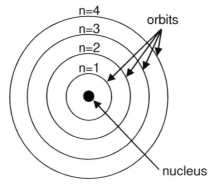

Figure 1 (Figure is NOT drawn to scale)

For three atoms containing only one electron, the energy (I, in electron volts, or eV) that is required to remove an electron and the energy (E, in eV) of a photon emitted when an electron falls from its initial orbit to the n = 1 orbit are shown in Figure 2.

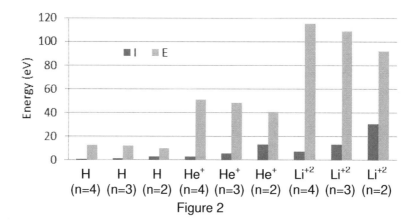

Figure 2

Table 1 contains data for the three atoms shown in Figure 2, including the number of protons (Z), the initial orbit (n), and the radius of the orbit (r).

Table 1			
Element	Z	n	r ($\times 10^{-8}$ cm)
H	1	4	8.5
H	1	3	4.8
H	1	2	2.1
He^+	2	4	4.2
He^+	2	3	2.4
He^+	2	2	1.1
Li^{+2}	3	4	2.8
Li^{+2}	3	3	1.6
Li^{+2}	3	2	0.7

1. According to Figure 2, as the value of n decreases for a given element, the values of I and E do which of the following?

	I	E
A.	increases only	increases only
B.	increases only	decreases only
C.	decreases only	decreases only
D.	decreases only	increases only

2. Based on the information in Figure 2, if n = 5, the value of E for the element He^+ would be closest to:

   F. less than 5.0 eV.
   G. between 5.0 and 40 eV.
   H. between 40 and 50 eV.
   J. greater than 50 eV.

3. According to Table 1 and the information provided in the passage, an atom has a net positive charge when:

   A. Z is greater than n.
   B. Z is less than n.
   C. Z is greater than the number of electrons.
   D. n is less than the number of electrons.

4. According to Figure 2 and Table 1, a photon with the most energy will be emitted when an electron falls from an orbit of what radius and from what element?

   F. 2.8×10^{-8} cm in Li^{+2}.
   G. 0.7×10^{-8} cm in Li^{+2}.
   H. 8.5×10^{-8} cm in H.
   J. 2.1×10^{-8} cm in H.

5. For a given value of n, the relationship between I and E for all single-electron elements can be approximated by the equation: $I \times c = E$, where c is a constant. Given this information, and the information in the passage, for the single-electron element Be^{+3} with n = 2, if I = 54.2 eV, the value for E would be closest to:

   A. less than 50 eV.
   B. between 50 eV and 75 eV.
   C. between 75 and 100 eV.
   D. greater than 100 eV.

Continued →

6. Based on the information in the passage, which of the following determines the net charge of an atom?

    F. The number of protons only.
    G. The number of electrons only.
    H. The number of neutrons only.
    J. Both the number of protons
        and the number of electrons.

7. For the atoms tested in the passage, which of the following forces kept the electrons in orbit around the nucleus?

    I.   Gravitational force
    II. Electromagnetic force
    III. Frictional force

    A. I only
    B. II only
    C. I and II only
    D. I, II, and III

III
RESEARCH SUMMARIES

Research Summaries passages present descriptions of scientific experiments or studies, along with tables and graphs showing the results. Some of the questions will ask you to evaluate the methods used in the experiment. Most of the questions ask you to interpret the results presented in tables and graphs, just like the Data Representation questions.

1. *RESEARCH SUMMARIES INTRO*

The last chapter showed us that Data Representation passages display *results* of experiments or investigations. Research Summaries passages display results too, but they also discuss the *experimental methods* used to obtain these results. This is the major difference between Research Summaries and Data Representation passages.

> The following clues should help you identify Research Summaries passages:
> - Research Summaries passages typically include "studies," "experiments," "activities," etc. These will usually be indicated with italicized headings within the passage.
> - Each passage typically has **6–7** questions (usually 7).
> - Besides tables and graphs showing results, you may also see figures that display equipment or other parts of the actual experiment.

To get a feel for what these passages look like, check out some of the Research Summaries passages in the ACT book. You should notice the following:

1. A short introduction, which usually explains the *purpose* of the experiments.
2. Two or more *experiments* (sometimes called *studies*, *activities*, etc.). Each experiment includes two things:

    - A description of the experimental method, often supported by a figure.

    - The results of the experiment, usually supported by graphs or tables.

Here's how we'll approach these passages:

READ (OR SKIM) THE INTRODUCTION

If the introduction is short, go ahead and read it. Otherwise, skim it. As with Data Representation passages, circle any identifiers or numbers in the text. These words or numbers should be easy to find, in case they show up later in the experiments or questions.

As you read (or skim) the introduction, try to identify the researcher's *purpose*. In other words, *why* were the experiments conducted? The purpose is often near the end of the introduction. When you spot it, underline it.

SKIM THE EXPERIMENTS

Just as with Data Representation passages, you should expect to *skim* the passage to get some idea of what the passage is about. As before, strive to get through the passage very quickly. Here are the steps:

1. Skim each experiment.

    *   Look for and circle identifiers and numbers in the text.

    *   See if you can note obvious differences between the experiments, especially in terms of the experimental methods. These differences may be found in the text or in the figures. For example, one experiment may be in a lab, and another in "the field." One experiment may test green lizards. Another may test brown lizards. And so on.

2. As with Data Representation passages, try to get a general idea of how information is presented in the figures (graphs, tables, etc.). In particular, read the *labels* and *units* for each figure.

3. Look for labels (and units) that are *repeated* in separate figures. Circle these labels and, if not too inconvenient, connect them with a line. This will clarify connections between the different experiments.

SHORT ON TIME?

Many of the questions on Research Summaries passages relate to only *one* of the experiments. If you're running short on time, you could try tackling these passages one experiment at a time. First, skim the introduction, and then quickly look over the questions for any that only test the introduction (there would be no mention of the specific experiments). Then skim Experiment 1 and look for questions that only mention Experiment 1. And so on.

Keep in mind, this "Short on Time?" approach is not ideal. Since you won't know in advance which questions are easier than others, the goal is always to at least get your eyes on every one. And jumping around in the questions will probably slow you down. But if you're running short on time, tackling the passages in parts will at least allow you to get to a few of the questions.

2. DATA REPRESENTATION: REVISITED

Great news! **About 75% of the questions on the Research Summaries passages are very similar to those on the Data Representation passages.** Questions will ask you to interpret data displayed in graphs, tables, and other figures. At this point, you should feel pretty comfortable with these kinds of questions, so be aggressive. Even if you are challenged by the other types of Research Summaries questions (ones that focus on experimental *methods* rather than *results*), most of the questions should feel very similar to the ones you saw in the last chapter.

UNDERLINE IMPORTANT PARTS OF THE QUESTION

We talked about this in the Data Representation section. You should underline the names of any figures and tables (Figure 1, Table 1, etc.), numbers and units, and any specific materials or test subjects, but now you must pay close attention to specific *experiments* (or *studies*, *activities*, etc.) mentioned in the question. Make sure to stay focused.

■

Go ahead and skim—and markup—the Research Summaries passage on the next page. We'll use this passage to introduce the types of questions you'll typically see with these passages.

Lesson Passage

Temperature plays an important role in plant growth. Three experiments were performed to measure the effects of temperature on corn and soybean plants. The experiments were performed concurrently in the same part of an open-air laboratory.

Experiment 1
A scientist planted 50 pots with 10 corn seeds each. In quantities of 10, pots were inserted into each of 5 temperature chambers. The temperature chambers were designed to maintain a constant temperature while allowing free exposure to sunlight and air. After 40 days, the plants were uprooted, oven-dried, and weighed. The experiment was also performed with soybean seeds. The results are shown in Table 1.

Table 1		
Temperature (°C)	Average mass of plants (g)	
	corn	soybean
0	0.0	0.9
10	5.1	2.8
20	12.2	6.5
30	12.8	2.2
40	5.8	1.0

Experiment 2
The *thermoperiod* is the range of daily temperature. The temperature of each chamber of Experiment 2 varied over 24 hours as shown in the figure below.

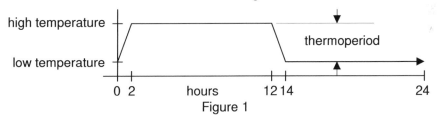

Figure 1

A scientist planted 70 pots with 10 corn seeds each. In quantities of 10, pots were inserted into each of 7 temperature chambers. Each temperature chamber had a low temperature of 20°C and was designed to allow free exposure to sunlight and air. After 40 days, the plants were uprooted, oven-dried, and weighed. The experiment was also performed with soybean seeds. The results are shown in Table 2.

Table 2		
Thermoperiod (°C)	Average mass of plants (g)	
	corn	soybean
0.0	12.2	6.5
2.5	14.8	7.5
5.0	18.2	9.4
7.5	22.5	12.4
10.0	28.0	14.8
12.5	34.1	13.1
15.0	37.0	12.0

Passage continues on next page →

Experiment 3

A scientist planted 10 corn seeds in each of 10 pots located in a location open to direct sunlight. The weights of the plants were measured after 40 days. The experiment was also performed with soybean seeds. During the 40 days, the average low temperature was 11.1°C and the average thermoperiod was 14.0°C. The results are shown in Table 3.

Table 3	
Average mass of plants (g)	
corn	soybean
35.8	12.7

■

(EX) The results of Experiment 1 indicate that, compared to corn plants, soybean plants likely thrive at a:

A. lower temperature because the weight of soybean plants is less than the weight of corn plants at all temperatures.
B. lower temperature because the temperature that yields the highest mass for soybean plants is lower than the temperature that yields the highest mass for corn plants.
C. higher temperature because the weight of soybean plants is greater than the weight of corn plants at 0°C.
D. higher temperature because the temperature that yields the highest mass for soybean plants is higher than the temperature that yields the highest mass for corn plants.

1. Based on the results of Experiment 2, if corn and soybean plants had been grown in a thermoperiod of 17.0°C, the average mass, in grams, of the plants would most likely be:

	corn	soybean
F.	less than 37.0	less than 12.0
G.	greater than 37.0	greater than 12.0
H.	less than 37.0	greater than 12.0
J.	greater than 37.0	less than 12.0

3. RESEARCH METHODS

TERMINOLOGY

In addition to the terms defined in the previous chapter (*independent* and *dependent variables*), you should be familiar with the following terms:

Hypothesis – a statement that explains a set of facts or principles, usually forming a basis for possible experiments to confirm its viability. A hypothesis is *not* yet proven.

Control – a group—sometimes called the *control group*—in a scientific experiment where the factor being tested is not applied. The control group serves as a standard for comparison against another group where the factor *is* applied. For example, if a drug tablet is tested on a group of subjects, another group—the control group—would receive drug-*free* tablets. Note: do not confuse the *control group* with a *controlled variable* (an independent variable).

Constant variable – a "variable" that is not changed throughout a series of experiments.

(EX) Which of the following sets of plants served as the control group in the experiments?

- **A.** The plants in the 0°C chamber of Experiment 1
- **B.** The plants in the 0°C chamber of Experiment 2
- **C.** The plants in Experiment 3
- **D.** There were no sets of plants that served as the control in the experiments.

2. Which of the following factors was NOT directly controlled in Experiment 2?

- **A.** The low temperature of the thermoperiod.
- **B.** The high temperature of the thermoperiod.
- **C.** The number of seeds planted in each pot.
- **D.** The amount of sunlight received by the plants.

THE EXPERIMENTAL METHOD

Most method questions ask about how the experiments were carried out. These questions often ask about *variables*. Why are some things varied and others held constant. For example, in the study of temperature and plants it was important to keep the soil concentrations constant in all experiments. Why? Because the study was testing the effects of *temperature*, not soil concentrations. Knowing what to vary (and, just as important, what *not* to) is one of the keys to conducting an effective experiment:

/ Vary what is being tested, and keep constant what is not.

Here's an example.

(EX) The experiments were performed concurrently in the same laboratory to ensure:

   A. identical planting methods for all samples.
   B. identical soil concentrations for all samples.
   C. that the plants were tested in an ideal growing season and location.
   D. identical sunlight and air conditions, other than temperature, for all samples.

BASIC METHOD QUESTIONS

Some questions simply ask about how the experiment was set up, or why it was set up in a particular way. Here's an example:

3. Which of the following temperature chambers presumably had the same variable effect on the corn and soybean plants?

   A. The 0°C chambers of Experiments 1 and 2.
   B. The 10°C chambers of Experiments 1 and 2.
   C. The 20°C chamber of Experiment 1 and the 0.0°C chamber of Experiment 2.
   D. The 0°C chamber of Experiment 1 and the 10.0°C chamber of Experiment 2.

MISTAKES

Some method questions focus on experimental *mistakes*. Typically, you'll be asked how a mistake might have affected the results.

(EX) In comparing the results of the three experiments, which of the following, if it had occurred, would probably have caused an error in interpreting these results?

    A. The eggs of an insect considered harmless to corn and soybean plants were found on some of the plants.

    B. The temperature chambers were found to reflect some incoming light.

    C. The weather conditions were cloudy for most of the 40 days of the experiments.

    D. The equipment used to control temperature in Experiment 1 was different from the equipment used in Experiment 2.

Try the following question:

4.   If the goal of Experiment 2 was to find the ideal thermoperiod for corn plants and soybean plants, did the scientist meet this goal?

    A. Yes, because the data shows the ideal thermoperiods for both corn plants and soybean plants.

    B. Yes, because the data shows that as thermoperiod increases, plant mass also increases.

    C. No, because the corn plants were not tested at high enough thermoperiods to find the maximum mass.

    D. No, because the soybean plants were not tested at high enough thermoperiods to find the maximum mass.

EQUIPMENT

Some questions focus on the *equipment* or *materials* used in the experiment. Usually, there is a scientific reason for the choice of equipment. These questions can usually be answered with a general scientific knowledge. Look at the following example:

(EX) The scientist in Experiment 1 likely used temperature chambers that allowed for free exposure to sunlight and air because:

- **A.** the plants in Experiment 1 were part of a control group.
- **B.** a transparent enclosure allowed for visual monitoring of the plants.
- **C.** plants would otherwise overheat at some of the temperatures tested in Experiment 1.
- **D.** plants require sunlight and carbon dioxide for photosynthesis to take place.

CHANGES TO EQUIPMENT OR CONDITIONS

Some method problems focus on *changes* to the equipment or materials used in the experiment. They ask how changes might affect the results of the experiment. Again, you can often answer these questions using a general understanding of science.

Try the following question:

5. If the plants used in Experiments 1 and 2 had been grown in an enclosure with artificial lighting, which of the following changes in procedure would be necessary?

- **A.** The lighting brightness would have to be measured and labeled in Tables 1 and 2.
- **B.** The lighting brightness would have to be varied depending on the temperature of the temperature chambers.
- **C.** The plants in Experiment 3 would also have to be grown in an enclosure with artificial lighting.
- **D.** The plants in Experiment 3 would have to be shaded when the artificial lighting is turned off.

LABORATORY EQUIPMENT

Some questions require you to identify types of equipment used in the experiment. You might want to review some of the typical laboratory apparatuses, including:

graduated container or beaker – a glass container marked with units of measurement.

test tube – a hollow cylinder of thin glass with one end closed.

flask – a bottle, usually of glass, having a rounded body and a narrow neck.

stopper – a plug, cork, or other piece for closing a bottle, tube, drain, or the like.

valve – any device for halting or controlling the flow of a liquid, gas, or other material through a passage.

syringe – a small device consisting of a glass tube, narrowed at its outlet, and fitted with a piston for drawing in a quantity of fluid or gas or for ejecting fluid or gas in a stream.

plunger – another name for the piston of a syringe.

dropper – a glass tube with a hollow rubber bulb at one end and a small opening at the other, for drawing in a liquid and expelling it in drops

If you have trouble visualizing any of the above equipment, you can find pictures online. Note that any less-common equipment introduced in a passage will be described for you.

4. *SCIENCE SENSE &*
SCIENCE KNOWLEDGE

SCIENCE SENSE

Some questions require a general understanding of science. In other words, the answers may not always be found directly in the passage, but if you have a good "science sense," the answer is usually clear. Here are some examples:

- Why would a scientist wait several minutes before analyzing the results of a chemical reaction?

    (To make sure the reaction has run to completion.)

- Why would a scale be *tared* (reset to zero) after a container is placed on it but before a substance is added to it?

    (To measure the weight of the substance alone, without the weight of the container.)

- Why are many subjects tested rather than just one?

    (To increase the accuracy of the results.)

If you can answer these questions, you're ahead of the game. Look at the following example:

(EX) Which of the following statements most likely describes an important reason for oven-drying the corn and soybean plants before weighing them?

- **A.** To test any variations in water storage of the plants.
- **B.** To remove any water found in the plants.
- **C.** To test the effects of high heat on the plants.
- **D.** To compare the effects of very high temperatures and relatively low temperatures on the plants.

SCIENCE KNOWLEDGE

You will in fact come across some problems that require specific knowledge of science. Some tests won't have any of these types of questions; other tests may have up to perhaps three or four. (A Science Knowledge example is on the following page.)

It's beyond the scope of this tutorial to get into the nitty gritty of all branches of science (we'd probably quadruple the size of the book). So if you're looking for the highest score possible, you might want to review some of the following basic scientific principles. All of these have shown up on recent ACTs:

CHEMISTRY:

- ☐ **Chemical equations**: Make sure you understand how chemical equations are balanced. You should know that the chemicals on each side of an equation will be the same (for example, if you have oxygen (O) on the left side, you'll see oxygen somewhere on the right side, too), and the number of *atoms* of each chemical on each side will be the same (for example, you might see $6O$ on the left side and $3O_2$ on the right side—in both cases, we have 6 oxygen atoms).
- ☐ **General behavior of gasses, liquids, and solids**: Especially make sure you understand phase diagrams, which show phases of substances in terms of pressure and temperature. Also, make sure you're comfortable with boiling and melting points.
- ☐ **Atomic structure**: You should know the locations and charges of the three basic elements of an atom: protons, neutrons, and electrons.
- ☐ **pH**: This is an important one. Some students think that the higher the pH, the more *acidic* the substance, but the opposite is true (the substance is more *basic*)! You might also memorize that the pH neutral point is 7.

PHYSICS:

- ☐ **Basic equation of motion**: These are sometimes called kinematic equations. They have to do with topics including acceleration and velocity, momentum, and the acceleration of gravity.
- ☐ **Newton's Laws of Motion**: Here's the important one: force = mass × acceleration ($F = ma$). Some students confuse force and mass, especially in regards to gravity.
- ☐ **Fluid mechanics**: Review density and buoyancy (Archimedes' Principle).

BIOLOGY:

- **Cellular biology**: Make sure you understand the common cellular structures and their general functions. Some examples include nuclei (genetics), ribosomes (protein manufacturing), mitochondria (energy production), and chloroplasts (photosynthesis).

- **Genetics**: Understand the following terms: DNA (and its structure), genes (dominant genes, recessive genes, and alleles), and chromosomes. To be safe, you might review the roll of mRNA in the transfer of genetic information.

■

Let's look at an example, similar to the previous question, that requires scientific knowledge:

(EX) The plants in the experiments were oven-dried to remove water. Prior to oven-drying, most of the water would likely be found in which of the following cell structures?

A. Mitochondrion
B. Chloroplast
C. Ribosome
D. Vacuole

■

RESEARCH SUMMARIES SUMMARY

The following outline summarizes the approaches to Research Summaries passages:

- As with Data Representation passages, *skim* the passage. Circle *identifiers* and *numbers* in the text. Also, underline the *purpose* of the experiments (found in the introduction).
- About 75% of the Research Summaries questions test information found in tables, graphs, and other figures, just like the Data Representation questions.
- Memorize terms that have to do with experimental methods (*hypothesis*, *control*, *constant variable*). You might also review *independent (controlled) variables* and *dependent variables* (see Chapter II).
- Be familiar with standard experimental methods, including likely consequences of procedural *mistakes*.
- Be familiar with experimental equipment.
    - Some questions focus on *changes* to the equipment or materials used in the experiment.
    - Review the common types of laboratory equipment.
- You will see a few questions that require some *science knowledge*. Stay aggressive, and try to use *science sense* and guess wisely if necessary.

CONFLICTING VIEWPOINTS PASSAGES

If you're following the **30-hour program**, you probably won't have time to cover the next chapter (Conflicting Viewpoints), but now that you've completed the Research Summaries chapter, you'll be ready to tackle at least 32 of the 40 questions on the Science Test . You should still plan to tackle the Conflicting Viewpoints questions when you take the test. As stated before, you can approach them as you would the passages on the Reading Test. These Conflicting Viewpoints passages tend to be less about tables, graphs, and numbers and more about *reading*. So give them a try. You'll hopefully get some of the easier ones correct.

5. *RESEARCH SUMMARIES PROBLEMS*

PRACTICE PROBLEMS

The Official ACT Prep Guide offers one Research Summaries passage in the "Improving Your Science Score" chapter. For additional practice, we'll use passages from Test 5. See the Tutoring Schedules in the Introduction for more on when to tackle these passages for different programs. Complete these passages *timed* (see the Science Introduction for single-passage timing estimates):

- **The Official ACT Prep Guide: "Improving Your Science Score" chapter:**
  - ☐ Passage II
- **The Official ACT Prep Guide: Test 5:**
  - ☐ Passage II
  - ☐ Passage V
  - ☐ Passage VI
- Additional Research Summaries practice passages (following pages):
  - ☐ Passage I
  - ☐ Passage II
  - ☐ Passage III

■

 PRACTICE TEST (30- and 40-hour programs): After completing practice passages (see the Tutoring Schedules in this tutorial's Introduction), take **Test 3** in the ACT book. You might want to first review Timing (see the Science Introduction). Make sure you have a timing strategy in place before you take the test.

Conflicting Viewpoints: Even though we haven't covered the Conflicting Viewpoints chapter, plan to tackle these questions if time permits. You may have to guess on some of them, but hopefully you can answer the more straightforward questions.

Corrections: And finally, don't forget to correct any missed questions after you grade the test (see below).

TEST CORRECTIONS

After each practice test is graded, you should correct questions related to this chapter that you missed or guessed on. See "Correcting Practice Tests" in the Introduction for more details. Here are the three steps to correcting practice tests:

1. Turn to the Techniques section at the end of this tutorial and circle the Research Summaries *questions* that you missed or guessed on for the test you are correcting. (Some of these may show up on Data Representation passages.)

2. Correct the problems in *The Official ACT Prep Guide*. As you correct the problems, go back to the tutorial and review the techniques. The idea is to: (1) identify techniques that have given you trouble, (2) go back to the tutorial so you can review and strengthen these techniques, and (3) apply these techniques to the specific problems on which you struggled.

3. If you have trouble identifying the best technique to use on a problem, or if you need a hint to head you in the right direction, see the Techniques section at the end of this tutorial.

RESEARCH SUMMARY PASSAGES

Passage I (7 questions = 6:00 min:sec)

Supercooled *sodium acetate* (CH_3COONa) is used in heating pads. A liquid is *supercooled* when it has been cooled below its freezing point without solidifying. When the supercooled liquid is disturbed with a seed crystal, it begins solidifying. The process is *exothermic* (heat is released). Students conducted the following experiments to study the formation and affects of CH_3COONa:

Experiment 1

CH_3COONa is produced when sodium bicarbonate ($NaHCO_3$) and acetic acid (CH_3COOH) are mixed together at a high temperature. Water (H_2O) and carbon dioxide (CO_2) are byproducts of the reaction. Students mixed 1.0 mol of $NaHCO_3$ and 2.0 mol of CH_3COOH in a graduated cylinder. The mixture was heated until boiling occurred. Once water vapor no longer was present, the cylinder was removed from the heat and the composition was analyzed. The procedure was repeated with different quantities of liquids, and the results were recorded in Table 1.

Table 1				
	Quantity (mol)			
Trial	Initial $NaHCO_3$	Initial CH_3COOH	Final $NaHCO_3$	Final CH_3COOH
1	1.0	2.0	0.0	1.0
2	1.0	1.5	0.0	0.5
3	1.5	2.0	0.0	0.5
4	2.0	1.0	1.0	0.0
5	2.0	1.5	0.5	0.0
6	2.0	2.0	0.0	0.0

Based on the data, the following equation was suggested:

$$NaHCO_3 + CH_3COOH + heat \rightarrow CH_3COONa + H_2O + CO_2$$

Experiment 2

The students poured 100 g of liquid CH_3COONa into a large Petri dish, placed the dish into an ice bath, and supercooled the liquid to a temperature T_c. The *velocity of crystallization* is the speed that crystallization expands from the point where a seed crystal is used to initiate the solidification process. Using a high-speed camera, the students measured the velocity of crystallization for various supercooled temperatures. The maximum temperature achieved was also recorded (Table 2).

Table 2		
T_c (°C)	Velocity of crystallization (mm/sec)	Maximum temperature (°C)
40	20	42.8
35	23	42.2
30	26	43.0
25	30	42.5
20	32	42.7

Experiment 3

The students placed 100 g of supercooled liquid CH_3COONa at 30°C in a Petri dish and introduced a seed crystal to begin the solidification process. They measured the maximum temperature achieved, the time to reach the maximum temperature, and the time until the CH_3COONa returned to 30°C. The procedure was repeated for different quantities of liquid CH_3COONa (see Table 3).

Table 3			
CH_3COONa (g)	Maximum temperature (°C)	Time to reach max temp. (sec)	Time to return to 30°C (sec)
100	42.5	42.4	183.9
150	43.5	46.3	191.5
200	43.2	51.0	198.0
250	42.3	54.5	206.2
300	42.9	58.2	212.0

1. Based on the results of Experiment 2, one can reasonably conclude that as the supercooled temperature (T_c) increased, the velocity of crystallization:

   A. decreased only.
   B. increased only.
   C. decreased, then stayed the same.
   D. stayed the same.

2. Based on the results of Experiments 2 and 3, which of the following variables affected the maximum temperature of CH_3COONa?

   F. Supercooled temperature of CH_3COONa
   G. Velocity of crystallization
   H. Weight of CH_3COONa
   J. None of the variables

3. The students measured the temperature of the CH_3COONa by taking the average reading of two thermometers, one at the center of the Petri dish where the seed crystal was introduced and one at the edge of the Petri dish. Based on the results of Experiments 2 and 3, at which mass and supercooled temperature of CH_3COONa would the temperatures of the two thermometers likely show the greatest variation 5 seconds after the solidification process had begun?

   A. 40°C and 300 g
   B. 20°C and 300 g
   C. 40°C and 100 g
   D. 20°C and 100 g

Continued →

4. Based on the results of Experiment 3, which of the following graphs best represents the likely temperature differences between 50 g and 500 g of supercooled CH_3COONa at 30°C when a seed crystal is introduced?

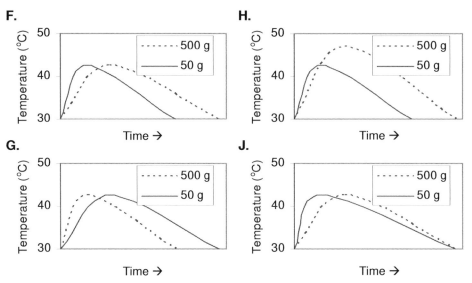

F.

Temperature (°C) vs Time → (500 g, 50 g)

H.

Temperature (°C) vs Time → (500 g, 50 g)

G.

Temperature (°C) vs Time → (500 g, 50 g)

J.

Temperature (°C) vs Time → (500 g, 50 g)

5. Based on the results of Experiment 1, if 3.0 mol of $NaHCO_3$ completely reacted with 3.5 mol CH_3COOH, what amount of $NaHCO_3$ would remain unreacted?

   A. 0.0 mol
   B. 0.5 mol
   C. 3.0 mol
   D. 3.5 mol

6. In Experiment 1, the students wanted to heat the solution until all H_2O and CO_2 had been removed, leaving pure CH_3COONa. Which of the following is the most likely reason why the students heated until no evidence of water vapor was present but did not measure the presence, if any, of CO_2?

   F. CO_2 has a significantly lower freezing point than H_2O.
   G. CO_2 has a significantly higher freezing point than H_2O.
   H. CO_2 has a significantly lower boiling point than H_2O.
   J. CO_2 has a significantly higher boiling point than H_2O.

Continued →

7. Based on the balanced chemical equation in the passage, if 4 moles of water molecules were produced in the reaction, which of the following could describe the chemical reaction that occurred?

   A. 2 moles of sodium acetate reacted with 2 moles of carbon dioxide

   B. 4 moles of sodium acetate reacted with 4 moles of carbon dioxide

   C. 2 moles of sodium bicarbonate reacted with 2 moles of acetic acid

   D. 4 moles of sodium bicarbonate reacted with 4 moles of acetic acid

Passage II (7 questions = 6:00 min:sec)

A *battery* is a device used to supply electricity. A *resistor* is a device that controls the flow of electricity by resisting the flow of current. A *capacitor* is a device that accumulates and stores a charge of electricity. Students set up an electrical circuit consisting of a 12-volt (V) battery, a resistor, a capacitor, and a switch (see Figure 1). The students used a *voltmeter*, a device that measures voltage across a circuit, to study several characteristics of the circuit.

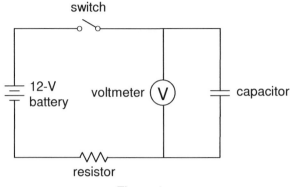

Figure 1

Experiment 1

A capacitor is measured by its *capacitance*, which is a measure of the maximum electrical charge and electrical energy that a capacitor can store. Students created a circuit as shown in Figure 1 with a 5×10^4 ohm (Ω) resistor and a 1×10^{-3} farad (F) capacitor. The switch was closed at time zero and the voltage across the capacitor was recorded. The results are shown in a best-fit curve (see Figure 2).

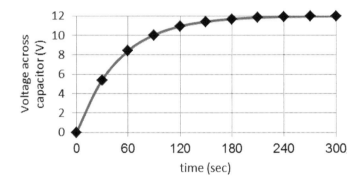

Figure 2

Experiment 2

Students set up the circuit shown in Figure 1 with a 5×10^4 Ω resistor and a 2.0×10^{-3} F capacitor. The students closed the switch and recorded the length of time until the voltage across the capacitor reached 12 V. They performed the experiment with several other capacitors. The results are shown in Table 1.

Table 1	
Capacitance ($\times 10^{-3}$ F)	Time to reach 12 V across capacitor (sec)
2.0	549
2.5	686
3.0	823
3.5	960

Experiment 3

Students set up the circuit shown in Figure 1 with a 4×10^4 Ω resistor and a 1.0×10^{-3} F capacitor. The students closed the switch and recorded the length of time until the voltage across the capacitor reached 12 V. They performed the experiment with several other resistors. The results are shown in Table 2.

Table 2	
Resistance ($\times 10^{14}$ Ω)	Time to reach 12 V across capacitor (sec)
4.0	220
3.0	165
2.0	110
1.0	55

1. The placement of the voltmeter in Figure 1 allowed the students to measure the voltage across the capacitor. Which of the following circuits would have most likely given the same results as those obtained in Experiments 1–3?

A.

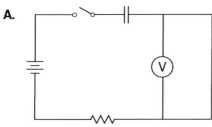

B.

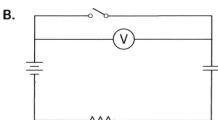

C.

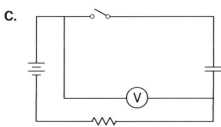

D.

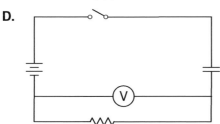

Continued →

2. According to Experiments 1 and 2, if a 1.5×10^{-3} F capacitor had been used, the time required for the voltage across the capacitor to reach 12 V would have been closest to:

    F. less than 300 sec.
    G. between 300 sec and
        549 sec.
    H. between 549 sec and
        960 sec.
    J. greater than 960 sec.

3. Based on Experiments 1 and 2, and assuming a circuit as shown in Figure 1 with a 5×10^4 Ω resistor, which of the following capacitances and times would yield the highest voltage across the capacitor?

    A. 1.0×10^{-3} F at 300 sec
    B. 2.0×10^{-3} F at 400 sec
    C. 3.0×10^{-3} F at 500 sec
    D. 4.0×10^{-3} F at 600 sec

4. The main purpose of Experiment 3 was to determine how varying the:

    F. capacitance affected the time required to reach a certain voltage across the capacitor.
    G. voltage across the capacitor affected the resistance at a given time.
    H. time to reach a certain voltage across the capacitor affected the resistance.
    J. resistance affected the time required to reach a certain voltage across the capacitor.

5. The *time constant* of a circuit is a measure of time equal to the product of the circuit resistance (in ohms) and the circuit capacitance (in farads). Which of the following is closest to the time constant for the circuit used in Experiment 1?

    A. 30 sec
    B. 50 sec
    C. 70 sec
    D. 90 sec

Continued →

6. The students claimed that they did not need to measure the voltage across the capacitor of Experiment 1 for longer than 300 seconds. Do the data in Experiment 1 support their claim?

   F. Yes; the time was sufficient to reach the minimum voltage across the capacitor.
   G. Yes; the time was sufficient to reach the maximum voltage across the capacitor.
   H. No; the time was not sufficient to reach the minimum voltage across the capacitor.
   J. No; the time was not sufficient to reach the maximum voltage across the capacitor.

7. The 12-V battery shown in Figure 1 is connected to the circuit with the positive terminal directly connected to the switch and the negative terminal directly connected to the resistor. When the switch is closed, the electrons flow in the direction(s) indicated by which of the following figures?

A.

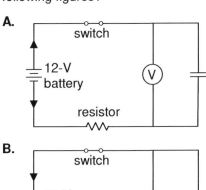

B.

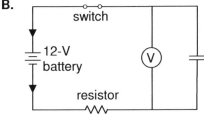

C.

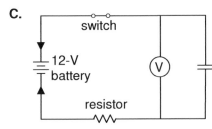

D.

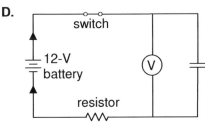

Passage III (6 questions = 5:15 min:sec)

A *top* is a cylindrical or conoidal device that spins on a tapering point. When a top spins, the rotating axis may display a rotational motion, called *precession*, around a line perpendicular to the surface at the point of contact with the top (see Figure 1). The following experiments were performed to study precession.

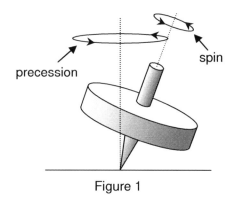

spin

precession

Figure 1

Experiment 1

Scientists used an electric motor to spin a top at a designated spin rate in revolutions per minute (rpm) and release it onto a smooth surface. Table 1 shows the measured precession rate (in rpm) for several spin rates.

Table 1	
Spin rate (rpm)	Precession rate (rpm)
250	16
500	8
800	5
2,000	2

Experiment 2

The height (*h*) of a top is defined as the distance from the point of the top where it meets the surface to the top's center of gravity. Scientists varied the height of the top shown in Figure 1 by extending a lightweight stem from the tip of the top. The electric motor was used to spin the top at a rate of 800 rpm for each trial. The precession rates are shown in Table 2.

Table 2	
h (inches)	Precession rate (rpm)
1	2.5
2	5.0
3	7.5
4	10.0

Experiment 3

Scientists used a falling platform to simulate a reduction of gravitational force acting on the top from Experiment 1. The gravitation force was reduced to 0.5 times the gravity of Earth. The scientists found that for a spin rate of 2,000 rpm, the precession rate was 1 rpm.

1. Which of the following graphs best represents the change in precession rate with the change in spin rate for the top tested in Experiment 1?

A.

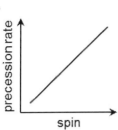

B.

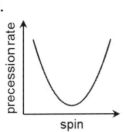

C.

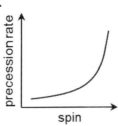

D.

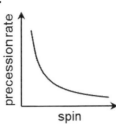

2. According to Experiment 2, a top with a height of 6 inches would have a precession rate of:

   F. 7.5 rpm.
   G. 10.0 rpm.
   H. 12.5 rpm.
   J. 15.0 rpm.

3. Which of the following experiments should a scientist perform to investigate the effect of a top's mass on the precession rate?

   A. Measure precession rates of tops of equal mass but different shapes, while keeping spin rate constant
   B. Measure precession rates of tops of equal mass but different shapes, while varying spin rates
   C. Measure precession rates of tops made from different metals, while keeping spin rate constant
   D. Measure precession rates of tops made from different metals, while varying spin rates

4. Based on the results of Experiment 2, what is the most likely value of h for the top used in Experiment 1?

   F. 5 inches
   G. 4 inches
   H. 3 inches
   J. 2 inches

Continued →

5. Given the information provided in Experiment 3, if a scientist wanted to test the hypothesis that precession rate is related to gravity, the scientist should repeat the experiment by:

    A. varying the acceleration of the falling platform.

    B. varying the velocity of the falling platform.

    C. varying the spin rate of the top.

    D. varying the height of the top.

6. In Experiment 1, the top was likely released onto a smooth surface in order to:

    F. maintain a constant precession rate while the spin rate was measured.

    G. maintain a constant spin rate while the precession rate was measured.

    H. accurately determine the difference between spin rate and precession rate.

    J. accurately measure the height of the top.

IV

CONFLICTING VIEWPOINTS

Conflicting Viewpoints passages present usually two viewpoints (occasionally more) on a given topic. The questions test your understanding of the topic and each viewpoint. Some questions will ask you to compare the viewpoints.

1. CONFLICTING VIEWPOINTS INTRODUCTION

At a glance, Conflicting Viewpoints passages look quite different from Data Representation and Research Summaries passages because they are typically mostly *text*, with few, if any, figures. This can make them more difficult, especially if the preceding chapters have you feeling comfortable interpreting the data found in figures. Conflicting Viewpoints passages usually don't display results. Rather, they introduce two or more theories or hypotheses based on some scientific topic.

The following clues should help you identify Conflicting Viewpoints passages:
- Conflicting Viewpoints passages typically include the viewpoints of different *people*, that is "scientists," "students," "researchers," etc., or you might see different "hypotheses." Generally, each viewpoint will be indicated with an italicized heading within the passage.
- While there are exceptions, these passages usually have few, if any, figures. Thus, most of a Conflicting Viewpoints passage is usually *text*.
- Each passage typically has **6-8** questions (usually 7).

Conflicting Viewpoints passages usually include the following:
1. An introduction, which will usually clearly explain what the scientists are debating.
2. Two or more *viewpoints*.

Here's how we'll approach these passages:

READ—YES, *READ*—THE PASSAGE

Unlike Data Representation and Research Summaries passages, most students should plan to actually *read* Conflicting Viewpoints passages. This does not mean that you'll have time to read *carefully*, and most students will probably have only a *blurry* understanding of what's going on. But, like the Reading section, it's important to actually get through the whole passage before turning to the questions.

/ **Read Conflicting Viewpoints passages before answering questions, but read *quickly*.**

Below are the steps:

1. Read the Introduction:
   - **Look for and circle identifiers.** Remember, identifiers are usually "interesting nouns." As with other science passages, words in italics are usually good identifiers. But since the actual text of Conflicting Viewpoints passages is more important than it is with the other passage types—and since you're actually *reading* the text, rather than just skimming—you should plan to circle additional identifiers. As with the Reading test, identifiers are the key to quickly finding information in the passage when you start answering the questions.
   - Identify the *purpose*, or central dilemma, of the passage. In other words, what are the scientists arguing about? The purpose is often near the end of the introduction. When you spot it, underline it.
2. Read the first viewpoint:
   - Once again, circle identifiers as you read.
   - The most important thing to look for is the scientist's *main argument*. What is the scientist's position on the subject? **Usually, the scientist's main point is found in the first sentence. Underline it.**
3. Read the second viewpoint (and so on):
   - As described above, look for and underline the main argument of the viewpoint and mark up identifiers and other important parts of the passage. In addition, now you can start to *compare* the two viewpoints. Ask yourself the following questions:
     - How are the main arguments different? How are they the same?
     - Do the scientists use different evidence or data?
     - Is some of the evidence or data the same but the scientists' *interpretations* different?

SHORT ON TIME?

As with Research Summaries passages, many of the questions on Conflicting Viewpoints passages relate to only *one* of the viewpoints. If you're running short on time, you could try tackling these passages one viewpoint at a time. For example, you might check the questions and notice that several questions only test Scientist 1's viewpoint. You could just focus on this one scientist, before running out of time.

We'll repeat what we said about this approach earlier: It's never great leaving questions blank, especially without at least *looking* at them. But if you're running short on time, tackling the Conflicting Viewpoints passage in parts will at least allow you to get to a few of the questions.

Go ahead and read—and markup—the Conflicting Viewpoints passage below. We'll use this passage to introduce the types of questions you'll typically see with these passages.

Lesson Passage

The Doppler effect describes the perceived shift in frequency of acoustic or electromagnetic radiation emitted by a source moving relative to an observer. The shift is to higher frequencies when the source approaches and to lower frequencies when it recedes. Two scientists discuss how the Doppler effect helps reveal the nature of the Universe.

Scientist 1

The Universe is expanding. Observations show that there is a Doppler shift in the light spectra from distant stars and galaxies. Just as the frequency of sound decreases as two objects depart, decreasing the sound's pitch, the frequency of light decreases, creating what is known as a red shift of the light. No matter what direction we aim our telescopes, the light from distant stars is "seen" at a lower frequency than what would be seen from a static star. So the Universe must have started as a point in space. And at this beginning, a "big bang" sent all matter expanding in all directions.

Scientist 2

The Universe is contracting. The idea of our three-dimensional Universe expanding indefinitely in all directions creates the uncomfortable mathematical notion of infinity. Also problematic is the idea that the Universe stops (what would be on the "other side"?). The most likely scenario is that our three-dimensional Universe is bent into a fourth dimension that we are unable to observe. To help imagine this scenario, consider a two-dimensional Universe in the shape of a globe, a Universe with a finite size and no ends. The tiny two-dimensional beings on this globe have no sense of the third-dimension (just as we have no sense of the fourth-dimension). Now imagine that a "big bang" occurred in the North Pole of this globe. All matter would begin heading to the South Pole. One might think that as an object approaches the South Pole, the objects around it would appear to draw closer together, but this in not the case. Because of the gravitational pull of the slowly accumulating objects in the South Pole, objects closer to the pole will accelerate faster than objects farther away. So in a contracting, post-"big bang" Universe, the Doppler effect would still show stars and galaxies moving away from us in all directions.

2. DIRECT QUESTIONS

As we said, most of the questions test just *one* part of the passage (one of the viewpoints or the introduction). These passages are similar to Reading Test passages in that you must answer questions using *context*, that is, the information given in the passage. Like most of the ACT Science Test, the subject will often sound confusing. But, again, don't worry about your knowledge of science. Just worry about the information given in the passage. The information you need to answer direct questions is found in the passage. Let's look at an example:

(EX) Which of the following figures best represents the relationship of movement and perceived frequency described by the Doppler effect?

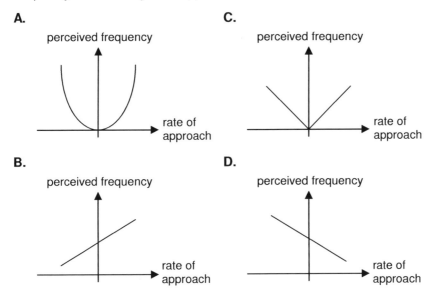

A.

B.

C.

D.

Now try Question 1:

1. Which of the following does Scientist 1 suggest is evidence of an expanding Universe?
   A. The light from nearby stars is perceived at a lower frequency than the light from more distant stars.
   B. The light from distant stars is perceived at a higher frequency than the light from closer stars.
   C. The light from distant stars is perceived at a lower frequency than the light from a theoretical star not moving away from the Earth.
   D. The light from distant stars is perceived at a higher frequency than the light from a theoretical star not moving away from the Earth.

3. INDIRECT QUESTIONS

Some questions will require you to interpret information given in the passage. These are similar to the Extended Reasoning questions found on the Reading Test. The information is still in the passage, but you might have to *interpret* that information to find the correct answer. Look at the following example:

(EX) Scientist 2 likely uses a two-dimensional world to illustrate his views because:

   A. the Earth-space is actually two-dimensional.
   B. all matter in the Universe moves only in two dimensions.
   C. a three-dimensional space would have to extend infinitely in all directions.
   D. readers would not be able to imagine the added dimension in a three-dimensional world.

Try the following question:

2. According to Scientist 2, which of the following affects the relative speed of two objects?

   A. The initial velocity of objects after a "big bang."
   B. The relative proximity to a gravitational pull.
   C. The distance between the two objects.
   D. The number of space dimensions in which the objects are found.

4. COMPARISONS

DIFFERENCES

The ACT calls these passages *Conflicting* Viewpoints, so it's no surprise that some of the questions will ask you to identify *differences* between the viewpoints. Some questions will ask about differences in the main arguments of the scientists. Harder questions will focus on specific details, such as the specific evidence used by the scientists. Look at the following example:

(EX) One of the primary differences between the two viewpoints is that:

    A. Scientist 1 uses direct observations while Scientist 2 uses a theoretical model.
    B. Scientist 1 uses evidence of a Doppler shift to explain his viewpoint while Scientist 2 considers the evidence false.
    C. Only Scientist 1 believes that all matter originated from a "big bang."
    D. Only Scientist 2 believes that a multi-dimensional Universe exists.

SIMILARITIES

Some questions will ask you to identify similarities in the viewpoints. Try the following question:

3. The views of both scientists are similar in that they both agree that:

    A. the Universe is expanding.
    B. the Universe is contracting.
    C. stars and galaxies appear to be moving away from us.
    D. because there is no observable fourth dimension, the Universe must be infinite.

5. CONFLICTING VIEWPOINTS ODDS & ENDS

NEW INFORMATION

We've covered questions that test new information in the Data Representation section. These types of questions are common on Conflicting Viewpoints passages. As discussed before, these questions provide new information in the question—perhaps a new material or test subject, perhaps a new definition or hypothesis—that is clearly not found in the passage. Sometimes these questions begin with the words "Suppose that . . ."

Typically the challenge to these is connecting the new information to the information given in the passage. We'll see an example of a question that tests new information below.

STRENGTHS

You might be asked to discuss the *strengths* of a viewpoint, or to identify evidence that *supports* a viewpoint. The following example also tests new information:

(EX) In 1965, two radio astronomers discovered a background "hiss" of stray microwaves in whatever direction they aimed their receiver. Scientists at the time said that these background microwaves were evidence of radiation left over from the "big bang." If this discovery were true, would it support the primary viewpoint of Scientist 1?

    A. Yes, because background microwaves would show measurable Doppler shifts just as light does.
    B. Yes, because the discovery provides evidence that all matter originated at a point in space.
    C. No, because Scientist 1 uses light waves, not microwaves, to provide evidence of a "big bang."
    D. No, because the discovery weakens the idea of an expanding Universe.

KEEP IT SIMPLE

Conflicting Viewpoints questions sometimes sound difficult, but try to *keep it simple*. For example, in the question above, did you really need to understand the idea of "background microwaves" and "radiation"? Probably not. Just ask yourself, does Scientist 1 support the idea of a big bang? The simple answer is *yes*.

WEAKNESSES

You might be asked to identify *weaknesses* in a viewpoint. These could be a result of *assumptions*, as discussed in the introduction, or you might be asked to look at *evidence* that weakens a viewpoint. Try the following question:

4. According to Scientist 2, a major flaw in Scientist 1's viewpoint is the notion that:
    - **A.** the shift in light frequency between departing objects is red.
    - **B.** the Universe must have started with a "big bang."
    - **C.** the Universe is infinite.
    - **D.** stars that appear static are actually moving away from us.

MORE THAN TWO VIEWPOINTS

Many Conflicting Viewpoints passages include more than two viewpoints. Sometimes the viewpoints may be relatively short, and the introduction will be relatively long. Turn to Passage I in the next section (page 734) to get a visual sense of what these passages look like.

Here are some important guidelines to remember when tackling these types of passages:
- The introductions to these passages are often harder to understand than the actual viewpoints. You should still read the introduction, but don't worry about understanding it completely. Look for "easy stuff" (see the Reading section), and circle your identifiers so you can find information later, if necessary.
- Don't forget to look for the purpose of the experiment(s) in the introduction.
- You'll probably see one or more questions that relate to the introduction only (no mention of the actual viewpoints). If the introduction is difficult, tackle these questions *last*. The questions that focus on the viewpoints are often easier.

■

CONFLICTING VIEWPOINTS SUMMARY

The following outline summarizes the approaches to Conflicting Viewpoints passages:

- *Read* the passage, looking for *identifiers* and the *main argument* for each viewpoint.
- Answer *direct questions* using context.
- Answer *indirect questions* by *interpreting* the context.
- Be prepared to *compare* the viewpoints. Think about *similarities* and *differences*.
- Expect to see questions that introduce *new information*.
- Be prepared to identify *strengths* and *weaknesses* in the viewpoints.
- Even when the passage and questions sound hard, always try to *keep it simple*.

6. CONFLICTING VIEWPOINTS PROBLEMS

PRACTICE PROBLEMS

The Official ACT Prep Guide offers one Conflicting Viewpoints passage in the "Improving Your Science Score" chapter. For additional practice, we'll use a passage from Test 5. See the Tutoring Schedules in the Introduction for more on when to tackle these passages for different programs. Complete these passages *timed* (see the Science Introduction for single-passage timing estimates):

- **The Official ACT Prep Guide: "Improving Your Science Score" chapter:**
  - ☐ Passage III
- **The Official ACT Prep Guide: Test 5***
  - ☐ Passage IV
- Additional Conflicting Viewpoints practice passages (following pages):
  - ☐ Passage I
  - ☐ Passage II
  - ☐ Passage III

■

> **PRACTICE TEST (40-hour program):** After completing several practice passages, as listed in the 40-hour Tutoring Schedule (see the Introduction), you should take **Test 3** in the ACT book. Don't forget to correct any missed questions after you grade the test (see below).

TEST CORRECTIONS

After each practice test is graded, you should correct questions related to this chapter that you missed or guessed on. See "Correcting Practice Tests" in the Introduction for more details. Here are the three steps to correcting practice tests:

1. Turn to the Techniques section at the end of this tutorial and circle the Research Summaries questions that you missed or guessed on for the test you are correcting.

2. Correct the problems in *The Official ACT Prep Guide*. As you correct the problems, go back to the tutorial and review the techniques. The idea is to: (1) identify techniques that have given you trouble, (2) go back to the tutorial so you can review and strengthen these techniques, and (3) apply these techniques to the specific problems on which you struggled.

3. If you have trouble identifying the best technique to use on a problem, or if you need a hint to head you in the right direction, see the Techniques section at the end of this tutorial.

■

Before tackling Passage I on the following pages, review "More Than Two Viewpoints" in the previous section.

CONFLICTING VIEWPOINTS PASSAGES

Passage I (7 questions = 6:00 min:sec)

Some bacteria contain small circular DNA molecules called *plasmids. Plasmid replication*, in which the plasmid produces a linear copy of itself, is not tied to chromosomal replication, but rather occurs autonomously by a method called *rolling-circle replication*. In rolling-circle replication, a replication initiator protein called *RepA* binds to a section of the plasmid called the *origin of replication*. The RepA recruits a *helicase* that unwinds the DNA. As the DNA unwinds it becomes coded by *single-strand DNA binding proteins*, until a replication of one strand of the original DNA is complete, with the genes in an identical order to that of the original plasmid. The single-stranded DNA can now in turn be replicated. A region of the DNA becomes looped, allowing *RNA polymerase* to access the DNA and act as a primer for the synthesis of DNA. The final double-stranded DNA is a replication of the original plasmid.

In an experiment, a particular plasmid with six genes (B, O, R, G, E, and S) was allowed to replicate. The six genes were equally spaced around the plasmid. The results of the experiment indicated that the entire plasmid was copied in 72 minutes and that the rate of gene transfer remained constant during the experiment. Four students were asked about the order in which the genes replicated. The students presented four models.

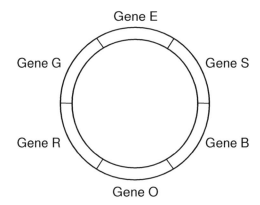

Student 1

Replication always begins between Gene S and Gene B, with Gene B replicated first and Gene S replicated last.

Student 2

Replication always begins between Gene S and Gene B, and replication may move in either direction, either beginning with Gene B and ending with Gene S or beginning with Gene S and ending with Gene B.

Student 3

Replication can begin between any two genes. Once initiated, the replication will always move in a clockwise direction (with respect to the figure).

Student 4

Replication can begin between any two genes and proceed in either direction.

1. Based on the information in the passage, if the replication process was interrupted after 24 minutes, how many genes would have been completely transferred?

   A. 2
   B. 3
   C. 4
   D. 5

2. Suppose the replication process was interrupted and only Genes G, E, and S had completely transferred. These results could agree with which of the following students?

   F. Student 1 only
   G. Student 2 only
   H. Students 3 and 4 only
   J. Students 2, 3, and 4 only

3. Suppose that a replication initiator bound to a section of the plasmid between Genes E and S. After 36 minutes, only Genes S, B, and O had NOT been transferred. This result agrees with the viewpoint of which of the following student(s)?

   A. Student 2 only
   B. Student 3 only
   C. Student 4 only
   D. Student 2 and 3 only

4. Suppose replication had been interrupted after 48 minutes and 4 Genes were completely transferred, including Gene E and Gene S. Based on the model presented by Student 3, which of the following could have been the first gene to transfer.

   F. Gene O
   G. Gene G
   H. Gene B
   J. Gene S

Continued →

5. Suppose replication was interrupted and the last gene to completely transfer was Gene R. Based on the model presented by Student 1, which of the following could be the time, in minutes, before replication was interrupted?

   A. 24
   B. 32
   C. 42
   D. 48

6. According to the passage, which of the following structures is required to replicate a single-stranded DNA into a double-stranded DNA?

   F. RepA
   G. helicase
   H. single-strand DNA
      binding proteins
   J. RNA polymerase

7. Suppose that plasmids only exist in prokaryotic cells. Based on this information, rolling circle replication most likely takes place in which of the following cell structures?

   A. Mitochondria
   B. Ribosomes
   C. Nuclei
   D. Cytoplasm

Page intentionally left blank.

Passage II (7 questions = 6:00 min:sec)

An experiment involving a frictionless pendulum was conducted to determine the final heights of two spheres of different masses.

In the first experiment, a 1 kg sphere, Sphere A, was released from rest at Point X (height h_i). The velocity of the sphere was measured at Point Y, and the final height h_f was measured after the sphere passed Point Y and reached the maximum height before swinging back toward Point Y. The experiment was repeated with a 2 kg sphere, Sphere B. See Figure 1.

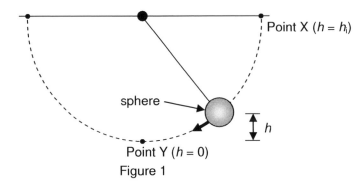

Point X ($h = h_i$)

sphere

h

Point Y ($h = 0$)

Figure 1

A teacher provided 3 students with the following definitions:

1. *PE*, the potential energy of a sphere due to the force of gravity, equals mgh, where m is the sphere's mass, g is the acceleration of the sphere due to the Earth's gravity, and h is the height of the sphere above Point Y. The *PE* of a sphere at Point X is notated as PE_X.
2. *KE*, the kinetic energy of a sphere, equals $\frac{1}{2}mv^2$, where v is the velocity of a sphere. The *KE* of a sphere at Point Y is notated as KE_Y.
3. *MO*, the momentum of a sphere, equals mv. The *MO* of a sphere at Point Y is notated as MO_Y.

The teacher asked the students to predict which sphere, if either, had the greatest maximum height, as measured in the experiments.

Student 1

When a sphere was released from Point X and began to fall by the acceleration of gravity g, its *PE* was converted to kinetic energy. When the sphere reached Point Y, all of the sphere's *PE* had been converted to kinetic energy. Based on Definition 1, because Sphere B had a greater mass m than did Sphere A (but equal g and h_i), Sphere B had a greater PE_X. Thus, Sphere B had a greater KE_Y than did Sphere A, and Sphere B reached a greater final height than did Sphere A.

Student 2

Because the two spheres had the same g and h_i, they had the same velocity at point Y. Based on Definition 3, because Sphere B had a greater m than did Sphere A, Sphere B had a greater MO_Y than did Sphere A, and Sphere B reached a greater final height than did Sphere A.

Student 3

Because the two spheres had the same g and h_i, they had the same velocity at point Y. Thus, the final height of Sphere A would equal that of Sphere B.

The results of the study are shown in Table 1.

Table 1					
Sphere	h_i (m)	PE_X (joules)	MO_Y (kg·m/s)	KE_Y (joules)	h_f (m)
A	1.0	9.8	4.4	9.8	1.0
B	1.0	19.6	8.8	19.6	1.0

1. Consider the statement "The mass of the sphere does not determine its final height." This statement is consistent with the prediction(s) of which of the following students?

   A. Student 1 only
   B. Student 3 only
   C. Students 2 and 3 only
   D. Students 1, 2, and 3

2. Suppose a third sphere, Sphere C, has a mass of 3.0 kg. Based on Definition 3 and Student 2's statements, will the momentum of Sphere C at Point Y be greater than, less than, or the same as the momentum of Sphere B at point Y?

   F. Greater, because the mass of Sphere C is greater than the mass of Sphere B.
   G. Greater, because the velocity at Point Y of Sphere C is greater than the velocity at Point Y of Sphere B.
   H. Less, because the velocity at Point Y of Sphere C is less than the velocity at Point Y of Sphere B.
   J. The same, because the velocity at Point Y of Sphere C is equal to the velocity at Point Y of Sphere B.

3. Based on Student 1's statements, which of following measurements is not dependent on a sphere's mass?

   A. h_i
   B. h_f
   C. PE_X
   D. KE_Y

4. Based on Table 1 and Definition 2, how did the velocity of Sphere A at Point Y compare to the velocity of Sphere B at Point Y? The velocity of Sphere A at Point Y was:

   F. ¼ as great.
   G. ½ as great.
   H. the same.
   J. 2 times as great.

Continued →

5. According to Table 1, PE_X equals KE_Y for each sphere. Which of following laws best explains this equality?

    A. Conservation of Gravity
    B. Conservation of Momentum
    C. Conservation of Mass
    D. Conservation of Energy

6. Consider the students' hypotheses about which sphere, if either, had the greatest maximum final height. Based on the results of the study, which of the students' predictions, if any, was (or were) correct?

    F. Student 1's only
    G. Student 1's and Student 2's only
    H. Student 3's only
    J. None of the students

7. Suppose that the study had been conducted on the Moon instead of on Earth. Based on Definition 1 and the statements of Student 1, would Sphere A have a greater KE_Y on Earth or on the Moon?

    A. The Earth, because the acceleration due to gravity on the Moon is greater than the acceleration due to gravity on Earth.
    B. The Earth, because the acceleration due to gravity on the Moon is less than the acceleration due to gravity on Earth.
    C. The Moon, because the acceleration due to gravity on the Moon is greater than the acceleration due to gravity on Earth.
    D. The Moon, because the acceleration due to gravity on the Moon is less than the acceleration due to gravity on Earth.

Page intentionally left blank.

Passage III (7 questions = 6:00 min:sec)

Bark beetles bore through the outer bark of trees and attract mates. The female beetles carve galleries in the inner bark to lay eggs. When the eggs hatch, the larvae burrow deeper into the inner bark and spread a fungus. Eventually, the fungus can spread to the *sapwood* of the inner tree, which is the part of the tree that conducts water from the roots to the leaves or needles. If the tree cannot fight off the beetles with enough resin to force them out or drown them, the fungus will eventually cut the veins that carry the water, and the tree dies. Two scientists discuss the impact of bark beetles on forests in the Western United States.

Scientist 1

Bark beetles increase the risk of wildfires by killing trees, leaving them dry and susceptible to wildfires. When trees die, they drop their needles to the ground. The risk may be short-lived, but as long as the needles still contain resin, the potential for surface fires is greatly increased. In addition, there is an increase in the potential for a crown fire in the early stages of a beetle epidemic, when the forest is a mixture of dead, dying, and living trees. Over the past twenty years, the beetles have spread across more than 100 million acres of forest, leaving dead and dying pine, spruce, and fir trees in their wake. These dead trees quickly lose moisture, and, combined with rising temperatures and less precipitation, leave the forests of the West in a state of great fire danger.

Scientist 2

Rather than increase the risk of wildfires, bark beetles actually reduce the risk by thinning tree crowns. As pine trees die, they drop their needles, needles that otherwise would fuel fast-moving wildfires from treetop to treetop. Without this tree-crown fuel, wildfires are slower-moving and easier to contain. Furthermore, there is no evidence to suggest that the fallen needles have any effect on wildfires. Wildfires feed on larger sources of fuel, such as fallen branches and larger limbs of the trees. To study the effects of bark beetles, scientists set up "dummy" trees to attract the beetles and then used computer models to predict fire behavior in the areas infested by the beetles. The models showed that the beetles actually reduced the threat of wildfires, even as surrounding areas, unaffected by bark beetles, showed greatly increased wildfire threats because of drought and higher temperatures.

1. One of the major points of difference between the two scientists is that:

   A. Scientist 1 is more concerned about the short-term effects of beetle infestation than is Scientist 2.
   B. Scientist 1 believes that beetles are killing trees while Scientist 2 does not.
   C. Scientist 1 discounts the role of crown fires in the spread of wildfires while Scientist 2 emphasizes the role of crown fires.
   D. Scientist 1 uses computer models as evidence while Scientist 2 references historical records.

2. According to the passage, which of the following would most likely help a tree survive during an infestation of bark beetles?

    F. Increased resin production

    G. Thicker outer layers of bark

    H. Reduced needles production

    J. Denser wood in the inner bark

3. New data suggests that the intensity and duration of wildfires in the Western United States has increased over the past twenty years even though the average temperature has remained the same and average precipitation has increased. Based on the information provided in the passage, this finding would most likely *weaken* the primary viewpoint(s) of:

    A. Scientist 1 only.

    B. Scientist 2 only.

    C. both Scientist 1 and Scientist 2.

    D. neither Scientist 1 nor Scientist 2.

4. According to Scientist 2, which of the following is NOT a factor in wildfire danger?

    F. Fallen tree limbs

    G. Drought and higher temperatures

    H. Fallen needles and leaves

    J. Thinning tree crowns

5. Scientist 2 would most likely agree that wildfire danger *decreases* as:

    A. tree foliage increases.

    B. bark beetle populations decrease.

    C. tree density decreases.

    D. dead-tree moisture decreases.

Continued →

6. According to the passage, both scientists would agree that the risk of wildfires, at least in part, is increased by:

   F. an increase of needles on the forest surface.
   G. the spread of fungus in trees' sapwood.
   H. environmental factors other than bark beetles.
   J. human's encroachment into previously protected forests.

7. Suppose that a tree dies and begins to drop its needles 100 days after the first bark beetle larvae are hatched. Based on the statements of Scientist 1, which of the following graphs best represents the risk of a surface fire over the following 200 days:

A.

C.

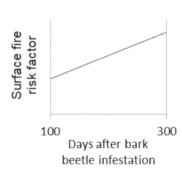

B.

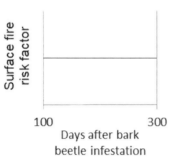

D.

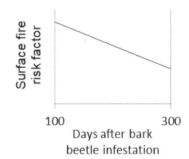

PART **5**

TECHNIQUES

TECHNIQUES

One of the keys to improving your ACT scores is learning from your mistakes. As stated throughout this tutorial, you should go back to practice tests and correct questions that relate to chapters, as these chapters are completed. These correction assignments, and the specific questions to (potentially) correct, are at the ends of chapters.

As you correct questions, you need to make sure that you're using the correct KlassTutoring techniques. The following pages list the techniques, as taught in this tutorial, for every question in *The Official ACT Prep Guide* (the most recent version, at the time of this writing).

Note that on the following pages, the actual answers are <u>not</u> given. The point of this section is to give you direction, by listing techniques and, often, hints. This will help you tackle problems using the techniques you've learned and give you an idea of what lessons to review in the tutorial.

Each subtest (English, Math, Reading, and Science) presents techniques differently, as described below.

ENGLISH

Eliminating answer choices is an important part of tackling the ACT English questions. Recognizing errors in the answer choices also gives you a good idea of what technique or techniques are being tested on a particular question. **For each question on the following pages, the given technique or techniques apply to *all incorrect answer choices*, unless labeled otherwise.** For example, look at the following question:

    1.   Run-ons / + Pronouns (Agreement) (B)

Here's what this means: <u>All three</u> incorrect answer choices have Run-on errors. *In addition*, answer choice B (and <u>only B</u>) has a Pronouns (Agreement) error.

Here's a similar example:

2. Run-ons (A, C) / Pronouns (Agreement) (B)

Now, <u>only A and C</u> have Run-on errors, and <u>only B</u> has a Pronouns (Agreement) error.

As you correct missed questions, look at your answer sheet, and make sure to focus on the technique or techniques associated with *your* incorrect answer.

MATH

You may be able to solve some math questions with more than one technique. Which technique is best is often a personal decision, based on your own strengths and weaknesses, and sometimes it may be a good idea to review *all* given techniques for a missed problem. Often, the more ways you can tackle a problem, the better.

THE PICK TRICKS

You will notice that the Pick Tricks (Pick Numbers or Pick Answers) show up frequently, either as preferred methods, or as optional ones. For most students, we recommend using a Pick Trick when one is given. It's good practice. These techniques are designed to get you out of jams, so make sure you're comfortable with them.

READING

The Reading techniques typically provided two pieces of information: question types and line numbers (context).

QUESTION TYPES

Knowing what type of question you're answering is an important part of the Reading Test. If you have trouble identifying any of these questions types, make sure to review the magnifying glass information in the Reading part of this tutorial. Of course, pay attention to the types of questions that you frequently miss, and review these sections in the tutorial.

LINE NUMBERS (CONTEXT)

The most important technique for Reading questions is the use of *context*. The answers must be clearly stated or supported by *the text*. If you miss a Reading question, you must find the part of the passage that contains the information or evidence that will lead you to the correct answer. The following pages display the pertinent line numbers for each question. When necessary, clarifying words or phrases are sometimes included.

For EXCEPT/NOT questions, we'll often list the line numbers for the *incorrect* answer choices.

Of course, finding the context is only part of it. You have to *understand* the context, not to mention the language in the questions and the answer choices. If you still have trouble with a question even after you have found the appropriate context in the passage, check the solutions in the ACT book.

Note that on the following pages we generally only refer to context related to *correct* answers. Of course, you may often choose to use context to *eliminate* answer choices. This is encouraged, especially when you are not sure of the correct answer. Again, the solutions in the ACT book may be helpful.

SCIENCE

As stated in the Science Introduction, each question is categorized by *question* type (Usage/Mechanics, Rhetorical Skills, and Conflicting Viewpoints), regardless of what type of *passage* the question shows up on.

As you review the solutions, you'll notice that we simply provide the name of the technique for many of the (easier) Science questions. We recommend reviewing related sections in the tutorial for the techniques you miss frequently. For most questions, we provide hints. It's always a good idea to attempt corrections on your own, before checking the solutions, but if you still have trouble with a question even after you have reviewed the technique in this tutorial and read our hint, if there is one, the solutions in the ACT book can be helpful.

1. TECHNIQUES: TEST 1

QUESTIONS BY SECTIONS/CHAPTERS

The following information lists every question on the test according to its relevant chapter or section in this tutorial. If you're correcting a test, circle the question numbers below that you missed or guessed on. Make sure to follow the Tutoring Schedule in the Introduction to know when to correct or tackle various types of questions.

ENGLISH	
Usage/Mechanics	Rhetorical Skills
[1, 2, 3, 5, 7, 8, 9, 10, 11, 12, 14] [16, 17, 18, 19, 20, 21, 22, 24, 25, 27, 28] [31, 33, 34, 35, 36, 38, 39, 41, 42, 43] [46, 47, 48, 49, 50, 51, 53, 56, 58] [61, 63, 64, 66, 67, 69, 71, 72, 73]	[4, 6, 13, 15] [23, 26, 29, 30] [32, 37, 40, 44, 45] [52, 54, 55, 57, 59, 60] [62, 65, 68, 70, 74, 75]

Brackets display separate passages.

MATH*							
Basic Concepts	Arith.	Algebra	Adv. Algebra	Geometry	Func-tions	Trig	Odds/ Ends
2, 25, 26	7, 12, 13, 28, 33, 41, 46, 54, 56, 60	1, 3, 9, 10, 23, 29, 38, 43, 51, 52, 53	15, 19, 47	4, 5, 6, 8, 11, 14, 16, 17, 21, 22, 31, 32, 34, 35, 36, 37, 45, 55, 59	18, 49	30, 39, 58	20, 27, 40, 42, 44, 48, 50, 57

*no KlassTutoring technique for #24

READING (by question type and passage)*							
Direct	Extended Reasoning	Purpose	Main Idea	Comparison	Tone	Words in Context
4, 5, 6, 7, 8, 10, 11, 16, 17, 23, 24, 25, 27, 29, 30, 33, 35, 36, 37, 38, 39, 40	9, 14, 15, 22, 26	2, 13, 21	1, 28, 31, 34	18, 19, 20	3	
Prose Fiction	Social Science	Humanities		Natural Science
1, 2, 3, 4, 5, 6, 7, 8, 9, 10	11, 12, 13, 14, 15, 16, 17, 18, 19, 20	21, 22, 23, 24, 25, 26, 27, 28, 29, 30		31, 32, 33, 34, 35, 36, 37, 38, 39, 40

Other: #12 and #32 (rhetorical devices: see Reading Introduction)

SCIENCE (by question type and passage)*		
Data Representation	Research Summaries	Conflicting Viewpoints
1, 2, 3, 4, 6, 7, 8, 11, 12, 21, 23, 25, 29, 30, 31, 33, 35, 36, 37, 38, 39, 40	5, 9, 10, 13, 22, 24, 26, 27, 28, 32, 34	14, 15, 16, 17, 18, 19, 20
[1, 2, 3, 4, 5, 6] [35, 36, 37, 38, 39, 40]	[7, 8, 9, 10, 11, 12, 13] [21, 22, 23, 24, 25, 26, 27] [28, 29, 30, 31, 32, 33, 34]	[14, 15, 16, 17, 18, 19, 20]

*For Reading and Science corrections, focus on *question type*. Use the *passage* categories only to identify trends, such as timing issues, or passage types that may need review.

TECHNIQUES AND HINTS

ENGLISH

PASSAGE I

1. Punctuation (A, B) / Apostrophes (D)

2. Adjectives & Adverbs (H, J) / Apostrophes & Confused Words (G): The word "then" should be "than."

3. Punctuation: Make sure you look for paired dashes (—); often, if there's one dash, there should be a second.

4. Main Ideas (additions): Watch out for redundancies. See "human encroachment" in the passage.

5. Punctuation: Often, the answer with no commas is best.

6. Transitions

7. Parallelism

8. Fragments

9. Idiom

10. Senseless (F) / Fragments (H, J): These answer choices are also missing commas.

11. Parallelism: See "a ten-year-old female."

12. Verb Tense / + Fragments & -ING (J)

13. Organization: clue word = "Ely" (he must have been introduced already)

14. Run-ons / + -ING (H)

15. Main Ideas (purpose): The aspect of animal behavior discussed in the passage is *learning*.

PASSAGE II

16. Misplaced Words: The first phrase (up to the comma) must modify the word "they," which refers to "'ghost signs.'" Only one answer choice creates a modifying phrase.

17. Redundancies

18. Punctuation

19. Run-ons (A, C) / Senseless (D)

20. Punctuation

21. Punctuation: We must have a comma after "apology," which is the last word in the independent clause (try the pause rule). Eliminate C and D. Next, does the sentence function grammatically without the word "instead"? If so, bind it with commas.

22. Misplaced Words / + Wordy & Passive Voice (J)

23. Answer the Question: Notice "ghost signs," "faded," "barely legible," etc. in the passage.

24. Fragments (F, G) / Wordy (H)

25. Senseless: For C, we have "evidently . . . of a hailstorm." For D, we have "vandalism or of a hailstorm." Choice A sounds somewhat awkward.

26. Transitions: The best answer on Transition questions is often the one with no transition.

27. Adjectives & Adverbs: The answer must be an adjective.

28. Punctuation

29. Organization: clue words = "Then there it was . . ." (¶3)

30. Main Ideas (purpose): If you don't spot the correct answer or aren't sure whether the answer is *yes* or *no*, try using POE (process off elimination). Main Ideas questions often have false answer choices, which are relatively easy to eliminate.

PASSAGE III

31. Fragments (A, D) / Punctuation (C)

32. Main Ideas (topic sentences): keywords = "the formation process" (Sentence 1 of paragraph)

33. Verb Tense

34. -ING, Wordy / + Run-ons (J)

35. Punctuation

36. Punctuation

37. Answer the Question

38. Redundancies

39. Run-ons (A, D) / Senseless (B)

40. Main Ideas (additions): keywords for this paragraph = "cave-creating process" (Sentence 2)

41. Adjectives & Adverbs

42. Pronouns (Agreement)

43. Fragments

44. Answer the Question: See "circular patch" in the passage.

45. Organization: clue words = "remains of" in ¶4

PASSAGE IV

46. Redundancies

47. Punctuation

48. Apostrophes & Confused Words

49. Fragments

50. Comparisons: Also note the confused words: "then" and "than" (see Apostrophes & Confused Words).

51. Misplaced Words: Read the question carefully; you must also "Answer the Question."

52. Transitions

53. Punctuation

54. Answer the Question

55. Main Ideas (transition sentences): Note Sentence 2 of this paragraph, which discusses the Servian Wall: "However . . ." The correct answer must contrast this second sentence.

56. Subject-Verb Agreement

57. Main Ideas (additions): Sentence 2 of this paragraph is the actual topic sentence (Sentence 1 is more of a transition sentence—see Question 55). Your primary keywords should be "Servian wall," and more specifically, the wall's "remnants."

58. Wordy

59. Answer the Question: The important word in the question is "irony."

60. Organization: clue words = "the two walls"

PASSAGE V

61. Punctuation

62. Main Ideas (topic/transition sentences): Forten's chances of surviving were "slim" (Sentence 1).

63. Subject-Verb Agreement (A, D) / Idiom (B, D)

64. Punctuation

65. Main Ideas (deletions): Note the flow of the passage: we go from "chances . . . were slim" to Forten became "successful." Use POE.

66. Verb Tense

67. Punctuation (C, D) / Pronouns (Case) (B)

68. Main Ideas (deletions): keywords = "Forten" (and his business) + "skilled apprentices"

69. Redundancies

70. Main Ideas (transition sentences): A keyword is "adapted."

71. Comparisons (B, C) / Punctuation (D)

72. Redundancies

73. Wordy

74. Organization: clue word = "newspaper" (¶6)

75. Main Ideas (purpose): Forten's business's "daily operations" were not described in detail.

MATH

1. Basic Algebra or Pick Numbers (type 1)

2. Calculators

3. Basic Algebra

4. Coordinates / Percent (*of–is*)

5. Lines: Find the equation of the line using the points (0, 620) and (10, 1,000). Note that 1985 corresponds with $x = 0$, and 1995 corresponds with $x = 10$.

6. Pick Answers / Calculators

7. Probability

8. Coordinates (midpoint)

9. Algebraic Word or Pick Answers: If you don't use the pick trick, you should have $116 = 8 + 2x$.

10. Algebraic Word: Your equation should be $500 + x(200) = 2,200$.

11. Pick Answers / Area & Perimeter

12. Tables & Graphs / Proportions (if necessary)

13. Tables & Graphs / Proportions

14. More Pick Numbers or Lines (equation of): If you use the Lines approach, pick any two points (n, c) from the table, and find the corresponding equation.

15. Factoring or Pick Answers

16. Angles

17. Solids & Volume

18. Basic Functions

19. Systems of Equations or Pick Answers: We recommend using the Pick Trick on this one.

20. Logarithms

21. Area & Perimeter

22. Lines (segments)

23. Pick Answers / Greatest Common Factors

24. No KlassTutoring technique: Hopefully you'll have a sense of the correct answer, especially if you've taken a statistics course. If not, make an educated guess.

25. Math Basics (least common multiples): The correct answer must be divisible by both 4 and 10. Check answers, starting with A.

26. Basic Concepts (absolute value) / Pick Numbers (type 1) (if necessary)

27. More Circles / Parabolas: If you're comfortable with parabolas, a quick sketch should be enough to answer the question.

28. Percent (of–is)

29. Basic Algebra

30. Basic Trigonometry

31. Area & Perimeter / Pick Answer or Basic Algebra

32. Area & Perimeter / Basic Algebra

33. Percent (of–is)

34. Triangles (Pythagorean Theorem)

35. Area & Perimeter

36. Coordinates

37. Coordinates: The "altitude" is just the height of the triangle. See the Area & Perimeter section for more on heights of triangles.

38. Algebraic Word: This is one of those relatively easy algebraic word questions where we just plug values into a given formula. Note, however, that $n!$ means $n \times (n - 1) \times . . . \times 1$ (see Permutations & Combinations).

39. Graphs of Sine & Cosine

40. Permutations & Combinations / Principle of Counting: Find the number of permutations for each group separately (note that letters and numbers CAN be repeated); then apply the Principle of Counting.

41. Averages, Medians, & Modes

42. Complex Numbers

43. Pick Answers or Basic Algebra

44. Direct & Inverse Variation

45. Lines (equations of)

46. Proportions

47. Factoring or Pick Numbers (type 1): Remember to factor common monomials from each expression first.

48. Matrices (multiplication): Review the $m \times n$ notation in the lesson. The number of columns of the first matrix (n) must equal the number of rows of the second matrix (m).

49. More Graphs of Functions (transformations) or Pick Answers: You can pick answers if you have a graphing calculator; just check the equations with $n = 1, 2,$ and 3, and stop when you find the one that looks correct.

50. Groups / Pick Answers: Start with F, since you're looking for the "minimum number." Here's the equation: $20 = 8 + 9 -$ both + neither.

51. Arithmetic Word Problems / Pick Answers: This is a very tricky problem (and a good one to skip for most students). A & C are easy to eliminate because they don't form perfect squares when added to 1. We can also eliminate D because 8 must pair with 17 (no other numbers less than 18

work with 17; by this same logic, 18 must pair with 7 and 16 must pair with 9)—so we have: 16 + 9, 17 + 8, and 18 + 7. Check the remaining answer choices. B: 15 + 1, 14 + 2, 13 + 3, 12 + 4, 11 + 5, 10 + 6. It worked!—all numbers (1–18) are accounted for. If you check E, you will end up, after pairing other numbers, with 13 + 15, which is not a perfect square. If necessary, see the solution in the ACT book for further explanation.

52. Pick Answers: You might have an easier time working in cents (look for 825 cents).

53. Exponents or Pick Answers: If you remember that anything raised to 0 is 1, and if you're comfortable with a little algebra, this question is straightforward. But you can also Pick Answers: be careful with your calculator—use parentheses.

54. Probability / Tables & Graphs

55. More Circles (revolutions) / Rates

56. Exponents (compare apples to apples) or Pick Numbers (type 2)

57. Patterns / Pick Numbers (type 3) (if necessary)

58. More Circles / Trigonometry Odds & Ends (inverse trigonometry): Make sure you use degrees in your calculations. Also, note that the answer choices are not simplified.

59. Area & Perimeter (SAS formula). You could also "Measure the Drawing" for this one (see Geometry Introduction).

60. Probability (distribution tables)

READING

PASSAGE I

1. Main Ideas: 3 ("the day I was born")

2. Purpose: 20 ("unceremoniously")

3. Tone: 50 ("ignoring"), 62 ("shuddered at the thought"), 65–68 ("I still have my name")

4. Direct: 54 ("Mama must not have . . . or who knows")

5. Direct: 67–68

6. Direct: 71–73

7. Direct: 78, 86: The word "sadness" shows up in both lines.

8. Direct: 60–61

9. Extended Reasoning: 79–80

10. Direct: 87–89

PASSAGE II

11. Direct: 1–5

12. Rhetoric: 13–14: A "monument" is typically a physical object. Here, it is used figuratively ("laws").

13. Purpose: 29–30: You must use logic for this one. Would you describe "bumpers, carburetors, and headlights" as necessary or optional ("accessories")? Quotes are often used to question the appropriateness or accuracy of a term.

14. Extended Reasoning: 87–91

15. Extended Reasoning: 44: The implication is that one or two varieties are typical. Eighteen must be extreme.

16. Direct: 84–85. See also 70–72.

17. Direct: 83–85 ("upscale car")

18. Comparison / Direct: See the copyright dates.

19. Comparison / Direct: 12–13, etc.

20. Comparison / Extended Reasoning: 67–68

PASSAGE III

21. Purpose: 11–13, 25–27, 49–51, 68–70: Watch out for answer choices that are too broad or too narrow.

22. Extended Reasoning: 85–86, etc.

23. Direct: 20–22

24. Direct: 26–27, 44–46

25. Direct: 33–35, 41–42

26. Extended Reasoning: 39–41

27. Direct: 11–13, 20–22

28. Main Idea: 68–70: Watch out for Eye Catchers in the answer choices.

29. Direct: 30–33

30. Direct: 66–67

PASSAGE IV

31. Main Idea (organization): 1–6, 18–21

32. Rhetoric: 23–27: You should probably use Process of Elimination (POE) for this one.

33. Direct: 6 ("strange"), 18–19 ("eager for a hint of the familiar")

34. Main Idea: 23–27

35. Direct: 35–37

36. Direct: 69–70, 74–76

37. Direct: 31–33

38. Direct: 65–66

39. Direct: 66–67

40. Direct: 78–80

SCIENCE

PASSAGE I (Data Representation)

1. Direct: Note that the description for Figure 2 discusses the relationship between "brightness" and "relative reflectance." Not surprisingly, they are directly related.

2. Direct

3. Direct: The greater the change, the steeper the line.

4. Direct

5. Science Sense: Interestingly, you don't actually need to go back to the passage for this one. Only one answer makes scientific sense. Just read them over.

6. Direct: The "standard" was assigned a 100% reflectance (see asterisk in Figure 2).

PASSAGE II (Research Summaries)

7. Interpolate

8. Make Connections: What is "concentration of dissolved nickel in the filtrate"? Check the text (see number 4 in Experiment 1). You might also need to check the text to see that Experiment 1 is "*standard filtration*" and Experiment 2 is "*vacuum filtration*." These are important connections to make early on for this passage. Hopefully you circled most of these words during your pre-question skim.

9. Research Methods / Science Sense: The only force acting on Experiment 1 (Trials 1–3) is gravity. Experiment 2 adds a vacuum pump. Use your science sense.

10. Research Methods: See Numbers 1 and 4 in Experiment 1.

11. Direct

12. Direct

13. Science Knowledge: Even if you're not great at chemical formulas, you can probably get this one. According to the formula in the passage, $2OH^-$ is a reactant (left of the $\rightarrow$) and $Ni(OH)_2 \cdot H_2O$ is a product (right of the $\rightarrow$). Note the numbers in front of each molecule: the ratio is 2:1. Take it from there.

PASSAGE III (Conflicting Viewpoints)

14. Direct: See the bullets in the introduction.

15. Direct: Scientist 2: "a disk . . . readily accrete."

16. Direct: Scientist 1: "Because stars . . . likely."

17. Direct: Skim for "M_s" for Scientists 1 and 2. Scientist 1 claims that the maximum mass of a protostar is 20 M_s, and Scientist 2 claims that the maximum mass of a protostar is 40 M_s. The question is now a matter of math: 20 $M_s \times x = 120$ M_s, etc. Note that Scientist 3 claims that the only limit to protostar size is "the amount of available gas."

18. New Information: See #17.

19. Direct: The key word is "rotates" (Scientist 2).

20. Direct: Note that the mass of the sun is 1 M_s (see Scientist 1), which is less than the maximum values given by all three scientists. See #17 for more on M_s.

PASSAGE IV (Research Summaries)

21. Direct

22. Research Methods (terminology): See Table 1: Mixture 1 is 100% potting soil.

23. Calculations & Math: Hint: there are 1,000 grams in a kilogram.

24. Research Methods: Quickly read the description for Study 2.

25. New Information: This passage does not make it easy to determine which study (and figure) is for tomato plants, and which is for pepper plants. You'll have to skim the introduction. Making connections with the text is an important part of answering Science questions.

26. Research Methods: Sometimes, you'll have to dig into the text a little. See Study 1: "On Day 28 . . . a single seedling in each pot."

27. Science Knowledge: How well do you understand photosynthesis?

PASSAGE V (Research Summaries)

28. Research Methods: identify the independent variables for Studies 1 and 2. Hopefully you circled italicized letters while skimming the passage; for this question, you need to know what E, V, and y mean.

29. Interpolation

30. Make Connections: Figure 2 displays a value for y. Identify this value, and then check the trials.

31. Learn / Make Connections: "Learn" from Study 1: note the relationship between the direction of E and the sign of y.

32. New Information / Research Methods: The students cannot vary L in any one CRT, so how many Ls are tested? Also, read the first sentence of each study.

33. Extrapolate / Trends: Determine the relationship between E and y (Study 1) and V and y (Study 2). Note that the relationship between E and y in Table 1 is linear (the differences between adjacent y values are equal).

34. Science Knowledge: You must know that electric charges of like sign repel each other (and, conversely, opposites attract). Since the cathode ray (the dotted line in Figure 1) is negative, and it since it bends up (see the figure), the bottom plate must be negative (the bottom plate is repelling, or pushing away, the cathode ray).

PASSAGE VI (Data Representation)

35. Direct

36. Calculations & Math: 200 nm → 100 nm

37. Learn: It's probably too difficult to extrapolate, so "learn" from Figure 1. For example, when $V = 10$ L, λ (for Kr) ≈ 100 nm, and when $V = 20$ L, $\lambda \approx 200$ nm. So what happens to λ as V doubles?

38. Calculations & Math

39. New Information / Science Sense / Trends: Note that λ is a measure of "the average distance a gas atom will travel between collisions" (see intro). Use your "science sense": If the average distance between collisions is shorter, will there be more collisions, or fewer?

40. New Information / Make Connections: Start with Table 1. Where does Rn fit in the table? Then connect this information to Figure 2. Try sketching a possible graph for Rn.

2. *TECHNIQUES: TEST 2*

QUESTIONS BY SECTIONS/CHAPTERS

The following information lists every question on the test according to its relevant chapter or section in this tutorial. If you're correcting a test, circle the question numbers below that you missed or guessed on. Make sure to follow the Tutoring Schedule in the Introduction to know when to correct or tackle various types of questions.

ENGLISH	
Usage/Mechanics	Rhetorical Skills
[1, 3, 5, 6, 7, 10, 11, 12] [16, 17, 19, 21, 23, 24, 25, 26, 28, 30] [31, 32, 33, 35, 36, 37, 38, 40, 41, 42, 44] [45, 46, 47, 48, 49, 50, 53, 54, 56, 57, 58] [61, 62, 63, 65, 66, 68, 69, 70, 71, 72, 73]	[2, 4, 8, 9, 13, 14, 15] [18, 20, 22, 27, 29] [34, 39, 43] [51, 52, 55, 59, 60] [64, 67, 74, 75]

Brackets display separate passages.

MATH							
Basic Concepts	Arith.	Algebra	Adv. Algebra	Geometry	Func-tions	Trig	Odds/ Ends
8	1, 3, 4, 5, 15, 29, 41, 45, 60	2, 12, 18, 26, 27, 31, 36, 37, 40, 44, 46, 47, 49, 58	9, 22, 28	6, 7, 10, 11, 13, 14, 16, 17, 19, 21, 25, 30, 33, 34, 38, 43, 50, 51, 52	23, 32, 54	20, 35, 48	24, 39, 42, 53, 55, 56, 57, 59

READING (by question type and passage)*						
Direct	Extended Reasoning	Purpose	Main Idea	Comparison	Tone	Words in Context
3, 5, 6, 9, 10, 11, 12, 17, 19, 20, 23, 24, 25, 33, 36, 37, 38, 39, 40	1, 2, 7, 8, 16, 18, 22, 26, 35	13, 14, 21, 31, 34		28, 29, 30	4, 27	15
Prose Fiction		Social Science		Humanities		Natural Science
1, 2, 3, 4, 5, 6, 7, 8, 9, 10		11, 12, 13, 14, 15, 16, 17, 18, 19, 20		21, 22, 23, 24, 25, 26, 27, 28, 29, 30		31, 32, 33, 34, 35, 36, 37, 38, 39, 40

Other: #32 (rhetorical devices: see Reading Introduction)

SCIENCE (by question type and passage)*		
Data Representation	Research Summaries	Conflicting Viewpoints
1, 3, 4, 6, 10, 13, 15, 17, 18, 19, 23, 24, 25, 26, 27, 35, 36, 38, 40	2, 5, 7, 8, 9, 11, 12, 14, 16, 20, 21, 22, 37, 39	28, 29, 30, 31, 32, 33, 34
[1, 2, 3, 4, 5, 6] [35, 36, 37, 38, 39, 40]	[7, 8, 9, 10, 11, 12, 13] [14, 15, 16, 17, 18, 19, 20] [21, 22, 23, 24, 25, 26, 27]	[28, 29, 30, 31, 32, 33, 34]

*For Reading and Science corrections, focus on *question type*. Use the *passage* categories only to identify trends, such as timing issues, or passage types that may need review.

TECHNIQUES AND HINTS

ENGLISH

PASSAGE I

1. Fragments

2. Answer the Question

3. Verb Tense

4. Main Ideas (additions): Note the clue words "the men" in the next sentence. A sentence must be added to introduce these men.

5. Verb Tense

6. Idiom

7. Wordy / + -*ING* (C)

8. Main Ideas (deletions): As always, look for answer choices that are false. The focus here is on Hay's fame (he "became famous . . .").

9. Main Ideas (deletions)

10. Parallelism

11. Verb Tense (A, D) / Subject-Verb Agreement (B, D)

12. Redundancies

13. Transitions

14. Organization: clue words = "For almost twenty years" (Sentence 5)

15. Main Ideas (purpose): The purpose must reflect the whole essay, not one small part.

PASSAGE II

16. Punctuation

17. Apostrophes & Confused Words

18. Transitions / + -*ING* (F)

19. Punctuation

20. Answer the Question

21. Misplaced Words

22. Main Ideas (topic sentences): Many of the words convey the *challenge* of "re-creating the past": "spent weeks" (¶2), "exhausting" (¶3), "physical demands" (¶3), "tiring months" (¶4), etc.

23. Fragments (A, D) / Run-ons (B)

24. Verb Tense

25. Pronouns (Case) (A, C) / Verb Tense (B)

26. Run-ons (F, G) / Senseless (H)

27. Main Ideas (additions): The subject of the added sentence is "theme park characters." Is this really topical at this point of the essay? Also note that this is the last sentence of the paragraph, a place of importance. Ask yourself if this sentence ties effectively to the paragraph's focus on the "exhausting" nature of the fair.

28. Wordy (F, G) / Style (J)

29. Transitions

30. Redundancies

PASSAGE III

31. Punctuation

32. Pronouns (Agreement)

33. Apostrophes & Confused Words (A, C) / Punctuation (D)

34. Transitions: The correct answer contrasts the words "for a time" (temporarily).

35. Verb Tense

36. Fragments

37. Redundancies

38. Punctuation: This question tests the use of commas with adjectives.

39. Main Ideas (deletions): Note the title of the essay.

40. Run-ons (F, J) / Fragments (C)

41. Idiom (B, D) / Pronouns (Agreement) (B, C)

42. Subject-Verb Agreement

43. Pronouns (Ambiguity) (A) / Style (B, D)

44. Redundancies

PASSAGE IV

45. Punctuation

46. Fragments, -*ING* (F, J) / Pronouns (Ambiguity) (G)

47. Punctuation

48. Subject-Verb Agreement

49. Fragments

50. Run-ons (F) / Fragments (G, H)

51. Organization: clue words = "*the* gas and dust" in ¶2 (italics added). The word *the* usually means that the noun or nouns (in this case, "gas and dust") have already been introduced.

52. Transitions

53. Verb Tense

54. Parallelism (F): See the end of the sentence. / Apostrophes & Confused Words (H) / Pronouns (Ambiguity) (J)

55. Main Ideas (deletions): Delete false answer choices. The keywords for this paragraph are "principle of averted vision."

56. Comparisons (F) / Wordy (G) / Punctuation (J)

57. Vocabulary

58. Apostrophes & Confused Words

59. Answer the Question

60. Main Ideas (purpose): Sometimes the stated goal is clearly true. Narrow it down to two answer choices, and focus on the second parts of these remaining choices. (One of the *yes* choices is false.)

PASSAGE V

61. Run-ons

62. Punctuation: Make sure the phrase between the dashes includes "all the shapes" (see the question).

63. Punctuation

64. Main Ideas (additions): This paragraph focuses on the "subject" (last sentence) of Little's paintings.

65. Redundancies

66. Vocabulary: The word "voluminous" usually refers to *volume*, not two-dimensional size.

67. Transitions: Even though there is some contrast here ("diagonal lines" in ¶2 → "a vertical . . . line" in ¶3), the author is not likely changing the subject. Rather, the author is giving an example of Little's work. (However, the author's use of the word "diagonal" is

questionable and should probably have been removed.)

68. Adjectives & Adverbs

69. Wordy (A) / Fragments (B) / Run-ons (D)

70. Redundancies: See the beginning of the sentence.

71. Subject-Verb Agreement (A, B) / Idiom (B, D)

72. Idiom

73. Wordy (A, B) / *-ING* (D)

74. Main Ideas (deletions): See "play" and "rhythm" in this paragraph.

75. Main Ideas (purpose): See the last sentence of the passage ("space," "shifts," "balance").

MATH

1. Proportions

2. Algebraic Word or Pick Answers: Here's the equation: $140 + 40x = 500$. Hopefully you're starting to get comfortable finding these on your own.

3. Arithmetic Word Problems: Either multiply how much each person overpaid ($0.75) by the number of people (27), or subtract how much they should have paid (27 × $8.50) from how much they did pay (27 × $9.25).

4. Probability

5. Averages, Medians, & Modes (*ANS*)

6. Angles

7. Triangles (similar)

8. Basic Concepts (absolute value)

9. Factoring or Pick Numbers (type 1)

10. Angles

11. Lines (segments) / Pick Answers or Basic Algebra: If you use algebra, you should get: $16 - x + 20 = 30$.

12. Basic Algebra

13. Area & Perimeter (shaded region)

14. Area & Perimeter (area fitting)

15. Arithmetic Word Problems / Percent (*of–is*)

16. Lines (equation of)

17. Lines (segments): You should be comfortable using your calculator on this problem.

18. Algebraic Word or Pick Answers: If you use algebra, your equation should be $180 - x = 160 - \frac{1}{2}x$.

19. Lines (equation of)

20. Basic Trigonometry

21. Coordinates: Feel free to "eyeball" this problem.

22. Algebraic Word / Factoring or Pick Answers: The inequality is $150 \le \frac{3(x^2+10x)}{40}$. After simplifying, you will either have to factor $x^2 + 10x - 200 \ge 0$, or Pick Answers.

23. Basic Functions

24. Principle of Counting

25. Lines (equation of)

26. Pick Answers

27. Algebraic Word: $15 - 5n < 0 \ldots$

28. Factoring or Pick Numbers (type 1)

29. Averages, Medians, & Modes / Pick Numbers (type 3) (if necessary)

30. Area & Perimeter (shaded region)

31. Averages, Medians, & Modes / Pick Numbers (type 3): Be careful with this question. If you pick, for example, $a = 2$ and $b = -3$, the average is negative ($-\frac{1}{2}$). But if you pick $a = 3$ and $b = -2$, the average is positive ($\frac{1}{2}$). You've passed the halfway point of the test (the questions are getting harder), so be cautious before going with your first answer.

32. Basic Functions

33. Triangles (Pythagorean Theorem)

34. Area & Perimeter

35. Laws of Sines & Cosines

36. Pick Numbers (type 1): Note that the answer choices can be viewed as only including the variable a: the "$c =$" in each choice could have been part of the question. So pick a number for a.

37. Algebraic Word: The equation for Sea Horse is: $255 = 50 \cdot (2 \text{ days}) + 0.25 \cdot (x$

miles). Ocean Blue follows similarly. Solve for x for both equations and compare.

38. Area & Perimeter (parallelogram)

39. Basic Concepts (terminology) / Complex Numbers: Use process of elimination if necessary: since I and IV are clearly true, the answer is apparent.

40. Calculators / More Pick Numbers: For example, pick a number with three digits (choice H): $x = 123 \rightarrow 123^2 = 15{,}129$. So our perfect square (15,129) has too many digits ($5 > 4$). Next, try a two-digit number (choice G) . . .

41. Probability (distribution tables): This problem involves two steps. First, find the expected occupancy rate (review probability distribution tables in the tutorial). Second, multiply this value by the number of rooms at the hotel (80). This will give you the expected number of occupied rooms.

42. Matrices (multiplication)

43. Angles / Basic Algebra or Pick Answers

44. Pick Numbers (type 3)

45. Proportions: Hint: use the final units in your "known relationship" (gallons and acres). Don't use your calculator (see the answer choices). Here's the proportion: $\frac{\text{gallons}}{\text{acres}} \quad \frac{\left(\frac{1}{128}\right)}{\left(\frac{40}{43{,}560}\right)} = \frac{x}{0.5}$. Solve for x. Yes, the numbers are ugly, but if you instead use your calculator to find a decimal answer, you'll have to check all of the answer choices, which will probably take too long.

46. Arithmetic Word Problems / Pick Answers: Use underlines to represent the tables, and write the number of people for each one. Start with K: $\underline{4}\,\underline{4}\,\underline{4}\,\underline{4}\,\underline{4}\,\underline{0}\,\underline{0}\,\underline{0}\,\underline{0}\,\underline{0} = 20$; this answer fails because some tables have 0 people. Move on to J . . .

47. Probability / Pick Numbers (type 3): This question looks harder than it is. Let's pick some numbers to give us something to worth with. $P(A) = 0.4$ and $P(B) = 0.2$. The probability that both events will occur is $0.4 \times 0.2 = 0.08$ (review probability of multiple events). Check the answer choices.

48. Trig & the Unit Circle

49. Pick Numbers (type 4)

50. Angles / Triangles (similar): You should know not to trust the drawing (it's too high a number for obvious answers).

51. Area & Perimeter

52. Area & Perimeter: This is a difficult question. The trick is to recognize that all triangles, with a common base, drawn between two parallel lines, will have the same area (because their heights will always equal). For example, the three triangles shown below (connect the dots) have equal areas:

In this question, since points A and B are stationary, segment AB is the common base. The slope of the line through C must equal that of line AB, thus giving us two parallel lines. (Hint: spin your book around, if necessary, so line AB is horizontal.)

53. Patterns or Calculators: For most students, the easiest approach is to simply type the numbers into your calculator: $24 + 29 + 34 + 39$ . . . Make sure you enter the numbers carefully, and don't forget to count—you might try entering 10 at a time. If you use the Patterns approach, use the arithmetic *sequence* formula (to find the 20th term, a_{20}) and then the arithmetic *series* formula (to find the sum).

54. Graphs of Functions / More Pick Numbers: If you're comfortable graphing piece-wise functions, you probably won't have to use the Pick Trick. Most students, however, will probably want to use the More Pick Numbers technique. Hint: Start with the first equation, for $x \le 1$; try $x = 0$ (eliminate G and H); then try $x = 1$ (eliminate F and J).

55. Permutations & Combinations

56. Complex Numbers

57. Vectors

58. Pick Numbers (type 3): Pick a number for t_1 (the time for Pendulum 1), and solve for L_1. Next, find t_2, which is just "triple" t_1, and calculate L_2. Compare L_1

and L_2. Note: even if you're quick with your math, this problem might take a while. A shortcut is to recognize that the numbers in the formula don't really matter (they'll all cancel out in the end, when you compare L_1 and L_2). So you can just use $t = \sqrt{L}$ for the formula. This saves considerable time.

59. Logarithms or Pick Numbers (type 1)

60. Percent (pick 100 / percent increase–decrease / difference-over-original)

READING

PASSAGE I

1. Extended Reasoning: 9–10, etc.

2. Extended Reasoning: 4–5, 17

3. Direct: 62–63

4. Tone: 72, (75): The first word of each answer choice make clear that this question tests tone.

5. Direct: 1–4

6. Direct: 33–34

7. Extended Reasoning: 42–43 ("numbers")

8. Extended Reasoning: 62–64, 65–67 ("old-fashioned")

9. Direct: 76–78

10. Direct: 81–82 ("*fading* brown photographs"—italics added)

PASSAGE II

11. Direct: The first mention of William after Caroline's discovery is in lines 89–93; no clear indication of his feelings are given.

12. Direct: 14

13. Purpose: 35 ("Caroline claimed these as her own"): You might use POE on this one.

14. Purpose: 79–80

15. Words in Context: See line 10 ("enormous") and the contrast signal "but" (line 11).

16. Extended Reasoning: 17–19: This question, despite its wording, is very close to direct.

17. Direct: 25–28

18. Extended Reasoning: 41–42

19. Direct: 61–66

20. Direct: 67–70

PASSAGE III

21. Purpose: 7

22. Extended Reasoning: See lines 19–20 ("neither Mama nor I could give satisfaction")

23. Direct: 31–32

24. Direct: 42

25. Direct: 55–56

26. Extended Reasoning: 65–67, 80–83: You might use POE on this one.

27. Tone: 86–88

28. Comparison / Direct: 24–30 ("only a select part"), 84–86

29. Comparison / Extended Reasoning: 39–41, 83–86

30. Comparison / Direct: 37–41

PASSAGE IV

31. Purpose: 1–3, 74–77, etc.: Try POE if necessary.

32. Rhetoric: 3–4 ("the hard way"), 27 ("guru of ant gurus"), 73 ("made bank"): Use POE—the incorrect answer choices are relatively easy to eliminate.

33. Direct: 4–5: The other answer choices can be found in lines 63–64 (A), 86–88 (B), and 25–57 (D).

34. Purpose: 41–42, 49

35. Extended Reasoning: 55–58 ("strange")

36. Direct: 1–3

37. Direct: 15–18

38. Direct: 52

39. Direct: 69–71

40. Direct: 78–79

SCIENCE

PASSAGE I (Data Representation)

1. Direct: Note "mating" (parents) and "offspring" (children) in the Key.

2. Science Sense: Look for individuals with the same parents.

3. Learn: Individuals 23 and 24 both possess Trait G. Look for other parents in the figure that both have Trait G, and observe their offspring.

4. Direct: Note that Individual 9 is <u>not</u> a grandchild of Individuals 1 and 2 (he "married into" the family).

5. Science Knowledge: A "sex-linked trait" is one that the mother passes to all sons. Even if you didn't know this (and, frankly, who would?), you should still eliminate A and C, which are false. Go with the more logical remaining answer choice. Science Knowledge questions can often be answered with a little "science sense."

6. Make Connections: First note the text at the end of ¶2 ("Based on this information, the scientists concluded that Trait G is a recessive trait.") This will allow you to eliminate two answer choices. Also note in ¶2 that Individual 21 is *Gg*. Look at the figure. Individual 21 does <u>not</u> have Trait G. This answers the question.

PASSAGE II (Research Summaries)

7. Research Methods (equipment) / Science Sense: Which answer choice is used to measure mass?

8. Research Methods: Always ask yourself what is being varied; note the variations in Groups 1–3 (see Table 1).

9. Research Methods: See the descriptions for Groups 1 and 2 in Table 1; also, note the asterisk (*) information.

10. Calculations & Math: Percent (part-over-whole)

11. Research Methods / Science Sense: Read the first sentence of the study ("Before pollination could occur . . .").

12. Research Methods: See the results for Group 4 (Figure 1).

13. Direct: Be careful: Figure 2 gives the "average mass per seed." We would need to know the total number of seeds to answer the question. Is this number given?

PASSAGE III (Research Summaries)

14. Research Methods / Science Sense: Note the two types of bacteria that are the focus of the study (see introduction).

15. Trends: The trends for CO_2 (left two bar graphs) and CH_4 (right two bar graphs) are clear.

16. Research Methods / Science Sense: Note the first sentence of ¶3 of the Study (". . . gas emissions from each soil section were measured . . ."). If scientists were measuring gas emissions, why would they have needed to keep the lid on each tank closed?

17. Make Connections: You must make connections with the text. First, note the mention of *aerobic bacteria* (which produce CO_2) and *anaerobic bacteria* (which produce CH_4) in the intro. Now, look at Figures 1 and 2. For the left two bar graphs, CO_2 levels are higher in fen soil (Figure 2) than in bog soil (Figure 1), and for the right two bar graphs, CH_4 levels are also higher in fen soil than in bog soil.

18. Make Connections: Again, you must make a connection with the text: In the intro, we learn that aerobic bacteria produce CO_2. Now look at the figures.

19. Calculations & Math: The graphs give values for *3* months (as mentioned in the question). The math is straightforward.

20. Research Methods: Hint: which answer choice displays a condition that would be difficult for the scientists to control?

PASSAGE IV (Research Summaries)

21. Science Sense: You should probably have a sense that weight and mass are directly proportional (as mass increases, weight increases). So find the answer choice with the heaviest weight (see Figure 2).

22. Research Methods: Simply read the descriptions of Studies 2 and 3.

23. Extrapolation: Start at $S = 50$ in, and extrapolate vertically up to $W = 90$ lb.

24. Direct: You might draw a vertical line up from $S = 30$ in (as always, make sure you're focusing on the correct figure).

25. Direct

26. Direct: If a variable is "independent of" another variable, the first variable will not change as the second variable is changed.

27. Direct / New Information: You might want to look back to the text to see that $F_{n, av}$ is the average net force per hinge (although you might note that no other forces are given in Figure 3). Find the data point where $F_{n, av} > 57$ lb.

PASSAGE V (Conflicting Viewpoints)

28. Weaknesses: Notice that argon is not mentioned in the passage. In addition, because argon only makes up "less than 1%" of air, we would not expect its existence to weaken any of the students' explanations.

29. Research Methods / Science Sense: I: See the first sentence of ¶2 of the intro. The contents are heated. II: All three students discuss chemical reactions; it's safe to assume they wouldn't want the silicone hoses to react with the chemicals in the experiment. III: Water is not mentioned in the passage.

30. Direct: Note that the question is asking about the change in percent of CO_2 and O_2. See the text: "the CO_2 in the air [formed] solid iron carbonate," and "almost all the gas remaining . . . was O_2."

31. Direct: The following percentages are given in the passage: Student 1: 20% N_2 ("almost all the gas remaining . . . was O_2"); Student 2: 80% O_2; Student 3: 20% O_2 ("almost all the gas remaining . . was N_2"); and Student 4: 20% CO_2 ("almost all the gas remaining . . . was O_2").

32. Direct: Student 3: ". . . the Fe . . . reacted with some of the O_2 . . . to form . . . (Fe_2O_3)."

33. Direct: Student 2: "25% N_2"; Student 3: "almost all the gas remaining . . was N_2."

34. New Information: Student 2 says that the Fe reacted with "*some* of the O_2" (italics added). In other words, the Fe

(iron) ran out before the O_2 did—the iron was the limiting reactant. (Note that the chemical symbol for iron is given in the first sentence of the passage.)

PASSAGE VI (Data Representation)

35. New Information / Calculations & Math: Find Λ° and Δ° in Table 2, note the "Quark spins," and add up the values given in the question. For example (Λ°): $\uparrow\downarrow\uparrow = (+\frac{1}{2}\hbar) + (-\frac{1}{2}\hbar) + (+\frac{1}{2}\hbar) = +\frac{1}{2}\hbar$.

36. Direct: If baryon is "electrically neutral," you probably could guess that its total charge is 0. Just add the values for each answer choice, using Table 1. Note that H and J can be immediately eliminated because they do not have "only 2 quark spins oriented in the same direction" (all three arrows point in the same direction for H and J).

37. Science Knowledge / Make Connections: You must know that protons have a charge of +1. Find "Proton" in Table 2, note its "Quark content," and finally check the charges in Table 1.

38. Make Connections: As with #37, use Table 2 to identify quark content, and Table 1 to find the charges.

39. Scientific Knowledge: You must know that atomic nuclei are made up of protons and neutrons. Check the quark content in Table 2.

40. Direct / New Information: The charges and masses of each quark are given in Table 1. Observe each pair given in the question's table. Can you find one pair of quarks where the positively charged quark is <u>not</u> more massive than the negatively charged quark?

3. TECHNIQUES: TEST 3

QUESTIONS BY SECTIONS/CHAPTERS

The following information lists every question on the test according to its relevant chapter or section in this tutorial. If you're correcting a test, circle the question numbers below that you missed or guessed on. Make sure to follow the Tutoring Schedule in the Introduction to know when to correct or tackle various types of questions.

ENGLISH	
Usage/Mechanics	Rhetorical Skills
[1, 3, 4, 7, 8, 9, 10, 12, 14] [16, 18, 19, 20, 21, 23, 24, 26, 27, 28, 29] [31, 32, 33, 34, 38, 39, 40, 41, 42, 43] [46, 47, 48, 50, 51, 52, 53, 56, 57, 58, 59] [61, 64, 65, 66, 67, 69, 71, 72]	[2, 5, 6, 11, 13, 15] [17, 22, 25, 30] [35, 36, 37, 44, 45] [49, 54, 55, 60] [62, 63, 68, 70, 73, 74, 75]

Brackets display separate passages.

MATH*							
Basic Concepts	Arith.	Algebra	Adv. Algebra	Geometry	Func-tions	Trig	Odds/Ends
4, 12	1, 2, 16, 22, 33, 35, 46, 50, 55, 60	6, 7, 9, 13, 15, 19, 21, 27, 31, 32, 48, 52	3, 23, 30, 39, 47	10, 14, 17, 18, 20, 24, 25, 26, 28, 29, 34, 38, 42, 43, 44, 45, 51	11, 56, 59	37, 40, 53	5, 8, 41, 49, 54, 57, 58

*no KlassTutoring technique for #5 and #36 (see notes on the following pages)

READING (by question type and passage)*						
Direct	Extended Reasoning	Purpose	Main Idea	Comp.	Tone	Words in Context
1, 4, 5, 7, 8, 9, 10, 12, 13, 14, 15, 16, 17, 23, 27, 28, 29, 30, 32, 34, 35, 36, 37, 38, 40	3, 19, 20, 24, 26, 33	2, 11, 31	21		6, 22	18, 25, 39

Prose Fiction	Social Science	Humanities	Natural Science
1, 2, 3, 4, 5, 6, 7, 8, 9, 10	11, 12, 13, 14, 15, 16, 17, 18, 19, 20	21, 22, 23, 24, 25, 26, 27, 28, 29, 30	31, 32, 33, 34, 35, 36, 37, 38, 39, 40

SCIENCE (by question type and passage)*		
Data Representation	Research Summaries	Conflicting Viewpoints
1, 2, 3, 4, 5, 7, 8, 9, 12, 13, 14, 18, 20, 21, 22, 23, 24, 25, 26, 34, 36, 39	6, 10, 11, 15, 16, 17, 19, 35, 37, 38, 40	27, 28, 29, 30, 31, 32, 33
[1, 2, 3, 4, 5, 6] [7, 8, 9, 10, 11, 12]	[13, 14, 15, 16, 17, 18, 19] [20, 21, 22, 23, 24, 25, 26] [34, 35, 36, 37, 38, 39, 40]	[27, 28, 29, 30, 31, 32, 33]

*For Reading and Science corrections, focus on *question type*. Use the *passage* categories only to identify trends, such as timing issues, or passage types that may need review.

TECHNIQUES AND HINTS
ENGLISH
Passage I

1. Punctuation (A, B) / Fragments (D)

2. Answer the Question: "grandmother's interests"

3. Redundancies

4. Fragments

5. Main Ideas (topic sentences): keywords = "Miami time." Only one answer choice refers to the (hint) "difficult concept" of Miami time.

6. Punctuation (F) / Transitions (H, J)

7. Wordy

8. Verb Tense: See "Recently"

9. Subject-Verb Agreement (A, B) / Nonsense (D)

10. Punctuation

11. Organization: clue word = "there," referring to "clearing"

12. Parallelism

13. Transitions

14. Comparisons: Watch out for the word "then" incorrectly used in a comparison (see Apostrophes & Confused Words).

15. Main Idea (purpose): The main focus of the essay is "Miami Time" (see the title).

Passage II

16. Run-ons

17. Transitions

18. Misplaced Words

19. Apostrophes & Confused Words (A, B) / Pronouns (Agreement) (D)

20. Punctuation

21. Misplaced Words

22. Transitions

23. Apostrophes & Confused Words

24. Subject-Verb Agreement

25. Answer the Question: keywords = "unity of purpose" (Sentence 2)

26. Redundancies

27. Misplaced Words (Improper Modifiers)

28. Punctuation

29. Run-ons

30. Main Ideas (deletions): keywords = "women's accomplishments" and "shared vision"

Passage III

31. Subject-Verb Agreement

32. Fragments (G): The second clause is a fragment. / Nonsense (H, J)

33. Pronouns Agreement / + Apostrophes & Confused Words (D)

34. Punctuation

35. Organization: clue word = "undaunted"; see "the public preferred . . ."

36. Main Ideas (deletions): keywords = "special effects"

37. Answer the Question: "skill and inventiveness"

38. Adjectives & Adverbs

39. Redundancies

40. Wordy

41. Run-ons

42. Verb Tense (F, H) / Idiom (Common Mistakes) (G)

43. Vocabulary

44. Answer the Question: "science fiction"

45. Main Ideas (purpose): keywords for the passage = "Méliès" and "science fiction films" (¶1)

Passage IV

46. Verb Tense (F, H) / Idiom (H, J): The phrase "out of style" is a common idiom.

47. Idiom (Common Mistakes) (A, C) / Verb Tense (D)

48. Punctuation (F, G) / Apostrophes & Confused Words (G, H)

49. Answer the Question: "specific information" / Style (A) / Idiom (Common Mistakes) (D)

50. Punctuation

51. Pronouns (Ambiguous)

52. Fragments (F, H) / -*ING* (H) / Verb Tense (J)

53. Punctuation

54. Answer the Question: "variety of settings" and "Liana's interest"

55. Main Ideas (additions): The focus of this paragraph is "Nancy Drew," not the "Nancy Drew Mystery Story series."

56. Parallelism

57. Transitions

58. Parallelism / + -*ING* (G, H)

59. Run-ons (A, B) / -*ING* (D)

60. Main Ideas: Which answer choice best describes "the stories themselves."

Passage V

61. Idiom: The phrase "from… to…" is a common idiom.

62. Answer the Question: The words "ill will and danger" = "spine-tingling" in H.

63. Main Ideas (transition/topic sentences): Try POE: eliminate off-topic answer choices.

64. Verb Tense / + Idiom (Common Mistakes) (F)

65. Run-ons (A) / Wordy (B) / Nonsense (D)

66. Run-ons

67. Punctuation

68. Main Ideas (additions): keyword = "cost" (Sentence 1 of the paragraph)

69. Nonsense

70. Answer the Question: What are "Mars Rovers"?

71. Redundancies (A, C) / Wordy (B)

72. Redundancies (F, H) / Adjectives & Adverbs ("age" is not an adjective) (G)

73. Transitions

74. Transitions

75. Main Ideas (passage): keywords for the passage = "Visiting Mars" (title) and the "cost" of doing so (see #68)

MATH

1. Proportions

2. Averages, Medians, & Modes (*ANS*)

3. Factoring or Basic Algebra: If you recognize that the numerator factors, with one expression canceling the denominator, you'll save some time.

4. Calculators

5. Try POE for this one. Note how easily the incorrect answers can be eliminated: for example, we know that Insect I is not an ant (given), so eliminate A and B. . . .

6. Basic Algebra / Calculators: If you use your calculator, make sure to use parentheses carefully.

7. Algebraic Word: You should have two equations: $6x + 8y = 2000$ and $x = 142$.

8. Principle of Counting

9. Basic Algebra / Calculators: As is often the case, if you're comfortable working with fractions, the calculator is optional.

10. Angles: Note that both triangles are isosceles: for each one, the base angles will equal.

11. Basic Functions

12. Basic Concepts (least common multiples): Just use your calculator, starting with F.

13. Pick Numbers (type 3): Pick a number for "a number" (see the question).

14. Area & Perimeter

15. Algebraic Word or Pick Answers / Percent (increase-decrease): Here's the inequality to solve: $8x(1.07) < 100$. (Note: the multiplier for a 7% increase is 1.07.)

16. Proportions

17. Lines (equation of)

18. Area & Perimeter

19. Algebraic Word: This problem is long and (thus) looks difficult, but if you're comfortable finding the expressions, it's not too bad. Set the following equal: Worker A: $20,000 + 800x$; Worker B: $15,200 + 2,000x$. Note the answer choices (do not solve for x!).

20. Triangles (Pythagorean Theorem)

21. Basic Algebra

22. Percent (*of–is*)

23. Working with Polynomials (*FOIL*)

24. Area & Perimeter (cutting): "Cut" the shape into a square and a rectangle.

25. Area & Perimeter (fitting)

26. Lines (equation of)

27. More Pick Numbers: Use your calculator to covert the radicals to decimals.

28. Triangles (similar)

29. Probability / Area & Perimeter

30. Algebraic Word / Factoring or Pick Answers: Your equation should be $x^2 - 23x = 50$. If you have any trouble finding or solving this equation, don't hesitate to Pick Answers.

31. Algebraic Word: The equation is given. Plug in the given numbers and solve.

32. Basic Algebra (inequalities) or More Pick Numbers: If you're not comfortable solving inequalities, use the Pick Tricks. Pick a number that is true for one (or more) of the answer choices, test it in the inequality, and eliminate answer choices accordingly. (Note: you obviously can't pick a number to test F—the "empty set" is the absence of all number, i.e. no solutions.)

33. Tables & Graphs / Ratios: Use the part-over-whole percent technique, but keep your answer in fraction (ratio) form.

34. Tables & Graphs / More Circles (sectors)

35. Averages, Medians, & Modes: Make sure you count all 20 data values (0, 0, 1, 1, 1, 1, 1 . . .).

36. There's no need for a "technique" on this one. Just carefully sketch your lines. Hint: count *while* you draw them; don't try to count afterward.

37. Basic Trigonometry: You could also "Measure the Drawing" using the given length (144) and check the answer choices with your calculator.

38. Coordinates (midpoint)

39. Systems of Equations (elimination method) or Basic Algebra (substitution)

40. Trig & the Unit Circle or Pick Answers: If you're not comfortable with the unit circle, just Pick Answers and use your calculator; make sure you're in radian mode. The faster approach, however, involves the *ASTC* initialism, which gives the positive trig functions for each quadrant:

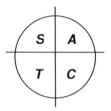

So, since Tangent is negative, θ must be in Quadrants II and IV.

41. Complex Numbers

42. Solids & Volume

43. Solids & Volume

44. Triangles (similar) or Measure the Drawing: You can simply eyeball this one; only one answer choice is close.

45. Triangles (special right): The given angles (30° and 45°) are clues that this problem is testing the 30-60-90 and 45-45-90 triangles. As is often the case, you must sketch the right triangles (they are not given):

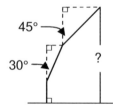

Note: The figure in the book is <u>not</u> drawn to scale. If you measure the drawing, none of the answer choices match perfectly. It's still better than guessing randomly, but using the triangles is the only sure way to get the question correct.

46. Probability (distribution tables): Watch out for the trap answer choice, the value of n with the greatest probability ($n = 0$).

47. Factoring or Graphs of Functions: If you're comfortable factoring, the zeros (or roots) of the function are the points

where the object touches the ground (only one of which occurs when $t > 0$). You could also use a graphing calculator.

48. Pick Numbers (type 1) or Exponents: The exponential approach is not easy (see the solution in the *Official ACT Prep Guide*). If you're comfortable quickly typing numbers into your calculator, use the Pick Trick. Otherwise, this is a good question to skip.

49. Logarithms: You should be able to convert the given logarithm to:

    $5^x = 5^{\frac{13}{2}}$. Solve for x (if necessary, see "Compare Apples to Apples" in the Exponents lesson).

50. Tables & Graphs / Percent (difference-over-original)

51. Area & Perimeter (fitting)

52. More Pick Numbers: Pick values for x (the "Size" of the unit), and check the areas using the table. For example, when $x = 1$, the area is $2 \times 4 = 8$. Eliminate answer choices accordingly.

53. Graphs of Sine & Cosine

54. Vectors

55. Exponents: Compare apples to apples, i.e. rewrite the equation so that the base numbers—3 and 9—are the same. Hint: $9 = 3^2$.

56. Area & Perimeter (SAS formula) / Functions: You will have to use the SAS formula for the area of a triangle: $A = \frac{1}{2}ab \sin \theta$. The initial area is $A_1 = \frac{1}{2}(20)(15) \cdot \sin \theta$. And the area in terms of t (which you will use to find the final area) is $A(t) = \frac{1}{2}(20)(15 - 2t)\sin \theta$. Set $A(t)$ equal to $\frac{1}{2}A_1$ and solve for t.

57. Permutations & Combinations: Note that the letters P and E show up twice, so you must divide by $(2!)(2!)$. Review permutations if necessary.

58. Pick Answers / Complex Numbers / Working with Polynomials: Use *FOIL* for the answer choices. Shortcut: Notice that the middle terms (the ones involving i) cancel for only one answer choice; since i is not part of $49x^2 + 81$, this must be the answer.

59. Graphs of Functions: This question sounds harder than it is. The "residual" is simply the difference between the data point and the y value predicted by the line of best fit. The data point with the greatest residual should be visually apparent (it's the one farthest from the line).

60. Probability: You might add the probabilities for 1–4 errors ("at least 1 error"), but the faster approach is to subtract the probability of 0 errors from the number 1, thus leaving you with the probability of one or more errors. (Note that the sum of the probabilities is 1, as we would expect.)

READING

PASSAGE I

1. Direct: 26–28

2. Purpose: 62 ("collective," "throughout the club")

3. Extended Reasoning: 10–12: There is no added set, but rather performances at "the end of the final set."

4. Direct: 35–37

5. Direct: 26–28

6. Tone: 35–37: The key words are "open disgust."

7. Direct: 75–77 ("bedrock")

8. Direct: 40–41

9. Direct: 65–67

10. Direct: 78–79

PASSAGE II

11. Purpose: 90–91: Like Main Idea questions, the answers to Purpose questions that relate to the whole passage are often found at the end of the last paragraph.

12. Direct: 87–88 ("The goal should be . . .")

13. Direct: 84–87, 90–91: See lines 6–10 for the "problem" mentioned in the correct answer.

14. Direct: G: 17–18; H: 73–74; J: last ¶.

15. Direct: A: 43–44; C: 46–47; D: 45–46

16. Direct: 74–79

17. Direct: 38–39

18. Words in Context: 51–52 ("in the middle of a grassy lawn")

19. Extended Reasoning: 64–66

20. Extended Reasoning: 67: There isn't much in the way of context for this one; you must use what you know about the term "mixed uses." How would you define *mixed* in this context?

PASSAGE III

21. Main Idea: 25–27, 61–63, 67–70

22. Tone: 7–9

23. Direct: 38–51

24. Extended Reasoning: 58–61

25. Words in Context: 56–58: The narrator wants to understand (or *get in* to) "the particulars"—she really wants to understand the subject of flower identification.

26. Extended Reasoning: 81–91: You might use POE on this one.

27. Direct: 25

28. Direct: 57 ("particulars"), 63 ("individuals")

29. Direct: 25–26, 52–54

30. Direct: 70–71

PASSAGE IV

31. Purpose: 12–14. Additional evidence can be found in lines 37–40, 52–56, 74–75, and 84–87.

32. Direct: 65–73: Note the mention of money in line 72 (a good identifier).

33. Extended Reasoning: 48–49 ("once on the ground")

34. Direct: 46–48: The answer is apparent, but not necessarily easy to find. Hopefully you had "scanning electron microscopy" circled as an identifier in lines 45–46.

35. Direct: 77–80

36. Direct: 3–5

37. Direct: 15–17

38. Direct: 31–32

39. Words in Context: 58–61

40. Direct: G: 84–85; H: 86; J: 85

SCIENCE

PASSAGE I (Data Representation)

1. New Information / Direct: See Figure 1; only one value is over 400 colonies.

2. Direct: Simply, which bars are higher in the two figures? Luckily, they are the same for both figures (the answer choices reverse the order of the figures, with water flow on the left, and *E. coli* on the right).

3. Trends: BI↑ Water quality↑

4. New Information / Trends / Make Connections: We could get into a series of trends, starting with the one given in the question (Quality↑ larvae↑), but we don't have to! Just look at the answer choices. Only one is true, according to Tables 1 and 2. This question serves as a good reminder to use the second parts of answer choices (after, for example, the Yes/No), especially on difficult-looking problems.

5. Make Connections (or Science Sense): You might have a "science sense" that as *E. coli* increases, water quality decreases. If not, look at the first sentence of ¶2.

6. New Information / Science Sense: Would large amounts of fertilizer increase or decrease water quality? Make sure to note the trend in Table 1 (see #3): BI↑ Water quality↑ (and, thus, as BI↓ Water quality↓).

PASSAGE II (Data Representation)

7. Tables: Just check a point or two, and eliminate answer choices accordingly.

8. Extrapolation

9. Direct / Calculations & Math: 133 – 81 = ?

10. Science Sense: This question sounds difficult, but just look at the chemical equation at the beginning of the passage. If one chemical "converts" into another, then the first one, a *reactant*, should be to the left of the arrow ($\rightarrow$) and the second, a *product*, should be to the right. Only one answer has the chemicals in the right places.

11. Science Knowledge: You must know that as pH increases, a substance becomes more basic (less acidic). See ¶2: "DMEA [is] an AWP ingredient that increases pH." Note that you can eliminate A and C whether you are familiar with the pH scale or not.

12. Make Connections: Start with Table 1: What is the volume of H_2 for AWP 3, Day 2? Now go to Figure 1, and find the day when EDTA gives that same volume. Note that EDTA is represented by the line with *one* dot between dashes, not two dots (cupferron). The *Key* can be confusing.

PASSAGE III (Research Summaries)

13. Direct: Restate the question: When do the scales display the same weight?

14. Direct: Figure 2 shows the weight of Scale A (using Scale B, in Trial 1) as spinning the hand about 90° clockwise. But how heavy is this? Look at Trial 2. You might also note that the scales are "identical" (see first sentence of the passage).

15. Science Sense / Trends: You might have a "science sense" that as a spring is compressed, its potential energy is increased, and the greater the weight, the more the spring is compressed. In other words, using our trends notation: weight↑ compression↑ potential energy↑.

16. Science Sense: Make sure you understand the introduction, especially Figure 1. Trial 1 gives away what the bottom scale will look like. But what about the top one? Since the top scale is upside down, it should show its own weight (since it's upside down, spin the book around if necessary).

17. Research Methods / Science Sense: Use POE. The correct answer may not be obvious, but the incorrect answer choices are either clearly incorrect (B: the board does not roll from side to side; C: the scales are weighing the 110.0 N weight, not the pencils—see #19) or somewhat ridiculous (D).

18. Trends

19. Research Methods: Note that the students are only measuring the 10.0 N block (not the board and pencils). See

Trial 5 for proof of this: the scales show a total of only 10.0 N (see Trial 2).

PASSAGE IV (Research Summaries)

20. Trends: Note the description of Experiment 3: EOR is the "minimum octane number . . ." Now check Table 2: Engine speed↑ EOR↓.

21. Interpolation

22. Calculations & Math: Pick a row from Table 1, and plug the values into the answer choices until you find one that works. Hint: To make the calculations easier, pick one of the rows that includes 0

23. Learn / Ratios / Make Connections: First, you must recognize that a heptane:isooctane ratio of 100:900 is equivalent to a ratio of 10:90 (review the Ratios section in the tutorial, under Data Representation Odds & Ends). This gives an octane number of 90. But what can we learn about the addition of TEL? Look at Figure 1. When 3 mL of TEL are added to isooctane (octane number = 100), the octane number increases to 125. So we've learned something. Apply this knowledge to the 10:90 mixture: In other words, if 100 → 125, then 90 → ?

24. Direct: Remember, EOR is the *minimum* octane number required for an engine to operate without damage (see #20). In other words, the actual octane number should be greater than or equal to the EOR.

25. Interpolation / Ratios: You might review Questions 19 and 20. It is not the amount of heptane or the amount of isooctane that is important; it is the *ratio* of heptane to isooctane that determines octane number. So 2:8 ~ 20:80. Interpolate (see Table 1).

26. New Information / Make Connections: Pure heptane has an octane number of 0 (see Table 1). We would expect the TEL to raise the octane number somewhat, but not to the value found when the sample was isooctane (which has an octane number of 100) (see Figure 1).

PASSAGE V (Conflicting Viewpoints)

27. Direct: Scientist B: "Short-period comets were once long-period comets."

28. Direct: Scientist A: "The KB has a *small inclination* . . . and is located in the solar system *between 30 A.U. and 50 A.U.*" (italics added).

29. Direct: Introduction: ". . . orbital planes [of short-period comets] have inclinations 30° or less."

30. Science Knowledge: You are looking for a "giant planet" (see Scientist B). Three of the choices are small planets.

31. Direct: You might use POE on this one. First of all, according to Scientist B, "the KB does not exist." Eliminate B and D. Next, Scientist B implies that short-period comets have orbital periods "less than 200 yr." So Comet Halley (76 yr.) is not a long-period comet. Eliminate C.

32. Direct: Scientist A refers to "much larger icy bodies" in comparison with "bodies with diameters between 10 km and 30 km."

33. Strengths & Weaknesses: Both viewpoints focus on our own solar system; see "Sun" in the first sentence of the introduction. The characteristics of a "nearby star" are off topic.

PASSAGE VI (Research Summaries)

34. Direct: See Table 3: Only two lines have no fruit (Fruit mass = 0 kg).

35. Science Knowledge: If you're familiar with the structures of cells, this one is straightforward. If not, take a guess.

36. Direct: The answer is given in the first sentence of the passage: "Tomato plants grow poorly in high-salt environments." You could also answer this one if you know (or guess) that NaCl is salt. What happens to mass as you go from Table 1 (low salt) to Table 3 (high salt)?

37. Research Methods (terms): Try POE on this one. Which answer choices are clearly *dependent* variables (the results of the experiment)? Hopefully you eliminated C and D. Since tomato plants were used in each line (they were not varied, and are thus not a variable of any kind), you can also eliminate B. *AtNHX1* was not incorporated into L4; it is thus an independent variable; the scientists *controlled* its inclusion in the experiment.

38. Science Sense: If you know what the prefixes hetero- and homo- mean, this question is easier than it sounds. The passage states that "two identical copies of this gene" were used for each line (¶3). Eliminate F and H, which mention "different" alleles. Lastly, which prefix means "the same"?

39. Tables (graphs from tables) / Calculations & Math: The relationship between height and mass is as expected (you can confirm by plotting a few points). You might need to review slope (see the Lines lesson in the Math part of this tutorial).

40. Research Methods (terms): At first glance, you might think there is no control group: all four lines are tested in varying salt concentrations (see Tables 1–3). However, one line did not receive an *AtNHX1* gene (read the introduction, ¶2, and see #37).

4. TECHNIQUES: TEST 4

QUESTIONS BY SECTIONS/CHAPTERS

The following information lists every question on the test according to its relevant chapter or section in this tutorial. If you're correcting a test, circle the question numbers below that you missed or guessed on. Make sure to follow the Tutoring Schedule in the Introduction to know when to correct or tackle various types of questions.

ENGLISH	
Usage/Mechanics	Rhetorical Skills
[1, 3, 6, 7, 8, 9, 10, 11, 12] [16, 17, 19, 21, 26, 27, 28] [30, 33, 34, 35, 36, 38, 40, 41, 42, 43] [45, 46, 47, 48, 49, 50, 51, 53, 54, 55, 56, 57, 58] [64, 65, 66, 67, 69, 70, 72, 73, 74]	[2, 4, 5, 13, 14] [15, 18, 20, 22, 23, 24, 25, 29] [31, 32, 37, 39, 44] [52, 59] [60, 61, 62, 63, 68, 71, 75]

Brackets display separate passages.

MATH							
Basic Concepts	Arith.	Algebra	Adv. Alg.	Geometry	Functions	Trig	Odds/ Ends
10, 14, 37, 47	2, 4, 9, 11, 15, 23, 27, 33, 34, 38, 39, 49, 54, 57	5, 8, 12, 16, 17, 19, 22, 26, 40, 53	7, 56	1, 6, 13, 18, 24, 25, 29, 30, 31, 36, 43, 46, 48, 52	20, 21, 32, 50, 59	42, 44	3, 28, 35, 41, 45, 51, 55, 58, 60

READING (by question type and passage)*						
Direct	Extended Reasoning	Purpose	Main Idea	Comp.	Tone	Words in Context
1, 4, 7, 15, 18, 20, 23, 25, 26, 27, 29, 30, 35, 38, 40	2, 3, 11, 12, 17, 21, 33, 34	6, 16, 22, 24	13, 14, 31	8, 9, 10	5, 32, 36, 37	19, 28, 39
Literary Narrative		Social Science		Humanities		Natural Science
1, 2, 3, 4, 5, 6, 7, 8, 9, 10		11, 12, 13, 14, 15, 16, 17, 18, 19, 20		21, 22, 23, 24, 25, 26, 27, 28, 29, 30		31, 32, 33, 34, 35, 36, 37, 38, 39, 40

SCIENCE (by question type and passage)*		
Data Representation	Research Summaries	Conflicting Viewpoints
8, 9, 10, 14, 15, 18, 20, 22, 24, 28, 30, 32, 33, 34, 35, 37, 38, 39, 40	11, 12, 13, 16, 17, 19, 21, 23, 25, 26, 27, 29, 31, 36,	1, 2, 3, 4, 5, 6, 7
[8, 9, 10, 11, 12, 13] [35, 36, 37, 38, 39, 40]	[14, 15, 16, 17, 18, 19, 20] [21, 22, 23, 24, 25, 26, 27] [28, 29, 30, 31, 32, 33, 34]	1, 2, 3, 4, 5, 6, 7

*For Reading and Science corrections, focus on *question type*. Use the *passage* categories only to identify trends, such as timing issues, or passage types that may need review.

TECHNIQUES AND HINTS
ENGLISH
Passage I

1. Redundancies: Read the beginning of the sentence carefully.

2. Answer the Question: The choice that gives the "most vivid description of iguanas on the floor" should be clear.

3. Wordy/Pronouns (Agreement) (A): The pronoun "which" is technically referring to "trees," clearly not the intended referent. / Run-on (B) / Fragment (D): Make sure you're comfortable with semicolons (see the Punctuations lesson).

4. Main Ideas (deletions): Consider the previous sentences; clearly a transition is needed before "I told the woman that I didn't mind."

5. Answer the Question: Only one choice describes the spikes' "pattern."

6. Nonsense: Make sure you get to the end of the sentence. You may be tempted especially by the two shorter choices, but neither makes sense with the words that follow (after the underline).

7. Pronouns (Agreement): See "her" near the end of the sentence.

8. Punctuation: Remember, *when in doubt, keep the commas out.*

9. Vocabulary

10. Wordy (G, H) / Subject-Verb Agreement (J): The verb "deliver" (plural) does not agree with "judge" (singular); this would be an unidiomatic construction in any case.

11. Punctuation: Once again, stay away from commas unless you are sure they are necessary.

12. Wordy

13. Organization: The placement should be clear if you consider the context prior to the point of insertion.

14. Main Ideas (purpose): The question itself is vague (no mention of *iguanas* or *vets*), so you may be tempted to answer "No." But focus on the second parts of the answer choices. Neither H

nor J works great (choice H isn't a primary focus of the essay, as suggested by its title). The answer must be "Yes." Of the two choices, hopefully the correct answer is apparent.

Passage II

15. Transitions: Even if you didn't understand the intended flow of the sentence, all three incorrect choices are Run-ons.

16. Punctuation

17. Idiom

18. Organization: This unusual Organization question, which asks you to change the order of the sentences, uses clue words, as with more typical Organization questions ("this event" in Sentence 2 and "His" in Sentence 3). So we know Sentence 1, which introduces both the runner and the event, must come first. From there, you must understand the intended flow of the sentences (note "however" in Sentence 2).

19. Punctuation: If you chose C or D, review the "One Comma Rule."

20. Main Ideas (transitions) / Answer the Question: Only one answer touches on the topic of the next paragraph (running).

21. Passive Voice

22. Main Ideas (topic sentences) / Answer the Question

23. Main Ideas (deletions): Mills was not *completely* unknown—he was *rather* unknown. The word *rather* here "softens" or minimizes the word *unknown*.

24. Answer the Question

25. Main Ideas (additions): The focus is on Mills and his preparation for the 1964 Olympics.

26. Vocabulary

27. Punctuation: The *who* phrase provides helpful information but is not completely necessary. Thus, as with *which* phrases (see the Pronouns lesson), it should be bound by commas.

28. Verb Tense: This one tests an irregular verb (*to run*): Mills *ran* today; Mills *had run* yesterday.

29. Main Ideas (deletions): Note the first two sentences of this paragraph.

Passage III

30. Run-ons

31. Transitions: Remember, correct answers to Transitions questions are often the ones with no transitions.

32. Answer the Question: Note the question's emphasis on the change happening "swiftly and dramatically."

33. Pronouns (Case): The pronoun refers to "Foley," who is a performer in the sentence (he "figured out . . ."); he is *not* an object of any action, so avoid *whom*.

34. Fragments

35. Confused Words: All of the words in question sound similar, but only one refers to something deceptive, or wrongly perceived by the senses. Note: an *allusion* is a reference to something (*an allusion to Shakespeare*), and *elusion*, a rare word, has to do with hiding or escaping (*to elude*).

36. Fragments / Wordy

37. Main Ideas (changes): This part of the paragraph focuses on how sounds are created in movies.

38. Verb Tense (G) / Idiom (H, J): Something *arises from* something else. / Subject-Verb Agreement (J): The subject is "need" (singular).

39. Main Ideas (deletions): Be careful of A: the role of a sound technician is not established by the underlined portion, although it is discussed later in the sentence.

40. Parallelism

41. Punctuation: Note the long dash after "props" later in the sentence.

42. Vocabulary: The correct choice is a common usage. If you didn't "hear" the best word, that's OK. On these Vocabulary and Idiom questions, just pick an answer and move on. Hopefully, as you take more tests (and

read more and more), you'll start to hear these correct uses.

43. Run-ons (A, B) / Nonsense (D)

44. Main Ideas (deletions): The second-to-last sentence ("The director . . .") doesn't focus on Foley or his work, so it would be a poor last sentence.

Passage IV

45. Punctuation: As explained in the Punctuation lesson, sometimes words that appear to be part of a noun phrase ("molecular biologist") are actually functioning as an adjective phrase (in this case, modifying "Bonnie Bassler"). Try removing the words to hear the error. Thus, the only correct comma is the one following the opening phrase.

46. Fragment (F) / Run-ons (G, H)

47. Punctuation: We must close the phrase that begins at the comma after "glow."

48. Apostrophes / + Wordy (F, G)

49. Punctuation: The correct answer displays a typical placement for a modifying phrase, at the end of the sentence, following a comma. You might review "Improper Modifiers" in the Misplaced Words lesson. / + Wordy (B): This choice is also missing a comma before "which" (see the Pronouns lesson).

50. Verb Tense: Note "releases" in the previous sentence.

51. Fragments (B, C) / Punctuation (D)

52. Transitions: Since the passage continues to discuss "quorum sensing," we're looking for a support transition. Do not be fooled by choice F: sure the bacterial species is different from that discussed in the previous paragraph, but the main topic of the passage remains quorum sensing—there is no contrast.

53. Punctuation: If you went with choice C, use the *and* rule between "related" and "bacterial" (see "Adjectives" in the Punctuation lesson).

54. Wordy / + Style (F): The phrase "neck of the woods" is too informal for this passage.

55. Pronouns (Case)

56. Subject-Verb Agreement: The subject is "strains."

57. Redundancies: Make sure to read to the end of the sentence.

58. Pronouns (Case) (F) / Pronouns (Ambiguity) (H, J): The word "them" is ambiguous.

59. Main Ideas (additions): The added sentence may seem off-topic—what does it have to do with "talking bacteria" (see the title)—but focus on the second parts of the answer choices. Neither of the *No* choices offers a good reason to not add the sentence. So focus on A and B. As you choose, note that the passage has already made clear that the research is focused on humans (read the first sentence of the last paragraph of the passage).

Passage V

60. Wordy (F) / Style (F, J): Words like "creeping" and "low-down" are too informal for this passage. If you narrow this one down to G and H, ask yourself what makes the most sense when referring to "subway lines."

61. Transitions: Remember, the choice with no transition is often the correct one.

62. Answer the Question: Note the words "highest degree of failure" in the question. Choice F is tempting, but there's a choice that's worse than *obscure*.

63. Main Ideas (additions): Note the first words of the next paragraph. We're clearly still in the past.

64. Comparisons: Note the word "More" at the beginning of the sentence. A comparison is being made: something is *more* this *than* that.

65. Fragments: Choice B appears to create a compound sentence, but the first part of the sentence (up to the comma) is not an independent clause (thus, we have a fragment).

66. Wordy / + -*ING* (F, H)

67. Run-ons: Since the second part of this sentence is an independent clause, the first part must be a phrase (or dependent clause). All three incorrect choices create comma-splice run-ons.

68. Answer the Question: Make sure to look for "the clearest example" of how Beck made the maps *simple*.

69. Vocabulary

70. Misplace Words (Improper Modifiers): It is the "board" that is "willing to try anything . . ." / Passive Voice: All three incorrect choices are in the passive voice.

71. Organization: Consider the flow of ideas. The paragraph begins with a discussion of the board's *resistance* to Beck's map (a negative tone). At Sentence 2 ("Still . . ."), the flow changes: the board becomes "willing to try" the map (a positive tone). Now, focus on the tone of Sentence 5: does it portray the map (in the board's eyes) as positive or negative?

72. Apostrophes & Confused Words

73. Punctuation: By now, you should be comfortable knowing when to keep out superfluous commas.

74. Pronouns (Ambiguity) (F) / Wordy (G, H)

75. Organization: Just look for the place where the passage discusses "distances." (To make these placement letters—[A], [B], etc.—easy to find, don't forget to circle them as you read the passage.)

MATH

1. Area & Perimeter

2. Probability

3. Principle of Counting

4. Arithmetic Word Problems: There's no shortcut to this one. For each item, calculate how many additional packages can be made. For example, Esteban has 30 pens remaining (3 boxes × 10 pens each). Since each package holds 5 pens, he can make 6 packages (30/5 = 6). After checking each item, whichever one makes the *least* number of packages will determine the number of additional packages that can be made.

Note: While this isn't a particularly hard question (note the number), it *is* laborious. Consider skipping it on your first pass, especially if time is a major concern.

5. Algebraic Word Problems: These Algebraic Word questions with given equations are usually straightforward. Just plug in carefully, and make sure you're comfortable with your calculator.

6. Angles (triangle / straight line): We can easily find $m\angle ABE$ (sum of angles in triangle is 180°). Then calculate the angle in question (sum of angles that form a straight line is 180°).

7. Working with Polynomials or Pick Numbers (type 1)

8. More Pick Numbers: Hint: Start with one of the higher numbers; typically, with these types of problems, the lower (easier) numbers (such as $t = 0$, $d = 15$) will give multiple correct "answers."

9. Percent (difference-over-original): Make sure you use the "original" number as your denominator.

10. Basic Concepts (absolute value)

11. Proportions: Using a proportion is straightforward: $\dfrac{\$}{\text{shares}} \dfrac{6{,}880}{160} = \dfrac{x}{70}$. You might also think in terms of ratios, with Samantha's share in the numerator and the total shares in the denominator: $\dfrac{70}{70 + 50 + 40} = \dfrac{7}{16}$ → $\dfrac{7}{16} \cdot 6{,}880 \ldots$

12. More Pick Numbers: If you're comfortable reading 2-D inequality graphs, you'll probably see the answer right away. The phrase "less than 30" means all numbers up to *but not including* 30. Note that an open circle on these graphs indicates that the number is *excluded* from the range (so choices F and H include 30 and choices G, J, and K do not). If you're unfamiliar with these graphs, use the Pick Trick (although you still need to understand the meanings of open and closed circles, as described above).

13. Triangles (similar): Focus on $\triangle ADE$ and $\triangle ABC$.

14. Calculator: Make sure you close the parentheses under the square root before dividing by 2. If you type $\sqrt{(50/2)}$, you'll get the wrong answer (5).

15. Ratios (shares)

16. Calculators or Pick Numbers (type 3): The easiest approach is to simply subtract the given fractions from 1 (use your calculator). You could also pick a number for the operating budget, preferably one divisible by 9 and 6 (such as 18). Once you find the amounts for library books and scholarships, subtract these values from the total budget, and use part-over-whole.

17. Basic Algebra or Pick Answers: Typically, when you see a variable in the denominator, cross multiply.

18. Area & Perimeter

19. Pick Answers: You could try graphing the inequalities (see "Systems of Linear Inequalities" in the Systems of Equations and Inequalities lesson), but the faster approach is to plug the answer choices into the given inequalities, eliminating appropriately.

20. More Graphs of Functions (range): This question looks hard, but if you understand range, just look at the greatest and least values of the graph. The answer is apparent.

21. Basic Functions: With composite functions, start on the inside and work out (so find $g(-3)$ first, and then plug the result into $f(x)$).

22. Algebraic Word Problems: This is one of those common "two equation–two unknown" algebraic word problems. If f is the price of a yard of flannel and c is the price of a yard of calico, the two equations are $3f + 4c = 25$ and $f + 2c = 11$. Review Systems of Equations and Inequalities if you need help solving the equations.

23. Averages, Medians, & Modes: Make sure you put the numbers in order before finding the median.

24. Area & Perimeter: If you're comfortable with parallelograms, which have two sets of equal sides, the answer should be straightforward. Did you choose K? This might feel like a problem with a

trick, but we're not yet halfway through the test. Choice K is an unlikely answer this early on.

25. Area & Perimeter: There are a couple ways to tackle this one. The answer choices expect you to find the lengths of the sides of the shaded rectangle, so we'll use this approach. To find the length of the side of each square, use the following equation (where x is the length of one square's side): $4x \cdot 6x = 1$. So each square has a side of length 1/24. Use this to find the sides of the shaded rectangle (keep your answer in fraction form—again, note the answer choices).

You could just as easily find the area of each of the 24 squares ($1 \div 24$), and count the shaded squares, but your answer won't match the form of the answer choices. Just simplify the answer choices with your calculator.

26. Probability / Pick Answers or Basic Algebra: We start with 16 red marbles and 42 total marbles. Since the number of additional red marbles (x) will also be added to the total number of marbles (the denominator of the probability ratio), we have: $\dfrac{16+x}{42+x} = \dfrac{3}{5}$. Solve by cross multiplying.

If you have trouble finding (or solving) the equation above, Pick Answers.

27. Exponents or Pick Numbers (type 1): While the Pick Trick will work fine, this one should be a snap if you understand negative exponents.

28. Sets & Groups: This is an unusual question, but not necessarily a difficult one. The important thing is to read the question carefully. $\triangle MNP$ "is a counterexample proving the claim false." Since the claim is that Set A does not contain isosceles triangles, $\triangle MNP$ must be an isosceles triangle in Set A.

29. Area & Perimeter (parallelogram)

30. Coordinates (slanted distances): If you use the Pythagorean triangle approach to finding the distance (as we recommend), you'll hopefully notice that the resulting triangle is a 3-4-5 one.

31. Lines (slope)

32. More Graphs of Functions (transformations)

33. Exponents or Calculator: "Compare apples to apples": Since $8 = 2^3$ and $4^{0.5} = 2$, we can write $8^2 \cdot 4^{0.5} = (2^3)^2 \cdot 2 = 2^6 \cdot 2$ . . . You could also plug the values into your calculator, and then check the answer choices.

34. Proportions: Make sure to read the question carefully. It's a straightforward Proportion problem, but what is given, and what is being asked, can be easy to miss.

35. Logarithms / Exponents: First simplify the log into its exponential form, and get the bases the same ("compare apples to apples"—see the Exponents lesson, and #33 above): $\log_2 \sqrt{8} = x \rightarrow$

$$2^x = \sqrt{8} \rightarrow 2^x = 8^{\frac{1}{2}} \rightarrow 2^x = (2^3)^{\frac{1}{2}} \rightarrow$$

$$2^x = 2^{\frac{3}{2}}.$$

You could also type the log directly into your calculator: $\log_2 \sqrt{8} = \dfrac{\log \sqrt{8}}{\log 2}$ (see the "base-change rule" in the Logarithm lesson).

36. Tables & Graphs / More Circles (sectors): First, find the number of students who picked bananas. Here's the math: $90 - 15 = 75$ (students who picked apples, bananas, or strawberries) $\rightarrow 75/3 = 25$ (students who picked bananas, since each of the three fruits was chosen by "an equal number of the remaining students"). Finally, apply the sector-of-circle ratios. Remember, these are always part (sector) to whole (circle). The first ratio is for students; the second is for degrees: $\dfrac{25}{90} = \dfrac{x}{360}$ . . .

37. Basic Concepts or Pick Numbers (type 1): If you're comfortable finding common denominators, use this approach. Otherwise, use the Pick Trick.

38. Tables & Graphs / Probability: Make sure you identify the *subgroup* and *target group*. Review "Probability and Tables" in the lesson if necessary.

39. Tables & Graphs / Probability: The challenge here might be finding the *target group* (numerator). Try changing the question by removing the NOTs: the target group includes all college or nonstudent residents (NOT high school) who approved or disapproved (NOT no opinion).

40. Tables & Graphs / Ratios / Basic Algebra: Remember that multi-question problems often quickly get harder as you go. Not surprisingly, this one can be tricky; it might be a good one to skip on your first pass. First, let's calculate how many (x) of the 15 incorrectly classified residents were college students, using the given 60% in the question and the information in the table (this is similar to the non–Pick Trick approach to #26): $\dfrac{14 + x}{30 + x} = 0.60$
→ cross multiply: $x = 10$. So the other 5 incorrectly classified residents must be high school students: $\dfrac{30 + 5}{45 + 5} = \dots$

41. Sets & Groups / Averages, Medians, & Modes (optional: Pick Numbers (type 3)): If you're comfortable with averages, medians, and modes, you should be able to identify the correct answer. If you had trouble, try picking easy numbers: For example, Set A: {1, 3, 3, 3, 3}, Set B: {2, 3, 3, 3, 3}. Clearly, the medians and modes of both sets are the same.

42. Trigonometry & the Unit Circle or Pick Numbers (type 1): If you're comfortable with trigonometry—especially the behavior of sine and cosine on a unit circle (or their graphs)—by all means go straight to the answer. Otherwise, use the Pick Trick. Don't forget to check every answer choice with Pick Numbers type 1.

43. Solids & Volume: A rather straightforward problem for #43. This is why it's important to look for easier problems in the last third of the test (on your first pass).

44. Triangles / Basic Trigonometry: As with many triangle problems, you must actually create the triangles. When you connect points *B* and *D*, you create two right triangles. Review the special

integer triangles in the lesson (3-4-5 and 5-12-13).

45. Patterns (repeating patterns): The magic number is 7 (7 days in a week). First, find a number close to 200 that is divisible by 7. Going back this many days will land on Tuesday. For example, 196 is divisible by 7, so if we go back 196 days from Tuesday, it's (again) Tuesday. If we go back 197 days, it's the day before Tuesday (Monday). And so on. . . .

46. Angles (vertical / complementary): The easiest approach is to see that angles 1 and 2 are *vertical*. Set the expressions equal and solve for *x*. Then note that angles 2 and 3 are *complementary*.

47. Basic Concepts (GCF / LCM): Note that 120 is a common multiple of choices C and D but not the *least* common multiple.

48. Triangles: You might not know what *scalene*, *acute*, or *obtuse* means, but you could still possibly eliminate some choices and take a guess. The trick is to investigate the hypotenuse of a right triangle with legs of 4 and 5. Here are the three possibilities:

- If the third side of the given triangle (7) *equals* the hypotenuse of the right triangle, then the given triangle is (perhaps obviously) a right triangle.

- If the third side is *less than* the hypotenuse, then the given triangle's largest angle is *less than* 90° (and the triangle is *acute*).

- Finally, if the third side is *greater* than the hypotenuse, then the given triangle's largest angle is *greater* than 90° (and the triangle is *obtuse*).

Review "Angle-Side Relationships" in the Triangles lesson if necessary. A *scalene* triangle is simply one with three sides of different lengths.

49. Probability (multiple events): The trick is to work with the probabilities of *losing* each game (40% and 65%).

50. More Graphs of Functions (domain) / Factoring or More Pick Numbers: If you're comfortable factoring, do so with the denominator, but remember that canceling like expressions in the numerator and denominator does *not* change the domain—it just creates a "hole" (note the open circle on the graph at $x = 3$) rather than an asymptote (review "Asymptotes" in the More Graphs of Functions lesson). You could also simply plug in the obvious numbers from the answer choices (-1, 2, 3, etc.) and eliminate choices accordingly.

51. Permutations & Combinations: Since order matters, this a permutation problem. Just focus on the last 4 numbers, each of which can be one of 10 numbers: So we have $10 \cdot 10 \cdot 10 \cdot 10$. As usual with these types of questions, the answers are in exponential form.

52. Coordinates (slanted distances): Of course, you should know that a circle is a set of points a certain distance (the radius) from a point. Just find the distance from the given center to the given point. The answer is hopefully clear (don't let the wordy answer choices confuse you).

53. Pick Answers or Logarithms: If you've never seen "ln" before, you might have to skip this one. But take a look at your calculator. See the "LN" key? If you look around, you should also see an "e" key. You could probably Pick Answers and get this one correct without really understanding the topic. Just carefully plug each answer into the equation for x, and stop when you find 7. A correct answer is a correct answer!

Here's the logarithmic/algebraic approach: The letters ln (or LN) represent something called the "natural log," which is simply $\log_e$. So we have $7 = \log_e(x - 2) + 3$ → $4 = \log_e(x - 2)$ → exponential form: $e^4 = x - 2 \ldots$

54. Tables & Graphs: Review #28 in the homework assignment from this lesson.

55. Algebraic Word Problems / Parabolas: Coming up with the correct equation can be tricky. We know that the store will sell 40 caps when the price is $22 each. Since for every $1 *decrease* ($x$) in price, the store will sell 4 *more* caps, we can write that the store sells $40 + 4x$ caps when the price is $22 - x$.

Revenue (y) is given as the number of caps sold times the price per cap, so we have $y = (40 + 4x)(22 - x)$. If you FOIL, you'll get a downward opening parabola: $y = -4x^2 + 48x + 880$. The y-value of the vertex will give you the maximum revenue (review the Parabolas & Ellipses lesson for finding the coordinates of the vertex).

56. Systems of Equations & Inequalities / Pick Numbers (type 2): While this isn't actually a "system" of inequalities, the lesson went over graphing inequalities. Pick simple numbers for a, b, and c (make sure $0 < a < b < c$) and quickly sketch your result. Note the slope, y-intercept, and shading of your graph as you eliminate answer choices.

57. Proportions: This is a long and relatively difficult problem (a good one to skip for many students), although it really only tests Proportions. We'll show you how to set up the equations for the *white* material:

The first proportion is for "exactly the right amount of material to make 500 banners" ($1/8 = 0.375$):

$$\frac{\text{banners}}{\text{yards}} \quad \frac{1}{0.375} = \frac{500}{w} \rightarrow \text{So we need } w$$

$= 187.5$ yards of white material.

If the club instead uses 12-yard bolts, the closest number greater than 187.5 that is divisible by 12 is 192, so we have our second proportion:

$$\frac{\text{banners}}{\text{yards}} \quad \frac{1}{0.375} = \frac{x}{192} \rightarrow \text{So we can}$$

make $x = 512$ banners.

If you go through the process above for *blue* material, you'll get 520 banners, so we're limited to 512 banners by the white bolts. Compare to the original 500 banners.

58. Complex Numbers and Working with Polynomials or Pick Numbers (type 1): We recommend using the Pick Trick. As mentioned in the Complex Numbers lesson, feel free to use your calculator. For example, if you pick $x = 2$ and type $(2 - 3i)^3$ into your calculator (make sure you can find the i key), you'll get $-46 -$

9*i* very quickly. Check the answer choices. If you're calculator doesn't have an *i* key, FOIL away. Don't forget that $i^2 = -1$.

59. More Graphs of Functions / More Pick Numbers: Since –4, 0, and 6 are factors (roots/zeroes) of the function, the polynomial must include $(x + 4)$, x, and $(x - 6)$. We also know that the *degree* of the polynomial must be *even* (the graph opens up to the right *and* to the left). Eliminate A, B, and C (by adding the exponents of x we know the degree of A is 3). Finally, pick a number and check the remaining two choices. Since the *y*-scale is not given in the graph, focus on the *sign* (+ or –) of your answer. Hint: try $x = 2$.

60. Matrices: In the lesson, review "Rule 1" in the "Multiplying Matrices" section. If you remember this rule, this turns out to be a straightforward question for a #60!

READING

PASSAGE I

1. Direct: 21–22

2. Extended Reasoning: 22–25: The "thing" must refer to something that the man can see in Palm Beach (eliminate G and J).

3. Extended Reasoning: 34–35: Remember that these fiction, or "literary narrative," passages often include metaphorical writing. It's unlikely that *actual* fireflies are perched in front of every home (eliminate A and C).

4. Direct: Line numbers not available: The passage never mentions that the girl pays any attention to the narrator.

5. Tone: 58–59 ("To blot her existence"), 62 ("Gazing coldly"), 87–89 (". . . unspeakable fatigue . . . tedious life.")

6. Purpose: 81–85: While Purpose questions typically ask about the author or narrator of a passage, this one asks about a *character*.

7. Direct: 44–46

8. Comparison: Note some of the similarities between "You" in Passage A and the narrator in Passage B: They

are both traveling (1–3, 39–41), they are confronted with a stranger with whom they do not want to make contact (5–7, 58–59) (you might even notice that both characters use *reading* as an excuse to avoid contact (9, 58–59)), and they are both struggling with unhappiness (35–38, 87–89).

9. Comparison / Direct: 5–11

10. Comparison / Extended Reasoning: 13–16, 52–57

PASSAGE II

11. Extended Reasoning: 1–5: The "rougher fringes" concerns a spirit of "the past," a turning away from "contraptions" and "progress." This same idea is discussed in relation to electricity in the fifth paragraph (see lines 68–70).

12. Extended Reasoning: 48–53, 56–58

13. Main Idea: 14–15, etc. Feel free to use POE (process of elimination) on this one. Only one choice is supported by context.

14. Main Idea: 64–68: One might question that the correct answer is actually the main idea of this paragraph (the main idea has more to do with Stevenson's dislike, not anticipation, of electric lighting), but only one answer is supported by context. Use POE.

15. Direct: The fact that Stevenson was a writer should be obvious. For the other answers, see 50 and 87–88.

16. Purpose: 1–6: The author is speaking metaphorically ("clashing swords" represent adventure and the past, while "telephone wires" represent "progress").

17. Extended Reasoning: 23–30. Watch out for C, which is too strong (and there is no mention of Stevenson "publicly" renouncing anything), and D, which has an eye-catcher ("consternation")—the "wringing of hands" primarily was a response to Stevenson's decision not to enter the family business, not specifically to his letters.

18. Direct: 35–38. Even though the question is worded like an Extended Reasoning one, the context is direct and clear.

19. WIC: Context is lacking for this one (you hopefully have a general knowledge of the phrase in question). We do know the author of the passage is traveling around in the footsteps of Stevenson (see 48–49). With this in mind, only one choice makes sense. Use POE if necessary. Note that both C and D take the phrase too literally.

20. Direct: 81–86

PASSAGE III

21. Extended Reasoning: 71–72, 83–85: Probably the hardest part of this question is its rather cumbersome wording. Here's the question made clearer: Which of the following is an example of how the author brings her own cultural intuition to her reading and research?

22. Purpose: 6–9 ("They matter—in significant ways . . .")

23. Direct: 39–44 (especially: ". . . it should remain true to the spirit . . . of the original"): The question is worded like an Extended Reasoning one, but the answer is fairly direct.

24. Purpose: The author mentions that her home pueblo is "very different" from other pueblos in lines 67–70, and then, in the next paragraph, discusses "problems" (79) with McDermott's book.

25. Direct: 88–92: Again, we have an Extended Reasoning–sounding question that has a very direct answer. The trick may be in finding context (did you have "elders" circled in the last paragraph?).

26. Direct: 15–17: Watch out for eye catchers in some of the incorrect answer choices ("lost hunters," "piñon-nut gatherers").

27. Direct: 65–67

28. WIC: 68 ("very different")

29. Direct 67–70

30. Direct: 84–85: It's worth noting that if you read carefully, these last three questions were relatively easy. This exemplifies why it's so important to get to the last few questions of a passage before running out of time, even if you have to skip some of the harder ones (e.g. #21) along the way.

PASSAGE IV

31. Main Idea: 49–51 . . . : The last half of the passage discusses how "weeds" survive in "derelict urban wastelands." Focus especially on the last paragraph. As you answer Main Idea questions, remember that the most important information in a passage is usually at its end.

32. Tone: 25–31: This question really tests the author's tone, or attitude, toward weeds. Hopefully you sensed that his tone is subtly positive (e.g. 18–21) and never negative. You may have an easier time using POE on this one: the groups in the three incorrect choices, for one reason or another, all view weeds negatively.

33. Extended Reasoning: 31–33. Make sure you read the question carefully (the word "unlike" is important). The "spontaneous vegetation" in line 4 refers to weeds, which are in "competition" with economic crops.

34. Extended Reasoning: 28–31

35. Direct: 22–23: In line 23, "such plants" refer to the "greenery" described in the first paragraph.

36. Tone: 54–70: This is similar to a Tone question. How do the two groups' observations relate? Note the word "Similarly" in line 63—this is enough to answer the question.

37. Tone: Note the author's descriptive words: "*flexible*" (72), "*opportunistic*" (literally speaking) (73), and "*tolerant*" (76). Are these words (especially the first and last) generally positive or negative? Does the author ever explicitly describe weeds negatively? See also Question 32.

38. Direct: 11–13

39. WIC: 11–16: Note the juxtaposition between the two sentences.

40. Direct: 20–21

SCIENCE

PASSAGE I (Conflicting Viewpoints)

1. Trends / Make Connections: Note the last sentence of Student 4. The order of

the atoms by size is the same as the order by atomic mass.

2. Direct: Students 1 and 3 clearly believe there is a lone pair (note the figures). For Student 4, read the first sentence.

3. Direct: Just skim through the viewpoints. Each of the first three students makes clear whether the atoms lie in a plane or not (you might skim for the word "plane"). For student 4, read the first sentence ("Student 3 is correct . . .").

4. Direct: Skim through the viewpoints, especially for for the words "unique bond angle(s)" or "unique angle(s)." The information is clearly stated.

5. Indirect: You'll have to do some easy arithmetic on this one. Start by looking at the figures for Students 1 and 2. Clearly, the three angles add to 360° (for Student 1: 180 + 90 + 90, and for Student 2: 120 + 120 + 120). To finish the problem, focus on Student 3.

6. New Information: As is often the case, these New Information questions might be good ones to skip if you're running short on time. Make sure you only focus on Students 1 and 2. Which student believes that the molecule has a *lone pair*? Answering this question will lead you to the correct answer.

7. Direct: Focus on the bond angles for each student. POE (process of elimination) should be straightforward. This is perhaps the easiest question for this passage, confirming the importance of getting your eyeballs on every question (even if you have to skip ones along the way).

PASSAGE II (Data Representation)

Important note: This is an especially difficult passage. If you've covered genetics in your biology class, you hopefully have some knowledge of genes, alleles, etc. Otherwise, try to identify the questions that do *not* test Science Knowledge, and use your "Science Sense" aggressively. Don't let this difficult passages drag on too long—easier ones are on the way. In fact, most students find this passage and the previous one the hardest passages on the test. Follow the timing

plan carefully so you can get your points on easier passages later.

8. New Information / Make Connections: Since all offspring of Cross 1 had black coats, it's possible (hypothetical) that both parents had the genotype *BBEE* (see Table 1). (Note how easily you can eliminate G and J.)

9. Direct: Just focus on Table 1. This is a relatively easy (and much welcome!) question on a hard passage.

10. Make Connections: First, recognize that, according to Table 1, brown or black coats require at least one *E* allele. (You might also note that yellow coats do not have any *E* alleles—only *e*.) Finally, focus on the Cross 3 row of Table 2.

11. Science Knowledge / Make Connections: If you know (or have a hunch) that "recessive alleles" are represented by lowercase letters, you have the science knowledge part of this question covered. According to Table 1, a lowercase phenotype (*bbee*) leads to a yellow coat, which is found in Crosses 2 and 3 only (Table 2).

12. New Information / Science Sense: If you're not comfortable with genetics, you might still have a "science sense" that if both parents have only *e* alleles (again, see yellow coats in Table 1), then the offspring will also only have *e* alleles.

13. Science Knowledge: In the words of the ACT: ". . . half of the gametes will contain the *B* allele and the other half will contain the *b* allele." Obviously, if you're not comfortable with this topic, take a guess and move on.

PASSAGE III (Research Summaries)

14. Direct

15. Trends

16. Research Methods (terminology): Knowing what "controls" means may help, but even if you don't, the text makes clear which PTs were controls (read Steps 1 and 3).

17. Research Methods: This one almost feels too easy, but the times are clearly listed in the passage ("18 hr" never shows up, even as an eye catcher).

18. Direct: A wordy question, but a relatively straightforward one, assuming you recognize that the different shades of each bar refer to the different times the PTs are submerged in water (see the "*Key*").

19. Research Methods / New Information: At first glance, it may appear that the strengths in Figure 1 (no GLA/zinc nitrate) are greater—or at least *often* greater—than the strengths in Figure 2 (GLA/zinc nitrate). But note the scales of the two graphs (*x*-axis): the strengths in Figure 2 are *always* greater.

20. Calculations & Math: You have to recognize that if W/D is between 0% and 100% (that is, a decimal between 0 and 1), then D (the dry strength) must be greater than W (the wet strength). (If W had been greater than D, the percent values would have been greater than 100%—try some sample values if you'd like.) In any case, you can use "science sense" on this one. What is likely stronger, a wet paper towel or a dry one?

PASSAGE IV (Research Summaries)

21. Research Methods (equipment)

22. Trends / Make Connections: Make sure you focus on the correct column and diets in Table 1.

23. Research Methods (equipment): Hint: Look at choice II: Why would one need a fine wire mesh to place the frogs into the tank? Eliminate choices accordingly.

24. Trends / Make Connections: As with Question 22, focus on the correct column and diets in Table 1.

25. Science Sense: If you're comfortable with standard "binomial nomenclature," this one's a snap. If not, the answer is rather sensible. Would the scientists want to use different types of frogs? (Hint: Read the introduction of the passage.)

26. Research Methods (basic)

27. Research Methods: The Experimental Method states that scientists should vary what is being tested and keep constant what is not. Which diets vary the number of calories per gram?

PASSAGE V (Research Summaries)

28. Direct

29. Research Methods (equipment): Skim the first paragraph of the "*Study*": "The slots . . . allowed only soil gas to enter the pipe."

30. Direct: Does the passage ever compare the "2 processes" (intro) of CO_2 production?

31. Research Methods: Read the description for Figure 2 (second paragraph of the "*Study*"): "Figure 2 shows the averaged results for CO_2 content *of the soil gas*, expressed in percent by volume . . ." (emphasis added).

32. Trends: It might be helpful to label each line with the correct date (see the "*Key*").

33. Extrapolation

34. New Information / Calculations & Math: Note the units of the *y*-axis of Figure 3. Once you find the correct percent, multiply this value by the sample weight (10 g) to find the water content.

PASSAGE VI (Data Representation)

35. Extrapolation

36. Science Sense: You probably know that gravity pulls *down* (eliminate H and J). In the first paragraph, the passage states that drag is a force that "opposes motion," so for a falling ball, drag must point *up*. POE will get you to the correct answer.

37. Direct

38. Combining Graphs: Make sure you keep track of which line refers to which vertical axis: speed (solid line) refers to the left axis, and drag (dotted line) refers the right axis.

39. Calculations & Math (proportions) / Make Connections: Your knowledge of proportions may help on this one, but you can just look at the second parts of the answer choices; only one is true.

40. Make Connections: A classic Make Connections problem. Start at Figure 3 (find the time, in msec). Then find the drag (in µN) for that time in Figure 1.

5. TECHNIQUES: TEST 5

QUESTIONS BY SECTIONS/CHAPTERS

The following information lists every question on the test according to its relevant chapter or section in this tutorial. If you're correcting a test, circle the question numbers below that you missed or guessed on. Make sure to follow the Tutoring Schedule in the Introduction to know when to correct or tackle various types of questions.

ENGLISH	
Usage/Mechanics	Rhetorical Skills
[2, 3, 4, 6, 7, 9, 10, 11, 12, 14] [16, 18, 19, 20, 21, 22, 25, 26, 27, 28] [31, 32, 34, 35, 36, 37, 39, 41, 42, 43] [46, 48, 49, 50, 51, 52, 53, 55, 56, 58] [62, 64, 65, 66, 68, 69, 70, 71]	[1, 5, 8, 13, 15] [17, 23, 24, 29, 30] [33, 38, 40, 44, 45] [47, 54, 57, 59, 60] [61, 63, 67, 72, 73, 74, 75]

Brackets display separate passages.

MATH							
Basic Concepts	Arithmetic	Algebra	Adv. Alg.	Geometry	Func-tions	Trig	Odds/Ends
4, 47, 57	2, 5, 6, 14, 17, 21, 25, 29, 34, 39, 40, 41, 50, 54, 56	1, 3, 11, 22, 37, 43, 48, 53, 55	13	7, 8, 9, 12, 19, 20, 23, 24, 26, 27, 28, 32, 33, 35, 36, 38, 51, 58, 59	10, 18, 31, 45, 60	16, 30, 49	15, 42, 44, 46, 52

READING (by question type and passage)*						
Direct	Extended Reasoning	Pur-pose	Main Idea	Comp.	Tone	Words in Context
3, 4, 7, 9, 10, 13, 17, 23, 26, 27, 28, 29, 33, 35, 36, 37	1, 2, 8, 14, 15, 24, 30, 38	11, 16, 21, 32, 39	5, 12, 31, 34	18, 19, 20	22	6, 25, 40

Literary Narrative	Social Science	Humanities	Natural Science
1, 2, 3, 4, 5, 6, 7, 8, 9, 10	11, 12, 13, 14, 15, 16, 17, 18, 19, 20	21, 22, 23, 24, 25, 26, 27, 28, 29, 30	31, 32, 33, 34, 35, 36, 37, 38, 39, 40

SCIENCE (by question type and passage)*		
Data Representation	Research Summaries	Conflicting Viewpoints
1, 2, 3, 4, 5, 6, 7, 8, 9, 11, 12, 13, 14, 15, 17, 27, 28, 29, 31, 35, 36	10, 16, 18, 19, 30, 32, 33, 34, 37, 38, 39, 40	20, 21, 22, 23, 24, 25, 26
[1, 2, 3, 4, 5, 6] [14, 15, 16, 17, 18, 19]	[7, 8, 9, 10, 11, 12, 13] [27, 28, 29, 30, 31, 32, 33] [34, 35, 36, 37, 38, 39, 40]	[20, 21, 22, 23, 24, 25, 26]

*For Reading and Science corrections, focus on *question type*. Use the *passage* categories only to identify trends, such as timing issues, or passage types that may need review.

TECHNIQUES AND HINTS
ENGLISH
Passage I

1. Main Ideas (deletions): Make sure to focus on the narrator, not his older sister.

2. Fragments (G, H) / Punctuation (J)

3. Apostrophes & Confused Words: The plural "houses" makes clear that there were more than one friend.

4. Run-ons (G, J) / Punctuation (H): The missing comma creates ambiguity: the word "playing" becomes linked with the first phrase of the sentence ("No matter where I was playing it . . .").

5. Answer the Question: *fervor* means *with an intense emotion*.

6. Pronouns (Case) (G, H) / Style (F): As always with Style questions, choose the simpler word ("me," not "myself") when there is no good reason not to.

7. Redundancies

8. Transitions

9. Idiom

10. Vocabulary

11. Fragments / + -*ING* (B, C)

12. Apostrophes & Confused Words (F, J): Do not confuse the words *than* and *then*. / Pronouns (Ambiguity) (H, J): What is "it" referring to?

13. Answer the Question: Note that "Hawaiian classics" is more specific (see the question) than "tropical tunes."

14. Idiom

15. Main Ideas / Answer the Question: Note the emphasis of "family" and "home" in the first two paragraphs.

Passage II

16. Redundancies

17. Main Ideas: Use POE (process of elimination) on this one, if necessary. All three incorrect answers are false.

18. Subject-Verb Agreement: Make sure to ignore prepositional phrases ("on one frequency") while identifying the subject.

19. Run-ons

20. Redundancies

21. Vocabulary

22. Punctuation / + Fragments (G)

23. Organization: Note the contrast transition ("however") in Sentence 5. Since Sentence 5 is positive, the previous sentence must be negative.

24. Answer the Question: Make sure your answer mentions "communication."

25. Punctuation

26. Fragments / + -*ING* (F)

27. Pronouns (Ambiguity): Starting a sentence with *It* (as in *It is . . .*) or *There* (as in *There are . . .*) is a common practice (the *It/There* is sometimes called a "dummy subject"). Good writers often try to avoid this usage, but it's grammatically fine (and not considered ambiguous).

28. Run-ons (F, G) / Fragments (H)

29. Transitions: Note that all three transitions (choices A, B, and C) are types of *contrast* transitions. This doesn't guarantee that they're all incorrect (since different transition of the same type may be used in different ways), but it's certainly a mark against them.

30. Main Ideas (purpose)

Passage III

31. Apostrophes & Confused Words (A, C) / Subject-Verb Agreement (C, D)

32. Subject-Verb Agreement / + -*ING* (G)

33. Transitions: Compare "simplify" in the previous sentence with "serious challenge" in this sentence.

34. Punctuation

35. Redundancies

36. Misplaced Words / Passive Voice

37. Idiom

38. Main Ideas (topic sentence): The keywords in the paragraph are "Precautions" and "safe" (both in the last sentence).

39. Fragments (A) / Run-ons (C, D)

40. Transitions

41. Punctuation: Note the comma after "training."

42. Subject-Verb Agreement: As is often the case with this technique, all three incorrect choices are of a different number (in this case, *singular*) than the number of the correct answer.

43. Parallelism / + -*ING* (C): This choice has an extra -*ING* word, a mark against it.

44. Answer the Question

45. Organization: You may have noticed the abrupt introduction of "Rock climbers" at the beginning of ¶2. While reading a passage the first time through, any time you "hear" awkwardness in a place marked for organization, make a note. You probably have the correct answer.

Passage IV

46. Subject-Verb Agreement: See note to Question 42 above.

47. Answer the Question

48. Punctuation

49. Redundancies (A, B) / Style (C)

50. Redundancies

51. Idiom

52. Wordy (G, H) / Nonsense (J): Christy is noting aspects (specifically color, texture, and design) of the furniture and fabrics. Combining all five words in the same list, as in choice J, is nonsensical.

53. Fragments / + -*ING* (A, B)

54. Organization: The clue words are "his trip" in the added sentence and "how the light falls" in Sentence 2. Note that "a visit" suggests that Sentence 2 introduces the trip to Philadelphia (eliminate choice F).

55. Fragments

56. Punctuation: If you went with J, remember, when in doubt, keep the comma out. The sentence sounds fine without pausing after "painting."

57. Answer the Question

58. Nonsense: Since we can assume that Franklin and Madison do not comprise *all* of the "Many of the assembled men," the incorrect choices are all nonsensical.

59. Organization: clue words: "Such measures" (first words of ¶3).

60. Main Ideas (purpose)

Passage V

61. Answer the Question: Like the other items listed, the correct answer should be specific and descriptive.

62. Apostrophes & Confused Words: The craft is many centuries old (eliminate F and J), and the centuries do not possess anything (eliminate H).

63. Main Ideas: keywords: "Pan Xiong" + "*paj ntaub*"; note: if you went with choice A, "*modern paj ntaub*" (emphasis on *modern*) is off-topic.

64. Fragments (F) / Verb Tense (H) / -*ING* ("having") (J)

65. Misplaced Words

66. Subject-Verb Agreement

67. Answer the Question: Note the mention of animals (elephant and snail).

68. Punctuation: You might try POE on this one: you should not separate two items in a list ("tiny, tight stitches" and "several complex techniques") with a comma (eliminate F and J), and you should not separate an adjective and its noun ("tight stitches") with a comma (eliminate G).

69. Pronouns (Agreement) (B): The missing comma before "which" is probably enough to eliminate this choice; it is also nonsense. / Noun Agreement (C): The sentence begins with a singular subject ("One technique"); remember, two nouns linked with *and* become collectively plural. / Run-ons (D)

70. Parallelism / + -*ING* (F)

71. Pronouns (Ambiguity)

72. Main Ideas: You might also consider that the word "regular" is ambiguous. Good writing tends to be clear and specific.

73. Transitions: Remember that no transition, when an option, is often the correct choice. If you went with B, note that what follows the (potential) transition ("she still wears . . .") is *not* an example of her clothing practices "When she was growing up."

74. Answer the Question: The important words in the question are "clearly and concisely."

75. Main Ideas: key word: "new generation" (next sentence).

MATH

1. Ratios / Probability / Pick Numbers (Type 4): To make this question easier, you might pick a convenient number for the total number of marbles: the obvious choice is 19 (the denominator in both given fractions). So we have 5 red marbles and 4 blue marbles. The probability of selecting a red *or* a blue marble is: $\frac{4+5}{19}$ . . .

2. Probability

3. Basic Algebra

4. Basic Concepts (absolute value)

5. Arithmetic Word Problems

6. Arithmetic Word Problems

7. Angles / Triangles / Area & Perimeter or Measure the Drawing: First, divide the hexagon into six triangles (connect the center with each vertex). Can you find the measure of one of the central angles? (Hint: divide 360° by the number of central angles.) What kind of triangles do we have?

   If you get stuck with the above approach, just "measure the drawing," using the given side (length = 4) as a ruler.

8. Area & Perimeter: Hint: divide the shape into two rectangles.

9. Area & Perimeter

10. Basic Functions: With composite functions, start on the inside, that is, calculate $g(4)$ first, and then plug your result into the function f.

11. Algebraic Word Problems: Review "Common Expressions" and "Inequality Word Problems" in the lesson.

12. Lines (equations of)

13. Systems of Equations

14. Proportions

15. Matrices

16. Basic Trigonometry

17. Rates, Times, & Distances: When you set up your $R \times T = D$ table, watch your units (the rate is give in miles per *hour*, so convert the given time to hours).

18. Basic Functions

19. Angles (straight lines): This question provides more information than you need (by now, you should be used to this on the ACT). Focus on $\triangle BDE$. Once you find the base angles, you can find $m\angle EBD$.

20. Lines (equation of): This is a wordy question, but it's straightforward. You're simply given two points, from which you can find the line's equation (review the lesson if necessary). Then plug in $x = n$.

21. Arithmetic Word Problems: From 8 a.m. to noon, 4 hours had passed (so increase the temperature by $\frac{1}{2} \times 4 = 2°$). Then subtract 1° for each hour until you fall below 49°. Keep track in your work space as you go.

22. Ratios / Pick Answers: Picking answers is probably easier than using algebra on this one. Don't forget to start with choice H. For example, with H (166), we have the following part-over-whole ratio: $\frac{(82+88+91+83)+166}{100 \cdot 4+200} = 0.85$. This works (so eliminate H), and keep checking. Hint: since we fell right in the middle of the allowable B range, you might jump to choice F or K.

23. Area & Perimeter

24. Area & Perimeter / Ratios

25. Averages, Medians & Mode: Use *ANS*.

26. Area & Perimeter / Algebraic Word Problems

27. Area & Perimeter: Note: remember that answers such as E ("Cannot be

determined . . .") are usually incorrect on mid- to high-level problems.

28. Area & Perimeter: Make sure to read the question carefully ("each direction").

29. Ratios: Solve this in two steps. Use the first ratio (4/10) with the total number of students (2,500). Then use the second ratio (3/8) with your result from the first step.

30. Trig & the Unit Circle

31. Basic Functions / Pick Answers: While we think the Pick Trick is easier, you could also solve this algebraically:

$$f(t) = \frac{2}{t+1} = t \;\rightarrow\; \text{solve for } t \text{ (see}$$

Factoring Quadratics in the Factoring lesson).

32. Triangles (Pythagorean Theorem)

33. Lines

34. Rates, Times, & Distances

35. Angles: If you have trouble with this one, just draw one or two triangles. Make sure to start with C "directly above" A.

36. Area & Perimeter / Percent (*of-is*)

37. Basic Algebra or Pick Answers

38. Area & Perimeter / Pick Numbers (Type 3): We recommend the Pick Trick, but there is an algebraic approach to this problem: Since the perimeter of the rectangle is 28, let the sides of the rectangle be x, x, $14 - x$, and $14 - x$ (you can confirm that the sum of these sides is 28). → Find the area, which is represented by a quadratic equation (parabola) ($y = -x^2 + 14x$). → Find the maximum value, the y value of the vertex (review the Parabolas lesson).

39. Averages, Medians, & Modes: This is an example of a wordy problem that (assuming you're comfortable with averages and medians) isn't too difficult. We don't cover standard deviation or range in our curriculum, but one of the other choices will definitely not change—this must be the answer.

40. Proportions: First, determine what fraction of the job Ruben completes in 2 hours: $1 - (2/5 + 1/3)$. This is your known relationship for a proportion

(your units should be *fraction of the job completed* and *hours*).

41. Exponents: You could solve this using Pick Numbers (type 1), but you should be able to tackle this algebraically, which is probably faster:

$$\frac{(2a^{-1}\sqrt{b})^4}{ab^{-3}} = \frac{2^4 a^{-1\cdot4} b^2}{ab^{-3}} \;\rightarrow\; \text{Next, move}$$

negative exponents to the opposite side

of the division line: $\dfrac{2^4 a^{-1\cdot4} b^2}{ab^{-3}} = \dfrac{16 b^3 b^2}{a^4 a}$

. . .

42. Probability / Permutations & Combinations: Since order matters ("youngest to oldest"), use a permutation to determine the total number of outcomes for the three positions in question: $\underline{3} \times \underline{2} \times \underline{1} = 6$. Now that you know the number of possible outcomes, you can determine the probability of guessing the correct order.

43. Pick Numbers (type 1) or Basic Algebra: We recommend the Pick Trick for this one. When you use your calculator, make sure to either solve the numerator and denominator separately, or use parentheses carefully.

If you'd like to solve algebraically, find the common denominators for the fractions in the numerator and the fractions in the denominator:

$$\frac{\frac{2x}{6} + \frac{3}{6}}{\frac{8}{12} - \frac{3}{12}} = \frac{\frac{2x+3}{6}}{\frac{8-3}{12}} = \frac{\frac{2x+3}{6}}{\frac{5}{12}}. \text{ Remember,}$$

dividing by a fraction is equivalent to multiplying by its inverse:

$$\frac{\frac{2x+3}{6}}{\frac{5}{12}} = \frac{2x+3}{6} \cdot \frac{12}{5} \ldots.$$

44. Permutations & Combinations: Note that the numbers and letters "can be repeated."

45. More Graphs of Functions (Transformations)

46. Logarithms

47. Calculators: Simply convert the given fractions to decimals and check the answer choices.

48. More Pick Numbers: Make sure to check every answer choice. If more

than one of them works, you'll have to pick new numbers.

49. The Laws of Sines & Cosines / Triangles (Angle-Side Relationships): First, use the angle-side relationship rules to determine which angle is the largest. Then plug values into the given Law of Cosines equation and solve for the angle. If you need help solving the equation, you might review "Inverse Trig Functions" in the Trigonometry Odds & Ends lesson.

50. Averages, Means, & Modes / Pick Numbers (Type 3): While you could solve this question algebraically, it's much easier to use the Pick Trick. For example, let $x = 10$ (the average of the first 4 tests):

$$\frac{A \times N = S}{10 \times 4 = 40}$$

The average for all five tests will be 10 + 2 (given), so we have:

$$\frac{A \times N = S}{12 \times 5 = 60}$$

The sum of the first 4 tests was 40, and the sum of all 5 tests is 60, so the score of the 5th test is 20. (Make sure to read the question carefully before choosing an answer.)

51. Angles: Since $m\angle A \neq m\angle B$, these angles are not vertical angles; they must form the two angles of a line (180°). For convenience, let $m\angle A = a$, and $m\angle B = b$. We have: $b = 3.5a$ (given) and $a + b = 180$. Solve for a using substitution (or Pick Answers).

52. Patterns (Recursive Series)

53. Calculators / Pick Numbers (Type 1): Pick an easy number, such as $a = -2$, and plug into your calculator carefully (if necessary).

54. Probability (Expected Value): These Expected Value problems usually give you a table of values and probabilities, but this one requires you to create your own table:

Score	Probability
1	1/10
2	2/10 = 1/5
3	3/10
4	4/10 = 2/5

Review the lesson to complete the problem.

55. Pick Numbers (Type 3): You could solve this one algebraically, but the problem is easily solved (especially for a #55!) if you pick numbers. Make sure your numbers are *consecutive odd integers*.

56. Averages, Medians, & Modes: Finding x should be straightforward (use *ANS* if necessary). Finding y can be trickier. We can write the three given numbers in order: {8, 29, 53}. Since the median is 38, and since the average of 29 and 53 is *not* 38, y must be the third number: {8, 29, y, 53}—no other placement could give the correct median. Now you can calculate y (review medians if necessary). Note: If you went with choice K, remember that this type of answer choice is rarely correct on medium- and high-level questions (see Question 27).

57. Basic Concepts (Factor Table) / Area & Perimeter: Using a factor table, find the integer factors of 144 (for example: 1 × 144, 2 × 72, etc.), and eliminate answer choices as you go. Remember, the answer choices are *perimeters*.

58. More Circles (Equation of) / Coordinates (Midpoint): The center of a circle is the midpoint of any diameter. In this case, we're given the y-coordinate of one endpoint ($y = 11$), and we know the y-coordinate of the midpoint (from the given equation: $y = 8$). Use the midpoint equation to find the other endpoint.

59. Solids & Volume / Percent: Use Percent Increase/Decrease to find the new dimensions. Then, after calculating the initial and final volumes, use Difference-over-Original. If you're comfortable with the Percent lesson, this is a fairly easy question for a #59!

60. Graphs of Functions / Calculators: This question is a snap if you're comfortable using a graphing calculator (see the Graphs of Functions lesson for more on graphing calculators). If you don't have, or are not comfortable using, a graphing calculator, you will have to use polynomial or synthetic division, neither of which is covered in our curriculum.

READING

PASSAGE I

1. Extended Reasoning: 31–32, 46–48

2. Extended Reasoning: "to smell a rat" is an idiomatic expression meaning to have suspicion about something (for example: *The offer seemed too good to be true—I smelled a rat*).

3. Direct: 19–21: Even though the question includes the word "suggests," the answer is *directly* supported by context.

4. Direct: 50–54

5. Main Idea: The keywords are "hard times," an idea only reflected in one choice. (If you are familiar with American history, you probably know that the Great Depression occurred in the 1930s.)

6. Words in Context: 14–16: Try Process of Elimination (POE) with this one.

7. Direct: 21–22

8. Extended Reasoning: 28–30

9. Direct: 39–42: If you went with choice B, note that while Jantzen may have "put in his own money" (40), choice B is not mentioned (and is too strong).

10. Direct: 65–66

PASSAGE II

11. Purpose: 15–16 ("stolid" means *unemotional* or *dull*)

12. Main Idea: 19–20, 25–26

13. Direct: 7–10

14. Extended Reasoning: 40–43

15. Extended Reasoning: In addition to the lines given in the question, see 74–78.

16. Purpose: 66–70

17. Direct: 70–74

18. Comparison / Direct: 6–8, 50–56, etc.

19. Comparison / Direct: 27–31, 62–64, etc.

20. Comparison / Direct: 38–39, 70–71

PASSAGE III

21. Purpose: 9–11

22. Tone: 41–48 ("miracle," "changed literature"), 87 ("master")

23. Direct: 31–32, 36–40

24. Extended Reasoning: 22–30

25. Words in Context: 23–26: Remember to come up with your own words using context; some words we came up with include *obliged*, *required*, and *duty-bound*. Notice that if you try to define *constrained* without context, you'll probably (incorrectly) go with choice A or D.

26. Direct: 34–35

27. Direct: 49–52

28. Direct: 52–58

29. Direct: 85–87

30. Extended Reasoning: 80–82 ("magical," "never sad"), 87 ("joking cheerfulness"). Martin's biography may focus on García Márquez's "sadness," but if we get "too depressed," we can always return to García Márquez himself, whose own autobiography is "never sad."

PASSAGE IV

31. Main Idea: Use POE: Each of the three wrong answer choices is too specific, each covering only one part of the passage.

32. Purpose: 1–2: Some of the choices may be difficult to eliminate, but the paragraph's topic sentence should help you spot the answer.

33. Direct: 9–10, 12–13, 17–18: Note that the question does not indicate the need to "extended your reasoning," so the answer should be directly supported (see the lines indicated; the important information follows "but" in each case).

34. Main Idea: 79–80

35. Direct: 10–12

36. Direct: 36–45: Watch out for eye catchers on this one.

37. Direct: 50–53

38. Extended Reasoning: 63–66

39. Purpose: 63–66: Try POE. Since Newton was "the first to perform such a calculation," we know his discovery was advanced. We also know that it occurred "[a] few years" (62) after Richer's work in 1672 (¶3). So Newton's calculations were performed some time ago.

40. Words in Context: 80–86: As always, think of your own words before looking at the answer choices. You may have come up with words such as *left* and *departed*.

SCIENCE

PASSAGE I (Data Representation)

1. Tables (Graphs from Tables)

2. Interpolation

3. Direct

4. Direct: Note the scale of the horizontal axis (gum concentration). There are *five* tick marks between 1.0 and 2.0, so each is worth 0.2. A common mistake is to go to the third tick mark, which is 1.6%, not 1.3%.

5. Interpolation: Always watch your units. For Question 2 above, we had to interpolate between 75 min and 120 min (since we were given 100 min). For this question, we must interpolate between 25°C and 45°C (since we are given 30°C).

6. Direct

PASSAGE II (Research Summaries)

7. Direct

8. Trends: From Figure 2: percent BD↑ A↑

9. Trends / Make Connections: Reversing the trend above, we have percent BD↓ A↓, so, to find the smallest A, find the sample (Table 1) with the smallest percent BD.

10. Science Sense: The first paragraph of the passage describes the reaction. Even if you're not familiar with chemical equations, the answer should be clear.

11. New Information / Learn: This one's a little tricky. First, we need to "learn" from the passage (using our "science sense") that the students measured A

at 1,746 cm^{-1} (Study 2) probably because A peaks at this wavenumber in Figure 1 (for BD). Thus, if the students stopped their measurements at 1,600 cm^{-1} in Study 1, they would have logically used the next highest wavenumber for BD (a little under 1,200 cm^{-1}) for Study 2.

You could also probably figure this one out by simply eliminating choices based on their second parts (after the word "because"); only one is true. This is often a good way to eliminate choices on difficult problems..

12. Make Connections: As always, don't forget to connect to the text when the figures don't provide enough information to answer the question. In this case, review the second and third sentences of the passage (hopefully you circled "FAMEs" when you skimmed the passage).

13. Calculations & Math: Use 5/100 for 5% (4.8% rounded). Then use the *of–is* technique: 5/100·10 L . . . . For the second column, hopefully you know that 1 L = 1,000 mL.

PASSAGE III (Data Representation)

14. Direct: A region's "thickness" is its radial distance, according to the "*x*"-axis of Figure 1. For example, the thickness of the "inner core" is about 1,200 km.

15. Direct

16. Science Sense: Note that in Figure 1, the Earth's surface is at the right side of the "upper mantle/crust." Beyond that we have "atmosphere/space."

17. Extrapolation / Make Connections: The "Earth's gravitational field" is defined in the text as g_E. To extrapolate, sketch carefully.

18. New Information / Science Sense: As suggested in Figure 1, and as you may know, the Earth's crust makes up the outermost layer of the Earth. But the important thing to recognize is that 30 km is a very small percent of the radius of the Earth (see Question 16). According to Figure 2, by the time we reach the crust, which would be just a sliver at the far right of the graph, we

have included nearly 100% of the Earth's mass.

19. New Information / Science Sense: Hopefully you have a "sense" that as g_E increases, the weight of an object also increases. So the rock located in the region with the smaller g_E will weigh less. If you went with choice B, note that weight is determined by mass (and the acceleration of the gravitational field), not density.

PASSAGE IV (Conflicting Viewpoints)

20. Direct

21. New Information

22. Science Knowledge: You must know that proteins, the molecules having to do with biological aging (according to Student 2), are composed of amino acids.

23. New Information: Hopefully you (quickly) read through the passage, circling identifiers such as "*cross-links.*" As with the questions on the Reading Test, quickly finding information is the key for many of the Conflicting Viewpoints questions.

24. Direct: Once again, if you circled a potential identifier such as "clumps," this one's a snap.

25. Strengths: Student 1 clearly states that antioxidants "eliminate ROS before they cause cell damage." If helpful, write the following trend: antioxidant↓ aging↑ (or vice versa).

26. New Information / Science Knowledge: None of the students mentions "genetic mutations," but one of the students discusses the fundamental material of genetics (a test of your "science knowledge").

PASSAGE V (Research Summaries)

27. Direct

28. Calculations & Math: Note that all values are greater than 30%, so the average must also be greater than 30%.

29. Make Connections

30. Research Methods: To find independent variables, always consider what is being changed or altered over the course of the experiment or experiments. You can often determine this just by looking at the figures. In each individual study, the *leachates* are being altered (maple, oak, pine, etc.). *Across* the studies, the *CM* (clay minerals) are being altered.

31. Direct: Note that in Study 3, the CM3 absorbed *exactly* 50% of the leachate DOC. (In Studies 1 and 2, the percent is clearly less than 50%.)

32. Science Knowledge: A *solution* is usually defined as a homogenous mixture of two or more substances. The key word here is *homogenous.* One substance must be dissolved in the other. Since the clay mineral particles are "filtered" out (see Study 1), the mixtures are not solutions.

33. New Information / Research Methods: The key words in the question are "visible wavelength range." This is the clue that the answer must have something to do with light (or *avoiding* light). So the answer is A or B. Check the second paragraph of the introduction.

PASSAGE VI (Research Summaries)

Note: Most students agree that this is the most difficult passage on this Science Test. Remember, if you're running short on time, try to identify the easier questions, even if you have to skip some of the harder ones. Also, by now you should know to skim these passages. There's a lot of data in this one. Get through it quickly, and circle identifiers, as usual.

34. Research Methods: See Figure 1. Note that you're looking for the petri dish's orientation *before* it was turned 90° (choice G is a trap).

35. Make Connections: Start with PD8 in Experiment 2. The passage makes clear that this petri dish held M seeds, and it was exposed to light. Which petri dish in Experiment 1 matches these two conditions?

36. Direct: We recommend you label Figure 1 in a way that is convenient to quickly see the following: PD1 and PD3 were placed *in the dark*, and PD2 and PD4 were place *in the light*. PD1 and PD2 held *WT seeds*, and PD3 and PD4 held *M seeds*. Once you have the

figure labeled accordingly, you'll see that two choices can be quickly eliminated (because they don't deal with M seeds in the absence of light). Finally, note the *radicles* (the roots) in the remaining PDs.

37. Science Sense: This one sounds confusing, but you can use "science sense." Do you think plants normally grow toward light or away from it? *Positive phototropism* vs. *negative phototropism* is discussed in the first paragraph. (Note: Figure 3 is for "radicle curvature," and the question is asking about "hypocotyls," so the figure should not be used to answer the question.)

38. Science Sense: This one sounds like a "science knowledge" question, but it's unlikely the ACT would really expect students to be familiar with words like *monocot*, *dicot*, and *cotyledons*. So we must make an educated guess. Did you notice the prefixes of monocot and dicot (*mono* = one, and *di* = two). Now look at PD2 (Figure 1). Note that the plants each have *two* leaves. Without much else to go on, take your guess.

39. Research Methods: Each petri dish is turned 90° *one time*. Much else happens in the experiment, but not in terms of the petri dish's *orientation*.

40. Research Methods (The Experimental Method): The WT seedlings should remain constant, and the light (or lack thereof) should be varied. If you carefully labeled the four drawings in Figure 1 (see Question 36), this one is straightforward.

6. TECHNIQUES: PRACTICE PROBLEMS

ENGLISH (Chapter 5)

Passage I

1. Redundancies

2. Wordy

3. Run-On

4. Fragment (F) / Wordy (G) / -*ING* (H)

5. Punctuation

6. Misplaced Words (Improper Modifiers)

7. Punctuation

8. Verb Tense: Tense should be *present* (see previous sentence).

9. Apostrophes and Confused Words

10. Main Ideas (additions): keywords = "waila," "history," and "influence"

11. Misplaced Words

12. Verb Tense (F & G)/-*ING* (G)/Passive Voice and Senseless (H)

13. Main Ideas: Keywords = "O'odham," "waila," and instruments (in general); note: a saxophone is a "woodwind" instrument.

14. Fragments / Punctuation

15. Organization: clue words = "Those same German influences"

Passage II

16. Vocabulary

17. Punctuation (A, C) / Fragments (C, D)

18. Main Ideas: keywords = "difference" (see #16) in the ways a person's age is computed

19. Vocabulary

20. Main Ideas (deletions)

21. Transitions

22. Idiom (prepositional)

23. Apostrophes & Confused Words (B, C) / Punctuation (D)

24. Pronouns (Agreement)

25. Fragments

26. Answer the Question: "positive attitude"

27. Pronouns (Case)

28. Main Ideas (deletions)

29. Redundancies

30. Vocabulary

Passage III

31. Answer the Question (A, D): "illustrate the term *dress code*" / Subject-Verb Agreement (B, D): "types" does not agree with "was" (B) or "is" (D).

32. Idiom (F): The word "inefficient" is awkward when followed by a preposition. / Style (G & H)

33. Main Ideas: keywords: "Kevin's case"

34. Punctuation

35. -*ING* / Idiom (prepositional)

36. Punctuation

37. Main Ideas: keyword = the "court" and "clothing" (watch out for off-topic answer choices)

38. Apostrophes & Confused Words

39. Pronouns (Case)

40. Transitions

41. Fragments (A, B) / -*ING* (D): The word "having" is usually incorrect.

42. Answer the Question: "convey the importance of the case"

43. Punctuation

44. Idiom (prepositional)

45. Main Ideas (purpose): Look for false answer choices.

SCIENCE (Chapter 8)

Sample Passage I (Data Representation):

1. Trends / Make Connections (Multiple Figures)

2. Trends / Graphs from Tables

3. Calculations & Math

4. Direct / Make Connections: Where is "sucrose"? You must *connect* to the text, which states that information about sucrose is given in Table 2 (read the intro paragraph). Hint: Make sure you compare the same *masses* of foods.

5. Learn / Make Connections / Calculations & Math: We don't have enough information in Table 1 to know what happens to 5.0 grams of potato, but can you *learn* something from the behavior of different masses of *sucrose* in Table 2?

Sample Passage II (Research Summaries):

6. Research Methods (mistakes)

7. Trends: Find a relationship between number of bulbs and *L*.

8. Research Methods: Consider what is being *varied* in each trial.

9. Science Sense: You should always take note of numbers given in descriptions (and headings), as described in the Data Representation Odds & Ends Section. The number 0.200 m is given in the description of the experiments, and in Figure 1. Hint: Can you find 0.446 m in the results?

10. Science Sense: Remember that *L* is found when the brightness of the Fixture-1 bulbs (see Figure 1) match the brightness of the Fixture-2 bulb ("the blocks looked equally bright"). So, if the Fixture 2 bulb is brighter, would the Fixture-1 bulbs have to move closer to the blocks or farther to show the same brightness?

Sample Passage III (Conflicting Viewpoints)

11. Calculations & Math: The time for each gene transfer is clearly given in the text.

12. Direct

13. Direct

14. Indirect: Consider the replication moving in either direction for 30 minutes.

15. Calculations & Math

Made in the USA
Las Vegas, NV
09 February 2021